fourth edition

1,001

low-fat vegetarian recipes

sue spitler WITH LINDA R. YOAKAM, R.D., M.S.

**SURREY
BOOKS**

CHICAGO

Fourth edition

Surrey Books is an imprint of Agate Publishing, Inc.
Art direction and book design: Joan Sommers Design, Chicago
Nutritional analyses: Linda R. Yoakam, R.D., M.S.
Printed in Canada

Library of Congress Cataloging-in-Publication data:
Spitler, Sue.
  1,001 low-fat vegetarian recipes / Sue Spitler, with Linda R. Yoakam.—4th ed.
  p. cm.
  Includes index.
  ISBN-13: 978-1-57284-083-6 (pbk.)
  ISBN-10: 1-57284-083-8 (pbk.)
  1. Vegetarian cookery. 2. Low-fat diet—Recipes. I. Yoakam, Linda R. II. Title. III. Title:
One thousand and one low-fat vegetarian recipes.

TX837.S698 2006
641.5'636—dc22

2006025885

10 9 8 7 6 5 4 3 2

CONTENTS

Introduction   v

1 *Appetizers*   1

2 *Soups*   51

3 *Stews and Casseroles*   115

4 *Vegetarian Entrées*   151

5 *Roasted and Grilled Dishes*   185

6 *Pasta*   219

7 *Loaves, Patties, and Sandwiches*   271

8 *Pizzas, Calzones, and Dinner Pies*   297

9 *Egg and Cheese Dishes*   337

10 *Bean Dishes*   357

11 *Grain Dishes*   391

12 *Smart Carb Entrées*   431

13 *Vegetable Side Dishes*   469

14 *Salads and Dressings*   511

15 *Breads*   537

16 *Sauces and Condiments*   581

17 *Desserts*   615

Index   682

ACKNOWLEDGMENTS

Kudos go to editor Perrin Davis and editorial assistants Rachel Hinton, Leona Pitej, and Christine Swinko for their enthusiasm and superb editing skills. Many thanks to associate Pat Molden for her willingness to help whenever and wherever needed. A thank you goes to Linda Yoakam for providing the nutritional information that is so necessary for recipe development, as well as its final documentation. I'm also grateful to publisher Susan Schwartz, for her encouragement in publishing the initial edition of this book, and to publisher Doug Seibold, for his support and encouragement in publishing this new fabulous fourth edition!

To my family and many friends who contribute so much to the world—this cookbook is a gift to nourish you and bring you joy.

INTRODUCTION

E ATING VEGETARIAN is possibly one of America's fastest growing food trends. *Vegetarian Times Magazine* reports that although 6% of the US population says they never eat meat, the most recent 2003 Vegetarian Resource Study survey confirms that 2.8% of the population is vegetarian. That translates to somewhere between 5.7 and 11.4 million people who are choosing a meatless lifestyle. Many restaurants offer vegetarian fare to meet the demand for meatless meals, and vegetarian restaurants are popping up in every city with the growth rate of alfalfa sprouts!

If you are already a vegetarian, this book will provide you with more than 1,000 delicious low-fat healthy recipes in 17 recipe categories from appetizers to desserts. If you are interested in becoming vegetarian but not quite sure how to approach the transition, this book will serve as a recipe encyclopedia to get you started! You'll also find the book helpful if you are a "sometimes vegetarian" who is interested in incorporating delicious meatless meals into current family meal patterns. There's no doubt about it: new vegetable recipes are welcome in any kitchen!

There are recipes for every meal occasion, with most being appropriate for casual entertaining as well as family dining.

Spinach and Cheese Mini-Quiches or Curried Onion Croustades will start any party in tasteful style. Tuscan Bean Soup, Mediterranean Curried Stew, and Cabbage and Sauerkraut Casserole entice with a travelogue of flavors. Tempeh Fajitas, Smoked Tofu Burgers, Moo Shu Tempeh, and Oriental Loaf are a few of the creative uses of the many soy products available today. Ever-popular pasta dishes entice as well; they include Artichoke Tortellini Bake, Rice Noodle Salad, and Ziti with Gremolata. Pizzas with pizzazz include Pizza Southwest-Style, Leek and Feta Cheese Pizza with Pesto, and Tuscan Potato Pizza, which is accented with a generous sprinkling of smoked mozzarella cheese.

Sweet Potato Hash and Poached Eggs is a delicious brunch or lunch offering. Adzuki Bean Pastitsio, Asian Fried Rice, Wheat Berry Waldorf, and Bean and Pasta Salad with White Bean Dressing are tempting dishes from the bean and grain chapters. Creative salads and side dishes include

Caribbean Potato Salad, Vegetable Salad with Millet, Smashed Potatoes and Greens, and Gulfport Okra. English Muffin Bread, Focaccia, or Lima Bean Wheat Bread are all perfect accompaniments to any meal. Healthful sweet endings such as low-fat Flourless Chocolate Cake, Rhubarb Streusel Cake, Rustic Fruit Tart, and Sugared Lemon Squares will have everyone scheming for second helpings!

Busy lifestyles allow precious little cooking time for many of us, so recipes are designed to get you in and out of the kitchen as quickly and effortlessly as possible. In fact, more than 500 of the recipes in this book can be prepared in 45 minutes or less! For easy identification, these recipes will have this symbol **45**. If the recipe requires baking, refrigeration, or freezing in addition to the actual preparation time, the symbols 🔥 and ❄ will also appear.

To prepare the designated recipes in 45 minutes, you'll want to assemble ingredients and equipment and read through the recipe to plan your preparation strategy. For example, you'll want to begin cooking pasta first and prepare other ingredients while the pasta is cooking. Or, start pizza dough and proceed with the recipe while the dough is rising. To aid in strategy planning, many recipes will include a 45 Minute Preparation Tip, located at the end of the recipe.

Eating vegetarian is extremely healthy. Medical research increasingly supports the health benefits of increasing the amounts of fruits, vegetables, grains, beans, breads, cereals, and pasta in our diets and limiting, if not totally eliminating, meat, poultry, fish, dairy foods, and fats. The new MyPyramid nutrition plan from the U.S. Department of Agriculture suggests eating at least 6 servings of grains, 4 servings of fruits and vegetables, 3 servings of dairy products and 5 ounces of protein sources or their equivalents each day, along with exercise.

It's commonly thought that vegetarian cooking is high in fat, due to ingredients such as nuts, cheese, or oil that are included as meat substitutes and for flavor and nutrition. We've proven here that vegetarian cooking *can* be low in fat without losing a bit of delicious flavor. To achieve optimal nutrition and low-fat percentages, we emphasize the use of fresh versus processed ingredients and use the many excellent fat-free, reduced-fat, and reduced-sodium products currently available. Flavors are fresh, with an integrity further enhanced by herbs and seasonings.

New in this edition is the Smart Carbs chapter, for those vegetarians who also are interested in wisely choosing their carbohydrates. But what is a low-carb diet? There is no standard definition. Registered dietitians recommend a minimum of 130 grams of total carbohydrate daily, which is the minimum that is required for normal functioning of the brain and nervous system. Because the long-term effects of following a very low-carbohydrate diet are still unknown, we do not advocate eating fewer than 130 grams of carbohydrate daily. This is still considered "low" compared to the Dietary Reference Intake recommended amount of 45-65% of total calories from carbohydrates (45% of a 2000 calorie diet is 225 grams of carbohydrate; 65% is 325 grams of carbohydrate).

For each of the recipes in this new chapter, you will find a net carbs value in the nutritional analysis. The net carbs value is based on the belief that fiber sources of carbohydrate are not absorbed by the body and therefore are calorie-free, do not affect blood sugars, and do not contribute to weight gain. Since this is the case, carbohydrates from fiber can be subtracted from the total carbohydrate count of a recipe or food. The total carbohydrates minus the fiber carbohydrates leaves the net carbs available for absorption into the body.

Although it's also commonly believed that low-carb recipes are high in fat, the recipes in the Smart Carbs chapter adhere to the low-fat guidelines in this book.

In accordance with American Heart Association guidelines, very few recipes in this book exceed 30 percent calories from fat, and almost all adhere to the following nutritional criteria:

Type of Recipe Maximum Amounts per Serving

	Calories	Cholesterol (mg)	Sodium (mg)
Soups, First Courses	200	50	600
Main-Dish Soups, Entrées, Salads, Sandwiches	400	100	800
Main-Dish Meals (including pasta, rice, grains)	500	125	800
Main-Dish Eggs, Cheese	400	450	800
Side-Dish Salads, Pasta, Grains, Vegetables	200	50	600
Sauces, Condiments	200	25	600
Breads	200	50	600
Desserts	350	90	600

Specific nutritional information is provided for each recipe (not including variations) in this book, but remember that nutritional data are not always infallible. The nutritional analyses are derived with computer software that is highly regarded by nutritionists and dietitians, but they are intended as guidelines only. The figures are based on actual laboratory values of ingredients, so results may vary slightly depending upon the brand or manufacturer of an ingredient that are used.

Ingredients noted as "optional," "to taste," or "as garnish" are not included in the nutritional analyses. When alternate choices or amounts of ingredients are given, the ingredient and amount listed first are used for analysis. Similarly, data is based on the first number of servings shown, where a range is given. Nutritional analyses are also based on the reduced-fat cooking methods used; the addition of margarine, oil, or other ingredients to the recipes will invalidate the data.

Other factors that can affect the accuracy of nutritional data include variability in sizes, weights, and measures of fruits, vegetables, and other foods. There is also a possible 20 percent error factor in the nutritional labeling of prepared foods.

If you have any health problems that require strict dietary requirements, it is important to consult a physician, dietitian, or nutritionist before using recipes in this or any other cookbook. Also, if you are a diabetic or require a diet that restricts calories, fat, or sodium, remember that the nutritional data may be accurate for the recipe as written, but not for the food you cooked due to the variables explained above.

Recipes are coded as follows so you can quickly tell if they are vegan, lacto-ovo vegetarian, lacto-vegetarian, or ovo-vegetarian.

V (vegan)—Recipes contain only plant-based food, with no dairy products or eggs.

LO (lacto-ovo vegetarian)—Recipes contain dairy products and eggs.

L (lacto-vegetarian)—Recipes contain dairy products, but no eggs.

O (ovo-vegetarian)—Recipes contain eggs, but no dairy products.

Variety abounds in this collection of more than 1,000 recipes. We hope you enjoy preparing and eating these dishes as much as we enjoyed creating them for you!

INGREDIENT INFORMATION

A LL THE INGREDIENTS in this book are readily available in supermarkets and health food stores. Following is helpful information on some of the ingredients we've used, with explanations of those you may not be very familiar with.

Bead Molasses Used mostly in Asian recipes, bead molasses is very dark and thick with an intense flavor. Like other molasses products, it is refined from the concentrated juice of sun-ripened sugar cane. It is readily available in Asian sections of supermarkets; other molasses products can be substituted.

Butter In non-vegan recipes, butter is suggested as an alternate for margarine for its lower trans-fat content and improved flavor.

Chili Oil As the name implies, this oil is *hot!* Use sparingly. The oil is found in the Asian section of supermarkets; store it at room temperature.

Cream Cheese The block-type of reduced-fat and fat-free cream cheese is usually specified in the recipes in this book; the tub-type is much softer in texture and does not always work the same in recipes. If substituting fat-free cream cheese in your favorite recipes for dips, use the block type and add any liquid ingredients gradually, as the cream cheese thins much more quickly than full-fat or reduced-fat cream cheese. Fat-free cream cheese can be used to make cake glaze but not frosting, as it thins with the addition of powdered sugar and cannot be thickened.

Cooking Sprays Vegetable and olive oil cooking sprays are used to greatly reduce the amounts of oil or fat needed in recipes. When a recipe calls for "sautéing in a lightly greased skillet," spray the skillet lightly with cooking spray or wipe the pan with a lightly oiled paper towel.

Fillo Pastry These paper-thin pastry sheets are found in the freezer section of supermarkets or in Mediterranean groceries; store them in the freezer. Before using, thaw the entire package of fillo overnight in the refrigerator, or for several hours at room temperature. After removing fillo from the package, always cover the unused sheets with a damp cloth to keep them soft, as they become dry and brittle very quickly. Unused fillo can be rolled or folded, sealed in plastic wrap, and refrozen.

Herbs and Spices In most recipes, dried or ground forms are called for, but where no such designation is made, fresh or whole items are intended. Fresh herbs may be substituted by using two to three times as much as indicated for the dried or ground version.

Margarine Use an all-vegetable product. Use regular rather than diet margarine, and be sure to shop for one of the new *trans* fat-free varieties.

Olive Oil As we have kept the use of oil to a minimum, we prefer using virgin olive oil to take advantage of its more intense flavor. Canola oil can be substituted, if desired.

Pasta, Grains, and Beans When a dried and uncooked ingredient is called for, the ingredient will read: "8 ounces spaghetti, uncooked." When a cooked ingredient is called for, the ingredient will read: "12 ounces cooked spaghetti." When dry pasta or rice noodles are called for, they are always egg-free and can be used in vegan dishes. Fresh pasta or refrigerated pasta such as ravioli, tortellini, wontons, and some flat noodles do contain eggs and are used in lacto-ovo- and ovo-vegetarian recipes.

Roasted Garlic See Roasted Garlic and Three-Cheese Spread, Step 1 (p. 22) for directions on roasting garlic. We suggest roasting several heads at a time to keep extra on hand for your favorite recipes. Roasted garlic can be refrigerated, wrapped in plastic wrap, up to 2 weeks. Purchased chopped roasted garlic can be used for convenience, but the flavor is less robust.

Sesame Oil We have specified Asian sesame oil in recipes, as this dark oil has an intense sesame flavor; it can be purchased in ethnic sections of supermarkets. There is also a light-colored sesame oil that can be found in the vegetable oil section of the supermarket; it can be substituted, but the sesame flavor is extremely subtle. Store at room temperature.

Shortening The manufacturing process of shortening usually creates *trans* fats; shop carefully for one of the new *trans* fat-free brands.

Tahini Paste This flavorful paste is made with ground toasted sesame seeds and is used in Greek hummus and other Mediterranean dishes. See our recipes for and Sun-Dried Tomato Hummus and Black Bean Hummus (pp. 15, 16). Store tahini in the refrigerator.

Tamari Soy Sauce This highly flavored soy sauce is naturally brewed and is made without sugar. It is available in regular or low-sodium varieties in Asian sections of supermarkets. Other soy sauce products can be substituted. Store in the refrigerator.

Tempeh A nutritious cultured product made from cooked soybeans, tempeh has its origins in Indonesia. The soybean mixture is pressed into cakes, sometimes being combined with grains and/or other ingredients, and has a texture that is firmer, or "meatier," than tofu. Like tofu, it readily absorbs flavors from soy sauce or marinades. Because of its firm texture, tempeh is great for grilling. Purchased in the produce section of super-markets, tempeh can be stored in the refrigerator or freezer.

Textured Vegetable Protein (TVP) This versatile product made from soy flour can be added as a meat substitute to recipes such as chili, Meatless Sloppy Joes (see p. 289), or Oriental Loaf, (see p. 272). Textured vegetable protein is dry and comes in either granular or chunk form; it must be reconstituted with water, vegetable broth, or liquid before using in recipes like loaves and patties. Like tofu and tempeh, textured vegetable protein takes on the flavor of whatever it is cooked with. Purchase in supermarkets or health food stores and store in an airtight package at room temperature.

Tofu, or Bean Curd Originating in China, tofu is made by coagulating soy milk, which is the liquid remaining from cooked ground soy beans. Pressed into cakes, tofu is made in a variety of textures — soft or silken, firm, and extra-firm. It is also available seasoned and in baked and smoked forms. Soft tofu has a very fine, delicate texture and is perfect for dips, sauces, soups, and dressings; the firmer textures are better for cooking, stir-frying, broiling, and baking. As tofu is extremely mild in flavor, it is generally marinated in soy sauce or other marinades before cooking. Tofu is extremely nutritious, but it is not low in fat, ranging between 40 and 45 percent calories from fat. We call for lower fat light tofu in most recipes. Purchase tofu in the produce section of supermarkets; it is most commonly packaged in liquid in plastic tubs. Once opened, tofu has a several-day limited storage time in the refrigerator; it should be stored covered in water, and the water should be changed daily. Tofu can also be frozen; it changes to an amber color in the freezer and when thawed is firmer in texture and somewhat crumbly. A few recipes in this book call for "pressed tofu." To press tofu, place it in a shallow dish such as a pie plate; place a plate over the tofu and one or two 16-ounce cans on top of the plate. Let it stand until the excess liquid has drained from the tofu (15 to 30 minutes). The resulting tofu is firmer in texture, and the process can be omitted if desired.

Vegetable Stocks   There are a variety of homemade vegetable stock recipes and a recipe for a quick-and-easy stock made with canned vegetable broth at the beginning of the soup chapter (see p. 51). A good-quality canned vegetable broth or reconstituted vegetarian vegetable bouillon cubes can be substituted for the homemade stocks, but we suggest diluting each can of broth or 2 cups of broth made from cubes with about ½ cup of water so that the flavor will be more subtle. Canned reduced-sodium vegetable broth and nicely flavored Asian broths are available in grocery or specialty stores, and can be substituted for homemade stocks. If you prefer the flavor of homemade stocks and enjoy making them, they can be used in any recipe in the book that calls for vegetable broth. For convenience, make stocks in large quantities and freeze.

Vegetarian Protein Products   A number of interesting and flavorful vegetarian protein products are available in the freezer section of the supermarket. Many are seasoned to resemble the flavors of beef, sausage, and chicken. They come in various forms, such as patties, links, strips, and crumbles. Usually soy-based, these products may also contain grains, vegetables, nuts, and cheese.

Check your local grocery store periodically for new vegetarian food items. Literally hundreds of fresh, frozen, canned, and packaged new food products find their way to grocery shelves each year. An occasional visit to a gourmet store may garner specialty items to keep in your pantry or freezer for interesting menu additions.

ONE

Appetizers

GORP, BY GOLLY!

V

45

The great snack mix for curing the munchies or for sharing with a gathering of friends.

16 servings (about ½ cup each)

3 cups low-fat granola

2 cups pretzel goldfish

½ cup sesame sticks, broken into halves

3 cups coarsely chopped mixed dried fruit

Butter-flavored cooking spray

1 teaspoon ground cinnamon

½ teaspoon ground nutmeg

Per Serving:
Calories: 172
% of calories from fat: 13
Fat (gm): 2.6
Saturated fat (gm): 0.2
Cholesterol (mg): 0
Sodium (mg): 82
Protein (gm): 2.7
Carbohydrate (gm): 37.8

Exchanges:
Milk: 0.0
Vegetable: 0.0
Fruit: 2.0
Bread: 0.5
Meat: 0.0
Fat: 0.5

1. Mix granola, pretzel goldfish, sesame sticks, and dried fruit on large jelly roll pan. Spray mixture generously with cooking spray; sprinkle with combined spices and toss. Bake at 350 degrees 15 to 20 minutes, stirring after 10 minutes; cool and store in covered container at room temperature.

HOT STUFF!

V

45

If this snack mix is not hot enough for you, add a few sprinkles of red pepper sauce! Use 2 cups of purchased plain pita chips, or make your own.

16 servings (about ½ cup each)

2 cups oyster crackers

Pita Chips (see p. 46)

½ cup dry-roasted smoked almonds

1 cup each: coarsely chopped mixed dried fruit, dried pineapple chunks

Butter-flavored cooking spray

1 teaspoon each: dried oregano leaves, garlic powder, chili powder, cayenne pepper, black pepper

Per Serving:
Calories: 120
% of calories from fat: 22
Fat (gm): 3.2
Saturated fat (gm): 0.2
Cholesterol (mg): 0
Sodium (mg): 160
Protein (gm): 3.2
Carbohydrate (gm): 21.7

Exchanges:
Milk: 0.0
Vegetable: 0.0
Fruit: 0.5
Bread: 1.0
Meat: 0.0
Fat: 0.5

1. Mix crackers, Pita Chips, almonds, and fruit on large jelly roll pan. Spray mixture generously with cooking spray; sprinkle with combined herbs and peppers and toss. Bake at 350 degrees 15 to 20 minutes, stirring after 10 minutes; cool and store in covered container at room temperature.

SOY NOSHERS

V

Healthy soy beans and dried cranberries star in this savory-sweet snack mix.

45

8 servings (about ⅓ cup each)

1½ cups roasted soy beans

Vegetable cooking spray

¾ teaspoon each: crushed dried rosemary and
  thyme leaves

½ cup each: cup wheat squares cereal, mini
  pretzel twists

1 cup dried cranberries, or blueberries

Garlic powder and salt, to taste

Per Serving:
Calories: 196
% of calories from fat: 28
Fat (gm): 6.4
Saturated fat (gm): 1
Cholesterol (mg): 0.0
Sodium (mg): 93
Protein (gm): 12
Carbohydrate (gm): 25

Exchanges:
Milk: 0.0
Vegetable: 0.0
Fruit: 0.5
Bread: 1.0
Meat: 1.0
Fat: 1.0

1. Place soy beans in large skillet; spray generously with cooking spray, sprinkle with herbs, and toss. Cook over medium heat 3 to 4 minutes; stir in remaining ingredients, except garlic powder, and cook until ingredients are toasted (about 5 minutes), stirring occasionally. Season to taste with garlic powder and salt; cool and store in covered container at room temperature.

FRUIT NUGGETS

V

45

These nuggets are bite-sized and perfect for high-energy snacking or for a sweet ending to a meal.

3 dozen

2 cups finely ground low-fat graham cracker crumbs

½ cup finely ground ginger snaps, or low-fat graham cracker crumbs

½ teaspoon each: ground cinnamon, nutmeg, ginger

½ cup each: finely chopped dried apples, dried apricots, dates, golden raisins

½ cup orange juice

2–3 tablespoons honey

3 tablespoons sugar

Per Nugget:
Calories: 57
% of calories from fat: 8
Fat (gm): 0.5
Saturated fat (gm): 0.1
Cholesterol (mg): 0
Sodium (mg): 29
Protein (gm): 0.8
Carbohydrate (gm): 12.8

Exchanges:
Milk: 0.0
Vegetable: 0.0
Fruit: 0.5
Bread: 0.5
Meat: 0.0
Fat: 0.0

1. Combine all ingredients, except sugar, in bowl, stirring until mixture holds together. Roll into 36 balls, each about 1 inch in diameter. Measure 1 tablespoon sugar into large plastic bag; add 1 dozen nuggets and shake until coated. Repeat with remaining sugar and nuggets. Store in covered container at room temperature.

EDAMAME SNACKERS

V

45

What snack could be healthier or easier!?

8 servings

1 pound fresh, or frozen, edamame in the shell

Kosher salt, to taste

Per Serving:
Calories: 38
% of calories from fat: 28
Fat (gm): 1.1
Saturated fat (gm): 0.2
Cholesterol (mg): 0.0
Sodium (mg): 5.7
Protein (gm): 3
Carbohydrate (gm): 3.4

Exchanges:
Milk: 0.0
Vegetable: 0.0
Fruit: 0.0
Bread: 0.5
Meat: 0.0
Fat: 0.0

1. Simmer edamame in 2 quarts water in large saucepan, covered, until tender, 5 to 8 minutes; drain. Serve edamame warm or at room temperature, sprinkled lightly with salt.

TOASTED ONION DIP

LO

45

This will bring back memories of the popular dip made with onion soup mix! Toasting the dried onion flakes is the flavor secret.

12 servings (about 2 tablespoons each)

3–4 tablespoons dried onion flakes

1 package (8 ounces) fat-free cream cheese

⅓ cup each: reduced-fat plain yogurt, fat-free mayonnaise

2 small green onions, chopped

2 cloves garlic, minced

¼ teaspoon crushed vegetable bouillon cube

2–3 tablespoons fat-free milk

½–1 teaspoon lemon juice

2–3 drops red pepper sauce

Salt and white pepper, to taste

Dippers: assorted vegetable relishes and bread sticks

Per Serving:
Calories: 32
% of calories from fat: 4
Fat (gm): 0.1
Saturated fat (gm): 0.1
Cholesterol (mg): 0.4
Sodium (mg): 223
Protein (gm): 3.3
Carbohydrate (gm): 3.9

Exchanges:
Milk: 0.0
Vegetable: 0.0
Fruit: 0.0
Bread: 0.0
Meat: 0.5
Fat: 0.0

1. Cook onion flakes in small skillet over medium to medium-low heat until toasted, 3 to 4 minutes, stirring frequently; remove from heat. Mix cream cheese, yogurt, mayonnaise, green onions, garlic, and bouillon in medium bowl until smooth, adding enough milk to thin the mixture to the desired dipping consistency. Stir in onions; season to taste with lemon juice, pepper sauce, salt, and white pepper. Serve with dippers (not included in nutritional data).

BAKED ARTICHOKE DIP

LO

Everyone's favorite, modified for healthful, low-fat goodness.

45

16 servings (about 3 tablespoons each)

1 can (15 ounces) artichoke hearts, rinsed, drained

½ package (8-ounce size) fat-free cream cheese, softened

½ cup each: grated fat-free Parmesan cheese, fat-free mayonnaise, fat-free sour cream

1–2 teaspoons lemon juice

1 green onion, thinly sliced

2 teaspoons minced garlic

2–3 drops red pepper sauce

Salt and cayenne pepper, to taste

Dippers: assorted vegetables, bread sticks, or crackers

Per Serving:
Calories: 39
% of calories from fat: 2
Fat (gm): 0.1
Saturated fat (gm): 0
Cholesterol (mg): 0
Sodium (mg): 190
Protein (gm): 3.5
Carbohydrate (gm): 6.8

Exchanges:
Milk: 0.0
Vegetable: 1.5
Fruit: 0.0
Bread: 0.0
Meat: 0.0
Fat: 0.0

1. Process artichoke hearts, cream cheese, Parmesan cheese, mayonnaise, sour cream, and lemon juice in food processor until smooth. Stir in green onion, garlic, and red pepper sauce. Season to taste with salt and cayenne pepper. Bake in small casserole, uncovered, at 350 degrees until lightly browned, 20 to 25 minutes. Serve warm with dippers (not included in nutritional data).

CURRY DIP

LO

Raw sweet potato slices and broccoli florets are particularly good with this dip.

45

12 servings (about 2 tablespoons each)

1½ cups fat-free mayonnaise

½ cup fat-free sour cream

¼ cup thinly sliced green onions

1½–2 teaspoons each: prepared horseradish, curry powder

2–3 teaspoons sugar

2–4 teaspoons lemon juice

Salt and white pepper, to taste

Dippers: assorted vegetable relishes, and Pita Chips (see p. 46)

Per Serving:
Calories: 34
% of calories from fat: 1
Fat (gm): 0
Saturated fat (gm): 0
Cholesterol (mg): 0
Sodium (mg): 393
Protein (gm): 0.7
Carbohydrate (gm): 8

Exchanges:
Milk: 0.0
Vegetable: 0.0
Fruit: 0.0
Bread: 0.5
Meat: 0.0
Fat: 0.0

1. Mix mayonnaise, sour cream, green onions, horseradish, curry powder, and sugar. Season to taste with lemon juice, salt, and white pepper. Refrigerate several hours for flavors to blend. Serve with dippers (not included in nutritional data).

TOMATILLO SALSA

V

45

Tomatillos (Mexican green tomatoes) contain natural pectin, so the salsa will thicken when refrigerated. You can thin it to the desired consistency with reserved cooking liquid or water.

16 servings (about 2 tablespoons each)

1½ pounds tomatillos, husks removed

½ cup finely chopped onion

2 cloves garlic, minced

¼ small jalapeño chili, seeds and veins discarded, very finely chopped

2 tablespoons finely chopped cilantro

½ teaspoon each: ground cumin and dried oregano leaves

⅛–¼ teaspoon sugar

Salt, to taste

Baked tortilla chips

Per Serving:
Calories: 17
% of calories from fat: 22
Fat (gm): 0.5
Saturated fat (gm): 0
Cholesterol (mg): 0
Sodium (mg): 2
Protein (gm): 0.5
Carbohydrate (gm): 3.1

Exchanges:
Milk: 0.0
Vegetable: 0.5
Fruit: 0.0
Bread: 0.0
Meat: 0.0
Fat: 0.0

1. Simmer tomatillos in water to cover in large saucepan until tender, 5 to 8 minutes. Cool and drain, reserving liquid.

2. Process tomatillos, onion, garlic, jalapeño chili, cilantro, cumin, and oregano in food processor or blender until almost smooth, adding enough reserved liquid to make medium dipping consistency; season to taste with sugar and salt. Serve with baked tortilla chips (not included in nutritional data).

RED TOMATO SALSA

V

45

Poblano chilies can be quite hot, so taste the salsa before adding them and adjust the amount specified, if necessary.

16 servings (about 2 tablespoons each)

2 large tomatoes, cut into wedges
¼ cup each: finely chopped onion, poblano chili
1 clove garlic, minced
¼ cup loosely packed cilantro, finely chopped
Salt, to taste
Baked tortilla chips

1. Process tomatoes, onion, chili, and garlic in food processor or blender until finely chopped. Mix in cilantro; season to taste with salt. Serve with tortilla chips (not included in nutritional data).

Per Serving:
Calories: 9
% of calories from fat: 10
Fat (gm): 0.1
Saturated fat (gm): 0
Cholesterol (mg): 0
Sodium (mg): 4
Protein (gm): 0.4
Carbohydrate (gm): 1.9

Exchanges:
Milk: 0.0
Vegetable: 0.5
Fruit: 0.0
Bread: 0.0
Meat: 0.0
Fat: 0.0

Variation

Med-Mex Fusion Salsa — Make salsa as above but substitute green bell pepper for the poblano chili and add ¼ cup coarsely crumbled fat-free feta cheese, ¾ teaspoon dried oregano leaves, and ¼ teaspoon red pepper flakes.

MEXICAN BEAN DIP

L

45

Nutritious black beans are a great source of folate.

12 servings (about 2 tablespoons each)

½ cup thinly sliced green onions
1–2 cloves garlic, minced
1 can (15 ounces) black beans, rinsed, drained
¾ cup (3 ounces) shredded reduced-fat
   Cheddar cheese
¼ teaspoon salt
⅓ cup vegetable broth, or water
1–2 tablespoons finely chopped cilantro
Baked tortilla chips

Per Serving:
Calories: 51
% of calories from fat: 31
Fat (gm): 2.4
Saturated fat (gm): 1.5
Cholesterol (mg): 7.4
Sodium (mg): 240
Protein (gm): 3.3
Carbohydrate (gm): 5.4

Exchanges:
Milk: 0.0
Vegetable: 0.0
Fruit: 0.0
Bread: 0.5
Meat: 0.0
Fat: 0.5

1. Sauté onions and garlic in lightly greased skillet until tender, about 3 minutes.

2. Process black beans, cheese, and salt in food processor or blender until almost smooth, adding enough broth to make desired dipping consistency. Mix in onion mixture and cilantro. Serve with tortilla chips (not included in nutritional data).

PINTO BEAN AND AVOCADO DIP

Avocado and tomato brighten this well-flavored bean dip. Increase the amount of jalapeño chili if you dare!

V

45

12 servings (about 2 tablespoons each)

1 can (15 ounces) pinto beans, rinsed, drained

¾ cup finely chopped onion

2 cloves garlic

½ jalapeño chili, minced

3 tablespoons finely chopped cilantro

1 large tomato, chopped

½ medium avocado, peeled, pitted, chopped

Salt and pepper, to taste

Baked tortilla chips

Per Serving:
Calories: 50
% of calories from fat: 25
Fat (gm): 1.4
Saturated fat (gm): 0.2
Cholesterol (mg): 0.0
Sodium (mg): 114
Protein (gm): 2.1
Carbohydrate (gm): 7.7

Exchanges:
Milk: 0.0
Vegetable: 0.0
Fruit: 0.0
Bread: 0.5
Meat: 0.0
Fat: 0.5

1. Process beans in food processor or blender until smooth; add onion, garlic, jalapeño chili, and cilantro and process until blended. Mix in tomato and avocado; season to taste with salt and pepper. Refrigerate 1 to 2 hours for flavors to blend. Serve with tortilla chips (not included in nutritional data).

CHILI CON QUESO

L

45

Our health-conscious version of this popular dip is made with reduced-fat pasteurized processed cheese for creamy texture and fat-free Cheddar cheese for accented flavor.

12 servings (about 2 tablespoons each)

5 medium anaheim, or 2 medium poblano, chilies, seeds and veins discarded, cut into halves

⅓ cup each: chopped onion, tomato

½ teaspoon dried oregano leaves

2 cups (8 ounces) shredded reduced-fat pasteurized processed cheese

1 cup (4 ounces) shredded fat-free Cheddar cheese

2–4 tablespoons fat-free milk

Baked tortilla chips

Per Serving:
Calories: 72
% of calories from fat: 26
Fat (gm): 2.8
Saturated fat (gm): 1.8
Cholesterol (mg): 9.1
Sodium (mg): 412
Protein (gm): 7.4
Carbohydrate (gm): 5.7

Exchanges:
Milk: 0.0
Vegetable: 0.0
Fruit: 0.0;
Bread: 0.5
Meat: 1.0
Fat: 0.0

1. Place chilies, skin sides up, on baking pan. Bake at 425 degrees until chilies are browned and soft, 20 to 25 minutes. Cool and cut into strips.

2. Sauté onion, tomato, and oregano in lightly greased skillet until onion is tender, about 5 minutes. Add cheeses and chili strips; cook over low heat until cheese is melted, stirring in milk for desired consistency. Serve warm with tortilla chips (not included in nutritional data).

QUESO FUNDIDO

L

45

The vegetarian chorizo recipe is easy, flavorful and can be used to inspire many of your Mexican dishes. Any extra Vegetarian Chorizo can be frozen for later use.

8 servings

¼ cup chopped red bell pepper

¾ cup (3 ounces) shredded fat-free Cheddar cheese

½ cup (2 ounces) cubed reduced-fat pasteurized processed cheese

¼–⅓ cup fat-free milk

8 corn tortillas, warm

½ cup (⅙ recipe) cooked, crumbled Vegetarian Chorizo (see p. 287)

2 tablespoons each: finely chopped green onion,
finely chopped cilantro

1. Sauté red bell pepper until tender in lightly
greased skillet, 2 to 3 minutes. Add cheeses;
cook over low heat until melted, stirring in milk
for desired consistency. Spoon about 2 tablespoons cheese mixture in the center of each
tortilla. Sprinkle with Vegetarian Chorizo, green
onion, and cilantro, and roll up.

Per Serving:
Calories: 112
% of calories from fat: 15
Fat (gm): 1.9
Saturated fat (gm): 0.7
Cholesterol (mg): 12.8
Sodium (mg): 274
Protein (gm): 8.7
Carbohydrate (gm): 15.2

Exchanges:
Milk: 0.0
Vegetable: 0.0
Fruit: 0.0
Bread: 1.0
Meat: 1.0
Fat: 0.0

SOMBRERO DIP

L

Use Florida avocados for the Guacamole, as they're lower in fat than the California variety.

6 servings

¼ cup each: chopped poblano chili, onion

½ recipe Vegetarian Chorizo (see p. 287)

4–5 leaves romaine lettuce

1 can (15 ounces) vegetarian refried beans

½ cup prepared medium or hot salsa

½ cup each: chopped romaine lettuce, tomato

Guacamole (recipe follows)

¼ cup (1 ounce) shredded fat-free Cheddar cheese

½ cup fat-free sour cream

1 green onion, thinly sliced

Baked tortilla chips

Per Serving:
Calories: 175
% of calories from fat: 16
Fat (gm): 3.2
Saturated fat (gm): 0.7
Cholesterol (mg): 23.7
Sodium (mg): 214
Protein (gm): 13.3
Carbohydrate (gm): 25

Exchanges:
Milk: 0.0
Vegetable: 2.0
Fruit: 0.0
Bread: 1.0
Meat: 1.0
Fat: 0.0

1. Sauté poblano chili and onion until tender in lightly greased
skillet, 3 to 5 minutes; stir in Vegetarian Chorizo.

2. Line a dinner-size serving plate with lettuce; cover with refried
beans to within 2 inches of edge of lettuce. Spoon salsa over beans,
leaving edge of bean layer showing. Spoon Vegetarian Chorizo mixture over salsa; sprinkle with chopped lettuce and tomato, leaving
edge of Vegetarian Chorizo showing. Spoon Guacamole over lettuce
and tomato and sprinkle with Cheddar cheese. Spoon sour cream
in large dollop on top; sprinkle with green onion. Serve with tortilla
chips (not included in nutritional data).

Guacamole

Makes about ⅔ cup

1 medium avocado, peeled, pitted
½ each: finely chopped small onion, jalapeno chili
1–2 tablespoons finely chopped cilantro
Salt and white pepper, to taste

1. Coarsely mash avocado in small bowl; mix in onion, jalapeño chili, and cilantro. Season to taste with salt and pepper.

Per Serving:
Calories: 169
% of calories from fat: 21
Fat (gm): 4
Saturated fat (gm): 0.7
Cholesterol (mg): 25.4
Sodium (mg): 703
Protein (gm): 11.6
Carbohydrate (gm): 23.3

Exchanges:
Milk: 0.0
Vegetable: 0.0
Fruit: 0.0
Bread: 1.5
Meat: 1.0
Fat: 0.0

PINE NUT SPINACH PÂTÉ

L

Toasted pine nuts provide flavor and texture accents in this unique dip.

45

❄

12 servings (about 2 tablespoons each)

1 package (10 ounces) frozen chopped spinach, thawed, well drained
¼ cup each: coarsely chopped onion, celery
1 clove garlic
2–3 teaspoons lemon juice
1 teaspoon dried dill weed
1–2 tablespoons toasted pine nuts, or slivered almonds
½ package (8-ounce size) fat-free cream cheese, softened
Salt and pepper, to taste
Bruschetta (see p. 46)

Per Serving:
Calories: 19
% of calories from fat: 21
Fat (gm): 0.5
Saturated fat (gm): 0.1
Cholesterol (mg): 0
Sodium (mg): 73
Protein (gm): 2.1
Carbohydrate (gm): 1.9

Exchanges:
Milk: 0.0
Vegetable: 0.5
Fruit: 0.0
Bread: 0.0
Meat: 0.0
Fat: 0.0

1. Process spinach, onion, celery, garlic, lemon juice, and dill weed in food processor until almost smooth; add pine nuts and process until coarsely chopped, using pulse technique. Stir in cream cheese; season to taste with salt and pepper. Refrigerate several hours for flavors to blend. Serve with Bruschetta (not included in nutritional data).

WILD MUSHROOM PÂTÉ

L

45

This pâté is most flavorful when made with wild mushrooms, though any type of mushrooms can be used.

8 servings (about 2 tablespoons each)

12 ounces coarsely chopped shiitake, or portobello, mushrooms

½ cup chopped onion

2–4 cloves garlic, minced

¼ cup dry sherry, or water

2 tablespoons grated fat-free Parmesan cheese

2–3 teaspoons lemon juice

Salt and pepper, to taste

Crusty bread or crackers

Per Serving:
Calories: 42
% of calories from fat: 2
Fat (gm): 0.1
Saturated fat (gm): 0
Cholesterol (mg): 0
Sodium (mg): 14
Protein (gm): 1.4
Carbohydrate (gm): 8.4

Exchanges:
Milk: 0.0
Vegetable: 1.5
Fruit: 0.0
Bread: 0.0
Meat: 0.0
Fat: 0.0

1. Add mushrooms, onion, garlic, and sherry to lightly greased skillet; cook, covered, over medium heat until mushrooms are wilted, about 5 minutes. Cook, uncovered, over medium heat until vegetables are very tender and all liquid absorbed, 8 to 10 minutes. Cool.

2. Process mushroom mixture and Parmesan cheese in food processor until smooth. Season to taste with lemon juice, salt, and pepper. Refrigerate 2 to 3 hours for flavors to blend. Serve in crock with bread or crackers (not included in nutritional data).

SOYBEAN AND VEGETABLE SPREAD

L

45

A delicious and nutritious spread for snacking, or to serve as party fare.

12 servings (about 3 tablespoons each)

½ cup each: chopped onion, carrot

2 cloves garlic, minced

2 tablespoons vegetable broth, or water

1½ cups cooked dried, or canned, soybeans

1 cup fat-free sour cream

2 tablespoons minced parsley

1–2 teaspoons lemon juice

Salt and pepper, to taste

Dippers: assorted vegetables, or crackers

Per Serving:
Calories: 56
% of calories from fat: 29
Fat (gm): 2
Saturated fat (gm): 0.3
Cholesterol (mg): 0
Sodium (mg): 17
Protein (gm): 5
Carbohydrate (gm): 5.6

Exchanges:
Milk: 0.0
Vegetable: 1.0
Fruit: 0.0
Bread: 0.0
Meat: 0.5
Fat: 0.0

1. Cook onion, carrot, garlic, and broth in small skillet, covered, over medium heat until vegetables are tender and liquid absorbed, 5 to 8 minutes; cool.

2. Process soybeans and sour cream in food processor until smooth. Stir in vegetable mixture and parsley; season to taste with lemon juice, salt, and pepper. Refrigerate several hours for flavors to blend. Serve with dippers (not included in nutritional data).

HERB CANNELLINI DIP

V

45

Another good-for-you dip that tastes terrific! Italian cannellini beans are white kidney beans that are similar in flavor and appearance to navy or Great Northern beans.

6 servings (about ¼ cup each)

1 can (15 ounces) cannellini, or Great Northern, beans, rinsed, drained

1 tablespoon each: olive oil, prepared horseradish

2 tablespoons minced chives

½ teaspoon each: dried oregano and basil leaves

2–3 drops red pepper sauce

2–3 teaspoons lemon juice

Salt and white pepper, to taste

Dippers: Pita Chips (see p. 46) and assorted vegetables

Per Serving:
Calories: 75
% of calories from fat: 25
Fat (gm): 2.8
Saturated fat (gm): 0.3
Cholesterol (mg): 0
Sodium (mg): 167
Protein (gm): 5.3
Carbohydrate (gm): 13.1

Exchanges:
Milk: 0.0
Vegetable: 0.0
Fruit: 0.0
Bread: 1.0
Meat: 0.0
Fat: 0.5

1. Process beans, olive oil, and horseradish in food processor until smooth. Mix in chives, herbs, and red pepper sauce. Season to taste with lemon juice, salt, and white pepper. Refrigerate 1 to 2 hours for flavors to blend. Serve with dippers (not included in nutritional data).

Variation

Roasted Garlic and Cannellini Dip — Cut ½ inch off tops of 2 garlic bulbs to expose cut cloves; drizzle each with 1 teaspoon olive oil. Wrap garlic in foil and bake at 400 degrees until soft when pressed, about 45 minutes; cool. Make dip as above; squeeze enough garlic from 1 head to make 1 tablespoon and stir into dip. Serve bean dip and remaining head of garlic on plate with crusty bread and vegetable relishes for dipping.

SUN-DRIED TOMATO HUMMUS

Sun-dried tomatoes and herbs embellish this Mediterranean favorite.

8 servings (about ¼ cup each)

1 can (15 ounces) chick peas, rinsed, drained

⅓ cup fat-free yogurt

2–3 tablespoons tahini (sesame seed paste)

3 cloves garlic

4 sun-dried tomato halves (not packed in oil),
   finely chopped

1 teaspoon each: dried oregano and mint leaves

2–3 teaspoons lemon juice

Salt and white pepper, to taste

Dippers: pita breads, cut into wedges, or Pita Chips
   (see p. 46)

Per Serving:
Calories: 73
% of calories from fat: 21
Fat (gm): 1.7
Saturated fat (gm): 0.2
Cholesterol (mg): 0.2
Sodium (mg): 256
Protein (gm): 3.6
Carbohydrate (gm): 11.4

Exchanges:
Milk: 0.0
Vegetable: 0.0
Fruit: 0.0
Bread: 1.0
Meat: 0.0
Fat: 0.0

1. Process chick peas, yogurt, tahini, and garlic in food processor until smooth. Stir in sun-dried tomatoes and herbs; season to taste with lemon juice, salt, and white pepper. Refrigerate 1 to 2 hours for flavors to blend. Serve with dippers (not included in nutritional data).

Variation

Parthenon Platter — Make hummus as above and spoon into a 6-inch flattened mound on serving platter. Combine 4 chopped canned artichoke hearts, ½ cup halved grape tomatoes, 6 sliced Greek olives, ⅓ cup crumbled fat-free feta cheese, 2 tablespoons olive oil, and ¾ teaspoon Italian seasoning; toss and spoon over hummus. Garnish plate with pepperoncini and serve with Pita Chips (see p. 46).

SPICY ORANGE HUMMUS

V *Another flavorful variation of traditional hummus.*

45 ❄

8 servings (about ¼ cup each)

1 can (15 ounces) chick peas, rinsed, drained

3 cloves garlic, minced

¼ cup orange juice

2 teaspoons soy sauce

1 teaspoon Dijon mustard

½ teaspoon each: curry powder, ground ginger

2 teaspoons grated orange zest

Salt and white pepper, to taste

Dippers: Pita Chips (see p. 46), or pita breads, cut into wedges

Per Serving:
Calories: 60
% of calories from fat: 15
Fat (gm): 1
Saturated fat (gm): 0.1
Cholesterol (mg): 0
Sodium (mg): 306
Protein (gm): 2.7
Carbohydrate (gm): 10.3

Exchanges:
Milk: 0.0
Vegetable: 0.0
Fruit: 0.0
Bread: 1.0
Meat: 0.0
Fat: 0.0

1. Process chick peas, garlic, orange juice, soy sauce, mustard, curry powder, and ginger in food processor until smooth; stir in orange zest. Season to taste with salt and white pepper. Refrigerate 1 to 2 hours for flavors to blend. Serve with dippers (not included in nutritional data).

BLACK BEAN HUMMUS

V *Tahini (ground sesame paste) and soy sauce season this unusual bean dip.*

45 ❄

6 servings (about ¼ cup each)

1 can (15 ounces) black beans, rinsed, drained

¼ cup reduced-sodium vegetable broth, or water

2–3 tablespoons tahini

3 cloves garlic

2–2½ tablespoons lemon juice

1½ tablespoons soy sauce

Salt and cayenne pepper, to taste

Dippers: Pita Chips (see p. 46), or pita breads, cut into wedges

Per Serving:
Calories: 100
% of calories from fat: 30
Fat (gm): 4
Saturated fat (gm): 0
Cholesterol (mg): 0
Sodium (mg): 480
Protein (gm): 7.6
Carbohydrate (gm): 13.9

Exchanges:
Milk: 0.0
Vegetable: 0.0
Fruit: 0.0
Bread: 1.0
Meat: 0.0
Fat: 0.5

1. Process beans, broth, tahini, garlic, lemon juice, and soy sauce in food processor until smooth; season to taste with salt and cayenne pepper. Refrigerate 1 to 2 hours for flavors to blend. Serve with dippers (not included in nutritional data).

EGGPLANT CAVIAR

L

Middle Eastern flavors will tempt you to second helpings!

6 servings (about 2 tablespoons each)

1 large eggplant (1½ pounds)

½ cup chopped tomato

¼ cup finely chopped onion

3 cloves garlic, minced

¼ cup fat-free yogurt

2 teaspoons extra-virgin olive oil

½ teaspoon dried oregano leaves

1–2 tablespoons lemon juice

4 pitted ripe olives, chopped

Salt and pepper, to taste

Dippers: lavosh, or pita bread wedges

Per Serving:
Calories: 59
% of calories from fat: 28
Fat (gm): 2.1
Saturated fat (gm): 0.3
Cholesterol (mg): 0.2
Sodium (mg): 19.1
Protein (gm): 1.8
Carbohydrate (gm): 10.1

Exchanges:
Milk: 0.0
Vegetable: 1.5
Fruit: 0.0
Bread: 0.0
Meat: 0.0
Fat: 0.5

1. Pierce eggplant in several places with fork; place in baking pan. Bake at 350 degrees until eggplant is soft, 45 to 50 minutes; cool. Cut eggplant in half; scoop out pulp with spoon. Mix eggplant, tomato, onion, garlic, yogurt, olive oil, and oregano in bowl; season to taste with lemon juice, salt, and pepper. Refrigerate 3 to 4 hours for flavors to blend. Serve with dippers (not included in nutritional data).

ROASTED ZUCCHINI AND GARLIC SPREAD

L

A great recipe for summer when garden zucchini are in generous supply.

45

12 servings (about 2 tablespoons each)

1¼ pounds zucchini, cut into 1-inch pieces
1 small onion, cut into wedges
2 garlic cloves, peeled
⅓ cup fat-free plain yogurt
2 tablespoons finely chopped parsley
Lemon juice, to taste
Salt and cayenne pepper, to taste
Dippers: Assorted vegetables and crackers

Per Serving:
Calories: 16
% of calories from fat: 6
Fat (gm): 0.1
Saturated fat (gm): 0.0
Cholesterol (mg): 0.1
Sodium (mg): 11
Protein (gm): 1.1
Carbohydrate (gm): 3.2

Exchanges:
Milk: 0.0
Vegetable: 0.5
Fruit: 0.0
Bread: 0.0
Meat: 0.0
Fat: 0.0

1. Arrange zucchini, onion, and garlic in single layer on a greased, foil-lined pan. Bake at 425 degrees until vegetables are very tender, about 15 to 20 minutes for garlic, 25 to 30 minutes for zucchini and onion. Cool.

2. Process vegetables in food processor until coarsely chopped. Stir in yogurt and parsley; season to taste with lemon juice, salt, and cayenne pepper. Serve with dippers (not included in nutritional data).

ARTICHOKE PÂTÉ

LO

For elegant presentation, spoon pâté on ends of Belgian endive leaves and arrange on a serving plate with vegetable garnishes.

45

16 servings (about 2 tablespoons each)

1 can (15 ounces) artichoke hearts, or bottoms, drained
½ package (8-ounce size) fat-free cream cheese, softened
⅓ cup grated fat-free Parmesan cheese
2–4 tablespoons fat-free mayonnaise
1–1½ teaspoons minced roasted garlic
2 tablespoons finely chopped parsley
1–2 teaspoons lemon juice

Per Serving:
Calories: 31
% of calories from fat: 13
Fat (gm): 0.5
Saturated fat (gm): 0.1
Cholesterol (mg): 0
Sodium (mg): 142
Protein (gm): 2.7
Carbohydrate (gm): 4.7

Exchanges:
Milk: 0.0
Vegetable: 1.0
Fruit: 0.0
Bread: 0.0
Meat: 0.0
Fat: 0.0

Salt and cayenne pepper, to taste

2 tablespoons each: chopped black olives, chopped roasted red bell peppers

Dippers: Assorted vegetables, lavosh, or melba toast

1. Process artichokes, cheeses, mayonnaise, and garlic in food processor until smooth. Stir in parsley; season to taste with lemon juice, salt, and cayenne pepper. Refrigerate several hours for flavors to blend. Spoon into crock and garnish with olives and red peppers; serve with dippers (not included in nutritional data).

GARDEN MUSHROOM SPREAD

Substitute zucchini, yellow summer squash, or bell peppers for the carrots in this flavor-fresh spread.

12 servings (about 2 tablespoons each)

¾ cup each: chopped onion, carrot

1–2 teaspoons grated lemon rind

2–3 cloves garlic, minced

12 ounces brown, or white, mushrooms, chopped

2 tablespoons dry sherry, or water

½ teaspoon each: dried thyme and savory leaves

½ package (8-ounce size) fat-free cream cheese

2 tablespoons each: grated fat-free Parmesan cheese, minced parsley

Salt, cayenne, and black pepper, to taste

Dippers: Assorted vegetables, whole wheat lavosh, or Bruschetta (see p. 46),

Per Serving:
Calories: 28
% of calories from fat: 5
Fat (gm): 0.2
Saturated fat (gm): 0
Cholesterol (mg): 0
Sodium (mg): 67
Protein (gm): 2.5
Carbohydrate (gm): 3.8

Exchanges:
Milk: 0.0
Vegetable: 1.5
Fruit: 0.0
Bread: 0.0
Meat: 0.0
Fat: 0.0

1. Sauté onion, carrot, lemon rind, and garlic in lightly greased skillet until tender, about 5 minutes; remove from skillet. Add mushrooms, sherry, and herbs to skillet; cook, covered, over medium heat until mushrooms are wilted, about 5 minutes. Cook, uncovered, until mushrooms are tender and liquid absorbed, about 5 minutes. Cool.

2. Process cream cheese, Parmesan cheese, and half the mushroom mixture in food processor until smooth. Stir in onion mixture, remaining mushroom mixture, and parsley. Season to taste with salt and peppers. Refrigerate 2 to 3 hours for flavors to blend. Serve with dippers (not included in nutritional data).

FAUX CHOPPED LIVER

O *This pâté boasts incredible texture and flavor.*

12 servings (about 2 tablespoons each)

1¾ cups reduced-sodium vegetable broth
½ cup dried lentils
1 cup finely chopped onion
1 clove garlic, minced
¼–½ teaspoon dried thyme leaves
¼–⅓ cup chopped walnuts
1 hard-cooked egg, chopped
Salt and pepper, to taste
24 slices cocktail rye bread, or crackers

Per Serving:
Calories: 152
% of calories from fat: 19
Fat (gm): 3.5
Saturated fat (gm): 0.4
Cholesterol (mg): 17.8
Sodium (mg): 194
Protein (gm): 7.8
Carbohydrate (gm): 25.5

Exchanges:
Milk: 0.0
Vegetable: 0.0
Fruit: 0.0
Bread: 0.0
Meat: 0.0
Fat: 0.5

1. Heat broth to boiling in medium saucepan; stir in lentils. Reduce heat and simmer, covered, until lentils are tender, but not mushy, and liquid is absorbed, about 45 minutes.

2. Sauté onion, garlic, and thyme in lightly greased skillet until onions are tender, 5 to 8 minutes. Process onion mixture, lentils and walnuts in food processor until almost smooth; stir in egg and season to taste with salt and pepper. Refrigerate 2 to 3 hours for flavors to blend. Serve with cocktail rye bread or crackers (not included in nutritional data).

EGGPLANT MARMALADE

V *A quick kitchen tip — gingerroot does not have to be peeled before using!*

12 servings (about 3 tablespoons each)

2 medium eggplant (1¼ pounds each), unpeeled, cubed (½-inch)
⅓ cup coarsely chopped onion
2 tablespoons minced roasted garlic
3 tablespoons each: minced gingerroot, light brown sugar
1½ teaspoons fennel seeds, crushed
2 tablespoons red wine vinegar

Per Serving:
Calories: 75
% of calories from fat: 21
Fat (gm): 1.9
Saturated fat (gm): 0.3
Cholesterol (mg): 0
Sodium (mg): 6
Protein (gm): 1.6
Carbohydrate (gm): 14.9

Exchanges:
Milk: 0.0
Vegetable: 2.0
Fruit: 0.5
Bread: 0.0
Meat: 0.0
Fat: 0.0

2 teaspoons Asian sesame oil

⅓ cup golden raisins

⅓ cup reduced-sodium vegetable broth

2–3 tablespoons toasted pine nuts, or slivered almonds

Whole wheat lavosh, or crackers

1. Combine eggplant, onion, garlic, gingerroot, brown sugar, and fennel; toss with vinegar and oil and arrange in single layer on a greased, foil-lined jelly roll pan.

2. Bake at 425 degrees until eggplant is browned and wrinkled, about 1½ hours, stirring every 30 minutes. Stir raisins and broth into mixture; bake until broth is absorbed, 10 to 15 minutes. Stir in pine nuts and cool. Refrigerate overnight for flavors to blend. Serve with lavosh (not included in nutritional data).

CHUTNEY CHEESE SPREAD

L

45

❄

Enjoy these flavors inspired by India. Ginger contributes "heat" as well as flavor to the spread, so adjust according to your taste. Make Pita Chips with curry powder or ground cumin.

8 servings (about 2 tablespoons each)

1 package (8 ounces) fat-free cream cheese, softened

1 cup (4 ounces) shredded reduced-fat Cheddar cheese

½ cup chopped mango chutney, divided

¼ cup finely chopped onion

2 tablespoons raisins, chopped

1–2 teaspoons finely chopped gingerroot

1 clove garlic, minced

½–1 teaspoon curry powder

1–2 tablespoons chopped dry-roasted cashews

Thinly sliced green onion tops, as garnish

Pita Chips (see p. 46), or assorted vegetables

Per Serving:
Calories: 116
% of calories from fat: 21
Fat (gm): 2.6
Saturated fat (gm): 1.1
Cholesterol (mg): 7.6
Sodium (mg): 367
Protein (gm): 7.4
Carbohydrate (gm): 14.6

Exchanges:
Milk: 0.0
Vegetable: 0.0
Fruit: 1.0
Bread: 0.0
Meat: 0.5
Fat: 0.5

1. Mix cheeses, 2 tablespoons chutney, onion, raisins, gingerroot, garlic, and curry powder until blended (do not beat, or fat-free cream cheese will become thin in texture). Refrigerate 1 to 2 hours for flavors to blend.

2. Mound spread on plate; spoon remaining 6 tablespoons chutney over or around spread. Sprinkle with cashews and onion tops; serve with Pita Chips (pp. 46) (not included in nutritional data).

ROASTED GARLIC AND THREE-CHEESE SPREAD

L

For best flavor, make this dip a day in advance.

45
❄

12 servings (about 2 tablespoons each)

1 small bulb garlic
Olive oil cooking spray
1 package (8 ounces) fat-free cream cheese, softened
1½–2 ounces goat cheese
¼ cup (2 ounces) grated fat-free Parmesan cheese
⅛ teaspoon white pepper
2–4 tablespoons fat-free milk
Dippers: Vegetable relishes and assorted crackers

Per Serving:
Calories: 43
% of calories from fat: 28
Fat (gm): 1.3
Saturated fat (gm): 0.9
Cholesterol (mg): 3.8
Sodium (mg): 142
Protein (gm): 4.7
Carbohydrate (gm): 2.5

Exchanges:
Milk: 0.0
Vegetable: 0.0
Fruit: 0.0
Bread: 0.0
Meat: 0.5
Fat: 0.5

1. Cut off top of garlic bulb to expose cloves. Spray garlic lightly with cooking spray and wrap in aluminum foil; bake at 400 degrees until very tender, 35 to 40 minutes. Cool; gently press cloves to remove from skins. Mash cloves with fork.

2. Mix cheeses, garlic, and white pepper in bowl, adding enough milk to make desired spreading consistency. Refrigerate 2 to 3 hours for flavors to blend. Serve with dippers (not included in nutritional data).

PEPPER-ONION RELISH AND CREAM CHEESE

L *Pepper-Onion Relish can be made and refrigerated 4 to 5 days in advance.*

45 **6 servings**

1 cup each: thinly sliced red and yellow bell pepper, onion

2 teaspoons minced jalapeño chili

1½ tablespoons olive oil

¼ cup packed light brown sugar

¼ cup each: cider vinegar, water

1 package (8 ounces) fat-free cream cheese, room temperature

Dippers: Assorted crackers

Per Serving:
Calories: 129
% of Calories from fat: 27
Fat (gm): 4.1
Saturated fat (gm): 0.8
Cholesterol (mg): 3
Sodium (mg): 212
Protein (gm): 6.3
Carbohydrate (gm): 18

Exchanges:
Milk: 0.0
Vegetable: 0.0
Fruit: 0.0
Bread: 1.0
Meat: 0.0
Fat: 1.0

1. Sauté bell pepper, onion and jalapeño chili in oil in large skillet until softened, 6 to 8 minutes. Stir in brown sugar, vinegar, and water and simmer, covered, over medium heat until very tender, about 5 minutes. Simmer, uncovered, until mixture is glazed and thickened, about 5 minutes; cool. Place cream cheese on serving plate and spoon pepper mixture over. Serve with crackers (not included in nutritional data).

CRANBERRY-PISTACHIO CREAM CHEESE

L *Substitute dried cherries or blueberries for the cranberries, or combine all three!*

45

6 servings

¼ cup thinly sliced onion

⅓ cup each: dried cranberries, chopped pistachios, apricot preserves, orange juice

1 package (8 ounces) fat-free cream cheese, room temperature

Dippers: Crusty bread or assorted crackers

Per Serving:
Calories: 145
% of calories from fat: 22
Fat (gm): 3.6
Saturated fat (gm): 0.8
Cholesterol (mg): 3
Sodium (mg): 271
Protein (gm): 7.2
Carbohydrate (gm): 22

Exchanges:
Milk: 0.0
Vegetable: 0.0
Fruit: 0.0
Bread: 1.5
Meat: 0.0
Fat: 1.0

1. Sauté onion in lightly greased medium skillet until tender, 3 to 4 minutes. Add cranberries, pistachios, preserves, and orange juice; cook over medium heat until mixture is thickened, but spoonable. Cool. Place cream cheese on serving plate and spoon cranberry mixture over. Serve with bread or crackers.

Variation

Raisin-Marmalade Cream Cheese — Make recipe above, substituting green onion for the onion, and raisins, pecans and orange marmalade for the cranberries, pistachios, and apricot preserves.

SESAME WONTON CUPS

V

45

These delicious snacks can also be served as a novel accompaniment to soups.

8 servings (2 each)

24 wonton wrappers

2 teaspoons Asian sesame oil

1 cup thinly sliced napa cabbage

½ cup each: broccoli sprouts, thinly sliced snow peas, shredded carrots

1 green onion, thinly sliced

Sweet Sesame Dressing (recipe follows)

Wasabi peas and toasted hemp or sesame seeds, as garnish

Per Serving:
Calories: 125
% of calories from fat: 27
Fat (gm): 4
Saturated fat (gm): 0.6
Cholesterol (mg): 1.5
Sodium (mg): 116
Protein (gm): 2.5
Carbohydrate (gm): 21.6

Exchanges:
Milk: 0.0
Vegetable: 0.0
Fruit: 0.5
Bread: 1.0
Meat: 0.0
Fat: 0.5

1. Lightly brush edges of wonton wrappers with Asian sesame oil. Press wontons, oil side up, in miniature muffin cups to form shells, using every other cup in muffin tin so that edges do not touch. Bake at 350 degrees until lightly browned, 6 to 7 minutes. Cool on wire racks.

2. Combine cabbage, sprouts, snow peas, carrots, and green onion in bowl; pour Sweet Sesame Dressing over and toss. Spoon mixture into wonton cups and garnish each with 2 or 3 wasabi peas and a sprinkling of hemp seeds.

Sesame Dressing

Makes about ½ cup

1 tablespoon Asian sesame oil

2–3 tablespoons rice wine vinegar

⅓ cup apricot preserves

1 teaspoon each: soy sauce, minced gingerroot

2–3 teaspoons peanut butter

1. Mix all ingredients.

GOAT CHEESE QUESADILLAS WITH TROPICAL FRUIT SALSA

L

Goat cheese and tropical fruits combine for a new flavor in quesadillas.

45 **8 servings**

4 ounces fat-free cream cheese, softened

2 ounces goat cheese

½ small jalapeño chili, minced

½ teaspoon each: dried marjoram and thyme leaves

⅛ teaspoon white pepper

8 whole wheat, or white, flour tortillas (6-inch)

Butter-flavored cooking spray

Tropical Fruit Salsa (see p. 604)

Per Serving:
Calories: 186
% of calories from fat: 25
Fat (gm): 5.2
Saturated fat (gm): 2.2
Cholesterol (mg): 7.5
Sodium (mg): 285
Protein (gm): 8
Carbohydrate (gm): 26.3

Exchanges:
Milk: 0.0
Vegetable: 1.0
Fruit: 0.5
Bread: 1.0
Meat: 0.5
Fat: 0.5

1. Combine cream cheese, goat cheese, jalapeño chili, herbs, and white pepper; spread about 3 tablespoons mixture on each of 4 tortillas. Top with remaining tortillas.

2. Cook 1 quesadilla in lightly greased skillet on medium to medium-low heat until browned on the bottom, 2 to 3 minutes. Spray top of quesadilla with cooking spray; turn and cook until browned on the bottom. Repeat with remaining quesadillas. Cut quesadillas into wedges; serve warm with Tropical Fruit Salsa.

BLACK BEAN QUESADILLAS

L

Substitute pinto beans for the black beans if you like, and vary the amount of jalapeño chili to taste.

12 servings

1 cup cooked dried black beans, or canned black beans, rinsed, and drained
1 cup mild, or hot, chili salsa, divided
¼ cup thinly sliced green onions
3 tablespoons finely chopped cilantro
2–3 teaspoons minced jalapeño chili
12 whole wheat, or white, flour tortillas (6-inch)
¾ cup (3 ounces) each: shredded reduced-fat Monterey Jack cheese, fat-free Cheddar cheese
Butter-flavored cooking spray

Per Serving:
Calories: 169
% of calories from fat: 21
Fat (gm): 3.9
Saturated fat (gm): 1.2
Cholesterol (mg): 5.1
Sodium (mg): 427
Protein (gm): 9
Carbohydrate (gm): 24.2

Exchanges:
Milk: 0.0
Vegetable: 0.0
Fruit: 0.0
Bread: 1.5
Meat: 0.5
Fat: 0.5

1. Mash beans slightly; combine with ¼ cup salsa, green onions, cilantro, and chili. Divide mixture on 6 tortillas, spreading almost to edges. Sprinkle with cheeses and top with remaining tortillas.

2. Cook 1 quesadilla on medium to medium-low heat in lightly greased skillet until browned on the bottom, 2 to 3 minutes. Spray top of quesadilla with cooking spray; turn and cook until browned on the bottom. Repeat with remaining quesadillas. Cut quesadillas into wedges; serve warm with remaining ¾ cup salsa.

POBLANO QUESADILLAS

L

45

Vegetarian chorizo (see p. 287) would be a flavorful addition to these quesadillas.

6 servings

1 small poblano chili, or green bell pepper, sliced
1 medium onion, finely chopped
1 teaspoon ground cumin
3 tablespoons finely chopped cilantro
1 cup (4 ounces) shredded reduced-fat Cheddar cheese
6 flour tortillas (6-inch)
Vegetable cooking spray

¾ cup Red Tomato, or Tomatillo, Salsa (see pp. 8, 7)
6 tablespoons fat-free sour cream

Per Serving:
Calories: 235
% of calories from fat: 28.4%
Fat (gm): 7.7
Saturated fat (gm): 3
Cholesterol (mg): 15.8
Sodium (mg): 385
Protein (gm): 10.4
Carbohydrate (gm): 33

Exchanges:
Milk: 0.0
Vegetable: 0.5
Fruit: 0.0
Bread: 2.0
Meat: 1.0
Fat: 1.0

1. Sauté poblano chili, onion, and cumin in lightly greased skillet until vegetables are tender, 3 to 5 minutes; stir in cilantro.

2. Sprinkle cheese on half of each tortilla; spoon vegetable mixture over. Fold tortillas in half. Cook 2 quesadillas in lightly greased large skillet over medium to medium-high heat until browned on the bottoms, 2 to 3 minutes. Spray tops of quesadillas with cooking spray; turn and cook until browned on the other side. Repeat with remaining quesadillas. Cut into wedges and serve warm with Red Tomato Salsa and sour cream.

TORTILLA WEDGES

LO

Fun to make and eat — our Mexican-style version of pizza!

45

12 servings (2 each)

Vegetarian Chorizo (see p. 287)
½ cup each: chopped green bell pepper, onion
Pepper, to taste
4 large flour tortillas (10-inch)
1 cup (4 ounces) each: shredded reduced-fat
   Monterey Jack cheese, fat-free Cheddar cheese
1 cup Red Tomato Salsa (see p. 8), or prepared salsa
¾ cup fat-free sour cream

Per Serving:
Calories: 206
% of calories from fat: 16
Fat (gm): 3.6
Saturated fat (gm): 1.4
Cholesterol (mg): 42.3
Sodium (mg): 551
Protein (gm): 25.2
Carbohydrate (gm): 18.4

Exchanges:
Milk: 0.0
Vegetable: 0.5
Fruit: 0.0
Bread: 0.5
Meat: 3.0
Fat: 0.0

1. Make Vegetarian Chorizo, but do not form into patties. Sauté Vegetarian Chorizo in lightly greased skillet until brown, crumbling with fork; add green pepper and onion and cook until tender, 2 to 3 minutes. Season to taste with pepper.

2. Place tortillas on baking sheets; sprinkle evenly with Monterey Jack cheese. Sprinkle with Vegetarian Chorizo mixture, and top with Cheddar cheese. Bake at 450 degrees until edges of tortillas are browned and cheese is melted, 6 to 8 minutes. Top with Red Tomato Salsa and sour cream. Cut each tortilla into 6 wedges.

NACHOS

L

45

Your favorite Mexican appetizer, without the guilt. Cooked, crumbled Vegetarian Chorizo (see p. 287) can be added to make these nachos "grandes"!

6 servings

Baked tortilla chips

1 can (15½ ounces) pinto beans, rinsed, drained, coarsely mashed

1 cup prepared mild, or hot salsa, divided

¾ teaspoon each: chili powder, dried oregano leaves

2–3 cloves garlic, minced

Salt, to taste

½ cup (2 ounces) shredded reduced-fat Cheddar, or Monterey Jack, cheese

1 medium tomato, chopped

½ small avocado, chopped

2 green onions, sliced

6 pitted ripe olives, sliced (optional)

¼ cup fat-free sour cream

Per Serving:
Calories: 182
% of calories from fat: 24
Fat (gm): 5.2
Saturated fat (gm): 1.2
Cholesterol (mg): 6.3
Sodium (mg): 376
Protein (gm): 7.7
Carbohydrate (gm): 28.8

Exchanges:
Milk: 0.0;
Vegetable: 0.0;
Fruit: 0.0;
Bread: 2.0;
Meat: 0.0;
Fat: 1.0

1. Spread tortilla chips in a single layer in jelly roll pan. Mix beans, ¼ cup salsa, chili powder, oregano, and garlic; season to taste with salt. Spoon bean mixture over tortilla chips; sprinkle with cheese. Bake at 350 degrees until beans are hot and cheese melted, 5 to 10 minutes. Sprinkle with tomato, avocado, onions, and olives; garnish with dollops of sour cream. Serve with remaining ¾ cup salsa.

JICAMA WITH LIME AND CILANTRO

 Very simple, and incredibly tasty!

45 **4 servings**

1 medium jicama, peeled, thinly sliced
Salt and lime juice, to taste
1–2 tablespoons finely chopped cilantro

1. Arrange jicama slices on large serving plate and sprinkle lightly with salt, lime juice, and cilantro.

Per Serving:
Calories: 17
% of calories from fat: 2
Fat (gm): 0
Saturated fat (gm): 0
Cholesterol (mg): 0
Sodium (mg): 0
Protein (gm): 0.5
Carbohydrate (gm): 3.8

Exchanges:
Milk: 0.0
Vegetable: 1.0
Fruit: 0.0
Bread: 0.0
Meat: 0.0
Fat: 0.0

FRIED RIPE PLANTAINS

V *When ripe, the plantain skin is black and the fruit is soft. If purchasing plantains when green, they will ripen more quickly if kept in a closed paper bag.*

45

4 servings

Canola, or peanut, oil
2 ripe plantains, peeled, diagonally cut into
  ¼-inch slices
Salt, to taste

1. Heat 1½ to 2 inches of oil to 375 degrees in large saucepan. Fry plantains until golden on both sides; drain well on paper toweling. Sprinkle with salt and serve hot.

Per Serving:
Calories: 119
% of calories from fat: 10
Fat (gm): 1.5
Saturated fat (gm): 0.3
Cholesterol (mg): 0
Sodium (mg): 4
Protein (gm): 1.2
Carbohydrate (gm): 28.6

Exchanges:
Milk: 0.0
Vegetable: 0.0
Fruit: 2.0
Bread: 0.0
Meat: 0.0
Fat: 0.0

Variation

Sweet Plantains — Make recipe as above, but do not use salt. Sprinkle plantains with sugar and cinnamon.

FRUIT EMPANADAS

L

Sweet empanadas can be served as an appetizer or dessert. They can be prepared and frozen up to 2 months; thaw overnight in the refrigerator and bake according to the recipe.

2 dozen

½ cup each: chopped dried apricots, raisins

½ cup water

¼ cup sugar

½ teaspoon ground cinnamon

⅛ teaspoon ground nutmeg

Empanada Pastry (recipe follows)

3 tablespoons fat-free milk

1 tablespoon sugar, for glaze

Per Empanada:
Calories: 64
% of calories from fat: 23
Fat (gm): 1.7
Saturated fat (gm): 0.4
Cholesterol (mg): 0
Sodium (mg): 16
Protein (gm): 1
Carbohydrate (gm): 11.8

Exchanges:
Milk: 0.0
Vegetable: 0.0
Fruit: 1.0
Bread: 0.0
Meat: 0.0
Fat: 0.0

1. Heat apricots, raisins, and water to boiling in small saucepan. Reduce heat and simmer, covered, until fruit is very soft, about 5 minutes. Mash fruit with fork until almost smooth; stir in ¼ cup sugar and spices; cool.

2. Roll half the Empanada Pastry on lightly floured surface until ⅛ inch thick; cut into circles with 3-inch cookie cutter. Place slightly rounded teaspoon of fruit mixture in center of each pastry circle; fold pastries in half and crimp edges with tines of fork. Make slit in top of each pastry with knife.

3. Bake on greased jelly roll pans at 350 degrees until golden, 12 to 15 minutes. Brush tops of pastries with milk and sprinkle with sugar; return to oven until glazed, 2 to 3 minutes.

Empanada Pastry

1¼ cups all-purpose flour

1 tablespoon sugar

¼ teaspoon baking powder

⅛ teaspoon salt

3 tablespoons vegetable shortening

1 teaspoon lemon juice, or distilled white vinegar

3–4 tablespoons fat-free milk, or water

1. Combine flour, sugar, baking powder, and salt in small bowl; cut in shortening until mixture resembles coarse crumbs. Mix in combined lemon juice and milk, a tablespoon at a time, to form soft dough. Refrigerate until ready to use.

RICOTTA-STUFFED SHELLS WITH SPINACH PESTO

Spinach Pesto can be made up to 1 week in advance and refrigerated; serve at room temperature.

4 servings (3 each)

¼ cup finely chopped onion

2–3 cloves garlic, minced

½ teaspoon dried basil leaves

½ cup chopped fresh spinach

¾ cup low-fat ricotta cheese

¼ teaspoon each: ground nutmeg, salt, pepper

12 conchiglie (jumbo pasta shells), about 4 ounces, cooked

Spinach Pesto (recipe p. 605)

Per Serving:
Calories: 178
% of calories from fat: 24
Fat (gm): 4.7
Saturated fat (gm): 0.8
Cholesterol (mg): 7.2
Sodium (mg): 216
Protein (gm): 9.5
Carbohydrate (gm): 24.6

Exchanges:
Milk: 0.0
Vegetable: 1.0
Fruit: 0.0
Bread: 1.5
Meat: 0.5
Fat: 0.5

1. Sauté onion, garlic, and basil in lightly greased skillet until onions are tender, 3 to 4 minutes. Add spinach and cook over medium heat until wilted, about 5 minutes. Stir spinach mixture into cheese; stir in nutmeg, salt, and pepper. Stuff mixture into shells; place in baking pan. Bake, covered, at 350 degrees until hot through, about 20 minutes. Serve with Spinach Pesto.

45-MINUTE PREP TIP: Begin cooking the pasta shells before preparing the rest of the recipe.

CHEESE AND SPINACH STUFFED MUSHROOMS

L

45

Perfect party fare, with good-for-you mushrooms and spinach! Garnish the serving platter with curly endive.

12 servings (3 each)

36 medium cremini, or white, mushrooms
½ cup chopped onion
5 ounces baby spinach, thinly sliced
1 package (3 ounces) fat-free cream cheese,
    room temperature
⅛ teaspoon ground nutmeg
Salt and pepper, to taste

Per Serving:
Calories: 22
% of calories from fat: 7
Fat (gm): 0.2
Saturated fat (gm): 0.1
Cholesterol (mg): 0.6
Sodium (mg): 51
Protein (gm): 2.5
Carbohydrate (gm): 3.3

Exchanges:
Milk: 0.0
Vegetable: 1.0
Fruit: 0.0
Bread: 0.0
Meat: 0.0
Fat: 0.0

1. Remove stems from mushrooms and chop finely. Sauté mushroom stems and onion in lightly greased small skillet until softened, about 5 minutes. Add spinach and stir until wilted, 1 to 2 minutes. Cool; mix in cheese and nutmeg; season to taste with salt and pepper.

2. Place mushroom caps in baking pan and fill with cheese mixture. Bake, uncovered, at 425 degrees until hot through, 5 to 8 minutes.

Variation

Orzo Stuffed Mushrooms — Make recipe as above, using 2 ounces baby spinach, adding ¾ cup cooked orzo and substituting ¾ teaspoon dried Italian seasoning for the nutmeg. Bake as above, loosely covered with foil.

CURRIED ONION CROUSTADES

L

The Croustades can be filled with the onion mixture and refrigerated several hours before baking.

8 servings (2 each)

2 cups chopped onions
2 cloves garlic, minced
1 teaspoon curry powder
½ teaspoon ground cumin
2 tablespoons flour

1 cup fat-free half-and-half, or fat-free milk

2 tablespoons dried fruit bits

1 tablespoon minced cilantro

Salt, cayenne, and black pepper, to taste

Croustades (see p. 47)

4 teaspoons chopped almonds

Per Serving:
Calories: 125
% of calories from fat: 13
Fat (gm): 1.8
Saturated fat (gm): 0.3
Cholesterol (mg): 0
Sodium (mg): 167
Protein (gm): 4.2
Carbohydrate (gm): 22.3

Exchanges:
Milk: 0.0
Vegetable: 1.0
Fruit: 0.0
Bread: 1.0
Meat: 0.0
Fat: 0.5

1. Sauté onions and garlic in lightly greased skillet 5 minutes; add spices and cook, covered, over low heat until onions are very soft, about 20 minutes. Stir in flour; cook 1 minute longer. Stir half-and-half and fruit into onion mixture; heat to boiling. Reduce heat and simmer, stirring, until thickened. Stir in cilantro; season to taste with salt, cayenne, and black pepper.

2. Place Croustades in baking pan and fill each with slightly rounded tablespoon of onion mixture; sprinkle with almonds. Bake, uncovered, at 425 degrees 10 minutes.

ARTICHOKE-STUFFED APPETIZER BREAD

L

45

❄

For easy entertaining, assemble this appetizer a day or two in advance. Bread pieces removed from the loaf can be used to make fresh breadcrumbs or croutons.

8 servings (2 each)

1 package (8 ounces) fat-free cream cheese, softened

1 can (14 ounces) artichoke hearts, drained, chopped

½ cup each: chopped red bell pepper, celery

¼ cup chopped pitted green, or black, olives

2 teaspoons drained capers

1 clove garlic, minced

½ teaspoon each: dried basil and oregano leaves

1–2 teaspoons white wine vinegar, or lemon juice

Salt and white pepper, to taste

1 loaf French bread (8 ounces, about 15 inches long)

Per Serving:
Calories: 151
% of calories from fat: 29
Fat (gm): 5.1
Saturated fat (gm): 0.3
Cholesterol (mg): 0
Sodium (mg): 600
Protein (gm): 6.9
Carbohydrate (gm): 20.9

Exchanges:
Milk: 0.0
Vegetable: 1.0
Fruit: 0.0
Bread: 1.0
Meat: 0.0
Fat: 1.0

1. Mix softened cream cheese, artichoke hearts, bell pepper, celery, olives, capers, garlic, and herbs; season to taste with vinegar, salt, and white pepper.

2. Slice bread lengthwise in half. Remove bread from centers of bread halves, using a paring knife or serrated grapefruit spoon, leaving ¾-inch shell of bread. Spoon filling into each bread half; press halves together firmly and wrap in plastic wrap. Refrigerate 2 hours or until serving time. Cut into 16 pieces.

CURRIED PINWHEELS

LO

45

❄

Make these easy appetizers up to 2 days in advance and refrigerate until ready to serve.

3 dozen

6 pieces luncheon-size lavosh (5-inch)

1½ packages (8 ounces each) fat-free cream cheese, softened

2 tablespoons fat-free mayonnaise

1–2 teaspoons spicy brown mustard

1 clove garlic, minced

1–1½ teaspoons curry powder

½ cup finely chopped cored apple

¼ cup each: finely chopped celery, green onions, dry-roasted peanuts

¾ cup chopped chutney

Per Pinwheel:
Calories: 38
% of calories from fat: 14
Fat (gm): 0.6
Saturated fat (gm): 0.1
Cholesterol (mg): 0
Sodium (mg): 79
Protein (gm): 1.9
Carbohydrate (gm): 6.2

Exchanges:
Milk: 0.0
Vegetable: 0.0
Fruit: 0.5
Bread: 0.0
Meat: 0.0
Fat: 0.0

1. Brush lavosh lightly with water and place between damp kitchen towels until softened enough to roll, 20 to 30 minutes.

2. Mix cream cheese, mayonnaise, mustard, garlic, and curry powder in bowl; spread about 3 tablespoons mixture on each lavosh. Combine remaining ingredients, except chutney, and sprinkle over cheese mixture. Roll lavosh tightly; wrap each roll in plastic wrap and refrigerate at least 4 hours. Cut each roll into 6 pieces; serve with chutney.

MUSHROOM BRUSCHETTA

L

45

Use any desired wild mushrooms and make this filling up to 2 days in advance. Heat briefly before assembling and broiling the bruschetta.

6 servings (2 each)

¼ cup each: chopped red, yellow bell pepper

2 green onions, thinly sliced

2 cloves garlic, minced

2 cups chopped wild mushrooms (portobello, shiitake, oyster, enoki, etc.)

1 teaspoon dried basil leaves

¼ teaspoon dried thyme leaves

2 tablespoons grated fat-free Parmesan cheese

Few drops balsamic vinegar

Salt and pepper, to taste

Bruschetta (see p. 46)

¼ cup (2 ounces) shredded reduced-fat mozzarella cheese

Per Serving:
Calories: 184
% of calories from fat: 17
Fat (gm): 3.4
Saturated fat (gm): 1.3
Cholesterol (mg): 5.1
Sodium (mg): 388
Protein (gm): 8.8
Carbohydrate (gm): 29.5

Exchanges:
Milk: 0.0
Vegetable: 0.5
Fruit: 0.0
Bread: 2.0
Meat: 0.5
Fat: 0.0

1. Sauté bell peppers, onions, and garlic 2 to 3 minutes in lightly greased skillet. Add mushrooms and cook, covered, over medium heat until wilted, about 5 minutes. Stir in herbs and cook until mushrooms are tender and all liquid is gone, 8 to 10 minutes. Stir in Parmesan cheese; season to taste with balsamic vinegar, salt, and pepper.

2. Spoon mushroom mixture on Bruschetta and sprinkle with mozzarella cheese; broil 6 inches from heat source until cheese is melted, 1 to 2 minutes. Serve warm.

SPINACH AND CHEESE MINI-QUICHES

LO

45

The tiny fillo shells, delicious and wonderfully crisp, are available in the frozen food section of supermarkets. You can also make small pastries in mini-muffin cups using a favorite pie pastry.

1½ dozen

1¼ cups fat-free cottage cheese

¼ cup grated fat-free Parmesan cheese

2 tablespoons each: fat-free milk, flour

½ cup finely chopped fresh spinach

½ teaspoon dried oregano leaves

¼ teaspoon dried thyme leaves

Salt and white pepper, to taste

2 eggs

1½ dozen frozen mini-fillo shells, thawed

Per Mini-Quiche:
Calories: 48
% of calories from fat: 30
Fat (gm): 1.6
Saturated fat (gm): 0.2
Cholesterol (mg): 23.7
Sodium (mg): 61
Protein (gm): 3.9
Carbohydrate (gm): 4.3

Exchanges:
Milk: 0.0
Vegetable: 0.0
Fruit: 0.0
Bread: 0.5
Meat: 0.0
Fat: 0.5

1. Mix cheeses, flour, spinach, oregano, and thyme; season to taste with salt and pepper. Stir in eggs. Spoon mixture into fillo shells on cookie sheet or in mini-muffin tins. Bake at 325 degrees until puffed and beginning to brown on the tops, about 20 minutes.

CHEESE AND SPINACH SQUARES

LO

45

Lots of cheese and spinach in these terrific appetizer squares! For variation, substitute fat-free Swiss or mozzarella cheese for the Cheddar.

12 servings (2 each)

Vegetable cooking spray

1–2 tablespoons unseasoned dry bread crumbs

2 cups fat-free cottage cheese

1½ cups (6 ounces) shredded fat-free Cheddar cheese

2 eggs

6 tablespoons whole wheat flour

1 package (10 ounces) frozen, chopped spinach, thawed, well drained

Per Serving:
Calories: 81
% of calories from fat: 11
Fat (gm): 1
Saturated fat (gm): 0.3
Cholesterol (mg): 35.5
Sodium (mg): 231
Protein (gm): 11.8
Carbohydrate (gm): 6.7

Exchanges:
Milk: 0.0
Vegetable: 1.0
Fruit: 0.0
Bread: 0.0
Meat: 1.0
Fat: 0.0

¼ cup each: thinly sliced green onions, chopped roasted red bell pepper or pimiento, finely chopped parsley

¼ teaspoon each: black pepper, cayenne pepper

⅛ teaspoon ground nutmeg

1. Spray 13 x 9-inch pan with cooking spray; coat bottom and sides of pan with bread crumbs. Combine cheeses and eggs in bowl; stir in remaining ingredients until blended. Pour into prepared pan and bake at 350 degrees until set and lightly browned, 35 to 40 minutes. Cool 10 minutes before cutting into squares.

BAKED SPINACH BALLS

LO

Often laden with butter, these savory treats are rich in flavor.

45

12 servings (2 each)

2 cups herb-seasoned bread stuffing cubes

¼ cup each: grated fat-free Parmesan cheese, chopped green onions

2 cloves garlic, minced

⅛ teaspoon ground nutmeg

1 package (10 ounces) frozen chopped spinach, thawed, well drained

¼–⅓ cup reduced-sodium vegetable broth

2 tablespoons margarine, or butter, melted

Salt and pepper, to taste

2 egg whites, lightly beaten

Mustard Sauce (see p. 612)

Per Serving:
Calories: 86
% of calories from fat: 24
Fat (gm): 2.4
Saturated fat (gm): 0.4
Cholesterol (mg): 0
Sodium (mg): 271
Protein (gm): 4.2
Carbohydrate (gm): 13

Exchanges:
Milk: 0.0
Vegetable: 1.0
Fruit: 0.0
Bread: 0.5
Meat: 0.0
Fat: 0.5

1. Combine stuffing cubes, Parmesan cheese, onions, garlic, and nutmeg in medium bowl. Mix in spinach, broth, and margarine; season to taste with salt and pepper. Mix in egg whites.

2. Shape mixture into 24 balls. Bake at 350 degrees on greased jelly roll pan until spinach balls are browned, about 15 minutes. Serve with Mustard Sauce.

WASABI POTATO SLICES

L

45
❄️

If you prefer, use 12 tiny red potatoes for this recipe, cutting them into halves and scooping a small amount of potato from the center of each half.

12 servings (2 each)

4 small red potatoes, cooked, chilled
Butter-flavor cooking spray
Salt and pepper, to taste
½ cup fat-free sour cream
½ teaspoon wasabi paste
Thinly sliced green onion tops, chopped hard-cooked
egg, as garnish

Per Serving:
Calories: 37
% of calories from fat: 1.3
Fat (gm): .1
Saturated fat (gm): 0
Cholesterol (mg): 1.7
Sodium (mg): 10.6
Protein (gm): 1.4
Carbohydrate (gm): 7.7

Exchanges:
Milk: 0.0
Vegetable: 0.0
Fruit: 0.0
Bread: 0.5
Meat: 0.0
Fat: 0.0

1. Cut each potato into 3 scant ½-inch slices, reserving ends for another use; scoop small amount of potato from center of each with melon baller. Spray tops of slices with cooking spray and sprinkle with salt and pepper; broil 4 inches from heat source in baking pan until lightly browned, 3 to 4 minutes. Cool.

2. Mix sour cream and wasabi paste; spoon into centers of potato slices and sprinkle with green onions and egg.

FIVE-SPICE POTSTICKERS

o

Purchased wonton wrappers make this recipe simple to prepare. Wonton wrappers can be cut into circles with a 2½-inch cutter, if you like. Assemble wontons up to 1 day in advance; dust lightly with flour and refrigerate, covered, in a single layer on a plate.

12 servings (4 each)

2 cups sliced Chinese, or napa, cabbage
½ cup shredded carrot
¼ cup each: thinly sliced green onions, celery
1–2 teaspoons minced gingerroot
1 clove garlic, minced
1 tablespoon reduced-sodium tamari soy sauce
¼–½ teaspoon each: hot chili paste, five-spice powder

Per Serving:
Calories: 130
% of calories from fat: 4
Fat (gm): 0.6
Saturated fat (gm): 0.1
Cholesterol (mg): 4
Sodium (mg): 431
Protein (gm): 5.2
Carbohydrate (gm): 25.9

Exchanges:
Milk: 0.0
Vegetable: 2.0
Fruit: 0.0
Bread: 1.0
Meat: 0.0
Fat: 0.0

2 ounces light tofu, cut into small cubes or coarsely crumbled

48 wonton, or gyoza, wrappers

1 egg white, beaten

Plum Sauce, and/or Tamari Dipping Sauce (see pp. 612, 613)

1. Stir-fry cabbage, carrot, green onions, celery, gingerroot, and garlic in lightly greased wok or large skillet over medium to medium-high heat until cabbage is wilted, 2 to 3 minutes. Remove from heat; stir in soy sauce, chili paste, and five-spice powder. Add tofu, toss lightly, and cool.

2. Spoon ½ tablespoon filling on wonton wrapper; brush edges of wrapper with egg white. Fold wrapper in half and press edges to seal. Repeat with remaining filling, wrappers, and egg white. Add 6 or 8 wontons to large saucepan of boiling water; simmer, uncovered, until wontons rise to the surface, 2 to 3 minutes. Remove with slotted spoon and drain. Repeat with remaining wontons.

3. Add single layer of wontons to lightly greased wok or large skillet and cook over medium heat until browned on the bottom, 2 to 3 minutes. Spray tops of wontons lightly with cooking spray; turn and cook until browned. Repeat with remaining wontons. Serve hot with Plum Sauce and/or Tamari Dipping Sauce.

CRANBERRY-CHEESE WONTONS

LO

Dried cranberries and gingerroot add a lively accent to these unusual cheese wontons. When fried at the correct temperature, deep-fried foods absorb almost no fat.

6 servings (4 each)

¾ package (8-ounce size) fat-free cream cheese

3 tablespoons chopped dried cranberries

2 tablespoons finely chopped chives

½–¾ teaspoon minced gingerroot

1 tablespoon minced parsley

Salt and white pepper, to taste

24 wonton wrappers

1 egg white, beaten

Canola, or peanut, oil, for frying

⅓ cup jalapeño jelly, heated, or Tamari Dipping Sauce (see p. 613)

Per Serving:
Calories: 182
% of calories from fat: 10
Fat (gm): 1.9
Saturated fat (gm): 0.3
Cholesterol (mg): 4
Sodium (mg): 368
Protein (gm): 7.9
Carbohydrate (gm): 31.6

Exchanges:
Milk: 0.0
Vegetable: 0.0
Fruit: 1.0
Bread: 1.0
Meat: 1.0
Fat: 0.0

1. Mix cream cheese, cranberries, chives, gingerroot, and parsley in small bowl; season to taste with salt and white pepper. Spoon ½ tablespoon filling on wonton wrapper; brush edges of wrapper with egg white. Fold wrapper in half and press edges to seal. Repeat with remaining filling, wrappers, and egg white.

2. Heat 2 inches of oil to 375 degrees in large saucepan. Fry wontons, 6 to 8 at a time, until golden, 1 to 2 minutes. Drain on paper toweling. Serve hot with jalapeño jelly or Tamari Dipping Sauce.

MIXED VEGETABLE EGG ROLLS

o *The Asian sesame oil in this recipe has a more distinctive sesame flavor than the light-colored domestic brands. Nutritious spinach, alfalfa sprouts, and black beans add a new dimension to these egg rolls.*

1 dozen

1 tablespoon sesame seeds

2–3 teaspoons Asian sesame oil

2 green onions, sliced

1 tablespoon minced gingerroot

2 cloves garlic, minced

2 cups sliced spinach

½ cup each: chopped water chestnuts, shredded carrot, sliced small mushrooms

1 can (15½ ounces) black beans, rinsed, drained

1–1½ teaspoons reduced-sodium tamari, or soy sauce

Salt and pepper, to taste

2 egg whites

1 cup alfalfa sprouts

12 egg roll wrappers

Peanut, or vegetable, oil

Plum Sauce, and/or Tamari Dipping Sauce (see pp. 612, 613)

Per Egg Roll:
Calories: 101
% of calories from fat: 12
Fat (gm): 1.6
Saturated fat (gm): 0.2
Cholesterol (mg): 0
Sodium (mg): 342
Protein (gm): 5.8
Carbohydrate (gm): 19

Exchanges:
Milk: 0.0
Vegetable: 1.5
Fruit: 0.0
Bread: 1.0
Meat: 0.0
Fat: 0.0

1. Sauté sesame seeds in Asian sesame oil in large skillet until beginning to brown, 1 to 2 minutes. Add green onions, gingerroot, and garlic; sauté until onions are tender, 1 to 2 minutes. Add spinach, water chestnuts, carrot, and mushrooms; cook, covered, over medium heat until spinach and mushrooms are wilted. Stir in beans and tamari sauce; season to taste with salt and pepper. Cool 5 to 10 minutes; stir in egg whites and alfalfa sprouts.

2. Spoon about ⅓ cup vegetable mixture near corner of 1 egg roll wrapper. Brush edges of wrapper with water. Fold bottom corner of egg roll wrapper up over filling; fold sides in and roll up. Repeat with remaining filling and wrappers.

3. Heat about 2 inches of oil to 375 degrees in deep skillet or large saucepan. Fry egg rolls until golden, 4 to 5 minutes. Drain on paper toweling. Serve hot with Plum Sauce and/or Tamari Dipping Sauce.

INDONESIAN-STYLE TOFU SATAY

V *Enjoy the lower fat benefits of light tofu in this many-flavored dish.*

8 servings

1 package (16 ounces) light extra-firm tofu

¼ cup reduced-sodium soy sauce, reduced-fat peanut butter, honey, lemon juice, and bead, or unsulphured, molasses

2 tablespoons finely chopped gingerroot

1 finely chopped serrano, or jalapeño, chili

3 cloves garlic, minced

2 teaspoons chili powder

1 tablespoon dark Asian sesame oil

3 tablespoons thinly sliced green onions

Per Serving:
Calories: 157
% of calories from fat: 28
Fat (gm): 5.2
Saturated fat (gm): 1
Cholesterol (mg): 0.0
Sodium (mg): 429
Protein (gm): 6.7
Carbohydrate (gm): 23

Exchanges:
Milk: 0.0
Vegetable: 0.0
Fruit: 0.0
Bread: 1.5
Meat: 0.0
Fat: 1.0

1. Press the tofu (see p. xi) to remove excess moisture. Cut tofu into ¾-inch cubes and arrange on 6 skewers. Place in single layer in baking dish. Process remaining ingredients, except green onions, in food processor or blender until smooth. Pour over tofu kabobs and refrigerate, covered, 1 hour; drain, reserving marinade.

2. Bake tofu kabobs at 400 degrees for 20 minutes. Mix green onions into reserved marinade and serve with kabobs.

TORTELLINI KABOBS WITH MANY-CLOVES GARLIC SAUCE

O

45

A fun party food, but also a great idea for a casual meal. Serve 4 skewers each for an entrée, and accompany with broiled tomato halves, a crisp green salad, and Garlic Bread (see p. 559).

8 servings (2 each)

1½ packages (9-ounces size) mushroom tortellini, cooked
5 cups each: assorted whole, cubed, and sliced vegetables (mushroom caps, cherry tomatoes, bell peppers, zucchini, broccoli florets, artichoke hearts, etc.)
Olive oil cooking spray
Many-Cloves Garlic Sauce (see p. 591)

Per Serving:
Calories: 146
% of calories from fat: 26
Fat (gm): 5
Saturated fat (gm): 1.8
Cholesterol (mg): 25.3
Sodium (mg): 171
Protein (gm): 7.4
Carbohydrate (gm): 23.3

Exchanges:
Milk: 0.0
Vegetable: 2.0
Fruit: 0.0
Bread: 1.0
Meat: 0.0
Fat: 0.5

1. Alternate tortellini and vegetables on 16 long skewers and arrange on broiler pan. Spray generously with cooking spray and broil 6 inches from heat source 4 minutes; turn kabobs, spray with cooking spray, and broil 3 to 4 minutes longer.

2. Make Many-Cloves Garlic Sauce using only 1 tablespoon olive oil; serve with kabobs.

NOTE: Partially cook firm vegetables such as broccoli, carrots, and zucchini until crisp-tender before using.

APPLE-CABBAGE STRUDELS

V

45

The strudels can be assembled several hours in advance; refrigerate, tightly covered. Spray tops of strudels generously with cooking spray before baking.

12 servings (2 each)

½ cup thinly sliced onion

2 cloves garlic, minced

3 cups thinly sliced cabbage

13 cup apple cider, or apple juice

1½ cups peeled, chopped, tart apples

¼ cup dark raisins

1–1½ teaspoons curry powder

Salt and pepper, to taste

8 sheets frozen fillo pastry, thawed

Butter-flavored cooking spray

Per Serving:
Calories: 34
% of calories from fat: 5
Fat (gm): 0.2
Saturated fat (gm): 0
Cholesterol (mg): 0
Sodium (mg): 8
Protein (gm): 0.6
Carbohydrate (gm): 8.5

Exchanges:
Milk: 0.0
Vegetable: 0.0
Fruit: 0.5
Bread: 0.0
Meat: 0.0
Fat: 0.0

1. Sauté onion and garlic in lightly greased skillet until tender, about 5 minutes. Add cabbage and apple cider; cook, covered, over medium heat until cabbage is wilted, about 5 minutes. Stir in apples, raisins, and curry powder; cook, uncovered, until apples are crisp-tender and mixture is almost dry, 5 to 8 minutes. Season to taste with salt and pepper. Cool.

2. Place 1 sheet fillo on clean surface; spray with lightly with butter-flavored cooking spray; top with second sheet of fillo and spray. Repeat with 3 more sheets of fillo. Spoon half the cabbage mixture evenly along short edge of fillo, leaving a 1-inch space from the edge. Roll up from short edge, tucking ends under. Place seam side down on greased cookie sheet. Repeat with remaining fillo, cooking spray, and cabbage mixture. Spray tops of strudels with cooking spray. Bake at 400 degrees until golden, about 15 minutes. Cool slightly; cut diagonally into 1-inch pieces with serrated knife. Serve warm or at room temperature.

ONION AND BLUE CHEESE FOCACCIA

L

Serve larger portions as a bread with entrée salads.

45

8 servings

2 cups thinly sliced onions
4 cloves garlic, minced
½ teaspoon dried rosemary leaves
Salt and pepper, to taste
1 focaccia (Italian flat bread, 10 ounces)
¼ cup chopped sun-dried tomatoes (not in oil)
2–3 ounces crumbled blue cheese
2 tablespoons grated fat-free Parmesan cheese

Per Serving:
Calories: 146
% of calories from fat: 21
Fat (gm): 3.5
Saturated fat (gm): 1.6
Cholesterol (mg): 5.2
Sodium (mg): 354
Protein (gm): 5.9
Carbohydrate (gm): 23.3

Exchanges:
Milk: 0.0
Vegetable: 2.0
Fruit: 0.0
Bread: 1.0
Meat: 0.0
Fat: 0.5

1. Cook onions and garlic in lightly greased skillet, covered, over medium heat until wilted. Cook, uncovered, over low heat until tender and lightly browned; stir in rosemary and season with salt and pepper. Arrange onions on bread; sprinkle with sun-dried tomatoes and cheeses. Bake at 350 degrees until bread is hot and cheese melted, about 15 minutes. Cut into 8 wedges.

CALZONES

L

These Italian-style pies filled with cheese and vegetables can also be served for a lunch or supper. A packaged mix makes a quick and easy dough.

16 servings

1 cup each: chopped zucchini, sliced mushrooms
½ cup each: chopped onion, green bell pepper
1 can (14½ ounces) diced tomatoes with roasted garlic, undrained
2 teaspoons Italian seasoning
1 cup fat-free ricotta cheese
2 cups (8 ounces) shredded reduced-fat mozzarella cheese
Salt and pepper, to taste
1 package (16 ounces) hot roll mix

Per Serving:
Calories: 185
% of calories from fat: 28
Fat (gm): 5.8
Saturated fat (gm): 1.6
Cholesterol (mg): 7.6
Sodium (mg): 379
Protein (gm): 9.4
Carbohydrate (gm): 23.6

Exchanges:
Milk: 0.0
Vegetable: 1.5
Fruit: 0.0
Bread: 1.0
Meat: 1.0
Fat: 0.5

1¼ cups hot water
1 tablespoon olive oil
Fat-free milk

1. Sauté zucchini, mushrooms, onion, and bell pepper in lightly greased skillet 5 minutes. Add tomatoes with liquid and Italian seasoning; simmer until vegetables are tender and excess liquid is gone, about 10 minutes. Cool slightly; stir in cheeses and season to taste with salt and pepper.

2. Make hot roll mix according to package directions, using hot water and oil. Divide dough into 8 parts; roll each into a 7-inch circle. Place about ½ cup vegetable mixture on each; fold in half and seal edges with tines of fork. Brush tops of pastries with fat-free milk. Bake on cookie sheet at 350 degrees until browned, about 15 minutes. Cut each calzone in half and arrange on serving platter. Serve warm.

EASY HERB LAVOSH

V

Quick, easy, delicious, and versatile!

45

◊

6 servings

1 Whole Wheat Lavosh (see p. 556), or purchased lavosh
Vegetable, or olive oil, cooking spray
½–¾ teaspoon caraway seeds, or other desired herbs

Per Serving:
Calories: 132
% of calories from fat: 3
Fat (gm): 0.6
Saturated fat (gm): 0.1
Cholesterol (mg): 0
Sodium (mg): 1
Protein (gm): 5
Carbohydrate (gm): 29.9

Exchanges:
Milk: 0.0
Vegetable: 0.0
Fruit: 0.0
Bread: 2.0
Meat: 0.0
Fat: 0.0

1. Spray top of lavosh lightly with cooking spray and sprinkle with herbs. Bake on a cookie sheet or piece of aluminum foil at 350 degrees until browned, 4 to 6 minutes (watch carefully as lavosh can burn easily).

NOTE: Use any herb you want, such as Italian seasoning, bouquet garni, creole seasoning, or a mix of herbs. Fat-free grated Parmesan cheese can be sprinkled over the lavosh, too.

PITA CHIPS

V

Perfect to serve with any dip, or to eat as a snack.

45

6 to 8 servings (6 to 8 each)

3 whole wheat pocket breads
Butter-flavored, or olive oil, cooking spray
3–4 teaspoons Italian seasoning, or other
  desired herbs

1. Open breads and separate each into 2 halves.
Stack halves and cut into 8 wedges. Arrange
wedges, soft sides up, in single layer on jelly
roll pan. Spray with cooking spray and sprinkle
with Italian seasoning. Bake at 425 degrees
until browned and crisp, 5 to 10 minutes.

Per Serving:
Calories: 86
% of calories from fat: 8
Fat (gm): 0.9
Saturated fat (gm): 0.1
Cholesterol (mg): 0
Sodium (mg): 171
Protein (gm): 3.2
Carbohydrate (gm): 17.7

Exchanges:
Milk: 0.0
Vegetable: 0.0
Fruit: 0.0
Bread: 1.0
Meat: 0.0
Fat: 0.0

Variation

Seasoned Pita Chips — 1 to 2 teaspoons chili powder, ground
cumin, or garlic powder; or 2 to 3 tablespoons grated fat-free
Parmesan cheese can be substituted for the Italian seasoning.

BRUSCHETTA

V

*These simple-to-make Italian garlic toasts are perfect for serving with any
kind of savory appetizer spread.*

45

12 servings (2 each)

1 loaf French bread (8 ounces, about 15 inches long)
Olive oil cooking spray
2 cloves garlic, cut into halves

1. Cut bread into 24 slices; spray both sides of
bread lightly with cooking spray. Broil on cookie
sheet 4 inches from heat source until browned,
2 to 3 minutes on each side. Rub top sides of
bread slices with cut sides of garlic.

Per Serving:
Calories: 53
% of calories from fat: 10
Fat (gm): 0.6
Saturated fat (gm): 0.1
Cholesterol (mg): 0.0
Sodium (mg): 115
Protein (gm): 1.7
Carbohydrate (gm): 10

Exchanges:
Milk: 0.0
Vegetable: 0.0
Fruit: 0.0
Bread: 0.5
Meat: 0.0
Fat: 0.0

NOTE: If desired, bread slices can be sprinkled with herbs, such as basil, oregano, or Italian seasoning, before broiling. Bread can also be sprinkled lightly with grated fat-free Parmesan cheese before broiling; watch carefully so cheese does not burn.

CROUSTADES

V

45

These crisp toast cups can be filled with just about any hot or cold, sweet or savory filling. Bake the Croustades up to a week in advance and store in an airtight container.

8 servings (2 each)

16 slices soft bread
Butter-flavored cooking spray

1. Cut 2½-inch rounds out of bread slices with cookie cutter (remaining bread can be used for croutons or soft or dry breadcrumbs).

2. Spray 16 mini-muffin tins with cooking spray; press 1 bread round firmly into each. Spray bread generously with cooking spray. Bake at 350 degrees until browned and crisp, 10 to 12 minutes.

Per Serving:
Calories: 67
% of calories from fat: 12
Fat (gm): 0.9
Saturated fat (gm): 0.2
Cholesterol (mg): 0
Sodium (mg): 135
Protein (gm): 2.1
Carbohydrate (gm): 12.4

Exchanges:
Milk: 0.0
Vegetable: 0.0
Fruit: 0.0
Bread: 1.0
Meat: 0.0
Fat: 0.0

TOFRUITY

V

45

A great sipping snack, or double the portion for a light, yet nutritious, meal on the go!

4 servings (about 1 cup each)

½ package (14-ounce size) light silken tofu, drained

1 cup cubed mango, or papaya

1 cup frozen, or fresh, raspberries, or strawberries

1½ cups orange juice

Honey, to taste

Per Serving:
Calories: 75
% of calories from fat: 8.6
Fat (gm): 0.8
Saturated fat (gm): 0.1
Cholesterol (mg): 0
Sodium (mg): 43.6
Protein (gm): 3.9
Carbohydrate (gm): 14.5

Exchanges:
Milk: 0.0
Vegetable: 0.0
Fruit: 1.0
Bread: 0.0
Meat: 0.5
Fat: 0.0

1. Process all ingredients, except honey, in blender or food processor until smooth, adding enough orange juice to make desired consistency; sweeten to taste with honey.

VERY BERRY SMOOTHIE

V

45

Perfect for a light meal or substantial snack when you need a pick-me-up. Nutrition-packed beans are a valuable source of protein and folate, and banana is a good source of potassium.

6 servings (about 1 cup each)

1½–2 cups orange juice

1 can (15 ounces) Great Northern, or navy, beans, rinsed, drained

1 cup frozen or fresh, hulled strawberries, and blueberries

1 small banana

1½ teaspoons ground cinnamon

⅛ teaspoon ground nutmeg

6–8 ice cubes

Honey, to taste

Per Serving:
Calories: 149
% of calories from fat: 3.7
Fat (gm): 0.7
Saturated fat (gm): 0.1
Cholesterol (mg): 0
Sodium (mg): 4.3
Protein (gm): 6.2
Carbohydrate (gm): 31.6

Exchanges:
Milk: 0.0
Vegetable: 0.0
Fruit: 1.0
Bread: 1.0
Meat: 0.5
Fat: 0.0

1. Process all ingredients, except ice cubes and honey, in blender or food processor until smooth. Add ice and blend until smooth; sweeten to taste with honey.

POMEGRANATE PASSION

V

45

Heart healthy pomegranate juice is an excellent source of antioxidants. Add a scoop or two of protein powder for a protein boost, if you like.

4 servings (about 1 cup each)

1 cup pomegranate juice
½ cup orange juice
1½ cups halved strawberries
1 large banana, sliced
Honey, to taste

Per Serving:
Calories: 95
% of calories from fat: 3
Fat (gm): 0.3
Saturated fat (gm): 0.1
Cholesterol (mg): 0.0
Sodium (mg): 3.6
Protein (gm): 1
Carbohydrate (gm): 23.4

Exchanges:
Milk: 0.0
Vegetable: 0.0
Fruit: 1.5
Bread: 0.0
Meat: 0.0
Fat: 0.0

1. Process pomegranate and orange juice, strawberries, and banana in blender or food processor until smooth; sweeten to taste with honey.

Variation

Blueberry Breeze — Make recipe as above, substituting blueberries for the strawberries and apple cider for the orange juice.

CANTALOUPE COOLER

V

45

Any ripe, flavorful melon can be used in this recipe.

4 servings (about 1 cup each)

1 quart peeled, seeded, cubed, ripe cantaloupe
½ cup orange juice
3–4 tablespoons lemon, or lime, juice
¼–½ cup fat-free milk
Honey, to taste

Per Serving:
Calories: 108
% of calories from fat: 3
Fat (gm): 0.4
Saturated fat (gm): 0.1
Cholesterol (mg): 0.3
Sodium (mg): 33
Protein (gm): 2.2
Carbohydrate (gm): 26.7

Exchanges:
Milk: 0.0;
Vegetable: 0.0
Fruit: 2.0
Bread: 0.0
Meat: 0.0
Fat: 0.0

1. Process cantaloupe, orange, and lemon juice, and milk in blender or food processor until smooth; sweeten to taste with honey.

TWO

Soups

BASIC VEGETABLE STOCK

V *As vegetables used in stocks are later discarded, they should be scrubbed but do not need to be peeled. This stock can be used in any of the soup recipes. Stocks can be refrigerated 3 to 4 days, or frozen up to 6 months.*

Makes about 2 quarts

1 large onion, coarsely chopped

1 each: thickly sliced leek, carrot, rib celery (1-inch)

½ teaspoon canola oil

8 cups water

1 cup dry white wine (optional)

4 cups mixed chopped vegetables (broccoli, green beans, cabbage, potatoes, tomatoes, summer, or winter squash, bell peppers, mushrooms, etc.)

6–8 parsley sprigs

1 bay leaf

4 whole allspice

1 tablespoon black peppercorns

2 teaspoons dried bouquet garni

Salt and pepper, to taste

Per Cup:
Calories: 12
% of calories from fat: 29
Fat (gm): 0.4
Saturated fat (gm): 0
Cholesterol (mg): 0
Sodium (mg): 12
Protein (gm): 0.4
Carbohydrate (gm): 1.8

Exchanges:
Milk: 0.0
Vegetable: 0.0
Fruit: 0.0
Bread: 0.0
Meat: 0.0
Fat: 0.0

1. Sauté onion, leek, carrot, and celery in oil in stock pot or large Dutch oven 5 minutes. Add water, wine, and chopped vegetables; add herbs, tied in cheesecloth bag. Heat to boiling; reduce heat and simmer, covered, 1½ to 2 hours. Strain stock, pressing lightly on vegetables to extract all juices; discard solids. Season to taste with salt and pepper.

ROASTED VEGETABLE STOCK

V *Roasting vegetables intensifies their flavors, adding richness to stock. The beet adds a subtle sweetness to the stock, but use only if you don't object to the pink color it creates!*

Makes about 2 quarts

1 each: coarsely chopped onion, garlic bulb, leek, carrot, zucchini, turnip, beet, tomato

½ small butternut, *or* acorn, squash, cut into 2-inch pieces

8 cups water

1 cup dry white wine, or water

3 cups coarsely chopped kale, or Swiss chard

6 sprigs parsley

1 bay leaf

1–2 teaspoons dried bouquet garni

1 teaspoon black peppercorns

4 whole allspice

Salt and pepper, to taste

Per Cup:
Calories: 25
% of calories from fat: 1
Fat (gm): 0
Saturated fat (gm): 0
Cholesterol (mg): 0
Sodium (mg): 12
Protein (gm): 0.2
Carbohydrate (gm): 1.5

Exchanges:
Milk: 0.0
Vegetable: 0.0
Fruit: 0.0
Bread: 0.0
Meat: 0.0
Fat: 0.0

1. Arrange onion, garlic, leek, carrot, tomato, zucchini, turnip, beet, and squash on greased, foil-lined pan; bake at 425 degrees until tender and browned, 35 to 40 minutes. Combine vegetables and all remaining ingredients, except salt and pepper, in stock pot or large Dutch oven; heat to boiling. Reduce heat and simmer, covered, 1½ to 2 hours. Strain, pressing lightly on vegetables to extract all juices; discard solids. Season to taste with salt and pepper.

MEDITERRANEAN STOCK

V *A lovely stock, scented with orange, fennel, and saffron.*

Makes about 2 quarts

1 each: thickly sliced large onion, leek, large carrot, sweet potato, zucchini, rib celery (1-inch)

½ each: sliced small fennel bulb, red bell pepper

2 teaspoons olive oil

8 cups water

Juice of 1 orange

1 cup dry white wine, or water

2 medium tomatoes, quartered

1 medium bulb garlic, cut crosswise in half

3 cups coarsely chopped spinach, or romaine lettuce

6 sprigs parsley

1 each: strip orange zest (3 x 1 inch), bay leaf

1–2 teaspoons bouquet garni

1 teaspoon black peppercorns

4 whole allspice

Pinch saffron

Salt and pepper, to taste

Per Cup:
Calories: 43
% of calories from fat: 24
Fat (gm): 1.2
Saturated fat (gm): 0.2
Cholesterol (mg): 0
Sodium (mg): 15
Protein (gm): 0.5
Carbohydrate (gm): 3.3

Exchanges:
Milk: 0.0
Vegetable: 0.5
Fruit: 0.0
Bread: 0.0
Meat: 0.0
Fat: 0.5

1. Sauté onion, leek, carrot, sweet potato, zucchini, celery, fennel, and bell pepper in oil in stock pot or large Dutch oven 8 to 10 minutes. Add remaining ingredients, except salt and pepper, and heat to boiling. Reduce heat and simmer, covered, 1½ to 2 hours. Strain, pressing lightly on vegetables to extract all juices; discard solids. Season to taste with salt and pepper.

RICH MUSHROOM STOCK

V *Dried shiitake mushrooms, also known as Chinese black mushrooms, add richness and depth of flavor to this stock.*

Makes about 2 quarts

1 each: sliced large onion, leek, rib celery

12 ounces cremini, or white, mushrooms

1 tablespoon minced garlic

1 teaspoon olive oil

7 cups water

¾ cup dry white wine, or water

1½–2 ounces dried shiitake mushrooms

6 sprigs parsley

¾ teaspoon each: dried sage and thyme leaves

1½ teaspoons black peppercorns

Salt and pepper, to taste

Per Cup:
Calories: 27
% of calories from fat: 22
Fat (gm): 0.7
Saturated fat (gm): 0.1
Cholesterol (mg): 0
Sodium (mg): 9
Protein (gm): 0.4
Carbohydrate (gm): 1.6

Exchanges:
Milk: 0.0
Vegetable: 0.0
Fruit: 0.0
Bread: 0.0
Meat: 0.0
Fat: 0.0

1. Sauté onion, leek, celery, cremini mushrooms, and garlic in oil in small stock pot or large Dutch oven 5 minutes. Add remaining ingredients, except salt and pepper, and heat to boiling; reduce heat and simmer, covered, 1½ hours. Strain, pressing lightly on vegetables to extract all juices; discard solids. Season to taste with salt and pepper.

ORIENTAL STOCK

V *A light, fragrant stock that can be used in Asian soups and entrées.*

Makes about 2 quarts

8 cups water

6 cups shredded bok choy, or Chinese cabbage

1¼ cups loosely packed cilantro, coarsely chopped

1 each: sliced large onion, carrot, small red bell
  pepper

⅓ cup sliced gingerroot

1 tablespoon minced garlic

3 dried shiitake mushrooms

4 teaspoons reduced-sodium tamari soy sauce

2 star anise

2 teaspoons five-spice powder

1½ teaspoons toasted Szechuan peppercorns

Salt and pepper, to taste

Per Cup:
Calories: 8
% of calories from fat: 11
Fat (gm): 0.1
Saturated fat (gm): 0
Cholesterol (mg): 0
Sodium (mg): 110
Protein (gm): 0.6
Carbohydrate (gm): 1.1

Exchanges:
Milk: 0.0
Vegetable: 0.0
Fruit: 0.0
Bread: 0.0
Meat: 0.0
Fat: 0.0

1. Combine all ingredients, except salt and pepper, in small stock pot or large Dutch oven; heat to boiling. Reduce heat and simmer, covered, 1 hour. Strain, pressing lightly on vegetables to extract all juices; discard solids. Season to taste with salt and pepper. Refrigerate or freeze.

CANNED VEGETABLE STOCK

V

45

A quick and easy solution for stock when you haven't the time or inclination to start from scratch.

Makes about 1½ quarts

1 each: coarsely chopped medium onion, tomato, carrot, rib celery

4 teaspoons minced garlic

1 teaspoon olive oil

2 cans (14½ ounces each) reduced-sodium vegetable broth

2 cups water

1 cup dry white wine, or water

4 sprigs parsley

2 bay leaves

Pepper, to taste

Per Cup:
Calories: 62
% of calories from fat: 11
Fat (gm): 0.8
Saturated fat (gm): 0.1
Cholesterol (mg): 0
Sodium (mg): 55
Protein (gm): 0.8
Carbohydrate (gm): 6.7

Exchanges:
Milk: 0.0
Vegetable: 1.0
Fruit: 0.0
Bread: 0.0
Meat: 0.0
Fat: 0.0

1. Sauté onion, tomato, carrot, celery, and garlic in oil in Dutch oven 5 minutes. Add broth and remaining ingredients, except pepper, and heat to boiling. Reduce heat and simmer, covered, 30 minutes. Strain, pressing lightly on vegetables to extract all juices; discard solids. Season with pepper.

VERY BERRY SOUP

L

45

A garden of berries in a bowl of soup! When fresh berries are out of season, frozen unsweetened berries can be substituted.

4 first-course servings (about 1 cup each)

1½ cups each: raspberries, quartered strawberries, water

¾ cup dry red wine, or cranberry juice

3–4 tablespoons sugar

½ cup fat-free half-and-half, or fat-free milk

4 tablespoons fat-free sour cream

¼ cup blueberries

Mint sprigs, as garnish

Per Serving:
Calories: 141
% of calories from fat: 3
Fat (gm): 0.5
Saturated fat (gm): 0
Cholesterol (mg): 0
Sodium (mg): 69
Protein (gm): 2.9
Carbohydrate (gm): 25.1

Exchanges:
Milk: 0.0
Vegetable: 0.0
Fruit: 2.0
Bread: 0.0
Meat: 0.0
Fat: 0.0

1. Heat raspberries, strawberries, water, wine, and sugar to boiling in large saucepan. Reduce heat and simmer, covered, until berries are tender, 5 to 8 minutes.

2. Process soup in food processor or blender until smooth. Strain mixture, discarding seeds. Mix in half-and-half; refrigerate until chilled. Top bowls of soup with a tablespoon each sour cream and blueberries; garnish with mint.

SWEET CHERRY SOUP

L

45

Serve as a first course — or a dessert! For year-round enjoyment, frozen cherries can be substituted for the fresh.

4 first-course servings (about 1 cup each)

1½ pounds dark sweet cherries, pitted

3–4 tablespoons sugar

3 cups plus 3 tablespoons water, divided

12 whole cloves

1 large cinnamon stick, broken into pieces

1½ tablespoons cornstarch

Ground nutmeg, as garnish

4 tablespoons fat-free sour cream

Per Serving:
Calories: 179
% of calories from fat: 8
Fat (gm): 1.6
Saturated fat (gm): 0.4
Cholesterol (mg): 0
Sodium (mg): 10
Protein (gm): 3
Carbohydrate (gm): 41.9

Exchanges:
Milk: 0.0
Vegetable: 0.0
Fruit: 3.0
Bread: 0.0
Meat: 0.0
Fat: 0.0

1. Combine cherries, sugar, and 3 cups water in medium saucepan; add spices, tied in cheesecloth bag. Heat to boiling; reduce heat and simmer, covered, until cherries are tender, 15 to 20 minutes. Remove and discard spices.

2. Process soup in food processor or blender until smooth. Strain, discarding cherry skins.

3. Return soup to saucepan and heat to boiling. Mix cornstarch and remaining 3 tablespoons water; whisk into boiling soup. Boil, whisking constantly, until thickened, about 1 minute; cool. Serve chilled; sprinkle each bowl of soup with nutmeg and top with a tablespoon of sour cream.

DILLED BEET SOUP

V   *It's not necessary to peel beets, as the skins slip off easily after cooking.*

8 first-course servings (about 1¼ cups each)

12 medium beets, tops trimmed, scrubbed (about 3 pounds)
3 cups water
2–3 vegetable bouillon cubes
Water
¾–1 cup dry red wine, or vegetable broth
1½–2 teaspoons dried dill weed
2–3 tablespoons red wine vinegar
Salt and pepper, to taste
Thin lemon slices, as garnish

Per Serving:
Calories: 63
% of calories from fat: 3
Fat (gm): 0.3
Saturated fat (gm): 0
Cholesterol (mg): 0
Sodium (mg): 318
Protein (gm): 1.8
Carbohydrate (gm): 10.6

Exchanges:
Milk: 0.0
Vegetable: 2.0
Fruit: 0.0
Bread: 0.0
Meat: 0.0
Fat: 0.0

1. Heat beets, 3 cups water, and bouillon cubes to boiling in large saucepan; reduce heat and simmer, covered, until beets are tender, 30 to 40 minutes. Drain, reserving cooking liquid. Slip skins off beets and cut into quarters.

2. Add enough water to reserved cooking liquid to make 6 cups. Process beets, wine, reserved cooking liquid, and dill weed in food processor or blender container until smooth. Season to taste with vinegar, salt, and pepper. Serve warm or chilled; garnish each bowl of soup with a lemon slice.

BEET BORSCHT

L *Several brands of soy-based vegetarian sausages are available, replacing the traditional Polish sausage often used in borscht.*

8 first-course servings (about 1¼ cups each)

4 medium beets, peeled, julienned

½–1 tablespoon margarine, or butter

6 cups Basic Vegetable Stock (see p. 52)

1 small head red cabbage, thinly sliced, or shredded

2 carrots, julienned

1 clove garlic, minced

1 bay leaf

2–3 teaspoons sugar

2 tablespoons cider vinegar

8 ounces vegetarian sausage links

Salt and pepper, to taste

Chopped dill weed, as garnish

Per Serving:
Calories: 104
% of calories from fat: 30
Fat (gm): 3.7
Saturated fat (gm): 0.6
Cholesterol (mg): 0
Sodium (mg): 230
Protein (gm): 6.2
Carbohydrate (gm): 12.9

Exchanges:
Milk: 0.0
Vegetable: 2.0
Fruit: 0.0
Bread: 0.0
Meat: 1.0
Fat: 0.0

1. Sauté beets in margarine in Dutch oven 3 to 4 minutes. Add stock, cabbage, carrots, garlic, bay leaf, sugar, and vinegar; heat to boiling. Reduce heat and simmer, covered, until vegetables are tender, 20 to 30 minutes.

2. Cook sausage links in lightly greased skillet over medium heat until browned on all sides, about 5 minutes. Cut links into 1-inch pieces and stir into soup; cook 5 minutes. Season to taste with salt and pepper; sprinkle each bowl of soup with dill weed.

CREAM OF BROCCOLI SOUP

L

Eat broccoli often — it's high in antioxidants and packed with nutrients. This soup can be served warm, or chilled.

6 first-course servings (about 1 cup each)

1 cup chopped onions

3 cloves garlic, minced

2 pounds broccoli, stalks peeled, cut into 2-inch pieces

½ teaspoon dried thyme leaves

⅛ teaspoon ground nutmeg

3½ cups Basic Vegetable Stock (see p. 52)

½ cup fat-free half-and-half, or fat-free milk

Salt and white pepper, to taste

6 tablespoons fat-free sour cream

1½ cups Croutons (½ recipe, see p. 560)

Per Serving:
Calories: 99
% of calories from fat: 9
Fat (gm): 1.1
Saturated fat (gm): 0.2
Cholesterol (mg): 0
Sodium (mg): 110
Protein (gm): 6.8
Carbohydrate (gm): 17.6

Exchanges:
Milk: 0.0
Vegetable: 2.0
Fruit: 0.0
Bread: 0.5
Meat: 0.0
Fat: 0.0

1. Sauté onions and garlic in lightly greased saucepan until tender, 3 to 5 minutes. Stir in broccoli, thyme, and nutmeg; cook 2 minutes longer. Add stock to saucepan and heat to boiling; reduce heat and simmer, covered, until broccoli is tender, about 10 minutes. Stir in half-and-half.

2. Process soup in food processor or blender until smooth; season to taste with salt and white pepper. Stir 1 tablespoon sour cream into each bowl of soup; sprinkle with Croutons.

Variations

Dilled Broccoli Soup — Make recipe as above, deleting thyme, nutmeg, and Croutons. Add ⅔ cup loosely packed fresh dill weed to soup when pureeing.

Broccoli-Kale Soup — Make recipe as above, increasing stock to 5 cups, adding ½ teaspoon dried marjoram leaves and deleting the half-and-half, Croutons, and nutmeg. Stir 2 cups lightly packed kale into the soup during the last 5 minutes of cooking time. Process as above, adding more stock as needed for desired consistency.

HERBED BROCCOLI AND PASTA SOUP

V

A versatile soup, as any vegetable in season and any choice of herb can be substituted for the broccoli and thyme.

4 entree servings (about 1½ cups each)

5½ cups Canned Vegetable Stock (see p. 56), or reduced-sodium vegetable broth

4 cloves garlic, minced

2 teaspoons dried thyme leaves

3 cups small broccoli florets

1 cup uncooked fusilli (spirals)

2–3 tablespoons lemon juice

¼ teaspoon salt

⅛ teaspoon pepper

Per Serving:
Calories: 151
% of calories from fat: 7.8
Fat (gm): 1.3
Saturated fat (gm): 0.1
Cholesterol (mg): 0.0
Sodium (mg): 801
Protein (gm): 6.4
Carbohydrate (gm): 29

Exchanges:
Milk: 0.0
Vegetable: 3.0
Fruit: 0.0
Bread: 1.0
Meat: 0.0
Fat: 0.0

1. Heat stock, garlic, and thyme to boiling in medium saucepan. Stir in broccoli and fusilli. Reduce heat and simmer, uncovered, until broccoli is tender and pasta is *al dente*, about 10 minutes. Season to taste with lemon juice, salt, and pepper.

FOUR-BEAN AND VEGETABLE SOUP

V *Any kind of dried beans can be used in the soup, or use prepackaged mixed dried beans.*

12 entree servings (about 1½ cups each)

8 ounces each: dried black, navy, pinto, and garbanzo beans

Water

2 cups chopped green bell pepper

1 cup chopped onion

6–8 cloves garlic, minced

2 tablespoons olive oil

6 cups Roasted Vegetable Stock (see p. 53)

2–3 teaspoons dried thyme leaves

3 bay leaves

2 cans (16 ounces each) reduced-sodium diced tomatoes, undrained

2 cups each: sliced carrots, cut green beans

Salt, cayenne, and black pepper, to taste

Per Serving:
Calories: 342
% of calories from fat: 11
Fat (gm): 4.3
Saturated fat (gm): 0.5
Cholesterol (mg): 0
Sodium (mg): 35
Protein (gm): 18.1
Carbohydrate (gm): 58.5

Exchanges:
Milk: 0.0
Vegetable: 3.0
Fruit: 0.0
Bread: 3.0
Meat: 1.0
Fat: 0.0

1. Cover dried beans with water in large saucepan; heat to boiling. Remove pan from heat; let stand 1 hour. Drain.

2. Sauté bell pepper, onion, and garlic in oil in Dutch oven until tender, 4 to 5 minutes. Add beans, stock, and herbs and heat to boiling; reduce heat and simmer, covered, until beans are tender, adding water if necessary, 1 to 1½ hours. Add tomatoes with liquid, carrots, and green beans during last 15 to 20 minutes of cooking time. Discard bay leaves; season to taste with salt, cayenne, and black pepper.

NAVY BEAN SOUP

V *A quick-soak method is used for the beans. If you prefer soaking the beans overnight, delete step 1 and proceed with step 2 in the recipe.*

6 entree servings (about 1¾ cups each)

8 ounces dried navy, or Great Northern, beans

Water

⅔ cup each: chopped onion, carrot, celery

2 cloves garlic, minced

1 tablespoon canola oil

1 tablespoon flour

4 cups Canned Vegetable Stock (see p. 56), or
    reduced-sodium vegetable broth

1 cup water

¼ teaspoon dried thyme leaves

1 bay leaf

Salt and pepper, to taste

Per Serving:
Calories: 312
% of calories from fat: 14
Fat (gm): 5.1
Saturated fat (gm): 0.8
Cholesterol (mg): 0
Sodium (mg): 79
Protein (gm): 14.3
Carbohydrate (gm): 47.8

Exchanges:
Milk: 0.0
Vegetable: 1.0
Fruit: 0.0
Bread: 3.0
Meat: 1.0
Fat: 0.5

1. Cover beans with 2 inches of water in large saucepan; heat to boiling and boil, uncovered, 2 minutes. Remove from heat and let stand, covered, 1 hour; drain.

2. Sauté onion, carrot, celery, and garlic in oil in large saucepan until vegetables are tender, 5 to 8 minutes. Stir in flour; cook over medium heat 1 minute. Add beans, stock, water, and herbs to saucepan; heat to boiling. Reduce heat and simmer, covered, until beans are tender, 1¼ to 1½ hours. Discard bay leaf; season to taste with salt and pepper.

WHITE BEAN AND SWEET POTATO SOUP WITH CRANBERRY COULIS

V *A most pleasing combination of colors and flavors!*

45 **6 entree servings** (about 1¼ cups each)

1 cup chopped onion
1 pound sweet potatoes, peeled, cubed
1 large tart cooking apple, peeled, cored, chopped
1½ teaspoons minced gingerroot
2 cans (15 ounces each) navy, or Great Northern
   beans, rinsed, drained
3 cups reduced-sodium vegetable broth
½ teaspoon dried marjoram leaves
Salt, cayenne, and white pepper, to taste
Cranberry Coulis (see p. 610)

Per Serving:
Calories: 310
% of calories from fat: 3
Fat (gm): 1.2
Saturated fat (gm): 0.3
Cholesterol (mg): 0
Sodium (mg): 650
Protein (gm): 12.6
Carbohydrate (gm): 64.6

Exchanges:
Milk: 0.0
Vegetable: 1.0
Fruit: 1.0
Bread: 3.0
Meat: 0.0
Fat: 0.0

1. Sauté onion, sweet potatoes, apple, and gingerroot in lightly greased large saucepan 5 minutes. Add beans, broth, and marjoram and heat to boiling; reduce heat and simmer, covered, until vegetables are tender, 10 to 15 minutes.

2. Process soup in food processor or blender until smooth; season to taste with salt, cayenne, and white pepper. Swirl 2 tablespoons Cranberry Coulis into each bowl of soup.

BEAN-THICKENED SOUP

V *Pureed beans contribute a hearty texture and subtle flavor to this soup.*

4 first-course servings (about 1⅓ cups each)

2 carrots, sliced
1 small onion, chopped
2 large cloves garlic, minced
1¾ cups Basic Vegetable Stock (see p. 52)
1 can (16 ounces) whole tomatoes, undrained, coarsely chopped
1 can (15 ounces) Great Northern beans, rinsed, drained, pureed
½ teaspoon each: dried thyme and sage leaves
Salt and pepper, to taste

1. Sauté carrots, onion, and garlic in lightly greased large saucepan until onion is tender, about 5 minutes. Stir in stock, tomatoes with liquid, pureed beans, and herbs. Heat to boiling; reduce heat and simmer, covered, until carrots are tender, about 10 minutes. Season to taste with salt and pepper.

Per Serving:
Calories: 176
% of calories from fat: 5
Fat (gm): 1
Saturated fat (gm): 0.2
Cholesterol (mg): 0
Sodium (mg): 208
Protein (gm): 9.8
Carbohydrate (gm): 34

Exchanges:
Milk: 0.0
Vegetable: 2.0
Fruit: 0.0
Bread: 1.5
Meat: 0.5
Fat: 0.0

TUSCAN BEAN SOUP

V

45

The Mediterranean Stock adds great flavor to this soup, but canned reduced-sodium vegetable broth can be used as well.

8 entree servings (about 1½ cups each)

1 cup chopped onion
½ cup each: chopped celery, green bell pepper
2 teaspoons minced roasted garlic
2 tablespoons olive oil
1 tablespoon flour
1½ teaspoons dried Italian seasoning
2 bay leaves
7 cups reduced-sodium vegetable broth
2 cans (15 ounces each) cannellini, or Great Northern, beans, rinsed, drained
2 tablespoons reduced-sodium tomato paste
½ cup quick-cooking barley
1 large Idaho potato, unpeeled, cut into ½-inch pieces
1 cup sliced carrots
1 cup packed baby spinach leaves
Salt and pepper, to taste

Per Serving:
Calories: 233
% of calories from fat: 18
Fat (gm): 5.6
Saturated fat (gm): 0.7
Cholesterol (mg): 0
Sodium (mg): 245
Protein (gm): 10.7
Carbohydrate (gm): 40.8

Exchanges:
Milk: 0.0
Vegetable: 2.0
Fruit: 0.0
Bread: 2.0
Meat: 0.0
Fat: 1.0

1. Sauté onion, celery, bell pepper, and garlic in oil in Dutch oven until tender, about 5 minutes. Add flour and herbs; cook 1 minute longer. Add broth, beans, and tomato paste and heat to boiling;

reduce heat and simmer, uncovered, 20 to 25 minutes, adding barley, potatoes, carrots, and spinach during last 10 minutes of cooking time. Discard bay leaves. Season to taste with salt and pepper.

BLACK BEAN SOUP WITH SUN-DRIED TOMATOES AND CILANTRO CREAM

L *Cilantro Cream adds a fresh accent to this south-of-the-border favorite.*

4 entree servings (about 1½ cups)

1 cup chopped onion
2 cloves garlic, minced
1 jalapeño chili, minced
3 cups Basic Vegetable Stock (see p. 52)
3 cups cooked dried black beans, or 2 cans
  (15 ounces each) black beans, rinsed, drained
¾ cup sun-dried tomatoes (not in oil)
¾ teaspoon ground cumin, dried oregano leaves
¼–½ teaspoon hot pepper sauce
Salt and pepper, to taste
¼ cup chopped cilantro
Cilantro Cream (recipe follows)

Per Serving:
Calories: 239
% of calories from fat: 5
Fat (gm): 1.5
Saturated fat (gm): 0.3
Cholesterol (mg): 0
Sodium (mg): 256
Protein (gm): 15.2
Carbohydrate (gm): 44.0

Exchanges:
Milk: 0.0
Vegetable: 1.0
Fruit: 0.0
Bread: 3.0
Meat: 0.0
Fat: 0.0

1. Sauté onion, garlic, and jalapeño chili in lightly greased large saucepan until tender, 5 to 8 minutes. Add stock, beans, sun-dried tomatoes, cumin, and oregano to saucepan; heat to boiling. Reduce heat and simmer, covered, 10 minutes.

2. Process soup in food processor or blender until smooth. Season to taste with hot pepper sauce, salt, and pepper; stir in cilantro. Garnish each bowl of soup with dollops of Cilantro Cream.

Cilantro Cream

Makes about ⅓ cup

⅓ cup fat-free sour cream
2 tablespoons minced cilantro
1 teaspoon lemon, or lime, juice
¾ teaspoon ground coriander
2–3 dashes white pepper

1. Combine all ingredients.

CLASSIC BLACK BEAN SOUP

L

The "quick" method of cooking dried beans saves time. Substitute 3 cans (15 ounces each) rinsed, drained black beans for the dried, if you prefer.

4 entree servings (about 1¼ cups each)

1½ cups dried black beans
1 large onion, chopped
4 cloves garlic, minced
1 tomato, chopped
1 teaspoon dried oregano leaves
½ teaspoon dried thyme leaves
Salt and pepper, to taste
4–6 tablespoons fat-free sour cream

Per Serving:
Calories: 289
% of calories from fat: 4
Fat (gm): 1.3
Saturated fat (gm): 0.3
Cholesterol (mg): 0
Sodium (mg): 23
Protein (gm): 18.1
Carbohydrate (gm): 53.7

Exchanges:
Milk: 0.0
Vegetable: 1.0
Fruit: 0.0
Bread: 3.0
Meat: 1.0
Fat: 0.0

1. Cover beans with 2 inches of water in large saucepan; heat to boiling and boil, uncovered, 2 minutes. Remove from heat and let stand, covered, 1 hour; drain.

2. Sauté onion and garlic 2 to 3 minutes in lightly greased large saucepan; add tomato and herbs and cook 2 to 3 minutes longer. Add beans, cover with 2 inches of water and heat to boiling. Reduce heat and simmer, covered, until beans are very tender, 1½ to 2 hours, adding water to cover beans if necessary.

3. Process soup in food processor or blender until smooth; season to taste with salt and pepper. Top each bowl of soup with a dollop of sour cream.

GARBANZO BEAN SOUP

L

Cumin adds a Mexican flavor to this soup; curry powder can be substituted to give an Indian flavor.

4 entree servings (about 1⅓ cups each)

2 medium onions, chopped

2 cloves garlic, minced

4 cups Basic Vegetable Stock (see p. 52)

2 cans (15 ½ ounces each) garbanzo beans, rinsed, drained

1 teaspoon ground cumin

½–¾ teaspoon dried thyme leaves

Salt and pepper, to taste

¼ cup fat-free sour cream

Paprika, or chili powder, as garnish

Per Serving:
Calories: 267
% of calories from fat: 15
Fat (gm): 4.6
Saturated fat (gm): 0.6
Cholesterol (mg): 0
Sodium (mg): 627
Protein (gm): 12.4
Carbohydrate (gm): 46.4

Exchanges:
Milk: 0.0
Vegetable: 1.0
Fruit: 0.0
Bread: 3.0
Meat: 0.0
Fat: 0.0

1. Sauté onions and garlic in lightly greased large saucepan until tender, about 5 minutes. Add stock, beans, cumin, and thyme and heat to boiling; reduce heat and simmer, covered, 10 minutes.

2. Process soup in food processor or blender until smooth; season to taste with salt and pepper. Top each bowl of soup with a dollop of sour cream and sprinkle with paprika.

RUSSIAN CABBAGE SOUP

L

Use red or green cabbage, fresh or canned beets in this savory soup.

8 first-course servings (about 1½ cups each)

2 medium onions, sliced

1 tablespoon margarine, or butter

7 cups Basic Vegetable Stock (see p. 52)

1 can (16 ounces) reduced-sodium whole tomatoes, undrained, coarsely chopped

6 cups thinly sliced red cabbage

4 large beets, peeled, cubed

1 cup each: sliced carrots, cubed turnip, potato

Per Serving:
Calories: 109
% of calories from fat: 17
Fat (gm): 2.2
Saturated fat (gm): 0.4
Cholesterol (mg): 0
Sodium (mg): 91
Protein (gm): 4
Carbohydrate (gm): 20.7

Exchanges:
Milk: 0.0
Vegetable: 3.0
Fruit: 0.0
Bread: 0.5
Meat: 0.0
Fat: 0.0

1 tablespoon cider vinegar

Salt and pepper, to taste

8 tablespoons fat-free sour cream

1. Sauté onions in margarine in Dutch oven until tender, about
5 minutes. Add stock, vegetables, and vinegar; heat to boiling.
Reduce heat and simmer, uncovered, 20 to 30 minutes; season to
taste with salt and pepper. Top each bowl of soup with a tablespoon
of sour cream.

DILLED CARROT SOUP

*Carrots team with dill for a fresh, clean flavor. Use canned reduced-sodium
vegetable broth, if you like.*

6 first-course servings (about 1½ cups each)

1½ cups chopped onions

2 cloves garlic, minced

6 cups Basic Vegetable Stock (see p. 52)

1 can (16 ounces) reduced-sodium diced
   tomatoes, undrained

2 pounds carrots, cut into 2-inch pieces

1 medium Idaho potato, peeled, cubed

2–3 tablespoons lemon juice

1–1½ teaspoons dried dill weed

Salt and white pepper, to taste

6 tablespoons fat-free plain yogurt

Shredded carrot, as garnish

Dill sprigs, as garnish

Per Serving:
Calories: 139
% of calories from fat: 6
Fat (gm): 1
Saturated fat (gm): 0.1
Cholesterol (mg): 0.3
Sodium (mg): 88
Protein (gm): 4.4
Carbohydrate (gm): 30.5

Exchanges:
Milk: 0.0
Vegetable: 6.0
Fruit: 0.0
Bread: 0.0
Meat: 0.0
Fat: 0.0

1. Sauté onions and garlic in lightly greased saucepan until tender,
about 5 minutes. Add stock, tomatoes and liquid, carrots, and
potato; heat to boiling. Reduce heat and simmer, covered, until
vegetables are tender, about 15 minutes.

2. Process soup in food processor or blender until smooth. Add
lemon juice and dill weed; season to taste with salt and white
pepper. Serve soup warm, or chilled. Top each bowl of soup with a
tablespoon of yogurt; garnish with shredded carrot and dill sprigs.

GINGER SPICED-ORANGE CARROT SOUP

V

This fragrant soup is scented with sweet spices, gingerroot, and orange.

45 **6 first-course servings** (about 1 cup each)

½ cup chopped onion

2 cloves garlic, minced

1 tablespoon margarine

1 tablespoon flour

1 cup reduced-sodium vegetable broth

1½ pounds carrots, sliced

2 teaspoons finely chopped gingerroot

¼ teaspoon ground cinnamon

1½–2 cups orange juice

Salt and pepper, to taste

Grated orange zest, as garnish

Per Serving:
Calories: 109
% of calories from fat: 19
Fat (gm): 2.4
Saturated fat (gm): 0.4
Cholesterol (mg): 0.0
Sodium (mg): 178
Protein (gm): 2
Carbohydrate (gm): 21

Exchanges:
Milk: 0.0
Vegetable: 0.0
Fruit: 0.0
Bread: 1.0
Meat: 0.0
Fat: 0.5

1. Sauté onion and garlic in margarine in large saucepan until tender, 3 to 4 minutes. Stir in flour; cook 1 minute longer. Add remaining ingredients, except orange juice, salt and pepper, and orange zest; heat to boiling. Reduce heat and simmer, covered, until carrots are tender, about 15 minutes.

2. Process soup and orange juice in blender or food processor until smooth. Season to taste with salt and pepper; garnish each bowl of soup with orange zest.

CREAM OF CAULIFLOWER SOUP WITH CHEESE

L

Fat-free half-and-half adds a rich creaminess to the soup.

6 first-course servings (about 1 cup each)

½ cup chopped onion

2 cloves garlic, minced

2 tablespoons flour

3½ cups Basic Vegetable Stock (see p. 52)

12 ounces cauliflower, cut into florets

1 large Idaho potato, peeled, cubed

¼–½ cup fat-free half-and-half, or fat-free milk

¾ cup (3 ounces) reduced-fat Cheddar cheese

Salt and white pepper, to taste

Ground mace, or nutmeg, as garnish

Per Serving:
Calories: 98
% of calories from fat: 22
Fat (gm): 2.4
Saturated fat (gm): 1.1
Cholesterol (mg): 7.6
Sodium (mg): 214
Protein (gm): 5.5
Carbohydrate (gm): 13.6

Exchanges:
Milk: 0.0
Vegetable: 1.0
Fruit: 0.0
Bread: 0.5
Meat: 0.5
Fat: 0.0

1. Sauté onion and garlic in lightly greased saucepan until tender, about 10 minutes. Stir in flour; cook about 1 minute longer. Add stock, cauliflower, and potato and heat to boiling; reduce heat and simmer, covered, until vegetables are tender, 10 to 15 minutes. Remove about half the vegetables from the soup with a slotted spoon and reserve. Puree remaining soup in food processor or blender until smooth.

2. Return soup to saucepan; stir in reserved vegetables, half-and-half, and cheese. Cook over low heat, stirring, until cheese is melted, 3 to 4 minutes. Season to taste with salt and white pepper; sprinkle each bowl of soup with mace.

HERBED CUCUMBER SOUP

L

This soup is very delicate in flavor. Use a serrated grapefruit spoon to seed cucumbers quickly and easily.

6 first-course servings (about 1⅓ cups each)

½ cup chopped onion

6 medium cucumbers (about 3 pounds), peeled, seeded, chopped

3 tablespoons flour

4 cups Basic Vegetable Stock (see p. 52), or reduced-sodium vegetable broth

1 teaspoon dried mint, or dill weed

½ cup fat-free half-and-half, or fat-free milk

Salt and white pepper, to taste

Paprika, and thin slices cucumber, as garnish

Per Serving:
Calories: 70
% of calories from fat: 8
Fat (gm): 0.6
Saturated fat (gm): 0.1
Cholesterol (mg): 0
Sodium (mg): 33
Protein (gm): 3.1
Carbohydrate (gm): 13.7

Exchanges:
Milk: 0.0
Vegetable: 1.0
Fruit: 0.0
Bread: 0.5
Meat: 0.0
Fat: 0.0

1. Sauté onion in lightly greased skillet until tender, 3 to 5 minutes. Add cucumbers and cook over medium heat 5 minutes; stir in flour and cook about 1 minute longer. Add stock and mint to saucepan; heat to boiling. Reduce heat and simmer, covered, 10 minutes.

2. Process soup in food processor or blender until smooth; stir in half-and-half and season to taste with salt and pepper. Serve warm, or chilled; garnish each bowl of soup with paprika and cucumber slices.

CUCUMBER AND SORREL SOUP

L

If cucumbers are mild in flavor, they do not need to be peeled. Spinach or kale can be substituted for the sorrel.

6 first-course servings (about 1¼ cups each)

¼ cup plus 2 tablespoons sliced green onions, divided

1 clove garlic, minced

3 cups (about 1½ pounds) peeled, seeded, chopped cucumbers

1 cup coarsely chopped sorrel

2 cups each: fat-free milk, Basic Vegetable Stock (see p. 52)

1 tablespoon cornstarch

2 tablespoons water

Salt and white pepper, to taste

1½ cups Herb Croutons (½ recipe, see p. 561)

Per Serving:
Calories: 70
% of calories from fat: 10
Fat (gm): 0.8
Saturated fat (gm): 0.2
Cholesterol (mg): 1.3
Sodium (mg): 94
Protein (gm): 4.5
Carbohydrate (gm): 11.7

Exchanges:
Milk: 0.0
Vegetable: 2.5
Fruit: 0.0
Bread: 0.0
Meat: 0.0
Fat: 0.0

1. Sauté ¼ cup green onions and garlic in lightly greased saucepan until tender, 3 to 4 minutes. Add cucumbers and sorrel, and cook over medium heat 5 minutes. Add milk and stock; heat to boiling. Reduce heat and simmer, covered, until cucumbers are tender, 5 to 10 minutes.

2. Process soup in food processor or blender until smooth; return to saucepan and heat to boiling. Whisk in combined cornstarch and water, whisking until thickened, about 1 minute. Season to taste with salt and white pepper. Serve chilled; top each bowl of soup with Herb Croutons and remaining green onions.

CREAMED CORN SOUP

L *For a flavor accent, garnish bowls of soup generously with finely chopped cilantro or parsley.*

4 entree servings (about 1 cup each)

½ cup chopped onion

1 medium Idaho potato, peeled, cubed

2 cloves garlic, minced

1 can (15½ ounces) whole kernel corn, drained

3 tablespoons all-purpose flour

½ teaspoon ground coriander

⅛ teaspoon cayenne pepper

3½ cups Canned Vegetable Stock (see p. 56)

1 cup fat-free milk

2 medium tomatoes, chopped

Salt and pepper, to taste

Paprika, as garnish

Per Serving:
Calories: 238
% of calories from fat: 8
Fat (gm): 2.3
Saturated fat (gm): 0.4
Cholesterol (mg): 1
Sodium (mg): 443
Protein (gm): 7.7
Carbohydrate (gm): 45.7

Exchanges:
Milk: 0.0
Vegetable: 3.0
Fruit: 0.0
Bread: 2.0
Meat: 0.0
Fat: 0.5

1. Sauté onion, potato, and garlic in lightly greased saucepan until onion is tender, about 5 minutes. Stir in corn, flour, coriander, and cayenne pepper; cook about 1 minute longer. Stir in stock and heat to boiling; reduce heat and simmer, covered, until potato is tender, about 10 minutes.

2. Process soup in food processor or blender until almost smooth; return to saucepan; stir in milk and tomatoes and heat to boiling. Reduce heat and simmer, uncovered, 5 minutes. Season to taste with salt and pepper; sprinkle each bowl of soup with paprika.

CORN SOUP WITH EPAZOTE

V *Epazote is a popular Mexican herb that can be purchased in Mexican groceries. It's easy to grow but must be planted annually in northern climates. A combination of fresh cilantro and oregano makes a flavorful substitute.*

4 entree servings (about 1½ cups each)

¾ cup chopped onion

1 each: minced medium jalapeño chili, clove garlic

1 tablespoon olive oil

3½ cups Roasted, or Basic, Vegetable Stock
   (see pp. 53, 52)

5 cups whole kernel corn

2 tablespoons chopped fresh, or 2 teaspoons dried
   epazote leaves

Salt, cayenne, and white pepper, to taste

¾ cup Roasted Red Pepper Sauce (½ recipe,
   see p. 590)

Per Serving:
Calories: 275
% of calories from fat: 12
Fat (gm): 4
Saturated fat (gm): 0.5
Cholesterol (mg): 0
Sodium (mg): 38
Protein (gm): 8.6
Carbohydrate (gm): 55.9

Exchanges:
Milk: 0.0
Vegetable: 2.5
Fruit: 0.0
Bread: 2.5
Meat: 0.0
Fat: 0.5

1. Sauté onion, jalapeño chili, and garlic in oil in large saucepan until tender, about 5 minutes. Add stock and corn; heat to boiling. Reduce heat and simmer, covered, 10 minutes.

2. Process soup in food processor or blender until almost smooth; stir in epazote and season to taste with salt, cayenne and white pepper. Serve warm or chilled; swirl about 3 tablespoons Roasted Red Pepper Sauce into each bowl of soup.

EGGPLANT SOUP WITH ROASTED RED PEPPER SAUCE

V *Grilling gives eggplant a distinctive smoky flavor. For indoor cooking, eggplant can be oven roasted. Pierce the eggplant in several places with a fork and place in a baking pan. Bake at 350 degrees until soft, 45 to 50 minutes.*

4 entree servings (about 1 cup each)

2 medium eggplants (about 2½ pounds)
¾ cup chopped onion

¼ cup chopped green bell pepper

2 cloves garlic, minced

1 tablespoon olive oil

4–5 cups Mediterranean Stock (see p. 54)

Salt and white pepper, to taste

Roasted Red Pepper Sauce (see p. 590)

Per Serving:
Calories: 250
% of calories from fat: 19
Fat (gm): 6
Saturated fat (gm): 0.7
Cholesterol (mg): 0
Sodium (mg): 25
Protein (gm): 6.8
Carbohydrate (gm): 44.8

Exchanges:
Milk: 0.0
Vegetable: 2.0
Fruit: 0.0
Bread: 2.0
Meat: 0.0
Fat: 1.0

1. Pierce eggplant in several places with fork. Grill over medium hot coals, turning frequently, until eggplant is very soft, about 30 minutes; cool slightly. Cut eggplant in half, scoop out pulp, and chop coarsely.

2. Sauté onion, pepper, and garlic in oil in large saucepan until tender, 5 to 8 minutes. Add stock and eggplant and heat to boiling. Reduce heat and simmer, covered, 10 minutes. Process soup in food processor or blender until smooth. Season to taste with salt and white pepper. Serve chilled; swirl about ¼ cup Roasted Red Pepper Sauce into each bowl of soup.

GARLIC SOUP WITH TOAST

V *Often a whole beaten egg is slowly stirred into this traditional soup just before serving.*

4 first-course servings (about 1 cup each)

4 slices firm bread (French or sourdough)

Vegetable cooking spray

6–8 cloves garlic, finely chopped

1 tablespoon olive oil

½ teaspoon ground cumin

¼ teaspoon each: dried oregano leaves,
   cayenne pepper

3½ cups Canned Vegetable Stock (see p. 56)

Salt, to taste

Chopped cilantro, as garnish

Per Serving:
Calories: 162
% of calories from fat: 28
Fat (gm): 5
Saturated fat (gm): 0.7
Cholesterol (mg): 0
Sodium (mg): 202
Protein (gm): 3.2
Carbohydrate (gm): 20.6

Exchanges:
Milk: 0.0
Vegetable: 1.0
Fruit: 0.0
Bread: 1.5
Meat: 0.0
Fat: 0.5

1. Spray both sides of bread slices generously with cooking spray; cook in large skillet, over medium heat, until golden, about 2 minutes on each side. Keep warm.

2. Sauté garlic in oil in medium saucepan lightly browned, about 5 minutes. Stir in herbs and cayenne pepper; cook about 1 minute longer. Add stock and heat to boiling; reduce heat and simmer, covered, 5 minutes. Season to taste with salt. Place slices of bread in bottoms of shallow bowls; ladle soup over and sprinkle with cilantro.

CREAM OF MUSHROOM SOUP

L *For a richer soup, use fat-free half-and-half instead of fat-free milk.*

4 first-course servings (about 1¼ cups each)

1 pound mushrooms

2 tablespoons margarine, or butter, divided

1 cup chopped onion

2½ cups Canned Vegetable Stock, or reduced-sodium vegetable broth (see p. 56)

2½ cups fat-free milk, divided

2 tablespoons plus 2 teaspoons cornstarch

Salt and pepper, to taste

Per Serving:
Calories: 207
% of calories from fat: 29
Fat (gm): 7
Saturated fat (gm): 1.4
Cholesterol (mg): 2.5
Sodium (mg): 185
Protein (gm): 8.6
Carbohydrate (gm): 25.3

Exchanges:
Milk: 0.5
Vegetable: 2.5
Fruit: 0.0
Bread: 0.5
Meat: 0.0
Fat: 1.5

1. Slice enough mushroom caps to make 2 cups; finely chop stems and remaining mushrooms. Sauté sliced mushrooms in 1 tablespoon margarine in large saucepan until browned, about 5 minutes; remove and reserve.

2. Sauté onion and chopped mushrooms in remaining 1 tablespoon margarine in saucepan until onion is tender, about 5 minutes. Add stock and 2 cups milk and heat to boiling. Mix remaining ½ cup milk and cornstarch and stir into boiling mixture; boil, stirring, until thickened, about 1 minute. Stir in reserved sliced mushrooms. Season to taste with salt and pepper.

SAVORY MUSHROOM AND BARLEY SOUP

V

45

Use of quick-cooking barley speeds preparation. Other grains, such as wild rice or oat groats, can be substituted for the barley; cook before adding to the soup.

4 first-course servings (about 1½ cups each)

1 cup each: chopped onion, celery, carrots

1 teaspoon dried savory leaves

¾ teaspoon fennel seeds, crushed

1 quart water

1 can (16 ounces) reduced-sodium whole tomatoes, undrained, coarsely chopped

½ cup quick-cooking barley

2 cups sliced cremini, or white, mushrooms

¼ cup chopped parsley

Salt and pepper, to taste

Per Serving:
Calories: 151
% of calories from fat: 8
Fat (gm): 1.4
Saturated fat (gm): 0.1
Cholesterol (mg): 0
Sodium (mg): 53
Protein (gm): 5.6
Carbohydrate (gm): 32.1

Exchanges:
Milk: 0.0
Vegetable: 2.0
Fruit: 0.0
Bread: 1.5
Meat: 0.0
Fat: 0.0

1. Sauté onion, celery, and carrots in lightly greased saucepan until onion is tender, about 5 minutes. Stir in herbs; cook about 1 minute longer. Add water, tomatoes with liquid, barley, and mushrooms to saucepan; heat to boiling. Cook, covered, until barley is tender, 10 to 15 minutes. Stir in parsley; season to taste with salt and pepper.

BLACK MUSHROOM SOUP

V

Chinese black mushrooms, also called shiitake mushrooms, add the fragrant, woodsy flavor to this soup.

6 first-course servings (about 1¼ cups each)

1½ ounces dried Chinese black mushrooms (shiitake)

1 ounce dried cloud ear mushrooms

2 cups boiling water

¼ cup each: chopped onion, green onions

5 cups Rich Mushroom, or Oriental, Stock (see pp. 54, 55)

3 cups sliced cremini mushrooms

Salt and white pepper, to taste

Per Serving:
Calories: 72
% of calories from fat: 16
Fat (gm): 1.4
Saturated fat (gm): 0.1
Cholesterol (mg): 0
Sodium (mg): 10
Protein (gm): 2.9
Carbohydrate (gm): 11.1

Exchanges:
Milk: 0.0
Vegetable: 3.0
Fruit: 0.0
Bread: 0.0
Meat: 0.0
Fat: 0.0

1. Place dried mushrooms in bowl; add boiling water. Let stand until mushrooms are softened, about 15 minutes. Drain, reserving liquid. Slice mushrooms, discarding tough stems from black mushrooms.

2. Sauté onions until tender in lightly greased saucepan, about 5 minutes. Add dried mushrooms, reserved liquid and stock; heat to boiling. Reduce heat and simmer, covered, 20 minutes, adding cremini mushrooms during last 10 minutes. Season to taste with salt and white pepper.

FRENCH ONION SOUP

L

This classic soup is topped with Bruschetta and fat-free cheese for healthful, delicious dining.

8 first-course servings (about 1¼ cups each)

6 cups (1½ pounds) thinly sliced Spanish onions

2 cloves garlic, minced

1 teaspoon sugar

6 cups reduced-sodium vegetable broth

2 bay leaves

Salt and white pepper, to taste

8 Bruschetta (⅓ recipe, see p. 46)

8 tablespoons (2 ounces) shredded fat-free Swiss, or mozzarella, cheese

Per Serving:
Calories: 126
% of calories from fat: 7
Fat (gm): 1
Saturated fat (gm): 0.1
Cholesterol (mg): 0.0
Sodium (mg): 542
Protein (gm): 4.9
Carbohydrate (gm): 25

Exchanges:
Milk: 0.0
Vegetable: 0.0
Fruit: 0.0
Bread: 1.5
Meat: 0.0
Fat: 0.0

1. Add onions and garlic to lightly greased Dutch oven and cook, covered, over medium-low heat until wilted, 8 to 10 minutes. Stir in sugar and continue cooking, uncovered, until onions are lightly browned. Stir in broth and bay leaves; heat to boiling. Reduce heat and simmer, covered, 30 minutes. Discard bay leaves; season to taste with salt and white pepper.

2. Top each Bruschetta with 1 tablespoon cheese; broil 6 inches from heat source until cheese is melted. Top each bowl of soup with a Bruschetta.

THREE-ONION SOUP WITH MUSHROOMS

V *Mushrooms are a flavorful addition to this onion soup. Substitute canned reduced-sodium vegetable broth to speed preparation.*

6 first-course servings (about 1½ cups each)

3 cups thinly sliced onions

1½ cups thinly sliced leeks

½ cup chopped shallots, or green onions

1 tablespoon margarine

1 teaspoon sugar

2 cups sliced mushrooms

6½ cups Rich Mushroom Stock (see p. 54)

Salt and pepper, to taste

Per Serving:
Calories: 119
% of calories from fat: 21
Fat (gm): 3
Saturated fat (gm): 0.5
Cholesterol (mg): 0
Sodium (mg): 45
Protein (gm): 2.7
Carbohydrate (gm): 18.5

Exchanges:
Milk: 0.0
Vegetable: 3.0
Fruit: 0.0
Bread: 0.0
Meat: 0.0
Fat: 0.5

1. Cook onions, leeks, and shallots in margarine in large saucepan, covered, over medium-low heat 15 minutes. Stir in sugar; continue cooking, uncovered, until onion mixture is golden, about 10 minutes longer. Stir in mushrooms; cook over medium heat until tender, about 5 minutes. Add stock and heat to boiling; reduce heat and simmer, uncovered, 15 minutes. Season to taste with salt and pepper.

SWEET POTATO CHIPOTLE CHILI

V

45

Chipotle chilies are dried, smoked jalapeño chilies. When canned, they are in adobo sauce, which is made with ground chilies and spices. The chilies add a distinctive smoky flavor to this robust dish; taste before adding a second chili, as they can be fiercely hot!

4 servings (1½ cups each)

1 cup frozen stir-fry pepper blend

2 teaspoons minced gingerroot

1 teaspoon each: minced garlic, cumin seeds

1 tablespoons peanut, or canola, oil

3 cups cubed, peeled sweet potatoes (½-inch)

2 cans (15 ounces each) black beans, rinsed, drained

1 can (14 ½ ounces) chili-style chunky tomatoes, undrained

1–2 chipotle chilies in adobo sauce, chopped

1 cup water, or vegetable broth

Salt, to taste

Per Serving:
Calories: 399
% of calories from fat: 12
Fat (gm): 5.4
Saturated fat (gm): 0.6
Cholesterol (mg): 0
Sodium (mg): 932
Protein (gm): 18.7
Carbohydrate (gm): 72.1

Exchanges:
Milk: 0.0
Vegetable: 2.0
Fruit: 0.0
Bread: 4.0
Meat: 0.0
Fat: 1.0

1. Sauté pepper blend, gingerroot, garlic, and cumin seeds in oil in large saucepan until tender, about 5 minutes. Add remaining ingredients, except salt, and heat to boiling. Reduce heat and simmer, covered, until sweet potatoes are tender, about 15 minutes. Season to taste with salt.

ONION AND LEEK SOUP WITH PASTA

L

Orzo, small shells, or bow ties can be alternate pasta choices.

4 entree servings (about 1¾ cups each)

4 cups sliced onions

2 cups sliced leeks

6 cloves garlic, minced

1 teaspoon sugar

7 cups Basic Vegetable Stock (see p. 52), or reduced-sodium vegetable broth

5 ounces uncooked small pasta rings

Salt and white pepper, to taste

6 teaspoons fat-free grated Parmesan cheese

Per Serving:
Calories: 288
% of calories from fat: 6
Fat (gm): 1.9
Saturated fat (gm): 0.2
Cholesterol (mg): 0
Sodium (mg): 66
Protein (gm): 9.7
Carbohydrate (gm): 59.9

Exchanges:
Milk: 0.0
Vegetable: 5.0
Fruit: 0.0
Bread: 2.0
Meat: 0.0
Fat: 0.0

1. Add onions, leeks, and garlic to lightly greased Dutch oven and cook, covered, over medium heat until wilted, 5 to 8 minutes. Stir in sugar; cook, uncovered, over medium-low heat until onion mixture is very soft and browned, 15 to 20 minutes. Add stock and heat to boiling. Add pasta, reduce heat, and simmer, uncovered, until pasta is *al dente*, 6 to 8 minutes. Season to taste with salt and white pepper; sprinkle each bowl of soup with Parmesan cheese.

VIDALIA ONION SOUP

V

The mild sweetness of Vidalia onions makes this soup special, but try it with other flavorful onion varieties too.

8 first-course servings (about 1¼ cups each)

6 cups (1½ pounds) thinly sliced Vidalia onions

2 cloves garlic, minced

1 teaspoon sugar

⅓ cup all-purpose flour

6 cups reduced-sodium vegetable broth

1½ teaspoons dried sage leaves

2 bay leaves

Salt, cayenne, and white pepper, to taste

Snipped chives, as garnish

Per Serving:
Calories: 88
% of calories from fat: 3
Fat (gm): 0.3
Saturated fat (gm): 0.1
Cholesterol (mg): 0
Sodium (mg): 13
Protein (gm): 2.2
Carbohydrate (gm): 16.4

Exchanges:
Milk: 0.0
Vegetable: 2.0
Fruit: 0.0
Bread: 0.5
Meat: 0.0
Fat: 0.0

1. Add onions and garlic to lightly greased saucepan and cook, covered, over medium-low heat until wilted, 8 to 10 minutes. Stir in sugar and continue cooking, uncovered, until onions are lightly browned. Stir in flour; cook about 1 minute longer. Add broth and herbs; heat to boiling. Reduce heat and simmer, covered, 30 minutes. Discard bay leaves.

2. Process half the soup in food processor or blender until smooth; return to saucepan and season to taste with salt, cayenne, and white pepper. Serve warm, or chilled; sprinkle each bowl of soup with chives.

CHILLED PEA SOUP

L

A refreshing soup for hot sultry days; serve with a ripe tomato salad and crusty bread or rolls.

45

4 entree servings (about 1½ cups each)

½ cup chopped onion

½ teaspoon each: dried marjoram and
thyme leaves

2 cups reduced-sodium vegetable broth

2 packages (20 ounces each) frozen peas

2 cups sliced romaine lettuce

Salt and white pepper, to taste

½ cup fat-free sour cream

Paprika, as garnish

Per Serving:
Calories: 257
% of calories from fat: 4
Fat (gm): 1.1
Saturated fat (gm): 0.2
Cholesterol (mg): 0
Sodium (mg): 274
Protein (gm): 17.4
Carbohydrate (gm): 46.6

Exchanges:
Milk: 0.0
Vegetable: 0.0
Fruit: 0.0
Bread: 3.0
Meat: 0.5
Fat: 0.0

1. Sauté onion and herbs in lightly greased large saucepan until onion is tender, about 5 minutes. Stir in broth, peas, and lettuce; heat to boiling. Reduce heat and simmer, covered, until peas are tender, 5 to 8 minutes. Process soup in food processor or blender until smooth; season to taste with salt and pepper. Serve chilled; stir sour cream into soup and sprinkle each bowl of soup with paprika.

SNOW PEA SOUP

L

Make this soup a day in advance so that flavors can blend.

45   **6 first-course servings** (about 1¼ cups each)

½ cup each chopped green onions, yellow onion

1 tablespoon margarine, or butter

1 pound snow peas, trimmed

4 cups coarsely chopped romaine lettuce

4 cups reduced-sodium vegetable broth

½ teaspoon each: dried tarragon and mint leaves

Salt and white pepper, to taste

6 tablespoons plain fat-free yogurt

Fresh mint, or tarragon, sprigs

Per Serving:
Calories: 76
% of calories from fat: 28
Fat (gm): 2.5
Saturated fat (gm): 0.5
Cholesterol (mg): 0.3
Sodium (mg): 47
Protein (gm): 4.3
Carbohydrate (gm): 9.8

Exchanges:
Milk: 0.0
Vegetable: 2.0
Fruit: 0.0
Bread: 0.0
Meat: 0.0
Fat: 0.5

1. Sauté onions in margarine in large saucepan until tender, about 5 minutes. Add snow peas and lettuce; sauté 3 to 4 minutes longer. Add broth, tarragon, and mint; heat to boiling.

2. Reduce heat and simmer, covered, 15 minutes or until snow peas are very tender. Process soup in food processor or blender until smooth; strain and discard solids. Season to taste with salt and white pepper. Serve warm, or chilled; garnish each bowl of soup with a tablespoon of yogurt and fresh mint.

SPLIT PEA SOUP

V *A perfect entree soup for hearty appetites on a crisp autumn or winter day. Serve with thick slices of Garlic Bread (see p. 559).*

6 entree servings (about 1⅓ cups each)

1½ cups chopped onions

1 cup chopped carrots

½ cup sliced celery

1 tablespoon canola oil

6 cups water

1¾ cups Canned Vegetable Stock (see p. 56)

1 pound dried split peas, rinsed and sorted

1 teaspoon dried marjoram leaves

Salt and pepper, to taste

Per Serving:
Calories: 321
% of calories from fat: 10
Fat (gm): 3.5
Saturated fat (gm): 0.5
Cholesterol (mg): 0
Sodium (mg): 44
Protein (gm): 19.6
Carbohydrate (gm): 53.4

Exchanges:
Milk: 0.0
Vegetable: 1.0
Fruit: 0.0
Bread: 3.0
Meat: 1.5
Fat: 0.0

1. Sauté onions, carrots, and celery in oil in large saucepan until tender, 8 to 10 minutes. Add water, stock, split peas, and marjoram; heat to boiling. Reduce heat and simmer, covered, until peas are tender, 1 to 1¼ hours. Season to taste with salt and pepper.

SWEET RED PEPPER SOUP

L

Use jarred roasted peppers for this soup, or roast 3 medium red bell (sweet) peppers. (See Roasted Red Pepper Sauce, p. 590).

4 first-course servings (about 1 cup each)

1 medium onion, chopped
½ small jalapeño chili, seeded, minced
1 clove garlic, minced
1 jar (15 ounces) roasted red bell peppers, drained
1 cup reduced-sodium tomato juice
1¾ cups Canned Vegetable Stock (see p. 56), or reduced-sodium vegetable broth
½ teaspoon dried marjoram leaves
Salt and pepper, to taste
¼ cup fat-free sour cream
Sliced green onion, as garnish

Per Serving:
Calories: 77
% of calories from fat: 5
Fat (gm): 0.4
Saturated fat (gm): 0.1
Cholesterol (mg): 0
Sodium (mg): 264
Protein (gm): 2.9
Carbohydrate (gm): 13.4

Exchanges:
Milk: 0.0
Vegetable: 3.0
Fruit: 0.0
Bread: 0.0
Meat: 0.0
Fat: 0.0

1. Sauté onion, jalapeño chili, and garlic in lightly greased saucepan until tender, about 5 minutes. Process onion mixture, bell peppers, and tomato juice in food processor or blender until smooth. Return mixture to saucepan and add stock and marjoram; heat to boiling. Reduce heat and simmer, covered, 15 minutes. Season to taste with salt and pepper. Serve warm or chilled; top each bowl of soup with a dollop of sour cream and sprinkle with green onion.

POTATO AND FRESH HERB POTAGE

L

For flavor variation, try another favorite garden herb such as rosemary, oregano, lemon thyme, marjoram, or sorrel.

6 first-course servings (about 1 cup each)

4 cups reduced-sodium vegetable broth
1 cup each firmly packed basil and parsley
½ cup chopped onion
1 teaspoon sugar
2 cups potatoes, peeled, cubed
1 cup fat-free milk

¼ cup all-purpose flour

1 tablespoon margarine, or butter

Salt and white pepper, to taste

Chopped parsley, as garnish

Per Serving:
Calories: 128
% of calories from fat: 17
Fat (gm): 2.5
Saturated fat (gm): 0.5
Cholesterol (mg): 0.8
Sodium (mg): 355
Protein (gm): 4
Carbohydrate (gm): 22.7

Exchanges:
Milk: 0.0
Vegetable: 0.0
Fruit: 0.0
Bread: 1.5
Meat: 0.0
Fat: 0.5

1. Heat broth, basil, parsley, onion, and sugar to boiling in medium saucepan. Simmer, covered, 30 minutes. Strain; return broth to saucepan. Add potatoes and heat to boiling; reduce heat and simmer, covered, until potatoes are tender, about 15 minutes. Mix milk and flour; stir into saucepan and heat to boiling. Boil, stirring, until thickened, about 1 minute; stir in margarine. Season to taste with salt and white pepper; sprinkle each bowl of soup with parsley.

VICHYSSOISE

L

45

This classic French potato soup is traditionally served chilled, although it's good warm too!

4 entree servings (about 1½ cups each)

¾ cup each: sliced leeks, or green onions, and celery

2 tablespoons margarine, or butter

6 cups reduced-sodium vegetable broth

2 pounds Idaho potatoes, peeled, cubed

¼ teaspoon dried thyme leaves

Salt and white pepper, to taste

6 tablespoons fat-free sour cream

Snipped chives, as garnish

Per Serving:
Calories: 282
% of calories from fat: 20
Fat (gm): 6.6
Saturated fat (gm): 1.2
Cholesterol (mg): 0
Sodium (mg): 134
Protein (gm): 6.2
Carbohydrate (gm): 51.5

Exchanges:
Milk: 0.0
Vegetable: 1.0
Fruit: 0.0
Bread: 3.0
Meat: 0.0
Fat: 1.0

1. Sauté leeks and celery in margarine in large saucepan until tender, about 8 minutes. Stir in broth, potatoes, and thyme and heat to boiling; reduce heat and simmer, covered, until potatoes are tender, about 15 minutes.

2. Process soup in food processor or blender until smooth; season to taste with salt and white pepper. Serve chilled; top each bowl of soup with 1 tablespoon sour cream and sprinkle with chives.

POTATO CHOWDER

L *A basic soup that is versatile: substitute any desired vegetables, such as carrots, zucchini, green beans, or corn, for part of the potatoes for a delectable vegetable chowder.*

4 entree servings (about 1½ cups each)

1 cup chopped onion

¼ cup thinly sliced celery

2 tablespoons margarine, or butter

3 tablespoons flour

2 cups Canned Vegetable Stock (see p. 56)

3½ cups peeled, cubed Idaho potatoes

¼–½ teaspoon celery seeds

2 cups fat-free milk

Salt and pepper, to taste

Per Serving:
Calories: 338
% of calories from fat: 17
Fat (gm): 6.6
Saturated fat (gm): 1.4
Cholesterol (mg): 2
Sodium (mg): 175
Protein (gm): 9.3
Carbohydrate (gm): 58.4

Exchanges:
Milk: 0.5
Vegetable: 1.0
Fruit: 0.0
Bread: 3.0
Meat: 0.0
Fat: 1.0

1. Sauté onion and celery in margarine in large saucepan until tender, 5 to 8 minutes; stir in flour and cook 1 minute longer. Add stock, potatoes, and celery seeds to saucepan; heat to boiling. Reduce heat and simmer, covered, until potatoes are tender, 10 to 15 minutes. Stir in milk and cook until hot, 2 to 3 minutes. Season to taste with salt and pepper.

HEARTY CORN AND POTATO CHOWDER

L *If a thicker soup is desired, mix 2 tablespoons flour with ⅓ cup water. Heat soup to boiling; stir in flour mixture and boil, stirring, until thickened, about 1 minute.*

4 entree servings (about 2 cups each)

2 cups whole kernel corn

1 medium onion, chopped

1 tablespoon canola oil

2 cups Basic Vegetable Stock (see p. 56)

2 cups unpeeled, cubed Idaho potatoes

½ cup sliced celery

½ teaspoon dried thyme leaves

1¾ cups fat-free half-and-half, or fat-free milk

Salt and pepper, to taste

Chopped parsley and chives, as garnish

Per Serving:
Calories: 298
% of calories from fat: 12
Fat (gm): 3.9
Saturated fat (gm): 0.5
Cholesterol (mg): 0
Sodium (mg): 134
Protein (gm): 9
Carbohydrate (gm): 57.0

Exchanges:
Milk: 1.0
Vegetable: 1.0
Fruit: 0.0
Bread: 2.5
Meat: 0.0
Fat: 0.5

1. Sauté corn and onion in oil in large saucepan until onion is tender, 5 to 8 minutes. Process ½ the vegetable mixture and the stock in food processor or blender until finely chopped; return mixture to saucepan.

2. Add potatoes, celery, and thyme to saucepan and heat to boiling; reduce heat and simmer, covered, until vegetables are tender, 10 to 15 minutes. Stir in half-and-half and cook 2 to 3 minutes. Season to taste with salt and pepper; sprinkle each bowl of soup with parsley and chives.

CHAYOTE SQUASH SOUP WITH CILANTRO SOUR CREAM

L

45

Chayote squash, often called a "vegetable pear," is native to Mexico and readily available here. The squash is light green in color and delicate in flavor.

6 first-course servings (about 1 cup each)

1 large onion, chopped

2 cloves garlic, minced

3 tablespoons flour

3 large chayote squash, peeled, seeded, sliced

6 cups reduced-sodium vegetable broth

Salt and white pepper, to taste

Cilantro Sour Cream (recipe follows)

Chopped cilantro, as garnish

Per Serving:
Calories: 68
% of calories from fat: 11
Fat (gm): 0.9
Saturated fat (gm): 0.1
Cholesterol (mg): 0.2
Sodium (mg): 27
Protein (gm): 2.9
Carbohydrate (gm): 13.3

Exchanges:
Milk: 0.0
Vegetable: 2.5
Fruit: 0.0
Bread: 0.0
Meat: 0.0
Fat: 0.0

1. Sauté onion and garlic in lightly greased saucepan until tender, about 5 minutes. Stir in flour; cook over medium heat 2 minutes, stirring constantly. Add squash and broth to saucepan; heat to boiling. Reduce heat and simmer, covered, until squash is tender, 15 to 20 minutes.

2. Process soup in food processor or blender until smooth; season to taste with salt and white pepper. Serve warm, or chilled; drizzle each bowl of soup with Cilantro Sour Cream and sprinkle with cilantro.

Cilantro Sour Cream

Makes about ½ cup

⅓ cup fat-free sour cream
1 tablespoon finely chopped cilantro
¼–⅓ cup fat-free milk

1. Mix sour cream and cilantro in small bowl, adding enough milk for desired consistency.

SUMMER SQUASH SOUP

Use any summer squash in this soup. To speed preparation, canned reduced-sodium vegetable broth can be substituted for the homemade.

6 first-course servings (about 1¼ cups each)

½ cup chopped shallots
¼ cup sliced green onions
2 cloves garlic, minced
4 medium zucchini, chopped
1 cup peeled, cubed Idaho potato
4 cups Basic Vegetable Stock (see p. 52)
1 cup chopped kale, or spinach leaves
1–½ teaspoons dried tarragon leaves
¼–½ cup fat-free half-and-half, or fat-free milk
Salt and white pepper, to taste
Cayenne pepper, as garnish
1½ cups Sourdough Croutons (½ recipe, see p. 560)

Per Serving:
Calories: 100
% of calories from fat: 7
Fat (gm): 0.8
Saturated fat (gm): 0.1
Cholesterol (mg): 0
Sodium (mg): 65
Protein (gm): 3.8
Carbohydrate (gm): 20.6

Exchanges:
Milk: 0.0
Vegetable: 1.0
Fruit: 0.0
Bread: 1.0
Meat: 0.0
Fat: 0.0

1. Sauté shallots, green onions, and garlic in lightly greased saucepan until tender, about 5 minutes. Add chopped zucchini and potato; sauté 5 to 8 minutes longer.

2. Add stock, kale, and tarragon to saucepan; heat to boiling. Reduce heat and simmer, covered, until vegetables are tender, 10 to 15 minutes.

3. Process soup in food processor or blender until smooth; stir in half-and-half and season to taste with salt and white pepper. Serve warm, or chilled. Sprinkle each bowl of soup with cayenne pepper and top with Sourdough Croutons.

DILLED ZUCCHINI AND BROCCOLI SOUP

| V |

Fresh dill and poblano chili add distinctive flavors to this velvet-textured soup.

| 45 |

6 first course servings (about 1¼ cups each)

1 each: chopped small poblano chili, or green bell pepper, and onion
2 teaspoons olive oil
3 cups reduced-sodium vegetable broth
3 medium zucchini, coarsely chopped
12 ounces broccoli, coarsely chopped
2 cups lightly packed dill weed
Salt and pepper, to taste

Per Serving:
Calories: 79
% of calories from fat: 23
Fat (gm): 2.3
Saturated fat (gm): 0.3
Cholesterol (mg): 0.0
Sodium (mg): 261
Protein (gm): 4
Carbohydrate (gm): 13

Exchanges:
Milk: 0.0
Vegetable: 2.0
Fruit: 0.0
Bread: 0.0
Meat: 0.0
Fat: 1.0

1. Sauté poblano chili and onion in oil in large saucepan until tender, 3 to 4 minutes. Add broth, zucchini, and broccoli and heat to boiling; reduce heat and simmer, covered, until vegetables are tender, about 10 minutes. Process soup and dill weed in blender or food processor until smooth; season to taste with salt and pepper. Serve warm or chilled.

CINNAMON-SPICED PUMPKIN SOUP

L

45

For convenience, 2 cans (16 ounces each) pumpkin can be substituted for the fresh pumpkin. Any yellow winter squash such as butternut, Hubbard, or acorn can also be used.

4 first-course servings (about 1¼ cups each)

4 cups cubed, seeded, peeled pumpkin

2 cups fat-free half-and-half, or fat-free milk

1–2 tablespoons light brown sugar

½ teaspoon ground cinnamon

¼–½ teaspoon ground nutmeg

Snipped chives, as garnish

Per Serving:
Calories: 125
% of calories from fat: 1
Fat (gm): 0.2
Saturated fat (gm): 0.1
Cholesterol (mg): 0
Sodium (mg): 122
Protein (gm): 5.2
Carbohydrate (gm): 23.2

Exchanges:
Milk: 1.0
Vegetable: 0.0
Fruit: 0.0
Bread: 0.5
Meat: 0.0
Fat: 0.0

1. Cook pumpkin in medium saucepan, covered, in 1 inch simmering water until tender, about 15 minutes; drain. Process pumpkin and half-and-half in food processor or blender; return to saucepan. Stir in brown sugar and spices and heat to boiling; reduce heat and simmer, uncovered, 5 minutes. Sprinkle each bowl of soup with chives.

CURRIED BUTTERNUT SQUASH SOUP

V

45

Acorn or Hubbard squash can also be used in this fragrant soup.

8 first-course servings (about 1 cup each)

½ cup chopped onion

1 clove garlic, mashed

2 teaspoons olive oil

4 cups reduced-sodium vegetable broth

2 pounds butternut squash, peeled, seeded, cubed

2 medium tomatoes, chopped

1½ teaspoons curry powder

1 cup coarsely chopped cilantro leaves and stems

Salt and pepper, to taste

Chopped cilantro, as garnish

Per Serving:
Calories: 80
% of calories from fat: 17
Fat (gm): 1.6
Saturated fat (gm): 0.2
Cholesterol (mg): 0.0
Sodium (mg): 236
Protein (gm): 2
Carbohydrate (gm): 16.3

Exchanges:
Milk: 0.0
Vegetable: 0.0
Fruit: 0.0
Bread: 1.0
Meat: 0.0
Fat: 0.0

1. Sauté onion and garlic in oil in large saucepan until tender, about 5 minutes. Add broth, squash, tomatoes, and curry powder and heat to boiling; reduce heat and simmer, covered, until squash is tender, about 10 minutes. Process soup and cilantro in blender or food processor until smooth; season to taste with salt and pepper. Serve warm; garnish each bowl of soup with cilantro sprigs.

Variation

Savory Herbed Squash Soup — Make recipe above, deleting tomatoes, curry powder and cilantro; add ¾ teaspoon each dried thyme and marjoram leaves and ¼–½ teaspoon ground mace.

ORANGE-SCENTED SQUASH SOUP

L

45

Subtly seasoned with orange and spices, this delicious soup can be served warm or chilled.

6 first-course servings (about 1⅓ cups each)

¾ cup chopped onion

1 teaspoon ground cinnamon

¼ teaspoon each: ground nutmeg, cloves

1½ cups water

3 pounds winter yellow squash (Hubbard, butternut, or acorn), peeled, cubed

1 large, tart cooking apple, peeled, cored, cubed

1 strip orange zest (3 x ½ inch)

¼–½ cup orange juice

1½–2 cups fat-free half-and-half, or fat-free milk

Salt and white pepper, to taste

6 thin orange slices

Snipped chives, as garnish

Per Serving:
Calories: 144
% of calories from fat: 8
Fat (gm): 1.4
Saturated fat (gm): 0.3
Cholesterol (mg): 0
Sodium (mg): 64
Protein (gm): 4.1
Carbohydrate (gm): 30.2

Exchanges:
Milk: 0.0
Vegetable: 0.0
Fruit: 0.0
Bread: 2.0
Meat: 0.0
Fat: 0.0

1. Sauté onion in lightly greased saucepan until tender, about 5 minutes. Stir in spices; cook about 1 minute longer. Add water, squash, apple, and orange zest to saucepan; heat to boiling. Reduce heat and simmer, covered, until squash is tender, 10 to 15 minutes.

2. Process soup in food processor or blender until smooth; add orange juice and half-and-half. Season to taste with salt and white pepper. Serve warm, or chilled. Top each bowl of soup with an orange slice and sprinkle with chives.

Variation

Winter Squash Soup — Make recipe as above, deleting cloves, orange zest, and orange juice. Add ¼ teaspoon each ground ginger and cumin, and 1 cup apple cider; reduce fat-free half-and-half to ½–1 cup.

CREAM OF TOMATO SOUP

L

45

A soup similar to the favorite-brand canned tomato soup we all remember eating as kids! Canned tomatoes are necessary for the flavor, so don't substitute fresh.

4 first-course servings (about 1¼ cups each)

2 cans (14½ ounces each) no-salt whole
  tomatoes, undrained
1–3 teaspoons vegetable bouillon crystals
2 cups fat-free milk
3 tablespoons cornstarch
⅛ teaspoon baking soda
2 teaspoons sugar
1–2 tablespoons margarine, or butter
Salt and pepper, to taste

Per Serving:
Calories: 142
% of calories from fat: 22
Fat (gm): 3.7
Saturated fat (gm): 0.8
Cholesterol (mg): 2
Sodium (mg): 395
Protein (gm): 6.3
Carbohydrate (gm): 22.6

Exchanges:
Milk: 0.5
Vegetable: 2.0
Fruit: 0.0
Bread: 0.5
Meat: 0.0
Fat: 0.5

1. Process tomatoes with liquid in food processor or blender until smooth; heat tomatoes and bouillon crystals in large saucepan to boiling. Mix milk and cornstarch; stir into boiling mixture. Boil, stirring, until thickened, about 1 minute. Add baking soda, sugar, and margarine to soup, stirring until margarine is melted. Season to taste with salt and pepper.

TWO-TOMATO SOUP

L *The concentrated flavor of sun-dried tomatoes enhances the taste of garden-ripe tomato soup.*

6 first-course servings (about 1¼ cups each)

1 cup chopped onion

½ cup each: chopped celery, carrot

2 teaspoons minced roasted garlic

4 cups Roasted Vegetable Stock (see p. 53)

4 cups chopped ripe tomatoes, or 2 cans (16 ounces each) reduced-sodium whole tomatoes, undrained, coarsely chopped

1 large Idaho potato, peeled, cubed

½ cup sun-dried tomatoes (not in oil)

½ teaspoons dried basil leaves

½ cup fat-free half-and-half, or fat-free milk

2–3 teaspoons sugar

Salt and pepper, to taste

Per Serving:
Calories: 117
% of calories from fat: 5
Fat (gm): 0.8
Saturated fat (gm): 0.1
Cholesterol (mg): 0
Sodium (mg): 150
Protein (gm): 3.7
Carbohydrate (gm): 22.6

Exchanges:
Milk: 0.0
Vegetable: 2.0
Fruit: 0.0
Bread: 1.0
Meat: 0.0
Fat: 0.0

1. Sauté onion, celery, carrot, and garlic in lightly greased large saucepan until tender, 5 to 8 minutes. Add stock, tomatoes with liquid, potato, sun-dried tomatoes, and basil; heat to boiling. Reduce heat and simmer, covered, until vegetables are tender, 10 to 15 minutes. Process soup in food processor or blender until smooth; return to saucepan. Stir in half-and-half and cook until hot, 3 to 5 minutes; season to taste with sugar, salt, and pepper.

RIPE TOMATO AND LEEK SOUP

L

Use summer's ripest tomatoes for this soup, cooking only briefly to maintain their sweetness. Peel the tomatoes or not, as you prefer.

6 first-course servings (about 1¼ cups each)

2 cups sliced leeks
3 cloves garlic, minced
1 tablespoon olive oil
6 large tomatoes (about 2½ pounds)
4 cups Basic Vegetable, or Mediterranean, Stock
   (see pp. 52, 54)
½–1 teaspoon dried basil leaves
Salt and white pepper, to taste
6 tablespoons fat-free sour cream, or plain yogurt
Basil sprigs, as garnish

Per Serving:
Calories: 99
% of calories from fat: 24
Fat (gm): 2.9
Saturated fat (gm): 0.5
Cholesterol (mg): 0
Sodium (mg): 64
Protein (gm): 3.5
Carbohydrate (gm): 17.3

Exchanges:
Milk: 0.0
Vegetable: 3.0
Fruit: 0.0
Bread: 0.0
Meat: 0.0
Fat: 0.5

1. Sauté leeks and garlic in oil in large saucepan until tender, about 8 minutes. Add tomatoes, stock, and basil to saucepan; heat to boiling. Reduce heat and simmer, covered, 10 minutes. Process soup in food processor or blender until smooth; season to taste with salt and white pepper. Serve soup warm or chilled; top each bowl of soup with a tablespoon of sour cream and garnish with basil sprigs.

GAZPACHO

L

Easy to make and served cold, Gazpacho is a wonderful soup to keep on hand in summer months.

45

6 first-course servings (about 1¼ cups each)

5 large tomatoes, halved, seeded
2 cups reduced-sodium tomato juice
2 cloves garlic
2 tablespoons lime juice
1 teaspoon dried oregano leaves
1 cup each: chopped yellow bell pepper, celery, cucumber
6 green onions, thinly sliced
2 tablespoons finely chopped cilantro

Salt and pepper, to taste
Avocado Sour Cream (recipe follows)
Hot pepper sauce

Per Serving:
Calories: 76
% of calories from fat: 17
Fat (gm): 1.6
Saturated fat (gm): 0.3
Cholesterol (mg): 0.1
Sodium (mg): 46
Protein (gm): 3.3
Carbohydrate (gm): 15.1

Exchanges:
Milk: 0.0
Vegetable: 2.0
Fruit: 0.0
Bread: 0.0
Meat: 0.0
Fat: 0.5

1. Chop tomatoes, reserving 1 cup. Process remaining tomatoes, tomato juice, garlic, lime juice, and oregano in food processor or blender until smooth. Mix tomato mixture, reserved tomatoes, bell pepper, celery, cucumber, green onions, and cilantro in large bowl; season to taste with salt and pepper. Serve chilled; top each bowl of soup with a dollop of Avocado Sour Cream. Serve with hot pepper sauce.

Avocado Sour Cream

Makes about ⅔ cup

½ medium avocado, chopped
¼ cup fat-free sour cream
2 tablespoons fat-free milk
Salt and white pepper, to taste

1. Process all ingredients in food processor until smooth; season to taste with salt and white pepper.

SUMMER MINESTRONE

L *Thick and savory, this traditional Italian soup is always a favorite.*

6 entree servings (about 1⅓ cups each)

2 cups each: cubed potatoes, sliced carrots

1 small zucchini, cubed

1 cup each: halved green beans, sliced zucchini, carrots cabbage, and chopped onion

½ cup sliced celery

3–4 cloves garlic, minced

2 teaspoons Italian seasoning

1 teaspoons dried oregano leaves

4 cups Mediterranean Stock (see p. 54), or reduced-sodium vegetable broth

1 can (15 ounces) each rinsed, drained kidney beans, and no-salt-added stewed tomatoes

2 cups water

1½ cups uncooked mostaccioli (penne)

½ teaspoon pepper

2 tablespoons grated Parmesan, or Romano, cheese

Per Serving:
Calories: 264
% of calories from fat: 9
Fat (gm): 2.7
Saturated fat (gm): 0.6
Cholesterol (mg): 1.6
Sodium (mg): 216
Protein (gm): 12.3
Carbohydrate (gm): 50.5

Exchanges:
Milk: 0.0
Vegetable: 3.0
Fruit: 0.0
Bread: 2.0
Meat: 1.0
Fat: 0.0

1. Sauté fresh vegetables in lightly greased large saucepan until crisp-tender, 10 to 12 minutes. Stir in Italian seasoning and oregano; cook 1 minute longer. Add stock, beans, tomatoes, and water; heat to boiling. Reduce heat and simmer, covered, 10 minutes. Heat soup to boiling and add pasta. Reduce heat and simmer, uncovered, until pasta is *al dente*, 10 to 12 minutes. Stir in pepper; sprinkle each bowl of soup with cheese.

VEGETABLE SOUP WITH ORZO

L *Escarole lends a unique taste to this hearty soup; kale or spinach can also be used.*

4 entree servings (about 2 cups each)

1 cup each: chopped onion, sliced carrots, celery

3 cloves garlic, minced

2 medium zucchini, or summer yellow squash, sliced

1 cup sliced mushrooms

½ teaspoon each: dried thyme and oregano leaves

5 cups Canned Vegetable Stock (see p. 56)

½ cup (4 ounces) uncooked orzo

½ cup frozen peas

6 medium leaves escarole, sliced or coarsely chopped

Salt and pepper, to taste

2 tablespoons grated Romano cheese

Per Serving:
Calories: 265
% of calories from fat: 10
Fat (gm): 2.9
Saturated fat (gm): 0.9
Cholesterol (mg): 3.6
Sodium (mg): 298
Protein (gm): 9.1
Carbohydrate (gm): 44.3

Exchanges:
Milk: 0.0
Vegetable: 3.0
Fruit: 0.0
Bread: 2.0
Meat: 0.0
Fat: 1.0

1. Sauté onion, carrots, celery, and garlic in lightly greased large saucepan until onion is tender, about 5 minutes. Add zucchini, mushrooms, and herbs; cook, covered, 2 to 3 minutes. Add stock and heat to boiling. Stir in orzo, peas, and escarole; reduce heat and simmer, uncovered, until orzo is *al dente*, about 7 minutes. Season with salt and pepper. Sprinkle each bowl of soup with cheese.

LIGHTLY CREAMED VEGETABLE SOUP

L

Fat-free milk, whipped with an immersion blender, lends a wonderful rich texture to this fragrant creamed soup. Or, if desired, just stir the milk into the soup near the end of the cooking time.

6 first-course servings (about 1⅓ cups each)

1 cup each: sliced onion, carrots, yellow summer
  squash

⅔ cup each: chopped green and red bell pepper, celery

1 clove garlic, minced

1½ tablespoons margarine, or butter

4 cups Basic Vegetable Stock (see p. 52)

4 peppercorns

3 whole cloves

1 bay leaf

⅓ cup all-purpose flour

⅔ cup water

Salt and pepper, to taste

½ cup fat-free milk

Ground nutmeg, as garnish

Per Serving:
Calories: 112
% of calories from fat: 27
Fat (gm): 3.6
Saturated fat (gm): 0.7
Cholesterol (mg): 0.3
Sodium (mg): 73
Protein (gm): 3.4
Carbohydrate (gm): 18

Exchanges:
Milk: 0.0
Vegetable: 2.0
Fruit: 0.0
Bread: 0.5
Meat: 0.0
Fat: 0.5

1. Sauté vegetables in margarine in large saucepan until onion is tender, 8 to 10 minutes. Add stock and herbs, tied in a cheesecloth bag; heat to boiling. Reduce heat and simmer, covered, until vegetables are tender, 10 to 15 minutes; discard herb bag. Heat soup to boiling; stir in combined flour and water. Boil, stirring, until thickened, about 1 minute. Season to taste with salt and pepper.

2. Just before serving, whip fat-free milk with an immersion blender, or process in blender at high speed 30 seconds; stir into soup. Sprinkle each bowl of soup with nutmeg.

LIME-SCENTED VEGETABLE SOUP

V *A soup with a fresh flavor, accented with lime and cilantro. Cubed light tofu can be added for a great protein boost.*

6 first-course servings (about 1¼ cups each)

2 cups sliced carrots

¾ cup each: chopped red bell pepper, sliced celery

½ cup sliced green onions

6 cloves garlic, minced

1 small jalapeño chili, finely chopped

6 cups Basic Vegetable Stock (see p. 52)

½–¾ cup lime juice

½ teaspoon ground cumin

1 cup chopped tomato

½ cup each: chopped cucumber, avocado

3–4 tablespoons finely chopped cilantro

1½ cups Herb Croutons (½ recipe, see p. 561)

Per Serving:
Calories: 106
% of calories from fat: 29
Fat (gm): 3.9
Saturated fat (gm): 0.1
Cholesterol (mg): 0
Sodium (mg): 100
Protein (gm): 3.3
Carbohydrate (gm): 17.6

Exchanges:
Milk: 0.0
Vegetable: 2.0
Fruit: 0.0
Bread: 0.5
Meat: 0.0
Fat: 0.5

1. Sauté carrots, bell pepper, celery, green onions, garlic, and jalapeño chili in lightly greased saucepan 5 minutes. Add stock, lime juice, and cumin to saucepan; heat to boiling. Reduce heat and simmer, covered, until vegetables are tender, 10 to 15 minutes. Add tomato, cucumber, and avocado to each bowl of soup; sprinkle with cilantro and Herb Croutons.

GARDEN HARVEST SOUP

V *Vary the vegetables according to your garden's or greengrocer's bounty.*

4 entree servings (about 2 cups each)

2 small onions, sliced

2 cloves garlic, minced

1 tablespoon olive oil

¾ cup each: sliced carrots, red and yellow bell pepper

½ cup whole kernel corn

5 cups Mediterranean, or Roasted Vegetable, Stock
(see pp. 54, 53)

1 cup each: cut green beans, sliced zucchini,
yellow summer squash

½ teaspoon each: dried basil and oregano leaves

Salt and pepper, to taste

⅓ cup fat-free half-and-half, or fat-free milk (optional)

Per Serving:
Calories: 241
% of calories from fat: 19
Fat (gm): 5.7
Saturated fat (gm): 0.7
Cholesterol (mg): 0
Sodium (mg): 40
Protein (gm): 6.8
Carbohydrate (gm): 41.5

Exchanges:
Milk: 0.0
Vegetable: 3.0
Fruit: 0.0
Bread: 1.5
Meat: 0.0
Fat: 1.0

1. Sauté onions and garlic in oil in large saucepan until tender, about 5 minutes. Add carrots, bell peppers, and corn and sauté 5 minutes. Add stock, remaining vegetables, and herbs; heat to boiling. Reduce heat and simmer, covered, until vegetables are tender, about 15 minutes; stir in half-and-half and simmer 2 minutes. Season to taste with salt and pepper.

VEGGIE BEAN AND BURGER SOUP

V

45

A quick and easy soup that kids will love — use their favorite vegetables and make enough for seconds!

8 entree servings (about 1¼ cups each)

12–16 ounces vegetarian ground beef

1 cup chopped onion

1 tablespoon olive oil

3 cups vegetable broth

1 can (14.5 ounces) petite-diced tomatoes, undrained

2 cups each: sliced carrots, broccoli florets

1 can each: (15 ounces each) black and navy beans, rinsed, drained

1 teaspoon dried thyme leaves

Salt and pepper, to taste

Per Serving:
Calories: 213
% of calories from fat: 10.6
Fat (gm): 2.7
Saturated fat (gm): 0.3
Cholesterol (mg): 0
Sodium (mg): 1065.6
Protein (gm): 17.0
Carbohydrate (gm): 33.7

Exchanges:
Milk: 0.0
Vegetable: 0.0
Fruit: 0.0
Bread: 2.0
Meat: 1.5
Fat: 0.0

1. Sauté vegetarian ground beef and onion in oil in large saucepan until onion is tender, about 5 minutes. Add remaining ingredients, except salt and pepper, and heat to boiling. Reduce heat and simmer, covered, until vegetables are tender, about 10 minutes. Season to taste with salt and pepper.

ALSATIAN PEASANT SOUP

L

Root vegetables, cabbage, and beans combine for a robust soup that is almost a stew. Serve with a crusty rye bread and a good beer.

6 entree servings (about 1½ cups each)

½ cup each: chopped onion, celery

1 tablespoon olive oil

1 cup each: cubed, unpeeled potato, parsnip, sliced carrots

1 teaspoon dried thyme leaves

½ teaspoon crushed caraway seeds

1 bay leaf

3 cups reduced-sodium vegetable broth

2 cups thinly sliced cabbage

2 cans (15 ounces each) Great Northern beans, rinsed, drained

Salt and pepper, to taste

¾ cup (3 ounces) shredded reduced-fat Swiss cheese

1½ cups Rye Caraway Croutons (½ recipe, see p. 560)

Per Serving:
Calories: 300
% of calories from fat: 13
Fat (gm): 4.3
Saturated fat (gm): 1
Cholesterol (mg): 5
Sodium (mg): 352
Protein (gm): 17
Carbohydrate (gm): 50

Exchanges:
Milk: 0.0
Vegetable: 1.0
Fruit: 0.0
Bread: 3.0
Meat: 1.0
Fat: 0.0

1. Sauté onion and celery in oil in large saucepan until tender, about 5 minutes. Add potato, parsnip, carrots, thyme, caraway, and bay leaf; cook over medium heat 5 minutes. Add broth, cabbage, and beans to saucepan; heat to boiling. Reduce heat and simmer, covered, until vegetables are tender, 10 to 15 minutes. Discard bay leaf; season to taste with salt and pepper. Sprinkle each bowl of soup with 2 tablespoons shredded cheese and Rye Caraway Croutons.

MEDITERRANEAN-STYLE VEGETABLE SOUP

V

A fragrant vegetable soup with a citrus accent.

6 first-course servings (about 1½ cups each)

2 cups sliced mushrooms

½ cup each: chopped onion, green bell pepper

3 cloves garlic, minced

3½ cups Mediterranean Stock (see p. 54)

1 can (16 ounces) reduced-sodium whole tomatoes, undrained, coarsely chopped

1 can (8 ounces) reduced-sodium tomato sauce

16 ounces light firm tofu, drained, cut into ¾-inch pieces

½ cup dry white wine (optional)

2 strips orange zest (3 x ½ inches)

2 bay leaves

¾ teaspoon each: dried marjoram and savory leaves

¼ teaspoon crushed fennel seeds

Salt and pepper, to taste

Per Serving:
Calories: 109
% of calories from fat: 15
Fat (gm): 2
Saturated fat (gm): 0.1
Cholesterol (mg): 0
Sodium (mg): 104
Protein (gm): 8.1
Carbohydrate (gm): 13.8

Exchanges:
Milk: 0.0
Vegetable: 2.5
Fruit: 0.0
Bread: 0.0
Meat: 0.5
Fat: 0.0

1. Sauté mushrooms, onion, bell pepper, and garlic in lightly greased large saucepan, covered, until vegetables are tender, 8 to 10 minutes. Add remaining ingredients, except salt and pepper, and heat to boiling; reduce heat and simmer, covered, 10 to 15 minutes. Remove bay leaves; season to taste with salt and pepper.

POBLANO CHILI SOUP

Poblano chilies give this soup extraordinary flavor. Taste the peppers, as they can vary in flavor from mild to very hot; if they are too hot for your taste, substitute some green bell peppers.

6 first-course servings (about 1 cup each)

2 medium onions, chopped

4 medium poblano chilies, seeded, chopped

½–1 small jalapeño chili, seeded, finely chopped

3½ cups Basic Vegetable Stock (see p. 52), or reduced-sodium vegetable broth

3 cups tomato juice

½ teaspoon ground cumin

½–1 cup water, divided

Salt and pepper, to taste

Chopped cilantro, as garnish

Per Serving:
Calories: 63
% of calories from fat: 6
Fat (gm): 0.4
Saturated fat (gm): 0
Cholesterol (mg): 0
Sodium (mg): 374
Protein (gm): 1.8
Carbohydrate (gm): 13.1

Exchanges:
Milk: 0.0
Vegetable: 2.5
Fruit: 0.0
Bread: 0.0
Meat: 0.0
Fat: 0.0

1. Sauté onions and chilies in lightly greased skillet until onions are tender, about 5 minutes. Add stock, tomato juice, and cumin and heat to boiling; reduce heat and simmer, covered, until chilies are very tender, about 10 minutes. Process in food processor or blender until smooth; season to taste with salt and pepper. Serve warm or chilled; sprinkle each bowl of soup with cilantro.

TOMATILLO SOUP WITH CILANTRO

L *Tomatillos, or Mexican green tomatoes, are not tomatoes at all, but instead are a member of the Cape gooseberry family. The papery husks must be removed before using.*

6 first-course servings (about 1¼ cups each)

23 cup chopped onion

1–2 small jalapeño chilies, finely chopped

2 cloves garlic, minced

2 pounds tomatillos, husks removed, rinsed, quartered

4 cups Basic Vegetable Stock (see p. 52), or reduced-sodium vegetable broth

¼–⅓ cup fat-free half-and-half, or fat-free milk

3 tablespoons finely chopped cilantro

Salt and white pepper, to taste

Baked Tortilla Strips (recipe follows)

Per Serving:
Calories: 92
% of calories from fat: 21
Fat (gm): 2.3
Saturated fat (gm): 0.1
Cholesterol (mg): 0
Sodium (mg): 58
Protein (gm): 2.9
Carbohydrate (gm): 16.2

Exchanges:
Milk: 0.0
Vegetable: 2.0
Fruit: 0.0
Bread: 0.5
Meat: 0.0
Fat: 0.0

1. Sauté onion, chilies, and garlic in lightly greased skillet until tender, about 5 minutes. Add tomatillos and stock and heat to boiling; reduce heat and simmer, covered, until tomatillos are very tender, 10 to 15 minutes. Process soup in food processor or blender until smooth; stir in half-and-half and cilantro and season to taste with salt and white pepper. Serve chilled; sprinkle each bowl of soup with Baked Tortilla Strips.

Baked Tortilla Strips

1 flour, or corn, tortilla, cut into strips, 2 x ¼-inches

Vegetable cooking spray

Salt, to taste

1. Arrange tortilla strips on cookie sheet; spray lightly with cooking spray and toss. Bake at 375 degrees until browned, about 10 minutes, stirring occasionally.

TORTILLA SOUP

V

Cubed tempeh can be added to the soup, if desired, to make this a more substantial dish.

8 first-course servings (about 1 cup each)

2 corn, *or* flour, tortillas, cut into 2 x ¼-inch strips
Vegetable cooking spray
¾ cup each: chopped onion, celery, tomato
½ teaspoon each: dried basil leaves, ground cumin
5 cups Basic Vegetable Stock (see p. 52)
1 can (15½ ounces) pinto beans, rinsed, drained
2 teaspoons finely chopped cilantro
1–2 teaspoons lime juice
Salt and cayenne pepper, to taste

Per Serving:
Calories: 93
% of calories from fat: 9
Fat (gm): 1
Saturated fat (gm): 0.1
Cholesterol (mg): 0
Sodium (mg): 237
Protein (gm): 5.1
Carbohydrate (gm): 18.1

Exchanges:
Milk: 0.0
Vegetable: 1.0
Fruit: 0.0
Bread: 1.0
Meat: 0.0
Fat: 0.0

1. Spray tortillas lightly with cooking spray and toss; cook in lightly greased medium skillet over medium heat until browned and crisp, about 5 minutes; reserve.

2. Sauté onion, celery, tomato, basil, and cumin in lightly greased saucepan until onion is tender, 3 to 5 minutes. Add stock and beans and heat to boiling; reduce heat and simmer, uncovered, 5 minutes. Stir in cilantro; season to taste with lime juice, salt and cayenne pepper. Add tortilla strips to soup bowls and ladle soup over.

POZOLE

V

45

Pozole always contains hominy; our vegetarian version is enhanced with a variety of crisp vegetable garnishes.

4 first-course servings (about 1⅓ cups each)

2 ancho chilies, stems, seeds, and veins discarded
1 cup boiling water
1 cup chopped onion
1 clove garlic, minced
2 cans (14½ ounces each) reduced-sodium vegetable broth
1 can (15½ ounces) hominy, rinsed, drained
1 can (14½ ounces) reduced-sodium tomatoes, drained, coarsely chopped

1 cup whole kernel corn

½ teaspoon dried oregano leaves

¼ teaspoon dried thyme leaves

Salt and pepper, to taste

4 lime wedges

⅓ cup each, thinly sliced: lettuce, cabbage, green onion, radish, and shredded carrot

Per Serving:
Calories: 186
% of calories from fat: 6
Fat (gm): 1.4
Saturated fat (gm): 0.2
Cholesterol (mg): 0
Sodium (mg): 323
Protein (gm): 5.3
Carbohydrate (gm): 40.8

Exchanges:
Milk: 0.0
Vegetable: 2.0
Fruit: 0.0
Bread: 2.0
Meat: 0.0
Fat: 0.0

1. Cover chilies with boiling water in small bowl of soup; let stand until softened, about 10 minutes. Process chilies and water in food processor or blender until smooth.

2. Sauté onion and garlic in lightly greased large saucepan until tender; add broth and heat to boiling. Reduce heat and simmer, covered, 10 to 15 minutes. Add hominy, tomatoes, corn, and herbs to saucepan; simmer, covered, 10 to 15 minutes. Season to taste with salt and pepper. Squeeze juice from one lime wedge into each bowl of soup. Pass fresh vegetables (not included in nutritional data) for each person to add to soup.

SUN-DRIED TOMATO AND LINGUINE SOUP

V

45

Great soup in less than 30 minutes! One-half cup uncooked orzo can be substituted for the linguine, if preferred.

4 first-course servings (about 1 cup each)

½ cup thinly sliced celery

2 tablespoons thinly sliced green onions

2 cloves garlic, minced

3½ cups reduced-sodium vegetable broth

3 ounces uncooked linguine, broken into 2- to 3-inch pieces

2 sun-dried tomatoes (not in oil), softened, chopped

1–2 teaspoons lemon juice

Salt and pepper, to taste

Per Serving:
Calories: 111
% of calories from fat: 10
Fat (gm): 1.3
Saturated fat (gm): 0.1
Cholesterol (mg): 0
Sodium (mg): 155
Protein (gm): 3.3
Carbohydrate (gm): 16.8

Exchanges:
Milk: 0.0
Vegetable: 1.0
Fruit: 0.0
Bread: 1.0
Meat: 0.0
Fat: 0.0

1. Sauté celery, onions, and garlic in lightly greased medium saucepan until tender, 5 to 7 minutes. Stir in broth and heat to boiling; add linguine and sun-dried tomatoes. Reduce heat and simmer, uncovered, until pasta is *al dente*, about 10 minutes. Season with lemon juice, salt and pepper.

CHICK PEA AND PASTA SOUP

V *Many fresh garden vegetables can be substituted for the zucchini and celery in this soup — carrots, cauliflower, broccoli florets, mushrooms, peas, and green beans are possible choices.*

4 entree servings (about 1¾ cups each)

¾ cup each: chopped onion, cubed zucchini

2 ribs celery, thinly sliced

3–4 cloves garlic, minced

1 teaspoon each: dried rosemary and thyme leaves

⅛ teaspoon dried crushed red pepper

4 cups Canned Vegetable Stock (see p. 56)

1 can each: (15 ounces) no-salt-added stewed tomatoes, and chick peas, rinsed, drained

1 cup (4 ounces) uncooked farfalle (bow ties)

Salt, to taste

2–3 teaspoons lemon juice

Per Serving:
Calories: 322
% of calories from fat: 10
Fat (gm): 3.7
Saturated fat (gm): 0.5
Cholesterol (mg): 0
Sodium (mg): 514
Protein (gm): 11.5
Carbohydrate (gm): 56.4

Exchanges:
Milk: 0.0
Vegetable: 3.0
Fruit: 0.0
Bread: 3.0
Meat: 0.0
Fat: 0.5

1. Sauté onion, zucchini, celery, and garlic in lightly greased large saucepan 5 minutes; stir in herbs and red pepper; cook about 1 minute longer. Add stock, tomatoes, and chick peas; heat to boiling. Reduce heat and simmer, covered, 10 minutes. Heat soup to boiling and add pasta; reduce heat and simmer, uncovered, until pasta is *al dente*, about 8 minutes; season to taste with salt and lemon juice.

TWO-BEAN AND PASTA SOUP

V *This substantial soup thickens upon standing; thin with additional stock or water, if necessary.*

6 entree servings (about 2 cups each)

1½ cups cubed carrots

1 medium green bell pepper, chopped

½ cup sliced green onions

3 cloves garlic, minced

2 teaspoons each: dried basil, and oregano leaves

4 cups Basic Vegetable Stock (see p. 52)

1 cup water

1 can (16 ounces) no-salt-added stewed tomatoes

1 can each (15 ounces) cannellini and pinto beans, rinsed, drained

1½ cups (4 ounces) uncooked rigatoni

2–3 teaspoons lemon juice

Salt and pepper, to taste

Per Serving:
Calories: 225
% of calories from fat: 7
Fat (gm): 2
Saturated fat (gm): 0
Cholesterol (mg): 0
Sodium (mg): 522
Protein (gm): 13.6
Carbohydrate (gm): 45.7

Exchanges:
Milk: 0.0
Vegetable: 2.0
Fruit: 0.0
Bread: 2.5
Meat: 0.0
Fat: 0.0

1. Sauté carrots, bell pepper, onions, and garlic in lightly greased large saucepan until vegetables are tender, about 7 minutes. Stir in basil and oregano; cook about 1 minute. Add stock, water, tomatoes, and both beans to saucepan; heat to boiling. Reduce heat and simmer, covered, 10 minutes. Heat soup to boiling and add pasta; reduce heat and simmer, uncovered, until pasta is *al dente*, 12 to 15 minutes. Season with lemon juice, salt, and pepper.

SPINACH AND TORTELLINI SOUP

LO *Pasta soups can be made 2 to 3 days in advance, enhancing flavors. If desired, cook pasta separately and add to the soup when reheating so it's fresh and perfectly cooked.*

4 entree servings (about 1½ cups each)

2 cups sliced carrots

¼ cup sliced green onions

2 cloves garlic, minced

1 teaspoon dried basil leaves

5 cups Canned Vegetable Stock (see p. 56)

1 package (9 ounces) fresh low-fat tomato-cheese tortellini

3 cups torn spinach leaves

2–3 teaspoons lemon juice

⅛–¼ teaspoon ground nutmeg

⅛ teaspoon pepper

Per Serving:
Calories: 290
% of calories from fat: 9
Fat (gm): 2.8
Saturated fat (gm): 1
Cholesterol (mg): 3.8
Sodium (mg): 395
Protein (gm): 12.1
Carbohydrate (gm): 48

Exchanges:
Milk: 0.0
Vegetable: 2.0
Fruit: 0.0
Bread: 2.5
Meat: 1.0
Fat: 0.0

1. Sauté carrots, green onions, garlic, and basil in lightly greased large saucepan until onions are tender, about 5 minutes. Add stock and heat to boiling; reduce heat and simmer, covered, 10 minutes. Heat soup to boiling; stir in tortellini and spinach; reduce heat and simmer, uncovered, until tortellini are *al dente*, about 5 minutes. Season with lemon juice, nutmeg, and pepper.

TORTELLINI SOUP WITH KALE

O *Fast and easy to make when there's little time to cook!*

45 **8 first-course servings** (about 1½ cups each)

1 cup sliced leek, or green onions

3 cloves garlic, minced

1 tablespoon olive oil

3 quarts reduced-sodium vegetable broth

2 cups (12 ounces) kale, coarsely chopped

1 cup sliced mushrooms

½ package (9 ounce-size) mushroom, or herb, tortellini

Salt and white pepper, to taste

1. Sauté leek and garlic in oil in large saucepan until leek is tender, 5 to 8 minutes. Add broth and heat to boiling; stir in kale and mushrooms. Reduce heat and simmer, covered, 5 minutes. Add tortellini and simmer, uncovered, until tortellini are *al dente*, about 7 minute; season to taste with salt and white pepper.

Per Serving:
Calories: 105
% of calories from fat: 24
Fat (gm): 3.1
Saturated fat (gm): 0.8
Cholesterol (mg): 8.4
Sodium (mg): 69
Protein (gm): 3
Carbohydrate (gm): 11.6

Exchanges:
Milk: 0.0
Vegetable: 2.0
Fruit: 0.0
Bread: 0.0
Meat: 0.0
Fat: 1.0

TORTELLINI AND MUSHROOM SOUP

LO *Porcini mushrooms, a Tuscan delicacy found fresh in the fall, are available in dried form year round. Porcini impart a wonderful earthy flavor to recipes. Other dried mushrooms, such as shiitake or Chinese black mushrooms, can be substituted for a similar flavor.*

6 first-course servings (about 1 cup each)

2 ounces dried porcini mushrooms

Hot water

8 ounces fresh white mushrooms, sliced

2 tablespoons finely chopped shallots, or green onions

2 cloves garlic, minced

½ teaspoon dried tarragon, or thyme, leaves

4 cups Rich Mushroom Stock (see p. 54), or reduced-sodium vegetable broth

¼ cup dry sherry (optional)

1 package (9 ounces) fresh low-fat tomato-and-cheese tortellini

Salt and pepper, to taste

Per Serving:
Calories: 110
% of calories from fat: 16
Fat (gm): 2
Saturated fat (gm): 0.4
Cholesterol (mg): 4.2
Sodium (mg): 184
Protein (gm): 5
Carbohydrate (gm): 17.1

Exchanges:
Milk: 0.0
Vegetable: 1.0
Fruit: 0.0
Bread: 1.0
Meat: 0.0
Fat: 0.5

1. Place dried mushrooms in bowl; pour hot water over to cover. Let stand until mushrooms are soft, about 15 minutes; drain. Slice mushrooms, discarding any tough parts.

2. Sauté dried and white mushrooms, shallots, garlic, and tarragon in lightly greased saucepan until mushrooms are tender, about 5

minutes. Add stock and sherry and heat to boiling; add tortellini, salt, and pepper. Reduce heat and simmer, uncovered, until tortellini are *al dente*, about 5 minutes; season to taste with salt and pepper.

GREEK LEMON-RICE SOUP

o *Nicely tart; use fresh lemon juice for the best flavor. If making this soup in advance, do not add egg until reheating for serving.*

4 first-course servings (about 1 cup each)

3½ cups Mediterranean Stock (see p. 54), or reduced-sodium vegetable broth
¼ cup long-grain rice
2 large cloves garlic, minced
¼–⅓ cup lemon juice
1 egg, lightly beaten
2 tablespoons chopped parsley
Salt and white pepper, to taste

Per Serving:
Calories: 106
% of calories from fat: 20
Fat (gm): 2.4
Saturated fat (gm): 0.5
Cholesterol (mg): 53.3
Sodium (mg): 31
Protein (gm): 3
Carbohydrate (gm): 14.4

Exchanges:
Milk: 0.0
Vegetable: 0.0
Fruit: 0.0
Bread: 1.0
Meat: 0.0
Fat: 0.5

1. Heat stock to boiling in medium saucepan; stir in rice and garlic. Reduce heat and simmer, covered, until rice is tender, about 25 minutes; reduce heat to low; Mix lemon juice and egg; slowly stir mixture into soup. Stir in parsley; season to taste with salt and white pepper.

ORIENTAL WATERCRESS SOUP

v *Spinach can be substituted for the watercress in this fragrant Cantonese offering.*

6 first-course servings (about 1 cup each)

6 cups Oriental Stock (see p. 55)
3 slices (scant ¼ inch thick) gingerroot
2 cups loosely packed torn watercress
Salt and white pepper, to taste
2 sliced green onions
2 tablespoons shredded carrot

1. Heat stock and gingerroot to boiling in large saucepan; reduce heat and simmer, covered, 5 minutes. Remove gingerroot with slotted spoon and discard. Add watercress and simmer, uncovered, 10 to 15 minutes. Season to taste with salt and white pepper. Sprinkle each bowl of soup with green onions and carrot.

Per Serving:
Calories: 11
% of calories from fat: 9
Fat (gm): 0.1
Saturated fat (gm): 0
Cholesterol (mg): 0
Sodium (mg): 116
Protein (gm): 0.9
Carbohydrate (gm): 1.8

Exchanges:
Milk: 0.0
Vegetable: 0.0
Fruit: 0.0
Bread: 0.0
Meat: 0.0
Fat: 0.0

CREAMY PEANUT BUTTER SOUP

L

African in origin, this soup will tempt peanut butter lovers! In our low-fat version, pureed beans contribute rich texture without detracting from the peanut flavor.

4 entree servings (about 1½ cups each)

½ cup each: chopped onion, carrot, celery
1 leek, cleaned, sliced
2 cloves garlic, minced
3 cups Canned Vegetable Stock (see p. 56)
1 can (15 ounces) Great Northern beans, rinsed, drained
½ cup reduced-fat peanut butter
½ cup fat-free half-and-half, or fat-free milk
½ teaspoon curry powder
2–3 teaspoons lemon juice
1–2 dashes red pepper sauce
Salt, cayenne, and black pepper, to taste
Sliced green onions, as garnish

Per Serving:
Calories: 379
% of calories from fat: 30
Fat (gm): 12.9
Saturated fat (gm): 2.7
Cholesterol (mg): 0
Sodium (mg): 88
Protein (gm): 19.2
Carbohydrate (gm): 48.6

Exchanges:
Milk: 0.0
Vegetable: 2.0
Fruit: 0.0
Bread: 2.5
Meat: 1.5
Fat: 1.5

1. Sauté onion, carrot, celery, leek, and garlic in lightly greased large saucepan 5 minutes. Add stock and beans and heat to boiling; reduce heat and simmer, covered, until vegetables are tender, 10 to 15 minutes.

2. Process soup and peanut butter in food processor or blender until smooth; return soup to saucepan, stir in half-and-half and curry powder and heat until hot. Season to taste with lemon juice, red pepper sauce, salt, cayenne, and black pepper. Sprinkle each bowl of soup with green onions.

VIETNAMESE CURRIED COCONUT SOUP

Rice stick noodles, made with rice flour, can be round or flat. They must be softened in water before cooking. Cooked angel hair pasta can be substituted.

6 first-course servings (about 1 cup each)

1 tablespoon minced garlic

3–4 tablespoons curry powder

3½ cups Basic Vegetable Stock (see p. 52)

3 cups reduced-fat coconut milk

2 tablespoons minced gingerroot

½ cup each: sliced green onions, yellow onion

2 tablespoons minced parsley

1 tablespoon grated lime zest

½–1 teaspoon oriental chili paste

2 tablespoons minced parsley

¼ cup each: lime juice, chopped cilantro

Salt and white pepper, to taste

8 ounces rice stick noodles

Per Serving:
Calories: 138
% of calories from fat: 27
Fat (gm): 4.3
Saturated fat (gm): 0
Cholesterol (mg): 0
Sodium (mg): 112
Protein (gm): 3.4
Carbohydrate (gm): 22.9

Exchanges:
Milk: 0.0
Vegetable: 1.0
Fruit: 0.0
Bread: 1.0
Meat: 0.0
Fat: 1.0

1. Sauté garlic in lightly greased large saucepan 1 minute; stir in curry powder and cook, stirring, 30 seconds. Add stock, coconut milk, gingerroot, onions, parsley, lime zest, and chili paste; heat to boiling. Reduce heat and simmer, covered, 15 minutes. Stir in lime juice and cilantro; season to taste with salt and white pepper.

2. Prepare noodles according to package directions. Spoon noodles into soup; ladle soup over noodles

COUNTRY LENTIL SOUP

L *A light soup that is wholesome in flavor and texture. This soup freezes well, so make extra.*

4 entree servings (about 1¾ cups each)

1½ cups chopped onions

1 cup each: sliced celery, carrots

2 teaspoons minced garlic

1 tablespoon olive oil

3 cups Roasted Vegetable Stock (see p. 53)

2 cups water

1 cup dried lentils

1 can (14½ ounces) reduced-sodium whole tomatoes, undrained, crushed

2 tablespoons chopped parsley

1 teaspoon dried marjoram leaves

½ teaspoon each: dried oregano and thyme leaves

Salt and pepper, to taste

4 tablespoons grated fat-free Parmesan cheese

Per Serving:
Calories: 275
% of calories from fat: 14
Fat (gm): 4.4
Saturated fat (gm): 0.6
Cholesterol (mg): 0
Sodium (mg): 109
Protein (gm): 15.8
Carbohydrate (gm): 42.8

Exchanges:
Milk: 0.0
Vegetable: 3.0
Fruit: 0.0
Bread: 2.0
Meat: 0.5
Fat: 0.5

1. Sauté onions, celery, carrots, and garlic in oil in large saucepan 5 to 8 minutes. Add stock, water, lentils, tomatoes, and herbs; heat to boiling. Reduce heat and simmer, covered, until lentils are tender, about 30 minutes. Season to taste with salt and pepper. Sprinkle each bowl of soup with 1 tablespoon cheese.

INDIAN LENTIL SOUP

L

45

This soup (Dal Shorba) from India is flavored with curry powder and sweet coriander. Red, green, or brown lentils can be used.

6 entree servings (about 1⅓ cups each)

½ cup chopped onion

1 clove garlic, minced

2 teaspoons curry powder

1 teaspoon each: crushed coriander and cumin seeds

½ teaspoon ground turmeric

¼ teaspoon crushed red pepper flakes

1 tablespoon olive oil

5 cups reduced-sodium vegetable broth

4 cups water

2 cups dried red, or brown, lentils

Salt and pepper, to taste

6 tablespoons fat-free plain yogurt

Per Serving:
Calories: 281
% of calories from fat: 11
Fat (gm): 3.6
Saturated fat (gm): 0.4
Cholesterol (mg): 0.3
Sodium (mg): 403
Protein (gm): 20
Carbohydrate (gm): 44

Exchanges:
Milk: 0.0
Vegetable: 0.0
Fruit: 0.0
Bread: 3.0
Meat: 1.0
Fat: 0.0

1. Sauté onion, garlic, curry powder, herbs, and red pepper in oil in large saucepan until onion is tender, about 5 minutes, stirring frequently. Add broth, water, and lentils; heat to boiling. Reduce heat and simmer, covered, until lentils are tender, about 30 minutes. Season to taste with salt and pepper. Top each bowl of soup with a tablespoon of yogurt.

THREE

Stews

and

Casseroles

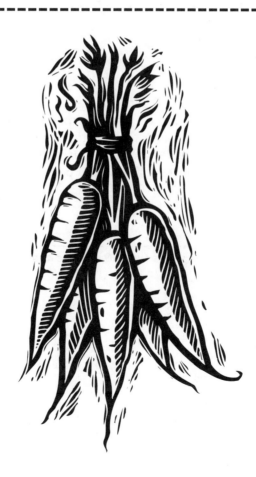

BEAN-THICKENED VEGETABLE STEW

V

Pureed beans provide the perfect thickening for this hearty stew.

45 **6 servings** (about 1¼ cups each)

3 carrots, sliced
1 medium onion, chopped
3 cloves garlic, minced
1¾ cups reduced-sodium vegetable broth
2 cups chopped tomatoes
1½ cups sliced mushrooms
1 yellow summer squash, sliced
1 can (15 ounces) black beans, rinsed, drained
1 can (15 ounces) navy beans, rinsed, drained, pureed
1 cup frozen peas
½ teaspoon each: dried thyme and oregano leaves
2 bay leaves
Salt and pepper, to taste
4 cups cooked noodles, warm

Per Serving:
Calories: 332
% of calories from fat: 6
Fat (gm): 2.4
Saturated fat (gm): 0.5
Cholesterol (mg): 35.2
Sodium (mg): 772
Protein (gm): 16.8
Carbohydrate (gm): 65

Exchanges:
Milk: 0.0
Vegetable: 0.0
Fruit: 0.0
Bread: 4.0
Meat: 1.0
Fat: 0.0

1. Sauté carrots, onion, and garlic in lightly greased large saucepan until tender, about 5 minutes. Stir in remaining ingredients, except salt, pepper, and noodles; heat to boiling. Reduce heat and simmer, uncovered, until vegetables are tender, 10 to 15 minutes. Discard bay leaves; season to taste with salt and pepper. Serve over noodles.

HASTY STEW

V

45

This stew is easily made in less than 30 minutes and boasts fresh flavors and textures.

4 servings (about 1 cup each)

2 medium onions, cut into wedges
8 ounces mushrooms, sliced
2 cloves garlic, minced
¼ cup finely chopped parsley
1 teaspoon dried savory leaves
1 bay leaf

3½ cups reduced-sodium vegetable broth

2 medium zucchini, sliced

2½ cups each: cubed unpeeled potatoes,
   cauliflower florets

1 large tomato, cut into wedges

Salt and pepper, to taste

3 cups cooked millet, or couscous, warm

Per Serving:
Calories: 404
% of calories from fat: 6
Fat (gm): 2.6
Saturated fat (gm): 0.4
Cholesterol (mg): 0
Sodium (mg): 116
Protein (gm): 13.4
Carbohydrate (gm): 84.6

Exchanges:
Milk: 0.0
Vegetable: 3.0
Fruit: 0.0
Bread: 4.5
Meat: 0.0
Fat: 0.0

1. Sauté onions, mushrooms, garlic, and herbs in lightly greased large saucepan until onions are tender, about 5 minutes. Add broth, zucchini, potatoes, and cauliflower and heat to boiling; reduce heat and simmer, covered, until vegetables are tender, about 10 minutes. Add tomato wedges during last 5 minutes of cooking time. Discard bay leaf; season to taste with salt and pepper. Serve with millet.

45-MINUTE PREP TIP: Begin cooking the millet before preparing the rest of the recipe.

VEGGIE STEW WITH DUMPLINGS

L

Dumplings that are soft, fluffy, and seasoned with herbs top this colorful stew.

45 **6 servings** (about 1½ cups each)

1 cup each: coarsely chopped onion, red bell pepper

1 tablespoon canola oil

3⅔ cups reduced-sodium vegetable broth, divided

⅓ cup all-purpose flour

3 medium potatoes, unpeeled, cut into 1-inch pieces

2 cups each: cubed butternut squash,
   unpeeled potatoes

1 medium zucchini, sliced

4 ounces halved cremini, or white, mushrooms

¾ cup frozen peas

1½ teaspoons dried Italian seasoning

Salt and pepper, to taste

Herb Dumplings (recipe follows)

Per Serving:
Calories: 328
% calories from fat: 13
Fat (gm): 5
Saturated fat (gm): 0.4
Cholesterol (mg): 0.4
Sodium (mg): 697
Protein (gm): 9.8
Carbohydrate (gm): 63.6

Exchanges:
Milk: 0.0
Vegetable: 3.0
Fruit: 0.0
Bread: 3.0
Meat: 0.0
Fat: 1.0

1. Sauté onion and bell pepper in oil in large saucepan until onion is tender, about 5 minutes. Stir in 3 cups broth and heat to boiling. Stir in combined remaining ⅔ cup broth and flour; boil, stirring, until thickened, about 1 minute. Stir in remaining ingredients, except salt, pepper, and Herb Dumplings; simmer covered until vegetables are just tender, about 10 minutes. Season to taste with salt and pepper.

2. Spoon dumpling dough on top of stew in 6 large spoonfuls; cook over low heat, uncovered, 10 minutes. Cook, covered, 10 minutes or until dumplings are tender and toothpick inserted in centers comes out clean.

Herb Dumplings

Makes 6

2 cups reduced-fat baking mix
¾ teaspoon dried Italian seasoning
⅔ cup fat-free milk

Combine biscuit mix and Italian seasoning in small bowl; stir in milk to form soft dough. Cook as directed in recipe.

VEGGIE MÉLANGE WITH BULGUR

V

Nutritious bulgur adds flavor and toothsome texture to this stew.

45 **4 servings** (about 1⅔ cups each)

¾ cup boiling water
½ cup uncooked bulgur
2 medium onions, coarsely chopped
2 cups carrots, cut into 1-inch pieces
1 cup each: cubed unpeeled Idaho potatoes, red bell pepper
2–3 cloves garlic, minced
1 can (14½ ounces) reduced-sodium tomato wedges, undrained
2–3 cups spicy tomato juice
2 cups each: cubed zucchini, halved cremini mushrooms
1 teaspoon each: dried thyme, oregano leaves
Salt and pepper, to taste

1. Stir boiling water into bulgur in bowl; let stand until bulgur is softened, about 20 minutes.

2. Sauté onions, carrots, potatoes, bell peppers, and garlic in lightly greased large saucepan until onions are tender, 8 to 10 minutes. Add bulgur and remaining ingredients, except salt and pepper; heat to boiling. Reduce heat and simmer, uncovered, until vegetables are tender and stew is thickened, 10 to 15 minutes. Season to taste with salt and pepper.

Per Serving:
Calories: 259
% of calories from fat: 5
Fat (gm): 1.4
Saturated fat (gm): 0.2
Cholesterol (mg): 0
Sodium (mg): 694
Protein (gm): 9.9
Carbohydrate (gm): 57.4

Exchanges:
Milk: 0.0
Vegetable: 5.0
Fruit: 0.0
Bread: 2.0
Meat: 0.0
Fat: 0.0

CABBAGE RAGOUT WITH REAL MASHED POTATOES

L

Fresh fennel, gingerroot, and apple lend aromatic highlights to this cabbage stew. If fresh fennel is not available, substitute celery and increase the amount of fennel seeds to 1½ teaspoons.

6 servings (about 1⅓ cups each)

1 medium eggplant (about 1¼ pounds), unpeeled, cut into scant 1-inch slices

1 cup chopped onion

½ cup thinly sliced fennel bulb

1 tablespoon each: minced garlic, gingerroot

1 teaspoon fennel seeds, crushed

8 cups thinly sliced cabbage

2 cups reduced-sodium vegetable broth

2 medium apples, cored, cubed

1 cup fat-free sour cream

Salt and pepper, to taste

Real Mashed Potatoes (see p. 493), or 4 cups cooked whole wheat noodles

Per Serving:
Calories: 249
% of calories from fat: 10
Fat (gm): 3
Saturated fat (gm): 0.5
Cholesterol (mg): 8.8
Sodium (mg): 255
Protein (gm): 8.5
Carbohydrate (gm): 50

Exchanges:
Milk: 0.0
Vegetable: 0.0
Fruit: 0.0
Bread: 3.0
Meat: 0.0
Fat: 0.5

1. Cook 5 or 6 eggplant slices over medium heat in lightly greased large skillet until browned on the bottom, 3 to 5 minutes. Spray tops of slices with cooking spray and turn; cook until browned, 3 to

5 minutes. Repeat with remaining eggplant. Cut eggplant into 1-inch cubes and reserve.

2. Sauté onion, fennel, garlic, gingerroot, and fennel seeds in lightly greased large saucepan until onion is tender, 3 to 5 minutes. Add cabbage and broth and heat to boiling; reduce heat and simmer, covered, until cabbage is wilted and crisp-tender, about 5 minutes. Stir in apples and cook, covered, until apples are tender, about 5 minutes. Stir in reserved eggplant and sour cream; cook over medium heat until hot through, 3 to 4 minutes. Season to taste with salt and pepper. Serve stew over potatoes or noodles.

BEAN AND SQUASH STEW

V

45

Stews don't have to be long-cooked to be good — this delicious stew is simmered to savory goodness in less than 30 minutes. Serve with Garlic Bread (see p. 559).

6 servings (about 1¼ cups each)

1½ cups each: chopped onions, green bell peppers

2 teaspoons minced roasted garlic

1 tablespoon flour

2 cups peeled, cubed, butternut, *or* acorn, squash (½-inch cubes)

2 cans (16 ounces each) reduced-sodium diced tomatoes, undrained

1 can (15 ounces) red kidney beans, rinsed, drained

1 can (13¼ ounces) baby lima beans, rinsed, drained

½–¾ teaspoon dried bouquet garni

Salt and pepper, to taste

Per Serving:
Calories: 239
% of calories from fat: 5
Fat (gm): 1.4
Saturated fat (gm): 0.2
Cholesterol (mg): 0
Sodium (mg): 160
Protein (gm): 14
Carbohydrate (gm): 50.5

Exchanges:
Milk: 0.0
Vegetable: 3.0
Fruit: 0.0
Bread: 2.0
Meat: 0.5
Fat: 0.0

1. Sauté onions, bell peppers, and garlic in lightly greased large saucepan until tender, about 8 minutes. Stir in flour; cook 1 minute longer. Add remaining ingredients, except salt and pepper, and heat to boiling; reduce heat and simmer 10 to 15 minutes. Season to taste with salt and pepper.

CHILI STEW

V | *A squeeze of lime adds a cooling touch to this veggie-packed chili.*

45 | **6 servings** (about 1⅓ cups each)

2 cups cubed butternut squash (1-inch)
1 cup each: chopped onions, celery, red bell pepper
½ jalapeño chili, finely chopped
2 cloves garlic, minced
1 can (15 ounces) each: reduced-sodium chunky
  tomato sauce, rinsed, drained red kidney beans
3 cups reduced-sodium tomato juice
½ package (12-ounce size) vegetarian ground beef
1 cup each: cubed zucchini, sliced mushrooms
1½ teaspoons each: chili powder, ground cumin
Salt and pepper, to taste
6 lime wedges

Per Serving:
Calories: 236
% of calories from fat: 4
Fat (gm): 1.1
Saturated fat (gm): 0.1
Cholesterol (mg): 0
Sodium (mg): 691
Protein (gm): 16.9
Carbohydrate (gm): 46

Exchanges:
Milk: 0.0
Vegetable: 3.0
Fruit: 0.0
Bread: 1.5
Meat: 1.0
Fat: 0.0

1. Sauté butternut squash onions, celery, bell pepper, jalapeño chili, and garlic in lightly greased Dutch oven or large saucepan until crisp-tender, 8 to 10 minutes. Add remaining ingredients, except salt, pepper, and lime wedges; heat to boiling. Reduce heat and simmer, uncovered, until vegetables are tender and stew is thickened, 10 to 15 minutes. Season to taste with salt and pepper. Serve with lime wedges.

HOT 'N' SPICY BEAN AND VEGETABLE STEW

| **V** |

Make this stew as fiery as you like with serrano or other hot chilies!

| **45** |

6 servings (about 1½ cups each)

1½ cups chopped onions

2–3 teaspoons each: minced serrano chilies, garlic

1 tablespoon flour

1½ teaspoons dried oregano leaves

1 teaspoon ground cinnamon

1 bay leaf

2 cans (16 ounces each) reduced-sodium diced
tomatoes, undrained

1½ cups reduced-sodium vegetable broth

1 tablespoon red wine vinegar

4 medium carrots, sliced

4 medium red potatoes, unpeeled, cubed

1 can (15 ounces) each: black beans, pinto beans, rinsed, drained

Salt and pepper, to taste

Per Serving:
Calories: 235
% of calories from fat: 3.7
Fat (gm): 1
Saturated fat (gm): 0.2
Cholesterol (mg): 0.0
Sodium (mg): 686
Protein (gm): 10
Carbohydrate (gm): 51

Exchanges:
Milk: 0.0
Vegetable: 1.0
Fruit: 0.0
Bread: 1.0
Meat: 0.0
Fat: 0.0

1. Sauté onions, chilies, and garlic in lightly greased Dutch oven or large saucepan 5 minutes; stir in flour and seasonings and cook 1 minute longer. Add remaining ingredients, except salt and pepper; heat to boiling. Reduce heat and simmer, covered, until vegetables are tender and stew thickened, 15 to 20 minutes. Discard bay leaf; season to taste with salt and pepper.

TEX-MEX VEGETABLE STEW

| **V** |

Poblano chilies range from mild to very hot in flavor, so taste a tiny bit before using. If the chili is very hot, you may want to substitute some green bell pepper.

| **45** |

6 servings (about 1½ cups each)

1 each: chopped medium red onion, poblano chili, seeded

3 cloves garlic, minced

3 cans (10 ounces each) tomatoes with green chilies, undrained

12 small new potatoes, cut into halves

4 medium carrots, cut into 1-inch pieces

3 ears corn, cut into 2-inch pieces

1 cup reduced-sodium vegetable broth

2 tablespoons balsamic vinegar

1 tablespoon chili powder

2 teaspoons ground cumin

½ teaspoon dried oregano leaves

1 can (15 ounces) black beans, rinsed, drained

2 cups frozen peas, thawed

½ cup finely chopped cilantro

Salt and pepper, to taste

Per Serving:
Calories: 423
% of calories from fat: 5
Fat (gm): 2.4
Saturated fat (gm): 0.2
Cholesterol (mg): 0
Sodium (mg): 793
Protein (gm): 16.7
Carbohydrate (gm): 92.5

Exchanges:
Milk: 0.0
Vegetable: 3.0
Fruit: 0.0
Bread: 5.0
Meat: 0.0
Fat: 0.0

1. Sauté onion, chili, and garlic in lightly greased large saucepan until softened, about 4 minutes. Add tomatoes, potatoes, carrots, corn, broth, vinegar, chili powder, cumin, and oregano; heat to boiling. Reduce heat and simmer, covered, until vegetables are tender, about 15 minutes. Stir in beans and peas and simmer 5 minutes. Stir in cilantro; season to taste with salt and pepper.

MEXICAN ANCHO CHILI STEW

V

45

This stew has lots of delicious sauce, so serve with warm tortillas, or serve over Black Beans and Rice (see p. 374). Vary the amount of ancho chilies to taste.

4 servings (about 1⅓ cups each)

4–6 ancho chilies, stems, seeds, and veins discarded

2 cups boiling water

4 medium tomatoes, cut into wedges

6–8 Mexican-style vegetarian burgers, crumbled

1 large onion, chopped

2 cloves garlic, minced

1 teaspoon minced serrano, or jalapeño, chili

1 teaspoon each: dried oregano leaves, crushed
   cumin seeds

2 tablespoons flour

Salt and pepper, to taste

Per Serving:
Calories: 275
% of calories from fat: 13
Fat (gm): 4.3
Saturated fat (gm): 0.1
Cholesterol (mg): 0
Sodium (mg): 735
Protein (gm): 11.9
Carbohydrate (gm): 50.9

Exchanges:
Milk: 0.0
Vegetable: 2.0
Fruit: 0.0
Bread: 2.5
Meat: 0.5
Fat: 0.5

1. Place ancho chilies in bowl; pour boiling water over. Let stand until chilies are softened, about 10 minutes. Process chilies and water, and tomatoes in food processor or blender until smooth.

2. Cook crumbled burgers, onion, garlic, serrano chili, and herbs in lightly greased large saucepan until onion is tender, about 5 minutes. Stir in flour; cook over medium heat 1 to 2 minutes more. Add chili and tomato mixture and heat to boiling. Reduce heat and simmer, covered, 15 to 20 minutes. Season to taste with salt and pepper.

VEGETARIAN MEATBALLS IN TOMATO CHILI SAUCE

v

Pasilla chilies are picante — use 2 only if you enjoy a truly hot sauce!

4 servings (4 meatballs each)

1–2 pasilla chilies
1 can (28 ounces) reduced-sodium diced tomatoes, undrained
1 package (12 ounces) vegetarian meatballs
Salt and pepper, to taste
3 cups cooked brown, or white, rice, warm

Per Serving:
Calories: 368
% of calories from fat: 15
Fat (gm): 6.4
Saturated fat (gm): 2.4
Cholesterol (mg): 63.4
Sodium (mg): 602
Protein (gm): 19
Carbohydrate (gm): 59.7

Exchanges:
Milk: 0.0
Vegetable: 2.0
Fruit: 0.0
Bread: 3.0
Meat: 1.5
Fat: 0.5

1. Cook pasilla chilies in lightly greased large saucepan over medium heat until softened; discard stems, seeds, and veins. Process chilies and tomatoes with liquid in blender until smooth. Heat tomato mixture to boiling in large saucepan; add vegetarian meatballs. Reduce heat and simmer, covered, 10 minutes. Season to taste with salt and pepper. Serve meatballs and sauce over rice.

MEXICAN-STYLE VEGETABLE STEW

V

45

A winter vegetable offering with a Mexican flair, spooned over strands of spaghetti squash. Serve with warm squares of Green Chili Corn Bread (see p. 561).

4 servings (about 1⅓ cups each)

1 medium spaghetti squash, halved, seeded

2 medium russet potatoes, cut into 1-inch pieces

1 each: chopped medium onion, large carrot

1 cup cubed rutabaga

½ cup chopped green bell pepper

2 cloves garlic, minced

1 tablespoon flour

1½ cups reduced-sodium vegetable broth (see p. xii)

1 can (14½ ounces) diced tomatoes and chilies, undrained

Salt and pepper, to taste

Cilantro, finely chopped, as garnish

Per Serving:
Calories: 188
% of calories from fat: 6
Fat (gm): 1.4
Saturated fat (gm): 0.2
Cholesterol (mg): 0.0
Sodium (mg): 523
Protein (gm): 5.5
Carbohydrate (gm): 42

Exchanges:
Milk: 0.0
Vegetable: 2.0
Fruit: 0.0
Bread: 2.0
Meat: 0.0
Fat: 0.0

1. Place squash halves, cut sides down, in baking pan; add ½ inch water. Bake, covered, at 350 degrees until tender, 30 to 40 minutes. Using fork, scrape squash to separate into strands.

2. While squash is cooking, sauté vegetables and garlic in lightly greased large skillet until lightly browned, 8 to 10 minutes. Stir in flour; cook 1 minute longer. Add broth and tomatoes with liquid; heat to boiling. Reduce heat and simmer, covered, until vegetables are tender, about 15 minutes. Season to taste with salt and pepper. Serve over spaghetti squash; sprinkle with cilantro.

ORANGE AND GINGER SQUASH STEW

L

45

Any winter squash, such as acorn, butternut, or Hubbard, is appropriate for this orange-and-ginger accented stew.

6 servings (about 1½ cups each)

2 each: chopped medium onions, green bell peppers

2 cloves garlic, minced

1 tablespoon olive oil

3 cups each: cubed peeled winter yellow squash, Idaho potatoes

1 can (14½ ounces) reduced-sodium diced tomatoes, undrained

2 cups reduced-sodium vegetable broth

½ cup orange juice

½ teaspoon ground ginger

1 cup fat-free sour cream

2 tablespoons minced parsley

1 tablespoon grated orange zest

Salt and pepper, to taste

4 cups cooked noodles, or brown basmati rice, hot

Per Serving:
Calories: 350
% of calories from fat: 11
Fat (gm): 4
Saturated fat (gm): 0.7
Cholesterol (mg): 42
Sodium (mg): 424
Protein (gm): 11
Carbohydrate (gm): 67

Exchanges:
Milk: 0.0
Vegetable: 0.0
Fruit: 0.0
Bread: 4.0
Meat: 0.0
Fat: 1.0

1. Sauté onions, peppers, and garlic in oil in large saucepan until tender, about 4 minutes. Add squash, potatoes, tomatoes with liquid, broth, orange juice, and ginger; heat to boiling. Reduce heat and simmer, uncovered, 30 minutes. Reduce heat to low and stir in sour cream, parsley, and orange zest; season to taste with salt and pepper. Serve over noodles.

CARIBBEAN SWEET-AND-SOUR STEW

V

45

Sweet-and-sour flavors team with tofu, pineapple, and beans in this island-inspired dish.

6 servings (about 1¼ cups each)

2 packages (10½ ounces each) light tofu, cut
  into 1-inch cubes

1 each: chopped medium onion, sliced medium
  red, and green, bell pepper

4 cloves garlic, minced

2 teaspoons minced gingerroot

1–2 jalapeño chilies, finely chopped

3 cups reduced-sodium vegetable broth (see p. xii)

1 can (20 ounces) pineapple chunks in juice,
  undrained

2 tablespoons light brown sugar

2–3 teaspoons curry powder

3 tablespoons apple cider vinegar

1 tablespoon cornstarch

1 can (15 ounces) black beans, rinsed, drained

4 cups cooked rice, warm

Per Serving:
Calories: 370
% of calories from fat: 6
Fat (gm): 2.5
Saturated fat (gm): 0.4
Cholesterol (mg): 0.0
Sodium (mg): 550
Protein (gm): 15
Carbohydrate (gm): 73

Exchanges:
Milk: 0.0
Vegetable: 1.0
Fruit: 0.0
Bread: 2.0
Meat: 1.0
Fat: 0.0

1. Add tofu to lightly greased large skillet and cook over medium heat until browned on all sides, 8 to 10 minutes; remove and reserve. Add onion, bell peppers, garlic, gingerroot, and jalapeño chilies to skillet; sauté until onions are tender, about 5 minutes. Stir in broth, pineapple with juice, sugar, curry powder, and reserved tofu; heat to boiling. Reduce heat and simmer, uncovered, 5 minutes.

2. Heat mixture to boiling; stir in combined vinegar and cornstarch, stirring until thickened, about 1 minute. Stir in beans and cook 2 to 3 minutes; serve over rice.

45-MINUTE PREP TIP: Begin cooking the rice before preparing the rest of the recipe.

GINGER BEAN AND BLACKEYE STEW

V *Fresh gingerroot accents the flavor contrasts in this colorful stew.*

6 servings (scant 1 cup each)

1 cup each: chopped onion, red bell pepper

1 tablespoon minced gingerroot

2 teaspoons each: minced garlic, jalapeño chili

1 tablespoon olive oil

½ teaspoon dried thyme leaves

1 can (15 ounces) each: black beans, black-eyed peas, rinsed, drained

¾ cup fresh, or frozen, cut okra

⅓ cup orange juice

⅓ cup jalapeño chili jelly, or orange marmalade

1 can (11 ounces) Mandarin orange segments, drained

Salt and pepper, to taste

3 cups cooked brown, or white, rice

Per Serving:
Calories: 294
% of calories from fat: 10.8
Fat (gm): 3.7
Saturated fat (gm): 0.6
Cholesterol (mg): 0.0
Sodium (mg): 490
Protein (gm): 10.0
Carbohydrate (gm): 59

Exchanges:
Milk: 0.0
Vegetable: 0.0
Fruit: 0.0
Bread: 4.0
Meat: 0.0
Fat: 1.0

1. Sauté onion, bell pepper, gingerroot, garlic, and jalapeño chili in oil in large skillet until tender, about 5 minutes; add thyme and cook 1 minute longer. Add black beans, black-eyed peas, okra, orange juice, and jelly; heat to boiling. Reduce heat and simmer, covered, until okra is tender, 5 to 10 minutes. Stir in orange segments; cook 1 to 2 minutes. Season to taste with salt and pepper. Serve over rice.

SWEET-SOUR SQUASH AND POTATO STEW

V

45

The vegetables are simmered in cider and seasoned with honey and vinegar for a refreshing sweet-sour flavor.

6 servings (about 1½ cups each)

½ cup chopped shallots

1 medium red bell pepper, chopped

2 cloves garlic, minced

1 tablespoon flour

1 can (14½ ounces) reduced-sodium diced
tomatoes, undrained

1 cup apple cider

2 cups each: cubed, peeled butternut, or acorn
squash, peeled sweet potato

1½ tablespoons each: honey, cider vinegar

1 bay leaf

¼ teaspoon ground nutmeg

1 large tart green apple, peeled, cubed

Salt and pepper, to taste

4 cups cooked basmati, or Jasmine, rice, warm

Per Serving:
Calories: 411
% of calories from fat: 4
Fat (gm): 1.8
Saturated fat (gm): 0.2
Cholesterol (mg): 0
Sodium (mg): 52
Protein (gm): 9.7
Carbohydrate (gm): 95.9

Exchanges:
Milk: 0.0
Vegetable: 3.0
Fruit: 1.0
Bread: 3.5
Meat: 0.0
Fat: 0.0

1. Sauté shallots, bell pepper, and garlic in lightly greased large
skillet until softened, about 4 minutes; stir in flour and cook 1
minute longer. Add tomatoes with liquid, cider, vegetables, honey,
vinegar, bay leaf, and nutmeg; heat to boiling. Reduce heat and
simmer, covered, 15 minutes; add apple and simmer until tender,
about 5 minutes. Discard bay leaf and season to taste with salt and
pepper; serve over rice.

TOFU AND VEGETABLE STEW

V

45

*As with most stews, vegetables in this dish can vary according to season and
availability; tempeh can be substituted for the tofu.*

4 servings (about 1¾ cups each)

½ cup each: sliced onion, celery

3 cloves garlic, minced

4 cups reduced-sodium vegetable broth

2 cups each: sliced carrots, unpeeled red potatoes

1 bay leaf

1 teaspoon ground cumin

½ teaspoon dried thyme leaves

½ package (10-ounce size) baby spinach

1 package (10½ ounces) firm light tofu, cubed
(½-inch)

Salt and pepper, to taste

Per Serving:
Calories: 239
% of calories from fat: 8
Fat (gm): 2.3
Saturated fat (gm): 0.2
Cholesterol (mg): 0
Sodium (mg): 182
Protein (gm): 11.1
Carbohydrate (gm): 43.8

Exchanges:
Milk: 0.0
Vegetable: 4.0
Fruit: 0.0
Bread: 1.5
Meat: 0.5
Fat: 0.0

1. Sauté onion, celery, and garlic in lightly greased large saucepan until softened, about 4 minutes. Add broth, carrots, potatoes, bay leaf, cumin, and thyme; heat to boiling. Reduce heat and simmer, covered, until vegetables are tender, about 15 minutes. Add spinach and tofu and simmer 3 to 4 minutes. Discard bay leaf; season to taste with salt and pepper.

THREE-BEAN STEW WITH POLENTA

V

45

Use any kind of canned or cooked dried beans; one 15-ounce can of drained beans yields 1½ cups.

4–6 servings (about 1–1½ cups each)

1 cup chopped onion

½ cup chopped red bell pepper

1 teaspoon minced, roasted garlic

1 tablespoon flour

1 can (15 ounces) each: black-eyed peas, black beans, red beans, rinsed, drained

1 can (16 ounces) reduced-sodium diced tomatoes, undrained

1½ teaspoons dried Italian seasoning

¾ cup reduced-sodium vegetable broth

Salt and pepper, to taste

Polenta (see p. 425)

Per Serving:
Calories: 299
% of calories from fat: 14
Fat (gm): 5.3
Saturated fat (gm): 0.6
Cholesterol (mg): 0
Sodium (mg): 587
Protein (gm): 17.5
Carbohydrate (gm): 56

Exchanges:
Milk: 0.0
Vegetable: 2.0
Fruit: 0.0
Bread: 3.0
Meat: 0.5
Fat: 0.0

1. Sauté onion, bell pepper, and garlic in lightly greased large saucepan until tender, about 5 minutes; stir in flour and cook 1 minute longer. Add black-eyed peas, beans, tomatoes with liquid, Italian seasoning, and broth to saucepan; heat to boiling. Reduce heat and simmer, covered, 10 minutes. Season to taste with salt and pepper. Serve stew over polenta.

SPICED BEAN STEW WITH FUSILLI

V

Use your favorite beans and any shaped pasta in this versatile stew.

45

8 servings (about 1¼ cups each)

2 cups chopped onions

½ cup sliced celery

1 cup sliced cremini, or white, mushrooms

2 cans (14½ ounces each) diced tomatoes with roasted garlic, undrained

1 can (15 ounces) each: garbanzo and dark red kidney beans, rinsed, drained

½ cup dry white wine, or water

1–2 tablespoons each: chili powder, ground cumin

½ teaspoon each: dried oregano and thyme leaves

8 ounces fusilli, cooked

Salt and pepper, to taste

3–4 tablespoons sliced green, or ripe, olives

Per Serving:
Calories: 269
% of calories from fat: 9
Fat (gm): 2.9
Saturated fat (gm): 0.3
Cholesterol (mg): 0
Sodium (mg): 761
Protein (gm): 12.3
Carbohydrate (gm): 50.4

Exchanges:
Milk: 0.0
Vegetable: 2.0
Fruit: 0.0
Bread: 2.5
Meat: 0.5
Fat: 0.0

1. Sauté onions, celery, and mushrooms in lightly greased large saucepan until onions are tender, 8 to 10 minutes. Add tomatoes with liquid, beans, wine, and herbs to saucepan; heat to boiling. Reduce heat and simmer, covered, until vegetables are tender, about 10 minutes. Add pasta and cook 2 to 3 minutes longer. Season to taste with salt and pepper; sprinkle with olives.

ITALIAN VEGETARIAN MEATBALL STEW

V

45

Italian-style vegetarian sausage links, cut into 1-inch pieces, can be substituted for the meatballs.

8 servings (about 1½ cups each)

1 each: medium chopped onion, sliced red, or green, bell pepper

2 cans (14½ ounces each) tomatoes with roasted garlic, undrained

1 cup reduced-sodium vegetable broth

1 can (15 ounces) cannellini, or Great Northern, beans, rinsed, drained

4 medium potatoes, unpeeled, cubed

8 ounces broccoli rabe, coarsely chopped

2 medium carrots, sliced

2 tablespoons balsamic vinegar

1 teaspoon each: dried oregano and basil leaves

1 package (12 ounces) vegetarian meatballs, warm

½ cup frozen peas

Salt and pepper, to taste

Grated Parmesan cheese, as garnish

Per Serving:
Calories: 204
% of calories from fat: 12
Fat (gm): 2.7
Saturated fat (gm): 0.5
Cholesterol (mg): 0.0
Sodium (mg): 520
Protein (gm): 11.2
Carbohydrate (gm): 35

Exchanges:
Milk: 0.0
Vegetable: 1.0
Fruit: 0.0
Bread: 2.0
Meat: 1.0
Fat: 0.0

1. Sauté onion and bell pepper in lightly greased large saucepan until tender, about 5 minutes. Add tomatoes with liquid, broth, beans, potatoes, broccoli rabe, carrots, vinegar, and herbs; heat to boiling. Reduce heat and simmer, covered, until vegetables are tender, about 20 minutes. Stir in meatballs and peas; cook until hot, about 5 minutes. Season to taste with salt and pepper; sprinkle each serving with Parmesan cheese.

GARDEN STEW WITH COUSCOUS

V

Take advantage of your garden's bounty with this quick and easy stew.

45

6 servings (about 1½ cups each)

2 medium onions, cut into 1-inch pieces
4 ounces each: sliced shiitake, cremini mushrooms
1 small jalapeño chili, finely chopped
1 tablespoon flour
2 cups reduced-sodium vegetable broth
1 medium turnip, cubed (½-inch)
8 ounces baby carrots
1 bay leaf
4 medium tomatoes, coarsely chopped
2 medium zucchini, sliced
½ cup loosely packed cilantro leaves
Salt and pepper, to taste
4 cups cooked couscous, warm

Per Serving:
Calories: 214
% of calories from fat: 3
Fat (gm): 0.8
Saturated fat (gm): 0.1
Cholesterol (mg): 0.0
Sodium (mg): 215
Protein (gm): 7.4
Carbohydrate (gm): 46

Exchanges:
Milk: 0.0
Vegetable: 0.0
Fruit: 0.0
Bread: 3.0
Meat: 0.0
Fat: 0.0

1. Sauté onions, mushrooms, and jalapeño chili in lightly greased large saucepan until tender, 5 to 8 minutes. Stir in flour; cook 1 minute longer. Add broth, turnip, carrots, and bay leaf; heat to boiling. Reduce heat and simmer, covered, until vegetables are tender, 10 to 15 minutes. Add tomatoes, and zucchini; simmer 5 minutes longer or until desired consistency; stir in cilantro. Discard bay leaf and season to taste with salt and pepper. Serve with couscous.

45-MINUTE PREP TIP: Cook couscous while the stew is simmering.

MEDITERRANEAN CURRIED STEW

V

Taste buds will be tantalized by the melding of cinnamon-spice and curry flavors this stew offers. Brightly colored Turmeric Rice completes the dish perfectly.

6 servings (about 1¼ cups each)

1 small eggplant (about 12 ounces), unpeeled, cut into 1-inch pieces

3 small onions, quartered

½ cup each: chopped green bell pepper, celery

2 cloves garlic, minced

2 tablespoons extra-virgin olive oil

1 tablespoon flour

½ teaspoon each: ground cinnamon, nutmeg, curry powder, cumin

⅛ teaspoon cayenne pepper

2 cans (14½ ounces, each) reduced-sodium diced tomatoes, undrained

½ cup reduced-sodium vegetable broth

1 cup each: cubed zucchini, butternut squash

1 can (15 ounces) garbanzo beans, rinsed, drained

Salt and pepper, to taste

Turmeric Rice (see p. 423)

3 tablespoons each: raisins, toasted slivered almonds

Per Serving:
Calories: 354
% of calories from fat: 22
Fat (gm): 8.8
Saturated fat (gm): 1.2
Cholesterol (mg): 0
Sodium (mg): 323
Protein (gm): 9.7
Carbohydrate (gm): 62.5

Exchanges:
Milk: 0.0
Vegetable: 3.0
Fruit: 0.0
Bread: 3.0
Meat: 0.0
Fat: 1.5

1. Sauté eggplant, onions, bell pepper, celery, and garlic in oil in large saucepan 10 minutes or until eggplant is beginning to brown. Stir in flour, spices, and cayenne pepper; cook 1 minute longer. Add tomatoes and liquid, broth, squash, and beans; heat to boiling. Reduce heat and simmer, covered, until vegetables are tender, 10 to 15 minutes. Season to taste with salt and pepper. Serve over Turmeric Rice and sprinkle with raisins and almonds.

OVEN-BAKED VEGETABLE TAJINE

V

45

A staple of Moroccan cuisine, tajines are traditionally cooked in earthenware pots. Serve with Pita Bread (see p. 556).

6 servings (about 1¼ cups each)

1 each: chopped medium onion, rib celery

1–2 teaspoons each: minced gingerroot, garlic

1 cinnamon stick

2 teaspoons each: paprika, ground cumin, coriander

2 cans (14½ ounces each) reduced-sodium diced
   tomatoes, undrained

½ cup reduced-sodium vegetable broth

1 can (16 ounces) garbanzo beans, rinsed, drained

1 cup each: chopped butternut squash, turnip

1 large carrot, sliced

1½ cups whole green beans, halved

1 cup pitted prunes

¼ cup pitted small black olives

Salt and pepper, to taste

4½ cups cooked couscous, warm

Per Serving:
Calories: 386
% of calories from fat: 10
Fat (gm): 4.6
Saturated fat (gm): 0.6
Cholesterol (mg): 0
Sodium (mg): 540
Protein (gm): 12.5
Carbohydrate (gm): 78.7

Exchanges:
Milk: 0.0
Vegetable: 3.0
Fruit: 1.0
Bread: 3.0
Meat: 0.0
Fat: 1.0

1. Sauté onion, celery, gingerroot, and garlic in lightly greased Dutch oven until onion is tender. Stir in spices; cook 1 minute longer. Add remaining ingredients, except salt, pepper, and couscous. Bake, covered, at 350 degrees, until vegetables are tender, 20 to 30 minutes. Season to taste with salt and pepper; serve over couscous.

MACARONI AND CHEESE

L

45

For kids of all ages — always a favorite! Any shaped pasta, such as rotini, fusilli, or orecchiette, can be substituted for the macaroni.

4 servings (about 1 cup each)

¼ cup finely chopped onion

2 tablespoons margarine, or butter

¼ cup all-purpose flour

2½ cups fat-free milk

2 ounces light pasteurized processed cheese, cubed

½ cup (2 ounces) shredded reduced-fat sharp, or mild, Cheddar cheese

1 teaspoon Dijon mustard

2 cups (10 ounces) elbow macaroni, cooked

Salt and cayenne pepper, to taste

2 tablespoons unseasoned dry bread crumbs

Paprika, as garnish

Per Serving:
Calories: 495
% of calories from fat: 21
Fat (gm): 11.6
Saturated fat (gm): 3.6
Cholesterol (mg): 17.7
Sodium (mg): 577
Protein (gm): 22
Carbohydrate (gm): 73.9

Exchanges:
Milk: 0.5
Vegetable: 0.0
Fruit: 0.0
Bread: 5.0
Meat: 1.0
Fat: 1.0

1. Sauté onion in margarine in medium saucepan until tender, 3 to 4 minutes. Stir in flour; cook over medium-low heat 1 minute, stirring constantly. Stir in milk and heat to boiling; boil, stirring, until thickened, about 1 minute. Add cheeses and mustard; stirring over low heat until melted.

2. Combine sauce and macaroni in 2-quart casserole. Season to taste with salt and cayenne pepper; sprinkle with bread crumbs and paprika. Bake, uncovered, at 350 degrees, until bubbly, 30 to 40 minutes.

Variation

Macaroni and Cheese Primavera — Stir 1 cup cooked broccoli florets, 1 cup sautéed sliced mushrooms, and ¼ cup sautéed chopped red bell pepper into the macaroni and sauce mixture; bake as above.

MIXED GRAIN AND VEGGIE CASSEROLE

L

45

Vegetables baked in a creamy casserole with mixed grains will satisfy the heartiest appetites.

6 servings (about 1¼ cups each)

2 cups each: cubed zucchini, coarsely chopped portobello, or shiitake, mushrooms

1 medium onion, chopped

3 cloves garlic, minced

1 can (11 ounces) whole kernel corn with red and green peppers

1 teaspoon dried marjoram leaves

Salt and pepper, to taste

2 cups each: cooked rice, oat groats

1 cup fat-free sour cream

¾ cup (3 ounces) shredded reduced-fat Colby, or Monterey Jack, cheese

2 sliced green onions

Per Serving:
Calories: 254
% of calories from fat: 13
Fat (gm): 3.9
Saturated fat (gm): 1.7
Cholesterol (mg): 10.1
Sodium (mg): 323
Protein (gm): 13.6
Carbohydrate (gm): 45.5

Exchanges:
Milk: 0.0
Vegetable: 1.0
Fruit: 0.0
Bread: 2.5
Meat: 0.5
Fat: 0.5

1. Sauté zucchini, mushrooms, onion, and garlic in lightly greased large skillet until tender, 8 to 10 minutes. Stir in corn and marjoram; season to taste with salt and pepper.

2. Combine rice and groats; season to taste with salt and pepper. Spoon ½ the grain mixture into 2-quart casserole; top with vegetable mixture and sour cream. Spoon remaining grain mixture on top. Bake, loosely covered, at 300 degrees until hot through, 30 to 40 minutes. Uncover, sprinkle with cheese, and bake until cheese is melted, about 5 minutes longer. Sprinkle with green onions.

VEGETABLE AND MIXED RICE CASSEROLE

L

Vary the vegetables according to season or preference.

45

6 servings (about 1⅓ cups each)

1½ cups sliced shiitake, or cremini, mushrooms

1 cup sliced zucchini

½ cup each: chopped onion, green and red bell pepper

1 teaspoon dried thyme leaves

1 package (6 ounces) brown and wild rice mix, cooked with spice packet

1 can (15 ounces) pinto beans, rinsed, drained

1 cup whole kernel corn

1 cup fat-free sour cream

1 cup (4 ounces) shredded reduced-fat Cheddar cheese, divided

Salt and pepper, to taste

Per Serving:
Calories: 307
% of calories from fat: 12
Fat (gm): 4.2
Saturated fat (gm): 1.4
Cholesterol (mg): 10.1
Sodium (mg): 708
Protein (gm): 16.9
Carbohydrate (gm): 54.7

Exchanges:
Milk: 0.0
Vegetable: 2.0
Fruit: 0.0
Bread: 3.0
Meat: 0.5
Fat: 0.5

1. Sauté mushrooms, zucchini, onion, bell peppers, and thyme in lightly greased medium skillet; cook, covered, over medium heat until vegetables are tender, 8 to 10 minutes. Combine rice, cooked vegetable mixture, beans, corn, sour cream, and ½ cup cheese in 2-quart casserole; season to taste with salt and pepper and sprinkle with remaining ½ cup cheese. Bake, uncovered, at 350 degrees until hot through, 30 to 40 minutes.

VEGETARIAN TETRAZZINI

L

A versatile dish—use any combination of vegetables or pasta.

8 servings

8 ounces mushrooms, sliced

1 cup each: sliced zucchini, red bell pepper, broccoli florets

½ cup chopped onion

1–2 tablespoons margarine, or butter

1¾ cups reduced-sodium vegetable broth

1 cup fat-free milk

½ cup dry white wine, or fat-free milk

2 tablespoons flour

16 ounces thin, or regular, spaghetti, cooked, warm

¼ cup (1 ounce) grated Parmesan cheese

¼ teaspoon each ground nutmeg, salt and pepper

Per Serving:
Calories: 344
% of calories from fat: 11
Fat (gm): 4.1
Saturated fat (gm): 1.2
Cholesterol (mg): 3
Sodium (mg): 176
Protein (gm): 12.9
Carbohydrate (gm): 60.3

Exchanges:
Milk: 0.0
Vegetable: 2.0
Fruit: 0.0
Bread: 3.5
Meat: 0.0
Fat: 1.0

1. Sauté mushrooms, zucchini, bell pepper, broccoli, and onion in margarine in large saucepan until tender, about 5 minutes. Add broth and milk and heat to boiling. Stir in combined wine and flour; boil, stirring, until thickened, about 1 minute (sauce will be very thin). Stir in remaining ingredients; spoon into 2-quart casserole or baking dish. Bake, uncovered, at 350 degrees until lightly browned and bubbly, about 45 minutes.

MEXICAN-STYLE LASAGNE

L *A lasagne with a difference! Add Vegetarian Chorizo (see p. 287), if you like.*

8 servings

2 cups each: fat-free ricotta cheese, shredded reduced-fat Monterey Jack cheese

1 can (15 ounces) each: pinto beans, black beans, drained

Chili-Tomato Sauce (recipe follows)

12 lasagne noodles (10 ounces), cooked

Per Serving:
Calories: 360
% of calories from fat: 18
Fat (gm): 8
Saturated fat (gm): 3.1
Cholesterol (mg): 26.3
Sodium (mg): 748
Protein (gm): 30.7
Carbohydrate (gm): 51

Exchanges:
Milk: 0.0
Vegetable: 3.0
Fruit: 0.0
Bread: 2.0
Meat: 2.5
Fat: 0.5

1. Combine cheeses; combine beans. Spread 1 cup Chili-Tomato Sauce on bottom of a 13 x 9-inch baking pan; top with 4 lasagne noodles, overlapping slightly. Spoon ⅓ of the cheese mixture over noodles, spreading lightly with rubber spatula; top with ⅓ of the beans and 1 cup Chili-Tomato Sauce. Repeat layers twice, ending with remaining 1 cup sauce. Bake at 350 degrees, loosely covered with foil, until bubbly, about 1 hour. Let stand 10 minutes before cutting.

Chili-Tomato Sauce

Makes about 5 cups

2 cups chopped onions
2–3 teaspoons each: minced garlic, jalapeño chili
2 cans (14½ ounces each) low-sodium stewed tomatoes
2 cans (8 ounces each) low-sodium tomato sauce
2 tablespoons chili powder
2 teaspoons ground cumin
1 teaspoon dried oregano leaves
Salt, to taste

1. Sauté onions, garlic, and jalapeño chili in lightly greased large skillet until onions are tender, 5 to 8 minutes. Stir in remaining ingredients, except salt; heat to boiling. Reduce heat and simmer, uncovered, until sauce is reduced to 5 cups, about 20 minutes. Season to taste with salt.

VEGGIE LASAGNE WITH EGGPLANT SAUCE

L

The hearty Eggplant Sauce is also wonderful served over shaped pastas, such as corkscrews or ziti, or over cheese or herb tortellini.

8 servings

1 cup each: sliced onion, zucchini, red bell pepper, mushrooms
3 cloves garlic, minced
2 cups fat-free ricotta cheese
¼ cup (1 ounce) grated Parmesan cheese
Eggplant Sauce (see p. 589)
12 lasagne noodles (10 ounces), cooked, room temperature
2 medium sweet potatoes, cooked until barely tender, sliced
2 cups (8 ounces) shredded reduced-fat mozzarella cheese

Per Serving:
Calories: 375
% of calories from fat: 24
Fat (gm): 10.4
Saturated fat (gm): 4.2
Cholesterol (mg): 2.3
Sodium (mg): 685
Protein (gm): 2.4
Carbohydrate (gm): 47

Exchanges:
Milk: 0.0
Vegetable: 3.0
Fruit: 0.0
Bread: 2.0
Meat: 2.5
Fat: 0.5

1. Sauté onion, zucchini, bell pepper, mushrooms, and garlic in lightly greased large skillet until tender, about 10 minutes. Mix ricotta and Parmesan cheese. Spread 1½ cups Eggplant Sauce in bottom of 13 x 9-inch baking pan; top with 4 lasagne noodles, overlapping slightly. Top with ⅓ each ricotta cheese mixture, sweet potatoes, sauteed vegetables, and 1½ cups Eggplant Sauce; sprinkle with ⅔ cup mozzarella cheese. Repeat layers 2 times. Bake, loosely covered, at 350 degrees until sauce is bubbly, about 1 hour. Let stand 10 minutes before cutting.

VEGETARIAN SAUSAGE LASAGNE

L

A skinny rendering of the classic lasagne we all love!

8 servings

Tomato and Vegetarian Meat Sauce (see p. 583)

1 package (8 ounces) vegetarian sausage patties, crumbled

1 can (6 ounces) reduced-sodium tomato sauce

2 cups fat-free ricotta cheese

¼ cup (1 ounce) grated Parmesan cheese

3 cups (12 ounces) shredded reduced-fat mozzarella cheese

12 lasagne noodles (10 ounces), cooked, room temperature

Per Serving:
Calories: 339
% of calories from fat: 29
Fat (gm): 11.1
Saturated fat (gm): 5.6
Cholesterol (mg): 25.3
Sodium (mg): 600
Protein (gm): 30.3
Carbohydrate (gm): 30

Exchanges:
Milk: 0.0
Vegetable: 2.0
Fruit: 0.0
Bread: 1.5
Meat: 3.0
Fat: 0.0

1. Make Tomato and Vegetarian Meat Sauce, substituting vegetarian sausage for the vegetarian ground beef, and adding tomato sauce. Combine cheeses. Spread 1 cup sauce on bottom of 13 x 9-inch baking pan; top with 4 lasagne noodles, overlapping slightly. Spoon ⅓ of the cheese mixture over noodles, spreading lightly with rubber spatula. Top with 1 cup sauce. Repeat layers 2 times, ending with layer of noodles, cheese, and remaining sauce.

2. Bake lasagne, loosely covered with aluminum foil, at 350 degrees until sauce is bubbly, about 1 hour. Let stand 10 minutes before cutting.

EGGPLANT LASAGNE

LO *Generous slices of eggplant replace the noodles in this flavorful version of lasagne.*

6 servings

1 large eggplant (about 1½ pounds), unpeeled,
   cut into ½-inch slices

3 egg whites, lightly beaten

½ cup unseasoned dry bread crumbs

¼ cup (1 ounce) grated, fat-free Parmesan cheese

2–4 tablespoons extra-virgin olive oil

Tomato and Veggie-Meat Sauce (see p. 583)

1 cup fat-free cottage cheese

¼–½ cup fat-free sour cream

¾–1 cup (3–4 ounces) shredded fat-free
   mozzarella cheese

Per Serving:
Calories: 256
% of calories from fat: 19
Fat (gm): 5.7
Saturated fat (gm): 0.8
Cholesterol (mg): 0
Sodium (mg): 491
Protein (gm): 24
Carbohydrate (gm): 29.8

Exchanges:
Milk: 0.0
Vegetable: 3.0
Fruit: 0.0
Bread: 1.0
Meat: 2.0
Fat: 0.0

1. Dip eggplant slices in egg whites; coat lightly with combined bread crumbs and Parmesan cheese. Sauté eggplant in oil in large skillet until browned, about 5 minutes on each side (if additional oil is needed, spray eggplant with olive oil cooking spray). Spoon ⅓ of the Tomato and Veggie-Meat Sauce into 12 x 7-inch baking dish; arrange ½ the eggplant slices over the sauce. Mix cottage cheese and sour cream; spread half the mixture over eggplant and spread with ⅓ of the sauce. Repeat layers, ending with remaining sauce.

2. Bake, uncovered, at 350 degrees until bubbly, about 45 minutes, sprinkling with mozzarella cheese during last 10 minutes.

BROCCOLI AND CHEESE ROTOLO WITH MANY-CLOVES GARLIC SAUCE

L *Some people prefer cutting lasagne noodles into halves before filling, as they are easier to handle when eating. If cut, spread each rotolo with 1½ to 2 tablespoons of the cheese mixture.*

6 servings

1½ cups chopped broccoli

¾ cup chopped red bell pepper

3 cloves garlic, minced

½ teaspoon each: dried marjoram, thyme leaves

1¼ cups reduced-fat ricotta cheese

Salt and pepper, to taste

12 lasagne noodles (10 ounces), cooked, room temperature

Many-Cloves Garlic Sauce (see p. 591)

Per Serving:
Calories: 210
% of calories from fat: 20
Fat (gm): 4.9
Saturated fat (gm): 0.2
Cholesterol (mg): 6.6
Sodium (mg): 104
Protein (gm): 10.1
Carbohydrate (gm): 31.7

Exchanges:
Milk: 0.0
Vegetable: 2.0
Fruit: 0.0
Bread: 1.5
Meat: 0.0
Fat: 1.0

1. Sauté broccoli, bell pepper, garlic, and herbs in lightly greased medium skillet until tender, about 8 minutes; cool. Stir in cheese; season to taste with salt and pepper. Spread 3 to 4 tablespoons of mixture evenly on each noodle and roll up; place, seam side down, in baking dish and spoon Many-Cloves Garlic Sauce over them. Bake, loosely covered with foil, at 350 degrees until hot and bubbly, 20 to 30 minutes.

SPINACH-MUSHROOM ROTOLO WITH MARINARA SAUCE

L *Add portobello or shiitake mushrooms to the filling for wonderful flavor and aroma.*

6 servings

2 cups sliced mushrooms

1 package (10 ounces) fresh spinach, cleaned, chopped

2 cloves garlic, minced

1 teaspoon each: dried basil and tarragon leaves

½ package (8-ounce size) reduced-fat cream cheese, room temperature

½ cup fat-free ricotta cheese

¼ teaspoon each: salt, pepper

12 lasagne noodles, cooked, room temperature

Marinara Sauce (see p. 582)

Per Serving:
Calories: 286
% of calories from fat: 30
Fat (gm): 10.3
Saturated fat (gm): 2.7
Cholesterol (mg): 8.7
Sodium (mg): 686
Protein (gm): 12.5
Carbohydrate (gm): 38

Exchanges:
Milk: 0.0
Vegetable: 3.0
Fruit: 0.0
Bread: 1.5
Meat: 0.0
Fat: 2.0

1. Cook mushrooms, spinach, garlic, and herbs in lightly greased large skillet, covered, until spinach is wilted, 2 to 3 minutes. Cook, uncovered, over medium to medium-high heat until liquid is gone, about 10 minutes; cool. Stir in cheeses, salt, and pepper. Spread 3 to 4 tablespoons mixture on each noodle and roll up; place in baking dish and spoon Marinara Sauce over. Bake, loosely covered with foil, at 350 degrees until hot and bubbly, 20 to 30 minutes.

SPAGHETTI AND EGGPLANT PARMESAN TORTE

L *Baked in a springform pan, the presentation of this dish is unusual and quite attractive.*

6 servings

1 large eggplant (about 3 pounds), unpeeled, cut into ¼-inch-thick slices

1 small onion, finely chopped

3 cloves garlic, minced

1 tablespoon olive oil

2 cans (8 ounces each) low-sodium tomato sauce

8 medium plum tomatoes, chopped

⅛ teaspoon crushed red pepper

3 tablespoons finely chopped fresh, or 2 teaspoons dried basil leaves

12 ounces spaghetti, cooked, room temperature

¼ cup (1 ounce) grated Parmesan cheese

2–3 tablespoons unseasoned dry bread crumbs

Per Serving:
Calories: 372
% of calories from fat: 13
Fat (gm): 5.4
Saturated fat (gm): 1.4
Cholesterol (mg): 3.3
Sodium (mg): 139
Protein (gm): 13.5
Carbohydrate (gm): 70

Exchanges:
Milk: 0.0
Vegetable: 3.0
Fruit: 0.0
Bread: 3.5
Meat: 0.0
Fat: 1.0

1. Cook eggplant slices in lightly greased large skillet until browned, about 4 minutes on each side; reserve. Add onion and garlic to skillet; sauté in oil until tender, 3 to 5 minutes. Add tomato sauce, tomatoes, and red pepper; heat to boiling. Reduce heat and simmer, uncovered, until mixture is of medium sauce consistency, about 15 minutes; stir in basil. Pour sauce over spaghetti and toss; sprinkle with Parmesan cheese and toss.

2. Coat greased 9-inch springform pan with bread crumbs. Line bottom and side of pan with ¾ of eggplant slices, overlapping slices and allowing those on side to extend 1 to 1½ inches above top of pan. Add spaghetti mixture and press into pan firmly. Fold eggplant slices at top of pan over spaghetti mixture. Overlap remaining eggplant slices on top, pressing firmly into place.

3. Bake, uncovered, at 350 degrees until hot through, about 30 minutes. Let stand 15 minutes; remove side of pan. Cut into wedges to serve.

EGGPLANT AND TOMATO SAUCE PARMESAN

L *Eggplant layered with Tomato and Vegetarian Meat Sauce and melted cheese, is baked to rich goodness.*

6–8 servings

3 pounds eggplant, unpeeled, cut into scant
  ½-inch slices
Salt
Olive oil cooking spray
Tomato and Vegetarian Meat Sauce (see p. 583)
6 ounces (¾ cup) each: shredded fat-free, and
  reduced-fat, mozzarella cheese
½ cup (2 ounces) grated fat-free Parmesan cheese

Per Serving:
Calories: 215
% of calories from fat: 15
Fat (gm): 3.7
Saturated fat (gm): 2.4
Cholesterol (mg): 11.4
Sodium (mg): 462
Protein (gm): 23.1
Carbohydrate (gm): 23.3

Exchanges:
Milk: 0.0
Vegetable: 3.0
Fruit: 0.0
Bread: 0.0
Meat: 2.5
Fat: 0.0

1. Sprinkle eggplant slices lightly with salt; let stand 30 minutes. Rinse well drain on paper toweling. Arrange eggplant on foil-lined greased jelly roll pan; spray generously with cooking spray. Bake at 425 degrees until tender, 20 to 30 minutes.

2. Layer ⅓ each eggplant slices, Tomato and Vegetarian Meat Sauce, and combined mozzarella cheeses in greased 13 x 9-inch baking pan. Repeat layers 2 times; sprinkle with Parmesan cheese. Bake, uncovered, at 350 degrees until bubbly, 30 to 40 minutes. Cool 10 minutes before cutting.

VEGETABLE-BARLEY MOUSSAKA

LO *This version of moussaka is filled with sumptuous vegetables and hearty barley, topped with a creamy custard.*

12 servings

1 large eggplant, unpeeled, sliced
Olive oil cooking spray
1 pound potatoes, unpeeled, sliced
3 cups chopped onions
2 cups each: chopped tomatoes, sliced mushrooms, carrots
1 small zucchini, sliced

3 cloves garlic, minced

1 teaspoon each: ground cinnamon, dried
    oregano leaves

½ teaspoon dried thyme leaves

¾ cup reduced-sodium vegetable broth

2 cups cooked barley

Salt and pepper, to taste

Custard Topping (recipe follows)

Ground nutmeg to taste

Per Serving:
Calories: 327
% of calories from fat: 25
Fat (gm): 9.3
Saturated fat (gm): 1.9
Cholesterol (mg): 28
Sodium (mg): 188
Protein (gm): 10.6
Carbohydrate (gm): 52.5

Exchanges:
Milk: 0.0
Vegetable: 3.0
Fruit: 0.0
Bread: 2.5
Meat: 0.0
Fat: 1.5

1. Spray eggplant slices on both sides with cooking spray. Bake on greased foil-lined jelly roll pan at 350 degrees until tender but still firm to touch, about 20 minutes. Arrange eggplant on bottom of 13 x 9 x 2-inch baking pan.

2. Heat potatoes, onions, tomatoes, mushrooms, carrots, zucchini, garlic, seasonings, and vegetable broth to boiling in large saucepan; reduce heat and simmer, uncovered, 10 minutes. Add barley; simmer, uncovered, until vegetables are tender and mixture is thick, about 10 minutes. Season to taste with salt and pepper. Spoon mixture over eggplant; pour Custard Topping over and sprinkle with nutmeg. Bake at 350 degrees until lightly browned, about 45 minutes. Cool 5 to 10 minutes before cutting.

Custard Topping

⅓ cup margarine, or butter

½ cup all-purpose flour

3 cups fat-free milk

1 egg

2 egg whites

Salt and pepper, to taste

1. Melt margarine in medium saucepan; stir in flour. Cook over medium heat until bubbly, about 2 minutes, stirring. Stir in milk; heat to boiling. Boil, stirring constantly, until thickened, about 1 minute.

2. Beat egg and egg whites in small bowl. Stir about 1 cup milk mixture into eggs; stir egg mixture back into saucepan. Cook over low heat until thickened, 1 to 2 minutes; season to taste with salt and pepper.

RATATOUILLE

V *We've baked this French vegetable stew in layers, the traditional way.*

4 side-dish servings

2 medium onions, sliced
½ large green bell pepper, sliced
4 cloves garlic, minced
3 medium tomatoes, coarsely chopped
1 teaspoon dried oregano and marjoram leaves
½ teaspoon each: dried thyme and savory leaves
Salt and pepper, to taste
1 medium eggplant (about 1¼ pounds), unpeeled
1 medium zucchini, sliced
Vegetable cooking spray
3 tablespoons minced parsley

Per Serving:
Calories: 103
% of calories from fat: 7
Fat (gm): 1
Saturated fat (gm): 0.2
Cholesterol (mg): 0
Sodium (mg): 20
Protein (gm): 4.2
Carbohydrate (gm): 23.5

Exchanges:
Milk: 0.0
Vegetable: 4.0
Fruit: 0.0
Bread: 0.0
Meat: 0.0
Fat: 0.0

1. Sauté onions, bell pepper, and garlic in lightly greased large skillet until tender, about 5 minutes. Add tomatoes and herbs and cook, covered, 5 minutes; cook uncovered until excess liquid is gone, about 5 minutes. Season to taste with salt and pepper. Transfer mixture to bowl and reserve.

2. Cut eggplant into strips measuring about 3 x ½ x ½ inches. Add eggplant and zucchini to skillet; spray with cooking spray. Cook over medium heat, stirring occasionally, until lightly browned; season to taste with salt and pepper. Layer half the eggplant mixture in ungreased 1½-quart casserole; layer with half the vegetable mixture. Repeat layers. Bake, uncovered, at 400 degrees until hot through, 15 to 20 minutes.

EGGPLANT CASSEROLE SOUFFLÉ

LO *Something different that's bound to please. Try Fresh Tomato and Herb Sauce or Fresh Tomato-Basil Sauce (see p. 584) as delicious alternatives to the sour cream sauce.*

8 side-dish servings

2 medium eggplants (1¼ pounds each), peeled,
   cut into ¾-inch slices
Vegetable cooking spray
¼ cup finely chopped onion
1 clove garlic, minced
¼ cup grated fat-free Parmesan cheese
2 tablespoons lemon juice
½–¾ teaspoon salt
¼ teaspoon pepper
4 eggs, separated
1 egg white
Minted Sour Cream (recipe follows)

Per Serving:
Calories: 105
% of calories from fat: 23
Fat (gm): 2.8
Saturated fat (gm): 0.8
Cholesterol (mg): 106.5
Sodium (mg): 218
Protein (gm): 7.7
Carbohydrate (gm): 14

Exchanges:
Milk: 0.0
Vegetable: 2.5
Fruit: 0.0
Bread: 0.0
Meat: 0.5
Fat: 0.5

1. Cook eggplant slices in lightly greased large skillet over medium heat until browned on the bottom, 3 to 5 minutes. Spray tops of slices with cooking spray and turn; cook until brown on the bottom. Cut eggplant into coarse pieces; mix with onion, garlic, cheese, lemon juice, salt, and pepper.

2. Beat egg yolks in small bowl until thick and lemon colored, about 5 minutes. With clean beaters and a large bowl, beat egg whites until stiff, but not dry, peaks form. Stir yolks into eggplant mixture; fold eggplant mixture into beaten egg whites.

3. Pour mixture into ungreased 2-quart soufflé dish. Bake at 350 degrees until puffed and brown, about 30 minutes. Serve with Minted Sour Cream.

Minted Sour Cream

Makes about 1 cup

1 cup fat-free sour cream
3–4 tablespoons fresh, or 1 teaspoon dried, mint leaves
Salt and white pepper, to taste

1. Mix sour cream and mint; season to taste with salt and white pepper. Refrigerate until serving time.

SWEET-SPICED CABBAGE WITH QUINOA

Cabbage is baked with a tomato sauce uniquely flavored with apricots, ginger, and sweet spices.

6 servings (about 1½ cups each)

¼ cup sliced green onions

2 cans (10 ounces each) diced tomatoes with chilies, undrained

3 tablespoons each: lemon juice, cider vinegar

¼ cup packed light brown sugar

½ teaspoon each: ground cinnamon, ginger

¾ cup reduced-sodium vegetable broth

¼ cup apricot nectar

½ cup chopped dried apricots

Salt and pepper, to taste

1 small cabbage (about 1 pound), sliced

½ cup gingersnap, or vanilla wafer, cookie crumbs

4 cups cooked quinoa, warm

Per Serving:
Calories: 282
% of calories from fat: 11
Fat (gm): 3.5
Saturated fat (gm): 0.4
Cholesterol (mg): 0
Sodium (mg): 396
Protein (gm): 7.5
Carbohydrate (gm): 58.9

Exchanges:
Milk: 0.0
Vegetable: 1.0
Fruit: 0.5
Bread: 3.0
Meat: 0.0
Fat: 0.5

1. Sauté green onions in lightly greased medium saucepan until tender, about 4 minutes. Stir in tomatoes with liquid, lemon juice, vinegar, brown sugar, cinnamon, ginger, broth, apricot nectar, and apricots; heat to boiling; reduce heat and simmer, covered, 10 minutes. Season to taste with salt and pepper.

2. Arrange cabbage in lightly greased large baking dish; pour tomato sauce over. Bake, covered, at 350 degrees 25 minutes. Sprinkle cookie crumbs over cabbage and bake, uncovered, 15 minutes or until cabbage is tender and crumbs are browned. Serve over quinoa.

FOUR

Vegetarian Entrées

SESAME ASPARAGUS STIR-FRY

O

45

Check the Asian section of your supermarket for the interesting selection of sauces available for noodles and rice.

4 servings (about 1 cup each)

8 ounces asparagus, cut into 1-inch pieces

¼ teaspoon dried pepper flakes

1 can (15 ounces) black beans, rinsed, drained

1 jar (14 ounces) Mandarin sesame sauce for noodles and rice

1 small tomato, coarsely chopped

1 package (16 ounces) Chinese egg noodles, cooked, warm

Per Serving:
Calories: 387
% of calories from fat: 14
Fat (gm): 6.2
Saturated fat (gm): 0.8
Cholesterol (mg): 0
Sodium (mg): 1187
Protein (gm): 9.3
Carbohydrate (gm): 74.6

Exchanges:
Milk: 0.0
Vegetable: 0.0
Fruit: 0.0
Bread: 5.0
Meat: 0.0
Fat: 0.5

1. Stir-fry asparagus over medium-high heat in lightly greased wok or medium skillet 3 to 4 minutes or until browned. Add red pepper flakes; cook 1 minute longer. Add beans and Mandarin sesame sauce and cook 2 to 3 minutes; stir in tomato. Serve over noodles.

45-MINUTE PREP TIP: Begin cooking the noodles before preparing the rest of the recipe.

WHITE BEAN MASHERS WITH SAUTÉED VEGETABLES

L

45

A quick and delicious dinner. Substitute cannelloni or lima beans for the Great Northern, if you prefer.

6 servings

1½ pounds Idaho potatoes, peeled, cubed

4 large cloves garlic, peeled

1 can (15 ounces) Great Northern beans, rinsed, drained

3–4 tablespoons each: fat-free milk, shredded Parmesan cheese

Salt and pepper, to taste

8 ounces sliced portobello mushrooms

Per Serving:
Calories: 145
% of calories from fat: 20
Fat (gm): 3.3
Saturated fat (gm): 0.9
Cholesterol (mg): 2.1
Sodium (mg): 218
Protein (gm): 8.1
Carbohydrate (gm): 24.9

Exchanges:
Milk: 0.0
Vegetable: 2.0
Fruit: 0.0
Bread: 1.0
Meat: 0.0
Fat: 0.5

1 cup small broccoli florets

2 green onions, sliced

1 tablespoon margarine, or butter

Salt and pepper, to taste

1. Cook potatoes and garlic, covered, in medium saucepan in 2 inches simmering water 10 minutes. Add beans and simmer until potatoes are tender, about 5 minutes; drain. Mash potatoes and beans with electric mixer or potato masher, adding milk, cheese, and salt and pepper to taste. Keep warm.

2. Sauté mushrooms, broccoli, and green onions in margarine in large skillet until tender and browned, about 8 minutes. Season to taste with salt and pepper. Serve over potatoes.

CABBAGE-FENNEL STRUDEL

V *If fresh fennel is not available, substitute sliced celery and add ½ teaspoon crushed fennel seeds to the recipe.*

4 servings

¾ cup each: chopped onion, sliced leek (white part only), or green onions

3 cloves garlic, minced

4 cups thinly sliced cabbage

1 cup sliced mushrooms

½ cup thinly sliced fennel bulb

1 cup reduced-sodium vegetable broth

½ cup dry white wine, or reduced-sodium vegetable broth

¾ teaspoon each: crushed anise, caraway seeds

¾ cup cooked brown rice

¼ cup dark raisins

Salt and pepper, to taste

5 sheets frozen fillo pastry, thawed

Vegetable cooking spray

Anise or caraway seeds, as garnish

Fresh Tomato-Basil Sauce (see p. 584)

Per Serving:
Calories: 315
% of calories from fat: 18
Fat (gm): 6.5
Saturated fat (gm): 1
Cholesterol (mg): 0.0
Sodium (mg): 583
Protein (gm): 8.4
Carbohydrate (gm): 55

Exchanges:
Milk: 0.0
Vegetable: 2.0
Fruit: 0.0
Bread: 3.0
Meat: 0.0
Fat: 1.0

1. Sauté onion, leek, and garlic in lightly greased large saucepan 3 to 5 minutes. Add cabbage, mushrooms, fennel, broth, wine, anise and caraway seeds; cook, covered, over medium heat until cabbage wilts, 5 to 10 minutes. Cook, uncovered, until cabbage begins to brown, about 10 minutes. Stir in rice and raisins; season to taste with salt and pepper. Cool.

2. Lay 1 sheet of fillo on clean surface; cover remaining fillo with damp towel to keep from drying. Spray fillo with cooking spray; top with 2 more sheets fillo, spraying each with cooking spray. Spoon ½ cabbage mixture across dough, 2 inches from short edge; roll up and place, seam-side down, on greased cookie sheet. Flatten roll slightly; spray with cooking spray and sprinkle with anise seeds. Repeat with remaining fillo and cabbage mixture.

3. Bake at 375 degrees until strudel is golden, 35 to 45 minutes. Cool 5 to 10 minutes before cutting; cut diagonally into halves. Serve with Fresh Tomato-Basil Sauce.

STUFFED CABBAGE WITH CHILI TOMATO SAUCE

V *This dish can be served in smaller portions as a side dish.*

6 servings

1 large head green cabbage
1 cup chopped onion
1 teaspoon each: minced jalapeño chili, garlic
1 tablespoon canola oil
1 can (15 ounces) black beans, rinsed, drained
2 medium tomatoes, chopped
½ teaspoon each:dried oregano and thyme leaves
½ cup each: raisins, cooked rice
1 tablespoon finely chopped cilantro
Salt and pepper, to taste
Chili Tomato Sauce (see p. 599)

Per Serving:
Calories: 228
% of calories from fat: 14
Fat (gm): 4
Saturated fat (gm): 0.4
Cholesterol (mg): 0
Sodium (mg): 313
Protein (gm): 11.9
Carbohydrate (gm): 45.5

Exchanges:
Milk: 0.0
Vegetable: 4.0
Fruit: 0.5
Bread: 1.0
Meat: 0.0
Fat: 0.5

1. Trim cabbage, discarding any wilted outside leaves. Place cabbage in large saucepan with water to cover; heat to boiling. Reduce heat and simmer, covered, 10 minutes. Drain cabbage; cool until warm enough to handle.

2. Sauté onion, jalapeño chili, and garlic in oil in large skillet until tender, about 5 minutes. Add beans, tomatoes, and herbs to skillet; lightly mash beans. Cook, covered, over medium heat, 10 minutes. Stir in raisins, rice, and cilantro; season to taste with salt and pepper.

3. Place cabbage on large square of double-thickness cheesecloth. Spread outer cabbage leaves as flat as possible without breaking them off. Cut out inner leaves of cabbage, chop finely, and add to rice mixture; remove and discard core of cabbage. Pack rice mixture in center of cabbage; fold outer leaves up over mixture, reshaping cabbage. Gather cheesecloth around cabbage and tie with string. Place cabbage in large saucepan and add water to cover; heat to boiling. Reduce heat and simmer, covered, 1 hour. Lift cabbage from saucepan and remove cheesecloth. Place cabbage on plate and cut into wedges; serve with Chili Tomato Sauce.

CABBAGE AND POTATO HASH

L

45

Serve with large dollops of fat-free sour cream and thick slices of a warm multigrain bread.

4 servings (about 1½ cups each)

1 large onion, chopped

1 small head cabbage, coarsely chopped (about 4 cups)

6 medium red potatoes, unpeeled, cubed

3 carrots, sliced

3 cloves garlic, minced

4–5 teaspoons gingerroot, minced

½ cup reduced-sodium vegetable broth

1½ teaspoons reduced-sodium tamari soy sauce

Salt and pepper, to taste

¼ cup fat-free sour cream

Per Serving:
Calories: 233
% of calories from fat: 2.7
Fat (gm): 0.7
Saturated fat (gm): 0.1
Cholesterol (mg): 2.5
Sodium (mg): 230
Protein (gm): 8.7
Carbohydrate (gm): 51.3

Exchanges:
Milk: 0.0
Vegetable: 1.0
Fruit: 0.0
Bread: 3.0
Meat: 0.0
Fat: 0.0

1. Sauté onion, cabbage, potatoes, carrots, garlic, and gingerroot in lightly greased large skillet until lightly browned, about 8 minutes. Add broth and soy sauce and cook, covered, over medium heat until vegetables are just tender, about 5 minutes. Season to taste with salt and pepper. Serve with sour cream.

EGGPLANT POLENTA STACK

LO

Packaged polenta comes in several flavors; choose your favorite for this dish.

45

4 servings

8 slices (¾-inch) eggplant
1 egg, lightly beaten
½ cup seasoned dry bread crumbs
¼ cup (1 ounce) grated Parmesan cheese
8 slices (½-inch) tomato
Salt and pepper, to taste
1 package (16 ounces) prepared Italian-herb polenta,
    cut into 8 slices
2–4 ounces reduced-fat feta, crumbled

Per Serving:
Calories: 222
% of calories from fat: 18
Fat (gm): 4.5
Saturated fat (gm): 2.4
Cholesterol (mg): 9
Sodium (mg): 624
Protein (gm): 10.9
Carbohydrate (gm): 35.1

Exchanges:
Milk: 0.0
Vegetable: 0.0
Fruit: 0.0
Bread: 2.0
Meat: 1.0
Fat: 0.0

1. Dip eggplant slices in egg and coat with combined bread crumbs and Parmesan cheese. Cook in lightly greased large skillet until browned, 6 to 8 minutes on each side. Arrange eggplant in baking pan; top with tomato slices and sprinkle lightly with salt and pepper. Top tomato slices with polenta and sprinkle with feta cheese. Bake at 500 degrees, loosely covered, until polenta is warm and cheese softened, about 5 minutes.

EGGPLANT AND VEGETABLE SAUTÉ

V

Another quick and easy recipe, guaranteed to get dinner on the table in record time!

45

4 servings (about 1 cup each)

1 large eggplant (about 1¼ pounds), unpeeled, cubed
2 medium onions, chopped
1 each: chopped yellow and red bell pepper
4 teaspoons minced roasted garlic
½ teaspoon each: dried savory, thyme, rosemary
    leaves
1 can (15 ounces) cannellini beans, or other white
    beans, rinsed, drained
Salt and pepper, to taste
8 ounces whole wheat spaghetti, cooked, warm

Per Serving:
Calories: 356
% of calories from fat: 5
Fat (gm): 2.3
Saturated fat (gm): 0.2
Cholesterol (mg): 0
Sodium (mg): 221
Protein (gm): 18.8
Carbohydrate (gm): 79.8

Exchanges:
Milk: 0.0
Vegetable: 3.0
Fruit: 0.0
Bread: 4.0
Meat: 0.0
Fat: 0.0

1. Cook eggplant, onions, bell peppers, and garlic over medium heat in lightly greased large saucepan, covered, 5 minutes; cook, uncovered, until vegetables are tender, 5 to 8 minutes. Stir in herbs and beans; cook until hot through, 3 to 5 minutes. Season to taste with salt and pepper. Serve over spaghetti.

45-MINUTE PREP TIP: Begin cooking the spaghetti before preparing the rest of the recipe.

STUFFED PORTOBELLO MUSHROOMS

These entrée-size mushrooms can also be served as appetizers: select a smaller size, or cut large mushrooms into halves or quarters.

4 servings (2 mushrooms each)

8 large portobello mushrooms (5 or more inches in diameter)

1 cup each: chopped red and yellow bell pepper

¼ cup each: chopped shallot, or onion, green onions

6 cloves garlic, minced

½ teaspoon each: dried basil, marjoram, and thyme leaves

Salt and pepper, to taste

6 ounces shredded fat-free mozzarella, or Cheddar, cheese

2 ounces goat cheese, crumbled

Per Serving:
Calories: 168
% of calories from fat: 19
Fat (gm): 3.9
Saturated fat (gm): 2.1
Cholesterol (mg): 6.5
Sodium (mg): 357
Protein (gm): 20.8
Carbohydrate (gm): 15.1

Exchanges:
Milk: 0.0
Vegetable: 2.0
Fruit: 0.0
Bread: 0.0
Meat: 2.0
Fat: 0.0

1. Remove mushroom stems, chop, and reserve. Bake mushrooms, smooth sides down, in greased jelly roll pan at 425 degrees for 15 minutes.

2. Sauté mushroom stems, bell peppers, shallot, green onions, and garlic in lightly greased large skillet until tender, 8 to 10 minutes. Stir in herbs and cook 1 to 2 minutes longer; season to taste with salt and pepper. Spoon onto mushrooms; sprinkle with cheeses. Bake at 425 degrees until mushrooms are tender and cheeses melted, about 10 minutes.

SWEET POTATO CAKES

O

45

Saucer-sized and topped generously with sour cream! The recipe is simple to double or triple, and the cakes can be kept warm in the oven.

2 servings

2 cups shredded sweet potatoes

½ cup each: shredded carrot, zucchini, Jerusalem artichoke, or potato

¼ cup finely chopped onion

½ teaspoon dried sage leaves

Salt and pepper, to taste

1 egg

2 egg whites

¼ cup all-purpose flour

Sour cream (optional)

Per Serving:
Calories: 303
% of calories from fat: 9
Fat (gm): 3.2
Saturated fat (gm): 0.9
Cholesterol (mg): 106.5
Sodium (mg): 116
Protein (gm): 12.1
Carbohydrate (gm): 56.8

Exchanges:
Milk: 0.0
Vegetable: 2.0
Fruit: 0.0
Bread: 2.5
Meat: 1.0
Fat: 0.0

1. Combine vegetables and sage in bowl; sprinkle lightly with salt and pepper. Mix in egg, egg whites, and flour.

2. Add ½ the vegetable mixture to lightly greased medium skillet, pressing down firmly to make a 7- to 8-inch cake. Cook over medium heat until browned on the bottom, 8 to 10 minutes. Loosen cake with spatula and invert onto plate. Slide cake back into skillet and cook until browned on the bottom, 8 to 10 minutes. Repeat with remaining potato mixture. Serve with sour cream, if desired.

SPAGHETTI SQUASH WITH VEGETABLE SAUTÉ

V

45

◊

Jerusalem artichokes, or sun chokes, add extra crunch to sautéed veggies.

4 servings

2 medium spaghetti squash, cut lengthwise into halves, seeded

2 cups peeled, cubed Jerusalem artichokes

1 medium onion, cubed

2 medium carrots, diagonally sliced

1½ cups quartered mushrooms

½ cup sliced celery

2 cloves garlic, minced

2 teaspoons flour

2 medium tomatoes, coarsely chopped

½ cup reduced-sodium vegetable broth

¾–1 teaspoon dried marjoram leaves

Salt and pepper, to taste

Per Serving:
Calories: 199
% of calories from fat: 9.3
Fat (gm): 2.3
Saturated fat (gm): 0.4
Cholesterol (mg): 0.0
Sodium (mg): 154
Protein (gm): 5.7
Carbohydrate (gm): 44.3

Exchanges:
Milk: 0.0
Vegetable: 2.0
Fruit: 0.0
Bread: 2.0
Meat: 0.0
Fat: 0.0

1. Place squash halves, cut sides down, in large baking pan; add ½ inch water. Bake, covered, at 350 degrees until squash is tender, 30 to 40 minutes. Scrape pulp into large bowl, separating strands with fork; reserve shells.

2. Sauté Jerusalem artichokes, onion, carrots, mushrooms, celery, and garlic in lightly greased large skillet until onion is transparent, about 5 minutes. Stir in flour and cook 1 minute longer. Add tomatoes, broth, and marjoram to skillet; heat to boiling. Cook, covered, until vegetables are tender, about 10 minutes. Season to taste with salt and pepper. Toss vegetable mixture with squash and spoon into reserved shells.

VEGETABLE CREPES

LO

Any favorite vegetables can be used in these versatile crepes.

4 servings (2 crepes each)

2 cups thinly sliced cabbage

1 cup thinly sliced celery

½ cup each: thinly sliced green bell pepper, mushrooms, green onions

2–3 teaspoons sugar

2 tablespoons water

2–3 teaspoons lemon juice

Salt and pepper, to taste

8 Crepes (see p. 575), warm

Mock Hollandaise Sauce (see p. 595)

Per Serving:
Calories: 215
% of calories from fat: 25
Fat (gm): 5.8
Saturated fat (gm): 1.4
Cholesterol (mg): 107.2
Sodium (mg): 530
Protein (gm): 14.7
Carbohydrate (gm): 25.1

Exchanges:
Milk: 0.5
Vegetable: 1.0
Fruit: 0.0
Bread: 1.0
Meat: 1.0
Fat: 0.5

1. Add cabbage, celery, bell pepper, mushrooms, green onions, sugar, and water to lightly greased large skillet. Cook, covered, over medium heat until cabbage and mushrooms are wilted, about 5 minutes. Cook, uncovered, until vegetables are tender, about 5 minutes longer. Season to taste with lemon juice, salt, and pepper. Spoon mixture along centers of crepes; roll up and arrange, seam sides down, on serving plates. Serve with Mock Hollandaise Sauce.

NIÇOISE PLATTER

A garden of vegetables on a plate, drizzled with vinaigrette and served with smooth-textured, garlic-spiked Tofu Aioli.

4 servings

12 small red potatoes (about 1¼ pounds), unpeeled, cooked

2 large beets, cooked

12 ounces green beans, ends trimmed, cooked

4 Braised Whole Artichokes (see p. 470)

2–4 hard-cooked eggs, halved

2 medium tomatoes, cut into wedges

3 cups mixed salad greens, torn into bite-size pieces

¼ cup halved ripe olives

4 teaspoons drained capers

½ cup salt-free, fat-free Italian dressing with herbs

1 small shallot, minced

1 clove garlic, minced

Salt and pepper, to taste

Tofu Aioli (recipe follows)

Per Serving:
Calories: 424
% of calories from fat: 26
Fat (gm): 12.5
Saturated fat (gm): 2
Cholesterol (mg): 106
Sodium (mg): 652
Protein (gm): 16.7
Carbohydrate (gm): 65.2

Exchanges:
Milk: 0.0
Vegetable: 4.0
Fruit: 0.0
Bread: 3.0
Meat: 1.0
Fat: 1.0

1. Cut potatoes into fourths; peel and slice beets. Arrange with Braised Whole Artichokes, eggs, and tomatoes on greens-lined plates; sprinkle with olives and capers. Drizzle with combined Italian dressing, shallot, and garlic and sprinkle lightly with salt and pepper. Serve with Tofu Aioli.

Tofu Aioli

Makes about ¾ cup

½ package (10½-ounce size) light firm tofu
1 tablespoon olive oil
¾ teaspoon each: tarragon vinegar, lemon juice
½ teaspoon Dijon-style mustard
3 cloves garlic, minced
Salt and white pepper, to taste

1. Process all ingredients, except salt and pepper, in food processor or blender; season to taste with salt and white pepper. Refrigerate, covered, until ready to use.

VEGETABLE STRUDEL WITH WILD MUSHROOM SAUCE

L

A special dish for festive occasions.

4 servings

½ cup each: chopped red and yellow bell pepper
¼ cup chopped shallot
2 cloves garlic, minced
1½ cups each: cubed, cooked butternut squash, cooked broccoli florets
Wild Mushroom Sauce (see p. 596), divided
¾ cup (3 ounces) shredded reduced-fat brick, or Swiss, cheese
Salt and pepper, to taste
6 sheets frozen fillo pastry, thawed
Butter-flavored vegetable cooking spray
Tarragon sprigs, as garnish

Per Serving:
Calories: 207
% of calories from fat: 19
Fat (gm): 4.6
Saturated fat (gm): 2.4
Cholesterol (mg): 15.2
Sodium (mg): 85
Protein (gm): 11.8
Carbohydrate (gm): 27.9

Exchanges:
Milk: 0.0
Vegetable: 3.0
Fruit: 0.0
Bread: 1.0
Meat: 1.0
Fat: 0.0

1. Sauté bell peppers, shallot, and garlic in lightly greased large skillet until tender, 5 to 8 minutes. Stir in squash, broccoli, and ½ the Wild Mushroom Sauce; cook until hot, 2 to 3 minutes. Remove from heat and stir in cheese. Season to taste with salt and pepper; cool.

2. Lay 1 sheet of fillo on clean surface; spray lightly with cooking spray. Cover with second sheet of fillo and spray with cooking spray; repeat with remaining fillo. Spoon vegetable mixture along long edge of fillo, 3 to 4 inches from the edge. Fold edge of fillo over filling and roll up, using towel to help lift and roll; place seam side down on greased cookie sheet. Spray top of fillo with cooking spray.

3. Bake at 375 degrees until golden, about 30 minutes. Let stand 5 minutes before cutting. Cut strudel into 4 pieces and arrange on plates; spoon remaining Wild Mushroom Sauce over and garnish with tarragon.

LEEK AND MUSHROOM STRUDEL

V

The strudel is scented with a combination of 3 herb seeds—anise, fennel, and caraway.

45

4 servings

½ cup chopped onion

2 cloves garlic, minced

2 pounds cleaned leeks (white part only), sliced

1 pound sliced shiitake, or portobello, mushrooms

½ cup reduced-sodium vegetable broth

½ teaspoon each: crushed caraway, fennel, and anise seeds

Salt and white pepper, to taste

5 sheets frozen fillo pastry, thawed

Vegetable cooking spray

Per Serving:
Calories: 225
% of calories from fat: 4
Fat (gm): 1.2
Saturated fat (gm): 0.2
Cholesterol (mg): 0
Sodium (mg): 66
Protein (gm): 5.8
Carbohydrate (gm): 52.5

Exchanges:
Milk: 0.0
Vegetable: 6.0
Fruit: 0.0
Bread: 1.0
Meat: 0.0
Fat: 0.0

1. Sauté onion and garlic in lightly greased large skillet 2 to 3 minutes. Add leeks, mushrooms, broth, and herbs to skillet; heat to boiling. Reduce heat and simmer, covered, until vegetables are tender, 10 to 15 minutes. Cook, uncovered, until excess liquid is gone, about 5 minutes. Season to taste with salt and white pepper; cool.

2. Lay 1 sheet of fillo on clean surface; spray with cooking spray. Cover with second sheet of fillo and spray with cooking spray; repeat with remaining fillo. Spoon vegetable mixture along long edge of fillo, 3 to 4 inches from the edge. Fold edge of fillo over filling and roll up, using towel to help lift and roll; place seam side down on greased cookie sheet. Spray top of fillo generously with cooking spray.

3. Bake at 375 degrees until golden, about 30 minutes. Let stand 5 minutes before cutting; cut into 4 pieces.

VEGETABLES PAPRIKASH

L

Your preference of hot or sweet paprika can be used in this recipe.

45   **4 servings**

2 cups thinly sliced cabbage
1 cup each: sliced onion, zucchini, carrots, green bell peppers
1½ cups sliced mushrooms
1 medium tomato, chopped
1 tablespoon olive oil
3 tablespoons flour
1 tablespoon paprika
¾ cup reduced-sodium vegetable broth
½ cup fat-free sour cream
Salt and pepper, to taste
12 ounces no-yolk noodles, cooked, warm

Per Serving:
Calories: 264
% of calories from fat: 17
Fat (gm): 5.2
Saturated fat (gm): 0.7
Cholesterol (mg): 0
Sodium (mg): 119
Protein (gm): 9.6
Carbohydrate (gm): 47.5

Exchanges:
Milk: 0.0
Vegetable: 3.0
Fruit: 0.0
Bread: 2.0
Meat: 0.0
Fat: 0.7

1. Sauté vegetables in oil in large skillet until tender, 5 to 8 minutes. Stir in flour and paprika; cook, stirring, 1 to 2 minutes. Stir in broth and heat to boiling; boil, stirring, until sauce thickens, about 1 minute. Stir in sour cream; season to taste with salt and pepper. Serve over noodles.

STUFFED GRAPEVINE LEAVES

L

The grapevine leaves are also excellent served with easy-to-make Mediterranean Roasted Eggplant and Tomatoes (see p. 204).

8 servings (about 5 each)

1 jar (16 ounces) grapevine leaves preserved in
 brine, drained

2 cups cooked rice

2–4 ounces pine nuts, toasted

½ cup currants, or chopped raisins

1½ teaspoons each: dried dill weed, mint leaves,
 ground allspice

2 teaspoons lemon juice

Salt and pepper, to taste

1½ cups reduced-sodium vegetable broth

2 cups (double recipe) Cucumber Yogurt (see p. 400)

Per Serving:
Calories: 200
% of calories from fat: 27
Fat (gm): 6.4
Saturated fat (gm): 0.6
Cholesterol (mg): 0.8
Sodium (mg): 1738
Protein (gm): 7.8
Carbohydrate (gm): 40.0

Exchanges:
Milk: 0.0
Vegetable: 0.0
Fruit: 0.0
Bread: 2.0
Meat: 0.0
Fat: 1.0

1. Boil grapevine leaves in 2 quarts boiling water in large saucepan 2 minutes; drain well on paper toweling. Trim and discard any tough stems or veins. Arrange leaves, vein sides up, on clean surface.

2. Combine rice, pine nuts, currants, dill weed, mint, allspice, and lemon juice; season to taste with salt and pepper. Spoon about 1 tablespoon mixture on a grape leaf; fold stem end over filling, fold in sides, and roll up. Repeat with remaining filling.

3. Line large skillet with torn and unused grape leaves; arrange filled grape leaves, seam sides down, in skillet. Pour broth into skillet and heat to boiling; reduce heat and simmer, covered, 45 minutes. Serve warm or room temperature with Cucumber Yogurt.

VEGETABLE CURRY

V

The fragrant curry seasoning is made with a blend of spices and herbs.

45

4 servings

½ cup chopped onion

2 cloves garlic, minced

1 large head cauliflower, cut into florets

2 medium potatoes, peeled, cut into ½-inch cubes

2 large carrots, cut into ½-inch slices

1½ cups reduced-sodium vegetable broth

¾ teaspoon ground turmeric

¼ teaspoon each: dry mustard, ground cumin, coriander

1 tablespoon flour

2 tablespoons cold water

1 large tomato, chopped

1–2 tablespoons lemon juice

Salt, cayenne, and black pepper, to taste

Per Serving:
Calories: 81
% of calories from fat: 6
Fat (gm): 0.6
Saturated fat (gm): 0
Cholesterol (mg): 0
Sodium (mg): 57.2
Protein (gm): 3.7
Carbohydrate (gm): 15.8

Exchanges:
Milk: 0.0
Vegetable: 2.0
Fruit: 0.0
Bread: 0.5
Meat: 0.0
Fat: 0.0

1. Sauté onion and garlic in lightly greased large saucepan 3 to 4 minutes. Add cauliflower, potatoes, carrots, broth, and herbs to saucepan; heat to boiling. Reduce heat and simmer, covered, until vegetables are tender, 10 to 15 minutes. Heat mixture to boiling; stir in combined flour and water, stirring until thickened, about 1 minute. Stir in tomato and lemon juice; simmer 2 to 3 minutes longer. Season to taste with salt, cayenne, and black pepper.

CURRIED TOFU AND VEGETABLES

V

Serve this quick curry with basmati rice.

45 **4 servings**

¼ cup chopped onion

2–3 teaspoons finely chopped gingerroot

1 tablespoon each: canola oil, curry powder

1 teaspoon ground cumin

1 small eggplant, cubed (1-inch)

2 cups cubed, peeled winter squash, or sweet potato
(½-inch)

1½ cups cut green beans

1 cup reduced-sodium vegetable broth

1 package (10 ounces) light firm tofu, cubed

Salt and pepper, to taste

¼ cup shredded unsweetened coconut

Per Serving:
Calories: 81
% of calories from fat: 6
Fat (gm): 0.6
Saturated fat (gm): 0
Cholesterol (mg): 0
Sodium (mg): 57.2
Protein (gm): 3.7
Carbohydrate (gm): 15.8

Exchanges:
Milk: 0.0
Vegetable: 2.0
Fruit: 0.0
Bread: 0.5
Meat: 0.0
Fat: 0.0

1. Sauté onion and gingerroot in oil in large saucepan 2 minutes;
add curry powder and cumin and sauté 1 minute longer. Add eggplant and squash; sauté until lightly browned, about 5 minutes. Stir
in green beans and broth. Heat to boiling; reduce heat and simmer,
covered, until vegetables are tender, about 15 minutes. Stir in tofu;
cook until hot, 3 to 4 minutes. Season to taste with salt and pepper;
sprinkle with coconut.

SPAGHETTI AND SPAGHETTI!

L

*Spaghetti squash is tossed with spaghetti and then with a medley of
flavorful vegetables.*

4 servings

1 medium spaghetti squash, halved, seeded

2 small eggplant, unpeeled, cut into ½-inch cubes

1½ cups each: chopped onions, mushrooms

4 cloves garlic, minced

1½ cups spicy tomato juice

4 medium tomatoes, chopped

½ cup loosely packed fresh, or 2 teaspoons dried, basil leaves

Salt and pepper, to taste

8 ounces thin spaghetti, cooked, warm

¼ cup (1 ounce) grated fat-free Parmesan cheese

Per Serving:
Calories: 442
% of calories from fat: 6
Fat (gm): 3
Saturated fat (gm): 0.5
Cholesterol (mg): 0
Sodium (mg): 557
Protein (gm): 17.7
Carbohydrate (gm): 91.6

Exchanges:
Milk: 0.0
Vegetable: 3.0
Fruit: 0.0
Bread: 5.0
Meat: 0.0
Fat: 0.0

1. Place squash halves, cut sides down, in baking pan; add ½ inch water. Bake, covered, at 350 degrees until tender, 30 to 40 minutes. Using fork, scrape squash to separate into strands.

2. Sauté eggplant, onions, mushrooms, and garlic in lightly greased Dutch oven or large saucepan 10 minutes. Add tomato juice, tomatoes, and basil; heat to boiling. Reduce heat and simmer, covered, until vegetables are tender, 10 to 15 minutes. Season to taste with salt and pepper. Toss spaghetti and squash in large serving bowl; add vegetable mixture and cheese and toss.

LENTIL RAVIOLI WITH GINGERED TOMATO RELISH

Delicate ravioli, bursting with myriad flavors!

4 servings (6 ravioli each)

¼ cup finely chopped fennel bulb, or celery

2 teaspoons grated gingerroot

¾ teaspoon each: curry powder, ground cumin

¼ teaspoon each: ground turmeric, cinnamon, and cayenne pepper

2⅔ cups water

⅔ cup dried lentils

2 tablespoons finely chopped cilantro

Salt, to taste

48 wonton wrappers

Gingered Tomato Relish (see p. 610)

Cilantro, as garnish

Per Serving:
Calories: 324
% of calories from fat: 5
Fat (gm): 1.8
Saturated fat (gm): 0.3
Cholesterol (mg): 12
Sodium (mg): 569
Protein (gm): 12.1
Carbohydrate (gm): 65.4

Exchanges:
Milk: 0.0
Vegetable: 2.0
Fruit: 0.0
Bread: 4.0
Meat: 0.0
Fat: 0.0

1. Sauté fennel and gingerroot in lightly greased large skillet 2 to 3 minutes; add spices and pepper and cook 1 minute longer. Add water and lentils to skillet; heat to boiling. Reduce heat and simmer, covered, until lentils are just tender, about 20 minutes. Simmer uncovered, until excess liquid is gone, about 5 minutes. Stir in cilantro; season to taste with salt.

2. Place 1 tablespoon lentil mixture in center of 1 wonton wrapper; brush edges of wrapper with water. Place second wonton wrapper on top and press edges to seal. Repeat with remaining wonton wrappers and filling. Add 4 to 6 ravioli to 3 quarts boiling water in large saucepan; reduce heat and simmer, uncovered, until ravioli float to surface and are *al dente,* 3 to 4 minutes. Remove with slotted spoon; repeat with remaining ravioli. Serve with Gingered Tomato Relish; garnish with cilantro.

CHEESE-STUFFED PASTA SHELLS WITH SIMPLE TOMATO SAUCE

LO *This dish can be made up to 2 days in advance of serving. Simply stuff the shells and refrigerate, covered. Add sauce when ready to bake.*

6 servings

1 package (15 ounces) fat-free ricotta cheese
1 cup (4 ounces) grated Parmesan cheese, divided
2 eggs
½ cup finely chopped parsley, divided
2 cloves garlic, minced
½ teaspoon salt
¼ teaspoon pepper
24 jumbo pasta shells, cooked
Simple Tomato Sauce (recipe follows)

Per Serving:
Calories: 356
% of calories from fat: 25
Fat (gm): 10.1
Saturated fat (gm): 4
Cholesterol (mg): 84.2
Sodium (mg): 747
Protein (gm): 25.8
Carbohydrate (gm): 43.6

Exchanges:
Milk: 0.0
Vegetable: 2.0
Fruit: 0.0
Bread: 2.0
Meat: 2.0
Fat: 1.0

1. Mix ricotta, ¾ cup Parmesan cheese, eggs, ¼ cup parsley, garlic, salt, and pepper. Stuff shells with mixture and arrange in baking pan. Spoon Simple Tomato Sauce over shells. Bake, covered, until hot through, 20 to 30 minutes. Sprinkle with combined remaining ¼ cup Parmesan cheese and parsley.

Simple Tomato Sauce

Makes about 3 cups

1 small onion, finely chopped

1 clove garlic, minced

1 tablespoon canola, or olive, oil

2 cans (14½ ounces each) low-sodium tomatoes, undrained, coarsely chopped

½ teaspoon each: sugar, dried basil, and oregano leaves

1 bay leaf

½ teaspoon salt

¼ teaspoon pepper

1. Sauté onion and garlic in oil in large skillet 2 to 3 minutes. Add tomatoes and remaining ingredients; heat to boiling. Reduce heat and simmer, covered, 20 minutes; discard bay leaf.

ITALIAN-STYLE VEGGIE MEATBALLS WITH POLENTA

L

45

Keep vegetarian meatballs in your freezer for cooking convenience. They cook quickly and have many uses.

4 servings

1 package (12 ounces) vegetarian meatballs

1 can (28 ounces) Italian-seasoned diced tomatoes, undrained

1 tablespoon minced roasted garlic

Polenta (see p. 425)

¼ cup (1 ounce) shredded Parmesan cheese

Per Serving:
Calories: 273
% of calories from fat: 21
Fat (gm): 6.5
Saturated fat (gm): 2
Cholesterol (mg): 3.9
Sodium (mg): 1412
Protein (gm): 18
Carbohydrate (gm): 37.7

Exchanges:
Milk: 0.0
Vegetable: 1.0
Fruit: 0.0
Bread: 2.0
Meat: 2.0
Fat: 0.0

1. Heat meatballs, tomatoes and liquid, and garlic to boiling in large skillet; reduce heat and simmer until meatballs are hot, 8 to 10 minutes. Simmer, uncovered, until tomato mixture is thickened to a medium consistency, about 10 minutes.

2. While meatballs are cooking, make Polenta. Serve meatballs and tomatoes over Polenta; sprinkle with cheese.

GREEN ON GREEN STIR-FRY WITH TOFU

V

The variety of green vegetables creates a beautiful presentation.

45 **6 servings** (about 1 cup each)

3 cups sliced leeks (white parts only)

1 cup sliced celery

1 teaspoon each: minced garlic, gingerroot

½ teaspoon crushed red pepper

3 cups each: snow peas, sliced bok choy

1 cup chopped green bell pepper

2 cups reduced-sodium vegetable broth

2 tablespoons cornstarch

2 teaspoons reduced-sodium soy sauce

Salt and pepper, to taste

1 package (10 ounces) light firm tofu, cubed

4 cups cooked rice, warm

Per Serving:
Calories: 236
% of calories from fat: 4.8
Fat (gm): 1.3
Saturated fat (gm): 0.2
Cholesterol (mg): 0.0
Sodium (mg): 319
Protein (gm): 9.3
Carbohydrate (gm): 47

Exchanges:
Milk: 0.0
Vegetable: 2.0
Fruit: 0.0
Bread: 2.0
Meat: 1.0
Fat: 0.0

1. Stir-fry leeks, celery, garlic, gingerroot, and crushed red pepper in lightly greased large wok or skillet 2 to 3 minutes. Add snow peas, bok choy, and bell pepper and stir-fry until crisp-tender, 3 to 5 minutes.

2. Stir combined broth, cornstarch, and soy sauce into wok and heat to boiling. Boil, stirring until thickened, about 1 minute. Season to taste with salt and pepper. Stir in tofu; cook 1 to 2 minutes longer. Serve over rice.

45-MINUTE PREP TIP: Begin cooking the rice before preparing the rest of the recipe.

SPRING VEGETABLE STIR-FRY

V

The best of spring's bounty, seasoned with fresh ginger, Asian sesame oil, and tamari soy sauce.

4 servings

1 cup each: sliced onion, mushrooms

8 small red potatoes, unpeeled, cut into ¼-inch slices

12 ounces asparagus, cut into 1½-inch pieces

½ cup chopped red bell pepper

2 cloves garlic, minced

1 tablespoon minced gingerroot

1½ cups reduced-sodium vegetable broth

4 teaspoons cornstarch

¼ cup cold water

1–2 teaspoons reduced-sodium tamari soy sauce

1 teaspoon Asian sesame oil

Salt and pepper, to taste

3 cups cooked unseasoned brown and wild rice blend

1 teaspoon sesame seeds

Per Serving:
Calories: 443
% of calories from fat: 7
Fat (gm): 3.4
Saturated fat (gm): 0.6
Cholesterol (mg): 0
Sodium (mg): 125
Protein (gm): 13.5
Carbohydrate (gm): 94

Exchanges:
Milk: 0.0
Vegetable: 2.0
Fruit: 0.0
Bread: 5.0
Meat: 0.0
Fat: 0.5

1. Stir-fry onion, mushrooms, and potatoes in lightly greased large wok or skillet 3 minutes. Add asparagus, bell pepper, garlic, and gingerroot; stir-fry 2 minutes. Add broth and heat to boiling; reduce heat and simmer, covered, until vegetables are crisp-tender, 3 to 5 minutes. Stir in combined cornstarch and water; boil, stirring, until thickened, about 1 minute. Stir in soy sauce and Asian sesame oil; season to taste with salt and pepper. Serve over rice; sprinkle with sesame seeds.

THAI STIR-FRY

V

45

An aromatic rice, such as basmati, or jasmine can be substituted for the Thai rice; cook with light coconut milk, if desired, or sprinkle with flaked coconut when serving.

4 servings

8 green onions, sliced

2 cups each: broccoli florets, thinly sliced carrots

½–1 cup Thai peanut sauce

½ cup reduced-sodium vegetable broth

2 teaspoons cornstarch

1 package (6.4 ounces) Thai coconut ginger rice, cooked, warm

¼ cup each: chopped cilantro, dry-roasted peanuts (optional)

Per Serving:
Calories: 238
% of calories from fat: 20
Fat (gm): 5.4
Saturated fat (gm): 1
Cholesterol (mg): 0
Sodium (mg): 1433
Protein (gm): 10.2
Carbohydrate (gm): 38.3

Exchanges:
Milk: 0.0
Vegetable: 2.0
Fruit: 0.0
Bread: 2.0
Meat: 0.0
Fat: 1.0

1. Sauté onions, broccoli, and carrots in lightly greased large skillet until crisp-tender, 4 to 5 minutes; stir in peanut sauce. Stir in combined vegetable broth and cornstarch; heat to boiling. Boil, stirring, until thickened, about 1 minute. Serve over rice; sprinkle with cilantro and peanuts, if using.

FIVE-SPICE STIR-FRY

V

Five-spice powder is a blend of spices and herbs that may vary according to the manufacturer. Fennel and anise seeds, anise and gingerroot, cinnamon, and cloves are usual ingredients.

4 servings (about 1 cup each)

2 pounds broccoli florets and sliced stems
3 cups sliced bok choy, or Chinese cabbage
1 each: sliced medium yellow bell pepper, onion
2–3 teaspoons Asian sesame oil
1 can (8 ounces) sliced water chestnuts, rinsed, drained
1⅓ cups reduced-sodium vegetable broth
4 teaspoons cornstarch
1 teaspoon five-spice powder
1 teaspoon ground ginger
2–3 teaspoons reduced-sodium tamari soy sauce
Salt and pepper, to taste
4 cups cooked brown rice, or thin spaghetti, warm
¼ cup finely chopped cilantro, or parsley

Per Serving:
Calories: 367
% of calories from fat: 12
Fat (gm): 5
Saturated fat (gm): 0.8
Cholesterol (mg): 0.0
Sodium (mg): 351
Protein (gm): 11.6
Carbohydrate (gm): 72.5

Exchanges:
Milk: 0.0
Vegetable: 2.0
Fruit: 0.0
Bread: 4.0
Meat: 0.0
Fat: 1.0

1. Stir-fry broccoli, bok choy, bell pepper, and onion in Asian sesame oil in wok or large skillet until crisp-tender, 8 to 10 minutes. Stir in water chestnuts. Stir in combined broth, cornstarch, five-spice powder, ginger, and soy sauce; heat to boiling. Boil, stirring, until thickened, about 1 minute. Season to taste with salt and pepper. Serve with rice; sprinkle with cilantro.

SZECHUAN VEGETABLE STIR-FRY

V *The hot chili oil and crushed red pepper are hot, so begin with less oil, adding more to taste. Asian sesame oil can be substituted for the hot chili oil.*

4 servings (about 1¼ cups each)

1 cup reduced-sodium vegetable broth, divided

¼ cup each: orange juice, reduced-sodium soy sauce

1–2 teaspoons hot chili oil

1–2 pinches crushed red pepper

1 package (8 ounces) tempeh, cut into ¾-inch cubes

8 ounces asparagus, cut into 1½-inch pieces

1 cup each: sliced carrots, green onions, red bell pepper, snow peas

2–3 teaspoons minced gingerroot

½ cup sliced shiitake, or cremini, mushrooms

4 cloves garlic, minced

2 tablespoons cornstarch

Salt and pepper, to taste

4 cups cooked brown rice, warm

¼ cup peanuts (optional)

Per Serving:
Calories: 455
% of calories from fat: 15
Fat (gm): 8.0
Saturated fat (gm): 1.3
Cholesterol (mg): 0
Sodium (mg): 663
Protein (gm): 23.3
Carbohydrate (gm): 75.8

Exchanges:
Milk: 0.0
Vegetable: 3.0
Fruit: 0.0
Bread: 4.0
Meat: 1.0
Fat: 1.0

1. Combine ½ cup broth, orange juice, soy sauce, hot chili oil, and red pepper; pour over tempeh in glass dish and let stand 30 minutes. Drain, reserving marinade.

2. Stir-fry tempeh in lightly greased large wok or skillet 2 to 3 minutes. Add vegetables; stir-fry until crisp-tender, 8 to 10 minutes. Add reserved marinade and heat to boiling; stir in combined cornstarch and remaining ½ cup broth. Boil, stirring, until thickened, about 1 minute. Season to taste with salt and pepper. Serve over rice; sprinkle with peanuts, if using.

CHOP SUEY

V *Bead molasses, a very dark molasses, adds the traditional flavor accent to this dish.*

6 servings

1½ packages (8 ounces each) tempeh, cut into strips, or pieces

1–2 tablespoons reduced-sodium tamari soy sauce

2 cups thinly sliced Chinese cabbage

1 cup each: chopped onion, red, or green, bell pepper, mushrooms

2 cloves garlic, minced

1½ cups reduced-sodium vegetable broth

2 tablespoons cornstarch

½–1 tablespoon bead molasses

2 cups fresh, or canned, rinsed, bean sprouts

1 can (8 ounces) bamboo shoots, or water chesnuts, rinsed, drained

Reduced-sodium soy sauce, to taste

Salt and pepper, to taste

6 cups cooked brown, or white, rice, warm

Per Serving:
Calories: 598
% of calories from fat: 18
Fat (gm): 12.6
Saturated fat (gm): 2.5
Cholesterol (mg): 0.0
Sodium (mg): 592
Protein (gm): 29
Carbohydrate (gm): 98

Exchanges:
Milk: 0.0
Vegetable: 0.0
Fruit: 0.0
Bread: 6.0
Meat: 3.0
Fat: 0.0

1. Brush tempeh with soy sauce; let stand 30 minutes. Stir-fry in lightly greased large wok or skillet 3 to 4 minutes; remove. Add cabbage, onion, bell pepper, mushrooms, and garlic; stir-fry until crisp-tender, 8 to 10 minutes. Add combined broth, cornstarch, and molasses and heat to boiling; boil, stirring, until thickened, about 1 minute. Stir in tempeh, bean sprouts, and bamboo shoots; stir-fry until hot, about 2 minutes. Season to taste with soy sauce, salt, and pepper. Serve over rice.

TEEM SEEM LOAF

o

Enjoy this flavorful loaf, topped with sweet-sour stir-fried vegetables. The mixture can also be shaped into small meatballs or burgers.

4 servings

Oriental Loaf (see p. 272)

8 ounces snow peas

¾ cup diagonally sliced carrots

1 can (8 ounces) water chestnuts, rinsed, drained, sliced

1 can (13¼ ounces) pineapple chunks in juice, drained, reserving ½ cup juice

1 tablespoon cornstarch

3 tablespoons each: sugar, cider vinegar, reduced-sodium tamari soy sauce

Salt and pepper, to taste

Per Serving:
Calories: 364
% of calories from fat: 11
Fat (gm): 4.6
Saturated fat (gm): 0.9
Cholesterol (mg): 53.3
Sodium (mg): 790
Protein (gm): 13.8
Carbohydrate (gm): 69

Exchanges:
Milk: 0.0
Vegetable: 2.0
Fruit: 2.5
Bread: 1.5
Meat: 1.0
Fat: 0.0

1. Make Oriental Loaf, shaping into round loaf, about 5 inches in diameter, in pie pan. Bake, uncovered at 350 degrees until hot in the center, about 1 hour.

2. Stir-fry snow peas and carrots in lightly greased large wok or skillet until crisp-tender, about 5 minutes. Add water chestnuts and pineapple chunks. Stir in combined cornstarch, reserved ½ cup pineapple juice, sugar, vinegar, and soy sauce and heat to boiling. Boil stirring, until thickened, about 1 minute. Season to taste with salt and pepper. Spoon vegetables over loaf on serving plate; cut into wedges.

MOO-SHU TEMPEH

O *Tempeh replaces pork in this Mandarin favorite. The Mandarin Pancakes are fabulous and can be made in advance. If short on time, however, flour tortillas can be substituted.*

6 servings (2 each)

1½ ounces dry Chinese mushrooms (shiitake)

Boiling water

2–3 tablespoons reduced-sodium tamari soy sauce

2 teaspoons Asian sesame oil

1 tablespoon minced gingerroot

1 teaspoon sugar

1 package (8 ounces) tempeh, julienned

2 eggs, lightly beaten

½ cup bamboo shoots, julienned

2 green onions, sliced

½ cup water

2 teaspoons cornstarch

Mandarin Pancakes (see pp. 575)

½–¾ cup oriental plum sauce

12 medium green onions

Per Serving:
Calories: 253
% of calories from fat: 23
Fat (gm): 6.5
Saturated fat (gm): 1.3
Cholesterol (mg): 71
Sodium (mg): 230
Protein (gm): 13.9
Carbohydrate (gm): 36.1

Exchanges:
Milk: 0.0
Vegetable: 1.0
Fruit: 0.0
Bread: 2.0
Meat: 1.0
Fat: 0.5

1. Place mushrooms in bowl; pour boiling water over to cover. Let stand until mushrooms are softened, about 15 minutes; drain. Slice mushrooms, discarding tough centers, and reserve.

2. Combine soy sauce, Asian sesame oil, gingerroot, and sugar; pour over tempeh in bowl. Let stand 30 minutes; do not drain.

3. Cook eggs in lightly greased large skillet over low heat until scrambled, breaking into small pieces with a fork; set aside. Add tempeh and marinade, reserved mushrooms, bamboo shoots, and green onions to skillet; cook over medium heat 2 to 3 minutes. Stir in combined water and cornstarch and heat to boiling; boil, stirring, until thickened, about 1 minute. Stir in reserved egg; cook 1 minute longer.

4. Spread each Mandarin Pancake with 2 to 3 teaspoons plum sauce; top with about ⅓ cup tempeh mixture and a green onion and roll up.

TEMPEH STEAK WITH RED AND GREEN STIR-FRY

V

If available, use red Swiss chard for its intense red and green color.

45

6 servings (about 1 cup each)

2 cups each: sliced red onions, red bell peppers
1 cup sliced celery
2 teaspoons minced garlic
1 teaspoon minced gingerroot
6 cups thinly sliced red, or green, Swiss chard, or
  spinach
2 cups reduced-sodium vegetable broth
2 tablespoons cornstarch
½–¾ teaspoon hot chili paste
Salt and pepper, to taste
16 ounces tempeh, cut into 6 pieces
4 teaspoons reduced-sodium tamari soy sauce

Per Serving:
Calories: 302
% of calories from fat: 26
Fat (gm): 9.4
Saturated fat (gm): 1.5
Cholesterol (mg): 0
Sodium (mg): 272
Protein (gm): 27.3
Carbohydrate (gm): 32

Exchanges:
Milk: 0.0
Vegetable: 3.0
Fruit: 0.0
Bread: 1.0
Meat: 2.0
Fat: 1.0

1. Stir-fry onions, bell peppers, celery, garlic, and gingerroot in lightly greased large wok or skillet until crisp-tender 5 to 8 minutes. Add Swiss chard and stir-fry until wilted, 1 to 2 minutes. Stir in combined broth, cornstarch, and chili paste; heat to boiling. Boil, stirring, until thickened, about 1 minute. Season to taste with salt and pepper.

2. Brush tempeh with tamari; cook in lightly greased wok over medium heat until browned, 2 to 3 minutes on each side. Serve vegetables over tempeh.

BURRITOS WITH POBLANO CHILI SAUCE

L

Brushed with sauce and cooked twice for extra flavor, these burritos are a beautiful adobe red color.

4 servings

3 arbol chilies, stems, seeds, and veins discarded

Hot water

¾ cup each: chopped zucchini, yellow summer squash

1 small onion, finely chopped

3 cloves garlic, minced

2 tablespoons finely chopped cilantro

1 teaspoon each: dried marjoram and oregano leaves

1 can (15 ounces) pinto beans, rinsed, drained

¼ cup water

1 cup chopped tomato

Salt and cayenne pepper, to taste

4 large (10-inch) flour tortillas

Poblano Chili Sauce (see p. 601)

½ cup fat-free sour cream

Medium, or hot, salsa, to taste

Per Serving:
Calories: 319
% of calories from fat: 10
Fat (gm): 3.7
Saturated fat (gm): 0.5
Cholesterol (mg): 0
Sodium (mg): 620
Protein (gm): 18.3
Carbohydrate (gm): 58.9

Exchanges:
Milk: 0.5
Vegetable: 2.0
Fruit: 0.0
Bread: 3.0
Meat: 0.5
Fat: 0.5

1. Cover arbol chilies with hot water in small bowl; let stand until softened, 10 to 15 minutes. Drain; chop finely.

2. Sauté zucchini, squash, onion, garlic, and herbs in lightly greased medium skillet until onion is tender, 8 to 10 minutes. Add beans, water, and arbol chilies to skillet; mash coarsely with fork. Stir in tomato; season to taste with salt and cayenne pepper. Spoon vegetable mixture along centers of tortillas; top each with ¼ cup Poblano Chili Sauce. Fold sides of tortillas in, overlapping filling; fold ends in, overlapping to make a square "package"; secure with toothpicks.

3. Cook burritos in lightly greased large skillet until browned on all sides, brushing with remaining Poblano Chili Sauce. Serve with sour cream and salsa.

ENCHILADAS MOLE

L *The Enchilada and Mole Sauces are fabulous, and worth the effort of making; a purchased mole sauce can be substituted, or bake the enchiladas topped with green or red salsa.*

4 servings (2 enchiladas each)

8–12 ounces tempeh, cut into strips (2 x ½ x ½ inches)

1 cup (½ recipe) Enchilada Sauce (see p. 599), or prepared salsa

8 corn, or flour, tortillas

½ cup (2 ounces) shredded fat-free Cheddar cheese

½ cup sliced green onions

4–8 tablespoons fat-free sour cream

¼ cup finely chopped cilantro

Mole Sauce (see p. 600)

Per Serving:
Calories: 388
% of calories from fat: 22
Fat (gm): 10.2
Saturated fat (gm): 1.5
Cholesterol (mg): 0
Sodium (mg): 235
Protein (gm): 26.2
Carbohydrate (gm): 53.8

Exchanges:
Milk: 0.0
Vegetable: 3.0
Fruit: 0.0
Bread: 2.5
Meat: 2.0
Fat: 1.0

1. Combine tempeh and Enchilada Sauce in glass baking dish; refrigerate 1 to 2 hours; drain, reserving Enchilada Sauce. Sauté tempeh in lightly greased medium skillet over medium heat until browned, 3 to 5 minutes.

2. Dip tortillas in reserved Enchilada Sauce to coat lightly. Spoon tempeh along centers of tortillas; top with cheese, green onions, sour cream, and cilantro. Roll up and place, seam sides down, in large baking pan; spoon Mole Sauce over. Bake, loosely covered, at 350 degrees until hot, 20 to 30 minutes.

VEGETABLE ENCHILADAS

L

8 to 12 ounces of tempeh or light firm tofu can be substituted for the vegetarian sausage; prepared enchilada sauce can be substituted for the homemade.

6 servings (2 enchiladas each)

2 cups chopped zucchini

1½ cups chopped tomatoes

¾ cup chopped carrots

¼ cup each: chopped poblano chili, green onions

4 cloves garlic, minced

1 teaspoon each: dried oregano leaves, ground cumin

1 package (12 ounces) frozen vegetarian sausage
   patties, crumbled

Salt and pepper, to taste

12 corn, or flour, tortillas

Enchilada Sauce (see p. 599)

¾ cup (3 ounces) shredded fat-free Cheddar cheese

3 tablespoons finely chopped cilantro

Per Serving:
Calories: 269
% of calories from fat: 6
Fat (gm): 1.8
Saturated fat (gm): 0.3
Cholesterol (mg): 0
Sodium (mg): 449
Protein (gm): 22.5
Carbohydrate (gm): 42.7

Exchanges:
Milk: 0.0
Vegetable: 2.0
Fruit: 0.0
Bread: 2.0
Meat: 1.5
Fat: 0.0

1. Sauté vegetables and herbs in lightly greased large skillet until vegetables are tender, about 10 minutes. Add vegetarian sausage; cook over medium heat until no excess juices remain, 5 to 8 minutes. Season to taste with salt and pepper.

2. Dip tortillas in Enchilada Sauce to coat lightly, and fill each with about ⅓ cup vegetable mixture. Roll up and place, seam sides down, in large baking pan. Spoon remaining Enchilada Sauce over enchiladas; sprinkle with cheese. Bake, uncovered, at 350 degrees, 15 to 20 minutes. Sprinkle with cilantro.

FLAUTAS WITH TOMATILLO SAUCE

L *Flautas are usually deep-fried; these are sautéed to achieve the same crisp goodness.*

4 servings (2 flautas each)

1 cup each: chopped zucchini, tomato, sliced
    mushrooms

½ cup each: chopped onion, poblano chili

½ teaspoon each: ground cumin, dried thyme leaves

2 tablespoons finely chopped cilantro

Salt and pepper, to taste

8 flour, or corn, tortillas

Vegetable cooking spray

1 cup (½ recipe) Tomatillo Sauce (see p. 602)

¼ cup crumbled Mexican white, or feta cheese

¼ cup fat-free sour cream

Per Serving:
Calories: 330
% of calories from fat: 22
Fat (gm): 8.1
Saturated fat (gm): 1.8
Cholesterol (mg): 5.1
Sodium (mg): 456
Protein (gm): 11
Carbohydrate (gm): 55.3

Exchanges:
Milk: 0.0
Vegetable: 2.0
Fruit: 0.0
Bread: 3.0
Meat: 0.0
Fat: 1.5

1. Sauté vegetables, cumin, thyme, and cilantro in lightly greased large skillet until tender, about 5 minutes; season to taste with salt and pepper. Spoon about ⅓ cup vegetable mixture on each tortilla; roll up and fasten with toothpicks. Spray flautas lightly with cooking spray; cook in skillet, over medium heat, until browned on all sides, 3 to 4 minutes. Spoon Tomatillo Sauce over flautas; sprinkle with cheese and top with dollops of sour cream.

TEMPEH FAJITAS

L

Fajitas are an American interpretation of soft tacos.

45

❄

4 servings (2 fajitas each)

8–12 ounces tempeh, cut into strips (2 x ½ x ½ -inch)
Fajita Marinade (recipe follows)
1 each sliced medium red bell pepper, onion
1 can (15 ounces) black beans, rinsed, drained
2 tablespoons finely chopped cilantro
1 teaspoon each: ground cumin, dried marjoram
  leaves
Salt and pepper, to taste
8 flour, *or* corn, tortillas, warm
1 cup hot or mild salsa
½ cup fat-free sour cream

Per Serving:
Calories: 441
% of calories from fat: 18
Fat (gm): 9.7
Saturated fat (gm): 1.4
Cholesterol (mg): 0
Sodium (mg): 601
Protein (gm): 29.1
Carbohydrate (gm): 70.8

Exchanges:
Milk: 0.0
Vegetable: 2.0
Fruit: 0.0
Bread: 4.0
Meat: 2.0
Fat: 0.0

1. Combine tempeh and Fajita Marinade in glass baking dish; refrigerate, covered, 1 to 2 hours; drain. Cook tempeh in lightly greased large skillet over medium heat until browned, 5 to 8 minutes; move tempeh to side of pan. Add bell pepper and onion; cook until tender, about 5 minutes. Add beans, cilantro, cumin, and marjoram; cook until hot, 2 to 3 minutes. Season to taste with salt and pepper; serve in tortillas with salsa and sour cream.

Fajita Marinade

Makes about ⅓ cup

⅓ cup lime juice
4 cloves garlic, minced
1½ teaspoons dried oregano leaves
½ teaspoon ground allspice
¼ teaspoon black pepper

1. Mix all ingredients.

THREE-CHILI TAMALES

V *Ancho chilies are fresh poblano chilies that have been dried. Ancho chilies, corn husks and masa harina (corn flour) can be purchased in large supermarkets or Mexican groceries.*

4 servings (3 tamales each)

2 ancho chilies, stems, seeds, and veins discarded
⅓ cup boiling water
1 large poblano chili, chopped
1 can (4 ounces) chopped green chilies, drained
½ teaspoon each: dried oregano, thyme leaves
Salt and pepper, to taste
Tamale Dough (recipe follows)
12 corn husks, softened in hot water, drained

Per Serving:
Calories: 187
% of calories from fat: 26
Fat (gm): 5.6
Saturated fat (gm): 1
Cholesterol (mg): 0
Sodium (mg): 396
Protein (gm): 3.7
Carbohydrate (gm): 29.9

Exchanges:
Milk: 0.0
Vegetable: 1.0
Fruit: 0.0
Bread: 1.5
Meat: 0.0
Fat: 1.0

1. Crumble ancho chilies into bowl; pour ⅓ cup boiling water over and let stand until softened, 15 to 20 minutes. Cook ancho chilies and liquid, poblano and green chilies, and herbs over medium heat in lightly greased medium skillet until chilies are tender, 5 to 8 minutes, stirring frequently. Season to taste with salt and pepper. Mix in Tamale Dough.

2. Spoon about ¼ cup of tamale mixture onto center of each corn husk; fold sides of husks over filling. Tie ends of tamales with string, making "bundles." Place tamales on steamer rack in saucepan with 2 inches of water. Steam, covered, 2 hours, adding more water to saucepan if necessary.

Tamale Dough

1 cup masa harina
¾ teaspoon baking powder
1½ tablespoons margarine, softened
¼–½ teaspoon salt
1 cup reduced-sodium vegetable broth

1. Combine masa harina, baking powder, margarine, and salt; gradually stir in broth (mixture will be soft).

VEGGIE TAMALES WITH BEANS

v *Tamales can be tied in "bundles," as in the preceding recipe, or in "envelopes," as in this recipe.*

4 servings (3 tamales each)

1 medium onion, chopped
½ cup chopped poblano chili
¾ cup frozen, whole kernel corn, chopped zucchini
3 cloves garlic, minced
¾ teaspoon dried marjoram leaves
¼ teaspoon ground allspice
½ can (15-ounce size) pinto beans, rinsed, drained, coarsely mashed
Salt and cayenne pepper, to taste
Tamale Dough (see p. 183)
12 corn husks, softened in hot water, drained

Per Serving:
Calories: 257
% of calories from fat: 20
Fat (gm): 6
Saturated fat (gm): 1
Cholesterol (mg): 0
Sodium (mg): 457
Protein (gm): 8.5
Carbohydrate (gm): 44.7

Exchanges:
Milk: 0.0
Vegetable: 2.0
Fruit: 0.0
Bread: 2.5
Meat: 0.0
Fat: 0.5

1. Sauté onion, poblano chili, corn, zucchini, garlic, marjoram, and allspice in lightly greased medium skillet until vegetables are tender, about 5 minutes. Stir in beans; season to taste with salt and cayenne pepper. Mix in Tamale Dough.

2. Spoon about ¼ cup of tamale mixture onto center of each corn husk. Fold sides of husks over filling; fold tops and bottoms of husks toward center and tie in the center with string. Place tamales on steamer rack in saucepan with 2 inches of water. Steam, covered, 2 hours, adding more water to saucepan if necessary.

FIVE

Roasted
and
Grilled Dishes

ROASTED CORN AND POTATO CHOWDER

L

45

Roasting enhances the natural flavors of vegetables, making this soup a favorite in our repertoire.

8 main-dish servings (about 1½ cups each)

6 ears corn, in the husks

2 pounds new red potatoes, halved

1 each: medium red bell pepper, onion, cut into ¾-inch pieces

3 cloves garlic, peeled

Olive oil cooking spray

2 teaspoons each: dried thyme and crushed rosemary leaves

6 cups reduced-sodium vegetable broth, divided

⅔ cup fat-free half-and-half, *or* fat-free milk

Salt and pepper, to taste

Per Serving:
Calories: 250
% of calories from fat: 6
Fat (gm): 1.6
Saturated fat (gm): 0.2
Cholesterol (mg): 0
Sodium (mg): 78
Protein (gm): 6.2
Carbohydrate (gm): 51.1

Exchanges:
Milk: 0.0
Vegetable: 1.0
Fruit: 0.0
Bread: 3.0
Meat: 0.0
Fat: 0.0

1. Soak corn in cold water to cover 30 minutes. Arrange corn and vegetables in single layer on 2 greased foil-lined jelly roll pans; spray with cooking spray and sprinkle with herbs. Roast at 425 degrees until browned and tender, about 40 minutes, removing garlic when soft, after about 30 minutes. Let vegetables stand until cool enough to handle. Remove and discard corn husks; cut kernels off cobs.

2. Process vegetables and 2 to 3 cups broth in food processor or blender until smooth. Heat vegetable mixture and remaining broth to boiling in large saucepan; reduce heat to medium. Stir in half-and-half and cook until hot, 3 to 4 minutes. Season to taste with salt and pepper.

HOT PEPPER VICHYSSOISE

LO *Potato soup will never be boring if served Tex-Mex style. This version, prepared with peppers, packs a punch!*

6 main-dish servings (about 1 cup each)

1 each: medium leek (white part only), large poblano and jalapeño chili

1 pound new red potatoes, unpeeled, halved

6 cloves garlic, peeled

Vegetable cooking spray

1½ teaspoons ground cumin

½ teaspoon each: chili powder, dried oregano leaves, pepper

4 cups reduced-sodium vegetable broth, divided

½–¾ cup fat-free half-and-half, or fat-free milk

¼ cup minced cilantro

Salt, to taste

6 pieces (⅔ recipe) Roasted Chili Corn Bread (see p. 216)

Per Serving:
Calories: 331
% of calories from fat: 7
Fat (gm): 2.5
Saturated fat (gm): 0.5
Cholesterol (mg): 24.7
Sodium (mg): 365
Protein (gm): 10
Carbohydrate (gm): 64.1

Exchanges:
Milk: 0.0
Vegetable: 4.0
Fruit: 0.0
Bread: 3.0
Meat: 0.0
Fat: 0.5

1. Cut leek and chilies into ¾-inch pieces. Arrange vegetables in single layer greased foil-lined jelly roll pan; spray with cooking spray and sprinkle with herbs and pepper. Roast at 425 degrees until browned and tender, about 40 minutes, removing garlic when tender, after about 30 minutes.

2. Process vegetables and 1 to 2 cups broth in food processor or blender until smooth. Heat vegetable mixture and remaining broth to boiling in large saucepan; reduce heat to medium. Stir in half-and-half and cook until hot, 3 to 4 minutes. Stir in cilantro; season with salt. Serve warm, or chilled, with Roasted Chili Corn Bread.

PUREED ROASTED VEGETABLE SOUP

L

45

The soup is served over rice, but it is also delicious served without rice and topped with Italian-Style Croutons (see p. 560).

6 main-dish servings (about 1½ cups each)

1 medium eggplant, peeled

2 patty pan squash, or small zucchini

1 each: medium red bell pepper, red onion, poblano chili

3 cloves garlic, peeled

Olive oil cooking spray

1½ tablespoons herbs de Provence

4 cups canned reduced-sodium vegetable broth, divided

1–2 tablespoons lemon juice

1 teaspoon grated lemon zest

Salt and pepper, to taste

3 cups cooked rice, warm

¾–1¼ cups fat-free plain yogurt

Per Serving:
Calories: 219
% of calories from fat: 4
Fat (gm): 1.1
Saturated fat (gm): 0.2
Cholesterol (mg): 0.5
Sodium (mg): 87
Protein (gm): 6.7
Carbohydrate (gm): 47.4

Exchanges:
Milk: 0.0
Vegetable: 3.0
Fruit: 0.0
Bread: 2.0
Meat: 0.0
Fat: 0.0

1. Cut vegetables, except garlic, into 1-inch pieces. Arrange vegetables in single layer on greased foil-lined pan; spray with cooking spray and sprinkle with herbs. Roast at 425 degrees until browned and tender, about 40 minutes, removing garlic when soft, after about 30 minutes.

2. Process vegetables and 1 cup broth in food processor or blender until smooth. Heat vegetable mixture, remaining 3 cups broth, lemon juice, and zest in large saucepan to boiling; reduce heat and simmer, uncovered, 5 minutes. Season to taste with salt and pepper. Serve soup over rice in bowls and top each with 2 to 3 tablespoons yogurt.

ROASTED VEGETABLE MINESTRONE

V

45

◊

Roasted vegetables can be made 1 to 2 days in advance; complete step 2 of recipe, simmering until hot, about 15 minutes.

8 main-dish servings (about 1¾ cups each)

1 each: medium eggplant, large unpeeled
   Idaho potato

2 each: medium zucchini, tomatoes

½ small butternut squash, peeled

1 each: large green and red bell pepper, large onion

4 cloves garlic, minced

Olive oil cooking spray

2 teaspoons dried Italian seasoning

1 can (15½ ounces) each: rinsed, drained cannellini,
   red kidney beans

7 cups reduced-sodium vegetable broth

2–3 tablespoons white balsamic vinegar

Salt and pepper, to taste

Per Serving:
Calories: 224
% of calories from fat: 7
Fat (gm): 2
Saturated fat (gm): 0.2
Cholesterol (mg): 0
Sodium (mg): 269
Protein (gm): 11.7
Carbohydrate (gm): 44.5

Exchanges:
Milk: 0.0
Vegetable: 3.0
Fruit: 0.0
Bread: 2.0
Meat: 0.0
Fat: 0.0

1. Cut fresh vegetables, except garlic, into ¾- to 1-inch pieces. Arrange vegetables in single layer on greased foil-lined jelly roll pan; spray with cooking spray and sprinkle with herbs. Roast at 425 degrees until browned and tender, about 40 minutes, removing garlic when soft, after about 30 minutes.

2. Heat beans and broth to boiling; add roasted vegetables, reduce heat, and simmer, covered, 10 minutes. Season to taste with vinegar, salt, and pepper.

ROASTED MANY-VEGGIE STEW

V

Serve this Italian-accented stew over Garlic Polenta (see pg. 425).

45

6 main-dish servings (about 2 cups each)

8 ounces new potatoes, unpeeled, quartered

1 cup each: cubed unpeeled eggplant, thickly sliced zucchini and cabbage, cauliflower florets, halved green beans

1 cup each: thinly sliced green bell peppers, onion

3 cloves garlic, minced

Olive oil cooking spray

¾–1 teaspoon dried Italian seasoning

1 cup each: reduced-sodium vegetable broth, dry red wine, or vegetable broth

¼ cup reduced-sodium tomato paste

2 tablespoons balsamic vinegar

1½ tablespoons brown sugar

2 medium tomatoes, cut into wedges

Salt and pepper, to taste

Per Serving:
Calories: 163
% of calories from fat: 3.2
Fat (gm): 0.6
Saturated fat (gm): 0.6
Cholesterol (mg): 0.0
Sodium (mg): 118
Protein (gm): 4.9
Carbohydrate (gm): 30.9

Exchanges:
Milk: 0.0
Vegetable: 0.0
Fruit: 0.0
Bread: 2.0
Meat: 0.0
Fat: 0.5

1. Arrange vegetables, except tomato wedges, in single layer on 2 greased foil-line jelly roll pans; spray with cooking spray and sprinkle with herbs. Roast at 475 degrees 15 to 20 minutes or until beginning to brown, stirring occasionally.

2. Heat broth, wine, tomato paste, vinegar, and sugar to boiling in small saucepan; pour over vegetables. Add tomato wedges to pan; reduce oven temperature to 350 degrees and bake, covered, 20 to 30 minutes or until vegetables are tender. Combine vegetables in bowl; season to taste with salt and pepper.

MESQUITE-SMOKED TOFU

V *Tofu, lightly smoked, is delicious! Tempeh can be substituted for the tofu.*

4 side-dish servings

2 packages (10½ ounces each) light firm tofu, *
halved lengthwise

1. Arrange hot charcoal around edges of grill and
place a shallow pan of water in center. Sprinkle
hot coals with mesquite chips that have been
soaked in water and well drained. Place tofu on
greased rack. Smoke, covered, 20 to 30 minutes,
or longer for a more intense smoky flavor.

Per Serving:
Calories: 54
% of calories from fat: 19.6
Fat (gm): 1.2
Saturated fat (gm): 0.2
Cholesterol (mg): 0.0
Sodium (mg): 125
Protein (gm): 9.3
Carbohydrate (gm): 1.6

Exchanges:
Milk: 0.0
Vegetable: 0.0
Fruit: 0.0
Bread: 0.0
Meat: 1.0
Fat: 0.0

NOTE: For range-top smoking, sprinkle 2 to 3 tablespoons mesquite
smoking bits (very small mesquite chips, available in canisters at
hardware and home improvement stores and some supermarkets)
or mesquite shavings in bottom of Dutch oven; place wire rack in
Dutch oven. Place tofu on greased pan on rack; heat, covered, over
high heat 5 minutes. Lift lid just enough to make sure pan is filled
with smoke; reduce heat to medium-low and cook, covered, 20 to
30 minutes.

JERK TEMPEH WITH BLACK BEANS AND RICE

V *A meal with island flavors! The Caribbean Jerk Seasoning is also excellent
on eggplant and portobello mushrooms.*

6 main-dish servings

2 packages (8 ounces each) tempeh, halved crosswise
1 tablespoon lime juice
Jerk Seasoning (recipe follows)
Black Beans and Rice (see p. 374)
Fried Ripe Plantains (see p. 29)

1. Brush tempeh pieces with lime juice;
sprinkle with Jerk Seasoning, pressing mixture

Per Serving:
Calories: 439
% of calories from fat: 16
Fat (gm): 8.3
Saturated fat (gm): 1.3
Cholesterol (mg): 0
Sodium (mg): 250
Protein (gm): 25.6
Carbohydrate (gm): 71.9

Exchanges:
Milk: 0.0
Vegetable: 1.0
Fruit: 1.0
Bread: 3.5
Meat: 2.0
Fat: 0.0

onto tempeh. Grill over medium-hot coals until browned and hot, about 5 minutes on each side, or roast at 425 degrees 20 to 30 minutes. Serve with Black Beans and Rice and Fried Plantains.

Jerk Seasoning

Makes about 2 tablespoons

1½ teaspoons each: onion and garlic powder

½ teaspoon each: dried thyme and oregano leaves, ground allspice and ginger, paprika, black pepper

¼ teaspoon each: ground nutmeg, cayenne pepper

1. Combine all ingredients; store in airtight container until ready to use.

TANDOORI TEMPEH WITH ORANGE CILANTRO RICE

L *Tempeh is marinated in a seasoned yogurt mixture, then grilled or roasted.*

4 main-dish servings

2 packages (8 ounces each) tempeh, halved crosswise

Tandoori Marinade (recipe follows)

Vegetable cooking spray

2½ cups (⅔ recipe) Orange Cilantro Rice (see p. 420)

Per Serving:
Calories: 363
% of calories from fat: 23
Fat (gm): 9.6
Saturated fat (gm): 1.6
Cholesterol (mg): 0.3
Sodium (mg): 37
Protein (gm): 28
Carbohydrate (gm): 44.1

Exchanges:
Milk: 0.0
Vegetable: 0.0
Fruit: 0.0
Bread: 3.0
Meat: 3.0
Fat: 0.0

1. Spread all surfaces of tempeh with Tandoori Marinade; refrigerate 3 to 4 hours or overnight.

2. Grill tempeh on greased rack over medium-hot coals until browned, 4 to 6 minutes on each side. Or, roast on greased foil-lined pan at 425 degrees until browned, 20 to 30 minutes. Serve with Orange Cilantro Rice.

Tandoori Marinade

Makes about ½ cup

⅓ cup fat-free plain yogurt
1 tablespoon each: finely chopped cilantro, jalapeno chili, garlic
1 teaspoon each: minced gingerroot, grated lime zest, ground coriander
1½ teaspoons each: paprika, ground cumin, and coriander

1. Combine all ingredients.

ROASTED VEGETABLES WITH MUSHROOM TORTELLINI

O

Substitute ravioli or a shaped pasta for the tortellini, if you want.

45

4 main-dish servings

3 medium Italian plum tomatoes, quartered
2 cups each: halved mushrooms, small okra
1 cup each: sliced zucchini, yellow summer
  squash, and broccoli rabe, or broccoli, cut
  into 3-inch pieces
Olive oil cooking spray
1½ teaspoons dried Italian seasoning
Salt and pepper, to taste
1 package (9 ounces) mushroom tortellini,
  cooked, warm
1–2 tablespoons olive oil

Per Serving:
Calories: 256
% of calories from fat: 19
Fat (gm): 5.6
Saturated fat (gm): 1.3
Cholesterol (mg): 3.8
Sodium (mg): 337
Protein (gm): 14.6
Carbohydrate (gm): 40.5

Exchanges:
Milk: 0.0
Vegetable: 2.0
Fruit: 0.0
Bread: 2.0
Meat: 1.0
Fat: 0.0

1. Arrange vegetables in single layer on greased foil-lined jelly roll pan; spray with cooking spray and sprinkle with Italian seasoning, salt and pepper. Roast at 425 degrees until tender and browned, about 40 minutes, removing broccoli rabe after about 20 minutes. Toss vegetables and tortellini with oil in bowl.

45-MINUTE PREP TIP: Begin cooking the tortellini 15 to 20 minutes before the vegetables are finished roasting.

FETTUCCINE WITH ROASTED VEGETABLE SAUCE

L   *A très trendy pasta sauce with fabulous flavor.*

45   **6 main-dish servings**

2 medium zucchini

1 each: peeled medium eggplant, red bell pepper,
   red onion

6 cloves garlic

Olive oil cooking spray

1½ teaspoons dried basil leaves

½ teaspoon each: dried oregano and marjoram leaves

¼ teaspoon crushed red pepper

4 cups reduced-sodium vegetable broth, divided

1–2 tablespoons lemon juice

1 teaspoon grated lemon zest

Salt and pepper, to taste

12 ounces fettuccine, cooked, warm

6 tablespoons fat-free grated Parmesan cheese

Per Serving:
Calories: 278
% of calories from fat: 9
Fat (gm): 3
Saturated fat (gm): 0.1
Cholesterol (mg): 0
Sodium (mg): 181
Protein (gm): 12.1
Carbohydrate (gm): 50.6

Exchanges:
Milk: 0.0
Vegetable: 3.0
Fruit: 0.0
Bread: 2.5
Meat: 0.5
Fat: 0.0

1. Cut vegetables, except garlic, into ¾ to 1-inch pieces; arrange in single layer on 2 greased foil-lined jelly roll pans. Spray with cooking spray and sprinkle with herbs and pepper. Roast at 425 degrees until browned and tender, about 40 minutes, removing garlic when soft, after about 20 minutes.

2. Process vegetables, garlic, and 1 to 2 cups broth in food processor or blender until smooth. Heat mixture and remaining broth to boiling in large saucepan; reduce heat and simmer, uncovered, 5 minutes. Stir in lemon juice and zest; season to taste with salt and pepper. Serve over pasta; sprinkle with cheese.

45-MINUTE PREP TIP: Begin cooking the fettuccine 15 to 20 minutes before the vegetables are finished roasting.

RISOTTO WITH ROASTED TOMATOES

L

45

The creamy texture of risotto comes from the short-grained arborio rice, which is available in Italian groceries and supermarkets.

6 main-dish servings

6 medium tomatoes, halved

Olive oil cooking spray

1½ teaspoons dried Italian seasoning

1 small onion, chopped

3 cloves garlic, minced

2 teaspoons olive oil

¾ cup arborio rice

3 cups reduced-sodium vegetable broth

2 tablespoons grated fat-free Parmesan cheese

Salt and pepper, to taste

Per Serving:
Calories: 278
% of calories from fat: 9
Fat (gm): 3
Saturated fat (gm): 0.1
Cholesterol (mg): 0
Sodium (mg): 181
Protein (gm): 12.1
Carbohydrate (gm): 50.6

Exchanges:
Milk: 0.0
Vegetable: 3.0
Fruit: 0.0
Bread: 2.5
Meat: 0.5
Fat: 0.0

1. Arrange tomatoes, cut sides up, on greased foil-lined jelly roll pan; spray with cooking spray and sprinkle with herbs. Roast at 425 degrees until tender, but not too soft, about 20 minutes. Cool; seed, if desired, and chop coarsely.

2. Sauté onion and garlic in oil in large saucepan until tender, about 5 minutes. Add rice and cook over medium heat until beginning to brown, 2 to 3 minutes.

3. Heat broth to boiling in small saucepan; reduce heat to medium-low to keep broth hot. Add broth to rice mixture, ½ cup at a time, stirring constantly, until broth is absorbed before adding another ½ cup. Continue process until rice is *al dente*, 20 to 25 minutes, adding tomatoes with last ½ cup broth. Stir in cheese; season to taste with salt and pepper.

ROASTED SQUASH, MOROCCAN STYLE

V

45

Roasted vegetables and pineapple, combined with couscous, create a perfect filling for oven-roasted acorn squash.

4 main-dish servings (about 2 cups each)

2 medium acorn squash, halved, seeded

1 medium pineapple, peeled, cored, cut into 1-inch pieces

2 cups quartered Brussels sprouts

2 medium onions, sliced

Olive oil cooking spray

¼ cup packed light brown sugar

⅛ teaspoon each: ground cinnamon, nutmeg

½ cup frozen whole-kernel corn, cooked

¼ cup each: dark raisins, finely chopped cilantro

⅔ cup couscous, cooked, warm

Salt and pepper, to taste

Per Serving:
Calories: 450
% of calories from fat: 3
Fat (gm): 1.5
Saturated fat (gm): 0.2
Cholesterol (mg): 0
Sodium (mg): 49
Protein (gm): 11.8
Carbohydrate (gm): 107

Exchanges:
Milk: 0.0
Vegetable: 2.5
Fruit: 1.5
Bread: 4.0
Meat: 0.0
Fat: 0.0

1. Arrange squash (cut sides up), pineapple, onions, and Brussels sprouts in single layer on greased foil-lined jelly roll pan; spray with cooking spray and sprinkle with combined brown sugar, cinnamon, and nutmeg. Bake at 425 degrees until vegetables are tender, about 40 minutes.

2. Arrange squash halves on plates. Stir remaining roasted vegetables, corn, raisins, and cilantro into couscous; season to taste with salt and pepper. Serve in squash halves.

45-MINUTE PREP TIP: Cook the couscous 10 minutes before the vegetables have finished roasting.

GRILL-ROASTED VEGETABLES WITH POLENTA

V *The vegetables can also be oven-roasted at 425 degrees for 30 to 40 minutes. For convenience, the Polenta can be made 2 to 3 days in advance.*

4 main-dish servings (about 1½ cups each)

4 each: medium tomatoes, red onions

2 each: medium red bell peppers, yellow summer squash

2 medium eggplant, unpeeled, cut in ½-inch rounds

1 large bulb garlic, top trimmed

2 tablespoons balsamic, or red wine, vinegar

1 tablespoon olive oil

1 teaspoon lemon juice

½ teaspoon each: dried rosemary, sage, and thyme leaves

Polenta (see p. 425)

4 slices Italian bread, toasted

Per Serving:
Calories: 473
% of calories from fat: 14
Fat (gm): 7.8
Saturated fat (gm): 1.2
Cholesterol (mg): 0
Sodium (mg): 513
Protein (gm): 13.5
Carbohydrate (gm): 91.9

Exchanges:
Milk: 0.0
Vegetable: 8.0
Fruit: 0.0
Bread: 3.0
Meat: 0.0
Fat: 1.0

1. Cut tomatoes and red onions into wedges; cut bell peppers and squash into 1-inch slices. Grill vegetables on greased rack over medium-hot coals, turning occasionally, until browned and tender, about 30 minutes. Combine vegetables, except garlic, in bowl; toss with combined vinegar, oil, lemon juice, and herbs.

2. Cut polenta into 8 wedges; cook in lightly greased large skillet until browned on both sides. Overlap 2 polenta wedges on each serving plate; spoon vegetables over. Serve roasted garlic to spread on bread.

ROASTED VEGETABLES WITH BEANS AND FRUIT

V

Serve with one of the grilled tofu or tempeh recipes in this chapter.

45

8 main-dish servings (generous 1 cup each)

2 each: peeled, sliced medium sweet potatoes, small parsnips, russet potatoes

3 medium onions, cut into wedges

1 each: thickly sliced yellow and red bell pepper, fennel bulb

1 can (15 ounces) each Great Northern and black beans, rinsed, drained

Vegetable cooking spray

1½ teaspoons dried marjoram leaves

½ teaspoon each: dried thyme leaves, crushed fennel seeds

¾ cup each: coarsely chopped dried apples, dried apricots

3 tablespoons white wine vinegar

2–3 tablespoons olive oil

Salt and pepper, to taste

Per Serving:
Calories: 321
% of calories from fat: 12
Fat (gm): 4.6
Saturated fat (gm): 0.6
Cholesterol (mg): 0
Sodium (mg): 192
Protein (gm): 11.9
Carbohydrate (gm): 65.7

Exchanges:
Milk: 0.0
Vegetable: 1.0
Fruit: 1.0
Bread: 3.0
Meat: 0.0
Fat: 0.5

1. Arrange vegetables, including beans, in single layer on greased foil-lined jelly roll pans; spray with cooking spray and sprinkle with combined herbs. Roast at 425 degrees until browned and tender, about 40 minutes, adding dried fruit the last 10 minutes. Combine in bowl; drizzle with vinegar and oil and toss. Season to taste with salt and pepper.

CASSEROLE OF ROASTED VEGETABLES AND BEANS

L

45

A great dish for tailgate parties or picnics. The casserole is also delicious served at room temperature.

6 main-dish servings

6 small zucchini

4 ribs celery

2 medium sweet onions

1 medium red, or green, bell pepper

Vegetable cooking spray

½ teaspoon dried oregano leaves

¼ teaspoon ground cinnamon

¾ teaspoon pepper

2 cans (15 ounces each) Great Northern beans, rinsed, drained

1 can (15 ounces) pinto beans, rinsed, drained

2 large tomatoes, coarsely chopped

Salt, to taste

¾ cup fresh whole wheat bread crumbs

½ cup (2 ounces) grated fat-free Parmesan cheese

⅓ cup finely chopped cilantro

¼ teaspoon paprika

Per Serving:
Calories: 329
% of calories from fat: 5
Fat (gm): 1.9
Saturated fat (gm): 0.3
Cholesterol (mg): 0
Sodium (mg): 386
Protein (gm): 21.9
Carbohydrate (gm): 62

Exchanges:
Milk: 0.0
Vegetable: 2.0
Fruit: 0.0
Bread: 3.0
Meat: 1.0
Fat: 0.0

1. Cut zucchini, celery, onions, and bell pepper into 1-inch pieces; arrange in single layer on greased foil-lined jelly roll pan. Spray with cooking spray and sprinkle with oregano, cinnamon, and pepper. Roast at 425 degrees until browned and tender, about 35 minutes.

2. Combine roasted vegetables, beans, and tomatoes in greased 2-quart casserole; season to taste with salt. Sprinkle combined bread crumbs, cheese, and cilantro over top of casserole; sprinkle with paprika. Bake, covered, at 350 degrees until casserole is browned and hot, about 20 minutes.

PORTOBELLO MUSHROOMS WITH GRILLED PEPPER RELISH AND POLENTA

V *Make this recipe with porcini mushrooms, if you're fortunate enough to find them in season.*

6 main-dish servings

6 large portobello mushrooms (4–5 inches
  in diameter)
Polenta (see p. 425)
Olive oil cooking spray
½ teaspoon dried thyme leaves
¼ teaspoon pepper
Salt, to taste
Grilled Pepper Relish (recipe follows)

Per Serving:
Calories: 171
% of calories from fat: 19
Fat (gm): 3.6
Saturated fat (gm): 0.4
Cholesterol (mg): 0
Sodium (mg): 217
Protein (gm): 6.8
Carbohydrate (gm): 26.4

Exchanges:
Milk: 0.0
Vegetable: 3.0
Fruit: 0.0
Bread: 1.0
Meat: 0.0
Fat: 0.5

1. Spray mushrooms and polenta wedges with cooking spray; sprinkle mushrooms with thyme and pepper. Grill over medium-hot coals until polenta is lightly browned and mushrooms are tender, about 8 minutes, turning mushrooms occasionally. Sprinkle mushrooms lightly with salt.

2. Place Polenta on serving plates, overlapping mushrooms on top. Spoon Grilled Pepper Relish over mushrooms.

Grilled Pepper Relish

Makes about 2 cups

1 each: medium red and yellow bell pepper
2 medium tomatoes
1 each: finely chopped green onion, minced garlic clove
2 tablespoons finely chopped fresh cilantro
½ teaspoon each: ground cumin, sugar
1 tablespoon each: balsamic vinegar, olive oil
Salt and pepper, to taste

1. Grill peppers and tomatoes on greased rack over medium-hot coals until browned and tender, 8 to 10 minutes, turning occasionally.

Cool vegetables; peel, core, seed, and chop coarsely. Combine vegetables and remaining ingredients, except salt and pepper, in bowl; toss gently. Season to taste with salt and pepper.

ROASTED VEGETABLES, MOO-SHU STYLE

V

45

For simplicity, we've substituted flour tortillas for the Mandarin Pancakes (see p. 575) traditionally served with moo-shu dishes.

6 main-dish servings (2 each)

1 pound each: green beans, or snow peas, sliced mushrooms

4 medium zucchini, halved lengthwise, sliced

1 medium onion, thinly sliced

Vegetable cooking spray

¾–1 teaspoon 5-spice powder

Salt and pepper, to taste

Plum Sauce (see p. 612)

12 flour tortillas (6-inch)

2 cups fresh bean sprouts

2 medium carrots, julienned

½ cup loosely packed cilantro

Per Serving:
Calories: 363
% of calories from fat: 14
Fat (gm): 5.8
Saturated fat (gm): 0.9
Cholesterol (mg): 0
Sodium (mg): 697
Protein (gm): 12.4
Carbohydrate (gm): 69.3

Exchanges:
Milk: 0.0
Vegetable: 4.0
Fruit: 0.0
Bread: 3.0
Meat: 0.0
Fat: 1.0

1. Arrange green beans, mushrooms, zucchini, and onion in single layer on greased foil-lined jelly roll pan. Spray vegetables with cooking spray and sprinkle with 5-spice powder. Roast at 425 degrees until crisp-tender, about 25 minutes; season to taste with salt and pepper.

2. Spread generous tablespoon Plum Sauce in center of each tortilla. Spoon roasted vegetables on tortillas; top with bean sprouts, carrots, and cilantro. Roll up, tucking up one end to hold and eat.

SPAGHETTI SQUASH WITH ROASTED TOMATO-HERB SAUCE AND ARTICHOKES

L   *The squash can also be grilled. Wrap squash halves in foil and grill over medium-hot coals until tender, 30 to 40 minutes, turning occasionally.*

4 main-dish servings

1 small spaghetti squash, halved, seeded

1 package (9 ounces) frozen artichoke hearts, thawed, halved

Roasted Tomato-Herb Sauce (recipe follows)

¼ cup grated fat-free Parmesan cheese

Per Serving:
Calories: 197
% of calories from fat: 7
Fat (gm): 1.8
Saturated fat (gm): 0.3
Cholesterol (mg): 0
Sodium (mg): 154
Protein (gm): 9.3
Carbohydrate (gm): 40.6

Exchanges:
Milk: 0.0
Vegetable: 5.0
Fruit: 0.0
Bread: 1.0
Meat: 0.0
Fat: 0.0

1. Place squash halves, cut sides down, in roasting pan and add 1 inch hot water. Bake, covered, on bottom oven rack at 400 degrees until tender, about 45 minutes. Using fork, scrape squash to separate into strands, leaving squash in shells to serve.

2. Stir artichoke hearts into Roasted Tomato-Herb Sauce and cook over medium heat until hot, about 5 minutes; spoon into squash halves. Sprinkle with cheese and toss.

Roasted Tomato-Herb Sauce

Makes about 3 cups

2½ pounds Italian plum tomatoes, halved

1 leek (white part only), cut into ¾-inch pieces

1 medium onion, cut into wedges

2 medium carrots, cut into ¾-inch pieces

2 cloves garlic, peeled

Vegetable cooking spray

½ teaspoon each: dried oregano and marjoram leaves

½ cup loosely packed basil leaves

Salt and pepper, to taste

1. Arrange vegetables in single layer on greased foil-lined jelly roll pan; spray with cooking spray and sprinkle with dried herbs. Roast at 425 degrees on top oven rack until vegetables are browned and tender, about 40 minutes. Process vegetables and basil in food processor or blender until almost smooth. Season to taste with salt and pepper.

ROASTED STUFFED PORTOBELLO MUSHROOMS WITH SPINACH-CILANTRO PESTO

L

Serve one mushroom as a hearty appetizer or first course.

45

4 main-dish servings

8 large portobello mushrooms (5–6 inches diameter)
1 cup each: finely chopped zucchini, shredded carrots
3 green onions, thinly sliced
¼ cup unseasoned dry bread crumbs
Spinach-Cilantro Pesto (see p. 608)
Salt and pepper, to taste
½ cup (2 ounces) shredded reduced-fat
   mozzarella cheese

Per Serving:
Calories: 185
% of calories from fat: 20
Fat (gm): 3.9
Saturated fat (gm): 1.8
Cholesterol (mg): 7.6
Sodium (mg): 206
Protein (gm): 16
Carbohydrate (gm): 19.1

Exchanges:
Milk: 0.0
Vegetable: 4.0
Fruit: 0.0
Bread: 0.5
Meat: 1.0
Fat: 0.0

1. Remove mushroom stems and chop. Sauté mushroom stems, zucchini, carrots, and green onions in lightly greased skillet until crisp-tender, about 8 minutes. Stir in bread crumbs and pesto; season to taste with salt and pepper. Spoon vegetable mixture onto mushrooms. Bake on greased jelly roll pan at 425 degrees until tender, about 20 minutes, sprinkling with cheese the last 5 minutes of roasting time.

GREEK EGGPLANT WITH FETA

L

45

Perfect for warm weather dining, as the dish is delicious served at room temperature.

4 main-dish servings (about 1½ cups each)

2 pounds eggplant, unpeeled
2 cups each: sliced red and yellow, bell
   peppers, onions
Olive oil cooking spray
1½ teaspoons dried rosemary leaves, crushed
¾ teaspoon each: dried marjoram, and thyme leaves
1 cup (4 ounces) crumbled feta cheese
Salt and pepper, to taste

Per Serving:
Calories: 275
% of calories from fat: 22
Fat (gm): 7.6
Saturated fat (gm): 4.4
Cholesterol (mg): 25
Sodium (mg): 332
Protein (gm): 10.7
Carbohydrate (gm): 48.2

Exchanges:
Milk: 0.0
Vegetable: 8.0
Fruit: 0.0
Bread: 0.0
Meat: 1.0
Fat: 0.5

1. Cut eggplant into ½-inch slices; cut slices into fourths. Arrange eggplant, bell peppers, and onions in single layer on greased foil-lined jelly roll pans. Spray with cooking spray and sprinkle with herbs. Roast at 425 degrees until browned and tender, about 40 minutes. Toss with cheese; season to taste with salt and pepper.

MEDITERRANEAN ROASTED EGGPLANT AND TOMATOES

V

45

Serve warm or at room temperature, with couscous or Polenta (see p. 425).

4 side-dish servings

1 small eggplant (about 1 pound), unpeeled
2 large tomatoes, cut into wedges
Olive oil cooking spray
½ teaspoon each: dried mint leaves, dill weed
Salt and pepper, to taste
½ tablespoon olive oil

Per Serving:
Calories: 49
% of calories from fat: 33
Fat (gm): 2
Saturated fat (gm): 0.3
Cholesterol (mg): 0.0
Sodium (mg): 5
Protein (gm): 1.5
Carbohydrate (gm): 8

Exchanges:
Milk: 0.0
Vegetable: 1.0
Fruit: 0.0
Bread: 0.0
Meat: 0.0
Fat: 0.5

1. Cut eggplant into ½-inch slices; cut slices into fourths. Arrange eggplant and tomatoes in single layer on greased foil-lined jelly roll pan;

spray cooking spray and sprinkle with herbs. Roast at 425 degrees until browned and tender, 30 to 40 minutes. Season to taste with salt and pepper; drizzle with olive oil and toss.

ROOT VEGGIES AND MASHED POTATOES

L

45

A selection of winter root vegetables roasted to perfection and served with garlic-spiked mashed potatoes.

6 main-dish servings (about 1½ cups each)

3 each: sliced, peeled medium beets, turnips, carrots

1 leek (white part only), cut into 1-inch pieces

2½ cups halved Brussels sprouts

Vegetable cooking spray

1 tablespoon caraway seeds

Salt, and pepper, to taste

1½ pounds Idaho potatoes, unpeeled, cubed

4 cloves garlic, peeled

¼ cup fat-free milk, hot

2 tablespoons margarine, or butter, cut into pieces

Per Serving:
Calories: 300
% of calories from fat: 19
Fat (gm): 6.7
Saturated fat (gm): 1.2
Cholesterol (mg): 0.3
Sodium (mg): 233
Protein (gm): 10
Carbohydrate (gm): 54.5

Exchanges:
Milk: 0.0
Vegetable: 2.0
Fruit: 0.0
Bread: 3.0
Meat: 0.0
Fat: 1.0

1. Arrange beets, turnips, carrots, leek, and Brussels sprouts in single layer on greased foil-lined pan in single layer; spray with cooking spray and sprinkle with caraway seeds; sprinkle lightly with salt and pepper. Roast at 400 degrees until vegetables are browned and tender, about 40 minutes.

2. Simmer potatoes and garlic in 2 inches water in covered saucepan until tender, 10 to 15 minutes; drain. Mash potatoes and garlic with masher or electric mixer, adding milk and margarine. Season to taste with salt and pepper. Spoon potatoes onto plates; spoon vegetables over.

ORIENTAL VEGETABLE SATAY

Vegetables are roasted with Fragrant Basting Sauce and served with a chunky Peanut Sauce.

V

45

4 main-dish servings

½ medium acorn squash, peeled, seeded, cut
   into 1-inch pieces

1 pound broccoli florets

½ pound fresh, or frozen, thawed, whole okra

2 medium yellow summer squash, cut into
   1-inch slices

4 ounces pearl onions, peeled

Fragrant Basting Sauce (see p. 614)

3 cups cooked rice, warm

Peanut Sauce (recipe follows)

Per Serving:
Calories: 452
% of calories from fat: 20
Fat (gm): 10.3
Saturated fat (gm): 1.8
Cholesterol (mg): 0
Sodium (mg): 775
Protein (gm): 13.4
Carbohydrate (gm): 78.9

Exchanges:
Milk: 0.0
Vegetable: 3.0
Fruit: 0.0
Bread: 4.0
Meat: 0.0
Fat: 2.0

1. Simmer acorn squash in 2 inches water in saucepan, covered, until beginning to soften, about 2 minutes; drain.

2. Arrange vegetables on skewers and place on lightly greased aluminum-foil-lined jelly roll pan. Roast at 425 degrees until lightly browned, about 10 minutes on each side, basting occasionally with Fragrant Basting Sauce. Serve kabobs on rice with Peanut Sauce.

Peanut Sauce

Makes about ⅔ cup

3 tablespoons each: reduced-sodium soy sauce, chunky peanut butter

2½ tablespoons sugar

¼ cup thinly sliced green onions

1 tablespoon minced gingerroot

1. Combine all ingredients.

45-MINUTE PREP TIP: Begin cooking the rice before preparing the rest of the recipe.

TOMATOES STUFFED WITH PEPPER-ROASTED WILD MUSHROOMS

V

45

A great accompaniment to Cajun Eggplant or Mesquite-Smoked Tofu (see pp. 208, 191).

6 side-dish servings

1 pound wild mushrooms (portobello, shiitake, oyster, cremini, etc.)

Olive oil cooking spray

½ teaspoon coarsely ground pepper

1 cup cooked basmati, or brown, rice

¼ cup unseasoned dry bread crumbs

2 tablespoons fat-free red wine vinaigrette

3 tablespoons each: finely chopped dill weed, chives

6 large tomatoes (10–12 ounces each)

Salt, to taste

Per Serving:
Calories: 136
% of calories from fat: 16
Fat (gm): 2.9
Saturated fat (gm): 0.2
Cholesterol (mg): 0
Sodium (mg): 143
Protein (gm): 6.4
Carbohydrate (gm): 26.6

Exchanges:
Milk: 0.0
Vegetable: 4.0
Fruit: 0.0
Bread: 0.5
Meat: 0.0
Fat: 0.0

1. Arrange mushrooms in single layer on greased foil-lined jelly roll pan; spray with cooking spray and sprinkle with pepper. Roast at 425 degrees until tender, about 20 minutes; cool slightly. Chop mushrooms and mix with rice, bread crumbs, vinaigrette, and herbs.

2. Slice tops from tomatoes and scoop out pulp with grapefruit spoon. Chop pulp and stir into mushroom mixture; season to taste with salt. Spoon mushroom mixture into tomatoes. Roast, lightly covered, in baking pan at 425 degrees until hot through, about 10 minutes.

45-MINUTE PREP TIP: Begin cooking the rice before preparing the rest of the recipe.

GRILLED BEET PUREE

L

Grilling adds a special flavor to beets, so do try it! Beets can also be roasted at 425 degrees until tender, about 40 minutes.

4 side-dish servings (about ⅓ cup each)

12 ounces beets
¼ cup orange juice
3 tablespoons fat-free sour cream
2 teaspoons grated orange zest
1½ tablespoons chopped cilantro
Salt and pepper, to taste

Per Serving:
Calories: 47
% of calories from fat: 2
Fat (gm): 0.1
Saturated fat (gm): 0
Cholesterol (mg): 0
Sodium (mg): 43
Protein (gm): 1.8
Carbohydrate (gm): 10.3

Exchanges:
Milk: 0.0
Vegetable: 2.0
Fruit: 0.0
Bread: 0.0
Meat: 0.0
Fat: 0.0

1. Grill beets on greased rack over medium-hot coals until tender, about 30 minutes, turning occasionally; cool and peel. Process beets, orange juice, sour cream, and orange zest in food processor or blender until smooth. Stir in cilantro; season to taste with salt and pepper.

CAJUN EGGPLANT

V

45

Packaged Cajun seasoning can be purchased, but we particularly like our homemade blend — also delicious on tempeh and portobello mushrooms.

4–6 side-dish servings

1 large eggplant (1¼–1½ pounds), unpeeled,
   cut into ½-inch slices
Vegetable cooking spray
Cajun Seasoning (recipe follows)

Per Serving:
Calories: 47
% of calories from fat: 9
Fat (gm): 0.5
Saturated fat (gm): 0.1
Cholesterol (mg): 0
Sodium (mg): 138
Protein (gm): 1.6
Carbohydrate (gm): 11

Exchanges:
Milk: 0.0
Vegetable: 2.0
Fruit: 0.0
Bread: 0.0
Meat: 0.0
Fat: 0.0

1. Lightly spray both sides of eggplant with cooking spray; sprinkle with Cajun Seasoning, pressing mixture onto eggplant. Grill on greased rack over medium-hot coals until tender, about 5 minutes per side, or roast in oven on greased foil-lined pan at 425 degrees until tender, about 30 minutes.

Cajun Seasoning

Makes about 2 tablespoons

2 teaspoons paprika

1 teaspoon each: onion and garlic powder

½ teaspoon each: dried thyme and oregano leaves, cayenne, and black pepper

¼ teaspoon salt

1. Mix all ingredients; store in airtight container.

ROASTED PEPERONATA

We've roasted this traditional Italian dish for more intense flavors — faster, and easier to cook, too! It's especially good as a topping on vegetarian burgers or sausages, or serve as a side dish with any favorite entrée.

V

45

8 side-dish servings (about ⅔ cup each)

1 pound each: sliced green, red, and yellow bell peppers

1½ pounds onions, sliced

Olive oil cooking spray

1 teaspoon dried oregano leaves

¾ teaspoon each: dried sage and thyme leaves

Salt and pepper, to taste

1. Arrange vegetables in single layer on greased foil-lined jelly roll pan; spray with cooking spray and sprinkle with herbs. Roast at 425 degrees until browned and tender, about 45 minutes; season to taste with salt and pepper.

Per Serving:
Calories: 83
% of calories from fat: 6
Fat (gm): 0.6
Saturated fat (gm): 0.1
Cholesterol (mg): 0
Sodium (mg): 4.7
Protein (gm): 3
Carbohydrate (gm): 19.3

Exchanges:
Milk: 0.0
Vegetable: 3.5
Fruit: 0.0
Bread: 0.0
Meat: 0.0
Fat: 0.0

ROASTED POTATO SALAD

LO

45

The potatoes are roasted until crusty and brown, lending a unique flavor to this salad.

6 side-dish servings (about 1½ cups each)

8–10 medium unpeeled Idaho potatoes,
  cut into eighths
Olive oil cooking spray
Salt and pepper, to taste
1 each: chopped medium onion, red and
  green bell pepper
½ cup each: thawed frozen peas, thinly sliced celery
Dilled Mayonnaise Dressing (recipe follows)

Per Serving:
Calories: 492
% of calories from fat: 4
Fat (gm): 2
Saturated fat (gm): 0.4
Cholesterol (mg): 0.3
Sodium (mg): 611
Protein (gm): 13.3
Carbohydrate (gm): 107.7

Exchanges:
Milk: 0.0
Vegetable: 1.0
Fruit: 0.0
Bread: 6.5
Meat: 0.0
Fat: 0.0

1. Arrange potatoes in single layer on greased foil-lined jelly roll pan; spray with cooking spray and sprinkle lightly with salt and pepper. Roast at 425 degrees until potatoes are browned, crusty, and tender, about 30 minutes; cool. Combine potatoes and vegetables; spoon Dilled Mayonnaise Dressing over and toss.

Dilled Mayonnaise Dressing

Makes about ¾ cup

¼ cup each: fat-free mayonnaise, plain yogurt
2 tablespoons Dijon-style mustard
1 tablespoon lemon juice
2 cloves garlic, minced
½ teaspoon dried dill weed

1. Mix all ingredients.

VEGETABLE AND WILD RICE SALAD

L *Other types of rice can be substituted for the wild rice, if desired, or use 1 package (6¼ ounces) long-grain white and wild rice mix, discarding the spice packet. Serve this dish warm or at room temperature.*

8 side-dish servings (about 1 cup each)

1 each: medium zucchini, yellow summer squash, eggplant, and red pepper

1 medium eggplant, peeled

1 medium red bell pepper

3 cloves garlic, peeled

Olive oil cooking spray

1 tablespoon herbs de Provence

½ cup fat-free honey-Dijon salad dressing

¼ cup fat-free plain yogurt

3 tablespoons orange juice

2 teaspoons grated orange zest

3 cups cooked wild rice

Salt and pepper, to taste

Per Serving:
Calories: 134
% of calories from fat: 4
Fat (gm): 0.6
Saturated fat (gm): 0.1
Cholesterol (mg): 0.1
Sodium (mg): 178
Protein (gm): 5
Carbohydrate (gm): 28.8

Exchanges:
Milk: 0.0
Vegetable: 2.5
Fruit: 0.0
Bread: 1.0
Meat: 0.0
Fat: 0.0

1. Cut vegetables, except garlic, into ¾ to 1-inch pieces. Arrange vegetables in single layer on greased foil-lined pan; spray with cooking spray and sprinkle with herbs. Roast at 425 degrees until browned and tender, about 40 minutes, removing garlic when soft, after about 20 minutes; cool.

2. Mash garlic and mix with salad dressing, yogurt, orange juice, and zest; drizzle over combined vegetables and rice and toss. Season to taste with salt and pepper.

ROASTED MUSHROOM SALAD

V *The varieties of mushrooms will vary according to season and availability.*

45 **6 side-dish servings** (about 1 cup each)

1½ pounds assorted mushrooms (portobello, cremini, shiitake, etc.)
Vegetable cooking spray
2 cups cooked orzo
1 medium tomato, chopped
2 tablespoons fat-free red wine vinaigrette
3 tablespoons each: finely chopped dill weed, chives
Salt and pepper, to taste

Per Serving:
Calories: 110
% of calories from fat: 18
Fat (gm): 2.5
Saturated fat (gm): 0.1
Cholesterol (mg): 0
Sodium (mg): 118
Protein (gm): 6.4
Carbohydrate (gm): 19.3

Exchanges:
Milk: 0.0
Vegetable: 3.0
Fruit: 0.0
Bread: 0.5
Meat: 0.0
Fat: 0.0

1. Arrange mushrooms in single layer on greased foil-lined jelly roll pan; spray with cooking spray. Roast at 425 degrees until tender, about 20 minutes; cool. Slice mushrooms and combine with orzo, tomato, vinaigrette, and herbs. Season to taste with salt and pepper.

45-MINUTE PREP TIP: Begin cooking the orzo before preparing the rest of the recipe.

SWEET ONION SALAD

L *An unusual salad that's bound to bring compliments to the cook!*

6 side-dish servings

12 ounces each: Vidalia, or Maui, and red onions
Vegetable cooking spray
1 teaspoon each: dried marjoram and thyme leaves
¼ teaspoon each: ground cloves, garlic powder
⅛–¼ teaspoon cayenne pepper
⅓ cup fat-free buttermilk salad dressing
4 teaspoons lemon juice
2 teaspoons grated lemon zest
Salt and pepper, to taste
3 cups each: torn leaf lettuce, curly endive
1½ cups (½ recipe) Croutons (see p. 560)

Per Serving:
Calories: 81
% of calories from fat: 7
Fat (gm): 0.7
Saturated fat (gm): 0.1
Cholesterol (mg): 0
Sodium (mg): 145
Protein (gm): 2.8
Carbohydrate (gm): 17.3

Exchanges:
Milk: 0.0
Vegetable: 2.0
Fruit: 0.0
Bread: 0.5
Meat: 0.0
Fat: 0.0

1. Cut onions into 2-inch wedges and arrange in single layer on greased foil-lined jelly roll pan; spray with cooking spray and sprinkle with herbs and pepper. Roast at 425 degrees until onions are tender, about 35 minutes. Toss with combined salad dressing, lemon juice, and lemon zest; season to taste with salt and pepper. Serve on greens-lined plates; sprinkle with Croutons.

ROASTED ORIENTAL SALAD

Hot chili oil is really hot, so use sparingly and taste before adding more.

6 main-dish servings

1 pound each: asparagus, shiitake mushrooms, stems removed

Vegetable cooking spray

8 ounces snow peas

3 cloves garlic, unpeeled

Salt and pepper, to taste

½ package (7-ounce size) rice noodles

1 medium carrot, shredded

1 small cucumber, seeded, chopped

2 green onions, thinly sliced

Oriental Vinaigrette (recipe follows)

Per Serving:
Calories: 183
% of calories from fat: 15
Fat (gm): 3.2
Saturated fat (gm): 0.5
Cholesterol (mg): 0
Sodium (mg): 223
Protein (gm): 5.4
Carbohydrate (gm): 36.5

Exchanges:
Milk: 0.0
Vegetable: 4.0
Fruit: 0.0
Bread: 1.0
Meat: 0.0
Fat: 0.5

1. Arrange asparagus and mushrooms in single layer on greased foil-lined jelly roll pan; spray with cooking spray. Roast at 425 degrees for 15 minutes. Add snow peas and garlic to pan; roast until vegetables are tender, about 20 minutes longer; cool. Reserve garlic for Oriental Vinaigrette; coarsely chop roasted vegetables and season to taste with salt and pepper.

2. Place noodles in large bowl; pour cold water over to cover. Let stand until noodles separate and are soft, about 10 minutes. Drain well and add to roasted vegetables in large bowl. Add carrot, cucumber, green onions, and Oriental Dressing and toss.

Oriental Vinaigrette

Makes about ½ cup

3 reserved roasted garlic cloves

2 tablespoons reduced-sodium tamari soy sauce

3 tablespoons rice wine vinegar

1 tablespoon vegetable oil

½–¾ teaspoon hot chili oil

2 teaspoons sugar

1 teaspoon minced gingerroot

⅓ cup chopped cilantro

1. Squeeze garlic cloves into small bowl; mix in remaining ingredients.

45-MINUTE PREP TIP: Soak and drain the rice noodles while the vegetables are roasting.

GRILLED VEGETABLE FAJITAS

L

Cactus "paddles" and poblano peppers are commonly available today in large supermarkets as well as Mexican groceries. Another vegetable, such as zucchini, can be substituted for the cactus, and green bell peppers and one jalapeño chili can replace the poblano chilies.

4 main-dish servings (2 fajitas each)

4 medium poblano chilies, cut into 1-inch slices

3 large tomatoes, cut into wedges

2 medium onions, cut into wedges

4 large cactus paddles (*nopales*), cut into 1-inch slices

Vegetable cooking spray

2 tablespoons each: olive oil, white distilled vinegar

1 tablespoon lime juice

2 cloves garlic, minced

Salt and cayenne pepper, to taste

8 flour, or corn, tortillas, warm

¼ cup chopped cilantro

8 tablespoons fat-free sour cream

4 avocado slices

Per Serving:
Calories: 414
% of calories from fat: 29
Fat (gm): 14.1
Saturated fat (gm): 2.3
Cholesterol (mg): 0
Sodium (mg): 47
Protein (gm): 12.6
Carbohydrate (gm): 64

Exchanges:
Milk: 0.0
Vegetable: 3.0
Fruit: 0.0
Bread: 3.5
Meat: 0.0
Fat: 2.0

1. Spray vegetables with cooking spray; grill on greased rack over medium-hot coals, turning occasionally, until vegetables are browned and tender, about 20 minutes (or bake on greased aluminum-foil-lined jelly roll pan at 400 degrees until brown and tender, about 30 minutes). Toss with combined oil, vinegar, lime juice, and garlic; season to taste with salt and cayenne pepper.

2. Spoon about ½ cup of vegetable mixture on each tortilla. Sprinkle with cilantro, top with 1 tablespoon sour cream and avocado slice and roll up.

GRILLED PORTOBELLO
MUSHROOM SANDWICHES

o *The sandwiches can also be made with pita bread: make a slit in the tops of 4 pita breads and fill.*

4 main-dish servings

1 each: medium red and yellow bell pepper

Salt and pepper, to taste

Olive oil cooking spray

4 large portobello, or porcini, mushrooms
    (4–5 inches diameter)

8 slices Italian bread

1 clove garlic, halved

¼ cup fat-free mayonnaise

3–4 tablespoons finely chopped basil

Per Serving:
Calories: 239
% of calories from fat: 10
Fat (gm): 2.6
Saturated fat (gm): 0.5
Cholesterol (mg): 0
Sodium (mg): 546
Protein (gm): 10.3
Carbohydrate (gm): 43.8

Exchanges:
Milk: 0.0
Vegetable: 3.0
Fruit: 0.0
Bread: 2.0
Meat: 0.0
Fat: 0.5

1. Grill bell peppers on greased rack over medium-hot coals, turning frequently, until peppers are blistered and blackened, 5 to 8 minutes. Place in plastic bag and let stand 10 minutes. Peel peppers, discarding skins. Cut peppers into ½-inch slices; sprinkle lightly with salt and pepper.

2. Spray both sides of mushrooms with cooking spray; grill, turning occasionally, until tender, about 8 minutes. Season to taste with salt and pepper.

3. Grill bread until toasted, 2 to 3 minutes on each side; rub tops of bread slices with cut sides of garlic. Mix mayonnaise and basil and spread on 4 bread slices; top with mushrooms, peppers, and remaining bread slices.

VEGGIE POCKET SANDWICHES

V

Also delicious as a sandwich with sourdough or multigrain bread!

45

4 main-dish servings

1 medium eggplant, unpeeled, cut into 1-inch cubes
1 each: large unpeeled, thickly sliced sweet potato, onion, green bell pepper
1 large tomato, cut into 8 wedges
Vegetable cooking spray
2 tablespoons balsamic, or red wine, vinegar
1 tablespoon olive oil, or vegetable oil
1 teaspoon lemon juice
2 cloves garlic, minced
1 teaspoon each: dried oregano and basil leaves
Salt and pepper, to taste
4 pita pockets, halved

Per Serving:
Calories: 292
% of calories from fat: 14
Fat (gm): 4.6
Saturated fat (gm): 0.6
Cholesterol (mg): 0
Sodium (mg): 334
Protein (gm): 7.9
Carbohydrate (gm): 56.3

Exchanges:
Milk: 0.0
Vegetable: 3.0
Fruit: 0.0
Bread: 2.5
Meat: 0.0
Fat: 1.0

1. Arrange vegetables in single layer on greased foil-lined pan and spray with cooking spray. Roast at 425 degrees until browned and tender, about 30 minutes. Toss with combined vinegar, oil, lemon juice, garlic, oregano, and basil; season to taste with salt and pepper. Spoon into pita pockets.

ROASTED CHILI CORN BREAD

LO

Roasted chilies and corn cut from the cob make this a bread to remember!

9 servings (1 piece each)

2 ears corn, in the husks
Vegetable cooking spray
1 each: halved small red bell pepper, poblano and jalapeño chili
3 green onions, white parts only
½ teaspoon each: ground cumin, dried oregano leaves
1½ cups all-purpose flour
½ cup yellow cornmeal

Per Serving:
Calories: 176
% of calories from fat: 8
Fat (gm): 1.6
Saturated fat (gm): 0.4
Cholesterol (mg): 24.7
Sodium (mg): 283
Protein (gm): 6.3
Carbohydrate (gm): 35

Exchanges:
Milk: 0.0
Vegetable: 1.0
Fruit: 0.0
Bread: 2.0
Meat: 0.0
Fat: 0.0

3 tablespoons light brown sugar
2¾ teaspoons baking powder
½–¾ teaspoon salt
2 eggs
1 cup buttermilk
3 tablespoons minced cilantro

1. Soak corn in water to cover for 30 minutes; drain. Arrange corn and vegetables in single layer on greased foil-lined jelly roll pan. Spray with cooking spray; sprinkle vegetables, except corn, with cumin and oregano. Roast at 425 degrees until browned and tender, about 40 minutes. Let corn stand until cool enough to handle; remove and discard husks and cut corn kernels off cobs. Chop remaining vegetables into ¼-inch pieces.

2. Combine flour, cornmeal, brown sugar, baking powder, and salt in medium bowl. Whisk eggs into buttermilk; add to flour mixture, stirring just until combined. Stir in vegetables and cilantro. Pour batter into greased and floured 8-inch baking pan. Bake at 350 degrees until corn bread is browned and toothpick comes out clean, 35 to 40 minutes. Cool on wire rack; serve warm.

SIX

Pasta

HOMEMADE PASTA

O

Fresh pasta dough is not difficult to make. A pasta machine is a very simple and expedient way of kneading, rolling, and cutting the dough, and it produces a high-quality pasta. Rolling and cutting the dough by hand is somewhat more difficult; it requires practice to make thin, delicate pasta. Follow cooking directions in Step 4 carefully. Fresh pasta cooks very quickly — much more quickly than purchased fresh or dried pasta.

4 main-dish servings

1½ cups all-purpose flour
2 large eggs

Per Serving:
Calories: 208
% of calories from fat: 13
Fat (gm): 3
Saturated fat (gm): 0.8
Cholesterol (mg): 106.5
Sodium (mg): 32
Protein (gm): 8
Carbohydrate (gm): 36.1

Exchanges:
Milk: 0.0
Vegetable: 0.0
Fruit: 0.0
Bread: 2.5
Meat: 0.0
Fat: 0.5

1. Mound flour on cutting board, making a well in center. Drop eggs into center of well.

Break egg yolks and mix eggs with fork. While mixing eggs, gradually start to incorporate flour into the eggs. As flour is incorporated, it will be necessary to move the mound of flour toward the center, using your hands. Continue mixing until all or almost all flour has been incorporated, forming a soft, but not sticky, ball of dough.

2. To knead dough with a pasta machine, set machine rollers on the widest setting. Cut dough into 2 equal pieces. Lightly flour outside of 1 piece, and pass it through the machine. Fold piece of dough into thirds; pass it through the machine again, inserting open edges (not the fold) of dough first. Repeat folding and rolling 8 to 12 times or until dough feels smooth and satiny; lightly flour dough only if it begins to feel sticky.

Move machine rollers to next narrower setting. Pass dough, without folding, through the machine, beginning to roll out and stretch dough. Move machine rollers to next narrower setting; pass dough through the machine. Continue process until pasta is as thin as desired. (Often the narrowest setting on machine makes pasta too thin; 1 or 2 settings from the end is usually best.) Lightly flour dough if it begins to feel even slightly sticky at any time. Repeat above procedures with second piece of dough.

To cut pasta with the machine, set cutting rollers for width of pasta desired; pass dough through cutters. Arrange cut pasta in single layer on lightly floured surface.

3. To knead dough by hand, knead on lightly floured surface until smooth and satiny, about 10 minutes. Cover dough lightly with damp towel and let rest 10 minutes.

Place dough on lightly floured surface. Starting in center of dough, roll with rolling pin from center to edge. Continue rolling, always from center to edge, keeping dough as round as possible, until dough is about $\frac{1}{16}$ inch thick. Lightly flour dough if it begins to feel even slightly sticky at any time.

To cut pasta by hand, flour top of dough lightly and roll up. Cut into desired widths with sharp knife. Immediately unroll cut pasta and arrange in single layer on lightly floured surface.

4. To cook fresh or dried pasta, heat 4 to 5 quarts lightly salted water to boiling. Add pasta and begin testing for doneness as soon as water returns to boil. Cooking time will vary from 0 to 2 minutes once water has returned to boil.

NOTES: Pasta can be cooked fresh, or it can be dried and frozen or stored in an airtight container to be cooked later. To dry pasta, let stand on floured surface (or hang over rack) until completely dried. (Be sure pasta is completely dried or it will turn moldy in storage.) Store at room temperature in airtight container, or freeze.

Fresh homemade pasta can be used with any recipe, but it will result in a higher cholesterol count than stated with the recipe, in some cases exceeding the guidelines shown on page vii.

LIGHT SUMMER PASTA SALAD

L

45

The fragrant aroma and flavor of fresh herbs accent summer's finest tomatoes in this salad.

6 side-dish servings

8 ounces spaghetti, cooked, room temperature
1 pound plum tomatoes, seeded, chopped
¾ cup (3 ounces) cubed reduced-fat mozzarella cheese (¼-inch)
¼ cup packed basil leaves, chopped
Garlic Vinaigrette (recipe follows)

1. Combine all ingredients and toss.

Per Serving:
Calories: 200
% of calories from fat: 30
Fat (gm): 7.6
Saturated fat (gm): 0.6
Cholesterol (mg): 5
Sodium (mg): 234
Protein (gm): 9.8
Carbohydrate (gm): 26.2

Exchanges:
Milk: 0.0
Vegetable: 1.0
Fruit: 0.0
Bread: 1.5
Meat: 0.0
Fat: 1.5

Garlic Vinaigrette

Makes about ⅓ cup

3 tablespoons red wine vinegar
2 tablespoons olive oil
3 cloves garlic, minced
⅛ teaspoon each salt and pepper

1. Mix all ingredients.

GARDEN VEGETABLE AND PASTA SALAD

L

45

The eggplant can be roasted and refrigerated 1 to 2 days in advance.

4 main-dish servings

1 medium eggplant, unpeeled, cut into ¾-inch pieces
Vegetable cooking spray
2 cups each: cauliflower and broccoli florets, cooked crisp-tender
10 cherry tomatoes, halved
½ medium green bell pepper, sliced
8 ounces fettuccine, or linguine, cooked
Basil Vinaigrette (recipe follows)

Salt and pepper, to taste

2 ounces feta cheese, crumbled

1. Arrange eggplant on greased foil-lined jelly roll pan; spray with cooking spray. Roast at 425 degrees until tender, about 20 minutes; cool. Combine eggplant, remaining vegetables, and linguine in bowl; toss with Basil Vinaigrette. Season to taste with salt and pepper; sprinkle with cheese.

Basil Vinaigrette

Makes about ⅓ cup

¼ cup balsamic vinegar

1 tablespoon olive oil

3 tablespoons chopped basil leaves

1. Mix all ingredients.

45-MINUTE PREP TIP: Cook the fettuccine while the eggplant is roasting.

Per Serving:
Calories: 304
% of calories from fat: 25
Fat (gm): 9
Saturated fat (gm): 2.7
Cholesterol (mg): 12.5
Sodium (mg): 423
Protein (gm): 12.8
Carbohydrate (gm): 47.2

Exchanges:
Milk: 0.0
Vegetable: 2.0
Fruit: 0.0
Bread: 2.5
Meat: 0.0
Fat: 1.5

PASTA AND PORTOBELLO MUSHROOMS VINAIGRETTE

V

45

For extra flavor, grill or smoke the whole portobello mushrooms, then slice and combine with the vegetables and vinaigrette.

4 main-dish servings

4 large portobello mushrooms, cut into ¾-inch slices

1 tablespoon olive oil

2 medium tomatoes, cut into wedges

1 each: sliced medium yellow summer squash, green bell pepper, large carrot, small red onion

3 cups rotini (corkscrews), cooked

Mixed Herb Vinaigrette (recipe follows)

Per Serving:
Calories: 422
% of calories from fat: 19
Fat (gm): 9.2
Saturated fat (gm): 1.2
Cholesterol (mg): 0
Sodium (mg): 326
Protein (gm): 12.7
Carbohydrate (gm): 73.9

Exchanges:
Milk: 0.0
Vegetable: 2.0
Fruit: 0.0
Bread: 4.0
Meat: 0.0
Fat: 2.0

1. Sauté mushrooms in oil in large skillet until tender, about 5 minutes; cool. Combine mushrooms, vegetables, and pasta in bowl; toss with Mixed Herb Vinaigrette.

Mixed Herb Vinaigrette

Makes about ⅓ cup

⅓ cup each: reduced-sodium vegetable broth, red wine vinegar

1 tablespoon olive oil

2 teaspoons each: sugar, Dijon mustard

1 teaspoon mustard seeds, crushed

3 cloves garlic, minced

1 tablespoon each: chopped fresh, or 1 teaspoon dried, marjoram, tarragon, thyme leaves

½ teaspoon each salt and pepper

Per Serving:
Calories: 422
% of calories from fat: 19
Fat (gm): 9.2
Saturated fat (gm): 1.2
Cholesterol (mg): 0
Sodium (mg): 326
Protein (gm): 12.7
Carbohydrate (gm): 73.9

Exchanges:
Milk: 0.0
Vegetable: 2.0
Fruit: 0.0
Bread: 4.0
Meat: 0.0
Fat: 2.0

1. Mix all ingredients.

SESAME PASTA SALAD WITH SUMMER VEGETABLES

V

The vegetables used in this salad can vary according to seasonal availability.

45

6 side-dish servings

1 small eggplant

1 cup each: sliced carrots, sliced yellow summer squash, broccoli florets, cooked until crisp-tender

1 medium red bell pepper, sliced

¼ cup sliced green onions

8 ounces thin spaghetti, cooked, room temperature

Sesame Dressing (recipe follows)

2 teaspoons toasted sesame seeds

Per Serving:
Calories: 220
% of calories from fat: 17.7
Fat (gm): 4.3
Saturated fat (gm): 0.6
Cholesterol (mg): 0
Sodium (mg): 136
Protein (gm): 6.7
Carbohydrate (gm): 38.8

Exchanges:
Milk: 0.0
Vegetable: 2.0
Fruit: 0.0
Bread: 2.0
Meat: 0.0
Fat: 1.0

1. Pierce eggplant 6 to 8 times with fork; place in greased baking pan. Roast, uncovered, until tender, about 30 minutes; cool. Cut eggplant in half; scoop out pulp, and into ¾-inch pieces. Combine eggplant, vegetables, and pasta in bowl; toss with Sesame Dressing and sprinkle with sesame seeds.

45-MINUTE PREP TIP: Cook the fettuccine while the eggplant is roasting.

Sesame Dressing

Makes about ⅓ cup

2 tablespoons each: reduced-sodium soy sauce, sesame oil
1 teaspoon hot chili oil (optional)
1 tablespoon balsamic, or red wine, vinegar
1½ tablespoons sugar
1 clove garlic, minced
1 tablespoon chopped cilantro, or parsley

1. Mix all ingredients.

BRUSSELS SPROUTS AND GNOCCHI SALAD

L

45

Use spinach or potato gnocchi, available in gourmet food shops, Italian groceries, or supermarkets. Pasta shells can be substituted, if preferred.

8 side-dish servings

8 ounces gnocchi, cooked, room temperature
8 ounces Brussels sprouts, halved, steamed, cooled
1 cup seeded, chopped tomato
1 medium purple, or green, bell pepper, sliced
¼ cup thinly sliced red onion
Sun-Dried Tomato and Goat Cheese Dressing
   (recipe follows)
2 tablespoons grated Romano cheese

Per Serving:
Calories: 172
% of calories from fat: 27
Fat (gm): 5.4
Saturated fat (gm): 0.9
Cholesterol (mg): 3.5
Sodium (mg): 179
Protein (gm): 6.3
Carbohydrate (gm): 26.3

Exchanges:
Milk: 0.0
Vegetable: 1.0
Fruit: 0.0
Bread: 1.5
Meat: 0.0
Fat: 1.0

1. Combine gnocchi and vegetables in bowl; top with Sun-Dried Tomato and Goat Cheese Dressing and sprinkle with cheese.

Sun-Dried Tomato and Goat Cheese Dressing

Makes about ⅓ cup

2 tablespoons each: olive oil, white wine vinegar, lemon juice

1 tablespoon goat cheese, or reduced-fat cream cheese, room temperature

3 sun-dried tomatoes (not in oil), softened, finely chopped

2 cloves garlic, minced

½ teaspoon each: dried marjoram and thyme leaves

¼ teaspoon salt

⅛ teaspoon pepper

1. Mix all ingredients.

RICE NOODLE SALAD

V

45

If you enjoy the flavor of sesame, substitute 1 tablespoon Asian sesame oil for 1 tablespoon of olive oil in the vinaigrette.

4 main-dish servings

1 package (7 ounces) rice noodles

1½ cups thinly sliced Chinese cabbage

2 cups snow peas, trimmed, cooked until crisp-tender

¾ cup each: sliced red and yellow bell pepper

1 cup each: sliced mushrooms and canned, drained lychee fruit, or pineapple chunks

½ cup fresh, or canned, bean sprouts, drained

Citrus Vinaigrette (recipe follows)

Per Serving:
Calories: 246
% of calories from fat: 26
Fat (gm): 7.5
Saturated fat (gm): 1
Cholesterol (mg): 0
Sodium (mg): 197
Protein (gm): 6.6
Carbohydrate (gm): 40.9

Exchanges:
Milk: 0.0
Vegetable: 2.0
Fruit: 0.0
Bread: 2.0
Meat: 0.0
Fat: 1.0

1. Place noodles in bowl; pour cold water over to cover. Let stand until noodles separate and are soft, about 5 minutes. Stir noodles into boiling water in large saucepan; reduce heat and simmer, uncovered, until tender, about 5 minutes. Drain and cool. Combine noodles, Chinese cabbage, snow peas, bell peppers, mushrooms, lychee fruit, and bean sprouts in large bowl; toss with Citrus Vinaigrette.

Citrus Vinaigrette

Makes about ⅓ cup

⅓ cup orange juice

2 tablespoons olive oil

2 cloves garlic, minced

½ teaspoon five-spice powder

¼ teaspoon each: salt and pepper

1. Mix all ingredients.

CREAMY FETTUCCINE PRIMAVERA

L

45

The sauce for this dish should be somewhat thin, as it thickens once removed from the heat. If reheating, the sauce will require additional milk.

4 main-dish servings

2 cups each: sliced mushrooms, broccoli florets

½ cup chopped red bell pepper

½ cup water

1 package (8 ounces) fat-free cream cheese

⅔–1 cup fat-free milk, divided

¼ cup sliced green onions

½ teaspoon dried Italian seasoning

2 tablespoons grated fat-free Parmesan cheese

Salt and white pepper, to taste

8 ounces fettuccine, cooked, warm

Per Serving:
Calories: 273
% of calories from fat: 8
Fat (gm): 2.5
Saturated fat (gm): 0.1
Cholesterol (mg): 0.7
Sodium (mg): 491
Protein (gm): 20.4
Carbohydrate (gm): 43.2

Exchanges:
Milk: 0.5
Vegetable: 2.0
Fruit: 0.0
Bread: 2.0
Meat: 0.5
Fat: 0.0

1. Sauté mushrooms, broccoli, and bell pepper in lightly greased large skillet 3 to 4 minutes. Add water and heat to boiling; reduce heat and simmer, covered, until broccoli is tender, about 8 minutes; drain.

2. Heat cream cheese, ⅔ cup milk, green onions, and Italian seasoning in small saucepan over low heat until cream cheese is melted, stirring frequently. Stir in Parmesan cheese and enough remaining milk to make a thin consistency. Season to taste with salt and pepper. Toss with fettuccine and vegetables.

45-MINUTE PREP TIP: Begin cooking the fettuccine before preparing the rest of the recipe.

FETTUCCINE WITH GREENS AND CARAMELIZED ONIONS

V

45

Cajun Eggplant or Mesquite Smoked Tofu (see pp. 208, 191) would be excellent with this pasta dish.

4 main-dish servings

4 medium onions, sliced
1 tablespoon olive oil
1 teaspoon sugar
1 can (14½ ounces) reduced-sodium vegetable broth
4 cups thinly sliced kale, mustard greens, Swiss
    chard, or spinach
Salt and pepper, to taste
8 ounces fettuccine, cooked, warm

Per Serving:
Calories: 281
% of calories from fat: 18
Fat (gm): 5.8
Saturated fat (gm): 0.5
Cholesterol (mg): 0
Sodium (mg): 151
Protein (gm): 10.3
Carbohydrate (gm): 49.9

Exchanges:
Milk: 0.0
Vegetable: 2.0
Fruit: 0.0
Bread: 2.5
Meat: 0.0
Fat: 1.0

1. Cook onions in oil over medium heat in large skillet 5 minutes; reduce heat to low and stir in sugar. Cook until onions are golden in color and very soft, about 20 minutes. Stir in broth; heat to boiling. Reduce heat and simmer, uncovered, until broth is reduced by ⅓, about 10 minutes. Add kale and simmer, covered, until wilted, 5 to 7 minutes. Simmer, uncovered, until broth is almost evaporated, about 5 minutes. Season to taste with salt and pepper. Toss with pasta.

45-MINUTE PREP TIP: Begin cooking the fettuccine before preparing the rest of the recipe.

FETTUCCINE WITH ROASTED GARLIC, ONIONS, AND PEPPERS

V

45

◊

Deceptively simple to make, and incredibly delicious to eat!

8 side-dish servings

2 bulbs garlic
Olive oil cooking spray
3 medium onions, cut into wedges
2 large red bell peppers, cut into ½-inch slices
2 tablespoons each: olive oil, lemon juice, chopped parsley
½ teaspoon salt

¼ teaspoon pepper

8 ounces fettuccine, cooked, warm

Per Serving:
Calories: 151
% of calories from fat: 26
Fat (gm): 4.5
Saturated fat (gm): 0.5
Cholesterol (mg): 0
Sodium (mg): 184
Protein (gm): 5
Carbohydrate (gm): 24.4

Exchanges:
Milk: 0.0
Vegetable: 1.5
Fruit: 0.0
Bread: 1.0
Meat: 0.0
Fat: 1.0

1. Cut a scant ½ inch off tops of garlic bulbs, exposing ends of cloves; spray with cooking spray. Wrap garlic bulbs loosely in aluminum foil. Arrange garlic, onions, and bell peppers in single layer on greased foil-lined jelly roll. Roast at 425 degrees until garlic is very soft and vegetables are tender, 30 to 40 minutes.

2. Cool garlic slightly; squeeze pulp into small bowl. Stir in oil, lemon juice, parsley, salt, and pepper. Toss with pasta and onion mixture.

45-MINUTE PREP TIP: Begin cooking the fettuccine before preparing the rest of the recipe.

FETTUCCINE WITH FRESH FENNEL AND BRUSSELS SPROUTS

L

If fennel is not available, substitute ½ cup thinly sliced celery, and add ½ teaspoon crushed fennel seeds to the sautéed vegetables.

45

4 main-dish servings

Per Serving:
Calories: 337
% of calories from fat: 32
Fat (gm): 12.3
Saturated fat (gm): 4.2
Cholesterol (mg): 78.1
Sodium (mg): 360
Protein (gm): 18.2
Carbohydrate (gm): 41.1

Exchanges:
Milk: 0.0
Vegetable: 0.0
Fruit: 0.0
Bread: 2.5
Meat: 2.0
Fat: 1.0

1 cup each: thinly sliced fennel bulb, onion

8 ounces small Brussels sprouts, halved

¼ cup water

1 tablespoon lemon juice

Salt and pepper, to taste

8 ounces spinach fettuccine, cooked, warm

½ cup (2 ounces) shredded Parmesan cheese

¼ cup toasted pine nuts, or slivered almonds

1. Sauté fennel and onion in lightly greased large skillet 3 to 4 minutes. Add Brussels sprouts and water and heat to boiling; reduce heat and simmer, covered, until sprouts are crisp-tender, 5 to 8 minutes. Stir in lemon juice; season to taste with salt and pepper. Serve over pasta; sprinkle with Parmesan cheese and pine nuts.

45-MINUTE PREP TIP: Begin cooking the fettuccine before preparing the rest of the recipe.

FETTUCCINE WITH EGGPLANT PERSILLADE

L

45

"Persillade" is a French term meaning "with lots of parsley," which this fragrant dish has.

4 main-dish servings

1 each: chopped medium onion, green and red
  bell pepper
1 small eggplant, unpeeled, cut into ½-inch cubes
2 teaspoons minced roasted garlic
½ cup canned reduced-sodium vegetable broth
Salt and pepper, to taste
½ cup finely chopped parsley
8 ounces whole wheat fettuccine, cooked, warm
2–4 tablespoons grated fat-free Parmesan cheese

Per Serving:
Calories: 246
% of calories from fat: 9
Fat (gm): 2.5
Saturated fat (gm): 0.1
Cholesterol (mg): 0
Sodium (mg): 136
Protein (gm): 11.0
Carbohydrate (gm): 48.7

Exchanges:
Milk: 0.0
Vegetable: 3.0
Fruit: 0.0
Bread: 2.0
Meat: 0.5
Fat: 0.0

1. Sauté onion, bell peppers, eggplant, and garlic in lightly greased large skillet 5 minutes, stirring occasionally. Add broth and heat to boiling; reduce heat and simmer, covered, until eggplant is tender and broth absorbed, about 5 minutes. Season to taste with salt and pepper. Toss vegetable mixture with parsley, pasta, and cheese.

45-MINUTE PREP TIP: Begin cooking the fettuccine before preparing the rest of the recipe.

LINGUINE WITH JULIENNED VEGETABLES AND RED PEPPER PESTO

L

Any of the pestos (see pp. 605–608) included in this cookbook would be excellent in this recipe.

4 main-dish servings

2 cups each: julienned zucchini, peeled, seeded
  yellow winter squash
½ cup julienned fennel bulb
¼ cup thinly sliced green onions
Salt and pepper, to taste
8 ounces linguine, cooked, warm
Red Pepper Pesto (see p. 607)
2 tablespoons grated fat-free Parmesan cheese

Per Serving:
Calories: 335
% of calories from fat: 32
Fat (gm): 12.6
Saturated fat (gm): 1.4
Cholesterol (mg): 0
Sodium (mg): 170
Protein (gm): 13
Carbohydrate (gm): 46.8

Exchanges:
Milk: 0.0
Vegetable: 1.0
Fruit: 0.0
Bread: 2.5
Meat: 0.5
Fat: 2.0

1. Sauté zucchini, squash, fennel, and green onions in lightly greased large skillet until tender, 8 to 10 minutes; season to taste with salt and pepper. Toss linguine with Red Pepper Pesto and vegetables; sprinkle with Parmesan cheese.

PASTA WITH GOAT CHEESE AND ONION CONFIT

L *Try this dish with flavored specialty pastas such as dried mushroom, herb, or black pepper.*

4 main-dish servings

4 cups thinly sliced onions

1 teaspoon minced garlic, sugar

½ teaspoon each: dried sage and rosemary leaves

½ cup dry white wine, or fat-free milk

2 ounces each: fat-free cream cheese, goat cheese

Salt and pepper, to taste

8 ounces whole wheat, or plain, thin spaghetti, cooked

2–3 tablespoons coarsely chopped walnuts

Per Serving:
Calories: 395
% of calories from fat: 15
Fat (gm): 6.7
Saturated fat (gm): 2.4
Cholesterol (mg): 6.5
Sodium (mg): 144
Protein (gm): 16
Carbohydrate (gm): 66.9

Exchanges:
Milk: 0.0
Vegetable: 2.0
Fruit: 0.0
Bread: 4.0
Meat: 0.5
Fat: 0.5

1. Sauté onions in lightly greased large skillet 3 to 4 minutes; reduce heat to medium-low and cook, covered, until onions are very soft, about 30 minutes. Stir in garlic, sugar, and herbs; cook, uncovered, until onions are caramelized, 15 to 20 minutes. Stir in wine; simmer 2 to 3 minutes longer. Add cream cheese and goat cheese, stirring until melted; season to taste with salt and white pepper. Toss with pasta; sprinkle with walnuts.

CURRIED PASTA AND VEGETABLES

V

This delicate curry dish is garnished with chopped peanuts and mango chutney for wonderful flavor and texture contrast.

4 main-dish servings

½ cup each: chopped red and yellow bell pepper

1 cup each: small cauliflower florets, peas, or cut green beans

½ teaspoon crushed red pepper

¼ cup water

Salt and pepper, to taste

2 cups (double recipe) Curry Sauce (see p. 594)

8 ounces angel hair pasta, cooked, warm

2–4 tablespoons chopped dry-roasted peanuts

¼ cup packed cilantro, chopped

¼ cup chopped mango chutney

Per Serving:
Calories: 390
% of calories from fat: 13
Fat (gm): 5.6
Saturated fat (gm): 1.1
Cholesterol (mg): 63.8
Sodium (mg): 84.7
Protein (gm): 13.6
Carbohydrate (gm): 68.7

Exchanges:
Milk: 0.0
Vegetable: 2.0
Fruit: 0.5
Bread: 3.5
Meat: 0.0
Fat: 1.0

1. Sauté bell peppers in lightly greased medium skillet until tender, 3 to 4 minutes. Add cauliflower, peas, crushed red pepper, and water; heat to boiling. Reduce heat and simmer, covered, until vegetables are tender, 5 to 8 minutes; cook, uncovered, until water has evaporated; season to taste with salt and pepper. Toss with Curry Sauce and pasta; sprinkle with peanuts and cilantro. Serve chutney on the side.

45-MINUTE PREP TIP: Begin cooking the pasta before preparing the rest of the recipe.

PASTA WITH GREENS AND BEANS

L

45

Mustard greens, Swiss chard, or other bitter greens are nutritious substitutes for the kale.

4 main-dish servings

1½ cups sliced onions

¾ cup chopped red bell pepper

1 tablespoon minced garlic

1–2 tablespoons olive oil

½–¾ teaspoon crushed red pepper

1 can (15 ounces) cannellini, or other white beans, rinsed, drained

5 cups loosely packed sliced kale

½ cup water

Salt and pepper, to taste

8 ounces mafalde, or other flat pasta, cooked, warm

¼ cup (1 ounce) grated fat-free Parmesan cheese

Per Serving:
Calories: 417
% of calories from fat: 12
Fat (gm): 5.9
Saturated fat (gm): 0.7
Cholesterol (mg): 0
Sodium (mg): 282
Protein (gm): 20.6
Carbohydrate (gm): 79.8

Exchanges:
Milk: 0.0
Vegetable: 3.0
Fruit: 0.0
Bread: 4.0
Meat: 0.5
Fat: 0.5

1. Sauté onions, bell pepper, and garlic in oil in large skillet until tender, 5 to 6 minutes; add crushed red pepper and cook 1 to 2 minutes longer. Add beans, kale, and water to skillet; cook, covered, over medium heat until kale is tender and liquid absorbed, about 10 minutes. Season to taste with salt and pepper. Toss with pasta and cheese.

45-MINUTE PREP TIP: Begin cooking the mafalde before preparing the rest of the recipe.

VERY SIMPLE PRIMAVERA

L

45

Very simple, and simply good! This primavera can take advantage of any fresh ingredients on hand.

6 main-dish servings

2 cups thinly sliced onions

4 teaspoons minced garlic

¾ teaspoon each: dried marjoram and basil leaves

1½ cups sliced mushrooms

1 cup each: thinly sliced green and red bell peppers

8 ounces sugar snap peas, halved

10–12 Italian plum tomatoes, quartered

Salt and pepper, to taste

12 ounces penne, or ziti, cooked, warm

¼ cup (1 ounce) grated fat-free Parmesan cheese

Per Serving:
Calories: 341
% of calories from fat: 6
Fat (gm): 2.2
Saturated fat (gm): 0.3
Cholesterol (mg): 0
Sodium (mg): 55
Protein (gm): 13.7
Carbohydrate (gm): 69.8

Exchanges:
Milk: 0.0
Vegetable: 4.0
Fruit: 0.0
Bread: 3.0
Meat: 0.0
Fat: 0.5

1. Sauté onions, garlic, and herbs in lightly greased large skillet 2 minutes. Add mushrooms and bell peppers; sauté 2 to 3 minutes. Add snap peas and tomatoes; cook, covered, over medium heat until tomatoes are wilted and peas are crisp-tender, 5 to 8 minutes. Season to taste with salt and pepper. Toss with pasta and cheese.

45-MINUTE PREP TIP: Begin cooking the penne before preparing the rest of the recipe.

GREAT GARLIC PASTA

L

45

Slow cooking gives a sweet, mellow flavor to the garlic. Using prepared peeled garlic will speed preparation.

4 main-dish servings

⅓ cup slivered, or thinly sliced, garlic

2–3 teaspoons olive oil

1 cup frozen tiny peas, thawed

2 tablespoons minced fresh parsley

1 tablespoon minced fresh, or 1 teaspoon crushed dried rosemary leaves

8 ounces (2 cups) orecchiette, or cappelletti, cooked, warm

¼ cup (1 ounce) freshly grated Parmesan cheese

Salt and pepper, to taste

Per Serving:
Calories: 302
% of calories from fat: 15
Fat (gm): 5
Saturated fat (gm): 1.4
Cholesterol (mg): 3.9
Sodium (mg): 132
Protein (gm): 12.1
Carbohydrate (gm): 52.2

Exchanges:
Milk: 0.0
Vegetable: 2.0
Fruit: 0.0
Bread: 3.0
Meat: 0.0
Fat: 1.0

1. Cook garlic over very low heat in oil in small skillet until very tender but not browned, about 10 minutes. Add peas and herbs and cook 2 minutes longer. Toss with pasta and cheese; season to taste with salt and pepper.

45-MINUTE PREP TIP: Begin cooking the orecchiette before preparing the rest of the recipe.

PENNE WITH ASPARAGUS AND PLUM TOMATOES

L

45

Uncooked tomatoes and crisp-tender asparagus are tossed with warm pasta for the freshest of spring flavors.

4 main-dish servings

¾ cup each: chopped onion, yellow bell pepper

1 teaspoon minced garlic

12 ounces fresh asparagus, cut into 1-inch pieces

3 tablespoons dry white wine, or water

2 cups seeded, chopped Italian plum tomatoes

8 ounces penne, cooked, warm

¼ cup chopped basil

Salt and pepper, to taste

2–4 tablespoons grated fat-free Parmesan cheese

Per Serving:
Calories: 295
% of calories from fat: 5
Fat (gm): 1.8
Saturated fat (gm): 0.3
Cholesterol (mg): 0
Sodium (mg): 45
Protein (gm): 12.1
Carbohydrate (gm): 58.0

Exchanges:
Milk: 0.0
Vegetable: 2.0
Fruit: 0.0
Bread: 3.0
Meat: 0.5
Fat: 0.0

1. Sauté onion, bell pepper, and garlic in lightly greased large skillet until tender, about 5 minutes. Add asparagus and wine; cook, covered, until asparagus is crisp-tender and wine evaporated, 3 to 5 minutes. Toss with tomatoes, pasta, and basil in bowl; season to taste with salt and pepper and sprinkle with cheese.

45-MINUTE PREP TIP: Begin cooking the penne before preparing the rest of the recipe.

"LITTLE EARS" WITH SMOKED TEMPEH AND VEGETABLES

V

45

Mesquite-Smoked Tofu (p. 191) can be used in place of the tempeh, if desired. Smoked tofu can also be purchased in health food and specialty stores.

4 main-dish servings

2 packages (8 ounces each) tempeh
3 cups broccoli florets, steamed
1 medium yellow, or green, bell pepper, sliced
12 cherry tomatoes, halved
2 cups (8 ounces) orecchiette ("little ears"), or small
    pasta shells, cooked
Mustard Seed Vinaigrette (recipe follows)

Per Serving:
Calories: 374
% of calories from fat: 27
Fat (gm): 11.7
Saturated fat (gm): 1.8
Cholesterol (mg): 0
Sodium (mg): 196
Protein (gm): 23.2
Carbohydrate (gm): 47.8

Exchanges:
Milk: 0.0
Vegetable: 2.0
Fruit: 0.0
Bread: 2.5
Meat: 2.0
Fat: 1.0

1. Smoke tempeh according to directions in Mesquite-Smoked Tofu recipe (see p. 191); cut tempeh into ¾-inch cubes. Combine tempeh, vegetables, and pasta in serving bowl; toss with Mustard Seed Vinaigrette.

Mustard Seed Vinaigrette

Makes about ⅓ cup

2 tablespoons each: olive oil, white wine vinegar, lemon juice
2 each: finely chopped medium shallots, cloves garlic
¾ teaspoon mustard seeds, crushed
½ teaspoon salt
¼ teaspoon pepper

1. Mix all ingredients.

45-MINUTE PREP TIP: Begin cooking the orecchiette before preparing the rest of the recipe.

FUSILLI WITH TOMATOES AND CORN

V

45

A perfect salad, especially when homegrown tomatoes, corn, and basil are available!

8 side-dish servings

2 cups chopped plum tomatoes
1 cup whole-kernel corn, cooked
½ cup sliced green onions
2⅔ cups (6 ounces) fusilli (spirals), or
   corkscrews, cooked
Fresh Basil Dressing (recipe follows)

Per Serving:
Calories: 135
% of calories from fat: 26
Fat (gm): 4
Saturated fat (gm): 0.6
Cholesterol (mg): 0
Sodium (mg): 141
Protein (gm): 4.1
Carbohydrate (gm): 21.8

Exchanges:
Milk: 0.0
Vegetable: 1.0
Fruit: 0.0
Bread: 1.0
Meat: 0.0
Fat: 1.0

1. Combine all ingredients and toss.

Fresh Basil Dressing

Makes about ⅓ cup

⅓ cup red wine vinegar
2 tablespoons olive, or canola oil
3 tablespoons finely chopped fresh, or 1½ teaspoons dried, basil leaves
2 cloves garlic, minced
½ teaspoon salt
¼ teaspoon pepper

1. Mix all ingredients.

45-MINUTE PREP TIP: Begin cooking the fusilli before preparing the rest of the recipe.

FARFALLE WITH ROASTED EGGPLANT AND SQUASH

This dish can also be served at room temperature, making it perfect potluck or picnic fare.

4 main-dish servings

4 cups each: unpeeled, cubed eggplant and butternut squash (1-inch)

6 Italian plum tomatoes, each cut lengthwise into 4 wedges

1 large green bell pepper, cut into 1-inch slices

Olive oil cooking spray

2 teaspoons dried rosemary leaves

1 teaspoon dried tarragon leaves

Salt and pepper, to taste

8 ounces farfalle (bow ties), or linguine, cooked, warm

2–3 tablespoon grated fat-free Parmesan cheese

Per Serving:
Calories: 376
% of calories from fat: 5
Fat (gm): 2.2
Saturated fat (gm): 0.3
Cholesterol (mg): 0
Sodium (mg): 51.3
Protein (gm): 12.9
Carbohydrate (gm): 81.7

Exchanges:
Milk: 0.0
Vegetable: 2.0
Fruit: 0.0
Bread: 4.5
Meat: 0.0
Fat: 0.0

1. Arrange vegetables in single layer on greased foil-lined jelly roll pan; spray with cooking spray and sprinkle with herbs. Roast at 425 degrees until tender and browned, about 40 minutes. Season to taste with salt and pepper. Toss with pasta and Parmesan cheese.

45-MINUTE PREP TIP: Begin cooking the farfalle before preparing the rest of the recipe.

BUCATINI WITH BRUSSELS SPROUTS AND WALNUTS

Bucatini is a spaghetti-type pasta with a hole in the center.

4 main-dish servings

12 ounces Brussels sprouts, cooked crisp-tender, halved

2 teaspoons minced garlic

8 ounces bucatini, or spaghetti, cooked, warm

2 cups seeded, chopped Italian plum tomatoes

⅔ cup minced parsley

¼ cup each: toasted unseasoned dry bread crumbs, chopped walnuts

2–4 tablespoons grated fat-free Parmesan cheese
Salt and pepper, to taste

1. Sauté Brussels sprouts and garlic in lightly greased skillet until hot, 3 to 4 minutes. Toss with remaining ingredients, except salt and pepper. Season to taste with salt and pepper.

45-MINUTE PREP TIP: Begin cooking the bucatini before preparing the rest of the recipe.

Per Serving:
Calories: 367
% of calories from fat: 16
Fat (gm): 6.7
Saturated fat (gm): 0.7
Cholesterol (mg): 0
Sodium (mg): 118
Protein (gm): 14.9
Carbohydrate (gm): 65.4

Exchanges:
Milk: 0.0
Vegetable: 3.0
Fruit: 0.0
Bread: 3.0
Meat: 0.5
Fat: 1.0

ZITI WITH GREMOLATA

V

45

The fresh lemon flavor of the Gremolata accents this tomato and pasta dish. Serve with Garlic Bread (see p. 559) and a robust red wine.

8 main-dish servings

½ cup chopped onion
8 ounces shiitake, or cremini, mushrooms, sliced
2 cans (14½ ounces each) diced tomatoes with
 Italian seasoning, undrained
Salt and pepper, to taste
1 pound ziti, or penne, cooked, warm
Gremolata (see p. 609)

Per Serving:
Calories: 268
% of calories from fat: 4
Fat (gm): 1.2
Saturated fat (gm): 0.2
Cholesterol (mg): 0
Sodium (mg): 227
Protein (gm): 9.3
Carbohydrate (gm): 53.8

Exchanges:
Milk: 0.0
Vegetable: 2.0
Fruit: 0.0
Bread: 3.0
Meat: 0.0
Fat: 0.0

1. Sauté onion and mushrooms in lightly greased large skillet until tender, 5 to 8 minutes. Add tomatoes with liquid and heat to boiling; reduce heat and simmer, uncovered, until thickened, about 10 minutes. Season to taste with salt and pepper. Toss with pasta and ½ the Gremolata; serve with remaining Gremolata.

45-MINUTE PREP TIP: Begin cooking the ziti before preparing the rest of the recipe.

STAR PASTA WITH CARROTS AND GINGER CREAM

L

45

Fresh gingerroot can be very hot in flavor; add more, or less, according to your taste preference. Gingerroot does not have to be peeled before using.

4 main-dish servings

1 medium shallot, finely chopped

1 tablespoon minced gingerroot

1 teaspoon margarine, or butter

1 cup finely chopped carrots

⅓ cup chopped red bell pepper

½ cup dry white wine

2 tablespoons flour

1 cup fat-free half-and-half, or fat-free milk

Salt and pepper, to taste

8 ounces stelline (small star-shaped pasta), or orzo, cooked, warm

Chopped cilantro, as garnish

Per Serving:
Calories: 322
% of calories from fat: 6
Fat (gm): 2.1
Saturated fat (gm): 0.3
Cholesterol (mg): 0
Sodium (mg): 84
Protein (gm): 10
Carbohydrate (gm): 58.0

Exchanges:
Milk: 0.5
Vegetable: 1.0
Fruit: 0.0
Bread: 3.0
Meat: 0.0
Fat: 1.0

1. Sauté shallot and gingerroot in margarine in medium skillet 2 minutes. Stir in carrots, bell pepper, and wine; heat to boiling. Reduce heat and simmer, covered, until vegetables are crisp-tender and wine evaporated, 8 to 10 minutes. Sprinkle with flour; cook 2 minutes longer. Add half-and-half; heat to boiling. Boil, stirring, until thickened, about 1 minute. Season to taste with salt and pepper. Toss with pasta; sprinkle generously with cilantro.

45-MINUTE PREP TIP: Begin cooking the pasta before preparing the rest of the recipe.

SOUTHWEST PASTA WITH CILANTRO PESTO

V

If poblano chilies are not available, substitute green bell peppers and add 1 to 2 teaspoons minced jalapeño chili to the onions when sautéing.

6 main-dish servings

3 cups each: peeled, cubed acorn squash, sliced zucchini

1 medium onion, sliced

3 poblano chilies, sliced

1–1½ teaspoons dried oregano leaves

¼–½ teaspoon ground cumin

1 tablespoon olive oil

¾ cup reduced-sodium vegetable broth

2 medium tomatoes, cut into wedges

Salt and pepper, to taste

12 ounces fettuccine, or other flat pasta,
cooked, warm

Cilantro Pesto (see p. 607)

Per Serving:
Calories: 408
% of calories from fat: 21
Fat (gm): 10
Saturated fat (gm): 2
Cholesterol (mg): 3.3
Sodium (mg): 196
Protein (gm): 13.8
Carbohydrate (gm): 69.5

Exchanges:
Milk: 0.0
Vegetable: 2.0
Fruit: 0.0
Bread: 4.0
Meat: 0.0
Fat: 1.5

1. Sauté acorn squash, zucchini, onion, poblano chilies, oregano, and cumin in oil in large skillet 3 minutes; add broth and heat to boiling. Reduce heat and simmer, covered, until acorn squash is crisp-tender, about 5 minutes. Add tomatoes; cook, covered, until softened, 3 to 4 minutes. Season to taste with salt and pepper. Toss fettuccine with Cilantro Pesto; top with vegetables.

45-MINUTE PREP TIP: Begin cooking the fettuccine before preparing the rest of the recipe.

PASTA SANTA FE

V

45

Flavors of the Southwest merge with pasta; this one is picante, with poblano chilies.

4 main-dish servings

1 medium onion, sliced

3 cloves garlic, minced

2 tablespoons canola oil

2 each: sliced medium zucchini, poblano chilies,
sliced tomatoes

1 cup whole-kernel corn

2 tablespoons chili powder

1 teaspoon dried oregano leaves

½ teaspoon ground cumin

2 tablespoons chopped cilantro

Salt and pepper, to taste

8 ounces trio maliano (combination of corkscrews,
shells, and rigatoni) pasta, cooked, warm

Per Serving:
Calories: 350
% of calories from fat: 24
Fat (gm): 9.6
Saturated fat (gm): 1.2
Cholesterol (mg): 0
Sodium (mg): 327
Protein (gm): 11.6
Carbohydrate (gm): 58

Exchanges:
Milk: 0.0
Vegetable: 2.0
Fruit: 0.0
Bread: 3.0
Meat: 0.0
Fat: 2.0

1. Sauté onion and garlic in oil in large skillet until tender, about 5 minutes. Add remaining vegetables, chili powder, oregano, and cumin. Cook, uncovered, over medium until vegetables are crisp-tender, about 10 minutes. Stir in cilantro; season to taste with salt, and pepper. Toss with pasta.

45-MINUTE PREP TIP: Begin cooking the pasta before preparing the rest of the recipe.

SESAME NOODLE SOUP WITH VEGETABLES

Asian sesame oil is dark in color and concentrated in flavor; light-colored sesame oil is very delicate in flavor. The fresh Chinese-style noodles are sometimes called soup noodles, chow mein noodles, or spaghetti. Caution: fresh noodles cook very quickly.

4 main-dish servings (about 2 cups each)

½ cup sliced green onions

4 cloves garlic, minced

1 tablespoon Asian sesame oil

2½ cups chopped or thinly sliced napa cabbage

1 cup each: chopped red bell peppers, julienned carrots, and sliced shiitake, or cremini mushrooms

3 cans (14½ ounces each) reduced-sodium vegetable broth

1 package (12 ounces) fresh Chinese-style noodles

Salt and pepper, to taste

Per Serving:
Calories: 281
% of calories from fat: 12
Fat (gm): 3.9
Saturated fat (gm): 0.5
Cholesterol (mg): 0
Sodium (mg): 150
Protein (gm): 4.1
Carbohydrate (gm): 60

Exchanges:
Milk: 0.0
Vegetable: 2.0
Fruit: 0.0
Bread: 3.0
Meat: 0.0
Fat: 0.5

1. Sauté green onions and garlic in sesame oil in large saucepan until tender, about 5 minutes. Add cabbage, bell peppers, carrots, and mushrooms; sauté until vegetables are crisp-tender, about 5 minutes. Add broth and heat to boiling. Stir in noodles, reduce heat and simmer, uncovered, until noodles are just tender, 1 to 2 minutes. Season to taste with salt and pepper.

45-MINUTE PREP TIP: Begin cooking the noodles before preparing the rest of the recipe.

ORIENTAL SOUP WITH NOODLES

V

45

The dried chow mein noodles are not the fried ones we have eaten with chop suey for many years. Be sure the correct noodles are used.

4 side-dish servings (about ¾ cup each)

1 ounce dried cloud ear, or shiitake, mushrooms

½ cup julienned carrots

2 cans (14½ ounces each) reduced-sodium vegetable broth

2 tablespoons dry sherry (optional)

1½ teaspoons reduced-sodium tamari soy sauce

½ teaspoon five-spice powder

2½ ounces snow peas, trimmed

1 cup sliced mushrooms

¼ cup sliced green onions

½ package (5-ounce size) dried chow mein noodles

Salt and pepper, to taste

Per Serving:
Calories: 146
% of calories from fat: 32
Fat (gm): 5.6
Saturated fat (gm): 0.8
Cholesterol (mg): 0
Sodium (mg): 259
Protein (gm): 3.6
Carbohydrate (gm): 21.3

Exchanges:
Milk: 0.0
Vegetable: 1.0
Fruit: 0.0
Bread: 1.0
Meat: 0.0
Fat: 1.0

1. Place dried mushrooms in bowl; pour hot water over to cover. Let stand until mushrooms are soft, about 15 minutes; drain. Slice mushrooms, discarding any tough parts.

2. Sauté dried mushrooms and carrots in lightly greased saucepan 3 to 4 minutes. Add vegetable broth, sherry, soy sauce, and five-spice powder. Heat to boiling; reduce heat and simmer, covered, 10 minutes. Stir in snow peas, mushrooms, and green onions; cook until peas are crisp-tender, about 4 minutes. Add noodles to saucepan; cook until just tender, about 10 minutes. Season to taste with salt and pepper.

VEGETABLE LO MEIN

o

45

Store gingerroot in a jar filled with dry sherry, cover, and refrigerate; the gingerroot will last at least 6 months. Gingerroot does not have to be peeled before using.

4 main-dish servings

4 Chinese dried black, or shiitake, mushrooms

1 tablespoon each: chopped gingerroot, minced garlic, Asian sesame oil

2 cups broccoli florets

1 cup sliced carrots

½ cup sliced leek (white part only)

1 cup each: chopped tomatoes, sliced kale, or bok choy

⅓ cup water

2 tablespoons dry sherry, or water

2 teaspoons cornstarch

1 tablespoon each: black bean paste, light soy sauce

1 package (12 ounces) fresh Chinese noodles, cooked

Per Serving:
Calories: 418
% of calories from fat: 9
Fat (gm): 4.2
Saturated fat (gm): 0.6
Cholesterol (mg): 0
Sodium (mg): 275
Protein (gm): 10.6
Carbohydrate (gm): 84.7

Exchanges:
Milk: 0.0
Vegetable: 4.0
Fruit: 0.0
Bread: 4.0
Meat: 0.0
Fat: 0.5

1. Place dried mushrooms in bowl; pour hot water over to cover. Let stand until mushrooms are soft, about 15 minutes; drain. Slice mushrooms, discarding tough parts. Stir-fry mushrooms, gingerroot, and garlic in sesame oil in large wok or skillet 2 minutes. Add remaining vegetables to wok and stir-fry until crisp-tender, 5 to 8 minutes. Stir in combined water, sherry, cornstarch, bean paste, and soy sauce and heat to boiling. Boil, stirring, until thickened, about 1 minute. Add noodles and stir-fry until hot, 2 to 3 minutes.

45-MINUTE PREP TIP: Begin cooking the noodles before preparing the rest of the recipe.

STIR-FRIED RICE NOODLES WITH VEGETABLES

V

45

Rice noodles are also called cellophane noodles, or "bihon." The dried noodles are soaked in cold water to soften, then drained before using.

4 main-dish servings (about 1½ cups each)

1 package (8 ounces) rice noodles

1 cup each: cut green beans, cubed yellow summer squash

½ cup each: thinly sliced celery, red bell pepper

4 green onions, thinly sliced

1 tablespoon finely chopped fresh gingerroot

1 tablespoon canola oil

2 cups shredded napa cabbage

1 cup reduced-sodium vegetable broth

2 tablespoons dry sherry (optional)

2–3 teaspoons light soy sauce

½–1 teaspoon Szechuan chili sauce

Per Serving:
Calories: 161
% of calories from fat: 20
Fat (gm): 3.8
Saturated fat (gm): 0.5
Cholesterol (mg): 0
Sodium (mg): 137
Protein (gm): 4.2
Carbohydrate (gm): 29.4

Exchanges:
Milk: 0.0
Vegetable: 1.0
Fruit: 0.0
Bread: 1.5
Meat: 0.0
Fat: 0.5

1. Place noodles in large bowl; pour cold water over to cover. Let stand until noodles separate and are soft, about 15 minutes; drain.

2. Stir-fry green beans, squash, celery, bell pepper, green onions, and gingerroot in oil in large wok or skillet until tender, 8 to 10 minutes. Add cabbage and stir-fry 1 minute. Stir in noodles and remaining ingredients. Heat to boiling; reduce heat and simmer, uncovered, until noodles have absorbed all liquid, about 5 minutes.

CHINESE NOODLES WITH SWEET POTATOES AND SNOW PEAS

O

Fresh Chinese noodles and oriental flavors make this pasta dish special.

45

4 main-dish servings

3 cups peeled, cubed, (½-inch) sweet potatoes

¾ cup diagonally sliced green onions

3 teaspoons minced garlic

1–2 teaspoons minced gingerroot

3 cups diagonally halved snow peas

½ cup chopped red bell pepper

¾ cup canned, reduced-sodium vegetable broth

1–2 teaspoons reduced-sodium tamari soy sauce

1½ teaspoons cornstarch

Salt and pepper, to taste

1 package (12 ounces) fresh Chinese egg noodles, cooked, warm

1–2 teaspoons toasted sesame seeds

Per Serving:
Calories: 447
% of calories from fat: 3
Fat (gm): 1.7
Saturated fat (gm): 0.3
Cholesterol (mg): 0
Sodium (mg): 108
Protein (gm): 9.1
Carbohydrate (gm): 100.8

Exchanges:
Milk: 0.0
Vegetable: 1.0
Fruit: 0.0
Bread: 6.0
Meat: 0.0
Fat: 0.0

1. Stir-fry potatoes, green onions, garlic, and gingerroot in lightly greased wok or large skillet 2 to 3 minutes; cook, covered, over low heat until potatoes are almost tender, 10 to 12 minutes, stirring occasionally. Add snow peas and bell pepper; stir-fry over medium heat until peas are crisp-tender, about 5 minutes.

2. Add combined vegetable broth, soy sauce, and cornstarch to wok and heat to boiling. Boil, stirring, until thickened, about 1 minute. Season to taste with salt and pepper. Serve with noodles and sprinkle with sesame seeds.

45-MINUTE PREP TIP: Begin cooking the noodles before preparing the rest of the recipe.

PASTA PEPERONATA

V

For a roasted version of this recipe, see Roasted Peperonata (p. 209).

45

4 main-dish servings

1½ each: sliced red, green, and yellow bell peppers

3 medium onions, sliced

1 large red onion, sliced

8 cloves garlic, minced

3 tablespoons each: olive oil, water

1 teaspoon sugar

Salt and pepper, to taste

8 ounces spaghetti, cooked, warm

¼ cup (1 ounce) grated Parmesan cheese

Per Serving:
Calories: 426
% of calories from fat: 25
Fat (gm): 11.8
Saturated fat (gm): 1.6
Cholesterol (mg): 0
Sodium (mg): 8
Protein (gm): 11.1
Carbohydrate (gm): 70.3

Exchanges:
Milk: 0.0
Vegetable: 3.0
Fruit: 0.0
Bread: 3.5
Meat: 0.0
Fat: 2.5

1. Sauté peppers, onions, and garlic in oil in large skillet 2 to 3 minutes. Add water; cook, covered, over medium to medium-high heat until soft, 2 to 3 minutes. Stir in sugar; cook, uncovered, over medium-low heat until mixture is very soft and browned, about 20 minutes. Season to taste with salt and pepper. Toss with spaghetti; sprinkle with cheese if desired.

45-MINUTE PREP TIP: Begin cooking the spaghetti before preparing the rest of the recipe.

PASTA WITH GREENS, RAISINS, AND PINE NUTS

V

45

Radicchio, escarole, curly endive, kale, or mustard greens can be substituted for the brightly colored oriental kale in this sweet-and-bitter Italian favorite.

4 main-dish servings

4 each: sliced medium onions, minced cloves garlic

1 tablespoon olive oil

1 teaspoon sugar

12 ounces oriental kale leaves, torn

⅓ cup dark raisins

½ cup reduced-sodium vegetable broth

Salt and pepper, to taste

8 ounces whole wheat spaghetti, or linguine, cooked, warm

2 tablespoons pine nuts, or slivered almonds

Per Serving:
Calories: 391
% of calories from fat: 17
Fat (gm): 8
Saturated fat (gm): 0.9
Cholesterol (mg): 0.0
Sodium (mg): 127
Protein (gm): 13
Carbohydrate (gm): 75

Exchanges:
Milk: 0.0
Vegetable: 0.0
Fruit: 0.0
Bread: 4.0
Meat: 0.0
Fat: 1.0

1. Sauté onions and garlic in oil in large skillet until tender, 3 to 5 minutes. Stir in sugar; cook over low heat until onions are golden,

10 to 15 minutes, stirring occasionally. Stir in kale, raisins, and broth; cook, covered, over low heat until kale is wilted, about 10 minutes. Season to taste with salt and pepper. Serve over spaghetti and toss; sprinkle with pine nuts.

45-MINUTE PREP TIP: Begin cooking the spaghetti before preparing the rest of the recipe.

"LITTLE EARS" WITH ARTICHOKE HEARTS, MUSHROOMS, AND PEPPERS

L

45

Because of their shape, orecchiette is named "little ears." Other pasta shapes such as cappelletti (little hats), farfalle (bow ties), or rotini (corkscrews) can be substituted.

4 main-dish servings

4 ounces shiitake, or cremini, mushrooms, sliced

1 each: coarsely chopped red and yellow bell pepper

4 cloves garlic, minced

2 teaspoons olive oil, or canola oil

½ can (15-ounce size) quartered artichoke hearts, rinsed, drained

Salt and pepper, to taste

3 cups (12 ounces) orecchiette, cooked, warm

¼ cup (1 ounce) crumbled feta cheese

2 tablespoons coarsely chopped walnuts

Per Serving:
Calories: 470
% of calories from fat: 18
Fat (gm): 9.7
Saturated fat (gm): 3.1
Cholesterol (mg): 14.1
Sodium (mg): 233
Protein (gm): 17.1
Carbohydrate (gm): 80.4

Exchanges:
Milk: 0.0
Vegetable: 2.0
Fruit: 0.0
Bread: 4.0
Meat: 0.5
Fat: 2.0

1. Sauté mushrooms, bell peppers, and garlic in oil in large skillet until tender, 3 to 5 minutes. Add artichoke hearts and cook until hot, 3 to 4 minutes. Season to taste with salt and pepper. Toss with pasta; sprinkle with feta cheese and walnuts.

45-MINUTE PREP TIP: Begin cooking the orecchiette before preparing the rest of the recipe.

MAFALDE WITH GARBANZO BEANS, TOMATOES, AND CROUTONS

O

This easy-to-make dish has many flavor and color contrasts.

45

4 main-dish servings

½ cup each: chopped onion, poblano chili, or green bell pepper
1 teaspoon minced garlic
1 can (15½ ounces) garbanzo beans, rinsed, drained
2 cups seeded, chopped Italian plum tomatoes
¼ cup each: chopped basil leaves, fat-free Italian salad dressing
8 ounces mafalde, or other flat pasta, cooked, warm
1 ½ cups (½ recipe) Italian-Style Croutons (see p. 560)
Grated fat-free Parmesan cheese, as garnish

Per Serving:
Calories: 397
% of calories from fat: 9
Fat (gm): 3.9
Saturated fat (gm): 0.6
Cholesterol (mg): 0
Sodium (mg): 717
Protein (gm): 14.8
Carbohydrate (gm): 76.3

Exchanges:
Milk: 0.0
Vegetable: 2.0
Fruit: 0.0
Bread: 4.5
Meat: 0.0
Fat: 0.5

1. Sauté poblano chili, onion, and garlic in lightly greased medium skillet until tender, 5 to 8 minutes. Add beans and cook, covered, over medium heat until hot, 3 to 4 minutes. Remove from heat and stir in tomatoes, basil, and salad dressing. Toss with pasta and croutons. Serve with Parmesan cheese.

45-MINUTE PREP TIP: Begin cooking the mafalde before preparing the rest of the recipe.

MAFALDE WITH SWEET POTATOES AND KALE

L

Sweet potatoes and kale add peak nutrition to this pasta dish. For an added nutritional boost, use whole wheat pasta.

45

4 main-dish servings

2 medium onions, each cut into 8 wedges, halved
3 cloves garlic, minced
2 medium sweet potatoes, peeled, cubed (¾-inch)
4 cups sliced kale, or Swiss chard
½ cup water
8 ounces mafalde, cooked, warm
2 tablespoons grated fat-free Parmesan cheese

Per Serving:
Calories: 338
% of calories from fat: 4
Fat (gm): 1.5
Saturated fat (gm): 0.2
Cholesterol (mg): 0
Sodium (mg): 51
Protein (gm): 11.8
Carbohydrate (gm): 69.5

Exchanges:
Milk: 0.0
Vegetable: 2.0
Fruit: 0.0
Bread: 4.0
Meat: 0.0
Fat: 0.0

1. Sauté onions and garlic in lightly greased large skillet 2 to 3 minutes. Add potatoes, kale, and water; heat to boiling. Reduce heat and simmer, covered, until kale and potatoes are tender and water absorbed, 10 to 12 minutes. Toss with pasta and cheese.

45-MINUTE PREP TIP: Begin cooking the mafalde before preparing the rest of the recipe.

PASTA FROM PESCIA

L

45

A hearty dish from the Tuscany region of Italy — any root vegetable you enjoy can be used in place of the potatoes.

4 main-dish servings

3 cups thinly sliced cabbage

1½ cups halved Brussels sprouts

2 medium carrots, diagonally sliced

2 cloves garlic, minced

½ teaspoon dried sage leaves

⅓ cup reduced-sodium vegetable broth

8 small new potatoes, unpeeled, cooked, halved

2 tablespoons grated Parmesan cheese

Salt and pepper, to taste

8 ounces rigatoni, or ziti, cooked, warm

Per Serving:
Calories: 486
% of calories from fat: 5
Fat (gm): 2.5
Saturated fat (gm): 0.9
Cholesterol (mg): 2.5
Sodium (mg): 144
Protein (gm): 16.9
Carbohydrate (gm): 102.3

Exchanges:
Milk: 0.0
Vegetable: 3.0
Fruit: 0.0
Bread: 6.0
Meat: 0.0
Fat: 0.0

1. Heat cabbage, Brussels sprouts, carrots, garlic, sage, and broth to boiling in large skillet. Reduce heat and simmer, covered, until cabbage is wilted, about 5 minutes. Add potatoes and cook, uncovered, until liquid is gone and cabbage is lightly browned, about 5 minutes. Stir in cheese; season to taste with salt and pepper. Toss with pasta.

45-MINUTE PREP TIP: Begin cooking the rigatoni before preparing the rest of the recipe.

PASTA WITH CABBAGE AND POTATOES

L

A nourishing entrée, perfect for cool-weather meals.

45

6 main-dish servings

6 cups thinly sliced cabbage

3 cups cubed, peeled Idaho potatoes (½-inch)

3 cloves garlic, minced

1 teaspoon each: dried rosemary and sage leaves

⅓ cup dry white wine, or vegetable broth

Salt and pepper, to taste

12 ounces pappardelle, or other wide pasta, cooked, warm

¼ cup (1 ounce) grated Parmesan cheese

Per Serving:
Calories: 349
% of calories from fat: 7
Fat (gm): 2.6
Saturated fat (gm): 1
Cholesterol (mg): 3.3
Sodium (mg): 279
Protein (gm): 11.9
Carbohydrate (gm): 67.9

Exchanges:
Milk: 0.0
Vegetable: 2.0
Fruit: 0.0
Bread: 4.0
Meat: 0.0
Fat: 0.0

1. Combine cabbage, potatoes, garlic, herbs, and wine in large skillet; heat to boiling. Cook, covered, over medium heat until potatoes are almost tender 8 to10 minutes; cook, uncovered, until potatoes are tender and excess liquid is gone, about 5 minutes, stirring occasionally. Season to taste with salt and pepper. Toss with pasta; sprinkle with Parmesan cheese.

45-MINUTE PREP TIP: Begin cooking the pappardelle before preparing the rest of the recipe.

ROTINI AND BEANS NIÇOISE

o *Italian green beans are sometimes called Romano, or flat, beans.*

45 **6 main-dish servings**

½ cup chopped shallots

2 cups chopped Italian plum tomatoes

1 teaspoon minced garlic

2 tablespoons drained capers

½ teaspoon dried tarragon leaves

2 teaspoons margarine, or butter

2 cups diagonally sliced Italian, or regular, green
 beans, cooked

1 can (13¼ ounces) baby lima beans, rinsed, drained

1 can (15 ounces) cannellini beans, rinsed, drained

4 cups cooked rotini, or other-shaped pasta, warm

Salt and pepper, to taste

Grated fat-free Parmesan cheese, as garnish

Per Serving:
Calories: 265
% of calories from fat: 7
Fat (gm): 2.4
Saturated fat (gm): 0.4
Cholesterol (mg): 0
Sodium (mg): 430
Protein (gm): 13.8
Carbohydrate (gm): 53.9

Exchanges:
Milk: 0.0
Vegetable: 2.0
Fruit: 0.0
Bread: 3.0
Meat: 0.0
Fat: 0.0

1. Sauté shallots, tomatoes, garlic, capers, and tarragon in margarine in large skillet 2 to 3 minutes; cook, covered, over medium heat until tomatoes are wilted, 3 to 5 minutes. Stir in beans; cook, covered, until hot, about 5 minutes. Stir in rotini; season to taste with salt and pepper. Sprinkle lightly with Parmesan cheese.

45-MINUTE PREP TIP: Begin cooking the rotini before preparing the rest of the recipe.

RIGATONI WITH VEGETARIAN SAUSAGE AND FENNEL PESTO

v *The aromatic flavor of fennel makes this dish very special!*

6 main-dish servings

1 package (12¾ ounces) vegetarian Italian-style sausages, crumbled

1½ cups thinly sliced fennel bulb, or celery

1 cup chopped onion

2 cloves garlic, minced

1 can (8 ounces) reduced-sodium whole tomatoes, drained, chopped

Fennel Pesto (see p. 606)

12 ounces rigatoni, or other tube pasta, cooked, warm

1. Sauté vegetarian sausage, fennel, onion, and garlic in lightly greased medium skillet until onion is tender, 5 to 8 minutes. Stir in tomatoes and Fennel Pesto. Heat to boiling; reduce heat and simmer, covered, until fennel is tender, about 15 minutes. Toss with pasta.

Per Serving:
Calories: 447
% of calories from fat: 26
Fat (gm): 12.8
Saturated fat (gm): 1.7
Cholesterol (mg): 0
Sodium (mg): 372
Protein (gm): 26.1
Carbohydrate (gm): 58

Exchanges:
Milk: 0.0
Vegetable: 2.0
Fruit: 0.0
Bread: 3.0
Meat: 2.0
Fat: 1.5

POTATO GNOCCHI WITH SAGE CREAM

L

Fat-free half-and-half is the secret to the rich creaminess of the sauce.

45 **6 main-dish servings**

2 cups fat-free half-and-half, or fat-free milk
16–20 medium sage leaves, thinly sliced, or 1 teaspoon dried sage leaves
2 tablespoons all-purpose flour
½ teaspoon ground nutmeg
¾ cup water, divided
1 cup chopped onion
2 teaspoons margarine, or butter
4 cups small broccoflower, or broccoli florets
1 package (16 ounces) potato gnocchi, cooked, warm
Salt and pepper, to taste
Shredded Parmesan cheese, as garnish

Per Serving:
Calories: 263
% of calories from fat: 2
Fat (gm): 0.6
Saturated fat (gm): 0.2
Cholesterol (mg): 0.9
Sodium (mg): 150
Protein (gm): 13.4
Carbohydrate (gm): 52.4

Exchanges:
Milk: 0.0
Vegetable: 2.0
Fruit: 0.0
Bread: 2.5
Meat: 0.0
Fat: 0.0

1. Heat half-and-half and sage (if using dried sage, tie leaves in small cheesecloth bag) to boiling in medium saucepan; reduce heat and simmer, covered, 10 minutes. Strain, discarding sage. Return half-and-half to saucepan and heat to boiling; whisk in combined flour, nutmeg, and ¼ cup water. Boil, whisking, until thickened, about 1 minute; keep warm.

2. Sauté onion in margarine in large skillet 2 to 3 minutes; add broccoflower and remaining ½ cup water and heat to boiling.

Reduce heat and simmer, covered, until broccoflower is crisp-tender, about 5 minutes; drain. Add sauce and gnocchi and cook 2 to 3 minutes; season to taste with salt and pepper. Sprinkle with cheese.

45-MINUTE PREP TIP: Begin cooking the gnocchi before preparing the rest of the recipe.

SPINACH GNOCCHI WITH GORGONZOLA SAUCE

LO *See the index for other delicious sauces to serve with the gnocchi.*

6 main-dish servings

½ cup chopped onion

2 cloves garlic, minced

3 packages (10 ounces each) frozen chopped spinach, thawed

1 cup all-purpose flour, divided

1 cup reduced-fat ricotta cheese

½ cup grated fat-free Parmesan cheese

1 egg

¼ teaspoon ground nutmeg

½ teaspoon each: salt, pepper

Gorgonzola Sauce (see p. 592)

Per Serving:
Calories: 314
% of calories from fat: 30
Fat (gm): 10
Saturated fat (gm): 4
Cholesterol (mg): 57
Sodium (mg): 616
Protein (gm): 19
Carbohydrate (gm): 33

Exchanges:
Milk: 0.0
Vegetable: 0.0
Fruit: 0.0
Bread: 2.0
Meat: 2.0
Fat: 1.5

1. Sauté onion and garlic in lightly greased large skillet until tender, about 5 minutes; stir in spinach. Cook over medium heat until spinach mixture is quite dry, about 8 minutes, stirring frequently; cool.

2. Stir ⅔ cup flour into spinach in bowl. Stir in cheeses, egg, nutmeg, salt, and pepper; cool. Spread remaining ⅓ cup flour on a plate. Drop 2 tablespoons spinach mixture into flour; roll into ball. Repeat with remaining spinach mixture, making 18 gnocchi. Add gnocchi to 3 quarts boiling water in large saucepan. Reduce heat and simmer, uncovered, until gnocchi float to surface, about 10 minutes. Toss with Gorgonzola Sauce.

MOLDED CAPELLINI CARBONARA

Thin spaghetti or linguine can be substituted for the angel hair pasta. The center of the mold can be filled with a mixture of vegetables, such as the asparagus and tomato mixture in Penne with Asparagus and Plum Tomatoes (see p. 235).

4 main-dish servings

¼ cup minced shallot

1 teaspoon minced garlic

1 cup seeded, chopped, Italian plum tomatoes

¼ teaspoon crushed red pepper

½ teaspoon dried oregano leaves

Salt and pepper, to taste

8 ounces capellini (angel hair pasta), cooked

3 eggs, lightly beaten

Per Serving:
Calories: 282
% of calories from fat: 16
Fat (gm): 5
Saturated fat (gm): 1
Cholesterol (mg): 157
Sodium (mg): 56
Protein (gm): 12
Carbohydrate (gm): 46

Exchanges:
Milk: 0.0
Vegetable: 0.0
Fruit: 0.0
Bread: 3.0
Meat: 1.0
Fat: 0.0

1. Sauté shallot and garlic in lightly greased skillet until tender, 3 to 4 minutes. Add tomatoes, crushed red pepper, and oregano. Cook, covered, over medium heat until tomatoes soften, about 5 minutes; season to taste with salt and pepper. Combine with pasta and eggs and spoon into greased 6-cup ring mold. Bake, uncovered, at 350 degrees until set, about 20 minutes. Invert onto serving plate.

45-MINUTE PREP TIP: Begin cooking the capellini before preparing the rest of the recipe.

SHELLS STUFFED WITH SPINACH AND TOFU

L

45

Firm tofu substitutes for usual ricotta cheese in this deliciously low-fat dish. Marinara Sauce or Tomato Sauce with Mushrooms and Sherry (see pp. 582, 585) can be substituted for the Fresh Tomato-Basil Sauce.

4 main-dish servings (5 shells each)

1½ cups chopped onions

6 cloves garlic, minced

1 package (10 ounces) baby spinach

¾ cup finely chopped parsley

1½ teaspoons dried basil leaves

½ package (14-ounce size) firm tofu, finely chopped

1½ cups (6 ounces) shredded fat-free
   mozzarella cheese

2 tablespoons grated fat-free Parmesan cheese

20 jumbo pasta shells (6 ounces), cooked, warm

2 cups (½ recipe) Fresh Tomato-Basil Sauce
   (see p. 584)

Per Serving:
Calories: 395
% of calories from fat: 9
Fat (gm): 4
Saturated fat (gm): 0.3
Cholesterol (mg): 0
Sodium (mg): 579
Protein (gm): 32.1
Carbohydrate (gm): 58.6

Exchanges:
Milk: 0.0
Vegetable: 3.0
Fruit: 0.0
Bread: 2.5
Meat: 2.5
Fat: 0.0

1. Sauté onions and garlic in lightly greased skillet until transparent, 3 to 5 minutes. Add spinach, parsley and basil and cook, covered, over medium heat until spinach is wilted, 3 to 5 minutes. Remove from heat and cool slightly; stir in tofu and cheeses.

2. Stuff each shell with about 3 tablespoons cheese mixture. Arrange shells in baking pan and spoon Fresh Tomato-Basil Sauce over. Bake at 350 degrees, loosely covered, until hot, 20 to 25 minutes.

45-MINUTE PREP TIP: Begin cooking the pasta shells before preparing the rest of the recipe.

VEGETABLE MANICOTTI WITH CREAMED SPINACH SAUCE

L *Three-Onion Sauce (see p. 592) is also an excellent accompaniment for this dish.*

4 main-dish servings (3 each)

½ cup chopped onion

3 cloves garlic, minced

2 cups loosely packed, chopped spinach leaves

½ cup each: chopped zucchini, yellow summer squash

1 teaspoon each: dried basil and oregano leaves

¾ cup fat-free ricotta cheese

Salt and pepper, to taste

1 package (8 ounces) manicotti, cooked, room temperature

Creamed Spinach Sauce (see p. 593)

Per Serving:
Calories: 476
% of calories from fat: 20
Fat (gm): 10.9
Saturated fat (gm): 3.6
Cholesterol (mg): 13.5
Sodium (mg): 431
Protein (gm): 26.1
Carbohydrate (gm): 72.4

Exchanges:
Milk: 1.0
Vegetable: 2.0
Fruit: 0.0
Bread: 3.0
Meat: 1.0
Fat: 1.5

1. Sauté onion and garlic in lightly greased large skillet until tender, about 3 minutes. Add remaining vegetables; sauté until tender, 5 to 8 minutes. Stir in herbs and cook 2 minutes longer. Stir in cheese; season to taste with salt and pepper.

2. Spoon about 3 tablespoons cheese and vegetable mixture into each manicotti; arrange in baking pan and spoon Creamed Spinach Sauce over. Bake at 350 degrees, loosely covered, until manicotti are hot and sauce is bubbly, 35 to 40 minutes.

MUSHROOM-BROCCOLI MANICOTTI

L *Any pasta that is going to be filled and baked should be cooked only until* al
dente *so the completed dish is not overcooked.*

4 main-dish servings (3 manicotti each)

4 shallots, or green onions, chopped

2 cloves garlic, minced

2 teaspoons dried basil leaves

1 teaspoon dried marjoram leaves

2 cups each: sliced mushrooms, finely chopped,
   cooked broccoli

1 cup reduced-fat ricotta cheese

¼ teaspoon each: salt, pepper

1 package (8 ounces) manicotti, cooked,
   room temperature

Tomato Sauce with Mushrooms and Sherry
   (see p. 585)

Per Serving:
Calories: 394
% of calories from fat: 17
Fat (gm): 7.8
Saturated fat (gm): 0.8
Cholesterol (mg): 7.9
Sodium (mg): 665
Protein (gm): 19.2
Carbohydrate (gm): 63.4

Exchanges:
Milk: 0.0
Vegetable: 4.0
Fruit: 0.0
Bread: 3.0
Meat: 0.0
Fat: 1.5

1. Cook shallots, garlic, herbs, and mushrooms in lightly greased
large skillet over medium heat, covered, until mushrooms release
juices, 3 to 5 minutes. Cook, uncovered, over medium to medium-
high heat, until liquid is evaporated, about 10 minutes. Stir in
broccoli, cheese, salt, and pepper.

2. Spoon about 3 tablespoons vegetable-cheese mixture into each
manicotti; arrange in baking pan and spoon Tomato Sauce with
Mushrooms and Sherry over. Bake at 350 degrees, loosely covered,
until manicotti are hot and sauce is bubbly, 30 to 35 minutes.

ARTICHOKE TORTELLINI BAKE

LO

45

◊

Refrigerated fresh tortellini and ravioli are convenient to have on hand for speedy meals — use any favorite in this dish.

4 main-dish servings

2 cups sliced mushrooms

1 small onion, sliced

1 teaspoon minced garlic

2 tablespoons flour

1 cup fat-free milk

Salt and cayenne pepper, to taste

1 can (14 ounces) artichoke hearts, drained

1 package (9 ounces) mozzarella-garlic tortellini, cooked, warm

½ cup (2 ounces) shredded reduced-fat Italian 6-cheese blend

1–2 tablespoons seasoned dry bread crumbs

Per Serving:
Calories: 267
% of calories from fat: 21
Fat (gm): 6.4
Saturated fat (gm): 3.4
Cholesterol (mg): 29.1
Sodium (mg): 523
Protein (gm): 16.9
Carbohydrate (gm): 37.4

Exchanges:
Milk: 0.0
Vegetable: 1.0
Fruit: 0.0
Bread: 2.0
Meat: 1.0
Fat: 0.5

1. Sauté mushrooms, onion, and garlic in lightly greased large saucepan until tender, about 5 minutes. Stir in flour; cook 1 to 2 minutes. Stir in milk and heat to boiling; boil, stirring, until thickened, 1 to 2 minutes. Season to taste with salt and cayenne pepper. Stir in artichokes, tortellini, and cheese. Spoon into greased 1½-quart casserole; sprinkle with bread crumbs. Bake, uncovered, at 375 degrees until bubbly, about 15 minutes.

45-MINUTE PREP TIP: Begin cooking the tortellini before preparing the rest of the recipe.

TORTELLINI AND 2-BEAN VEGETABLE SOUP

LO

45

Make this soup a day or two in advance so flavors can develop; add the tortellini when reheating.

6 main-dish servings (about 1¼ cups each)

½ cup sliced leek (white part only), or green onions

3 cloves garlic, minced

2 tablespoons finely chopped cilantro leaves

2 teaspoons each: dried basil, and oregano leaves

2 cans (14½ ounces each) vegetable broth

1 cup water

1 cup each: quartered Brussels sprouts, sliced
    yellow summer squash, chopped tomato

1 can (15 ounces) each: black-eyed peas,
    dark red kidney beans, rinsed, drained

½ package (9-ounce size) fresh reduced-fat
    cheese tortellini

Salt and pepper, to taste

Per Serving:
Calories: 160
% of calories from fat: 5.5
Fat (gm): 1.0
Saturated fat (gm): 0.1
Cholesterol (mg): 0.4
Sodium (mg): 777
Protein (gm): 8.1
Carbohydrate (gm): 30.1

Exchanges:
Milk: 0.0
Vegetable: 0.0
Fruit: 0.0
Bread: 2.0
Meat: 0.0
Fat: 0.0

1. Sauté leek, garlic, and herbs in lightly greased large saucepan until leek is tender, 3 to 5 minutes. Add broth, water, vegetables, beans, and tortellini; heat to boiling. Reduce heat and simmer, covered, until vegetables are tender and tortellini are *al dente*, about 10 minutes. Season to taste with salt and pepper.

CURRIED TORTELLINI WITH BEANS AND SQUASH

O

Coconut milk adds a subtle Asian flavor to this colorful pasta combination.

6 main-dish servings

1⅓ cups coarsely chopped onions

⅔ cup red bell pepper

2 teaspoons minced garlic

1 teaspoon curry powder

2 cups diagonally sliced Italian, or regular, green beans

2 cups julienned, peeled, seeded butternut, or acorn, squash

¼ cup water

1 cup reduced-fat coconut milk

2 packages (9 ounces each) mushroom, or herb, tortellini, cooked, warm

Salt and pepper, to taste

3 tablespoons chopped cilantro

Per Serving:
Calories: 269
% of calories from fat: 25
Fat (gm): 8.3
Saturated fat (gm): 3
Cholesterol (mg): 30
Sodium (mg): 220
Protein (gm): 11.4
Carbohydrate (gm): 44.1

1. Sauté onions, bell pepper, garlic, and curry powder in lightly greased large skillet until tender, onions are tender, 3 to 4 minutes. Add beans, squash, and water; heat to boiling. Reduce heat and simmer, covered, until vegetables are tender and water absorbed, 6 to 8 minutes. Stir in coconut milk and tortellini; cook until hot, 2 to 3 minutes. Season to taste with salt and pepper; sprinkle with cilantro.

Exchanges:
Milk: 0.0
Vegetable: 2.0
Fruit: 0.0
Bread: 2.0
Meat: 0.0
Fat: 1.5

45-MINUTE PREP TIP: Begin cooking the tortellini before preparing the rest of the recipe.

20-MINUTE RAVIOLI

0

Use any favorite kind of fresh ravioli in this quick and nutritious dish.

45

4 main-dish servings

¾ cup chopped onion

2 teaspoons minced garlic

1 tablespoon olive oil

¾ cup canned kidney beans, rinsed, drained

1 package (9 ounces) sun-dried tomato ravioli, cooked, warm

1 large tomato, cubed

½ teaspoon dried thyme leaves

Salt and pepper, to taste

Per Serving:
Calories: 234
% of calories from fat: 35
Fat (gm): 9.4
Saturated fat (gm): 3.8
Cholesterol (mg): 32.8
Sodium (mg): 320
Protein (gm): 9.5
Carbohydrate (gm): 29.1

Exchanges:
Milk: 0.0
Vegetable: 0.0
Fruit: 0.0
Bread: 2.0
Meat: 1.0
Fat: 1.0

1. Sauté onion and garlic in oil in large skillet until tender, about 5 minutes. Stir in beans, ravioli, tomato, and thyme; cook until mixture is hot, about 5 minutes. Season to taste with salt and pepper.

45-MINUTE PREP TIP: Begin cooking the ravioli before preparing the rest of the recipe.

WINE-GLAZED RAVIOLI AND ASPARAGUS

A reduction of vegetable broth, white wine, and orange juice creates an elegant and fragrant sauce for pasta.

4 main-dish servings

2 cups reduced-sodium vegetable broth

1 cup each: dry white wine, orange juice

¼ teaspoon crushed red pepper

1 pound asparagus, cut into 1-inch pieces

1 package (9 ounces) mushroom ravioli, cooked, warm

2 tablespoons margarine

Salt and pepper, to taste

Per Serving:
Calories: 290
% of calories from fat: 32
Fat (gm): 10.6
Saturated fat (gm): 3.6
Cholesterol (mg): 26.8
Sodium (mg): 254
Protein (gm): 8.2
Carbohydrate (gm): 33

Exchanges:
Milk: 0.0
Vegetable: 1.0
Fruit: 0.0
Bread: 2.0
Meat: 0.0
Fat: 1.5

1. Heat vegetable broth, white wine, orange juice, and red pepper to boiling in large skillet; boil, uncovered, 10 minutes or until liquid is reduced to about ½ cup. Add asparagus and cook, covered, over medium heat until crisp-tender, 3 to 4 minutes. Add ravioli and margarine; cook 2 to 3 minutes longer. Season to taste with salt and pepper.

45-MINUTE PREP TIP: Begin cooking the ravioli before preparing the rest of the recipe.

SWEET POTATO RAVIOLI WITH CURRY SAUCE

A light curry-flavored sauce is a delicate accompaniment to this unusual ravioli.

4 main-dish servings (4 each)

1 cup mashed, cooked, sweet potatoes

2 small cloves garlic, minced

½–¾ teaspoon ground ginger

Salt and pepper, to taste

32 wonton wrappers

Curry Sauce (see p. 594)

Per Serving:
Calories: 323
% of calories from fat: 4
Fat (gm): 1.5
Saturated fat (gm): 0.3
Cholesterol (mg): 8
Sodium (mg): 387
Protein (gm): 8.9
Carbohydrate (gm): 65.7

Exchanges:
Milk: 0.0
Vegetable: 0.5
Fruit: 0.0
Bread: 4.0
Meat: 0.0
Fat: 0.0

1. Mix sweet potatoes, garlic, and ginger; season to taste with salt and pepper. Spoon about 1 tablespoon mixture onto wonton wrapper; brush edges of wrapper with water. Top with second wonton wrapper and press edges together to seal. Repeat with remaining wonton wrappers and potato mixture.

2. Add 4 to 6 ravioli to 2 quarts boiling water in large saucepan; reduce heat and simmer, uncovered, until ravioli float to surface and are *al dente*, 3 to 4 minutes; remove with slotted spoon. Repeat with remaining ravioli. Serve with Curry Sauce.

HERBED CHEESE RAVIOLI WITH WILD MUSHROOM SAUCE

LO

4 main-dish servings (4 each)

¼ package (8-ounce size) vegetarian Italian-style sausage patties, crumbled

1 small onion, minced

2 cloves garlic, minced

1 cup reduced-fat ricotta cheese

1 teaspoon dried rosemary leaves

32 wonton wrappers

Wild Mushroom Sauce (see p. 596)

Per Serving:
Calories: 313
% of calories from fat: 26.2
Fat (gm): 9.1
Saturated fat (gm): 3.5
Cholesterol (mg): 27
Sodium (mg): 466
Protein (gm): 13.2
Carbohydrate (gm): 42.9

Exchanges:
Milk: 0.0
Vegetable: 0.0
Fruit: 0.0
Bread: 3.0
Meat: 1.0
Fat: 1.0

1. Sauté vegetarian sausage, onion, and garlic in lightly greased small skillet until onion is tender, about 5 minutes. Remove from heat and mix in ricotta cheese and rosemary.

2. Place about 1 tablespoon cheese mixture on wonton wrapper; brush edges of wrapper with water. Top with a second wonton wrapper and press edges together to seal. Repeat with remaining wonton wrappers and cheese mixture.

3. Cook 4 to 6 ravioli in 2 quarts water in large saucepan; reduce heat and simmer, uncovered, until ravioli float to surface and are *al dente*, 3 to 4 minutes; remove with slotted spoon. Repeat with remaining ravioli. Serve with Wild Mushroom Sauce.

EGGPLANT RAVIOLI

LO

The ravioli are easily made with wonton wrappers. Assemble 2 to 3 hours ahead for convenience, and refrigerate in a single layer, covered with plastic wrap.

6 main-dish servings (4 each)

Eggplant Filling (recipe follows)
48 wonton wrappers
Fresh Tomato and Herb Sauce (see p. 584)

Per Serving:
Calories: 306
% of calories from fat: 10
Fat (gm): 3.6
Saturated fat (gm): 0.6
Cholesterol (mg): 8
Sodium (mg): 493
Protein (gm): 15.9
Carbohydrate (gm): 54.6

Exchanges:
Milk: 0.0
Vegetable: 3.0
Fruit: 0.0
Bread: 2.5
Meat: 1.0
Fat: 0.0

1. Place about 1½ tablespoons eggplant mixture on wonton wrapper; brush edges of wrapper with water. Top with second wonton wrapper and press edges together to seal. Repeat with remaining wonton wrappers and eggplant mixture.

2. Cook 4 to 6 ravioli in 2 quarts boiling water in large saucepan; reduce heat and simmer, uncovered, until ravioli float to the surface and are *al dente*, 3 to 4 minutes; remove with slotted spoon. Repeat with remaining ravioli. Serve with Fresh Tomato and Herb Sauce.

Eggplant Filling

Makes about 2 cups

½ cup each: minced onion, green bell pepper
2 teaspoons minced garlic
1 small eggplant, peeled, coarsely chopped
1 teaspoon dried Italian seasoning
½ cup water
1–2 teaspoons light brown sugar
1 teaspoon balsamic vinegar
½ cup (2 ounces) each: shredded fat-free mozzarella cheese, fat-free ricotta cheese
¼ cup (1 ounce) grated fat-free Parmesan cheese
Salt and pepper, to taste

1. Sauté onion, bell pepper, and garlic in lightly greased large skillet until tender, about 5 minutes. Add eggplant and sauté 1 to 2 minutes.

Stir in herbs and water; heat to boiling. Reduce heat and simmer, covered, until vegetables are tender, about 10 minutes. Stir in sugar and vinegar; cook, uncovered, until liquid is almost gone, about 5 minutes. Cool; stir in cheeses and season to taste with salt and pepper.

Variation

Eggplant Loaf with Simple Tomato Sauce — Make Eggplant Filling as above; spoon into greased 8 x 4-inch loaf pan. Bake, loosely covered, at 350 degrees until set, about 30 minutes. Loosen sides of loaf with sharp knife and unmold; serve with Simple Tomato Sauce (see p. 169).

FETA CHEESE AND SUN-DRIED TOMATO RAVIOLI

LO *Other sauces, such as Roasted Red Pepper Sauce, Many-Cloves Garlic Sauce, or Creamed Spinach Sauce (see pp. 590, 591, 593) are also excellent with these versatile ravioli.*

4 main-dish servings (4 each)

½ package (8-ounce size) fat-free cream cheese

¼ cup (1 ounce) crumbled fat-free feta cheese

1 ounce sun-dried tomatoes (not in oil), softened, chopped

½ teaspoon grated lemon zest

1 teaspoon dried oregano leaves

32 wonton wrappers

Mediterranean Tomato-Caper Sauce, warm (see p. 590)

Per Serving:
Calories: 327
% of calories from fat: 6
Fat (gm): 2.2
Saturated fat (gm): 0.9
Cholesterol (mg): 10.5
Sodium (mg): 728
Protein (gm): 15.3
Carbohydrate (gm): 61.4

Exchanges:
Milk: 0.0
Vegetable: 2.0
Fruit: 0.5
Bread: 3.0
Meat: 0.5
Fat: 0.0

1. Mix cheeses, tomatoes, lemon zest, and oregano. Spoon about 1 tablespoon cheese mixture on wonton wrapper; brush edges of wrapper with water. Top with second wonton wrapper and press edges together to seal. Repeat with remaining wonton wrappers and cheese mixture.

2. Cook ravioli in 2 quarts boiling water in large saucepan; reduce heat and simmer, uncovered, until ravioli float to the surface and are *al dente*, 3 to 4 minutes; remove with slotted spoon. Repeat with remaining ravioli. Serve with Mediterranean-Caper Sauce.

SQUASH AND MUSHROOM LASAGNE

L *A white sauce and tomato sauce are combined in this delicate lasagne.*

8 main-dish servings

1 cup sliced onion

1 tablespoon minced garlic

1 pound portobello, or cremini, mushrooms, sliced

½ cup dry white wine, or canned reduced-sodium
  vegetable broth

Salt and pepper, to taste

¼ cup finely chopped shallots, or green onions

2 teaspoons margarine, or butter

¼ cup all-purpose flour

1 teaspoon dried rosemary leaves

½ teaspoon dried thyme leaves

2 cups fat-free milk

4 cups jarred reduced-sodium spaghetti sauce

½ package (8-ounce size) fat-free cream cheese,
  cubed

¾ cup (3 ounces) grated fat-free Parmesan
  cheese, divided

12 lasagne noodles (10 ounces), cooked

1 pound winter yellow squash (acorn, butternut,
  Hubbard, etc.), peeled, thinly sliced

Per Serving:
Calories: 306
% of calories from fat: 14
Fat (gm): 4.8
Saturated fat (gm): 1
Cholesterol (mg): 4
Sodium (mg): 226
Protein (gm): 15
Carbohydrate (gm): 49.6

Exchanges:
Milk: 0.0
Vegetable: 1.0
Fruit: 0.0
Bread: 3.0
Meat: 1.0
Fat: 0.5

1. Sauté onion and garlic in lightly greased large skillet 3 to 4 minutes; add mushrooms and sauté 5 minutes. Add wine to skillet and heat to boiling; cook over medium heat until mixture is dry, about 5 minutes, stirring occasionally. Season to taste with salt and pepper.

2. Sauté shallots in margarine in medium saucepan until tender, 2 to 3 minutes. Stir in flour and herbs; cook 1 to 2 minutes, stirring constantly. Whisk in milk and heat to boiling; boil, whisking constantly, until thickened, about 1 minute. Mix in spaghetti sauce, cream cheese, and ½ cup Parmesan cheese; cook, stirring frequently, until sauce is hot and cream cheese melted, 5 to 7 minutes. Season to taste with salt and pepper.

3. Stir 1 cup sauce into mushroom mixture. Spread about ¾ cup remaining sauce in bottom of 13 x 9-inch baking pan; arrange 4 noodles in pan, overlapping edges. Spoon ½ of mushroom mixture and squash slices over noodles and spread with ¾ cup sauce. Repeat layers; top with layer of remaining 4 noodles and ¾ cup sauce. Sprinkle with remaining ¼ cup Parmesan cheese. Bake at 350 degrees, loosely covered, until noodles and squash are tender, 50 to 60 minutes. Let stand 10 minutes before serving.

ROASTED RED PEPPER AND SPINACH LASAGNE

For convenience, the recipe uses jarred roasted red peppers, but you can roast your own using the method in Roasted Red Pepper Sauce (see p. 590).

8 main-dish servings

1 cup chopped onion

2 teaspoons minced roasted garlic

¾ teaspoon each: dried marjoram and oregano leaves

3 cups fat-free milk, divided

¼ cup plus 2 tablespoons all-purpose flour

1 cup (4 ounces) grated fat-free Parmesan cheese

½ package (8-ounce size) fat-free cream cheese, cubed

⅔ cup finely chopped parsley

Salt and pepper, to taste

2 packages (10 ounces each) frozen, thawed, chopped spinach, very well drained

⅔ cup fat-free ricotta cheese

12 lasagne noodles (10 ounces), cooked

1 jar (15 ounces) roasted red peppers, drained, cut into 1-inch slices

1 cup (4 ounces) reduced-fat mozzarella cheese

Per Serving:
Calories: 261
% of calories from fat: 13
Fat (gm): 3.8
Saturated fat (gm): 1.7
Cholesterol (mg): 9.1
Sodium (mg): 386
Protein (gm): 21.4
Carbohydrate (gm): 36.8

Exchanges:
Milk: 0.5
Vegetable: 2.0
Fruit: 0.0
Bread: 1.5
Meat: 1.0
Fat: 0.0

1. Sauté onion, garlic, and herbs in lightly greased large saucepan until tender, 5 to 8 minutes; stir in herbs and cook 1 minute longer. Add 2 cups milk and heat to boiling. Mix remaining 1 cup milk and flour and whisk into boiling mixture; boil, whisking, until thickened, about 1 minute. Remove from heat; mix in Parmesan and cream cheese, and parsley, stirring until cream cheese is melted.

Season with salt and pepper. Mix spinach and ricotta cheese; season to taste with salt and pepper.

2. Spread ¾ cup sauce in bottom of 13 x 9-inch baking pan. Arrange 4 noodles in pan, overlapping edges. Top with ½ of the spinach mixture and red pepper slices; spread with generous 1 cup sauce. Repeat layers; top with remaining 4 noodles and spread with remaining 1¼ cups sauce. Sprinkle with mozzarella cheese. Bake at 350 degrees, loosely covered, until hot, about 45 minutes. Let stand 10 minutes before serving.

ARTICHOKE LASAGNE

L

The lasagne can be assembled up to a day in advance and refrigerated, covered. Bake as directed below, increasing baking time by 15 to 20 minutes.

8 main-dish servings

1½ cups each: shiitake mushrooms, chopped onions

1 cup chopped red bell pepper

2 teaspoons minced garlic

8 cups loosely packed baby spinach

2 packages (9 ounces each) frozen, thawed, artichoke hearts, cut into bite-sized pieces

Salt and pepper, to taste

3 cups fat-free milk, divided

¼ cup plus 2 tablespoons flour

1 cup (4 ounces) grated fat-free Parmesan cheese

½ package (8-ounce size) fat-free cream cheese, cubed

⅔ cup finely chopped parsley

1 teaspoon dried thyme leaves

1 teaspoon lemon juice

12 lasagne noodles (10 ounces), cooked

1 cup (4 ounces) shredded reduced-fat mozzarella cheese

Per Serving:
Calories: 278
% of calories from fat: 7
Fat (gm): 2.1
Saturated fat (gm): 0.2
Cholesterol (mg): 1.5
Sodium (mg): 438
Protein (gm): 22.5
Carbohydrate (gm): 46.4

Exchanges:
Milk: 0.0
Vegetable: 3.0
Fruit: 0.0
Bread: 2.0
Meat: 1.0
Fat: 0.0

1. Sauté mushrooms, onions, bell pepper, and garlic in lightly greased large skillet 3 minutes; add spinach and artichoke hearts. Cook, covered, over medium heat until spinach is wilted, about 5 minutes. Cook, uncovered, until mixture is dry. Remove from heat; season to taste with salt and pepper.

2. Heat 2 cups milk to boiling in large saucepan. Mix remaining 1 cup milk and flour; whisk into boiling milk. Boil, whisking, until thickened, about 1 minute. Remove from heat; mix in Parmesan and cream cheese, parsley, thyme, and lemon juice, stirring until cream cheese is melted. Season to taste with salt and pepper.

3. Spread 1 cup sauce in bottom of 13 x 9-inch baking pan; arrange 4 noodles in pan, overlapping edges. Spoon ½ of the artichoke mixture over noodles and spread with 1 cup sauce. Repeat layers; top with remaining 4 noodles and spread with 1 cup sauce. Sprinkle with mozzarella cheese. Bake at 350 degrees, loosely covered, until hot, about 45 minutes. Let stand 10 minutes before cutting.

SEVEN

Loaves, Patties,
and
Sandwiches

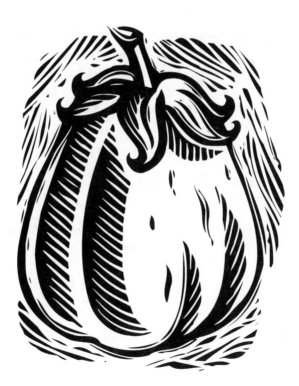

ORIENTAL LOAF

o *Stir-fry vegetables are a perfect accompaniment to this flavorful loaf.*

4 servings

1 cup textured vegetable protein

1 cup reduced-sodium vegetable broth

2 ½ cups cooked brown, or white, rice

¼ cup each: sliced green onions, water chestnuts

2 teaspoons each: minced gingerroot, chili sesame oil, reduced-sodium tamari soy sauce

1 clove garlic, minced

⅓–½ cup unseasoned dry bread crumbs

¼ cup all-purpose flour

½ teaspoon five-spice powder

Salt and pepper, to taste

1 egg

Per Serving:
Calories: 205
% of calories from fat: 19
Fat (gm): 4.5
Saturated fat (gm): 0.9
Cholesterol (mg): 53.3
Sodium (mg): 227
Protein (gm): 18.6
Carbohydrate (gm): 24.9

Exchanges:
Milk: 0.0
Vegetable: 0.0
Fruit: 0.0
Bread: 1.5
Meat: 2.0
Fat: 0.0

1. Combine vegetable protein and broth in bowl; let stand until broth is absorbed. 5 to 10 minutes. Mix in remaining ingredients, except salt, pepper, and egg. Season mixture to taste with salt and pepper; mix in egg. Pack into greased 7 x 4-inch loaf pan. Bake, uncovered, at 350 degrees 1 hour. Loosen sides of loaf with sharp knife and unmold.

MESQUITE-SMOKED TOFU AND BROWN RICE LOAF

o *If you should want to smoke your own tofu, see Mesquite-Smoked Tofu, p. 191. This mixture makes delicious burgers, too.*

6–8 servings

1 cup coarsely chopped broccoli

½ cup chopped onion

2 cloves garlic, minced

1½–2 teaspoons dried rosemary leaves

2 cups each: loosely packed chopped spinach, cooked brown rice

3 Italian plum tomatoes, coarsely chopped

6 ounces smoked tofu, finely chopped, or crumbled

¼ cup all-purpose flour

½ cup reduced-sodium vegetable broth

Salt and pepper, to taste

1 egg

Per Serving:
Calories: 145
% of calories from fat: 13
Fat (gm): 2.2
Saturated fat (gm): 0.4
Cholesterol (mg): 35.5
Sodium (mg): 69
Protein (gm): 6.8
Carbohydrate (gm): 25.9

1. Sauté broccoli, onion, garlic, and rosemary in lightly greased medium skillet until broccoli is crisp- tender, 8 to 10 minutes. Mix in remaining ingredients, except salt, pepper, and egg. Season to taste with salt and pepper; mix in egg. Pack into greased 9 x 5-inch loaf pan. Bake, uncovered, at 350 degrees 1 hour. Loosen sides of loaf with knife and unmold.

Exchanges:
Milk: 0.0
Vegetable: 2.0
Fruit: 0.0
Bread: 1.0
Meat: 0.5
Fat: 0.0

KASHA LOAF BAKED IN SQUASH HALVES

You'll enjoy this unique combination of flavors and textures, attractively served in squash halves.

4 servings

½ cup each: sliced celery, carrots

1 teaspoon minced jalapeño chili

1 cup each: cooked kasha (roasted buckwheat),
   corn bread stuffing crumbs

½ cup each: chopped dried apricots, pitted prunes

1 cup reduced-sodium vegetable broth

Salt and pepper, to taste

2 eggs, lightly beaten

2 small acorn squash, halved, seeded

Per Serving:
Calories: 319
% of calories from fat: 6
Fat (gm): 2.4
Saturated fat (gm): 0.6
Cholesterol (mg): 53.3
Sodium (mg): 196
Protein (gm): 9.6
Carbohydrate (gm): 72.1

Exchanges:
Milk: 0.0
Vegetable: 1.0
Fruit: 1.5
Bread: 2.5
Meat: 0.5
Fat: 0.0

1. Sauté celery, carrots, and jalapeño chili in lightly greased small skillet until tender, 5 to 8 minutes. Stir in kasha, stuffing crumbs, dried fruit, and broth; season to taste with salt and pepper. Mix in eggs. Spoon mixture into squash halves and place in baking pan; add 1-inch hot water to pan. Bake, covered, at 350 degrees until squash is fork-tender, about 1 hour.

STUFFED POBLANO CHILIES

LO

45

A south-of-the-border loaf baked inside one of Mexico's favorite chilies.
Poblano chilies can be very hot in flavor; sweet bell peppers may
be substituted.

4–6 servings

1 cup textured vegetable protein

½ cup corn bread stuffing crumbs

1¼ cups reduced-sodium vegetable broth

1 cup cooked brown rice

¾ cup each: shredded reduced-fat mozzarella cheese
   (3 ounces), whole-kernel corn, chopped zucchini

⅓ cup each: chopped red and green bell pepper

1–1½ teaspoons dried oregano leaves, minced
   jalapeno chili

½ teaspoon ground cumin

Salt and pepper, to taste

1 egg

6 large poblano chilies, halved lengthwise, seeded

Per Serving:
Calories: 293
% of calories from fat: 19
Fat (gm): 6
Saturated fat (gm): 3
Cholesterol (mg): 64
Sodium (mg): 662
Protein (gm): 20
Carbohydrate (gm): 41

Exchanges:
Milk: 0.0
Vegetable: 1.0
Fruit: 0.0
Bread: 2.0
Meat: 2.0
Fat: 0.0

1. Combine vegetable protein, stuffing crumbs, and broth in bowl;
let stand until broth is absorbed, 5 to 10 minutes. Mix in rice,
cheese, vegetables, and herbs; season to taste with salt and pepper.
Mix in egg.

2. Cook poblano chilies in boiling water to cover until beginning to
soften, about 3 minutes; drain. Pack stuffing into chili halves and
place in baking pan. Bake, loosely covered, at 350 degrees until
stuffing is hot and peppers tender, about 45 minutes.

VEGETARIAN BURGER BONANZA

O

45

Veggie burgers need never be boring. Enjoy one of the tempting versions below using this basic recipe, or one of your favorite purchased vegetarian burgers.

6 servings

1 package (12 ounces) vegetarian
   ground beef
1 egg, lightly beaten
¼ cup each: unseasoned dry bread crumbs, finely
   chopped onion
½ teaspoon salt
¼ teaspoon pepper
6 whole wheat hamburger buns, toasted

Per Serving:
Calories: 233
% of calories from fat: 12.1
Fat (gm): 3.6
Saturated fat (gm): .3
Cholesterol (mg): 35.3
Sodium (mg): 627
Protein (gm): 19
Carbohydrate (gm): 40

Exchanges:
Milk: 0.0
Vegetable: 1.0
Fruit: 0.0
Bread: 2.0
Meat: 2.0
Fat: 0.0

1. Combine all ingredients, except buns; shape into 6 burgers. Cook in lightly greased skillet over medium heat until browned, about 5 minutes on each side. Serve in buns.

Variations

Smothered Onion-Garlic Veggie Burgers — Thinly slice 1 large onion and 4 large cloves garlic; cook in 1 tablespoon vegetable oil in large skillet over medium heat until very soft, 15 to 20 minutes; season to taste with salt and pepper. Spoon over burgers in toasted buns.

Wild Mushroom Veggie Burgers — Sauté 2 to 3 cups sliced wild mushrooms in 1 tablespoon vegetable oil in large skillet until tender, 5 to 8 minutes; season to taste with dried thyme leaves, salt, and pepper. Spoon over cooked burgers in toasted sesame buns.

Gourmet Cheese Veggie Burgers — Top each cooked burger with ½-ounce slice each reduced-fat Cheddar, Swiss, and Pepper-Jack Jack cheese; cook, covered, over medium heat until cheeses are melted, 3 to 4 minutes. Serve in toasted buns.

Blues Veggie Burgers — Top each cooked burger with 2 slices crisp vegetarian bacon and 1 ounce crumbled blue cheese; cook, covered, over medium heat until cheese is melted, 2 to 3 minutes. Serve in toasted onion buns.

Swiss-Kraut Veggie Burgers — Spread 1 tablespoon reduced-fat 1,000 Island salad dressing on each cooked burger and top with 1 slice reduced-fat Swiss cheese and 2–3 tablespoons sauerkraut; cook, covered, over medium heat until cheese is melted, 2 to 3 minutes. Serve in toasted rye buns.

Mediterranean Veggie Burgers — Spray both sides of eggplant slices with olive oil cooking spray; sauté in skillet until browned, 3 to 4 minutes on each side. Season to taste with salt and pepper. Top each cooked burger with eggplant slice; serve in toasted Italian bread slices with roasted red pepper strips and crumbled fat-free feta cheese.

Mexi-Veggie Burgers — Sauté 1 each small sliced poblano chili and onion in lightly greased skillet until tender, about 5 minutes; season to taste with oregano, salt, and pepper. Mix with cooked crumbled burgers; roll in flour tortillas with chopped tomato and chopped cilantro.

Greek Isle Veggie Burgers — Sauté ¾ cup each chopped tomato and zucchini in lightly greased skillet until tender, about 5 minutes; season to taste with dried mint and oregano, salt and pepper. Serve with cooked burgers and crumbled fat-free feta cheese in pita pockets.

VEGGIE-TOFU BURGERS

V

45

Healthy vegetables, tofu, and crunchy walnuts combine in these honey-sweetened burgers.

4 servings

⅔ cup each: finely chopped onion, shredded carrots

2 teaspoons minced roasted garlic

2 cups firmly packed chopped spinach

1 package (10½ ounces) light tofu, well drained, crumbled

2 sun-dried tomatoes (not in oil), softened, chopped

2 tablespoons reduced-sodium tamari soy sauce

1 tablespoon honey

½ cup coarsely chopped walnuts

¾ cup unseasoned dry bread crumbs, divided

Salt and pepper, to taste

4 whole wheat buns, toasted

Spicy brown mustard, or mayonnaise

Per Serving:
Calories: 364
% of calories from fat: 30
Fat (gm): 12.5
Saturated fat (gm): 1.4
Cholesterol (mg): 0
Sodium (mg): 778
Protein (gm): 17.9
Carbohydrate (gm): 48.6

Exchanges Exchanges:
Milk: 0.0
Vegetable: 1.0
Fruit: 0.0
Bread: 3.0
Meat: 1.0
Fat: 1.5

1. Sauté onion, carrots, and garlic in lightly greased large skillet 2 to 3 minutes. Add spinach, tofu, sun-dried tomatoes, soy sauce, and honey to skillet. Cook, covered, over medium heat until vegetables are tender, about 5 minutes. Cook, uncovered, until mixture is dry, about 5 minutes, stirring occasionally. Process in food processor until finely chopped; stir in walnuts and ½ cup bread crumbs; season to taste with salt and pepper.

2. Shape mixture into 4 burgers and coat with remaining ¼ cup bread crumbs; cook in lightly greased skillet until browned, about 5 minutes on each side. Serve in buns with mustard or mayonnaise.

SMOKED TOFU BURGERS

0

45

Use our recipe for Mesquite-Smoked Tofu (see pg. 191), or purchase smoked tofu at a health food store.

4 servings

¼ cup finely chopped red, or green, bell pepper

2 tablespoons finely chopped onion

2 cloves garlic, minced

¼ jalapeño chili, minced

1 tablespoon Asian sesame oil

4 ounces cremini mushrooms, finely chopped

1–1½ tablespoons reduced-sodium tamari soy sauce

1 package (10 ½ ounces) smoked tofu, mashed

¾ cup cooked brown rice

½–⅔ cup unseasoned dry bread crumbs

Salt and pepper, to taste

1 egg white

4 whole wheat hamburger buns, toasted

1 small onion, sliced

Per Serving:
Calories: 300
% of calories from fat: 24
Fat (gm): 8.2
Saturated fat (gm): 1.3
Cholesterol (mg): 0
Sodium (mg): 558
Protein (gm): 14.6
Carbohydrate (gm): 43.8

Exchanges:
Milk: 0.0
Vegetable: 0.5
Fruit: 0.0
Bread: 2.5
Meat: 1.0
Fat: 1.0

1. Sauté bell pepper, chopped onion, garlic, and jalapeño chili in sesame oil in large skillet until tender, about 5 minutes. Add mushrooms and soy sauce; sauté, uncovered, until mushrooms are tender, 3 to 4 minutes. Stir in tofu, rice, and bread crumbs; season to taste with salt and pepper. Mix in egg white.

2. Shape mixture into 4 burgers; cook in lightly greased skillet over medium heat until browned, about 5 minutes on each side. Serve in buns with sliced onion.

SQUASH AND TEMPEH PATTIES

L

45

Serve these sweet-flavored patties with accompaniments of sour cream and/or applesauce.

4 servings

½ cup each: chopped onion, red bell pepper

½ jalapeño chili, minced

2 teaspoons minced garlic

1 package (8 ounces) tempeh, crumbled

1½ cups mashed, cooked acorn squash

2 tablespoons apricot jam

1 cup corn bread stuffing crumbs, crushed, divided

Salt and pepper, to taste

½ cup each: applesauce, fat-free sour cream

Per Serving:
Calories: 262
% of calories from fat: 16
Fat (gm): 5
Saturated fat (gm): 0.8
Cholesterol (mg): 0
Sodium (mg): 124
Protein (gm): 16.4
Carbohydrate (gm): 42.4

Exchanges Exchanges:
Milk: 0.0
Vegetable: 1.0
Fruit: 0.0
Bread: 2.5
Meat: 1.0
Fat: 0.0

1. Sauté onion, bell pepper, jalapeño chili, and garlic in lightly greased skillet 2 to 3 minutes. Add tempeh and cook until vegetables are tender, 5 to 8 minutes. Stir in squash, jam, and ⅔ cup stuffing crumbs; season to taste with salt and pepper.

2. Shape mixture into 4 patties and coat with remaining ⅓ cup crumbs; cook in lightly greased skillet over medium heat until browned, about 5 minutes on each side. Serve warm with applesauce and sour cream.

VEGETARIAN FALAFEL BURGERS

L

45

The falafel mixture can also be shaped into 1-inch balls, cooked as the recipe directs, and served with Yogurt Cucumber Sauce as appetizers.

4 servings

1 package (6 ounces) falafel mix
½ cup shredded carrots
¼ cup sunflower kernels
2 tablespoons thinly sliced green onions
Yogurt Cucumber Sauce (recipe follows)

Per Serving:
Calories: 258
% of calories from fat: 32
Fat (gm): 8.4
Saturated fat (gm): 1
Cholesterol (mg): 3.5
Sodium (mg): 582
Protein (gm): 11.4
Carbohydrate (gm): 28.1

Exchanges:
Milk: 0.0
Vegetable: 0.0
Fruit: 0.0
Bread: 2.0
Meat: 1.0
Fat: 1.5

1. Prepare falafel mix with water according to package directions; mix in carrots, sunflower kernels, and green onions.

2. Shape mixture into 8 burgers about ½ inch thick; cook in lightly greased large skillet until browned, 4 to 5 minutes on each side. Serve with Yogurt Cucumber Sauce.

Yogurt-Cucumber Sauce

Makes about 1⅓ cups

1 cup each: reduced-fat plain yogurt, finely chopped cucumber
½ teaspoon each: dried dill weed, or mint leaves
Salt and white pepper, to taste

1. Mix yogurt, cucumber, and herbs; season to taste with salt and pepper.

45-MINUTE PREP TIP: Make Yogurt Cucumber Sauce before preparing the rest of the recipe.

FALAFEL PITAS WITH TAHINI DRESSING

L

45

The falafel mixture can also be shaped into meatballs, coated lightly with unseasoned dry bread crumbs, sprayed with cooking spray and baked at 375 degrees until browned, about 15 minutes. Serve in pitas.

4 servings

1½ cups cooked dried, or drained, canned
    garbanzo beans, coarsely pureed
¼ cup finely chopped parsley
2 tablespoons chopped onion
2 cloves garlic, minced
1–2 tablespoons lemon juice
¼ cup all-purpose flour
1¼ teaspoons ground cumin
Salt and pepper, to taste
2 pita breads, halved
Tahini Dressing (recipe follows)
¼ cup each: chopped tomato, cucumber,
    thinly sliced green onions

Per Serving:
Calories: 291
% of calories from fat: 23
Fat (gm): 7.6
Saturated fat (gm): 0.3
Cholesterol (mg): 0.3
Sodium (mg): 194
Protein (gm): 13.2
Carbohydrate (gm): 45.0

Exchanges:
Milk: 0.0
Vegetable: 2.0
Fruit: 0.0
Bread: 2.5
Meat: 0.5
Fat: 1.0

1. Mix garbanzo beans, parsley, onion, garlic, lemon juice, flour, and cumin in bowl; season to taste with salt and pepper.

2. Shape mixture into 4 burgers and cook in lightly greased skillet until browned, 3 to 4 minutes on each side. Arrange burgers in pitas; drizzle 2 tablespoons Tahini Dressing over each burger. Spoon combined tomato, cucumber, and sliced green onions into pitas.

Tahini Dressing

Makes about 1⅓ cups

⅓ cup fat-free yogurt
2–3 tablespoons tahini (sesame seed paste)
1 small clove garlic, minced
½–1 teaspoon lemon juice

1. Mix all ingredients; refrigerate until ready to use..

45-MINUTE PREP TIP: Make Tahini Dressing before preparing the rest of the recipe.

HERBED VEGGIE BURGERS

LO

45

Serve with Greens-Stuffed Baked Tomatoes and Sweet Potato Pone (see pp. 509, 501).

4 servings

¾ cup each: finely chopped broccoflower florets, mushrooms

¼ cup finely chopped onion

2 cloves garlic, minced

2 teaspoons each: dried bouquet garni, basil leaves, divided

⅔ cup cooked wild, or brown, rice

⅓ cup each: quick-cooking oats, coarsely chopped toasted walnuts

½ cup each: shredded fat-free Cheddar cheese (2 ounces), 1% fat cottage cheese

Salt and pepper, to taste

1 egg

3 multigrain, or whole wheat, buns, toasted

⅓ cup fat-free mayonnaise

Lettuce leaves

Per Serving:
Calories: 313
% of calories from fat: 26
Fat (gm): 9.5
Saturated fat (gm): 1.3
Cholesterol (mg): 1.3
Sodium (mg): 700
Protein (gm): 19.6
Carbohydrate (gm): 40

Exchanges:
Milk: 0.0
Vegetable: 0.0
Fruit: 0.0
Bread: 2.5
Meat: 2.0
Fat: 0.5

1. Sauté broccoflower, mushrooms, onion, garlic, and bouquet garni in lightly greased medium skillet until tender, 8 to 10 minutes. Mix in rice, oats, walnuts, and cheeses; season to taste with salt and pepper. Mix in egg.

2. Shape mixture into 4 burgers; cook in lightly greased skillet over medium to medium-low heat until browned, 3 to 4 minutes on each side. Serve in buns with mayonnaise and lettuce.

KASHA-VEGGIE BURGERS

L

45

Though the list of ingredients is lengthy, these burgers are well worth the effort to make. Prepare double the recipe, and freeze some of the burgers for future use.

4 servings

¾ cup each: finely chopped zucchini, mushrooms

¼ cup each: finely chopped onion, green bell pepper

2 cloves garlic, minced

½ teaspoon each: dried dill weed, basil, and thyme leaves

2 cups loosely packed spinach, finely chopped

1 medium tomato, seeded, chopped

⅔ cup cooked kasha, or brown rice

1 cup fresh whole wheat bread crumbs

½ cup each: fat-free ricotta cheese, shredded fat-free mozzarella cheese (2 ounces)

Salt and pepper, to taste

4 whole wheat buns, toasted

Per Serving:
Calories: 247
% of calories from fat: 12
Fat (gm): 3.6
Saturated fat (gm): 0.8
Cholesterol (mg): 0
Sodium (mg): 398
Protein (gm): 17.3
Carbohydrate (gm): 40.2

Exchanges:
Milk: 0.0
Vegetable: 2.0
Fruit: 0.0
Bread: 2.0
Meat: 1.0
Fat: 0.0

1. Sauté zucchini, mushrooms, onion, bell pepper, garlic, and herbs in lightly greased medium skillet until tender, about 8 minutes. Add spinach and tomato; cook, covered, over medium heat until spinach is wilted, 2 to 3 minutes. Mix in kasha, bread crumbs, and cheeses; season to taste with salt and pepper.

2. Shape mixture into 4 burgers; cook in lightly greased skillet over medium heat until browned, 3 to 4 minutes on each side. Serve in buns.

45-MINUTE PREP TIP: Begin cooking kasha before preparing the rest of the recipe.

GREEK-STYLE GARBANZO BURGERS WITH FENNEL GOAT CHEESE RELISH

LO

The burgers can also be served with Spinach Cilantro Pesto (see p.608).

45

4 servings

¼ cup each: finely chopped onion, red, or green, bell pepper

1½ teaspoons minced roasted garlic

2 sun-dried tomatoes (not in oil), softened, chopped

¾ teaspoon each: dried oregano and thyme leaves, ground cumin

1½ cups cooked dried, or drained, canned garbanzo beans, coarsely pureed

Salt, cayenne, and black pepper, to taste

1 egg white

¼–⅓ cup fresh whole wheat bread crumbs

2 pita breads, halved, or 4 whole wheat hamburger buns

Fennel Goat Cheese Relish (recipe follows)

Per Serving:
Calories: 302
% of calories from fat: 28
Fat (gm): 9.9
Saturated fat (gm): 2.7
Cholesterol (mg): 7.5
Sodium (mg): 458
Protein (gm): 13.2
Carbohydrate (gm): 43.5

Exchanges:
Milk: 0.0
Vegetable: 1.0
Fruit: 0.0
Bread: 2.5
Meat: 0.5
Fat: 1.5

1. Sauté onion, bell pepper, garlic, sun-dried tomatoes in lightly greased medium skillet until tender, about 5 minutes; stir in garbanzo beans; season to taste with salt, cayenne, and black pepper. Mix in egg white and enough bread crumbs for mixture to hold together.

2. Shape mixture into 4 burgers; cook in lightly greased skillet over medium heat until brown, about 5 minutes on each side. Arrange burgers in pita halves; spoon Fennel Goat Cheese Relish inside.

Fennel Goat Cheese Relish

Makes about 1 cup

⅓ cup each: thinly sliced fennel bulb, green onions

1 tablespoon each: olive oil, balsamic vinegar

¼ cup each: crumbled goat cheese (1 ounce), sliced pitted green, or ripe olives

1. Combine all ingredients.

45-MINUTE PREP TIP: Make Fennel Goat Cheese Relish before preparing the rest of the recipe.

CANNELLINI BEAN PATTIES WITH FRESH TOMATO RELISH

V

45

Patties can be lightly coated with cornmeal before cooking for an added bit of "crunch."

4 servings

1 can (15 ounces) cannellini beans, or other white beans, rinsed, drained, coarsely pureed

½ cup finely chopped tomato

¼ cup each: finely chopped onion, green bell pepper

1 ½ teaspoons minced garlic

2–4 tablespoons yellow cornmeal

1–1½ teaspoons Italian seasoning

Salt and pepper, to taste

4 slices Italian bread, or 4 whole wheat hamburger buns, toasted

1 clove garlic, cut in half

Fresh Tomato Relish (recipe follows)

Per Serving:
Calories: 231
% of calories from fat: 19
Fat (gm): 5.7
Saturated fat (gm): 0.8
Cholesterol (mg): 0
Sodium (mg): 395
Protein (gm): 11.7
Carbohydrate (gm): 42.9

Exchanges:
Milk: 0.0
Vegetable: 2.0
Fruit: 0.0
Bread: 2.0
Meat: 0.0
Fat: 1.0

1. Combine beans, tomato, onion, bell pepper, garlic, cornmeal, and Italian seasoning; season to taste with salt and pepper.

2. Shape mixture into 4 patties; cook in lightly greased large skillet over medium heat until browned, about 5 minutes on each side. Rub tops of bread slices with cut sides of garlic; top with patties and serve with Fresh Tomato Relish.

Fresh Tomato Relish

Makes about 1 cup

1 cup chopped tomato

1 tablespoon finely chopped fresh , or 1 teaspoon dried basil leaves

1 tablespoon each: olive oil, red wine vinegar

Salt and pepper, to taste

1. Mix tomato, basil, oil, and vinegar; season to taste with salt and pepper.

45-MINUTE PREP TIP: Make Fresh Tomato Relish before preparing the rest of the recipe.

SOYBEAN-VEGGIE BURGERS

O

45

These burgers pack a hefty nutritional punch and taste as good as they are good for you! Just so you know, soybeans triple in volume when cooked.

4 servings

½ cup each: finely chopped onion, carrots

¼ cup finely chopped red bell pepper

4 cloves garlic, minced

1 cup cooked soybeans, coarsely pureed

1 cup cooked basmati rice

½ cup seasoned dry bread crumbs

Hot pepper sauce, to taste

Salt and pepper, to taste

1 egg

4 whole wheat buns, toasted

4 teaspoons spicy brown, or horseradish mustard

Lettuce leaves

Per Serving:
Calories: 317
% of calories from fat: 20
Fat (gm): 7.3
Saturated fat (gm): 1.3
Cholesterol (mg): 53.3
Sodium (mg): 695
Protein (gm): 16.9
Carbohydrate (gm): 49.6

Exchanges:
Milk: 0.0
Vegetable: 1.0
Fruit: 0.0
Bread: 3.0
Meat: 1.0
Fat: 0.5

1. Sauté onion, carrots, bell pepper, and garlic in lightly greased medium skillet until tender, about 8 minutes. Mix in soybeans, rice, and bread crumbs; season to taste with red pepper sauce, salt, and pepper. Mix in egg.

2. Shape mixture into 4 burgers; cook in lightly greased skillet over medium heat until browned, 3 to 4 minutes on each side. Serve in buns with mustard and lettuce.

EGGPLANT PARMESAN SANDWICHES

LO

45

Try crumbled feta cheese as a delicious substitute for the mozzarella.

4 servings

4 thick slices eggplant (scant ¾ inch)

1 egg, beaten

⅓ cup seasoned dry bread crumbs

2 tablespoons grated fat-free Parmesan cheese

4 ounces sliced fat-free mozzarella cheese

4 French rolls, or hoagie buns, toasted

2 roasted small red peppers, halved

Pizza Sauce (see p. 582)

1. Dip eggplant slices in egg and coat with combined bread crumbs and Parmesan cheese. Cook in lightly greased large skillet over medium heat until tender and browned, about 5 minutes on each side. Top each eggplant slice with 1 ounce cheese; cook, covered, until cheese is melted, 2 to 3 minutes. Serve in buns with roasted red peppers and Pizza Sauce.

Per Serving:
Calories: 255
% of calories from fat: 13
Fat (gm): 3.6
Saturated fat (gm): 1
Cholesterol (mg): 58
Sodium (mg): 588
Protein (gm): 17
Carbohydrate (gm): 37.6

Exchanges:
Milk: 0.0
Vegetable: 0.0
Fruit: 0.0
Bread: 2.5
Meat: 1.0
Fat: 0.0

45-MINUTE PREP TIP: Make Pizza Sauce before preparing the rest of the recipe.

VEGETARIAN CHORIZO

LO
45

This well seasoned version of chorizo is made with vegetarian ground beef. Make into patties, or crumble to serve in quesadillas, nachos, and enchiladas.

6 servings

½–1 teaspoon each: coriander and cumin seeds, crushed

1–2 dried ancho chilies

1 package (12 ounces) vegetarian ground beef

2 eggs

2 tablespoons cider vinegar

2 cloves garlic, minced

2 tablespoons paprika

1–1½ teaspoons dried oregano leaves

½ teaspoon salt

1 cup mild or hot salsa

6 tablespoons fat-free sour cream

Per Serving:
Calories: 123
% of calories from fat: 20
Fat (gm): 3
Saturated fat (gm): 0.6
Cholesterol (mg): 71
Sodium (mg): 600
Protein (gm): 15
Carbohydrate (gm): 11

Exchanges:
Milk: 0.0
Vegetable: 2.0
Fruit: 0.0
Bread: 0.0
Meat: 0.5
Fat: 0.0

1. Heat seeds in small skillet over medium heat until toasted, 2 to 3 minutes, stirring frequently; remove from skillet. Add ancho chili to skillet; cook over medium heat until softened, turning frequently so chili doesn't burn, 1 to 2 minutes. Remove and discard stem, veins, and seeds; chop chili finely.

2. Combine all ingredients except salt, salsa, and sour cream. Shape mixture into 6 patties; cook in lightly greased large skillet over medium to medium-low heat until browned, 3 to 4 minutes on each side. Serve with salsa and sour cream.

PICANTE BLACK BEAN TOSTADAS

LO

45

These bean patties can also be served in buns, topped with Red Tomato Salsa (see pg. 8).

6 servings

2 cans (15 ounces each) black beans, rinsed, drained, coarsely pureed

1 cup (4 ounces) shredded reduced-fat Monterey Jack cheese

½ cup each: very finely chopped onion, zucchini

4 cloves garlic, minced

1–2 serrano, or jalapeño, chilies, minced

1–1½ teaspoons each: dried oregano leaves, ground cumin

¼–½ teaspoon crushed red pepper

Salt and pepper, to taste

1 egg white

¼–⅓ cup unseasoned dry bread crumbs

6 corn, or flour, tortillas

1½ cups each: thinly sliced iceberg lettuce, chopped tomatoes

Guacamole (see p. 12)

6 tablespoons fat-free sour cream

Per Serving:
Calories: 308
% of calories from fat: 20
Fat (gm): 8
Saturated fat (gm): 2.6
Cholesterol (mg): 13.5
Sodium (mg): 715
Protein (gm): 22.5
Carbohydrate (gm): 48.5

Exchanges:
Milk: 0.0
Vegetable: 1.0
Fruit: 0.0
Bread: 2.5
Meat: 1.0
Fat: 1.0

1. Mix beans, cheese, onion, zucchini, garlic, serrano chili, herbs, and crushed red pepper; season to taste with salt and pepper. Mix in egg white and enough bread crumbs to hold together a firm mixture.

2. Shape mixture into 6 patties; cook in lightly greased skillet over medium heat until browned, about 5 minutes on each side. Cook tortillas in lightly greased large skillet over medium heat until crisp and browned, about 1 minute on each side. Top tortillas with lettuce, tomatoes, and patties. Serve with Guacamole and sour cream.

45-MINUTE PREP TIP: Make Guacamole before preparing the rest of the recipe.

MEATLESS SLOPPY JOES

V

45

A great sandwich for kids of all ages! Serve with lots of pickles and fresh vegetable relishes.

4 servings

¾ cup sliced mushrooms

½ cup each: chopped onion, green, or red, bell pepper

1 teaspoon minced garlic

½ cup each: reduced-sodium catsup, textured vegetable protein

⅔ cup water

2 tablespoons light brown sugar

1 tablespoon prepared mustard

1 teaspoon celery seeds

½ teaspoon chili powder

Salt and pepper, to taste

4 whole wheat hamburger buns, toasted

8 sweet, or dill, pickle spears

Per Serving:
Calories: 264
% of calories from fat: 11
Fat (gm): 3.5
Saturated fat (gm): 0.7
Cholesterol (mg): 0
Sodium (mg): 428
Protein (gm): 15.1
Carbohydrate (gm): 48.9

Exchanges:
Milk: 0.0
Vegetable: 1.0
Fruit: 0.0
Bread: 2.0
Meat: 2.0
Fat: 0.0

1. Sauté mushrooms, onion, bell pepper, and garlic in lightly greased medium saucepan until tender, 5 to 8 minutes. Stir in remaining ingredients, except salt, pepper, buns, and pickles; heat to boiling. Reduce heat and simmer, covered, 10 minutes. Season to taste with salt and pepper. Serve in buns with pickles.

VEGGIE JOES

L

45

We recommend using frozen tofu for this recipe, as the texture of frozen, thawed, tofu is firmer. Tempeh can be substituted for the tofu.

6 servings

2 packages (10½ ounces each) frozen light firm tofu, thawed

½ cup chopped green bell pepper

¼ cup sliced green onions

2 cloves garlic, minced

¾ cup each: sliced carrots, small broccoli florets, whole-kernel corn

3 cans (8 ounces each) reduced-sodium tomato sauce

1½–2 tablespoons cider vinegar

3–4 teaspoons brown spicy mustard

2–3 teaspoons sugar

½ teaspoon celery seeds

Salt and pepper, to taste

6 sesame seed hamburger buns, toasted

¾ cup (3 ounces) shredded fat-free Cheddar cheese

Per Serving:
Calories: 270
% of calories from fat: 13
Fat (gm): 3.9
Saturated fat (gm): 0.6
Cholesterol (mg): 0
Sodium (mg): 513
Protein (gm): 18.7
Carbohydrate (gm): 41.2

Exchanges:
Milk: 0.0
Vegetable: 3.0
Fruit: 0.0
Bread: 2.0
Meat: 1.0
Fat: 0.0

1. Press excess liquid from tofu with paper toweling. Crumble tofu, or mash coarsely with a fork. Sauté tofu, bell pepper, green onions, and garlic in lightly greased large skillet 3 to 4 minutes. Add remaining vegetables and cook, covered, over medium heat until crisp-tender, about 5 minutes. Add tomato sauce, vinegar, mustard, sugar, and celery seeds and heat to boiling. Reduce heat and simmer, covered, 5 to 10 minutes. Season to taste with salt and pepper. Serve in buns; sprinkle with cheese.

MOCK CHICKEN SALAD SANDWICHES

O

45

If you prefer a softer texture, cook the tempeh in simmering water 5 to 10 minutes; drain and cool. The salad mixture is also excellent served in scooped-out tomatoes.

4 servings

1 package (8 ounces) tempeh, crumbled

⅓ cup each: chopped onion, celery, green bell pepper

2–4 tablespoons sliced green, or black, olives

⅓–½ cup fat-free mayonnaise

1–2 teaspoons each: Dijon mustard, lemon juice

Salt and pepper, to taste

8 slices whole wheat, or light rye, bread, toasted

Lettuce leaves, as garnish

1 medium tomato, sliced

Per Serving:
Calories: 293
% of calories from fat: 22
Fat (gm): 7.7
Saturated fat (gm): 1.4
Cholesterol (mg): 0
Sodium (mg): 690
Protein (gm): 18.1
Carbohydrate (gm): 42.1

Exchanges:
Milk: 0.0
Vegetable: 1.0
Fruit: 0.0
Bread: 2.5
Meat: 1.5
Fat: 0.5

1. Combine tempeh, onion, celery, bell pepper, and olives in a bowl. Mix in combined mayonnaise, mustard, and lemon juice; season to taste with salt and pepper. Spoon mixture on 4 bread slices; top with lettuce, tomato, and remaining bread.

GOAT CHEESE HOAGIES

L

45

A sandwich full of surprise flavors!

4 servings

4 cups sliced onions

2 cups sliced green bell peppers

2 teaspoons minced garlic

⅓ cup water

¼ cup raisins

1–1½ tablespoons balsamic vinegar

Salt and pepper, to taste

½ package (8-ounce size) fat-free cream cheese, room temperature

½ cup (2 ounces) goat cheese

4 French rolls, or hoagie buns

16 spinach leaves

Per Serving:
Calories: 284
% of calories from fat: 16
Fat (gm): 5.2
Saturated fat (gm): 2.5
Cholesterol (mg): 6.5
Sodium (mg): 382
Protein (gm): 11.5
Carbohydrate (gm): 50.2

Exchanges:
Milk: 0.0
Vegetable: 4.0
Fruit: 0.0
Bread: 2.0
Meat: 0.5
Fat: 0.5

1. Cook onions, bell peppers, and garlic in lightly greased large skillet over medium to medium-low heat, covered, until softened and beginning to brown, 15 to 20 minutes. Add water, raisins, and vinegar; heat to boiling. Reduce heat and simmer, covered, until water has evaporated, 5 to 8 minutes. Season to taste with salt and pepper.

2. Mix cheeses and spread on tops and bottoms of rolls; fill with spinach leaves and onion mixture.

PORTOBELLO MONTE CRISTO GRILL

LO *A fabulous sandwich, dipped in egg batter and grilled to golden goodness.*

45 **4 servings**

4 large portobello mushrooms, stems removed

2 tablespoons olive oil

1 teaspoon Italian seasoning

Salt and pepper, to taste

8 slices sourdough bread

1 roasted red pepper, cut into 1-inch strips

3–4 ounces fat-free feta cheese, sliced

1 egg

¼ cup fat-free milk

Per Serving:
Calories: 252
% of calories from fat: 34
Fat (gm): 9.6
Saturated fat (gm): 1.6
Cholesterol (mg): 63.4
Sodium (mg): 674
Protein (gm): 11.7
Carbohydrate (gm): 30.2

Exchanges:
Milk: 0.0
Vegetable: 0.0
Fruit: 0.0
Bread: 2.0
Meat: 1.0
Fat: 1.0

1. Sauté mushrooms in oil in large skillet just until tender, 5 to 8 minutes, turning once. Sprinkle with Italian seasoning and season to taste with salt and pepper. Place mushrooms on 4 slices bread; top with roasted red pepper, feta cheese, and remaining bread.

2. Beat egg and milk until blended in pie plate. Dip sandwiches in egg mixture; cook in greased large skillet over medium heat until browned, 3 to 4 minutes on each side.

CUCUMBER CHEESE MELT

L

A marvelous combination of flavors that will keep you coming back for more!

45 **4 servings**

¼ package (8-ounce size) fat-free cream
   cheese, room temperature
2 tablespoons crumbled blue cheese
8 slices multigrain bread
¼ cup apricot jam
16 cucumber slices
4 slices (3 ounces) fat-free Swiss cheese
Vegetable cooking spray

Per Serving:
Calories: 249
% of calories from fat: 11
Fat (gm): 3.1
Saturated fat (gm): 1.1
Cholesterol (mg): 2.6
Sodium (mg): 673
Protein (gm): 13.6
Carbohydrate (gm): 42.9

Exchanges:
Milk: 0.0
Vegetable: 2.0
Fruit: 0.0
Bread: 2.0
Meat: 1.0
Fat: 0.0

1. Mix cheeses and spread on 4 slices of bread; spread each with 1 tablespoon jam and top with 4 cucumber slices, a slice of Swiss cheese, and remaining bread. Spray both sides of sandwiches lightly with cooking spray; cook in large skillet over medium heat until browned, about 5 minutes on each side.

BLUE CHEESE AND PEAR MELT

L

Blue cheese and pears are perfect flavor companions, any way they are served.

45 **4 servings**

8 slices honey wheat, or light rye, bread
4 slices (3 ounces) fat-free Swiss cheese
¼ cup mango chutney
1 medium pear, cored, cut into ¼-inch slices
½ cup (2 ounces) crumbled blue cheese
Vegetable cooking spray

Per Serving:
Calories: 284
% of calories from fat: 20
Fat (gm): 6.6
Saturated fat (gm): 3.2
Cholesterol (mg): 10.5
Sodium (mg): 780
Protein (gm): 13.6
Carbohydrate (gm): 44.6

Exchanges:
Milk: 0.0
Vegetable: 0.0
Fruit: 1.0
Bread: 2.0
Meat: 1.0
Fat: 0.5

1. Top 4 slices bread with Swiss cheese, and spread each with 1 tablespoon chutney; arrange pears on chutney, sprinkle with blue cheese and top with remaining bread. Spray both sides of sandwiches with cooking spray; cook in large skillet until browned, about 5 minutes on each side.

PEANUTTY AND JELLY SANDWICHES

V

45

You won't believe the rich, peanut butter flavor of this creamy, low-fat sandwich spread! Great on raisin bread or crackers, topped with sliced banana or apple.

6 servings

¾ cup drained canned Great Northern beans

⅓ cup reduced-fat smooth, or chunky, peanut butter

2 tablespoons halved raisins

1–2 tablespoons honey

12 slices whole wheat, or multigrain, bread

¾ cup grape, or other flavor, jam

Per Serving:
Calories: 384
% of calories from fat: 18
Fat (gm): 7.9
Saturated fat (gm): 1.7
Cholesterol (mg): 0
Sodium (mg): 389
Protein (gm): 11.9
Carbohydrate (gm): 70.6

Exchanges:
Milk: 0.0
Vegetable: 0.0
Fruit: 0.0
Bread: 4.0
Meat: 1.0
Fat: 1.0

1. Process beans in food processor until smooth; mix in peanut butter, raisins, and honey. Spread on 6 slices bread; top with jam and remaining bread.

SWISS CHEESE AND SPINACH PINWHEELS

L

45

These fabulous sandwiches can be made in advance and refrigerated up to 2 days — always ready for hungry appetites!

8 servings (2 slices each)

1 large whole wheat lavosh (16 inches diameter)

1 package (8 ounces) fat-free cream cheese, room
    temperature

1 tablespoon fat-free sour cream

2 tablespoons minced onion

1 teaspoon fennel seeds, crushed

10 slices (7½ ounces) fat-free Swiss cheese

4 cups loosely packed spinach leaves

2 medium tomatoes, thinly sliced

⅓ cup drained, sliced olives

Per Serving:
Calories: 177
% of calories from fat: 29
Fat (gm): 5.8
Saturated fat (gm): 0.9
Cholesterol (mg): 0
Sodium (mg): 782
Protein (gm): 13.4
Carbohydrate (gm): 18.4

Exchanges:
Milk: 0.0
Vegetable: 1.0
Fruit: 0.0
Bread: 1.0
Meat: 1.0
Fat: 0.5

1. Place lavosh between 2 damp clean kitchen towels; let stand until lavosh is softened enough to roll, 10 to 15 minutes.

2. Mix cream cheese, sour cream, onion, and fennel seeds in small bowl; spread on lavosh. Arrange Swiss cheese, spinach, tomatoes, and olives on top. Roll lavosh tightly; wrap in plastic wrap and refrigerate at least 4 hours, but no longer than 2 days. Trim ends and cut into 1-inch slices.

SLICED MUSHROOM PINWHEELS

L

45

Easy to make and carry, lavosh sandwiches are great for picnics, as well as home dining.

8 servings (2 slices each)

1 large whole wheat lavosh (16 inches diameter)

4 ounces mushrooms

1 package (8 ounces) fat-free cream cheese, room temperature

1 tablespoon fat-free sour cream

1 teaspoon minced garlic

1–2 teaspoons Dijon mustard

1 medium onion, thinly sliced

⅓ cup red bell pepper, thinly sliced

3 tablespoons fat-free Italian salad dressing

Per Serving:
Calories: 122
% of calories from fat: 27
Fat (gm): 3.7
Saturated fat (gm): 0.7
Cholesterol (mg): 0
Sodium (mg): 309
Protein (gm): 6.5
Carbohydrate (gm): 16

Exchanges:
Milk: 0.0
Vegetable: 1.0
Fruit: 0.0
Bread: 1.0
Meat: 0.0
Fat: 0.5

1. Place lavosh between 2 damp clean kitchen towels; let stand until lavosh is softened enough to roll, 10 to 15 minutes.

2. Remove mushroom stems and chop; slice mushroom caps. Mix cream cheese, chopped mushroom stems, sour cream, garlic, and mustard in small bowl; spread mixture on lavosh. Toss sliced mushrooms, onion, and bell pepper with salad dressing; arrange over cheese mixture. Roll lavosh tightly; wrap in plastic wrap and refrigerate at least 4 hours, but no longer than 2 days. Trim ends and cut into 1-inch slices.

EIGHT

Pizzas, Calzones,

and

Dinner Pies

Pizza can be served as an appetizer, snack, entrée, or even a bread, so the number of servings in each pizza recipe will vary depending upon how the pizza is used in a meal. For this reason, the yield for the recipes has been given in slices, with nutritional information provided per slice.

For those pizzas that have the 45-minute symbol, make Pizza Dough and begin the rest of recipe while the dough is rising.

BASIC PIZZA DOUGH

V | *Quick and easy to make, this dough uses fast-rising yeast.*

45 | **Makes one 12-inch crust** (6 large slices)

1¼ cups all-purpose flour, divided
1 package fast-rising yeast
½ teaspoon sugar
¼ teaspoon salt
½ cup very hot water (120 degrees)

Per Slice Slice:
Calories: 99.5
% of calories from fat: 2
Fat (gm): 0.3
Saturated fat (gm): 0
Cholesterol (mg): 0
Sodium (mg): 89
Protein (gm): 3.2
Carbohydrate (gm): 20.7

Exchanges:
Milk: 0.0
Vegetable: 0.0
Fruit: 0.0
Bread: 1.5
Meat: 0.0
Fat: 0.0

1. Combine ¾ cup flour, yeast, sugar, and salt in bowl; add hot water, stirring until smooth. Mix in enough remaining ½ cup flour to make a soft dough. Knead on floured surface until smooth and elastic, 3 to 5 minutes. Cover dough with bowl and let stand 15 minutes. Spread on pan according to directions in pizza recipes.

CORNMEAL PIZZA DOUGH

V | *Another fast and easy-to-make, no-rise pizza dough!*

45 | **Makes one 12-inch crust** (6 large slices)

1 cup all-purpose flour, divided
¼ cup yellow cornmeal
1 package fast-rising yeast
½ teaspoon sugar
½ cup very hot water (120 degrees)

Per Slice:
Calories: 99
% of calories from fat: 4
Fat (gm): 0.4
Saturated fat (gm): 0.1
Cholesterol (mg): 0
Sodium (mg): 2.3
Protein (gm): 3.1
Carbohydrate (gm): 20.7

Exchanges:
Milk: 0.0
Vegetable: 0.0
Fruit: 0.0
Bread: 1.5
Meat: 0.0
Fat: 0.0

1. Combine ½ cup flour, cornmeal, yeast, and sugar in bowl; add hot water, stirring until smooth. Mix in enough remaining ½ cup flour to make a soft dough. Knead on floured surface until smooth and elastic, 3 to 5 minutes. Cover dough with bowl and let stand 15 minutes. Spread on pan according to directions in pizza recipes.

WHOLE WHEAT PIZZA DOUGH

V

Whole wheat flour enhances the nutritional qualities of this crust.

45

Makes one 12-inch crust (6 large slices)

¾ cup all-purpose flour, divided
1 package fast-rising yeast
¼ teaspoon salt
½ cup very hot water (120 degrees)
2 teaspoons honey
½ cup whole wheat flour

1. Combine all-purpose flour, yeast, and salt in bowl; add hot water and honey, stirring until smooth. Mix in enough whole wheat flour to make a soft dough. Knead on floured surface until smooth and elastic, 3 to 5 minutes. Cover dough with bowl and let stand 15 minutes. Spread dough on pan according to directions in pizza recipes.

Per Slice:
Calories: 101
% of calories from fat: 3
Fat (gm): 0.3
Saturated fat (gm): 0.1
Cholesterol (mg): 0
Sodium (mg): 90
Protein (gm): 3.5
Carbohydrate (gm): 21.6

Exchanges:
Milk: 0.0
Vegetable: 0.0
Fruit: 0.0
Bread: 1.5
Meat: 0.0
Fat: 0.0

Variation

Rye Pizza Dough — Make dough as above, substituting rye flour for the whole wheat, and adding ½ teaspoon lightly crushed caraway seeds.

CHEESE PIZZA DOUGH

L

45

Two cheeses flavor this crust; fat-free Monterey Jack or Swiss cheese can be substituted for the Cheddar.

Makes one 12-inch crust (6 large slices)

1¼ cups all-purpose flour, divided
1 package fast-rising yeast
½ teaspoon sugar
⅔ cup very hot water (120 degrees)
2 tablespoons grated fat-free Parmesan cheese
¼ cup (1 ounce) shredded fat-free Cheddar cheese

Per Slice:
Calories: 112
% of calories from fat: 2
Fat (gm): 0.3
Saturated fat (gm): 0
Cholesterol (mg): 0
Sodium (mg): 49
Protein (gm): 5.4
Carbohydrate (gm): 21.7

Exchanges:
Milk: 0.0
Vegetable: 0.0
Fruit: 0.0
Bread: 1.5
Meat: 0.0
Fat: 0.0

1. Combine ¾ cup flour, yeast, and sugar in bowl; add hot water, stirring until smooth. Mix in Parmesan cheese and enough remaining ½ cup flour to make smooth dough. Knead on floured surface until smooth, kneading in Cheddar cheese. Cover dough with bowl and let stand 15 minutes. Spread dough on pan according to directions in pizza recipes.

SPINACH AND 4-CHEESE PIZZA

L

Enjoy the combination of 4 cheeses on this flavorful pizza.

45

6 slices

2 cups sliced mushrooms

1 medium onion, sliced

3 cloves garlic, minced

Olive oil cooking spray

Basic Pizza Dough (see p. 298)

1 cup fat-free ricotta cheese

½ cup (2 ounces) shredded fat-free mozzarella cheese

¼ cup (1 ounce) grated fat-free Parmesan cheese

1 package (10 ounces) frozen spinach, thawed, well drained

3 tablespoons fat-free sour cream

1 tablespoon lemon juice

Salt and pepper, to taste

2 ounces sun-dried tomatoes (not in oil), softened

¼ cup (1 ounce) crumbled blue cheese

Per Slice:
Calories: 230
% of calories from fat: 10.6
Fat (gm): 2.7
Saturated fat (gm): 1.4
Cholesterol (mg): 17.3
Sodium (mg): 652
Protein (gm): 16.4
Carbohydrate (gm): 35.5

Exchanges:
Milk: 0.0
Vegetable: 1.0
Fruit: 0.0
Bread: 2.0
Meat: 1.0
Fat: 0.0

1. Cook mushrooms, onion, and garlic in lightly greased large skillet over medium heat, covered, until mushrooms are wilted, about 5 minutes. Cook, uncovered, until vegetables are tender and excess liquid evaporated, about 5 minutes.

2. Spread dough on greased 12-inch pizza pan, making rim around edge; bake at 425 degrees 10 minutes. Combine ricotta, mozzarella, and Parmesan cheese, spinach, sour cream, and lemon juice; season to taste with salt and pepper. Spread evenly on baked crust; top with mushroom mixture, sun-dried tomatoes, and blue cheese. Bake until crust is browned, about 15 minutes.

DEEP-PAN SPINACH PIZZA

L

45

We've made this pizza in a springform pan, but use a deep-dish pizza pan if you have one.

6 slices

¼ cup finely chopped onion

1 clove garlic, minced

1 package (10 ounces) frozen chopped spinach, thawed, well drained

Salt and pepper, to taste

Cornmeal Pizza Dough (see p. 298)

¼ cup reduced-sodium tomato sauce

1½ cups fat-free ricotta cheese

2 tablespoons each: grated fat-free Parmesan cheese, fat-free sour cream

1 teaspoon dried Italian seasoning

1 medium tomato, sliced

½ cup (2 ounces) shredded reduced-fat mozzarella cheese

Per Slice:
Calories: 195
% of calories from fat: 8
Fat (gm): 1.9
Saturated fat (gm): 1.1
Cholesterol (mg): 5.1
Sodium (mg): 151
Protein (gm): 16.3
Carbohydrate (gm): 30.5

Exchanges:
Milk: 0.0
Vegetable: 1.0
Fruit: 0.0
Bread: 1.5
Meat: 1.0
Fat: 0.0

1. Sauté onion and garlic in lightly greased medium skillet until tender, 2 to 3 minutes; add spinach and cook until mixture is very dry. Season to taste with salt and pepper.

2. Roll dough on floured surface to circle 13 inches in diameter; ease dough into greased 9-inch springform pan, covering bottom and 2 inches up side of pan. Spread tomato sauce on bottom of dough. Spoon combined ricotta and Parmesan cheese, sour cream and Italian seasoning; top with spinach mixture. Fold edge of dough over edge of filling; top center of pizza with tomato slices and mozzarella cheese. Bake at 400 degrees until dough is browned, about 20 to 30 minutes. Let stand 5 to 10 minutes before cutting.

BREAKFAST PIZZA

LO

45

Great for breakfast, brunch, or a light supper. The egg is added last and quickly cooked in the oven.

6 slices

Cheese Pizza Dough or Cornmeal Pizza Dough
(see pp. 299, 298)
1 cup Pizza Sauce (see p. 582)
½ cup each: sliced green bell pepper, onion
1 cup (4 ounces) shredded fat-free mozzarella cheese
3 slices cooked, crumbled vegetarian bacon
1 egg

Per Slice:
Calories: 197
% of calories from fat: 9
Fat (gm): 1.9
Saturated fat (gm): 0.4
Cholesterol (mg): 35.5
Sodium (mg): 287
Protein (gm): 15.1
Carbohydrate (gm): 29.5

Exchanges:
Milk: 0.0
Vegetable: 1.0
Fruit: 0.0
Bread: 1.5
Meat: 1.0
Fat: 0.0

1. Spread dough on greased 12-inch pizza pan, making rim around edge. Spread sauce on dough and sprinkle with bell pepper, onion, cheese, and vegetarian bacon. Bake at 425 degrees until crust is browned, 15 to 20 minutes. Remove from oven and break egg into center of pizza. Stir egg with fork and quickly spread over pizza. Return to oven and bake until egg is cooked, 1 to 2 minutes.

RANCH-STYLE PIZZA

L

45

A skinny version of a pizza from our favorite pizzeria.

6 slices

Basic Pizza Dough (see p. 298)
½ cup fat-free ranch salad dressing, divided
1 cup (4 ounces) shredded fat-free mozzarella cheese
½ cup (2 ounces) shredded reduced-fat mozzarella
cheese
1 cup thinly sliced spinach
½ cup sliced mushrooms

Per Slice:
Calories: 171
% of calories from fat: 9
Fat (gm): 1.7
Saturated fat (gm): 1.1
Cholesterol (mg): 5.1
Sodium (mg): 378
Protein (gm): 12.9
Carbohydrate (gm): 25

Exchanges:
Milk: 0.0
Vegetable: 0.5
Fruit: 0.0
Bread: 1.5
Meat: 1.0
Fat: 0.0

1. Spread dough on greased pan, making rim around edge. Brush dough with ¼ cup salad dressing; sprinkle with cheeses. Mound spinach and mushrooms in center of pizza. Bake at 425 degrees until crust is browned, 15 to 20 minutes. Drizzle pizza with remaining ¼ cup salad dressing.

REUBEN PIZZA

LO

45

Sauerkraut, 1,000 Island salad dressing, and vegetarian bacon-flavored bits create a pizza that rivals the sandwich!

6 slices

12 ounces cabbage, thinly sliced

½ cup red onion, thinly sliced

1 teaspoon caraway seeds, crushed

2 tablespoons water

½ can (14½-ounce size) sauerkraut, rinsed, well drained

½–1 cup (2–4 ounces) shredded fat-free mozzarella cheese

1–2 tablespoons crumbled cooked vegetarian bacon

Rye Pizza Dough (see p. 299)

¼ cup fat-free 1,000 Island salad dressing

Per Slice:
Calories: 185
% of calories from fat: 4
Fat (gm): 0.9
Saturated fat (gm): 0.1
Cholesterol (mg): 0
Sodium (mg): 402
Protein (gm): 8.8
Carbohydrate (gm): 36.9

Exchanges:
Milk: 0.0
Vegetable: 1.0
Fruit: 0.0
Bread: 2.0
Meat: 0.5
Fat: 0.0

1. Sauté cabbage, onion, and 1 teaspoon caraway seeds in lightly greased large skillet 2 to 3 minutes. Add water; cook, covered, over medium heat until cabbage is wilted, 5 to 8 minutes. Stir in sauerkraut; cook, uncovered, over medium heat until cabbage is very tender, 15 to 20 minutes. Cool; stir in cheese and vegetarian bacon.

2. Spread dough on greased 12-inch pizza pan, making rim around edge. Spread salad dressing on dough. Spread cabbage mixture evenly over dough; sprinkle with cheese and vegetarian bacon. Bake at 425 degrees until crust is browned, 15 to 20 minutes.

ASIAN-STYLE PIZZA

Stir-fried vegetables create new flavor interest as a pizza topping!

6 slices

1 cup each: sliced shiitake, or cremini, mushrooms
   and bok choy

½ cup small broccoli florets, snow peas, sliced
   onion, green bell pepper

2 teaspoons minced gingerroot

1 clove garlic, minced

1–2 teaspoons reduced-sodium tamari soy sauce

Salt and pepper, to taste

Basic Pizza Dough (see p. 298)

1 package (10 ounces) smoked tofu,
   cubed (½-inch)

¾ cup (3 ounces) shredded fat-free mozzarella cheese

Per Slice
Calories: 174
% of calories from fat: 5
Fat (gm): 1
Saturated fat (gm): 0.1
Cholesterol (mg): 0
Sodium (mg): 276
Protein (gm): 13.2
Carbohydrate (gm): 28.6

Exchanges:
Milk: 0.0
Vegetable: 1.0
Fruit: 0.0
Bread: 1.5
Meat: 1.0
Fat: 0.0

1. Stir-fry vegetables, gingerroot, and garlic in lightly greased large
skillet until tender, 8 to 10 minutes. Season to taste with soy sauce,
salt, and pepper; cool.

2. Spread dough on greased 12-inch pizza pan, making rim around
edge. Arrange vegetables and tofu on dough; sprinkle with cheese.
Bake at 425 degrees until crust is browned, 15 to 20 minutes.

FRENCH-STYLE ONION PIZZA

*Called a "Pissaladiere" in France, this onion pizza is more traditionally
made on a pastry rather than a pizza crust.*

6 slices

6 cups thinly sliced onions

2 medium tomatoes, coarsely chopped

¼ cup finely chopped parsley

½ teaspoon each: dried oregano and thyme leaves

Salt and pepper, to taste

Basic Pizza Dough (see p. 298)

2–4 tablespoons sliced ripe olives

Per Slice:
Calories: 165
% of calories from fat: 9
Fat (gm): 1.6
Saturated fat (gm): 0.2
Cholesterol (mg): 0
Sodium (mg): 191
Protein (gm): 5.1
Carbohydrate (gm): 33.5

Exchanges:
Milk: 0.0
Vegetable: 2.0
Fruit: 0.0
Bread: 1.5
Meat: 0.0
Fat: 0.0

1. Cook onions in lightly greased large skillet over medium to medium-low heat until very tender, about 15 minutes. Add tomatoes and herbs; cook over medium heat until mixture is thick, about 15 minutes. Season to taste with salt and pepper; cool.

2. Spread dough on greased 12-inch pizza pan, making rim around edge. Spread onion mixture over dough and sprinkle with olives. Bake at 425 degrees until crust is browned, 15 to 20 minutes.

FRESH TOMATO AND BASIL PIZZA

One of the simplest yet most flavorful pizzas you've ever tasted! Use fresh basil if you possibly can.

6 slices

Basic Pizza Dough (see p. 298)
Pizza Sauce (see p. 582)
1–2 teaspoons minced plain, or roasted, garlic
1 cup (4 ounces) fat-free mozzarella cheese
½ cup (2 ounces) reduced-fat mozzarella cheese
2 medium tomatoes, thinly sliced
18 basil leaves, or 1 teaspoon dried basil leaves
Salt and pepper, to taste

Per Serving:
Calories: 450
% of calories from fat: 10
Fat (gm): 2
Saturated fat (gm): 1
Cholesterol (mg): 8.4
Sodium (mg): 466
Protein (gm): 11.6
Carbohydrate (gm): 22.6

Exchanges:
Milk: 0.0
Vegetable: 0.0
Fruit: 0.0
Bread: 1.5
Meat: 1.0
Fat: 0.0

1. Spread dough on greased 12-inch pizza pan, making rim around edge. Mix Pizza Sauce and garlic; spread over dough. Sprinkle with cheeses and top with tomato slices and basil; sprinkle tomatoes lightly with salt and pepper. Bake at 425 degrees until crust is browned, 15 to 20 minutes.

ARTICHOKE AND ROASTED PEPPER PIZZA

L

45

Roasted green bell peppers add a unique flavor; roasted red peppers can be substituted.

6 slices

1 medium green bell pepper, cut into ½-inch slices

Basic Pizza Dough (see p. 298)

½ can (15-ounce size) reduced-sodium whole tomatoes, drained, coarsely chopped

½ can (15-ounce size) quartered artichoke hearts, rinsed, drained

½ teaspoon dried Italian seasoning

½ cup (2 ounces) shredded fat-free mozzarella cheese

¼ cup (1 ounce) shredded reduced-fat mozzarella cheese

2 tablespoons grated fat-free Parmesan cheese

Per Slice:
Calories: 169
% of calories from fat: 18
Fat (gm): 3.6
Saturated fat (gm): 0.6
Cholesterol (mg): 2.5
Sodium (mg): 311
Protein (gm): 9
Carbohydrate (gm): 26.8

Exchanges:
Milk: 0.0
Vegetable: 1.0
Fruit: 0.0
Bread: 1.5
Meat: 0.5
Fat: 0.0

1. Arrange bell pepper in greased foil-lined baking pan; roast at 425 degrees until pepper is tender and browned, 20 to 30 minutes.

2. Spread dough on greased 12-inch pizza pan, making rim around edge. Arrange bell pepper, tomatoes, and artichoke hearts on dough; sprinkle with Italian seasoning and cheeses. Bake at 425 degrees until crust is browned, 15 to 20 minutes.

ROASTED RED PEPPER AND CHEESE PIZZA

L

45

For color and flavor variation, try a yellow or green bell pepper.

6 slices

1 large red bell pepper, cut into ¾-inch slices

Cornmeal Pizza Dough (see p. 298)

1 cup fat-free ricotta cheese

½ cup (2 ounces) shredded fat-free mozzarella cheese

¼ cup (1 ounce) shredded fat-free Parmesan cheese

3 tablespoons fat-free sour cream

1 tablespoon lemon juice

Per Slice:
Calories: 172
% of calories from fat: 3
Fat (gm): 0.6
Saturated fat (gm): 0.1
Cholesterol (mg): 0
Sodium (mg): 124
Protein (gm): 14.4
Carbohydrate (gm): 29.4

Exchanges:
Milk: 0.0
Vegetable: 1.0
Fruit: 0.0
Bread: 1.5
Meat: 1.0
Fat: 0.0

1 clove garlic, minced

12–18 fresh basil leaves

2 green onions, thinly sliced

1. Arrange bell pepper slices in greased foil-lined pan. Roast at 425 degrees until peppers are tender and browned, 20 to 30 minutes.

2. Spread dough on greased 12-inch pizza pan, making rim around edge; bake dough at 425 degrees 15 to 20 minutes. Spread combined cheeses, sour cream, lemon juice, and garlic evenly on crust; top with roasted red pepper slices, basil leaves, and green onions. Bake at 425 degrees until crust is browned, 15 to 20 minutes.

TUSCAN POTATO PIZZA

L

A hearty pizza with robust country flavor.

45

6 slices

🔥

8 ounces small russet potatoes, unpeeled, cut into
   ¼-inch slices

1 medium red onion, thinly sliced

Vegetable cooking spray

Salt and pepper, to taste

Whole Wheat Pizza Dough (see p. 299)

2 teaspoons minced garlic

1 teaspoon dried sage leaves

½ teaspoon dried thyme leaves

2 sun-dried tomatoes (not in oil), softened, chopped

1 cup (4 ounces) shredded fat-free mozzarella cheese

½ cup (2 ounces) shredded smoked mozzarella cheese

Per Slice:
Calories: 225
% of calories from fat: 8
Fat (gm): 2.1
Saturated fat (gm): 0.1
Cholesterol (mg): 5
Sodium (mg): 301
Protein (gm): 14.4
Carbohydrate (gm): 38.2

Exchanges:
Milk: 0.0
Vegetable: 0.0
Fruit: 0.0
Bread: 2.5
Meat: 1.0
Fat: 0.0

1. Arrange potatoes and onion on greased foil-lined jelly roll pan; spray with cooking spray. Roast at 425 degrees until almost tender, about 10 minutes. Season to taste with salt and pepper; cool.

2. Spread dough on greased 12-inch pizza pan, making rim around edge. Sprinkle garlic on crust. Arrange potatoes and onions on crust; sprinkle with remaining ingredients. Bake at 425 degrees until crust is browned, 15 to 20 minutes.

PIZZA ON PASTA

LO

A fun pizza, with a crust made of spaghetti!

45   **6 slices**

1 package (8 ounces) vegetarian sausage patties, or
links, crumbled

1 cup each: sliced mushrooms, zucchini

½ cup sliced red bell pepper

¼ cup sliced green onions

1½ teaspoons minced garlic

8 ounces thin spaghetti, cooked

1½ teaspoons dried Italian seasoning

Salt and pepper, to taste

1 egg, lightly beaten

1 medium tomato, sliced

¾–1 cup (3–4 ounces) shredded reduced-fat
muenster, or mozzarella, cheese

Pizza Sauce (see p. 582), warm

Per Slice:
Calories: 305
% of calories from fat: 20
Fat (gm): 6.8
Saturated fat (gm): 2.1
Cholesterol (mg): 9
Sodium (mg): 359
Protein (gm): 18.6
Carbohydrate (gm): 42.7

Exchanges:
Milk: 0.0
Vegetable: 2.0
Fruit: 0.0
Bread: 2.0
Meat: 2.0
Fat: 0.0

1. Sauté vegetarian sausage, mushrooms, zucchini, bell pepper, green onions, and garlic in lightly greased large skillet until vegetables are tender, about 8 minutes. Stir in spaghetti and Italian seasoning; season to taste with salt and pepper. Stir in egg whites.

2. Pat spaghetti mixture into even layer in lightly greased large skillet with pancake turner. Cook, covered, over medium to medium-low heat until browned on the bottom, about 5 minutes. Loosen side and bottom of "pizza" with pancake turner; invert onto large plate. Slide "pizza" back into skillet; top with tomatoes and sprinkle with cheese. Cook, covered, over medium heat until cheese is melted, about 5 minutes. Slide onto serving plate; cut into wedges and serve with Pizza Sauce.

LEEK AND FETA PIZZA WITH PESTO

L *Use your choice of pesto recipes (see Index), or used a purchased pesto.*

6 slices

4 cups sliced leeks (white parts only)
1 teaspoon dried basil leaves
Salt and pepper, to taste
Basic Pizza Dough (see p. 298)
Sun-Dried Tomato Pesto (see p. 606)
½ cup (2 ounces) each: shredded fat-free mozzarella, and crumbled reduced-fat feta cheese
2 tablespoons (½ ounce) grated fat-free Parmesan cheese

Per Slice:
Calories: 288
% of calories from fat: 27
Fat (gm): 8.9
Saturated fat (gm): 1.9
Cholesterol (mg): 3.4
Sodium (mg): 428
Protein (gm): 12.1
Carbohydrate (gm): 41.9

Exchanges:
Milk: 0.0
Vegetable: 3.0
Fruit: 0.0
Bread: 1.5
Meat: 1.0
Fat: 1.0

1. Sauté leeks and basil in lightly greased large skillet until leeks are tender, 8 to 10 minute. Season to taste with salt and pepper; cool.

2. Spread dough on greased 12-inch pizza pan, making rim around edge. Spread Sun-Dried Tomato Pesto on dough; top with leeks and sprinkle with cheeses. Bake at 425 degrees until crust is browned, 15 to 20 minutes.

TACO PIZZA

L *Top this baked pizza with your choice of taco ingredients before eating!*

45

6 slices

Cornmeal Pizza Dough (see p. 298)
⅓ package (12-ounce size) vegetarian ground beef
1–2 tablespoons taco seasoning mix
⅔ cup water
½ cup (2 ounces) each: shredded fat-free Cheddar and reduced-fat Monterey Jack cheese
½ large green bell pepper, sliced
1 cup chopped lettuce
½ cup chopped tomato
6 tablespoons each: fat-free sour cream, salsa

Per Slice:
Calories: 190
% of calories from fat: 10
Fat (gm): 2.2
Saturated fat (gm): 1.1
Cholesterol (mg): 6.8
Sodium (mg): 370
Protein (gm): 14.9
Carbohydrate (gm): 27.8

Exchanges:
Milk: 0.0
Vegetable: 0.5
Fruit: 0.0
Bread: 1.5
Meat: 1.5
Fat: 0.0

1. Spread dough on lightly greased 12-inch pizza pan, making rim around edge. Combine vegetarian ground beef, taco seasoning mix, and water in medium saucepan; heat to boiling. Reduce heat and simmer, uncovered, until mixture is dry, about 5 minutes. Sprinkle mixture over dough; top with cheeses, and bell pepper.

2. Bake pizza at 425 degrees until crust is browned, 15 to 20 minutes. Sprinkle with lettuce and tomato and serve immediately with sour cream and salsa.

BLACK BEAN AND JALAPEÑO PIZZA

L

45

For quick and easy individual pizzas, assemble ingredients as below, using 4 flour tortillas; bake at 350 degrees until beans are hot and cheese melted, about 10 minutes.

6 slices

Cornmeal, or Cheese Pizza Dough (see pp. 298, 299)
1 cup mild, or hot salsa, divided
1 cup cooked dried, or rinsed, drained, canned, black beans
¼–⅓ cup drained, pickled, sliced jalapeño chilies
1 cup (4 ounces) shredded reduced-fat Cheddar cheese

1. Spread dough on pan, making rim around edge. Spread ¾ cup salsa on dough. Lightly mash black beans with remaining ¼ cup salsa; spoon over pizza. Sprinkle with jalapeño chilies and cheese. Bake at 425 degrees until crust is browned, 15 to 20 minutes.

Per Slice:
Calories: 191
% of calories from fat: 16
Fat (gm): 3.3
Saturated fat (gm): 1.5
Cholesterol (mg): 10.1
Sodium (mg): 334
Protein (gm): 9.9
Carbohydrate (gm): 30.3

Exchanges:
Milk: 0.0
Vegetable: 1.0
Fruit: 0.0
Bread: 2.0
Meat: 0.5
Fat: 0.0

HUEVOS RANCHEROS PIZZA

LO *Pizza crust replaces tortillas in this version of the popular Mexican dish.*

6 slices

1 large poblano chili, sliced

½ large red bell pepper, sliced

1 small onion, sliced

2 cloves garlic, minced

Salt and pepper, to taste

Cornmeal, or Cheese Pizza Dough
(see pp. 298, 299)

1 cup mild or hot salsa, or pizza sauce

Vegetarian Chorizo (see p. 287)

1 cup (4 ounces) shredded fat-free Cheddar cheese

1 egg

Per Slice:
Calories: 225
% of calories from fat: 10
Fat (gm): 2.4
Saturated fat (gm): 0.6
Cholesterol (mg): 71
Sodium (mg): 382
Protein (gm): 18.8
Carbohydrate (gm): 32.5

Exchanges:
Milk: 0.0
Vegetable: 1.0
Fruit: 0.0
Bread: 1.5
Meat: 1.5
Fat: 0.0

1. Sauté poblano chili, bell pepper, onion, and garlic in lightly greased large skillet until tender, about 8 minutes. Season to taste with salt and pepper.

2. Spread dough on greased 12-inch pizza pan, making rim around edge. Spread salsa on dough; top with sautéed vegetables, Vegetarian Chorizo, and cheese. Bake at 425 degrees until crust is browned, 15 to 20 minutes. Remove from oven; break egg into center of pizza. Stir egg with fork and quickly spread over pizza. Return to oven and bake until egg is cooked, 1 to 2 minutes.

PIZZA WITH YELLOW AND GREEN SQUASH

L *A pizza with garden-fresh flavors and colors!*

45 6 slices

1 each: sliced medium zucchini, yellow summer
squash, onion
2 cloves garlic, minced
Salt and pepper, to taste
Cheese Pizza Dough (see p. 299)
1 medium tomato, thinly sliced
¾ teaspoon dried Italian seasoning
1 cup (4 ounces) shredded reduced-fat
mozzarella cheese

Per Slice:
Calories: 189
% of calories from fat: 16
Fat (gm): 3.2
Saturated fat (gm): 2.1
Cholesterol (mg): 10.1
Sodium (mg): 188
Protein (gm): 11.8
Carbohydrate (gm): 27.5

Exchanges:
Milk: 0.0
Vegetable: 1.0
Fruit: 0.0
Bread: 1.5
Meat: 1.0
Fat: 0.0

1. Sauté squash, onion, and garlic in lightly greased large skillet
until crisp-tender, about 3 minutes; season to taste with salt
and pepper.

2. Spread dough on greased 12-inch pizza pan, making rim around
edge. Arrange tomato slices on dough and top with squash mixture;
sprinkle with herbs and cheese. Bake at 425 degrees until browned,
15 to 20 minutes.

BROCCOLI AND MUSHROOM PIZZA

L *Smoked mozzarella cheese gives this pizza its wonderful smoky flavor.*

45 6 slices

1 cup each: broccoli florets, sliced cremini
mushrooms, onion
2 cloves garlic, finely chopped
⅛ teaspoon red pepper flakes
Vegetable cooking spray
Whole Wheat Pizza Dough (see p. 299)
1 cup fat-free ricotta cheese
3 tablespoons fat-free sour cream
½ teaspoon dried sage leaves
½ cup each: shredded smoked and fat-free
mozzarella cheese (2 ounces each)

Per Slice:
Calories: 201
% of calories from fat: 9
Fat (gm): 2.2
Saturated fat (gm): 1.1
Cholesterol (mg): 6.8
Sodium (mg): 265
Protein (gm): 16.5
Carbohydrate (gm): 32

Exchanges:
Milk: 0.0
Vegetable: 1.0
Fruit: 0.0
Bread: 1.5
Meat: 1.5
Fat: 0.0

1. Sauté broccoli, mushrooms, onion, and garlic in lightly greased large skillet until crisp-tender, 5 to 8 minutes. Stir in red pepper flakes; season to taste with salt and pepper.

2. Spread dough on greased 12-inch pan, making rim around edge. Spray dough with cooking spray; bake at 425 degrees 10 minutes. Spread dough with combined ricotta cheese, sour cream, sage, and smoked mozzarella cheese; top with vegetable mixture and sprinkle with mozzarella cheese. Bake at 425 degrees until crust is browned, about 15 minutes.

ZUCCHINI AND MUSHROOM PIZZA WITH FILLO CRUST

L

45

Any kind of mushrooms can be used, but the wild varieties have the fullest flavor.

8 slices

1 cup sliced leeks (white part only)

4 cups sliced wild mushrooms (cremini, shiitake, portobello, oyster, etc.)

1 teaspoon minced garlic

2 medium zucchini, thinly sliced

½ teaspoon dried thyme leaves

Salt and pepper, to taste

Olive oil cooking spray

8 sheets frozen, fillo pastry, thawed

1 cup (4 ounces) crumbled reduced-fat feta cheese

¼ cup (1 ounce) grated fat-free Parmesan cheese

Per Slice:
Calories: 69
% of calories from fat: 29
Fat (gm): 2.4
Saturated fat (gm): 1.3
Cholesterol (mg): 5.1
Sodium (mg): 223
Protein (gm): 5.1
Carbohydrate (gm): 8.1

Exchanges:
Milk: 0.0
Vegetable: 0.5
Fruit: 0.0
Bread: 0.5
Meat: 0.5
Fat: 0.0

1. Cook leeks, mushrooms, and garlic in lightly greased large skillet, covered, over medium heat until wilted, 3 to 4 minutes. Add zucchini and thyme and cook, uncovered, until vegetables are tender, 5 to 8 minutes; season to taste with salt and pepper.

2. Spray jelly roll pan with cooking spray; place sheet of fillo on pan and spray lightly. Repeat with remaining fillo. Spoon vegetable mixture evenly over fillo; sprinkle with cheeses. Bake at 375 degrees until fillo is browned and cheese melted, about 15 minutes.

TOMATO FILLO PIZZA

L

Use summer's ripest tomatoes for this delectable pizza.

45

8 slices

Olive oil cooking spray
8 sheets frozen fillo pastry, thawed
2 cups (8 ounces) shredded fat-free mozzarella cheese
½ cup thinly sliced onion
1 pound tomatoes, thinly sliced
Salt and pepper, to taste
¼ cup (1 ounce) grated Parmesan cheese
¾ teaspoon each: dried dill weed, basil leaves

Per Slice:
Calories: 79
% of calories from fat: 14
Fat (gm): 1.2
Saturated fat (gm): 0.6
Cholesterol (mg): 2.5
Sodium (mg): 270
Protein (gm): 12
Carbohydrate (gm): 5.4

Exchanges:
Milk: 0.0
Vegetable: 0.0
Fruit: 0.0
Bread: 0.5
Meat: 1.0
Fat: 0.0

1. Spray jelly roll pan with cooking spray; place sheet of fillo on pan and spray generously with spray. Repeat with remaining fillo. Sprinkle mozzarella cheese and onion over fillo; arrange tomato slices on top. Sprinkle with salt and pepper, Parmesan cheese, and herbs. Bake at 375 degrees until fillo is browned and cheese melted, about 15 minutes.

GARDEN PATCH PIZZA

L

Pick the best from the season's bounty for this good-for-you pizza!

45

8 slices

1¼ packages (8-ounce size) fat-free cream
   cheese, room temperature
2 tablespoons fat-free sour cream
1 teaspoon dried Italian seasoning
1 large whole wheat lavosh (5¼ ounces)
1 cup each: broccoli florets, chopped,
   seeded cucumber
2–3 marinated artichoke hearts, drained, sliced
¼ cup each: sliced carrot, sliced green onion
1–2 tablespoons sliced ripe olives
½ cup (2 ounces) shredded reduced-fat Havarti cheese
¼ cup French, or other, fat-free salad dressing

Per Slice:
Calories: 149
% of calories from fat: 28
Fat (gm): 4.6
Saturated fat (gm): 0.8
Cholesterol (mg): 5.1
Sodium (mg): 419
Protein (gm): 9.3
Carbohydrate (gm): 17.2

Exchanges:
Milk: 0.0
Vegetable: 2.0
Fruit: 0.0
Bread: 0.5
Meat: 0.5
Fat: 0.5

1. Mix cream cheese, sour cream, and Italian seasoning; spread on lavosh. Arrange vegetables and cheese on top. Serve immediately, or refrigerate no longer than 1 hour. Drizzle with salad dressing before serving.

SPINACH SALAD PIZZA

LO

45

This salad on a pizza is made with a large, crisp lavosh cracker. Serve with any salad dressing you like.

8 slices

1½ packages (8-ounce size) fat-free cream cheese, room temperature

5 tablespoons fat-free sweet-sour salad dressing, divided

1 large whole wheat lavosh (5¼ ounces)

2 cups packed spinach leaves, torn into bite-sized pieces

1 cup sliced mushrooms

½ cup thinly sliced red onion

2 hard-cooked eggs, sliced

2 tablespoons cooked, crumbled vegetarian bacon

Per Slice:
Calories: 162
% of calories from fat: 25
Fat (gm): 4.6
Saturated fat (gm): 0.5
Cholesterol (mg): 53.3
Sodium (mg): 405
Protein (gm): 10.2
Carbohydrate (gm): 19.9

Exchanges:
Milk: 0.0
Vegetable: 1.5
Fruit: 0.0
Bread: 1.0
Meat: 0.5
Fat: 0.5

1. Mix cream cheese and 2 tablespoons sweet-sour dressing; spread on lavosh. Top with spinach, mushrooms, onion, hard-cooked eggs, and vegetarian bacon. Serve immediately, or refrigerate no longer than 1 hour. Drizzle with remaining 3 tablespoons sweet-sour dressing before serving.

GAZPACHO PIZZA

LO *Gazpacho, chilled and refreshing, served on a crust!*

45 **8 slices**

1¼ packages (8-ounce size) fat-free cream
  cheese, room temperature
2 tablespoons fat-free mayonnaise
½ teaspoon dry mustard
1 tablespoon chopped chives
1 large whole wheat lavosh (16 inches)
1 cup each: chopped seeded tomato, cucumber
½ cup each: chopped onion, yellow and green bell
  pepper, avocado
1 teaspoon each: minced garlic, jalapeño chili
¼ cup fat-free Italian salad dressing

Per Slice:
Calories: 153
% of calories from fat: 29
Fat (gm): 5.1
Saturated fat (gm): 0.4
Cholesterol (mg): 0
Sodium (mg): 415
Protein (gm): 7.4
Carbohydrate (gm): 19.9

Exchanges:
Milk: 0.0
Vegetable: 1.5
Fruit: 0.0
Bread: 1.0
Meat: 0.0
Fat: 1.0

1. Mix cream cheese, mayonnaise, dry mustard, and chives; spread on lavosh. Combine remaining ingredients and spoon onto lavosh; serve immediately.

FRUIT ORCHARD PIZZA

L *Select the season's ripest fruit for this pizza. In the winter season, canned or frozen, thawed fruits can be used.*

45 **8 slices**

1½ packages (8-ounce size) fat-free cream cheese,
  room temperature
2 tablespoons maple syrup, or honey
1 teaspoon ground cinnamon
1 large whole wheat lavosh (16 inches)
5–6 cups assorted fresh fruit (strawberries, raspberries,
  blueberries, sliced peaches, pears, plums, kiwi, etc.)
Raspberry Sauce (see p. 662)

Per Slice:
Calories: 195
% of calories from fat: 14
Fat (gm): 3.2
Saturated fat (gm): 0
Cholesterol (mg): 0
Sodium (mg): 295
Protein (gm): 8.2
Carbohydrate (gm): 34.2

Exchanges:
Milk: 0.0
Vegetable: 0.0
Fruit: 1.0
Bread: 1.5
Meat: 0.0
Fat: 0.5

1. Mix cream cheese, maple syrup, and cinnamon; spread on lavosh. Arrange fruit attractively on top. Serve immediately, or refrigerate no longer than 1 hour. Drizzle with Raspberry Sauce before serving.

PEAR DESSERT PIZZA

L

45

Serve as a dessert, or when in the mood for something a little bit different and wonderful.

6 slices

Basic Pizza Dough (see p. 298)

¼ cup plus 2 tablespoons sugar, divided

2 tablespoons honey

2 large ripe pears, cored, sliced

Vegetable cooking spray

½ teaspoon ground cinnamon

¼ cup (1 ounce) crumbled blue cheese

2 tablespoons raisins

2–4 tablespoons coarsely chopped walnuts

Per Slice Slice:
Calories: 244
% of calories from fat: 12
Fat (gm): 3.3
Saturated fat (gm): 1
Cholesterol (mg): 3.5
Sodium (mg): 156
Protein (gm): 5.2
Carbohydrate (gm): 50.2

Exchanges:
Milk: 0.0
Vegetable: 0.0
Fruit: 1.5
Bread: 2.0
Meat: 0.0
Fat: 0.5

1. Make Basic Pizza Dough, adding 2 tablespoons sugar to flour. Spread dough on greased pizza pan, making rim around edge. Drizzle dough with honey; arrange pears on top. Spray pears lightly with cooking spray and sprinkle with remaining ¼ cup sugar and cinnamon and remaining ingredients. Bake at 425 degrees until crust is browned, 15 to 20 minutes.

APPLE SALAD PIZZA

L

45

◊

Use your favorite sweet or tart apple for this pizza and serve as a light lunch or side dish.

6 slices

Basic Pizza Dough (see p. 298)

2 cups each: baby spinach, chopped, red apples

2 tablespoons lemon juice

¼ cup each: raisins, chopped walnuts, or pecans

½ teaspoon curry powder (optional)

½ cup (2 ounces) shredded fat-free Cheddar cheese

¼ cup (1 ounce) crumbled blue cheese

Per Slice:
Calories: 218
% of calories from fat: 19
Fat (gm): 4.9
Saturated fat (gm): 1.2
Cholesterol (mg): 3.5
Sodium (mg): 204
Protein (gm): 7.9
Carbohydrate (gm): 37.7

Exchanges:
Milk: 0.0
Vegetable: 1.0
Fruit: 1.0
Bread: 1.5
Meat: 0.0
Fat: 0.5

1. Spread dough on greased 12-inch pizza pan, making rim around edge. Arrange spinach on dough. Toss apples with remaining ingredients; arrange on spinach. Bake at 425 degrees until dough is browned, 15 to 20 minutes.

FRUIT FOCACCIA

L *Serve as a dessert or a meal accompaniment.*

8 servings

½ cup each: dried cranberries, or cherries, dried
   fruit bits
1 cup boiling water
1 Focaccia (½ recipe; see p. 557)
2 tablespoons granulated sugar
1 tablespoon melted margarine, or butter
⅓ cup packed light brown sugar

Per Serving:
Calories: 253
% of calories from fat: 8
Fat (gm): 2.4
Saturated fat (gm): 0.6
Cholesterol (mg): 1.2
Sodium (mg): 188
Protein (gm): 6.6
Carbohydrate (gm): 52.6

Exchanges:
Milk: 0.0
Vegetable: 0.0
Fruit: 0.5
Bread: 3.0
Meat: 0.0
Fat: 0.0

1. Pour boiling water over combined dried fruits in bowl; let stand until softened, 10 to 15 minutes. Drain.

2. Make Focaccia, adding granulated sugar to the flour mixture. After first rising, spread dough in greased baking pan, 11 x 7 inches. Let rise until double in size, about 30 minutes.

3. Make ¼-inch indentations with fingers to "dimple" dough. Spread margarine over dough; sprinkle with fruit and brown sugar. Bake at 425 degrees until browned, 20 to 25 minutes.

LEEK AND ONION FOCACCIA

L *This recipe can also be made as a pizza, using Basic Pizza Dough (see p. 298).*

8 servings

1 Focaccia (½ recipe; see p. 557)
½ cup each: thinly sliced leek (white part only),
   yellow and red onion

½ teaspoon crumbled dried sage leaves

1–2 teaspoons olive oil

Salt and pepper, to taste

1–2 tablespoons grated fat-free Parmesan cheese

1. Make Focaccia; after first rising, spread dough in greased jelly roll pan, 15 x 10 inches. Let stand until dough is doubled in size, about 30 minutes. Make ¼-inch indentations with fingers to "dimple" the dough. Toss leek, onion, and sage with oil and spread over dough. Sprinkle with salt, pepper, and Parmesan cheese. Bake at 425 degrees until golden, 20 to 25 minutes.

Per Serving:
Calories: 193
% of calories from fat: 7
Fat (gm): 1.6
Saturated fat (gm): 0.4
Cholesterol (mg): 1.2
Sodium (mg): 171
Protein (gm): 7.1
Carbohydrate (gm): 38.4

Exchanges:
Milk: 0.0
Vegetable: 1.0
Fruit: 0.0
Bread: 2.5
Meat: 0.0
Fat: 0.0

VEGETARIAN SAUSAGE CALZONES

L

Hot roll mix makes these calzones fast and easy to prepare. The filling can be prepared a day in advance and refrigerated; heat until warm before assembling calzones.

8 servings

1 cup each: sliced carrots, onion, zucchini

½ cup each: chopped red bell pepper, sliced mushrooms

4 cloves garlic, minced

1 package (8 ounces) vegetarian sausages, or patties, crumbled

¾ teaspoon each: dried Italian seasoning, crushed fennel seeds

1½ cups chopped tomatoes

1 cup rinsed, drained, canned cannellini, or Great Northern, beans

¼ cup sliced ripe olives

Salt and pepper, to taste

1 package (16 ounces) hot roll mix

1¼ cups very hot water (120 degrees)

1 tablespoon olive oil

¾ cup each: shredded fat-free, and reduced-fat mozzarella cheese (3 ounces each)

2 tablespoons fat-free milk

Per Serving:
Calories: 398
% of calories from fat: 24
Fat (gm): 11
Saturated fat (gm): 2.6
Cholesterol (mg): 9.2
Sodium (mg): 757
Protein (gm): 20.8
Carbohydrate (gm): 55.8

Exchanges:
Milk: 0.0
Vegetable: 2.0
Fruit: 0.0
Bread: 3.0
Meat: 2.0
Fat: 0.5

1. Cook carrots, onion, zucchini, bell pepper, mushrooms, and garlic in lightly greased large skillet over medium heat, covered, 5 minutes. Add vegetarian sausage, herbs, tomato, beans, and olives; cook, covered, until vegetables are just tender, 5 to 8 minutes, stirring occasionally. Season to taste with salt and pepper.

2. Make hot roll mix according to package directions for pizza crust, using 1¼ cups very hot water and 1 tablespoon oil. Divide dough into 8 equal pieces. Roll 1 piece dough on floured surface into circle 7 inches in diameter. Spoon about ¾ cup filling on dough and sprinkle with 3 tablespoons combined cheeses. Brush edge of dough with milk and fold in half. Flute edge of dough or press with tines of fork. Place on greased cookie sheet. Repeat with remaining dough, filling, and cheese.

3. Brush tops of calzones with milk. Bake at 375 degrees until browned, about 15 minutes. Cool on wire rack 5 minutes.

CHEESE AND MUSHROOM CALZONES

L *Use any mushrooms you like — the wild varieties lend a woodsy, rich flavor.*

8 servings

6 cups sliced porcini, or portobello, mushrooms

½ cup each: chopped broccoli, onion

2 teaspoons minced roasted garlic

1 teaspoon dried basil leaves

1 cup each: fat-free ricotta, and shredded fat-free mozzarella cheese (4 ounces each)

2 tablespoons grated Parmesan cheese

¼ cup fat-free sour cream

Salt and pepper, to taste

1 package (16 ounces) hot roll mix

1¼ cups water, very hot (120 degrees)

1 tablespoon olive oil

2 tablespoons fat-free milk

Per Serving:
Calories: 312
% of calories from fat: 16
Fat (gm): 5.8
Saturated fat (gm): 1.1
Cholesterol (mg): 4.6
Sodium (mg): 387
Protein (gm): 18
Carbohydrate (gm): 48.4

Exchanges:
Milk: 0.0
Vegetable: 1.0
Fruit: 0.0
Bread: 3.0
Meat: 1.0
Fat: 0.5

1. Cook mushrooms, broccoli, onion, garlic, and basil in lightly greased large skillet, covered, over medium heat until mushrooms are wilted, about 5 minutes. Cook, uncovered, until vegetables are tender, 5 to 8 minutes. Cool; mix in cheeses and sour cream; season to taste with salt and pepper.

2. Make hot roll mix according to package directions for pizza, using 1¼ cups hot water and 1 tablespoon olive oil. Divide dough into 8 equal pieces. Roll 1 piece dough on floured surface into 6- to 7-inch circle; spoon about ⅔ cup mushroom mixture on dough. Brush edge of dough with milk and fold in half. Flute edges of dough or press together with tines of fork. Place on greased cookie sheet. Repeat with remaining dough and filling.

3. Brush tops of calzones with milk. Bake at 375 degrees until browned, 15 to 20 minutes. Let cool on wire rack 5 minutes before serving.

SWEET FENNEL CALZONES

Fresh fennel, onion, sour cream, and melted cheese are combined in these golden calzones.

8 servings

6 cups thinly sliced fennel bulb

1½ cups chopped onion

⅔ cup chopped red bell pepper

2 cloves garlic, minced

1 cup (4 ounces) shredded fat-free mozzarella cheese

½ cup fat-free sour cream

Salt and pepper, to taste

1 package (16 ounces) hot roll mix

1¼ cups very hot water (120 degrees)

1 tablespoon olive oil

2 tablespoons fat-free milk

Per Serving:
Calories: 307
% of calories from fat: 15
Fat (gm): 5.3
Saturated fat (gm): 0.8
Cholesterol (mg): 3.4
Sodium (mg): 378
Protein (gm): 13.8
Carbohydrate (gm): 52

Exchanges:
Milk: 0.0
Vegetable: 1.5
Fruit: 0.0
Bread: 3.0
Meat: 0.5
Fat: 0.5

1. Cook fennel, onion, bell pepper, and garlic in lightly greased large skillet, covered, over medium heat until tender, 15 to 20 minutes, stirring occasionally. Cool; stir in cheese and sour cream. Season to taste with salt and pepper.

2. Make hot roll mix according to package directions for pizza, using 1¼ cups hot water and 1 tablespoon olive oil. Divide dough into 8 equal pieces. Roll 1 piece dough on floured surface into 6- to 7-inch circle; spoon about ⅔ cup fennel mixture on dough. Brush edge of dough with milk and fold in half. Flute edges of dough or press together with tines of fork. Place on greased cookie sheet. Repeat with remaining dough and filling.

3. Brush tops of calzones with milk. Bake at 375 degrees until browned, 15 to 20 minutes. Let cool on wire rack 5 minutes.

TORTA RUSTICA

LO

An Italian pizza in a crust-lined deep-dish pie.

45

8 servings

1½ cups chopped onions

1½ teaspoons minced roasted garlic

1 package (8 ounces) vegetarian sausages, or patties, crumbled

1 can (16 ounces) reduced-sodium whole tomatoes, undrained, coarsely chopped

3 cups each: sliced zucchini, mushrooms

Salt and pepper, to taste

1 package (16 ounces) hot roll mix

1 cup very hot water (120 degrees)

1 egg

1–1½ cups (4 ounces) shredded reduced-fat mozzarella cheese

2 tablespoons fat-free milk

Per Serving:
Calories: 368
% of calories from fat: 27
Fat (gm): 11.2
Saturated fat (gm): 2.2
Cholesterol (mg): 34.2
Sodium (mg): 668
Protein (gm): 17
Carbohydrate (gm): 50.4

Exchanges:
Milk: 0.0
Vegetable: 2.0
Fruit: 0.0
Bread: 2.0
Meat: 2.0
Fat: 1.0

1. Sauté onions, garlic, and vegetarian sausages in lightly greased large skillet until onions are tender, about 5 minutes. Stir in tomatoes and liqiud, zucchini, and mushrooms; heat to boiling. Reduce heat and simmer, covered, 5 minutes. Simmer, uncovered, until excess liquid is gone, about 10 minutes. Season to taste with salt and pepper.

2. Make hot roll mix according to package directions, using hot water and egg. Roll ⅔ of dough on floured surface to fit 2-quart casserole or soufflé dish. Ease dough into casserole, allowing dough to extend 1 inch over edge. Spoon half the vegetable mixture into casserole; sprinkle with half the cheese. Top with remaining vegetable mixture and cheese.

3. Roll remaining dough into circle to fit top of casserole. Bring outside edges of dough together and crimp. Cut 1 or 2 slits in top of dough with sharp knife. Brush top of dough with milk. Bake at 400 degrees until crust is browned, about 30 minutes. Let stand 10 minutes before serving.

ITALIAN VEGGIE BURGER PIE

LO

45

Vegetarian Italian-style burgers and vegetables bake into a wonderful pie in no time at all!

6 servings

½ package (16-ounce size) frozen Italian-style vegetarian burgers, crumbled

1 cup chopped tomato

½ cup each: chopped onion, zucchini, red bell pepper

1 teaspoon dried Italian seasoning

¾ cup reduced-fat baking mix

1 cup (4 ounces) shredded fat-free mozzarella cheese

1 tablespoon grated fat-free Parmesan cheese

1 cup fat-free milk

2 eggs

Per Serving:
Calories: 205
% of calories from fat: 22
Fat (gm): 5.1
Saturated fat (gm): 0.9
Cholesterol (mg): 36.2
Sodium (mg): 679
Protein (gm): 18.7
Carbohydrate (gm): 21.7

Exchanges:
Milk: 0.0
Vegetable: 1.0
Fruit: 0.0
Bread: 1.0
Meat: 2.0
Fat: 0.0

1. Combine vegetarian burgers, tomato, onion, zucchini, bell pepper, and Italian seasoning; spoon into lightly greased 9-inch pie pan.

2. Combine baking mix and cheeses in small bowl; mix in combined milk and eggs; pour over mixture in pie pan. Bake at 400 degrees until set and browned on the top, 35 to 40 minutes. Let stand 5 minutes before cutting.

VEGGIE POT PIE

V *This skinny version of a family favorite sports only a top crust.*

4 servings (about 1¼ cups each)

½ cup each: sliced leek (white part only),
  chopped green onions
¾ cup sliced red bell pepper
2 cloves garlic, minced
½ teaspoon each: dried rosemary and
  marjoram leaves
2 cups reduced-sodium vegetable broth
1½ cups each: cubed peeled sweet potato,
  yellow summer squash
1 cup cut green beans
½ cup broccoflower, or cauliflower florets
3 tablespoons flour
⅓ cup cold water
Salt and pepper, to taste
Pot Pie Pastry (recipe follows)
Fat-free milk

Per Serving:
Calories: 366
% of calories from fat: 30
Fat (gm): 12.6
Saturated fat (gm): 2.4
Cholesterol (mg): 0.0
Sodium (mg): 541
Protein (gm): 8.3
Carbohydrate (gm): 57

Exchanges:
Milk: 0.0
Vegetable: 0.0
Fruit: 0.0
Bread: 4.0
Meat: 0.0
Fat: 2.0

1. Sauté leek, green onions, bell pepper, garlic, and herbs in lightly greased large saucepan until tender, 5 to 8 minutes. Add broth and remaining vegetables; heat to boiling. Reduce heat and simmer, covered, until vegetables are tender, about 10 minutes. Heat to boiling and stir in combined flour and cold water; boil, stirring, until thickened, about 1 minute. Season to taste with salt and pepper; pour into 1½-quart souffle dish.

2. Roll pastry on floured surface into circle 1 inch larger than top of soufflé dish and place on top of dish. Flute edge of pastry. Brush top of pastry with milk. Bake at 425 degrees until pastry is browned, about 20 minutes. Cool on wire rack 5 minutes.

Pot Pie Pastry

1 cup all-purpose flour
¼ teaspoon each: baking powder, salt
4 tablespoons cold margarine, or butter, cut into pieces
4–5 tablespoons ice water

1. Combine flour, baking powder, and salt in small bowl; cut in margarine with pastry blender until mixture resembles coarse crumbs. Mix in water, 1 tablespoon at a time, to form dough. Refrigerate, covered, until ready to use.

AUTUMN VEGETABLE PIE

L *Choose ingredients from your garden or produce market for this savory pie.*

4 servings (about 1¼ cups each)

½ cup each: chopped onion, sliced celery,
   red bell pepper
2 cloves garlic, minced
½ teaspoon each: dried sage and thyme leaves
2 cups reduced-sodium vegetable broth
1 cup each: cubed peeled sweet potato, unpeeled
   russet potato, turnip, halved Brussels sprouts
½ cup each: lima beans, halved small mushrooms
3 tablespoons flour
⅓ cup cold water
Salt and pepper, to taste
Pot Pie Pastry (see p. 325)
Fat-free milk

Per Serving:
Calories: 374
% of calories from fat: 29
Fat (gm): 12
Saturated fat (gm): 2.4
Cholesterol (mg): 0.0
Sodium (mg): 573
Protein (gm): 9
Carbohydrate (gm): 58

Exchanges:
Milk: 0.0
Vegetable: 2.0
Fruit: 0.0
Bread: 3.0
Meat: 0.0
Fat: 2.5

1. Sauté onion, celery, bell pepper, garlic, and herbs in lightly greased large saucepan until vegetables are tender, about 5 minutes. Add broth and remaining vegetables; heat to boiling. Reduce heat and simmer, covered, until vegetables are tender, about 10 minutes. Heat to boiling and stir in combined flour and cold water; boil, stirring, until thickened, about 1 minute. Season to taste with salt and pepper. Spoon into 1½-quart casserole.

2. Roll pastry on floured surface into circle 1 to 1½ inches larger than top of soufflé dish and place on top of casserole. Flute pastry. Brush top of pastry with milk. Bake at 425 degrees until pastry is browned, about 20 minutes. Cool on wire rack 5 minutes.

SHEPHERD'S VEGGIE POT PIE

L

Topped with mashed potatoes instead of pastry, this comfort food is sure to please.

4 servings (about 1¼ cups each)

1 cup chopped onion

½ cup each: chopped green bell pepper, sliced celery

1 clove garlic, minced

½ teaspoon each: dried savory and thyme leaves

2 cups reduced-sodium vegetable broth

1 cup each: thinly sliced cabbage, carrots, cubed
   unpeeled potatoes

¾ cup each: fresh, or frozen, peas, sliced mushrooms

3 tablespoons flour

⅓ cup cold water

Salt and pepper, to taste

2 cups (½ recipe) Real Mashed Potatoes (see p. 493)

1 tablespoon margarine, or butter, melted

Paprika, as garnish

Per Serving:
Calories: 243
% of calories from fat: 19
Fat (gm): 5
Saturated fat (gm): 1
Cholesterol (mg): 1.6
Sodium (mg): 358
Protein (gm): 6.8
Carbohydrate (gm): 44

Exchanges:
Milk: 0.0
Vegetable: 0.0
Fruit: 0.0
Bread: 3.0
Meat: 0.0
Fat: 1.0

1. Sauté onion, bell pepper, celery, garlic, and herbs in lightly greased large saucepan until vegetables are tender, 5 to 8 minutes. Stir in broth and remaining vegetables and heat to boiling; reduce heat and simmer, covered, until vegetables are tender, 10 to 15 minutes. Heat to boiling; stir in combined flour and cold water; boil, stirring, until thickened, about 1 minute. Season to taste with salt and pepper. Spoon mixture into 1½-quart soufflé dish.

2. Spoon or pipe potatoes around edge of souffle;soufflé; drizzle with margarine and sprinkle with paprika. Bake, uncovered, at 350 degrees until lightly browned, 20 to 30 minutes.

USE-IT-UP PIE

LO

45

So named because any little tidbits left in the fridge can be used in this tasty pie. Reduced-fat baking mix makes the recipe easy.

6 servings

1 cup sliced mushrooms

½ cup each: chopped onion, green bell pepper, sliced zucchini, broccoli florets

1 teaspoon minced garlic

1 teaspoon each: dried basil and oregano leaves

¼–½ teaspoon crushed red pepper

1 cup coarsely chopped tomato

½ cup rinsed, drained, canned kidney, or black, beans

½ cup (2 ounces) shredded reduced-fat Cheddar cheese

Salt and pepper, to taste

1¼ cups reduced-fat baking mix

2 tablespoons grated fat-free Parmesan cheese

2 eggs

1 cup fat-free milk

Per Serving:
Calories: 203
% of calories from fat: 20
Fat (gm): 4.5
Saturated fat (gm): 1.3
Cholesterol (mg): 76.7
Sodium (mg): 675
Protein (gm): 10.7
Carbohydrate (gm): 31

Exchanges:
Milk: 0.0
Vegetable: 2.0
Fruit: 0.0
Bread: 1.5
Meat: 0.5
Fat: 0.5

1. Sauté mushrooms, onion, bell pepper, zucchini, broccoli, garlic, and herbs in lightly greased large skillet until vegetables are tender, 5 to 8 minutes. Stir in tomato, beans, and cheese; season to taste with salt and pepper. Spoon into greased 9-inch pie pan.

2. Mix baking mix, Parmesan cheese, eggs, and milk; spread over vegetables in pan. Bake at 400 degrees until set and browned, 25 to 30 minutes. Let stand 5 minutes.

MEXICALI PIE

LO

Another easy-to-make pie, perfect for brunch, lunch, or a light supper.

45

6 servings

½ cup chopped onion

½ can (15-ounce size) dark red kidney beans, rinsed, drained

1 cup whole kernel corn

1 zucchini, halved, thinly sliced

¼ cup chopped yellow bell pepper

1 tablespoon canned chopped green chilies

1½ teaspoons chili powder, divided

¼ teaspoon ground cumin

¾ cup reduced-fat baking mix

1 cup (4 ounces) shredded reduced-fat taco cheese

1 cup fat-free milk

2 eggs

Per Serving:
Calories: 209
% of calories from fat: 19
Fat (gm): 4.7
Saturated fat (gm): 0.3
Cholesterol (mg): 46.2
Sodium (mg): 531
Protein (gm): 14.6
Carbohydrate (gm): 29.3

Exchanges:
Milk: 0.0
Vegetable: 1.0
Fruit: 0.0
Bread: 1.5
Meat: 1.5
Fat: 0.0

1. Spoon combined onion, beans, corn, zucchini, bell pepper, chilies, 1 teaspoon chili powder, and cumin into greased 9-inch pie pan.

2. Combine baking mix, remaining ½ teaspoon chili powder, and cheese in bowl; mix in milk and eggs. Pour batter over vegetables. Bake at 400 degrees until set and browned on the top, 35 to 40 minutes. Let stand 5 minutes.

ARTICHOKE PIE

LO

The ingredients of the baked artichoke dip we all love, made into a wonderful rich and cheesy pie.

45

8 servings

1 package (8 ounces) fat-free cream cheese, room temperature

1 cup (4 ounces) shredded fat-free mozzarella cheese

¼ cup (1 ounce) grated fat-free Parmesan cheese

1 can (14 ounces) artichoke hearts, drained, sliced

2 teaspoons minced roasted garlic

¾ cup reduced-fat baking mix

1 cup fat-free milk

¼ cup each: fat-free mayonnaise and fat-free
sour cream

2 eggs

Per Serving:
Calories: 169
% of calories from fat: 24
Fat (gm): 4.7
Saturated fat (gm): 0.2
Cholesterol (mg): 27.1
Sodium (mg): 755
Protein (gm): 14.2
Carbohydrate (gm): 18.8

1. Mix cheeses and spread in bottom of greased
10-inch pie pan; top with artichoke hearts and
roasted garlic.

2. Mix baking mix and combined milk, mayonnaise, sour cream, and eggs; pour over artichoke.
Bake at 400 degrees until set and browned on
the top, 35 to 40 minutes. Let stand 5 minutes.

Exchanges:
Milk: 0.0
Vegetable: 1.0
Fruit: 0.0
Bread: 1.0
Meat: 1.5
Fat: 0.0

RICH TOMATO TART

LO *Rich in flavor, this tart has a texture similar to a quiche.*

6 servings

½ cup chopped onion

2 teaspoons minced garlic

1 can (14¼ ounces) reduced-sodium diced
tomatoes, drained

2 tablespoons finely chopped chives

½ teaspoon each: dried marjoram and thyme leaves

1 tablespoon sugar

Salt and pepper, to taste

3 eggs, lightly beaten

½ cup fat-free sour cream

¾ cup each: cooked brown rice, shredded fat-free
mozzarella, or Cheddar, cheese (3 ounces)

Baked Tart Crust (recipe follows)

1 medium tomato, sliced

Per Serving:
Calories: 319
% of calories from fat: 30
Fat (gm): 11
Saturated fat (gm): 2
Cholesterol (mg): 113
Sodium (mg): 317
Protein (gm): 14
Carbohydrate (gm): 42

Exchanges:
Milk: 0.0
Vegetable: 0.0
Fruit: 0.0
Bread: 2.5
Meat: 1.0
Fat: 1.5

1. Sauté onion and garlic in lightly greased large skillet until tender,
about 5 minutes. Add canned tomatoes, herbs, and sugar; cook
over medium heat until mixture is dry, about 5 minutes; season to
taste with salt and pepper. Mix in remaining ingredients, except

Baked Tart Crust and tomato. Spoon evenly into Baked Tart Crust and top with sliced tomato. Bake, uncovered, at 350 degrees until filling is set, 25 to 30 minutes. Let stand 5 minutes.

Baked Tart Crust

1½ cups all-purpose flour
½ teaspoon baking powder
Pinch salt
4 tablespoons cold margarine, or butter, cut into pieces
5–6 tablespoons ice water

1. Combine flour, baking powder, and salt in medium bowl; cut in margarine until mixture resembles coarse crumbs. Add water a tablespoon at a time, mixing lightly with a fork after each addition, until dough just holds together. Refrigerate, covered, at least 30 minutes.

2. Roll dough on lightly floured surface into circle 1 inch larger than 9-inch tart pan. Ease pastry into pan and trim. Line bottom of pastry with aluminum foil and fill with a single layer of pie weights or dried beans. Bake at 400 degrees 15 minutes; remove weights and pierce bottom of crust with tines of fork. Bake until pastry is browned, 10 to 15 minutes longer. Cool on wire rack.

MUSHROOM TART

LO   *Be prepared for compliments when serving this attractive tart!*

6 servings

2 pounds medium cremini, or white, mushrooms
2 tablespoons minced shallots
2 cloves garlic, minced
½ teaspoon dried thyme leaves
1–2 pinches ground nutmeg
Salt and pepper, to taste
3 eggs, lightly beaten
⅔ cup fat-free sour cream

¾ cup each: cooked brown rice, shredded fat-free
mozzarella cheese (3 ounces)
Baked Tart Crust (see p. 330)
Vegetable cooking spray

Per Serving:
Calories: 323
% of calories from fat: 29
Fat (gm): 11
Saturated fat (gm): 2.4
Cholesterol (mg): 113
Sodium (mg): 303
Protein (gm): 17
Carbohydrate (gm): 41

Exchanges:
Milk: 0.0
Vegetable: 0.0
Fruit: 0.0
Bread: 2.5
Meat: 1.0
Fat: 1.5

1. Remove stems from 12 ounces mushrooms; reserve caps. Slice stems and remaining mushrooms. Cook sliced mushrooms, shallots, garlic, thyme, and nutmeg in lightly greased large skillet, covered, over medium heat until mushrooms wilt and release moisture, about 5 minutes. Cook, uncovered, until mushrooms are tender and liquid is evaporated, 5 to 7 minutes; season to taste with salt and pepper. Mix in eggs, sour cream, rice, and cheese.

2. Spread mushroom mixture evenly in Baked Tart Crust; arrange reserved mushroom caps on top and spray with cooking spray. Bake at 350 degrees until filling is set, 25 to 30 minutes. Let stand 5 minutes.

LEEK PIE

LO *A wonderful pie to make when leeks are in season.*

6 servings

2 pounds leeks, trimmed to 14 inches
¾ teaspoon dried dill weed
2–3 pinches ground nutmeg
Salt and pepper, to taste
3 eggs
½ cup fat-free sour cream
Baked Tart Crust (see p. 330)
Vegetable cooking spray

Per Serving:
Calories: 334
% of calories from fat: 29
Fat (gm): 11
Saturated fat (gm): 2.4
Cholesterol (mg): 109
Sodium (mg): 251
Protein (gm): 10
Carbohydrate (gm): 50

Exchanges:
Milk: 0.0
Vegetable: 0.0
Fruit: 0.0
Bread: 3.0
Meat: 0.5
Fat: 2.0

1. Cook leeks in boiling water to cover in large skillet until limp, 5 to 7 minutes; drain well. Cut 5 inches off green part of leeks and reserve; thinly slice remaining leeks. Cook sliced leeks in lightly greased large skillet, covered, over medium-low heat until very soft, about 20 minutes. Stir in dill and nutmeg; season to taste with salt and pepper. Mix in eggs and sour cream.

2. Spread leek mixture evenly in Baked Tart Crust; arrange reserved green tops in spoke pattern on top and spray with cooking spray. Bake at 350 degrees until filling is set, 30 to 35 minutes. Let stand 5 minutes.

SWEET ONION TARTE TATIN

V *You'll win raves when you serve this beautiful upside-down tart! For best flavor, use a sweet onion, such as Vidalia.*

6–8 servings

1 tablespoon granulated, or light brown, sugar

2½ pounds small sweet onions, peeled, halved crosswise

Salt and pepper, to taste

⅓ cup dark, or light, raisins

1 teaspoon dried thyme leaves

¼ teaspoon ground allspice

1½ cups reduced-sodium vegetable broth

2 teaspoons balsamic vinegar

Baked Tart Crust (see p. 330)

Per Serving:
Calories: 291
% of calories from fat: 25
Fat (gm): 8.3
Saturated fat (gm): 1.6
Cholesterol (mg): 0
Sodium (mg): 126
Protein (gm): 5.9
Carbohydrate (gm): 49.8

Exchanges:
Milk: 0.0
Vegetable: 3.0
Fruit: 0.5
Bread: 1.5
Meat: 0.0
Fat: 1.5

1. Heat lightly greased 12-inch skillet with ovenproof handle over medium heat until hot; sprinkle bottom evenly with sugar. Place onion halves, cut sides down, in skillet, fitting in as many as possible. Cut remaining onion halves into pieces, or chop coarsely, and fill in any spaces between onion halves. Sprinkle lightly with salt and pepper; sprinkle with raisins, thyme, and allspice. Cook, uncovered, over medium heat until onions begin to brown on the bottoms, 8 to 10 minutes.

2. Add broth and vinegar to skillet; heat to boiling. Reduce heat and simmer, covered, until onions are tender, 20 to 25 minutes. Heat to boiling; reduce heat and simmer rapidly, uncovered, until liquid is almost gone.

3. Make Baked Tart Crust, but do not bake. Roll pastry on floured surface into 13-inch circle. Ease pastry over onions; tucking pastry around edges. Bake at 375 degrees until pastry is browned and juices are bubbly, 30 to 35 minutes. Cool in pan on wire rack 10 minutes; place large serving plate over skillet and invert tart onto plate. Serve warm or room temperature.

CURRIED ONION BAKLAVA

V *A unique baklava that is not a dessert! Serve in small pieces as an appetizer, or in larger pieces for an entrée or side dish.*

8 servings

2 pounds onions, thinly sliced

3 tablespoons curry powder

¼ cup all-purpose flour

½ cup orange juice

¼ cup each: chopped mango chutney, dried apricots

Salt and pepper, to taste

¼ cup ground almonds

½ cup ground ginger snaps

½ teaspoon ground cinnamon

Butter-flavored vegetable cooking spray

10 sheets frozen fillo, thawed

½ cup water

3 tablespoons each: sugar and honey

Per Serving:
Calories: 198
% of calories from fat: 15
Fat (gm): 3.4
Saturated fat (gm): 0.4
Cholesterol (mg): 0
Sodium (mg): 57
Protein (gm): 3.6
Carbohydrate (gm): 40.8

Exchanges:
Milk: 0.0
Vegetable: 3.0
Fruit: 0.5
Bread: 1.0
Meat: 0.0
Fat: 0.5

1. Sauté onions in lightly greased large skillet 5 minutes; cook, covered, over medium-low heat until onions are very tender, 15 to 20 minutes. Sprinkle with curry powder and flour and cook, stirring, 1 minute. Stir in orange juice, chutney, and apricots; heat to boiling. Reduce heat and simmer, uncovered, until apricots are softened and mixture thickened, about 5 minutes. Season to taste with salt and pepper; cool.

2. Combine almonds, ginger snaps, and cinnamon. Spray bottom of 13 x 9-inch baking pan with cooking spray. Fold 1 sheet of fillo in half crosswise and place in pan; spray with cooking spray and sprinkle with 4 teaspoons almond mixture. Repeat with fillo and almond mixture four times, ending with fillo.

3. Spread onion mixture over fillo. Add remaining fillo and almond mixture in layers, as in Step 2, ending with fillo. Spray fillo with cooking spray and score with sharp knife into serving pieces. Bake at 350 degrees 45 minutes, covering loosely with foil if becoming too brown. Cut into pieces while hot.

4. Heat water, sugar, and honey to boiling in small saucepan, stirring to dissolve sugar. Pour mixture over hot baklava. Cool 10 to 15 minutes before serving, or cool completely and serve at room temperature.

SQUASH AND MUSHROOM GALETTE

LO | *The Galette Pastry Dough, made with yeast, is quite special.*

4–6 servings

½ cup thinly sliced leek

½ cup each: chopped onion, medium red bell pepper

2 medium portobello mushrooms, sliced

8 cloves garlic, minced

1½ teaspoons dried sage leaves

1 tablespoon olive oil

½ cups 1½ cups cooked mashed acorn, or butternut, squash

Salt and pepper, to taste

Galette Pastry Dough (recipe follows)

½ cup (2 ounces) shredded fat-free Cheddar cheese

2 tablespoons grated Parmesan cheese

1 egg white, beaten

Per Serving:
Calories: 339
% of calories from fat: 18
Fat (gm): 7.1
Saturated fat (gm): 1.7
Cholesterol (mg): 58.3
Sodium (mg): 338
Protein (gm): 16.5
Carbohydrate (gm): 54

Exchanges:
Milk: 0.0
Vegetable: 1.0
Fruit: 0.0
Bread: 3.0
Meat: 1.0
Fat: 1.0

1. Sauté leek, onion, bell pepper, mushrooms, garlic, and sage in oil in large skillet until tender, about 5 minutes. Mix in squash; season to taste with salt and pepper.

2. Roll Galette Pastry Dough on lightly floured surface to 14-inch circle; transfer to greased cookie sheet or large pizza pan. Spoon vegetable mixture evenly on dough, leaving 2-inch border around edge. Sprinkle with cheeses. Fold edge of dough over edge of vegetable mixture, pleating to fit; brush dough with egg white.

Bake at 400 degrees until crust is golden, about 25 minutes. Cut into wedges; serve warm.

Galette Pastry Dough

1 teaspoon active dry yeast
⅓ cup warm water (115 degrees)
1 egg, beaten
3 tablespoons fat-free sour cream
1½ cups all-purpose flour
¼ teaspoon salt

1. Stir yeast into warm water in medium bowl; let stand 5 minutes. Add egg and sour cream, mixing until smooth. Stir in flour and salt, making a soft dough. Knead dough on lightly floured surface until smooth, about 10 minutes.

Variation

Roasted Peperonata Galette — Make Roasted Peperonata (see p. 209). Roll Galette Pastry Dough as directed in Step 3 above. Spoon peperonata mixture evenly on dough, leaving a 2-inch border around edge; sprinkle with ½ cup (2 ounces) shredded fat-free mozzarella cheese and 1 tablespoon shredded Parmesan cheese. Fold edge of dough over edge of vegetable mixture, pleating to fit. Brush dough with egg white. Bake as above.

NINE

Egg
and
Cheese Dishes

EGGS BENEDICT

LO

45

A popular brunch dish comes to the table in healthy vegetarian style. Six slices of English Muffin Bread (see p. 551) can be substituted for the English muffins.

6 servings

3 English muffins, halved, toasted
Spinach leaves, as garnish
6 each: tomato slices, poached eggs
Mock Hollandaise Sauce (see p. 595)
Paprika and chopped parsley, as garnish

Per Serving:
Calories: 180
% of calories from fat: 29
Fat (gm): 5.6
Saturated fat (gm): 1.6
Cholesterol (mg): 212.1
Sodium (mg): 461
Protein (gm): 13.7
Carbohydrate (gm): 17.1

Exchanges:
Milk: 0.0
Vegetable: 0.0
Fruit: 0.0
Bread: 1.5
Meat: 1.0
Fat: 0.5

1. Top English muffin halves with spinach, tomato slices, and eggs. Spoon Mock Hollandaise Sauce over eggs; sprinkle with paprika and parsley.

45-MINUTE PREP TIP: Make Mock Hollandaise Sauce before preparing the rest of the recipe.

PIPERADE

LO

45

Eggs are gently scrambled with a bell pepper and onion mixture in the Basque tradition. Serve with warm Focaccia (see p. 557).

4 servings

Peperonata (see p. 492)
1 large tomato, chopped
4 eggs, lightly beaten
4 egg whites
2 tablespoons fat-free milk
Salt and pepper, to taste

Per Serving:
Calories: 173
% of calories from fat: 28
Fat (gm): 5.6
Saturated fat (gm): 1.6
Cholesterol (mg): 213.1
Sodium (mg): 129
Protein (gm): 12.9
Carbohydrate (gm): 19.2

Exchanges:
Milk: 0.0
Vegetable: 4.0
Fruit: 0.0
Bread: 0.0
Meat: 1.0
Fat: 0.5

1. Make Peperonata, adding chopped tomato during last 10 minutes of cooking time. Move Peperonata to side of skillet; add combined eggs, egg whites, and milk. Cook until eggs are set, stirring occasionally. Gently stir eggs into Peperonata; season to taste with salt and pepper.

HASH AND EGGS

O

45

You'll enjoy the variety of vegetables in this hearty hash.

4 servings

1 cup chopped onion
4 medium Idaho potatoes, unpeeled, cooked, cubed
Vegetable cooking spray
1 cup each: frozen peas, whole kernel corn
½ teaspoon dried thyme leaves
Salt and pepper, to taste
4 eggs

Per Serving:
Calories: 180
% of calories from fat: 29
Fat (gm): 5.6
Saturated fat (gm): 1.6
Cholesterol (mg): 212.1
Sodium (mg): 461
Protein (gm): 13.7
Carbohydrate (gm): 17.1

Exchanges:
Milk: 0.0
Vegetable: 0.0
Fruit: 0.0
Bread: 1.5
Meat: 1.0
Fat: 0.5

1. Sauté onion and potatoes in lightly greased large skillet 2 to 3 minutes; spray with cooking spray and cook until potatoes are browned, about 5 minutes. Add peas, corn, and thyme; cook 2 to 3 minutes longer. Season to taste with salt and pepper. Move hash to side of skillet; add eggs and cook, covered, over low heat until cooked, 3 to 4 minutes. Season to taste with salt and pepper.

Variation

Herbed Bean and Sweet Potato Hash — Make recipe as above, substituting sweet potatoes for the Idaho potatoes, 1 can (15 ounces) drained dark kidney beans for the peas and corn, and adding 1 teaspoon crushed dried rosemary leaves.

SWEET POTATO HASH WITH POACHED EGGS

| **0** | *A colorful hash dish that's perfect for a breakfast, brunch, or light supper.* |

| **45** | **4 servings** (scant 1 cup each) |

2 cups each: cubed peeled cooked sweet potatoes,
   Idaho potatoes (½-inch)
½ cup each: chopped onion, red bell pepper
1 teaspoon dried rosemary leaves
½ teaspoon dried thyme leaves
Vegetable cooking spray
Salt and pepper, to taste
4 poached, or fried, eggs

Per Serving:
Calories: 393
% of calories from fat: 13
Fat (gm): 5.8
Saturated fat (gm): 1.7
Cholesterol (mg): 212
Sodium (mg): 171
Protein (gm): 12.3
Carbohydrate (gm): 74.4

Exchanges:
Milk: 0.0
Vegetable: 0.5
Fruit: 0.0
Bread: 4.5
Meat: 1.0
Fat: 0.0

1. Sauté vegetables and herbs in lightly greased large skillet 5
minutes; spray with cooking spray and cook until potatoes are
browned, about 5 minutes. Season to taste with salt and pepper.
Top each serving of hash with an egg.

EGGS AND MUSHROOMS À LA KING

| **LO** | *A brunch or light supper favorite that's fast and easy to make. For a special* |
| **45** | *touch, add 1 to 2 tablespoons of dry sherry to the sauce.* |

4 servings

2 cups sliced cremini mushrooms
½ cup chopped onion
1–2 tablespoons margarine, or butter
¼ cup all-purpose flour
½ teaspoon dried thyme leaves
3 cups fat-free milk
4 hard-cooked eggs, chopped
Salt and pepper, to taste
4 English muffins, split, toasted, or waffles
2–4 tablespoons crumbled, cooked vegetarian bacon

Per Serving:
Calories: 355
% of calories from fat: 26
Fat (gm): 10.2
Saturated fat (gm): 2.6
Cholesterol (mg): 216.2
Sodium (mg): 520
Protein (gm): 20.5
Carbohydrate (gm): 44.5

Exchanges:
Milk: 1.0
Vegetable: 0.0
Fruit: 0.0
Bread: 2.0
Meat: 1.0
Fat: 1.5

1. Sauté mushrooms and onion in margarine until onion is tender
and mushrooms are beginning to brown, 8 to 10 minutes. Sprinkle

with flour and thyme; cook 1 to 2 minutes longer. Stir in milk and heat to boiling; boil, stirring, until thickened, about 1 minute. Reduce heat and stir in eggs; season to taste with salt and pepper. Serve over English muffins; sprinkle with vegetarian bacon.

PASTA EGG SALAD

Serve this delicious salad on lettuce-lined plates, garnished with tomato wedges.

4 servings (about 1 cup each)

4 ounces pasta rings, cooked, room temperature
5 hard-cooked eggs, coarsely chopped
½ cup sliced snow peas
¼ cup each: finely chopped onion, red bell pepper
Mayonnaise Dressing (recipe follows)
Salt and pepper, to taste

Per Serving:
Calories: 257
% of calories from fat: 25
Fat (gm): 7.3
Saturated fat (gm): 2.1
Cholesterol (mg): 266.3
Sodium (mg): 516
Protein (gm): 13.2
Carbohydrate (gm): 34.9

Exchanges:
Milk: 0.0
Vegetable: 1.0
Fruit: 0.0
Bread: 2.0
Meat: 1.0
Fat: 0.5

1. Combine all ingredients, except salt, and pepper, in bowl; season to taste with salt and pepper.

Mayonnaise Dressing

Makes about ⅔ cup

½ cup fat-free mayonnaise
3 tablespoons white wine vinegar
1 tablespoon Dijon-style mustard
¼ cup each finely chopped parsley and chives

1. Mix all ingredients.

45-MINUTE PREP TIP: Make Mayonnaise Dressing before preparing the rest of the recipe.

PASTA FRITTATA

LO | *A pasta frittata is a delicious way to use leftover pasta and vegetables.*

45 | **4 servings**

2 cups cooked thin spaghetti

2 eggs, lightly beaten

2 tablespoons grated Parmesan cheese

½ teaspoon salt

¼ teaspoon pepper

1 cup cauliflower florets

¾ cup each: sliced carrots, red bell peppers

½ cup each: sliced zucchini, chopped tomato

¼ cup sliced green onions

2 cloves garlic, minced

¾ teaspoon each: dried basil, oregano, and
marjoram leaves

1 tablespoon olive oil, or canola oil

Salt and pepper, to taste

Per Serving:
Calories: 228
% of calories from fat: 26
Fat (gm): 7
Saturated fat (gm): 1.4
Cholesterol (mg): 106
Sodium (mg): 83
Protein (gm): 10
Carbohydrate (gm): 34

Exchanges:
Milk: 0.0
Vegetable: 1.0
Fruit: 0.0
Bread: 2.0
Meat: 0.0
Fat: 1.0

1. Mix spaghetti, eggs, cheese, ½ teaspoon salt, and ¼ teaspoon pepper; spread evenly in lightly greased medium skillet. Cook, uncovered, over medium to medium-low heat until browned on bottom, about 5 minutes. Turn and cook until browned on other side, about 5 minutes; keep warm on low heat.

2. While frittata is cooking, sauté vegetables and herbs in oil in large skillet until tender, 8 to 10 minutes; season to taste with salt and pepper. Slide frittata onto serving plate; spoon vegetables over.

45-MINUTE PREP TIP: Begin cooking spaghetti before preparing the rest of the recipe.

VEGETABLE FRITTATA WITH PARMESAN TOAST

LO *This Italian-style omelet is quick and easy to prepare, and delicious to eat!*

4 servings

2 cups sliced mushrooms

½ cup each: sliced poblano chili, onion

2 cloves garlic, minced

6 eggs, lightly beaten

¼ cup fat-free milk

½ cup each: cooked brown rice, shredded fat-free
   Cheddar cheese

¼ teaspoon salt

⅛ teaspoon pepper

4 slices Italian, or French, bread

4 teaspoons grated Parmesan cheese

Per Serving:
Calories: 285
% of calories from fat: 30
Fat (gm): 9.5
Saturated fat (gm): 3
Cholesterol (mg): 319
Sodium (mg): 732
Protein (gm): 19
Carbohydrate (gm): 30

Exchanges:
Milk: 0.0
Vegetable: 0.0
Fruit: 0.0
Bread: 2.0
Meat: 2.0
Fat: 1.0

1. Sauté vegetables in lightly greased medium ovenproof skillet until tender, about 8 minutes. Pour combined eggs, milk, rice, cheese, salt, and pepper over vegetables; cook, without stirring, over medium-low heat until egg is set and lightly browned on bottom, about 10 minutes.

2. Sprinkle bread with Parmesan cheese. Broil bread and frittata 6 inches from heat source until bread is browned and frittata is cooked on top, 2 to 4 minutes. Slide frittata onto plate; serve with bread.

VEGETABLE PUFF

LO

45

Perfect for brunch or lunch, sautéed vegetables are baked with eggs in a casserole.

6 servings

2 cups each: sliced mushrooms, coarsely chopped broccoli florets

1 cup shredded carrots

½ cup each: chopped red bell pepper, shallots, or green onions

2 cloves garlic, minced

¼ cup whole kernel corn

2 teaspoons lemon juice

¾ teaspoon dried thyme leaves

Salt and pepper, to taste

1 cup fat-free half-and-half, or fat-free milk

2 tablespoons flour

4 eggs, lightly beaten

4 large egg whites

½ teaspoon cream of tartar

Per Serving:
Calories: 139
% of calories from fat: 27
Fat (gm): 4.3
Saturated fat (gm): 1.4
Cholesterol (mg): 143
Sodium (mg): 169
Protein (gm): 10
Carbohydrate (gm): 16

Exchanges:
Milk: 0.0
Vegetable: 3.0
Fruit: 0.0
Bread: 0.0
Meat: 1.0
Fat: 5.0

1. Sauté mushrooms, broccoli, carrots, bell pepper, shallots, and garlic in lightly greased large skillet until tender, about 8 minutes. Stir in corn, lemon juice, and thyme; season to taste with salt and pepper. Transfer mixture to large bowl.

2. Whisk half-and-half and flour until blended in small saucepan; heat to boiling. Boil, whisking, until thickened, about 1 minute. Whisk about half the mixture into beaten eggs; whisk egg mixture back into half-and-half. Stir into vegetable mixture.

3. Beat egg whites in large bowl to soft peaks. Add cream of tartar and beat until stiff, but not dry, peaks form; fold into vegetable mixture and spoon into greased 1½-quart casserole. Place casserole in a large roasting pan on center oven rack; add 2 inches hot water to pan. Bake, uncovered, at 375 degrees until puffed and browned, about 35 minutes. Serve immediately.

OMELET PUFF WITH VEGETABLE MÉLANGE

O

Made with beaten egg whites, this oven-baked omelet soars to new heights.

45

2 servings

2 eggs
¼ teaspoon each: dried tarragon leaves, salt, pepper
5 egg whites
¼ cup water
Vegetable Mélange (recipe follows)
2 slices crusty Italian bread, warm

Per Serving:
Calories: 265
% of calories from fat: 22
Fat (gm): 7
Saturated fat (gm): 2
Cholesterol (mg): 212
Sodium (mg): 722
Protein (gm): 21
Carbohydrate (gm): 31

Exchanges:
Milk: 0.0
Vegetable: 0.0
Fruit: 0.0
Bread: 2.0
Meat: 2.0
Fat: 0.0

1. Beat eggs, tarragon, salt, and pepper at high speed in small bowl until thick and lemon colored, about 5 minutes. Beat egg whites in large bowl with clean beaters until foamy; mix in water at high speed, beating until stiff, but not dry, peaks form. Fold into beaten eggs.

2. Spread egg mixture evenly in lightly greased ovenproof 10-inch skillet; cook over medium heat until bottom of omelet is lightly browned, about 5 minutes. Bake at 325 degrees, uncovered, until puffed and lightly browned. Loosen edge of omelet with spatula; slide onto serving plate, carefully folding omelet in half. Spoon Vegetable Mélange over omelet and serve with bread.

Vegetable Mélange

Makes about 3 cups

1 cup each: sliced zucchini, onion, small whole okra, tomato wedges
½ cup sliced green bell pepper
1 teaspoon dried Italian seasoning
Salt and pepper, to taste

1. Sauté vegetables and Italian seasoning in lightly greased large skillet until tender, 5 to 7 minutes. Season to taste with salt and pepper.

45-MINUTE PREP TIP: Make Vegetable Melange before preparing the rest of the recipe.

NOODLES FLORENTINE

LO

45

Cut into generous squares and serve with a vegetable salad and warm multigrain bread.

4 servings

¾ cup each: finely chopped red onion, red
  bell pepper

2 cloves garlic, minced

1 package (10 ounces each) frozen chopped
  spinach, thawed, drained

4 eggs, lightly beaten

4 ounces spinach noodles, cooked

1 cup fresh whole wheat bread crumbs

2 teaspoons sugar

½ teaspoon each: ground nutmeg, salt, pepper

½ cup (2 ounces) shredded reduced-fat Swiss cheese

Per Serving:
Calories: 359
% of calories from fat: 20
Fat (gm): 8.6
Saturated fat (gm): 2.7
Cholesterol (mg): 242.8
Sodium (mg): 414
Protein (gm): 20.3
Carbohydrate (gm): 48.7

Exchanges:
Milk: 0.0
Vegetable: 1.0
Fruit: 0.0
Bread: 3.0
Meat: 2.0
Fat: 0.0

1. Sauté onion, bell pepper, and garlic in lightly greased medium skillet until tender, about 4 minutes; transfer to large bowl and stir in spinach. Mix in remaining ingredients, except cheese, and spoon into greased 11 x 7-inch baking dish. Bake, uncovered, at 325 degrees 30 minutes. Sprinkle with cheese; bake until sharp knife inserted near center comes out clean, about 10 minutes. Cool on wire rack 5 minutes.

45-MINUTE PREP TIP: Begin cooking noodles before preparing the rest of the recipe.

VEGGIE KUGEL

LO

45

This kugel, with lots of veggies, is high in protein and low in fat.

6 servings

¾ cup each: chopped red bell pepper, onion

2 tablespoons margarine, or butter

2 cups each: halved Brussels sprouts, cubed peeled sweet potatoes, cooked

¾ teaspoon each: dried thyme, marjoram leaves

1 can (12 ounces) evaporated fat-free milk

2 tablespoons flour

1 package (10 ounces each) frozen chopped spinach, thawed, well drained

12 ounces no-yolk noodles, cooked

3 eggs, lightly beaten

½ teaspoon each: salt, pepper

Per Serving:
Calories: 432
% of calories from fat: 21
Fat (gm): 10.3
Saturated fat (gm): 2.7
Cholesterol (mg): 217
Sodium (mg): 463
Protein (gm): 20.7
Carbohydrate (gm): 64.7

Exchanges:
Milk: 0.0
Vegetable: 1.0
Fruit: 0.0
Bread: 4.0
Meat: 1.0
Fat: 1.5

1. Sauté bell pepper and onion in margarine in large skillet until tender, about 5 minutes; add Brussels sprouts, sweet potatoes, and herbs. Stir in combined evaporated milk and flour; heat to boiling. Boil, stirring, until thickened, about 1 minute; cool. Mix in remaining ingredients. Spoon into greased 13 x 9-inch baking dish. Bake, uncovered, at 350 degrees 35 minutes, or until sharp knife inserted near center comes out clean. Cool on wire rack 5 minutes.

45-MINUTE PREP TIP: Begin cooking noodles before preparing the rest of the recipe.

HUEVOS RANCHEROS

Everyone loves Mexican "country-style eggs" for a hearty breakfast! To speed preparation, canned vegetarian refried beans can be used.

6 servings

6 corn tortillas

Vegetable cooking spray

6 eggs, fried

Serrano Tomato Sauce (p. 602)

Refried Beans (p. 374)

Per Serving:
Calories: 252
% of calories from fat: 22
Fat (gm): 6.2
Saturated fat (gm): 1.7
Cholesterol (mg): 213
Sodium (mg): 109
Protein (gm): 14.3
Carbohydrate (gm): 35.6

Exchanges:
Milk: 0.0
Vegetable: 1.0
Fruit: 0.0
Bread: 2.0
Meat: 1.5
Fat: 0.0

1. Spray tortillas lightly on both sides with cooking spray; cook in large skillet over medium heat until browned, about 1 minute on each side. Place on plates and top with eggs; spoon Serrano Tomato Sauce over eggs. Serve with Refried Beans.

EGGS RANCHEROS WITH BLACK BEANS AND 2 SALSAS

O *A Mexican breakfast favorite, served with 2 salsas, black beans, and rice.*

45 **4 servings**

6 eggs, lightly beaten
Salt and pepper, to taste
4 corn, or flour, tortillas, warm
½ cup each: red, and green salsa
Seasoned Mashed Black Beans (see p. 373)
3 cups cooked rice, warm

1. Scramble eggs in lightly greased medium skillet over medium heat; season to taste with salt and pepper. Spoon eggs over tortillas on plates; spoon salsas over eggs. Serve with Seasoned Mashed Black Beans and rice.

45-MINUTE PREP TIP: Begin cooking rice and make Seasoned Mashed Black Beans before preparing the rest of the recipe.

Per Serving:
Calories: 514
% of calories from fat: 15
Fat (gm): 9
Saturated fat (gm): 2.5
Cholesterol (mg): 317
Sodium (mg): 1814
Protein (gm): 24
Carbohydrate (gm): 89.5

Exchanges:
Milk: 0.0
Vegetable: 0.0
Fruit: 0.0
Bread: 6.0
Meat: 1.0
Fat: 1.0

BREAKFAST BURRITOS

LO *A delicious alternative to standard breakfast fare!*

45 **6 servings** (1 burrito each)

3 cups cubed, unpeeled Idaho potatoes, cooked
1 cup each: chopped red, or green, bell peppers, chopped green onions
4 cloves garlic, minced
1½ cups cubed zucchini
¼ cup whole kernel corn
8 eggs
¼ cup finely chopped cilantro
¾ teaspoon dried oregano leaves
Salt and pepper, to taste
6 flour tortillas (10-inch)

Per Serving:
Calories: 478
% of calories from fat: 28
Fat (gm): 14.5
Saturated fat (gm): 5
Cholesterol (mg): 292
Sodium (mg): 785
Protein (gm): 20
Carbohydrate (gm): 65

Exchanges:
Milk: 0.0
Vegetable: 1.0
Fruit: 0.0
Bread: 4.0
Meat: 2.0
Fat: 1.0

1 cup (4 ounces) shredded reduced-fat
   mozzarella, or Cheddar, cheese

1–1½ cups mild, or hot, salsa

1. Sauté potatoes, bell peppers, green onions, and garlic in lightly
greased large skillet until potatoes are browned, about 10 minutes.
Add zucchini and corn; cook, covered, until zucchini is tender,
about 5 minutes.

2. Beat eggs, cilantro, and oregano; add to skillet and cook over
medium heat until set, stirring occasionally. Season to taste with
salt and pepper. Spoon mixture onto tortillas and sprinkle with
cheese. Fold 2 sides of each tortilla in about 2 inches, then roll up
from other side to enclose filling; serve with salsa.

SCRAMBLED EGGS WITH VEGETARIAN CHORIZO

LO *Crumbled vegetarian sausage patties or links can be substituted for the
Vegetarian Chorizo.*

6 servings

1 large tomato, chopped

½ cup sliced green onions

2–3 teaspoons finely chopped serrano, or
   jalapeño, chilies

2 small cloves garlic, minced

Vegetarian Chorizo (see p. 287), crumbled

9 eggs, lightly beaten

¼ cup fat-free milk

Salt and pepper, to taste

Tomatillo Sauce, warm (see p. 602)

6 corn, or flour, tortillas

Per Serving:
Calories: 347
% of calories from fat: 31
Fat (gm): 12
Saturated fat (gm): 3
Cholesterol (mg): 388
Sodium (mg): 724
Protein (gm): 28
Carbohydrate (gm): 34

Exchanges:
Milk: 0.0
Vegetable: 0.0
Fruit: 0.0
Bread: 2.0
Meat: 3.0
Fat: 0.5

1. Sauté tomato, green onions, chilies, and garlic in lightly greased
large skillet until tender, about 5 minutes. Add Vegetarian Chorizo
and cook 3 to 4 minutes. Add combined eggs and milk and cook
over medium heat until eggs are set, stirring occasionally; season to
taste with salt and pepper. Serve with Tomatillo Sauce and tortillas.

EGGS SCRAMBLED WITH CRISP TORTILLA STRIPS

LO *This is a good recipe to use with day-old or slightly stale tortillas.*

6 servings

6 corn tortillas, cut into 2 x ½-inch strips

Vegetable cooking spray

9 eggs, lightly beaten

3 tablespoons fat-free milk

Salt and pepper, to taste

3 tablespoons each: crumbled Mexican white, or farmer's, cheese and finely chopped cilantro

1½ cups Poblano Chili Sauce, warm (see p. 601), or salsa

Black Beans and Rice (see p. 374)

Per Serving:
Calories: 374
% of calories from fat: 24
Fat (gm): 10
Saturated fat (gm): 3
Cholesterol (mg): 322
Sodium (mg): 641
Protein (gm): 18
Carbohydrate (gm): 55

Exchanges:
Milk: 0.0
Vegetable: 0.0
Fruit: 0.0
Bread: 4.0
Meat: 1.0
Fat: 1.0

1. Spray tortilla strips lightly with cooking spray; cook in skillet over medium to medium-high heat until browned and crisp. Add combined eggs and milk and cook over medium heat until set, stirring occasionally; season to taste with salt and pepper. Sprinkle with cheese and cilantro. Serve eggs with Poblano Chili Sauce and Black Beans and Rice.

EGGS SCRAMBLED WITH CACTUS

LO

45 *Cactus paddles, or "nopales," are available canned as well as fresh; the canned cactus do not have to be cooked. Poblano chilies or sweet bell peppers can be substituted, if preferred.*

4 servings

1 quart water

8 ounces cactus paddles, sliced

1 teaspoon salt

¼ teaspoon baking soda

¾ cup each: chopped onion, tomato

1 teaspoon finely chopped jalapeño chili

6 eggs, lightly beaten

2 tablespoons fat-free milk

Per Serving:
Calories: 182
% of calories from fat: 29
Fat (gm): 6
Saturated fat (gm): 2
Cholesterol (mg): 212
Sodium (mg): 292
Protein (gm): 13
Carbohydrate (gm): 20

Exchanges:
Milk: 0.0
Vegetable: 0.0
Fruit: 0.0
Bread: 1.0
Meat: 2.0
Fat: 0.0

Salt and pepper, to taste

4 corn, or flour, tortillas, warm

1. Heat water to boiling in medium saucepan; add cactus, 1 teaspoon salt, and baking soda. Reduce heat and simmer, uncovered, until cactus is crisp-tender, about 20 minutes. Rinse in cold water; drain.

2. Sauté cactus, onion, tomato, and jalapeño chili in lightly greased large skillet until onion is tender, 3 to 4 minutes. Add combined eggs and milk and cook over medium heat until set, stirring occasionally; season to taste with salt and pepper. Serve with tortillas.

BEAN AND CHEESE CHILES RELLENOS

L *Chiles rellenos are normally coated with a beaten egg-white mixture and deep-fried in oil; our healthful version uses only 1 tablespoon of oil.*

6 servings

6 large poblano chilies, or green bell peppers

2 quarts water

½ small jalapeño chili, minced

4 cloves garlic, minced

1 teaspoon dried oregano leaves

2 packages (8 ounces each) fat-free cream cheese, room temperature

½ cup (2 ounces) Mexican white (*queso blanco*), or farmer's, cheese, crumbled

1½ cups cooked, or rinsed, drained canned pinto beans

1 tablespoon vegetable oil

Per Serving:
Calories: 204
% of calories from fat: 25
Fat (gm): 5.5
Saturated fat (gm): 0.4
Cholesterol (mg): 22.3
Sodium (mg): 520
Protein (gm): 17.2
Carbohydrate (gm): 19.4

Exchanges:
Milk: 0.0
Vegetable: 1.0
Fruit: 0.0
Bread: 1.0
Meat: 1.5
Fat: 0.5

1. Cut stems from tops of poblano chilies; remove and discard seeds and veins. Heat water to boiling in large saucepan; add peppers. Reduce heat and simmer, uncovered, 2 to 3 minutes, until peppers are slightly softened. Drain and cool.

2. Sauté jalapeño chili, garlic, and oregano in lightly greased small skillet until chili is tender, 2 to 3 minutes; cool slightly and mix with cheeses, and beans. Stuff poblano chilies with mixture; sauté in oil over medium heat until peppers are tender and browned on all sides, 6 to 8 minutes.

BLACK BEAN CHEESECAKE WITH SALSA

LO

45

❄

🔥

This unusual entrée can also be served in smaller pieces as an appetizer or first course. It can be served at room temperature, or heated as the recipe directs. Make it a day in advance, as overnight chilling is essential.

8 servings

4 flour tortillas

3 packages (8 ounces each) fat-free cream cheese, room temperature

6 eggs

1 can (15 ounces) black beans, rinsed, drained

½ jalapeño chili, finely chopped

2 tablespoons finely chopped onion

2 cloves garlic, minced

2 teaspoons dried cumin

½ teaspoon each: dried oregano leaves, chili powder, salt, cayenne pepper

1 cup hot or milk salsa

Per Serving:
Calories: 249
% of calories from fat: 25
Fat (gm): 7
Saturated fat (gm): 2
Cholesterol (mg): 165
Sodium (mg): 797
Protein (gm): 21.5
Carbohydrate (gm): 25

Exchanges:
Milk: 0.0
Vegetable: 0.0
Fruit: 0.0
Bread: 1.5
Meat: 2.5
Fat: 0.0

1. Line greased 9-inch springform pan with overlapping tortillas.

2. Beat cream cheese in large bowl until fluffy; beat in eggs. Mix in remaining ingredients, except salsa; pour into prepared springform pan. Bake, uncovered, at 300 degrees until center is set and sharp knife inserted halfway between center and edge of cheesecake comes out almost clean, 1¾ to 2 hours. Cool on wire rack; refrigerate 8 hours or overnight.

3. Cook wedges of cheesecake in lightly greased large skillet over medium-low heat until browned on both sides. Serve with salsa.

CHEDDAR CHEESE SOUFFLÉ

LO

This spectacular soufflé soars above the soufflé dish!

45

4 servings

1–2 tablespoons grated fat-free Parmesan cheese

1 cup fat-free milk

3 tablespoons flour

½ teaspoon each: dry mustard, dried marjoram leaves

¼ teaspoon cayenne pepper

2 pinches ground nutmeg

3 egg yolks

¼ cup (1 ounce) shredded fat-free Cheddar cheese

Salt and white pepper, to taste

3 egg whites

¼ teaspoon cream of tartar

Per Serving:
Calories: 162
% of calories from fat: 23
Fat (gm): 4.1
Saturated fat (gm): 1.3
Cholesterol (mg): 160.8
Sodium (mg): 340
Protein (gm): 19.3
Carbohydrate (gm): 11.2

Exchanges:
Milk: 0.0
Vegetable: 0.0
Fruit: 0.0
Bread: 0.5
Meat: 2.5
Fat: 0.0

1. Coat lightly greased 1-quart soufflé dish with Parmesan cheese. Attach a foil collar, extending foil 3 inches above top of dish; lightly grease inside of collar.

2. Mix milk and flour until blended in small saucepan; mix in mustard, marjoram, cayenne, and nutmeg. Heat to boiling, whisking; boil, whisking, until thickened, about 1 minute. Whisk about ½ cup mixture into egg yolks in small bowl; whisk mixture back into saucepan. Add cheese and whisk over low heat until melted; season to taste with salt and white pepper.

3. Beat egg whites and cream of tartar in medium bowl to stiff, but not dry, peaks. Stir about ⅓ the egg whites into cheese mixture; fold cheese mixture into remaining whites. Spoon into prepared soufflé dish. Bake at 350° until soufflé is puffed, browned, and just set in the center, 35 to 40 minutes. Serve immediately.

CHEESE FONDUE

L

45

Flavorful with wine and a hint of garlic, this creamy fondue is made with fat-free cheese!

8 servings (¼ cup each)

1½ cups dry white wine

2–3 large cloves garlic, peeled

2 packages (3 ounces each) fat-free cream cheese

2 cups (8 ounces) shredded fat-free Swiss cheese

1 tablespoon flour

Salt, cayenne, and black pepper, to taste

French bread, cubed, for dipping

Per Serving:
Calories: 100
% of calories from fat: 0
Fat (gm): 0
Saturated fat (gm): 0
Cholesterol (mg): 0
Sodium (mg): 547
Protein (gm): 10.8
Carbohydrate (gm): 5

Exchanges:
Milk: 0.0
Vegetable: 0.0
Fruit: 0.0
Bread: 0.0
Meat: 1.5
Fat: 0.0

1. Heat wine and garlic to boiling in medium saucepan; reduce heat and simmer rapidly, uncovered, until reduced to ¾ cup, about 15 minutes; discard garlic. Add cream cheese and cook over low heat, stirring until melted and smooth. Toss shredded Swiss cheese with flour; add to saucepan and stir until melted. Season to taste with salt, cayenne, and black pepper. Serve in fondue pot or bowl with bread cubes (not included in nutritional analysis) for dipping.

NOTES: Instead of wine, ¾ cup fat-free milk can be substituted. Simmer with garlic 5 minutes, then proceed with recipe as above.

If fondue becomes too thick, it can be thinned with white wine, fat-free milk, or water.

WELSH RAREBIT

L

45

Perhaps you know this dish as Welsh Rabbit. Whatever the name, the distinctively flavored sauce is rich and delicious.

6 servings (about ½ cup sauce each)

¼ cup very finely chopped onion

2 tablespoons margarine, or butter

¼ cup all-purpose flour

2 cups fat-free milk

½ cup white wine, or fat-free milk

2 ounces light pasteurized processed cheese, cubed

½ cup (2 ounces) reduced-fat sharp Cheddar cheese

¼–½ teaspoon dry mustard

White and cayenne pepper, to taste

6 slices sourdough, or multigrain, bread

Butter-flavored vegetable cooking spray

6 thick slices tomato

Paprika, as garnish

Per Serving:
Calories: 219
% of calories from fat: 31
Fat (gm): 7.6
Saturated fat (gm): 3.4
Cholesterol (mg): 11.5
Sodium (mg): 502
Protein (gm): 9.9
Carbohydrate (gm): 24.1

Exchanges:
Milk: 0.0
Vegetable: 0.0
Fruit: 0.0
Bread: 1.5
Meat: 1.0
Fat: 1.0

1. Sauté onion in margarine in medium saucepan until tender, 2 to 3 minutes. Stir in flour and cook over medium-low heat, stirring, 1 minute. Whisk in milk and wine; heat to boiling. Boil, whisking, until thickened, about 1 minute. Stir in cheeses and dry mustard; whisk over low heat until cheeses are melted. Season to taste with white and cayenne pepper.

2. Spray both sides of bread with cooking spray; cook over medium heat in large skillet until browned, 2 to 3 minutes on each side. Sauté tomato slices in lightly greased medium skillet until hot, 2 to 3 minutes. Arrange bread on plates; top with tomato slices, and spoon cheese sauce over. Sprinkle with paprika.

Variation

Cheese and Vegetable Rarebit — Make recipe as above, stirring ½ cup each sautéed broccoli florets, chopped portobello mushrooms, and chopped yellow summer squash into the cheese sauce in step 1; delete tomato in step 2.

QUICHE LORRAINE

LO

45

Enjoy the rich texture and flavor of this classic quiche, modified to low-fat goodness by using a combination of fat-free and evaporated fat-free milk.

6 servings

¼ cup finely chopped onion

¾ cup fat-free milk

½ can (12-ounce size) evaporated fat-free milk

2 eggs, lightly beaten

¼ cup fat-free sour cream

2 tablespoons crumbled, cooked vegetarian bacon

¼ teaspoon salt

⅛ teaspoon each: cayenne pepper, ground nutmeg

1 cup (4 ounces) shredded fat-free Swiss cheese

1 tablespoon flour

Basic Pie Crust, baked in 8-inch pie pan

Per Serving:
Calories: 293
% of calories from fat: 32
Fat (gm): 10
Saturated fat (gm): 2
Cholesterol (mg): 74
Sodium (mg): 690
Protein (gm): 14
Carbohydrate (gm): 35

Exchanges:
Milk: 0.0
Vegetable: 0.0
Fruit: 0.0
Bread: 2.0
Meat: 2.0
Fat: 1.0

1. Sauté onion in lightly greased small skillet until tender, 3 to 5 minutes; cool. Mix onion and remaining ingredients, except cheese and flour, in medium bowl until smooth. Toss cheese with flour; stir into milk mixture and pour into pie crust. Bake at 350 degrees until set and a sharp knife inserted near center comes out clean, about 40 minutes. Cover edge of pie crust with aluminum foil if becoming too brown. Cool on wire rack 5 minutes.

Variation

Spinach Quiche — Make recipe as above, adding ½ package (10-ounce size) frozen, thawed, well drained spinach to sautéed onion in step 1; cook over medium heat until mixture is quite dry, 3 to 4 minutes. Complete recipe as above.

TEN

Bean Dishes

FAVA BEAN BRUSCHETTA

L

45

Assembled on Italian bread halves, these bruschetta can be cut into large pieces for a light entrée, or into small pieces for appetizers.

8 main-dish servings

1 loaf Italian bread, halved lengthwise
Olive oil cooking spray
2 cloves garlic, halved
Fava Bean Spread (recipe follows)
2–3 medium tomatoes, thinly sliced
1 medium onion, thinly sliced
1 cup (4 ounces) each: shredded fat-free mozzarella
    cheese, crumbled reduced-fat feta cheese
¼ cup sliced, pitted black olives
Chopped parsley, as garnish

Per Serving:
Calories: 307
% of calories from fat: 22
Fat (gm): 7.7
Saturated fat (gm): 2.2
Cholesterol (mg): 5.1
Sodium (mg): 761
Protein (gm): 16.9
Carbohydrate (gm): 43.2

Exchanges:
Milk: 0.0
Vegetable: 0.0
Fruit: 0.0
Bread: 3.0
Meat: 1.0
Fat: 1.0

1. Spray cut sides of bread with cooking spray; broil 4 inches from heat source until toasted. Rub bread with cut sides of garlic cloves; spread with Fava Bean Spread. Top with tomato and onion slices and sprinkle with cheeses, olives, and parsley. Bake on cookie sheet at 450 degrees until bean mixture is hot and cheese melted, 8 to 10 minutes. Cut into serving pieces.

Fava Bean Spread

Makes about 2 cups

2 cups cooked fresh, or dried, fava beans, or 1 can (19 ounces) fava beans, rinsed, drained
1 tablespoon each: olive oil, lemon juice
¼ cup each: packed parsley and basil leaves
Salt and cayenne pepper, to taste

1. Process all ingredients, except salt and cayenne pepper, in food processor until smooth; season to taste with salt and pepper.

45-MINUTE PREP TIP: Make Fava Bean Spread before preparing the rest of the recipe.

GARLICKY LIMA BEAN SOUP

L

45

For those who love garlic! The garlic, of course, can be reduced in amount if you prefer a more subtle dish.

6 side-dish servings (about 1 cup each)

2 cups coarsely chopped onions

10 large cloves garlic, peeled, quartered

1 teaspoon each: dried thyme leaves, crushed red pepper

2 cans (17 ounces each) lima beans, rinsed, drained

3 cups reduced-sodium vegetable broth

½ cup fat-free half-and-half, or fat-free milk

Salt and white pepper, to taste

Per Serving:
Calories: 169
% of calories from fat: 5
Fat (gm): 0.9
Saturated fat (gm): 0.2
Cholesterol (mg): 0
Sodium (mg): 429
Protein (gm): 9.2
Carbohydrate (gm): 31.8

Exchanges:
Milk: 0.0
Vegetable: 1.0
Fruit: 0.0
Bread: 2.0
Meat: 0.0
Fat: 0.0

1. Sauté onions, garlic, thyme, and red pepper in lightly greased large saucepan, covered, until onions are tender, 8 to 10 minutes. Add beans and broth and heat to boiling; reduce heat and simmer, covered, 10 minutes.

2. Process in food processor or blender until smooth; return to saucepan. Stir in half-and-half; cook, covered, over medium heat 5 minutes. Season to taste with salt and white pepper.

EASIEST BLACK-EYED PEA AND LENTIL SOUP

v *This soup will thicken if refrigerated, so stir in additional broth when reheating. The soup freezes well, too.*

6 main-dish servings (about 1⅔ cups each)

¾ cup dried black-eyed peas

¾ cup each: chopped carrots, onion

½ cup sliced celery

1 teaspoon minced garlic

2 tablespoons olive oil

6–8 cups canned reduced-sodium vegetable broth

3 medium tomatoes, chopped

1½ cups dried lentils

½ teaspoon each: dried marjoram, oregano, and thyme leaves

1 bay leaf

Salt and pepper, to taste

Per Serving:
Calories: 356
% of calories from fat: 14
Fat (gm): 5.9
Saturated fat (gm): 0.9
Cholesterol (mg): 0
Sodium (mg): 119
Protein (gm): 20.7
Carbohydrate (gm): 58.3

Exchanges:
Milk: 0.0
Vegetable: 2.0
Fruit: 0.0
Bread: 3.0
Meat: 1.0
Fat: 1.0

1. Cover black-eyed peas with 2 inches water in medium saucepan; heat to boiling and boil, covered, 2 minutes. Remove from heat and let stand 1 hour; drain.

2. Sauté carrots, onion, celery and garlic in oil in large saucepan 5 minutes. Add 6 cups broth, tomatoes, lentils, black-eyed peas, and herbs to saucepan; heat to boiling. Reduce heat and simmer, covered, until black-eyed peas are tender, 45 to 60 minutes, adding additional broth if necessary. Discard bay leaf; season to taste with salt and pepper.

CURRIED BEAN SOUP

L

45

Use any white bean, such as cannellini, navy, soy, lima, or garbanzo in this creamy, rich soup.

6 main-dish servings (about 1¼ cups each)

1 cup each: chopped onion, sliced leek
   (white part only)
3 teaspoons each: minced garlic, curry powder
2 tablespoons olive oil
2 cans (15½ ounces each) Great Northern beans,
   rinsed, drained
3½ cups reduced-sodium vegetable broth
½ cup fat-free half-and-half, or fat-free milk
Salt and pepper, to taste
6 tablespoons fat-free sour cream, or plain yogurt
3 tablespoons finely chopped cilantro
2 tablespoons finely chopped red bell pepper

Per Serving:
Calories: 263
% of calories from fat: 16
Fat (gm): 4.9
Saturated fat (gm): 1
Cholesterol (mg): 0
Sodium (mg): 393
Protein (gm): 13.7
Carbohydrate (gm): 42.5

Exchanges:
Milk: 0.0
Vegetable: 1.5
Fruit: 0.0
Bread: 2.5
Meat: 0.5
Fat: 0.5

1. Sauté onion, leek, garlic, and curry powder in oil in large saucepan until tender, 5 to 8 minutes. Add beans and broth and heat to boiling. Reduce heat and simmer, covered, 5 minutes.

2. Process bean mixture in food processor or blender until smooth; return to saucepan. Stir in half-and-half; cook over medium heat 2 to 3 minutes. Season to taste with salt and pepper. Top each bowl of soup with a tablespoon of sour cream. Sprinkle with cilantro and bell pepper.

YELLOW AND WHITE BEAN CHILI

V *For convenience, 1 can (15 ounces each) drained, rinsed beans can be substituted for each kind of cooked dried beans.*

6 main-dish servings (about 1¼ cups each)

1 cup each: chopped onion, thinly sliced leek
(white part only), yellow bell pepper

1 jalapeño chili, finely chopped

2 teaspoons each: minced garlic, cumin seeds

1 tablespoon olive oil

¾ cup each: cubed yellow summer squash, peeled
red potatoes

1½ cups each: cooked, dried Great Northern,
garbanzo, soy beans

1 can (14½ ounces) reduced-sodium vegetable broth

½ cup dry white wine

1 teaspoon each: dried oregano leaves, chili powder

½ teaspoon each: ground coriander, cinnamon

1 bay leaf

Salt and pepper, to taste

1 small tomato, finely chopped

2 green onions, thinly sliced

3 tablespoons finely chopped cilantro

Per Serving:
Calories: 319
% of calories from fat: 22
Fat (gm): 8
Saturated fat (gm): 1.1
Cholesterol (mg): 0
Sodium (mg): 56.9
Protein (gm): 17.2
Carbohydrate (gm): 45.5

Exchanges:
Milk: 0.0
Vegetable: 0.0
Fruit: 0.0
Bread: 3.0
Meat: 1.0
Fat: 0.5

1. Sauté onion, leek, bell pepper, jalapeño chili, garlic, and cumin seeds in oil in large saucepan until tender, about 8 minutes. Add squash, potatoes, beans, broth, wine, herbs, and spices and heat to boiling. Reduce heat and simmer, covered, until vegetables are tender, about 15 minutes. Simmer, uncovered, until thickened, 5 to 10 minutes. Season to taste with salt and pepper; discard bay leaf. Sprinkle each bowl of soup with tomato, green onions, and cilantro.

TEXAS STEW WITH CHILI-CHEESE DUMPLINGS

L

With only 30 minutes cooking time, this is a stew you'll prepare often. One green bell pepper and one jalapeño chili can be substituted for the poblano chili.

6 main-dish servings (about 1½ cups each)

2 cups chopped onions

1 cup each: coarsely chopped poblano chili, red and yellow bell peppers

3 cloves garlic, minced

2–3 tablespoons chili powder

1½–2 teaspoons ground cumin

¾ teaspoon each: dried oregano and marjoram leaves

2 tablespoons olive oil

2 cans (15 ounces each) reduced-sodium whole tomatoes, undrained, coarsely chopped

1 can (15 ounces) each: black-eyed peas and red beans, rinsed, drained

1½ cups cubed, peeled butternut, or acorn, squash

1 cup fresh, or frozen, thawed, okra

Salt and pepper, to taste

Chili-Cheese Dumplings (recipe follows)

Per Serving:
Calories: 433
% of calories from fat: 29
Fat (gm): 14.9
Saturated fat (gm): 2.7
Cholesterol (mg): 3.7
Sodium (mg): 713
Protein (gm): 17.4
Carbohydrate (gm): 65.9

Exchanges:
Milk: 0.0
Vegetable: 3.0
Fruit: 0.0
Bread: 3.0
Meat: 1.0
Fat: 2.0

1. Sauté onions, poblano chili, bell peppers, garlic, and herbs in oil in large saucepan until tender, about 10 minutes. Stir in remaining ingredients, except salt and pepper and Chili-Cheese Dumplings; heat to boiling. Reduce heat and simmer, covered, until okra and squash are tender, 8 to 10 minutes. Season to taste with salt and pepper.

2. Spoon dumpling dough into 6 mounds on top of stew. Cook, uncovered, 5 minutes. Cook, covered, until dumplings are dry, 5 to 10 minutes longer.

Chili-Cheese Dumplings

Makes 6 dumplings

⅔ cup all-purpose flour

⅓ cup yellow cornmeal

1½ teaspoons baking powder

1 teaspoon chili powder

½ teaspoon salt

2 tablespoons vegetable shortening

¼ cup (1 ounce) shredded reduced-fat
   Monterey Jack cheese

1 tablespoon finely chopped cilantro

½ cup fat-free milk

Per Serving:
Calories: 433
% of calories from fat: 29
Fat (gm): 14.9
Saturated fat (gm): 2.7
Cholesterol (mg): 3.7
Sodium (mg): 713
Protein (gm): 17.4
Carbohydrate (gm): 65.9

Exchanges:
Milk: 0.0
Vegetable: 3.0
Fruit: 0.0
Bread: 3.0
Meat: 1.0
Fat: 2.0

1. Combine flour, cornmeal, baking powder, chili powder, and salt in medium bowl; cut in shortening with pastry blender until mixture resembles coarse crumbs. Mix in cheese and cilantro; stir in milk, forming a soft dough.

VERY QUICK BEAN AND VEGETABLE STEW

O

45

Pureed beans provide a perfect thickening for the stew, and canned vegetables speed preparation.

6 main-dish servings (about 1¼ cups each)

3 carrots, sliced

¾ cup chopped onion

2 teaspoons minced garlic

1 can (15 ounces) navy beans, rinsed, drained, pureed

2 cups vegetable broth

2 cans (16 ounces each) Italian-style zucchini with
   mushrooms in tomato sauce

1 can (15 ounces) black beans, rinsed, drained

1 cup frozen peas

1½ teaspoons dried Italian seasoning

Salt and pepper, to taste

8 ounces egg noodles, cooked, warm

Per Serving:
Calories: 365
% of calories from fat: 7
Fat (gm): 3
Saturated fat (gm): 0.5
Cholesterol (mg): 32.6
Sodium (mg): 1479
Protein (gm): 18.1
Carbohydrate (gm): 69.7

Exchanges:
Milk: 0.0
Vegetable: 2.0
Fruit: 0.0
Bread: 4.0
Meat: 0.0
Fat: 0.5

1. Sauté carrots, onion, and garlic in lightly greased large saucepan 5 minutes. Stir in pureed navy beans and broth; add remaining ingredients, except salt, pepper, and noodles; heat to boiling. Reduce heat and simmer, covered, 10 minutes; season to taste with salt and pepper. Serve over noodles.

45-MINUTE PREP TIP: Cook noodles before preparing the rest of the recipe.

WINTER BEAN AND VEGETABLE STEW

V

Serve this satisfying stew with Multigrain Batter Bread (see p. 552).

45

6 main-dish servings (about 1⅓ cups each)

1 cup each: chopped onion, cubed peeled Idaho potato, sweet potato, (½-inch)

½ cup each: sliced carrot, parsnip, chopped green bell pepper

2 cloves garlic, minced

2 tablespoons olive oil

1 tablespoon flour

1½ cups reduced-sodium vegetable broth

1 can (15 ounces) black beans, rinsed, drained

1 can (13¼ ounces) baby lima beans, rinsed, drained

1 large tomato, cut into wedges

½ teaspoon each: dried sage and thyme leaves

Salt and pepper, to taste

Per Serving:
Calories: 238
% of calories from fat: 20
Fat (gm): 5.7
Saturated fat (gm): 0.7
Cholesterol (mg): 0
Sodium (mg): 399
Protein (gm): 10.8
Carbohydrate (gm): 42.4

Exchanges:
Milk: 0.0
Vegetable: 2.0
Fruit: 0.0
Bread: 2.0
Meat: 0.0
Fat: 1.0

1. Sauté onion, potatoes, carrot, parsnip, bell pepper, and garlic in oil in large saucepan 5 minutes; stir in flour and cook 1 minute longer. Add remaining ingredients, except salt and pepper, and heat to boiling. Reduce heat and simmer, covered, until vegetables are tender, 15 to 20 minutes; season to taste with salt and pepper.

ADZUKI BEAN PASTITSIO

LO *Any cooked bean, or lentils, can be substituted for the adzuki beans. Mafalde or fusilli are other pasta choices.*

8 main-dish servings

½ cup each: chopped onion, green bell pepper

1 cup cooked adzuki beans

1 cup Mediterranean Tomato-Caper Sauce (see p. 590)

1 teaspoon dried mint leaves

Salt and pepper, to taste

2 cups elbow macaroni, cooked, divided

½ cup (2 ounces) grated fat-free Parmesan cheese, divided

2⅓ cups fat-free milk

2 tablespoons margarine, or butter

4 eggs, lightly beaten

Ground nutmeg, as garnish

Per Serving:
Calories: 273
% of calories from fat: 20.7
Fat (gm): 6.2
Saturated fat (gm): 1.7
Cholesterol (mg): 109
Sodium (mg): 206
Protein (gm): 14.8
Carbohydrate (gm): 39.3

Exchanges:
Milk: 0.0
Vegetable: 0.0
Fruit: 0.0
Bread: 2.5
Meat: 2.0
Fat: 1.0

1. Sauté onion and bell pepper in lightly greased medium saucepan until tender, about 5 minutes. Stir in beans, Mediterranean Tomato-Caper Sauce, and mint; cook over medium heat until hot, about 5 minutes. Season to taste with salt and pepper.

2. Spoon half the pasta into 13- x 9-inch baking pan. Spoon sauce over; sprinkle with ¼ cup Parmesan cheese. Spoon remaining pasta over the top.

3. Heat milk and margarine in small saucepan over medium heat until hot, but not boiling. Whisk hot milk into eggs in bowl; pour over casserole and sprinkle with remaining ¼ cup cheese and nutmeg. Bake at 350 degrees until topping is set and browned, 50 to 60 minutes.

EGGPLANT AND BEAN CURRY STEW

v *The flavorful curry seasoning is created by making a simple paste of onion, garlic, and herbs.*

4 main-dish servings (about 1 cup each)

2 medium red potatoes, peeled, cubed (¾-inch)

1 small eggplant, cubed (¾-inch)

¼ cup chopped onion

1 teaspoon each: minced garlic, ground coriander

½ teaspoon ground cumin

¼ teaspoon ground turmeric

1 tablespoon olive oil

1 can (16 ounces) reduced-sodium whole tomatoes, undrained, coarsely chopped

1 can (15 ounces) garbanzo beans, rinsed, drained

½ cup water

⅛–¼ teaspoon crushed red pepper

Salt, to taste

¼ cup finely chopped cilantro

Per Serving:
Calories: 242
% of calories from fat: 21
Fat (gm): 6
Saturated fat (gm): 0.8
Cholesterol (mg): 0
Sodium (mg): 446
Protein (gm): 8.2
Carbohydrate (gm): 41.8

Exchanges:
Milk: 0.0
Vegetable: 2.0
Fruit: 0.0
Bread: 2.0
Meat: 0.0
Fat: 1.0

1. Sauté potatoes, eggplant, onion, garlic, herbs, and in oil in large saucepan until potatoes are lightly browned, 5 to 8 minutes. Add remaining ingredients, except salt and cilantro; heat to boiling. Reduce heat and simmer, covered, until eggplant is tender, 20 to 25 minutes. Season to taste with salt; stir in cilantro.

NEW ENGLAND BAKED BEANS

V *Long-baked and savory, these beans are the best! If you prefer soaking beans overnight, delete step 1 and proceed with step 2.*

4 main-dish servings (about 1 cup each)

8 ounces dried navy, or Great Northern, beans

¾ cup chopped onion

1 clove garlic, minced

3 tablespoons each: reduced-sodium tomato paste, dark molasses, light brown sugar, crumbled cooked vegetarian bacon

½ teaspoon each: dry mustard, dried thyme leaves, salt

Per Serving:
Calories: 299
% of calories from fat: 5
Fat (gm): 1.8
Saturated fat (gm): 0.3
Cholesterol (mg): 0
Sodium (mg): 385
Protein (gm): 14.6
Carbohydrate (gm): 58.9

Exchanges:
Milk: 0.0
Vegetable: 0.0
Fruit: 0.0
Bread: 4.0
Meat: 0.0
Fat: 0.0

1. Cover beans with 2 inches water in large saucepan; heat to boiling and boil, uncovered, 2 minutes. Remove from heat and let stand, covered, 1 hour. Add enough water to beans to cover, if necessary. Heat to boiling; reduce heat and simmer, covered, until beans are tender, about 1¼ hours. Drain; reserve liquid.

2. Mix beans and remaining ingredients in 1½-quart casserole; add enough reserved liquid to cover beans. Bake, covered, at 325 degrees 3 hours, stirring occasionally. Bake, uncovered, until beans are desired consistency, 45 to 60 minutes.

GINGER-BAKED BEANS

V *Slow baking adds goodness to this special ginger and sweet-spiced bean dish.*

8 main-dish servings (about 1 cup each)

1½ cups chopped onions

¼ cup finely chopped gingerroot

4 cloves garlic, minced

2 tablespoons vegetable oil

6 cups cooked dried, or 4 cans (15 ounces each) Great Northern, Beans, rinsed, drained

½ cup packed light brown sugar

1 can (6 ounces) reduced-sodium tomato sauce

½ cup light molasses

1 teaspoon each: dry mustard, ground ginger, dried thyme leaves

¼ teaspoon each: ground cinnamon and allspice

2 bay leaves

Salt and pepper, to taste

½ cup coarsely ground gingersnap crumbs

1. Sauté onions, gingerroot, and garlic in oil in medium skillet until tender, 5 to 8 minutes. Mix with remaining ingredients, except salt, pepper, and gingersnap crumbs, in 2-quart casserole; season to taste with salt and pepper. Bake, covered, at 300 degrees 2 hours. Sprinkle top of beans with gingersnap crumbs; bake, uncovered, until beans are thickened to desired consistency, about 30 minutes. Discard bay leaves.

Per Serving:
Calories: 341
% of calories from fat: 12
Fat (gm): 4.8
Saturated fat (gm): 0.8
Cholesterol (mg): 0
Sodium (mg): 60
Protein (gm): 12.5
Carbohydrate (gm): 64.9

Exchanges:
Milk: 0.0
Vegetable: 1.0
Fruit: 0.0
Bread: 4.0
Meat: 0.0
Fat: 0.5

JUST PEACHY BEAN POT

V

45

Peaches and nectar, dried fruit, and mango chutney add special flavor to this bean combo.

6 main-dish servings (about 1⅓ cups each)

1 cup chopped onion

1 clove garlic, minced

1–1½ teaspoons curry powder

½ teaspoon each: ground allspice, crushed red pepper

1 tablespoon margarine

1 can (15 ounces) navy beans, rinsed, drained

2 cans (15 ounces each) red kidney beans, rinsed, drained

1½ cups diced peaches

½ cup each: coarsely chopped mixed dried fruit, mango chutney

½–¾ cup peach nectar

2 tablespoons cider vinegar

Salt and pepper, to taste

Per Serving:
Calories: 332
% of calories from fat: 8
Fat (gm): 3.4
Saturated fat (gm): 0.5
Cholesterol (mg): 0
Sodium (mg): 621
Protein (gm): 17.5
Carbohydrate (gm): 68.8

Exchanges:
Milk: 0.0
Vegetable: 0.0
Fruit: 1.5
Bread: 3.0
Meat: 0.5
Fat: 0.0

1. Sauté onion, garlic, herbs, and crushed red pepper in margarine in small skillet until tender, about 5 minutes. Mix with remaining ingredients, except salt and pepper, in 2½-quart casserole; season to taste with salt and pepper. Bake, covered, at 350 degrees 30 minutes; bake, uncovered, if thicker consistency is desired, about 15 minutes.

SANTA FE BAKED BEANS

L *These baked beans boast flavors of the great Southwest.*

4 main-dish servings (about 1⅓ cups each)

1 cup chopped onion

½ cup chopped poblano chili, or green bell pepper

½–1 serrano, or jalapeño, chili, finely chopped

1 tablespoon olive oil

3 cups cooked dried pinto beans, or 2 cans
   (15 ounces each) pinto beans, rinsed, drained

2 cups whole kernel corn

6 sun-dried tomatoes (not in oil), softened, sliced

2–3 tablespoons honey

½ teaspoon each: ground cumin, dried thyme leaves

3 bay leaves

Salt and pepper, to taste

½ cup (2 ounces) crumbled Mexican white, or
   farmer's, cheese

¼ cup finely chopped cilantro

Per Serving:
Calories: 400
% of calories from fat: 17
Fat (gm): 8.1
Saturated fat (gm): 2.7
Cholesterol (mg): 12.7
Sodium (mg): 364
Protein (gm): 17.9
Carbohydrate (gm): 69.4

Exchanges:
Milk: 0.0
Vegetable: 1.0
Fruit: 0.0
Bread: 4.0
Meat: 0.5
Fat: 1.0

1. Sauté onion and chilies in oil in small skillet until tender, about 5 minutes. Combine with remaining ingredients, except salt, pepper, cheese, and cilantro, in 1½-quart casserole; season to taste with salt and pepper and sprinkle with cheese. Bake, covered, at 350 degrees until bean mixture is hot, about 30 minutes; bake, uncovered, if thicker consistency is desired, about 15 minutes. Discard bay leaves. Sprinkle with cilantro.

TUSCAN BEAN BAKE

V *Easy to make, these beans are lemon-scented and seasoned with sun-dried tomatoes, garlic, and herbs.*

4 main-dish servings (about 1 cup each)

1 cup dried cannellini, or Great Northern, beans

1 cup reduced-sodium vegetable broth

½ cup each: chopped onion, red bell pepper

2 teaspoons minced garlic

1 teaspoon each: dried sage and rosemary leaves

2–3 teaspoons grated lemon zest

6 sun-dried tomatoes (not in oil), softened, sliced

Salt and pepper, to taste

1 cup fresh whole wheat bread crumbs

¼ cup minced parsley

Per Serving:
Calories: 250
% of calories from fat: 6
Fat (gm): 1.7
Saturated fat (gm): 0.3
Cholesterol (mg): 0
Sodium (mg): 220
Protein (gm): 14.3
Carbohydrate (gm): 45.4

Exchanges:
Milk: 0.0
Vegetable: 1.5
Fruit: 0.0
Bread: 2.5
Meat: 0.5
Fat: 0.0

1. Cover beans with 2 inches water in large saucepan; heat to boiling and boil, uncovered, 2 minutes. Remove from heat and let stand, covered, 1 hour; drain.

2. Combine beans and remaining ingredients, except bread crumbs and parsley, in 1 ½-quart casserole. Bake, covered, at 350 degrees, until beans are tender, about 1 hour; season to taste with salt and pepper. Sprinkle combined bread crumbs and parsley over top, pressing lightly onto beans to moisten. Bake, uncovered, until thickened, about 20 minutes.

BRAZILIAN BLACK BEAN BAKE

V

Festive flavors of Brazil combine in this irresistible dish!

45

Makes 8 main-dish servings (about 1 cup each)

2 cups chopped onions

1–2 tablespoons each: minced jalapeno chili, gingerroot

4 cans (15 ounces each) black beans, rinsed, drained

2 cans (14½ ounces each) petite diced tomatoes, undrained

½ cup each: honey, packed light brown sugar

¾ teaspoon each: dried thyme leaves, ground cumin

Salt and pepper, to taste

½ cup each: sliced mango, banana

Per Serving:
Calories: 336
% of calories from fat: 0.5
Fat (gm): 0.2
Saturated fat (gm): 0.0
Cholesterol (mg): 0.0
Sodium (mg): 1009
Protein (gm): 12
Carbohydrate (gm): 73

Exchanges:
Milk: 0.0
Vegetable: 2.0;
Fruit: 0.0
Bread: 4.0
Meat: 0.0
Fat: 0.0

1. Sauté onions, jalapeno chili, and gingerroot in lightly greased skillet until onions are tender, about 5 minutes. Mix with remaining ingredients, except salt, pepper, mango, and banana, in 3-quart casserole; season to taste with salt and pepper. Bake, covered, at 350 degrees 45 minutes; uncover and bake to desired thickness, about 30 minutes. Top with mango and banana before serving.

FRIED LENTILS

V

Fried lentils, or "dal," are a staple of Indian cooking. They are normally cooked in a large quantity of clarified, browned butter, or "ghee," but we have substituted a small amount of vegetable oil to keep the dish low in fat.

8 side-dish servings (about ½ cup each)

1½ cups dried red lentils

1 cup chopped onion

1 teaspoon each: ground turmeric, crushed cumin seeds

¼ teaspoon crushed red pepper

2 tablespoons vegetable oil

½ cup chopped cilantro

Salt, to taste

2 teaspoons grated lemon zest

1. Cover lentils with 2 inches water and heat to boiling; reduce heat and simmer, covered, until very soft, 30 to 40 minutes. Drain well.

2. Sauté onion, turmeric, cumin seeds, and crushed red pepper in oil in large skillet until onions are tender, 5 to 8 minutes; reserve ¼ cup mixture. Add lentils to skillet; cook over low heat, stirring frequently to prevent burning, until mixture is thickened, 10 to 20 minutes. Stir in cilantro; season to taste with salt. Sprinkle with reserved ¼ cup onion mixture and lemon zest.

Per Serving:
Calories: 171
% of calories from fat: 20
Fat (gm): 4
Saturated fat (gm): 0.5
Cholesterol (mg): 0
Sodium (mg): 4.4
Protein (gm): 10.5
Carbohydrate (gm): 24.6

Exchanges:
Milk: 0.0
Vegetable: 1.0
Fruit: 0.0
Bread: 1.5
Meat: 0.0
Fat: 1.0

SEASONED MASHED BLACK BEANS

V

Black beans at their flavorful best — quick and easy too!

45

6 side-dish servings (about ⅔ cup each)

2 medium onions, chopped
4 cloves garlic, minced
1–2 small jalapeño chilies, minced
2 cans (15 ounces each) black beans, rinsed, drained
2 cups reduced-sodium vegetable broth
¾–1 teaspoon dried cumin
⅓ cup chopped cilantro leaves
Salt and pepper, to taste

Per Serving:
Calories: 109
% of calories from fat: 2
Fat (gm): 0.3
Saturated fat (gm): 0.0
Cholesterol (mg): 0.0
Sodium (mg): 691
Protein (gm): 6.5
Carbohydrate (gm): 25

Exchanges:
Milk: 0.0
Vegetable: 0.0;
Fruit: 0.0
Bread: 1.5
Meat: 0.0
Fat: 0.0

1. Sauté onions, garlic, and jalapeño chili in lightly greased large skillet until tender, 3 to 4 minutes. Add beans and broth and cook over medium heat, coarsely mashing beans with fork. Stir in cumin and cilantro. Season to taste with salt and pepper.

REFRIED BEANS

V *Two cans (15 ounces each) pinto beans, rinsed and drained, can be substituted for the dried beans. Delete step 1 in recipe, and use 2 cups reduced-sodium vegetable broth for the cooking liquid.*

6 side-dish servings (about ½ cup each)

1¼ cups dried pinto beans

Water

1 medium onion, coarsely chopped

Salt and pepper, to taste

Per Serving:
Calories: 106
% of calories from fat: 3
Fat (gm): 0.4
Saturated fat (gm): 0.1
Cholesterol (mg): 0
Sodium (mg): 2
Protein (gm): 6.1
Carbohydrate (gm): 20

Exchanges:
Milk: 0.0
Vegetable: 0.0
Fruit: 0.0
Bread: 1.5
Meat: 0.0
Fat: 0.0

1. Cover beans with 2 inches of water in a large saucepan; heat to boiling and boil, uncovered, 2 minutes. Remove from heat; let stand, covered, 1 hour. Drain beans; cover with 2 inches of water and heat to boiling. Reduce heat and simmer, covered, until beans are tender, 1½ to 2 hours. Drain, reserving 2 cups liquid.

2. Sauté onion in lightly greased large skillet until tender, 3 to 5 minutes. Add 1 cup beans and 1 cup reserved liquid to skillet. Cook over high heat, mashing beans with end of meat mallet or potato masher until almost smooth. Add half the remaining beans and liquid; continue cooking and mashing beans. Repeat with remaining beans and liquid. Season to taste with salt and pepper.

BLACK BEANS AND RICE

V *If fresh epazote is available, add a sprig or two to the rice while cooking.*

45 **6 side-dish servings** (about ⅔ cup each)

¼ cup each: chopped onion, sliced green onions

4 cloves garlic, minced

1 cup long-grain rice

2½ cups reduced-sodium vegetable broth

1 can (15 ounces) black beans, rinsed, drained

2 tablespoons finely chopped cilantro

Salt and pepper, to taste

Per Serving:
Calories: 171
% of calories from fat: 2
Fat (gm): 0.4
Saturated fat (gm): 0.1
Cholesterol (mg): 0.0
Sodium (mg): 462
Protein (gm): 6
Carbohydrate (gm): 38

Exchanges:
Milk: 0.0
Vegetable: 0.0
Fruit: 0.0
Bread: 2.5
Meat: 0.0
Fat: 0.0

1. Sauté onion, green onions, and garlic in lightly greased medium saucepan until tender, about 5 minutes. Add rice and cook over medium heat until lightly browned, 2 to 3 minutes, stirring frequently. Add broth and heat to boiling; reduce heat and simmer, covered, until rice is tender, 20 to 25 minutes, adding beans during last 5 minutes. Stir in cilantro; season to taste with salt and pepper.

MEXI-BEANS, GREENS, AND RICE

V

Hotly spiced, the chilies and cayenne pepper in this dish can be decreased if less hotness is desired. Four cans (15 ounces each) pinto beans, rinsed and drained, can be substituted for the dried beans; delete step 1 in recipe.

8 main-dish servings (about 1¼ cups each)

2 cups dried pinto beans

1 each: chopped onion, poblano chili, red bell pepper

4 cloves garlic, minced

1 tablespoon each: finely chopped gingerroot, serrano chilies

2 tablespoons olive oil

2 cups reduced-sodium vegetable broth, or water

2–3 teaspoons chili powder

2 teaspoons dried oregano leaves

1 teaspoon ground cumin

¼ teaspoon cayenne pepper

1 can (15 ounces) diced tomatoes, undrained

2 cups coarsely chopped turnip, or mustard, greens

Salt, to taste

5 cups cooked rice, warm

Cilantro, finely chopped, as garnish

Per Serving:
Calories: 361
% of calories from fat: 12
Fat (gm): 4.7
Saturated fat (gm): 0.7
Cholesterol (mg): 0
Sodium (mg): 103
Protein (gm): 14.4
Carbohydrate (gm): 66.7

Exchanges:
Milk: 0.0
Vegetable: 2.0
Fruit: 0.0
Bread: 3.5
Meat: 0.5
Fat: 0.5

1. Cover beans with 2 inches water in large saucepan; heat to boiling and boil, uncovered, 2 minutes. Remove from heat and let stand, covered, 1 hour; drain.

2. Sauté onion, poblano chili, bell pepper, garlic, gingerroot, and serrano chilies in oil in large saucepan until tender, 8 to 10 minutes. Add beans, broth and seasonings; heat to boiling. Reduce heat and simmer, covered, until beans are tender, 1 to 1¼ hours, adding water if necessary. Stir in tomatoes and greens; simmer, uncovered, to desired thickness, 15 to 30 minutes. Season to taste with salt. Serve over rice; sprinkle generously with cilantro.

BOURBON STREET RED BEANS AND RICE

v *The New Orleans favorite, at its healthy, low-fat best!*

4 main-dish servings (about 1¼ cups each)

1 cup dried red beans

2–3 cups reduced-sodium vegetable broth

1 cup each: chopped onion, green bell peppers, celery

½–1 jalapeño chili, finely chopped

1 teaspoon each: dried thyme and oregano leaves

½ teaspoon each: dried sage leaves, ground cumin

2 bay leaves

¼ teaspoon each: red pepper sauce, cayenne pepper

4–6 drops liquid smoke

Salt, to taste

4 cups cooked rice, warm

Per Serving:
Calories: 431
% of calories from fat: 3
Fat (gm): 1.7
Saturated fat (gm): 0.3
Cholesterol (mg): 0
Sodium (mg): 73
Protein (gm): 16.4
Carbohydrate (gm): 85.2

Exchanges:
Milk: 0.0
Vegetable: 2.0
Fruit: 0.0
Bread: 5.0
Meat: 0.5
Fat: 0.0

1. Cover beans with 2 inches water in large saucepan; heat to boiling and boil 2 minutes. Remove from heat and let stand 1 hour; drain and return to saucepan.

2. Add 2 cups broth to beans and heat to boiling; simmer, covered, 30 minutes. Add vegetables and herbs; simmer, covered, until beans are tender, 30 to 45 minutes, adding more broth if necessary (beans should be moist but without excess liquid). Discard bay leaves. Stir in red pepper sauce, cayenne pepper, and liquid smoke; season to taste with salt. Serve over rice.

HOPPING JOHN

V *Be sure to eat your portion of Hopping John before noon on January 1 to guarantee a new year of good luck!*

6 main-dish servings (about 1 cup each)

1 ½ cups chopped onions

½ cup chopped celery

3 cloves garlic, minced

1 cup long-grain white rice

3 cups reduced-sodium vegetable broth

1 teaspoon dried oregano leaves

1 bay leaf

2 cans (15 ounces each) black-eyed peas, rinsed, drained

2–3 dashes each: red pepper sauce, liquid smoke (optional)

Salt and pepper, to taste

Per Serving:
Calories: 306
% of calories from fat: 21
Fat (gm): 7
Saturated fat (gm): 1
Cholesterol (mg): 0
Sodium (mg): 447
Protein (gm): 9.6
Carbohydrate (gm): 50.7

Exchanges:
Milk: 0.0
Vegetable: 1.0
Fruit: 0.0
Bread: 3.0
Meat: 0.5
Fat: 1.0

1. Sauté onions, celery, and garlic in lightly greased large saucepan until tender, 5 to 8 minutes. Add rice, broth, oregano, and bay leaf; heat to boiling. Reduce heat and simmer, covered, until rice is tender, about 25 minutes. Stir in black-eyed peas, red pepper sauce, and liquid smoke. Cook, covered, over medium-low heat 5 minutes; discard bay leaf. Season to taste with salt and pepper.

ITALIAN-STYLE BEANS AND VEGETABLES

V *This colorful mélange can also be served over pasta, rice, or squares of warm corn bread.*

6 servings (about 1¼ cups each)

1½ cups each: chopped onions, portobello
   mushrooms
4 cloves garlic, minced
2 tablespoons olive oil
2 cups broccoli florets and sliced stems
1 cup sliced yellow summer squash
1 can (15 ounces) each: garbanzo and red kidney
   beans, rinsed, drained
1 can (14½ ounces) reduced-sodium whole tomatoes,
   undrained, coarsely chopped
1 teaspoon dried basil leaves
½ teaspoon each: dried oregano and thyme leave
¼–½ teaspoon crushed red pepper
Salt and pepper, to taste
Polenta (see p. 425)

Per Serving:
Calories: 304
% of calories from fat: 21
Fat (gm): 7.7
Saturated fat (gm): 1
Cholesterol (mg): 0
Sodium (mg): 641
Protein (gm): 13.3
Carbohydrate (gm): 50.2

Exchanges:
Milk: 0.0
Vegetable: 2.0
Fruit: 0.0
Bread: 2.5
Meat: 0.5
Fat: 1.0

1. Sauté onions, mushrooms, and garlic in oil in large saucepan until tender, about 10 minutes. Add broccoli and squash; cook, covered, over medium heat 5 minutes. Stir in remaining ingredients, except salt, pepper, and Polenta; heat to boiling. Reduce heat and simmer, covered, until broccoli is tender, about 5 minutes; season to taste with salt and pepper. Serve over polenta.

STIR-FRIED BEANS AND GREENS

o

45

Oriental foods and flavors combine with beans in this sesame-accented main course.

6 main-dish servings (about 1¼ cups each)

8 ounces snow peas, diagonally halved

1 each: sliced onion, bell pepper

1 tablespoon each: finely chopped gingerroot, garlic, serrano, or jalapeño, chili

1 tablespoon sesame oil

3 cups thinly sliced bok choy, or Chinese cabbage

2 cans (15 ounces each) black-eyed peas, rinsed, drained

1–2 tablespoons each: reduced-sodium tamari soy sauce, black bean sauce

Pepper, to taste

4 cups Chinese-style egg noodles, or rice, cooked, warm

2 teaspoons toasted sesame seeds

Per Serving:
Calories: 367
% of calories from fat: 23
Fat (gm): 9.6
Saturated fat (gm): 1.3
Cholesterol (mg): 0
Sodium (mg): 541
Protein (gm): 12.6
Carbohydrate (gm): 58.4

Exchanges:
Milk: 0.0
Vegetable: 2.0
Fruit: 0.0
Bread: 3.5
Meat: 0.5
Fat: 1.0

1. Stir-fry snow peas, onion, bell pepper, gingerroot, garlic, and serrano chili in sesame oil in large wok or skillet, 5 to 8 minutes. Stir in bok choy; cook, covered, over medium heat until wilted, 2 to 3 minutes. Add black-eyed peas and stir-fry until hot, about 5 minutes. Stir in soy sauce and black bean sauce; season to taste with pepper. Serve over noodles; sprinkle with sesame seeds.

45-MINUTE PREP TIP: Cook noodles before preparing the rest of the recipe.

BUTTER BEAN AND SPROUTS STIR-FRY

O

45

A mix of beans and fresh vegetables are seasoned with fennel, anise, and gingerroot and accented with a hint of sherry.

6 main-dish servings (about 1 cup each)

1 ½ cups halved Brussels sprouts

1 cup sliced onion

½ cup chopped red bell pepper

½ jalapeño chili, minced

1 tablespoon finely chopped gingerroot

½ teaspoon each: dried fennel and anise seeds

1 tablespoon olive oil

1 can (15 ounces) butter beans, or baby lima beans,
rinsed, drained

2 cups thinly sliced savoy cabbage, or
Chinese cabbage

1 large tomato, diced

2 tablespoons each: dry sherry, water

1 tablespoon reduced-sodium tamari soy sauce

2 teaspoons cornstarch

Salt and pepper, to taste

1 package (12 ounces) Chinese-style egg noodles,
cooked, warm

6 tablespoons chopped cashews

Per Serving:
Calories: 369
% of calories from fat: 15
Fat (gm): 6.7
Saturated fat (gm): 1.1
Cholesterol (mg): 0
Sodium (mg): 383
Protein (gm): 12.6
Carbohydrate (gm): 69.9

Exchanges:
Milk: 0.0
Vegetable: 2.0
Fruit: 0.0
Bread: 3.5
Meat: 0.5
Fat: 1.0

1. Stir-fry Brussels sprouts, onion, bell pepper, jalapeno chili, ginger-root, and fennel and anise seeds in oil in large wok or skillet 5 minutes. Add butter beans, cabbage and tomato; cook, covered, over medium to medium-low heat until Brussels sprouts and cabbage are tender, about 5 minutes, stirring occasionally.

2. Stir combined sherry, water, soy sauce, and cornstarch into vegetable mixture and heat to boiling. Cook, stirring constantly, until thickened, about 1 minute. Season to taste with salt and pepper. Serve over noodles; sprinkle with cashews.

45-MINUTE PREP TIP: Cook noodles before preparing the rest of the recipe.

ADZUKI BEAN STIR-FRY

V *Sweet-and-sour in flavor, this colorful stir-fry can be made with any kind of canned or cooked dried bean you like.*

4 main-dish servings (about 1 cup each)

½ cup each: sliced onion, red bell pepper

2 cups halved snow peas

2 teaspoons each: minced garlic, gingerroot

2 cups cooked dried adzuki beans

1 cup water

⅔ cup orange juice

2 tablespoons each: reduced-sodium tamari soy
sauce, rice wine vinegar, honey

½ teaspoon chili paste

4 teaspoons cornstarch

3 cups cooked brown rice, or Chinese-style noodles

Per Serving:
Calories: 443
% of calories from fat: 4
Fat (gm): 1.9
Saturated fat (gm): 0.3
Cholesterol (mg): 0
Sodium (mg): 349
Protein (gm): 17
Carbohydrate (gm): 91.4

Exchanges:
Milk: 0.0
Vegetable: 0.0
Fruit: 0.0
Bread: 6.0
Meat: 0.0
Fat: 0.0

1. Stir-fry onion, bell pepper, snow peas, garlic, and gingerroot in lightly greased large wok or skillet 5 minutes. Add beans and water and heat to boiling; reduce heat and simmer, covered, until vegetables are crisp-tender, 3 to 5 minutes. Stir in combined remaining ingredients, except rice; heat to boiling. Boil, stirring constantly, until thickened, about 1 minute. Serve over rice.

ASPARAGUS AND WHITE BEANS, ITALIAN-STYLE

L

45

Imagine yourself in a medieval town in Tuscany while enjoying this spring sauté.

4 main-dish servings

1 pound asparagus, cut into 2-inch pieces

2 teaspoons minced garlic

2 teaspoons olive oil

2 cups chopped Italian plum tomatoes

1 can (15 ounces) cannellini, or Great Northern, beans, rinsed, drained

1 teaspoon dried rosemary leaves, or Italian seasoning

1 cup canned reduced-sodium vegetable broth

Salt and pepper, to taste

8 ounces linguine, or thin spaghetti, cooked, warm

¼–½ cup (1–2 ounces) shredded Parmesan cheese

Per Serving:
Calories: 339
% of calories from fat: 16
Fat (gm): 6.1
Saturated fat (gm): 1.4
Cholesterol (mg): 3.9
Sodium (mg): 458
Protein (gm): 15.8
Carbohydrate (gm): 58.7

Exchanges:
Milk: 0.0
Vegetable: 2.0
Fruit: 0.0
Bread: 3.0
Meat: 0.5
Fat: 1.0

Sauté asparagus and garlic in oil in large skillet until crisp-tender, 3 to 4 minutes. Stir in tomatoes, beans, rosemary, and broth; heat to boiling. Reduce heat and simmer rapidly until mixture has thickened, 3 to 5 minutes. Season to taste with salt and pepper. Serve over pasta; sprinkle with cheese.

45-MINUTE PREP TIP: Cook pasta before preparing the rest of the recipe.

CURRIED SOYBEANS AND POTATOES

V

Make this recipe a day in advance to allow flavors to fully develop. The curry seasoning is a combination of 4 aromatic spices.

4 main-dish servings (about 1 cup each)

¾ cup each: chopped onion, red bell pepper

2 teaspoons minced garlic

1 jalapeno chili, finely chopped

2 teaspoons ground turmeric

1 teaspoon ground cumin

½ teaspoon each: ground coriander, ginger

4 medium russet potatoes, peeled, cubed

2½ cups cooked dried, or rinsed, drained soy beans

1 medium tart cooking apple, peeled, cored, cubed

1 cup water

2 teaspoons lemon juice

2 tablespoons finely chopped cilantro

Salt and pepper, to taste

Per Serving:
Calories: 368
% of calories from fat: 24
Fat (gm): 10.4
Saturated fat (gm): 1.5
Cholesterol (mg): 0
Sodium (mg): 28
Protein (gm): 22
Carbohydrate (gm): 52.7

Exchanges:
Milk: 0.0
Vegetable: 2.0
Fruit: 0.0
Bread: 2.5
Meat: 1.5
Fat: 1.0

1. Sauté onion, bell pepper, garlic, jalapeño chili, and spices in lightly greased large skillet until tender, about 5 minutes. Add potatoes, soy beans, apple, and water; heat to boiling. Reduce heat and simmer, covered, until potatoes are tender, about 15 minutes. Simmer, uncovered, until almost dry, 5 to 10 minutes. Stir in lemon juice and cilantro; season to taste with salt and pepper.

BLACK BEAN MEATBALLS

Nicely picante and spiced, these meatballs will have everyone asking for more!

6 main-dish servings (5 each)

2 cans (15 ounces each) black beans, rinsed, drained

1 medium jalapeño chili, chopped

2 teaspoons finely chopped gingerroot

1 cup loosely packed cilantro leaves

¼ cup flaked unsweetened coconut

½ teaspoon curry powder

Salt and pepper, to taste

4 cups cooked kasha, cracked wheat, or couscous, warm

2 cups (double recipe) Cucumber Yogurt (see p. 400)

Per Serving:
Calories: 284
% of calories from fat: 9
Fat (gm): 3.4
Saturated fat (gm): 1.2
Cholesterol (mg): 0.9
Sodium (mg): 503
Protein (gm): 19.4
Carbohydrate (gm): 55.9

Exchanges:
Milk: 0.0
Vegetable: 0.0
Fruit: 0.0
Bread: 3.5
Meat: 1.0
Fat: 0.0

1. Process beans, jalapeño chili, gingerroot, cilantro, coconut, and curry powder in food processor until smooth. Season to taste with salt and pepper. Shape mixture into 30 balls and place in baking pan. Bake at 350 degrees until hot, 15 to 20 minutes. Serve on kasha; spoon Cucumber Yogurt over.

45-MINUTE PREP TIP: Begin cooking the kasha and make the Cucumber Yogurt before preparing the rest of the recipe.

MEAN BEAN PASTA

L

45

Chock full of beans and highly seasoned with herbs, this hearty dish packs a high-protein nutritional punch.

6 main-dish servings (about 1 cup each)

1 cup each: chopped green bell peppers, onion

4 teaspoons minced garlic

2 tablespoons olive oil

4 cups thinly sliced cabbage

2 medium yellow summer squash, sliced

2 teaspoons dried rosemary leaves

1 teaspoon each: dried sage and savory leaves

1 can (15 ounces) each: black and garbanzo beans, rinsed, drained

Salt and pepper, to taste

12 ounces whole wheat fettuccine, cooked, warm

¼ cup (1 ounce) grated fat-free Parmesan cheese

Per Serving:
Calories: 391
% of calories from fat: 19
Fat (gm): 8.9
Saturated fat (gm): 0.8
Cholesterol (mg): 0
Sodium (mg): 644
Protein (gm): 19.7
Carbohydrate (gm): 67.3

Exchanges:
Milk: 0.0
Vegetable: 1.5
Fruit: 0.0
Bread: 4.0
Meat: 0.5
Fat: 1.0

1. Sauté bell peppers, onion, and garlic in oil in large saucepan until tender, about 5 minutes. Add cabbage, squash, and herbs; cook, covered, over medium heat until cabbage is wilted, about 5 minutes. Stir in beans; cook until hot about 5 minutes, stirring occasionally. Season to taste with salt and pepper. Serve over pasta; sprinkle with Parmesan cheese.

45-MINUTE PREP TIP: Begin cooking the fettuccine before preparing the rest of the recipe.

BEAN AND PASTA SALAD WITH WHITE BEAN DRESSING

L

Pureed beans, fat-free sour cream, and seasonings combine to make a rich, delicious salad dressing — use on green salads too!

6 side-dish servings (about 1 cup each)

4 ounces tri-color radiatore, or rotini, cooked

1 can (14¼ ounces) baby lima beans, rinsed, drained

½ can (15-ounce size) Great Northern beans, rinsed, drained

½ package (9-ounce size) frozen artichoke hearts, cooked, halved

2 cups cut green beans, cooked

¼ cup each: sliced red bell pepper, pitted black olives

½ cup (2 ounces) julienned reduced-fat brick cheese

White Bean Dressing (recipe follows)

Per Serving:
Calories: 314
% of calories from fat: 19
Fat (gm): 6.7
Saturated fat (gm): 1.4
Cholesterol (mg): 5.1
Sodium (mg): 522
Protein (gm): 16.2
Carbohydrate (gm): 50.1

Exchanges:
Milk: 0.0
Vegetable: 2.0
Fruit: 0.0
Bread: 2.5
Meat: 1.0
Fat: 0.5

1. Combine all ingredients in large bowl and toss.

White Bean Dressing

Makes about 1½ cups

½ can (15-ounce size) Great Northern beans, rinsed, drained

½ cup fat-free sour cream

1 tablespoon olive oil

2–3 tablespoons red wine vinegar

2 cloves garlic

1 teaspoon dried oregano leaves

2 tablespoons each: sliced green onions, chopped parsley

Salt and pepper, to taste

Per Serving:
Calories: 314
% of calories from fat: 19
Fat (gm): 6.7
Saturated fat (gm): 1.4
Cholesterol (mg): 5.1
Sodium (mg): 522
Protein (gm): 16.2
Carbohydrate (gm): 50.1

Exchanges:
Milk: 0.0
Vegetable: 2.0
Fruit: 0.0
Bread: 2.5
Meat: 1.0
Fat: 0.5

1. Process beans, sour cream, olive oil, vinegar, garlic, and oregano in food processor or blender until smooth. Stir in green onions and parsley; season to taste with salt and pepper. Refrigerate several hours for flavors to blend.

PASTA, WHITE BEAN, AND RED CABBAGE SALAD

LO

45

The salad can be made in advance, but stir in the cabbage just before serving for fresh color.

6 main-dish servings (about ⅔ cup each)

2¼ cups (6 ounces) rotini (corkscrews), cooked
1 cup each: sliced red cabbage, rinsed, drained,
    canned Great Northern beans
¼ cup each: chopped onion, green bell pepper
Caraway Dressing (recipe follows)

1. Combine all ingredients in salad bowl
and toss.

Per Serving:
Calories: 185
% of calories from fat: 5
Fat (gm): 1.1
Saturated fat (gm): 0.2
Cholesterol (mg): 0
Sodium (mg): 268
Protein (gm): 8.7
Carbohydrate (gm): 35.9

Exchanges:
Milk: 0.0
Vegetable: 1.5
Fruit: 0.0
Bread: 2.0
Meat: 0.0
Fat: 0.0

Caraway Dressing

Makes about 1 cup

½ cup each: fat-free mayonnaise, fat-free sour cream
2 teaspoons lemon juice
2 cloves garlic, minced
1 teaspoon caraway seeds, crushed
¼ teaspoon each: salt, pepper

1. Mix all ingredients.

45-MINUTE PREP TIP: Begin cooking rotini
and make the Caraway Dressing before preparing the rest of the
recipe.

BEAN, TOMATO, AND BREAD SALAD

L *Use summer ripe tomatoes for best flavor. Any favorite bean can be used.*

4 main-dish servings (about 1½ cups each)

3 cups cubed sourdough bread (½-inch)

Olive oil cooking spray

2 large tomatoes, cubed

½ small red onion, thinly sliced

1½ cups cooked dried, or 1 can (15 ounces) anasazi, beans, rinsed, drained

¾ cup cooked, dried navy beans, or soybeans, or ½ can (15-ounce size) navy beans, or soybeans, rinsed, drained

1 cup chopped roasted red peppers

Parmesan Vinaigrette (recipe follows)

Salt and pepper, to taste

Per Serving:
Calories: 282
% of calories from fat: 26
Fat (gm): 8.3
Saturated fat (gm): 1.1
Cholesterol (mg): 0
Sodium (mg): 161
Protein (gm): 12.1
Carbohydrate (gm): 42.3

Exchanges:
Milk: 0.0
Vegetable: 1.0
Fruit: 0.0
Bread: 2.5
Meat: 0.5
Fat: 1.0

1. Spray bread cubes generously with cooking spray; arrange in single layer on jelly roll pan. Bake at 350 degrees until golden, 10 to 15 minutes, stirring occasionally. Cool.

2. Combine tomatoes, onion, beans, and roasted red peppers in bowl; pour Parmesan Vinaigrette over and toss. Season to taste with salt and pepper. Let stand 15 to 30 minutes; add bread cubes toss. Serve immediately.

Parmesan Vinaigrette

Makes about ½ cup

2–4 tablespoons each: olive oil, red wine vinegar

2 tablespoons each: grated fat-free Parmesan cheese, chopped basil and parsley leaves

1 tablespoon chopped fresh, or ½ teaspoon dried oregano leaves

1 teaspoon minced garlic

1. Mix all ingredients.

VEGETABLE SALAD WITH 2 BEANS

V

45

Enjoy the fresh flavors of cilantro and orange and the accent of jalapeño chili in this great salad.

4 main-dish servings (about 1½ cups each)

1 package (10 ounces) frozen baby lima beans, cooked
1 can (15 ounces) garbanzo beans, rinsed, drained
1 large Idaho potato, peeled, cubed, cooked
1 cup each: peeled, seeded, chopped cucumber, sliced zucchini,
½ cup chopped green pepper
¼ cup chopped cilantro
Citrus Vinaigrette (recipe follows)

Per Serving:
Calories: 341
% of calories from fat: 24
Fat (gm): 9.4
Saturated fat (gm): 1.3
Cholesterol (mg): 0
Sodium (mg): 463
Protein (gm): 12.6
Carbohydrate (gm): 54.8

Exchanges:
Milk: 0.0
Vegetable: 2.0
Fruit: 0.0
Bread: 3.0
Meat: 0.0
Fat: 1.5

1. Combine all ingredients in salad bowl and toss.

Citrus Vinaigrette

Makes about ⅔ cup

¼ cup each: fresh orange juice, lime juice
2 tablespoons olive oil
1 teaspoon each: dried cumin, minced jalapeño chili
¼ teaspoon each: paprika, salt, cayenne pepper

1. Mix all ingredients.

ORANGE-MARINATED BEAN SALAD

V

45

A medley of beans is enhanced with a fresh accent of orange.

6 main-dish servings (about ⅔ cup each)

1 can (15 ounces) each: adzuki and red kidney beans, rinsed, drained
1 cup thinly sliced cabbage
⅓ cup each: thinly sliced green onions, yellow bell pepper, celery, carrot
Orange Dressing (recipe follows)
Salt and white pepper, to taste

3 large red bell peppers, halved

Shredded lettuce, as garnish

1. Combine beans, cabbage, green onions, sliced bell pepper, celery, and carrot; pour Orange Dressing over and toss; season to taste with salt and white pepper. Spoon salad into bell pepper halves; serve on lettuce-lined plates.

Orange Dressing

Makes about ½ cup

⅓ cup orange juice

¼ cup white wine vinegar

2 tablespoons olive oil

2 cloves garlic, minced

1 tablespoon finely chopped cilantro

2 teaspoons grated orange zest

1. Mix all ingredients.

BLACK BEAN AND RICE SALAD

V

45

Use your favorite variety of sweet or tart apple to lend flavor accent to this salad.

4 main-dish servings (about 2 cups each)

1 cup cooked rice

1 can (15 ounces) black beans, rinsed, drained

1½ cups each: sliced bok choy, or Chinese cabbage, red cabbage

1 cup cubed, seeded, peeled cucumber

2 tablespoons each: sliced green onions, celery

1 medium apple, unpeeled, cubed

2 tablespoons dark raisins

¼ cup finely chopped cilantro

3 tablespoons each: balsamic vinegar, olive oil

1½ teaspoons Dijon mustard

Salt and pepper, to taste

Per Serving:
Calories: 334
% of calories from fat: 14
Fat (gm): 5.5
Saturated fat (gm): 0.6
Cholesterol (mg): 0
Sodium (mg): 297
Protein (gm): 11
Carbohydrate (gm): 67.1

Exchanges:
Milk: 0.0
Vegetable: 2.0
Fruit: 0.0
Bread: 3.0
Meat: 0.5
Fat: 1.0

Per Serving:
Calories: 409
% of calories from fat: 24
Fat (gm): 11.9
Saturated fat (gm): 1.5
Cholesterol (mg): 0
Sodium (mg): 376
Protein (gm): 13.6
Carbohydrate (gm): 69.8

Exchanges:
Milk: 0.0
Vegetable: 0.0
Fruit: 0.5
Bread: 4.0
Meat: 0.0
Fat: 2.0

1. Combine rice, beans, vegetables, apple, raisins, and cilantro in bowl; drizzle with combined vinegar, oil, and mustard and toss. Season to taste with salt and pepper.

FAVA BEAN SALAD PLATTER

V *Use the season's most abundant vegetables on this colorful and versatile salad platter.*

4 main-dish servings

Fava Bean Spread (see p. 358)

4 cups torn escarole, or curly endive

2 cups each: cooked green beans, cauliflower florets

4 small tomatoes, cut into wedges

1 cup frozen artichoke hearts, cooked

¼ cup pitted Greek olives

4 each: sliced green onions, lemon wedges

2–4 tablespoons olive oil

Salt and pepper, to taste

¼ cup each: finely chopped fresh basil and oregano leaves

1¼ pita breads, halved, warm

Per Serving:
Calories: 363
% of calories from fat: 30
Fat (gm): 13.3
Saturated fat (gm): 1.9
Cholesterol (mg): 0
Sodium (mg): 411
Protein (gm): 15.5
Carbohydrate (gm): 53.5

Exchanges:
Milk: 0.0
Vegetable: 3.0
Fruit: 0.0
Bread: 2.5
Meat: 0.0
Fat: 2.5

1. Spoon Fava Bean Spread on lettuce-lined plates; arrange vegetables and lemon wedges around the spread. Drizzle vegetables with oil; sprinkle with salt, pepper, and herbs. Serve with pita breads.

ELEVEN

Grain Dishes

BARLEY-VEGETABLE CHOWDER

L *A perfect soup for crisp autumn days; substitute any desired vegetables.*

45 **4 main-dish servings** (about 1¾ cups each)

2 small onions, chopped

1 leek, sliced

2 cloves garlic, minced

2 cans (14½ ounces each) reduced-sodium
  vegetable broth,

1 cup each: lima beans, whole kernel corn, chopped
  cabbage, sliced carrots

¾ teaspoon each: dried savory and thyme leaves

1 bay leaf

⅔ cup quick-cooking barley

2 tablespoons flour

½ cup fat-free milk

Salt and pepper, to taste

Per Serving:
Calories: 312
% of calories from fat: 4
Fat (gm): 1.3
Saturated fat (gm): 0.3
Cholesterol (mg): 0.5
Sodium (mg): 121
Protein (gm): 12.7
Carbohydrate (gm): 66

Exchanges:
Milk: 0.0
Vegetable: 2.0
Fruit: 0.0
Bread: 3.5
Meat: 0.0
Fat: 0.0

1. Sauté onions, leek, and garlic in lightly greased large saucepan until tender, about 5 minutes. Add broth, remaining vegetables, herbs, and barley; heat to boiling; reduce heat and simmer, covered, until vegetables and barley are tender, about 20 minutes. Heat to boiling; stir in combined flour and milk; boil, stirring, until thickened, about 1 minute. Season to taste with salt and pepper, discard bay leaf.

WHEAT BERRY AND LENTIL STEW WITH DUMPLINGS

L *Use trans-fat free vegetable shortening in the dumplings.*

8 main-dish servings (about 1⅛ cups each)

1 cup wheat berries

2 medium onions, chopped

½ cup each: chopped celery, sliced carrots

4 cloves garlic, minced

1 teaspoon dried savory leaves

3 cups reduced-sodium vegetable broth

2 pounds russet potatoes, unpeeled, cubed

1½ cups cooked lentils

Salt and pepper, to taste

Herb Dumplings (recipe follows)

Per Serving:
Calories: 414
% of calories from fat: 10
Fat (gm): 4.7
Saturated fat (gm): 0.6
Cholesterol (mg): 0.3
Sodium (mg): 259
Protein (gm): 16.8
Carbohydrate (gm): 78.6

Exchanges:
Milk: 0.0
Vegetable: 1.0
Fruit: 0.0
Bread: 5.0
Meat: 0.0
Fat: 0.5

1. Cover wheat berries with 2 to 3 inches water in saucepan; let stand 8 hours or overnight. Heat to boiling; reduce heat and simmer, covered, until wheat berries are tender, 45 to 55 minutes. Drain.

2. Sauté onions, celery, carrots, garlic, and savory in lightly greased large saucepan until onions are tender, 3 to 5 minutes. Add broth, potatoes, and carrots and heat to boiling; reduce heat and simmer, covered, until vegetables are tender, 10 to 15 minutes. Stir in wheat berries and lentils; cook until hot, about 5 minutes. Season to taste with salt and pepper.

3. Spoon dumpling dough on top of stew; cook, uncovered, 5 minutes. Cook, covered, until dumplings are dry, 5 to 10 minutes longer.

Herb Dumplings

½ cup each: all-purpose flour, yellow cornmeal

1½ teaspoons baking powder

½ teaspoon each: dried sage and thyme leaves, salt

2 tablespoons vegetable shortening

½ cup fat-free milk

1. Combine flour, cornmeal, baking powder, herbs, and salt in bowl. Cut in shortening with pastry blender until mixture resembles coarse crumbs. Stir in milk to make a soft dough.

BARLEY WITH PEPPERS AND POTATOES

V

Enjoy this delicious variation of the Mexican "rajas con papas." If poblano chilies are not available, substitute green bell peppers and 1 to 2 teaspoons of minced jalapeños.

4 main-dish servings (about 1½ cups each)

6 large poblano chilies, sliced

2 medium onions, chopped

1 tablespoon olive, or canola oil

3 cups cooked, cubed, unpeeled potatoes

2 cups cooked barley

2 tablespoons finely chopped cilantro leaves

1 teaspoon dried cumin

Salt and cayenne pepper, to taste

Per Serving:
Calories: 313
% of calories from fat: 13
Fat (gm): 5
Saturated fat (gm): 0.6
Cholesterol (mg): 0.0
Sodium (mg): 20
Protein (gm): 8
Carbohydrate (gm): 64

Exchanges:
Milk: 0.0
Vegetable: 0.0
Fruit: 0.0
Bread: 4.0
Meat: 0.0
Fat: 1.0

1. Sauté chilies and onions in oil in large skillet until crisp-tender, about 5 minutes. Add potatoes; sauté until browned, 5 to 8 minutes. Add barley and cook over medium heat until hot, 3 to 4 minutes. Stir in cilantro and cumin; season to taste with salt and cayenne pepper.

WHEAT AND BARLEY BOWL

V

45

Grains and greens are cooked together, then combined with tomatoes and toasted nuts.

4 main-dish servings (about 1 cup each)

¾ cup quick-cooking barley

2 cups reduced-sodium vegetable broth

¼ cup bulgur

½ teaspoon dried thyme leaves

3 cups thinly sliced turnip greens, kale, or spinach

½ cup thinly sliced green onions

1 large tomato, coarsely chopped

¼ cup coarsely chopped walnuts, toasted

1–2 tablespoons lemon juice

Salt and pepper, to taste

Per Serving:
Calories: 257
% of calories from fat: 20
Fat (gm): 6
Saturated fat (gm): 0.6
Cholesterol (mg): 0
Sodium (mg): 66
Protein (gm): 8.6
Carbohydrate (gm): 41.7

Exchanges:
Milk: 0.0
Vegetable: 1.0
Fruit: 0.0
Bread: 2.5
Meat: 0.0
Fat: 1.0

1. Add barley to lightly greased large saucepan and cook over medium heat, stirring occasionally, until golden, about 5 minutes. Add broth, bulgur, and thyme and heat to boiling: reduce heat and simmer, covered, until barley is tender, about 10 minutes. Stir in greens and green onions; cook, covered, until all liquid is gone, about 10 minutes. Stir in tomato, walnuts, and lemon juice; cook 5 minutes longer. Season to taste with salt and pepper.

BARLEY AND VEGETABLE MÉLANGE

Topped with an egg, this hearty dish is perfect for any meal.

4 main-dish servings

3 cups reduced-sodium vegetable broth

1 cup quick-cooking barley

⅓ cup sliced green onions

1 cup sliced mushrooms

2 cloves garlic, minced

1 ½ cups each: sliced zucchini, halved cherry tomatoes

Salt and pepper, to taste

4 fried, or poached, eggs

Per Serving:
Calories: 265
% of calories from fat: 27
Fat (gm): 8.4
Saturated fat (gm): 2.1
Cholesterol (mg): 211.1
Sodium (mg): 517
Protein (gm): 12.6
Carbohydrate (gm): 37.4

Exchanges:
Milk: 0.0
Vegetable: 1.0
Fruit: 0.0
Bread: 2.0
Meat: 1.0
Fat: 1.0

1. Heat broth to boiling in medium saucepan; stir in barley. Reduce heat and simmer, covered, until barley is tender, 10 to 12 minutes. Remove from heat and let stand 5 minutes.

2. Sauté onions, mushrooms, and garlic in lightly greased large skillet until tender, about 5 minutes. Add zucchini and tomatoes; sauté until zucchini is lightly browned, 5 to 8 minutes. Stir in barley; season to taste with salt and pepper. Top each serving with an egg.

KASHA WITH GREEN VEGGIES

O

45

Kasha are buckwheat groats that have been roasted. Traditionally, kasha is mixed with raw egg and cooked in a skillet until dry; this keeps the grains separate while cooking. Buckwheat groats can be substituted in the recipe; if using, delete egg and begin with step 2.

6 main-dish servings

1½ cups kasha

1 egg, beaten

1 large green bell pepper, chopped

½ cup sliced green onions

2 cloves garlic, minced

1 tablespoon olive oil

4 cups reduced-sodium vegetable broth

½ teaspoon each: dried marjoram and thyme leaves

8 ounces broccoli rabe, cut into 1-inch pieces

½ cup frozen, thawed baby lima beans

Salt and pepper, to taste

Per Serving:
Calories: 217
% of calories from fat: 18
Fat (gm): 4.7
Saturated fat (gm): 0.9
Cholesterol (mg): 35.5
Sodium (mg): 40
Protein (gm): 8.6
Carbohydrate (gm): 38.8

Exchanges:
Milk: 0.0
Vegetable: 1.0
Fruit: 0.0
Bread: 2.0
Meat: 0.0
Fat: 1.0

1. Mix kasha and egg in bowl; cook over medium heat in large lightly greased large skillet until kasha is dry and grains are separated.

2. Sauté bell pepper, green onions, and garlic in oil in large saucepan until tender, about 5 minutes. Add kasha, broth, and herbs to saucepan; heat to boiling. Reduce heat and simmer, covered, 20 minutes; add broccoli rabe and lima beans and simmer until kasha and broccoli rabe are tender and liquid absorbed, about 10 minutes. Season to taste with salt and pepper.

BLACK-EYED PEAS AND GREENS WITH MILLET

V

45

A new twist to Hopping John! Your preference in greens might also be kale or mustard greens.

4 main-dish servings (about 1½ cups each)

1 medium onion, sliced

2 cloves garlic, minced

1 can (14½ ounces) reduced-sodium vegetable broth

3 tablespoons red wine vinegar

6 cups coarsely chopped turnip greens

2 large tomatoes, cut in wedges

1 can (15 ounces) black-eyed peas, rinsed, drained

1 cup millet

2 tablespoons finely chopped cilantro leaves

Salt and pepper, to taste

Red pepper sauce, to taste

Per Serving:
Calories: 322
% of calories from fat: 6
Fat (gm): 2.3
Saturated fat (gm): 1.1
Cholesterol (mg): 0
Sodium (mg): 385
Protein (gm): 12.4
Carbohydrate (gm): 63.9

Exchanges:
Milk: 0.0
Vegetable: 2.0
Fruit: 0.0
Bread: 3.5
Meat: 0.5
Fat: 0.0

1. Sauté onion and garlic in lightly greased large saucepan until tender, about 5 minutes. Add broth and vinegar and heat to boiling; add greens and tomatoes. Reduce heat and simmer, covered, until greens are wilted, about 5 minutes. Add black-eyed peas and millet; simmer, covered, until liquid is absorbed, about 20 minutes. Stir in cilantro; season to taste with salt, pepper, and red pepper sauce.

MEXICAN-STYLE GRAIN AND VEGETABLE CASSEROLE

Rice and millet combine with vegetables and south-of-the-border flavors. Toast the millet in a skillet over medium heat, about 5 minutes, to maximize flavor.

L

45

6 main-dish servings (about 1¼ cups each)

⅔ cup each: chopped red bell pepper, onion

3 cloves garlic, minced

1 jalapeño chili, finely chopped

2 cups each: cubed peeled chayote squash, halved small cremini mushrooms

1 cup whole kernel corn

½ teaspoon each: dried oregano leaves, ground cumin, chili powder

Salt and pepper, to taste

2 cups each: cooked white, or brown, rice, and millet

1 cup fat-free sour cream

¾ cup (3 ounces) shredded reduced-fat Monterey Jack cheese

2 green onions, sliced

Per Serving:
Calories: 293
% of calories from fat: 12
Fat (gm): 4.1
Saturated fat (gm): 1.7
Cholesterol (mg): 10.1
Sodium (mg): 156
Protein (gm): 14
Carbohydrate (gm): 52.6

Exchanges:
Milk: 0.0
Vegetable: 2.0
Fruit: 0.0
Bread: 3.0
Meat: 0.5
Fat: 0.0

1. Sauté bell pepper, onion, garlic, and jalapeño chili in lightly greased large skillet 5 minutes; add squash, mushrooms, corn, and herbs. Cook, covered, over medium heat until squash and mushrooms are tender, about 8 minutes, stirring occasionally. Season to taste with salt and pepper.

2. Combine rice and millet; spoon half the mixture into greased 2-quart casserole. Top with vegetable mixture and sour cream; spoon remaining grain mixture on top. Bake, loosely covered, at 300 degrees until hot, 30 to 40 minutes. Sprinkle with cheese, and bake, uncovered, until cheese is melted, 5 to 10 minutes; sprinkle with green onions.

45-MINUTE PREP TIP: Begin cooking rice and millet before preparing the rest of the recipe.

MILLET WITH ARTICHOKE HEARTS AND VEGETABLES

V *Deeply browned artichoke hearts, seasoned with garlic, add robust flavor to this grain and vegetable combination.*

4 main-dish servings (about 1½ cups each)

½ cup millet

1¾ cups reduced-sodium vegetable broth, divided

2 cans (15 ounces each) artichoke hearts, drained, halved

1 tablespoon margarine

½ cup each: chopped onion, green bell pepper

2 cloves garlic, minced

1 medium eggplant, unpeeled, cut into 1-inch pieces

1 cup each: chopped tomato, zucchini

1 bay leaf

Salt and pepper, to taste

Per Serving:
Calories: 327
% of calories from fat: 13
Fat (gm): 5.3
Saturated fat (gm): 0.9
Cholesterol (mg): 0
Sodium (mg): 287
Protein (gm): 13.6
Carbohydrate (gm): 65.3

Exchanges:
Milk: 0.0
Vegetable: 7.0
Fruit: 0.0
Bread: 1.5
Meat: 0.0
Fat: 1.0

1. Cook millet in large saucepan over medium heat until toasted, 2 to 3 minutes. Add 1¼ cups broth and heat to boiling; reduce heat and simmer, covered, until millet is tender and broth absorbed, about 15 minutes.

2. Sauté artichoke hearts in margarine in large skillet until well browned on all sides, 5 to 7 minutes; remove from skillet and reserve. Add onion, bell pepper, and garlic to skillet; sauté until tender, 3 to 5 minutes. Add remaining ½ cup broth, vegetables, and bay leaf; heat to boiling. Reduce heat and simmer, covered, until eggplant is tender, 15 to 20 minutes. Add millet and artichoke hearts; cook until hot, 3 to 4 minutes. Discard bay leaf; season to taste with salt and pepper.

CURRIED COUSCOUS

L

Couscous, a staple in Mediterranean countries, is one of the fastest, easiest grains to cook. Serve with a selection of condiments so the dish can be enjoyed with a variety of flavor accents.

4 main-dish servings (about 1½ cups each)

8 ounces fresh, or frozen, thawed, whole okra

1 medium onion, chopped

2 cloves garlic, chopped

1 cup each: whole kernel corn, sliced mushrooms

2 medium carrots, sliced

1½ teaspoons curry powder

1 cup reduced-sodium vegetable broth

⅔ cup couscous

1 medium tomato, chopped

Salt and pepper, to taste

Cucumber Yogurt (recipe follows)

Onion-Chutney Relish (recipe follows)

¼ cup each: chopped unsalted peanuts, dark raisins

Per Serving:
Calories: 304
% of calories from fat: 11
Fat (gm): 3.9
Saturated fat (gm): 0.6
Cholesterol (mg): 0.5
Sodium (mg): 55
Protein (gm): 9.5
Carbohydrate (gm): 60.1

Exchanges:
Milk: 0.0
Vegetable: 3.0
Fruit: 1.0
Bread: 2.0
Meat: 0.0
Fat: 0.5

1. Sauté okra, onion, and garlic in lightly greased large saucepan until onion is tender, about 5 minutes. Stir in corn, mushrooms, carrots, and curry powder; cook 2 minutes. Add broth and heat to boiling; reduce heat and simmer, covered, until vegetables are tender, 8 to 10 minutes. Stir in couscous and tomato; remove from heat and let stand, covered, until couscous is tender and broth absorbed, about 5 minutes. Season to taste with salt and pepper. Serve with Cucumber Yogurt, Onion-Chutney Relish, peanuts, and raisins.

Cucumber Yogurt

Makes about 1 cup

⅔ cup each: fat-free plain yogurt, seeded, finely chopped cucumber
1 teaspoon dried dill weed

1. Combine all ingredients.

Onion-Chutney Relish

Makes about 1 cup

4 medium onions, chopped
½ cup chopped mango chutney
1–1½ teaspoons dried mint leaves

1. Sauté onions in lightly greased large skillet 3 to 4 minutes; reduce heat to low and cook until very soft and golden, about 15 minutes. Mix in chutney and mint; cool.

CURRIED SWEET POTATO COUSCOUS

| V | *Versatile couscous blends easily with a variety of vegetable flavors.* |

45 **4 main-dish servings**

¼ cup sliced onion
2 cloves garlic, minced
1–2 tablespoons olive oil
2 medium sweet potatoes, cooked, diced
1–1½ teaspoons curry powder
¼ cup each: raisins, walnuts
1 cup reduced-sodium vegetable broth
⅔ cup couscous
1 cup thinly sliced kale
Salt and pepper, to taste

Per Serving:
Calories: 317
% of calories from fat: 25
Fat (gm): 9
Saturated fat (gm): 1
Cholesterol (mg): 0
Sodium (mg): 136
Protein (gm): 7.5
Carbohydrate (gm): 53.3

Exchanges:
Milk: 0.0
Vegetable: 0.0
Fruit: 0.0
Bread: 3.0
Meat: 0.0
Fat: 2.0

1. Sauté onion and garlic in olive oil in large saucepan until tender, 2 to 3 minutes. Add sweet potatoes; cook until lightly browned, about 5 minutes. Stir in curry powder, raisins, walnuts, and broth; heat to boiling. Add couscous and kale, stirring with a fork; remove from heat and let stand, covered, until couscous is tender and broth is absorbed, about 5 minutes. Season to taste with salt and pepper.

FRUITED COUSCOUS WITH SMOKED TOFU

L *Make Mesquite-Smoked Tofu (see p. 191) a day in advance, as the flavor will heighten. Purchased smoked tofu can also be used.*

6 main-dish servings (about 1 cup each)

½ cup each: finely chopped onion, red bell pepper, celery

1½ teaspoons minced garlic

1 tablespoon olive oil

1¼ cups reduced-sodium vegetable broth

1½ teaspoons curry powder

1 package (10 ounces) couscous (spice packet discarded)

Mesquite-Smoked Tofu (see p. 191), cubed

1 can (11 ounces) Mandarin orange segments, drained

Salt and pepper, to taste

6 tablespoons (1½ ounces) crumbled reduced-fat feta cheese

Per Serving:
Calories: 303
% of calories from fat: 15
Fat (gm): 5.1
Saturated fat (gm): 1
Cholesterol (mg): 2.5
Sodium (mg): 216
Protein (gm): 15.6
Carbohydrate (gm): 48

Exchanges:
Milk: 0.0
Vegetable: 0.5
Fruit: 0.5
Bread: 2.5
Meat: 1.0
Fat: 0.5

1. Sauté onion, bell pepper, celery, and garlic in oil in medium saucepan until tender, about 5 minutes. Add broth and curry powder and heat to boiling and stir in couscous; remove from heat and let stand, covered, 5 minutes. Stir in tofu and orange segments; cook over medium heat until hot, 3 to 4 minutes. Season to taste with salt and pepper; sprinkle with cheese.

QUINOA WITH ROASTED EGGPLANT AND SQUASH

V

45

Grain recipes are versatile, as almost any grain can be used in them. Couscous, millet, or kasha also would be excellent choices in this recipe.

4 main-dish servings (about 1½ cups each)

1 small butternut squash, peeled, cubed
1 medium eggplant, unpeeled, cubed
1 cup each: thickly sliced bell pepper, onions
Vegetable cooking spray
1 teaspoon dried rosemary leaves
½ teaspoon each: dried savory and thyme leaves
2 cups reduced-sodium vegetable broth
1 cup quinoa
Salt and pepper, to taste

Per Serving:
Calories: 282
% of calories from fat: 10
Fat (gm): 3.4
Saturated fat (gm): 0.4
Cholesterol (mg): 0
Sodium (mg): 46
Protein (gm): 8.6
Carbohydrate (gm): 54.8

Exchanges:
Milk: 0.0
Vegetable: 3.0
Fruit: 0.0
Bread: 2.5
Meat: 0.0
Fat: 0.5

1. Arrange vegetables in single layer on greased foil-lined jelly roll pan. Spray vegetables with cooking spray; sprinkle with herbs. Roast at 425 degrees until vegetables are tender, 35 to 45 minutes.

2. Heat broth to boiling in medium saucepan; stir in quinoa. Reduce heat and simmer, covered, until quinoa is tender and broth absorbed, about 15 minutes. Combine quinoa and warm vegetables; season to taste with salt and pepper.

QUINOA AND WHEAT BERRY PILAF

V

The two grains are a contrast in appearance, texture, and flavor. Any favorite cooked grains can be substituted.

4 main-dish servings (about 1½ cups each)

½ cup wheat berries
1 cup reduced-sodium vegetable broth
½ cup quinoa
1 cup chopped shiitake, or portobello, mushrooms
⅔ cup each: chopped green onions, red bell pepper
3 cloves garlic, minced

1 tablespoon olive oil

½ cup peas

Salt and pepper, to taste

Per Serving:
Calories: 248
% of calories from fat: 19
Fat (gm): 5.4
Saturated fat (gm): 0.7
Cholesterol (mg): 0
Sodium (mg): 43
Protein (gm): 8.1
Carbohydrate (gm): 43.8

1. Cover wheat berries with 2 inches water in small saucepan and soak overnight. Heat to boiling; reduce heat and simmer, covered, until tender, 15 to 20 minutes. Drain.

Exchanges:
Milk: 0.0
Vegetable: 1.0
Fruit: 0.0
Bread: 2.5
Meat: 0.0
Fat: 1.0

2. Heat broth to boiling in small saucepan; add quinoa. Reduce heat and simmer until quinoa is tender and broth absorbed, about 15 minutes.

3. Sauté mushrooms, green onions, bell pepper, and garlic in oil in large skillet until tender, 5 to 8 minutes. Add peas and grains; cook, covered, until hot, 2 to 3 minutes. Season to taste with salt and pepper.

GARDEN QUINOA

V

45

An attractive and tasteful collaboration of heart-healthy quinoa and vegetables!

2 main-dish servings (about 1 ½ cups each)

Per Serving:
Calories: 304
% of calories from fat: 23
Fat (gm): 8
Saturated fat (gm): 1
Cholesterol (mg): 0.0
Sodium (mg): 46
Protein (gm): 9
Carbohydrate (gm): 51

¾ cup each: julienne carrots, thinly sliced
   red onion, red bell pepper
2 teaspoons olive or canola oil
2 cups cooked quinoa
¼ cup finely chopped cilantro
Salt and pepper, to taste

Exchanges:
Milk: 0.0
Vegetable: 1.0
Fruit: 0.0
Bread: 3.0
Meat: 0.0
Fat: 1.5

1. Sauté vegetables in oil in large skillet until crisp-tender, about 5 minutes. Stir in quinoa and cook until hot through, 2 to 3 minutes; stir in cilantro and season to taste with salt and pepper.

ASIAN FRIED RICE

o

The combination of wild and white rice adds a new dimension to an Asian favorite. Lightly scrambled egg is a traditional addition to many fried rice recipes; it can be omitted, if desired.

4 main-dish servings (about 1½ cups each)

2 cups broccoli florets and sliced stalks

1 cup halved snow peas

¾ cup each: bean sprouts, sliced carrots, shiitake mushrooms, chopped celery, green bell pepper

1 teaspoon each: minced garlic, finely chopped gingerroot

½ cup reduced-sodium vegetable broth

2 tablespoons reduced-sodium soy sauce

1½ cups each: cooked white and wild rice

1 egg, lightly scrambled, crumbled

Salt and pepper, to taste

Per Serving:
Calories: 236
% of calories from fat: 8
Fat (gm): 2.1
Saturated fat (gm): 0.5
Cholesterol (mg): 53.3
Sodium (mg): 340
Protein (gm): 10.2
Carbohydrate (gm): 46.9

Exchanges:
Milk: 0.0
Vegetable: 2.0
Fruit: 0.0
Bread: 2.5
Meat: 0.0
Fat: 0.0

1. Stir-fry vegetables and gingerroot in lightly greased large wok or skillet until crisp-tender, 5 to 8 minutes. Add broth and soy sauce; stir in rice and scrambled egg and stir-fry 2 to 3 minutes longer. Season to taste with salt and pepper.

MUSHROOM AND ASPARAGUS PILAF

V

45

The dried Chinese black or shiitake mushrooms impart a hearty, woodsy flavor to this pilaf.

8 main-dish servings (about 1½ cups each)

3⅓ cups reduced-sodium vegetable broth, divided

2 cups dried Chinese mushrooms

2 cups chopped onions

4 cloves garlic, minced

2 teaspoons dried basil leaves

½ teaspoon each: dried thyme and savory leaves

1½ pounds asparagus, cut into 1½-inch pieces

¼ cup dry sherry, or water

2 packages (6 ounces each) tabbouleh wheat salad mix (spice packet discarded)

¼ teaspoon red pepper sauce

Salt and pepper, to taste

4 green onions, thinly sliced

¼ cup toasted pecan halves

Per Serving:
Calories: 224
% of calories from fat: 11
Fat (gm): 3
Saturated fat (gm): 0.3
Cholesterol (mg): 0.0
Sodium (mg): 603
Protein (gm): 8
Carbohydrate (gm): 45

Exchanges:
Milk: 0.0
Vegetable: 0.0
Fruit: 0.0
Bread: 3.0
Meat: 0.0
Fat: 0.5

1. Heat 2 cups broth to boiling; pour over mushrooms in bowl and let stand until mushrooms are softened, 10 to 15 minutes. Drain; reserve broth. Slice mushrooms, discarding tough stems.

2. Sauté mushrooms, onions, garlic, and herbs in lightly greased large skillet until onions are tender, about 5 minutes. Add asparagus, sherry, reserved mushroom broth, and remaining 1⅓ cups broth; heat to boiling. Stir in tabbouleh; reduce heat and simmer, covered, until tabbouleh is tender and broth absorbed, 3 to 5 minutes. Stir in red pepper sauce; season to taste with salt and pepper. Sprinkle with green onions and pecans.

FRUIT PILAF

V   *An easy pilaf, with dried fruit and nuts, that is simply good.*

4 main-dish servings (about 1 cup each)

½ cup sliced green onions

¼ cup thinly sliced celery

1 tablespoon margarine

⅔ cup brown rice

⅓ cup wild rice

2½ cups reduced-sodium vegetable broth

½ teaspoon each: dried marjoram and thyme leaves

1 large tart, or sweet, apple, peeled, cubed

⅓ cup each: chopped dried apricots, dried pears

4–6 tablespoons pecan, or walnut, halves, toasted

Salt and pepper, to taste

Per Serving:
Calories: 353
% of calories from fat: 23
Fat (gm): 9.2
Saturated fat (gm): 1.2
Cholesterol (mg): 0
Sodium (mg): 80
Protein (gm): 6.4
Carbohydrate (gm): 60.9

Exchanges:
Milk: 0.0
Vegetable: 0.0
Fruit: 1.5
Bread: 2.5
Meat: 0.0
Fat: 2.0

1. Sauté green onions and celery in margarine in large saucepan until celery is tender, about 5 minutes. Add brown and wild rice and cook 2 minutes longer. Stir in broth and herbs and heat to boiling; reduce heat and simmer, covered, 45 minutes. Stir in apple, apricots, and pears; simmer, covered, until rice is tender and broth absorbed, about 10 minutes. Stir in pecans; season to taste with salt and pepper.

SWEET BULGUR PILAF

V

A pilaf with sweet accents of yellow squash, raisins, and pie spice.

45 **4 main-dish servings** (about 1 cup each)

⅔ cup each: finely chopped onion, sliced
   green onions
1 large clove garlic, minced
1 cup bulgur
2¼ cups reduced-sodium vegetable broth
½–¾ teaspoon ground cinnamon
2 cups cubed, peeled butternut, or acorn, squash
¼ cup each: currants, or raisins, toasted pine nuts
Salt and pepper, to taste

Per Serving:
Calories: 263
% of calories from fat: 19
Fat (gm): 6.2
Saturated fat (gm): 1
Cholesterol (mg): 0
Sodium (mg): 44
Protein (gm): 8.7
Carbohydrate (gm): 46.1

Exchanges:
Milk: 0.0
Vegetable: 0.0
Fruit: 0.0
Bread: 3.0
Meat: 0.0
Fat: 1.0

1. Sauté onion, green onions, garlic, and bulgur in lightly greased large saucepan until onions are tender, 5 to 6 minutes. Stir in broth and cinnamon and heat to boiling; reduce heat and simmer, covered, 10 minutes. Stir in squash and currants; simmer, covered, until squash is tender, about 15 minutes. Stir in pine nuts; season to taste with salt and pepper.

ORIENTAL PILAF

V

45

Snow peas, water chestnuts, oriental seasonings, and a combination of brown rice and millet make this pilaf a favorite.

4 main-dish servings (about 1¼ cups each)

⅓ cup each: chopped onion, celery

2–3 teaspoons finely chopped gingerroot

2 cloves garlic, minced

1 tablespoon Asian sesame oil

½ cup each: brown rice, millet

2½ cups reduced-sodium vegetable broth

1½ cups halved snow peas

½ can (6-ounce size) water chestnuts, rinsed, drained, sliced

½ cup thinly sliced green onions

2–3 tablespoons reduced-sodium tamari soy sauce

Salt and pepper, to taste

Per Serving:
Calories: 273
% of calories from fat: 18
Fat (gm): 5.4
Saturated fat (gm): 0.8
Cholesterol (mg): 0
Sodium (mg): 387
Protein (gm): 8.2
Carbohydrate (gm): 47.9

Exchanges:
Milk: 0.0
Vegetable: 1.0
Fruit: 0.0
Bread: 3.0
Meat: 0.0
Fat: 0.5

1. Sauté onion, celery, gingerroot, and garlic in sesame oil in large saucepan until onion is tender, about 10 minutes. Add rice and millet and cook 2 minutes longer; add broth and heat to boiling. Reduce heat and simmer, covered, 15 minutes. Stir in snow peas, water chestnuts, and green onions; simmer, covered, until grains and snow peas are tender and broth absorbed, about 10 minutes. Season to taste with soy sauce, salt, and pepper.

WINTER VEGETABLE RISOTTO

L *Arborio rice is a short-grain rice grown in the Arborio region of Italy. It's especially suited for making risotto, as it cooks to a wonderful creaminess. Other longer-grained rices can be used, but the texture of the risotto will be less creamy.*

4 main-dish servings (about 1¼ cups each)

1 small onion, chopped

3 cloves garlic, minced

1 cup sliced cremini, or white, mushrooms

1 teaspoon each: dried rosemary and thyme leaves

1½ cups arborio rice

6 cups reduced-sodium vegetable broth

1 cup each: halved Brussels sprouts, cubed,
    peeled sweet potato, cooked until crisp-tender

¼ cup (1 ounce) grated Parmesan cheese

Salt and pepper, to taste

Per Serving:
Calories: 384
% of calories from fat: 8
Fat (gm): 3.3
Saturated fat (gm): 1.4
Cholesterol (mg): 4.9
Sodium (mg): 153
Protein (gm): 11
Carbohydrate (gm): 77.3

Exchanges:
Milk: 0.0
Vegetable: 3.0
Fruit: 0.0
Bread: 4.0
Meat: 0.0
Fat: 0.5

1. Sauté onion and garlic in lightly greased large saucepan until tender, about 5 minutes. Add mushrooms and herbs; cook until mushrooms are tender, 5 to 7 minutes. Stir in rice; cook over medium heat until rice begins to brown, 2 to 3 minutes, stirring frequently.

2. Heat broth just to boiling in medium saucepan; reduce heat to medium-low to keep broth hot. Add broth to rice mixture, ½ cup at a time, stirring constantly over medium heat until broth is absorbed before adding next ½ cup. Continue process until rice is *al dente* and mixture is creamy, 20 to 25 minutes, adding Brussels sprouts and sweet potato during last 10 minutes of cooking time. Stir in cheese; season to taste with salt and pepper.

ALL-SEASON RISOTTO

L *A blending of summer and winter squash provides color and flavor to this creamy risotto dish.*

6 main-dish servings (about 1⅓ cups each)

2 cups each: peeled, cubed acorn, or
   butternut, squash
1 cup each: sliced zucchini, cremini mushrooms,
   chopped red bell pepper
6 plum tomatoes, quartered
2 teaspoons dried oregano leaves
2 tablespoons olive oil, divided
1 cup chopped onion
2 cloves garlic, minced
1½ cups arborio rice
1 ½ quarts reduced-sodium vegetable broth
2 cups water
¼ cup (1 ounce) grated fat-free Parmesan cheese
1 can (15½ ounces) black beans, rinsed, drained
½ cup frozen peas, thawed
Salt and pepper, to taste

Per Serving:
Calories: 391
% of calories from fat: 13
Fat (gm): 6.2
Saturated fat (gm): 0.8
Cholesterol (mg): 0
Sodium (mg): 328
Protein (gm): 14.7
Carbohydrate (gm): 75.9

Exchanges:
Milk: 0.0
Vegetable: 2.0
Fruit: 0.0
Bread: 4.0
Meat: 0.0
Fat: 1.0

1. Sauté squash, zucchini, mushrooms, bell pepper, tomatoes, and oregano in 1 tablespoon oil in large skillet until tender, about 8 minutes; reserve. Sauté onion and garlic in remaining tablespoon oil in large saucepan until tender, 3 to 4 minutes. Add rice; cook 2 to 3 minutes, stirring occasionally.

2. Heat broth and water to simmering in medium saucepan; reduce heat to low and keep warm. Add broth to rice mixture, ½ cup at a time, stirring constantly over medium heat until broth is absorbed before adding next ½ cup. Continue process until rice is *al dente* and mixture is creamy, 20 to 25 minutes. Stir in cheese, beans, peas, and reserved vegetables; cook 2 to 3 minutes longer. Season to taste with salt and pepper.

PORCINI RISOTTO

L *Use dried shiitake or Chinese black mushrooms if porcini are not available.*

4 main-dish servings (about 1 cup each)

1 cup boiling water

¼–½ ounce dried porcini mushrooms

1 small onion, chopped

3 cloves garlic, minced

1 small tomato, seeded, chopped

1 teaspoon dried sage leaves

1½ cups arborio rice

1½ quarts reduced-sodium vegetable broth

¼ cup (1 ounce) grated Parmesan cheese

Salt and pepper, to taste

2 tablespoons each: toasted pine nuts, finely
   chopped fresh sage

Per Serving:
Calories: 389
% of calories from fat: 14
Fat (gm): 6.1
Saturated fat (gm): 1.9
Cholesterol (mg): 4.9
Sodium (mg): 135
Protein (gm): 10.2
Carbohydrate (gm): 68

Exchanges:
Milk: 0.0
Vegetable: 2.0
Fruit: 0.0
Bread: 4.0
Meat: 0.0
Fat: 1.0

1. Pour boiling water over mushrooms in bowl; let stand until mushrooms are soft, about 15 minutes; drain, reserving liquid. Slice mushrooms, discarding tough stems.

2. Sauté mushrooms, onion, and garlic in lightly greased large saucepan until tender, about 5 minutes. Stir in tomato and sage; cook 2 minutes longer. Stir in rice and cook over medium heat until rice begins to brown, 2 to 3 minutes, stirring frequently.

3. Heat broth and reserved porcini liquid to boiling in medium saucepan; reduce heat to medium-low to keep broth hot. Add broth to rice mixture, ½ cup at a time, stirring constantly over medium heat until broth is absorbed before adding another ½ cup. Continue process until rice is *al dente* and mixture is creamy, 20 to 25 minutes; stir in cheese. Season to taste with salt and pepper; sprinkle with pine nuts and sage.

BROCCOLI RISOTTO

L *A flavorful risotto, abundantly seasoned with herbs.*

6 main-dish servings (about 1¼ cups each)

1 small onion, chopped

2 cloves garlic, minced

½ teaspoon each: crushed fennel seeds, dried sage and oregano leaves

⅛ teaspoon each: ground allspice, mace

1½ cups arborio rice

1½ quarts reduced-sodium vegetable broth

8 ounces vegetarian sausage, thawed, crumbled

2 cups broccoli florets, cooked crisp-tender

½ cup raisins

2 tablespoons grated Parmesan cheese

Salt and pepper, to taste

Per Serving:
Calories: 351
% of calories from fat: 20.2
Fat (gm): 8.1
Saturated fat (gm): 1.4
Cholesterol (mg): 1.5
Sodium (mg): 833
Protein (gm): 13.1
Carbohydrate (gm): 59

Exchanges:
Milk: 0.0
Vegetable: 0.0
Fruit: 0.0
Bread: 4.0
Meat: 1.0
Fat: 0.5

1. Sauté onion and garlic in lightly greased large saucepan until tender, about 5 minutes. Stir in herbs, spices, and rice; cook over medium heat until rice begins to brown, 2 to 3 minutes, stirring frequently.

2. Heat broth to boiling in medium saucepan; reduce heat to medium-low to keep broth hot. Add broth to rice mixture, ½ cup at a time, stirring constantly over medium heat until broth is absorbed before adding another ½ cup. Continue process until rice is *al dente* and mixture is creamy, 20 to 25 minutes, adding vegetarian sausage, broccoli, and raisins during last 10 minutes of cooking time. Stir in cheese; season to taste with salt and pepper.

SUMMER SQUASH RISOTTO

L

A perfect risotto for summer, when squash and tomatoes are fresh from the garden.

4 main-dish servings (about 1 cup each)

1 cup each: sliced zucchini, summer yellow squash

1 tablespoon olive oil

1 medium onion, chopped

3 cloves garlic, minced

8 Italian plum tomatoes, quartered

1½ teaspoons dried oregano leaves

1½ cups arborio rice

1½ quarts reduced-sodium vegetable broth

¼ cup (1 ounce) grated Romano cheese

Salt and pepper, to taste

Per Serving:
Calories: 423
% of calories from fat: 15
Fat (gm): 7.4
Saturated fat (gm): 2
Cholesterol (mg): 7.2
Sodium (mg): 128
Protein (gm): 11.1
Carbohydrate (gm): 79.5

Exchanges:
Milk: 0.0
Vegetable: 3.0
Fruit: 0.0
Bread: 4.0
Meat: 0.0
Fat: 1.5

1. Sauté zucchini and yellow squash in oil in lightly greased medium skillet until crisp-tender, 5 to 7 minutes; reserve. Sauté onion and garlic in lightly greased saucepan until tender, about 5 minutes. Add tomatoes and oregano; cook until tomatoes are soft, about 3 minutes. Add rice; cook over medium heat until rice begins to brown, 2 to 3 minutes, stirring frequently.

2. Heat broth to boiling in small saucepan; reduce heat to medium-low to keep broth hot. Add broth to rice mixture, ½ cup at a time, stirring constantly over medium heat until broth is absorbed before adding another ½ cup. Continue process until rice is *al dente* and mixture is creamy, 20 to 25 minutes, adding reserved vegetables during last 5 minutes of cooking time. Stir in cheese; season to taste with salt and pepper.

TWO-CHEESE RISOTTO

L

45

This risotto is quickly prepared with a simplified method that requires little stirring.

4 main-dish servings (about 1 cup each)

½ cup finely chopped onion

1 cup arborio rice

2½ cups vegetable broth

½ cup dry white wine

1 cup (4 ounces) shredded Parmesan cheese

¼–½ cup (1 to 2 ounces) crumbled blue cheese

2–3 tablespoons chopped chives, or parsley

Salt and pepper, to taste

Per Serving:
Calories: 345
% of calories from fat: 22
Fat (gm): 8.3
Saturated fat (gm): 5.2
Cholesterol (mg): 21.1
Sodium (mg): 525
Protein (gm): 13.9
Carbohydrate (gm): 47.3

Exchanges:
Milk: 0.0
Vegetable: 0.0
Fruit: 0.0
Bread: 3.0
Meat: 1.0
Fat: 1.5

1. Sauté onion in lightly greased large saucepan 1 to 2 minutes. Add rice, vegetable broth, and wine and heat to boiling. Reduce heat and simmer, covered, until rice is *al dente* and liquid absorbed, 20 to 25 minutes, stirring occasionally. Stir in cheeses and chives. Season to taste with salt and pepper.

RISI BISI

L

45

Opinions vary as to whether Risi Bisi is a risotto or a thick soup. If you agree with the latter definition, use an additional ½ to 1 cup of broth to make the mixture a thick-soup consistency.

4 main-dish servings (about 1 cup each)

1 small onion, chopped

3 cloves garlic, minced

1½ cups arborio rice

2 teaspoons dried basil leaves

1½ quarts reduced-sodium vegetable broth

8 ounces frozen tiny peas, thawed

¼ cup (1 ounce) grated Parmesan cheese

Salt and pepper, to taste

Per Serving:
Calories: 407
% of calories from fat: 6
Fat (gm): 2.5
Saturated fat (gm): 1.3
Cholesterol (mg):
4.9Sodium (mg): 291
Protein (gm): 12.2
Carbohydrate (gm): 82.1

Exchanges:
Milk: 0.0
Vegetable: 1.0
Fruit: 0.0
Bread: 5.0
Meat: 0.0
Fat: 0.5

1. Sauté onion and garlic in lightly greased large saucepan until tender, about 5 minutes. Stir in rice and basil. Cook over medium heat until rice begins to brown, 2 to 3 minutes, stirring frequently.

2. Heat broth to boiling in medium saucepan; reduce heat to medium-low to keep broth hot. Add broth to rice mixture, ½ cup at a time, stirring constantly over medium heat until broth is absorbed before adding another ½ cup. Continue process until rice is *al dente* and mixture is creamy, 20 to 25 minutes. Stir in peas during last 10 minutes of cooking time. Stir in Parmesan cheese; season to taste with salt and pepper.

RISOTTO-VEGETABLE CAKES

LO *A great way to use leftover risotto!*

4 main-dish servings

1 medium onion, finely chopped

2 cloves garlic, minced

1 teaspoon dried oregano leaves

1 cup arborio rice

3 cups reduced-sodium vegetable broth

¼ cup (1 ounce) each: shredded reduced-fat Cheddar, or Monterey Jack, cheese, grated fat-free Parmesan cheese

½ cup each: chopped zucchini, carrots, red bell pepper, celery

1 egg, lightly beaten

⅔ cup Italian-seasoned dry bread crumbs

8 beefsteak tomatoes, thickly sliced

Salt and pepper, to taste

Per Serving:
Calories: 409
% of calories from fat: 12
Fat (gm): 5
Saturated fat (gm): 2
Cholesterol (mg): 59
Sodium (mg): 1142
Protein (gm): 16
Carbohydrate (gm): 77

Exchanges:
Milk: 0.0
Vegetable: 3.0
Fruit: 0.0
Bread: 4.0
Meat: 0.0
Fat: 1.0

1. Sauté onion, garlic, and oregano in lightly greased large saucepan until tender, about 3 minutes. Add rice; cook 2 to 3 minutes, stirring frequently.

2. Heat broth to simmering in medium saucepan; reduce heat to low to keep broth warm. Add broth to rice mixture, ½ cup at a time, stirring constantly over medium heat until broth is absorbed before adding next ½ cup. Continue process until rice is *al dente*

and mixture is creamy, 20 to 25 minutes; stir in cheeses. Cool to room temperature.

3. Sauté zucchini, carrots, bell pepper, and celery in lightly greased large skillet until tender, 5 to 8 minutes. Stir into rice mixture; stir in egg and bread crumbs. Form mixture into 8 patties, each a scant ¾ inch thick. Broil 6 inches from heat source, until browned, 2 to 4 minutes each side. Top each patty with tomato slice and sprinkle lightly with salt and pepper; broil until tomato is browned, 2 to 3 minutes.

TABBOULEH

Always a favorite — this version includes finely chopped mint as well as parsley.

4 side dish servings (about 1 cup each)

¾ cup bulgur

1½ cups coarsely chopped seeded tomatoes

¾ cup each: thinly sliced green onions,
   finely chopped parsley

¼ cup finely chopped mint

⅓–⅔ cup fat-free plain yogurt

¼–⅓ cup lemon juice

1½–2 tablespoons olive oil

Salt and pepper, to taste

Per Serving:
Calories: 176
% of calories from fat: 28
Fat (gm): 5.9
Saturated fat (gm): 0.8
Cholesterol (mg): 0.3
Sodium (mg): 34
Protein (gm): 5.7
Carbohydrate (gm): 28.2

Exchanges:
Milk: 0.0
Vegetable: 1.0
Fruit: 0.0
Bread: 1.5
Meat: 0.0
Fat: 1.0

1. Pour boiling water over bulgur to cover; let stand 15 minutes or until bulgur is tender but slightly chewy; drain. Mix bulgur, tomatoes, green onions, parsley, and mint; stir in yogurt, lemon juice, and oil. Season to taste with salt and pepper. Refrigerate 1 to 2 hours for flavors to blend.

TABBOULEH AND VEGETABLE SALAD MEDLEY

L

Two salads—tabbouleh dressed with Lemon-Cinnamon Vinaigrette, and a mixed vegetable salad with chunky Cucumber-Sour Cream Dressing—are lightly combined for a contrast of flavors. Or, if desired, the salads can be served side by side.

4 main-dish servings

1 package (5¼ ounces) tabbouleh wheat salad mix (spice packet discarded)

1 cup cold water

⅓ cup each: finely chopped celery, sliced green onions

8 prunes, pitted, chopped

1 tablespoon finely chopped fresh, or 1 teaspoon dried, basil leaves

1 clove garlic, minced

Lemon-Cinnamon Vinaigrette (recipe follows)

Salt and pepper, to taste

2 cups cauliflower florets

⅔ cup each: chopped red bell pepper, diagonally sliced carrots, halved cherry tomatoes

Cucumber-Sour Cream Dressing (recipe follows)

Salad greens, as garnish

¼ cup (1 ounce) crumbled feta cheese

Per Serving:
Calories: 382
% of calories from fat: 28
Fat (gm): 12.5
Saturated fat (gm): 2.5
Cholesterol (mg): 6.5
Sodium (mg): 600
Protein (gm): 11.4
Carbohydrate (gm): 61.6

Exchanges:
Milk: 0.0
Vegetable: 3.0
Fruit: 1.5
Bread: 1.5
Meat: 0.0
Fat: 2.5

1. Mix tabbouleh and cold water in medium bowl; let stand until water is absorbed, about 30 minutes. Stir in celery, green onions, prunes, basil, and garlic; add Lemon-Cinnamon Vinaigrette and toss. Season to taste with salt and pepper.

2. Combine cauliflower, bell pepper, carrots, and tomatoes in large bowl; spoon Cucumber-Sour Cream Dressing over and toss. Season to taste with salt and pepper. Add tabbouleh salad and toss lightly. Serve on lettuce-lined plates; sprinkle with feta cheese.

Lemon-Cinnamon Vinaigrette

Makes about ½ cup

⅓ cup lemon juice
3 tablespoons olive oil, or canola oil
¼ teaspoon dried cinnamon

1. Combine all ingredients.

Cucumber-Sour Cream Dressing

Makes about 1 cup

½ cup fat-free sour cream
¼ cup fat-free plain yogurt
1 teaspoon each: white wine vinegar, dried dill weed
½ medium cucumber, peeled, seeded, chopped

1. Combine all ingredients.

VEGETABLE SALAD WITH MILLET

V

45

Serve this salad in bowls, in beefsteak tomato halves, or use it as a filling for warm pita pockets.

6 main-dish servings (about 1⅓ cups each)

1¼ cups millet
3⅓ cups water
½ cup each: sliced celery, red bell pepper
¼ cup each: sliced green onions, carrot, parsley
and basil leaves
½ small head iceberg lettuce, sliced
1 medium tomato, coarsely chopped
Oregano Vinaigrette (recipe follows)
Salt and pepper, to taste
4 pita breads

Per Serving:
Calories: 350
% of calories from fat: 24
Fat (gm): 9.2
Saturated fat (gm): 1.3
Cholesterol (mg): 0.0
Sodium (mg): 237
Protein (gm): 9.3
Carbohydrate (gm): 57.0

Exchanges:
Milk: 0.0
Vegetable: 0.0
Fruit: 0.0
Bread: 4.0
Meat: 0.0
Fat: 1.5

1. Cook millet in large saucepan over medium heat until toasted, 2 to 3 minutes, stirring frequently. Add water and heat to boiling;

reduce heat and simmer, covered, until millet is tender and liquid absorbed, about 15 minutes. Remove from heat and let stand, covered, 10 minutes; cool.

2. Process celery, bell pepper, green onions, carrot, parsley, and basil in food processor until finely chopped; transfer to large bowl. Process lettuce until finely chopped; add to vegetables. Add tomatoes, millet, and Oregano Vinaigrette; toss. Season to taste with salt and pepper. Serve with pitas.

Oregano Vinaigrette

Makes about 1/3 cup

3 tablespoons each: olive oil, white wine vinegar
1 teaspoon dried oregano leaves

1. Mix all ingredients.

WHEAT BERRY WALDORF

Bulgur can be substituted for the wheat berries; soak bulgur in 1 1/3 cups water until tender and proceed with recipe.

4 main-dish servings (about 1 1/2 cups each)

1 1/4 cups wheat berries
1 1/2 cups peeled, cored, cubed pineapple
2 medium oranges, peeled, cut into segments
1 cup each: unpeeled, cubed apple, thinly sliced
   fennel bulb
3 tablespoons coarsely chopped walnuts
1/3 cup fat-free mayonnaise
2 1/2 teaspoons Dijon mustard
1 1/2 tablespoons lemon juice
2 teaspoons sugar
3/4 teaspoon crushed fennel seeds

Per Serving:
Calories: 319
% of calories from fat: 12
Fat (gm): 4.6
Saturated fat (gm): 0.3
Cholesterol (mg): 0
Sodium (mg): 310
Protein (gm): 7.8
Carbohydrate (gm): 65.8

Exchanges:
Milk: 0.0
Vegetable: 0.0
Fruit: 1.5
Bread: 3.0
Meat: 0.0
Fat: 0.5

1. Cover wheat berries with 2 to 3 inches water in saucepan; let stand overnight. Heat to boiling; reduce heat and simmer, covered, until wheat berries are tender, 45 to 55 minutes. Drain and cool.

2. Combine wheat berries, fruit, fennel, and walnuts in bowl. Spoon combined remaining ingredients over salad and toss.

WHEAT BERRY AND GARDEN TOMATO SALAD

L

The texture of wheat berries is a perfect complement to crisp cucumbers and sun-ripened tomatoes. Kamut is an excellent grain to substitute.

4 main-dish servings (about 1⅔ cups each)

3 cups cooked wheat berries
4 cups coarsely chopped ripe tomatoes
1½ cups cubed, seeded cucumber
⅓ cup each: sliced green onions, chopped parsley
½ cup (2 ounces) crumbled reduced-fat feta cheese
Roasted Garlic Vinaigrette (recipe follows)
Salt and pepper, to taste

Per Serving:
Calories: 281
% of calories from fat: 30
Fat (gm): 10
Saturated fat (gm): 2.4
Cholesterol (mg): 5.1
Sodium (mg): 221
Protein (gm): 9.4
Carbohydrate (gm): 42.7

Exchanges:
Milk: 0.0
Vegetable: 2.0
Fruit: 0.0
Bread: 2.0
Meat: 0.0
Fat: 2.0

1. Combine all ingredients and toss; season to taste with salt and pepper.

Roasted Garlic Vinaigrette

Makes about ⅓ cup

2–4 tablespoons olive oil
¼ cup balsamic vinegar
2 teaspoons minced roasted garlic
1 teaspoon each: dried mint and oregano leaves

1. Mix all ingredients.

ORANGE CILANTRO RICE

V

A perfect accompaniment to grilled or roasted tofu, tempeh, or vegetables.

45 **6 side-dish servings** (about ⅔ cup each)

½ cup sliced green onions
1 cup long-grain rice
Grated zest of 1 small orange
2¼ cups water
2 tablespoons finely chopped cilantro
Salt and pepper, to taste

1. Sauté onions in lightly greased medium saucepan until tender, 3 to 5 minutes. Add rice and orange zest; cook over medium heat until rice is lightly browned, 2 to 3 minutes. Add water and heat to boiling; reduce heat and simmer, covered, until rice is tender, 20 to 25 minutes. Stir in cilantro; season to taste with salt and pepper.

Per Serving:
Calories: 118
% of calories from fat: 1
Fat (gm): 0.2
Saturated fat (gm): 0
Cholesterol (mg): 0
Sodium (mg): 2
Protein (gm): 2.3
Carbohydrate (gm): 26

Exchanges:
Milk: 0.0
Vegetable: 0.0
Fruit: 0.0
Bread: 1.5
Meat: 0.0
Fat: 0.0

YELLOW SALSA RICE

V

Ground turmeric contributes subtle flavor and an attractive yellow color to the rice.

45

6 side-dish servings (about ⅔ cup each)

1 can (14½ ounces) reduced-sodium vegetable broth
½ teaspoon ground turmeric
1 cup long-grain rice
¼ cup prepared medium, or hot, salsa
1 medium tomato, chopped
Salt and pepper, to taste
Chopped cilantro, as garnish

1. Heat broth and turmeric to boiling in medium saucepan; stir in rice and salsa. Reduce heat and simmer, covered, until rice

Per Serving:
Calories: 130
% of calories from fat: 2
Fat (gm): 0.3
Saturated fat (gm): 0.1
Cholesterol (mg): 0
Sodium (mg): 103
Protein (gm): 2.7
Carbohydrate (gm): 28.4

Exchanges:
Milk: 0.0
Vegetable: 1.0
Fruit: 0.0
Bread: 1.5
Meat: 0.0
Fat: 0.0

is tender and liquid absorbed, 20 to 25 minutes; stir in tomato during last 5 minutes of cooking time. Season to taste with salt and pepper; sprinkle with cilantro.

MEXICAN RED RICE

V

45

The tomatoes are pureed in the traditional version of this recipe. We've chosen to chop the tomato for more attractive color and flavor.

6 side-dish servings (about ⅔ cup each)

1 large tomato, chopped

½ cup chopped onion

1 clove garlic, minced

½ teaspoon each: dried oregano leaves, ground cumin

1 cup long-grain rice

1 can (14½ ounces) reduced-sodium vegetable broth

⅓ cup water

1 carrot, cooked, chopped

½ cup frozen peas, thawed

Salt and pepper, to taste

Per Serving:
Calories: 149
% of calories from fat: 2
Fat (gm): 0.4
Saturated fat (gm): 0.1
Cholesterol (mg): 0
Sodium (mg): 45
Protein (gm): 3.7
Carbohydrate (gm): 32.5

Exchanges:
Milk: 0.0
Vegetable: 0.0
Fruit: 0.0
Bread: 2.0
Meat: 0.0
Fat: 0.0

1. Sauté tomato, onion, garlic, and herbs in lightly greased large saucepan until onion is tender, 3 to 5 minutes. Add rice; cook over medium heat until rice is lightly browned, 2 to 3 minutes, stirring frequently. Add broth and water and heat to boiling; reduce heat and simmer, covered, until rice is tender, about 25 minutes, adding carrot and peas during last 5 minutes. Season to taste with salt and pepper.

SPICY RICE

L

45

This aromatic spiced dish of East Indian origins will complement many meals. The turmeric lends a beautiful yellow color to the rice.

8 side-dish servings (about ½ cup each)

1 medium onion, sliced

1 clove garlic, minced

1 tablespoon olive oil

1 cup uncooked basmati rice

½ cup reduced-fat plain yogurt

1–2 cardamom pods, crushed

¼ teaspoon each: ground turmeric, ginger

⅛ teaspoon crushed red pepper

2 cups reduced-sodium vegetable broth

Salt and pepper, to taste

1 small tomato, cut into 8 wedges

1 tablespoon finely chopped cilantro

Per Serving:
Calories: 166
% of calories from fat: 19
Fat (gm): 3.6
Saturated fat (gm): 0.5
Cholesterol (mg): 1.2
Sodium (mg): 54
Protein (gm): 4.4
Carbohydrate (gm): 27.9

Exchanges:
Milk: 0.0
Vegetable: 1.0
Fruit: 0.0
Bread: 1.5
Meat: 0.0
Fat: 0.5

1. Sauté onion and garlic in oil in large saucepan until tender, about 8 minutes. Stir in rice; cook over medium heat until beginning to brown about 5 minutes, stirring frequently. Stir in yogurt, spices, and crushed red pepper; cook over medium-high heat 5 minutes, stirring frequently. Add broth and heat to boiling; reduce heat and simmer, covered, until rice is tender, about 25 minutes. Season to taste with salt and pepper. Garnish with tomato wedges; sprinkle with cilantro.

TURMERIC RICE

| V |

Use this rice whenever the yellow color will enhance a meal.

| 45 |

6 side-dish servings (about ⅔ cup each)

2¼ cups reduced-sodium vegetable broth
½ teaspoon each: ground turmeric, salt
1 cup long-grain rice
2–3 tablespoons finely chopped cilantro, or parsley

1. Heat broth, turmeric, and salt to boiling in small saucepan; stir in rice. Reduce heat and simmer, covered, until rice is tender and broth absorbed, 20 to 25 minutes. Stir in parsley.

Per Serving:
Calories: 120
% of calories from fat: 3
Fat (gm): 0.3
Saturated fat (gm): 0.1
Cholesterol (mg): 0
Sodium (mg): 7
Protein (gm): 2.3
Carbohydrate (gm): 26

Exchanges:
Milk: 0.0
Vegetable: 0.0
Fruit: 0.0
Bread: 1.5
Meat: 0.0
Fat: 0.0

THAI FRIED RICE

| O |

Although coconut ginger rice is delicious, any leftover rice can be used, making this speedy dish even faster!

| 45 |

2 main-dish servings

1 package (16 ounces) frozen vegetable stir-fry blend with sugar snap peas
6 green onions, sliced
½–1 teaspoon hot chili sesame oil
2 eggs, lightly beaten
1 package (6.4 ounces) Thai coconut ginger rice, cooked, warm
2–3 tablespoons Thai peanut sauce (see Note)
1–2 tablespoons reduced-sodium tamari sauce

Per Serving:
Calories: 337
% of calories from fat: 20
Fat (gm): 7.6
Saturated fat (gm): 0.9
Cholesterol (mg): 212
Sodium (mg): 483
Protein (gm): 19.6
Carbohydrate (gm): 47.4

Exchanges:
Milk: 0.0
Vegetable: 3.0
Fruit: 0.0
Bread: 2.0
Meat: 1.0
Fat: 1.5

1. Stir-fry frozen vegetables and green onions in sesame oil in large skillet until tender, 3 to 4 minutes; move vegetables to side of skillet. Add eggs; cook over medium heat until set, stirring occasionally, about 2 minutes. Break up eggs with spatula and mix with vegetables; stir in rice and peanut and tamari sauces.

NOTE: If you cannot find Thai peanut sauce in your supermarket, mix 1 to 2 tablespoons reduced-fat peanut butter, 2 to 3 teaspoons reduced-sodium tamari soy sauce, and ½ to 1 teaspoon minced gingerroot.

45-MINUTE PREP TIP: Begin cooking the rice before preparing the rest of the recipe.

WILD RICE SOUFFLÉ

LO *When you're in the mood for something new and different, try this great soufflé!*

4 main-dish servings

⅓ cup wild rice

1 cup each: reduced-sodium vegetable broth, fat-free milk

¼ cup all-purpose flour

½ cup (2 ounces) shredded reduced-fat Cheddar cheese

¼ cup thinly sliced green onions

¼–½ teaspoon each: paprika, dried savory and thyme leaves

White pepper, to taste

3 egg yolks

3 egg whites, beaten to stiff peaks

Per Serving:
Calories: 210
% of calories from fat: 28
Fat (gm): 6.5
Saturated fat (gm): 2.4
Cholesterol (mg): 168.3
Sodium (mg): 288
Protein (gm): 13
Carbohydrate (gm): 23

Exchanges:
Milk: 0.0
Vegetable: 0.0
Fruit: 0.0
Bread: 1.5
Meat: 1.5
Fat: 0.5

1. Heat rice and broth to boiling in small saucepan; reduce heat and simmer, covered, until rice is tender and broth absorbed, 45 to 55 minutes.

2. Mix milk and flour in medium saucepan; heat to boiling. Boil, whisking, until thickened, about 1 minute. Remove from heat; add cheese and stir until melted (sauce will be very thick). Stir in green onions, paprika, and herbs. Season to taste with white pepper.

3. Beat egg yolks in small bowl until thick and lemon colored, about 5 minutes; mix into cheese mixture. Fold in egg whites; fold in rice. Spoon into greased 1-quart soufflé dish. Bake at 350 degrees until knife inserted halfway between center and edge comes out clean, 45 to 55 minutes.

POLENTA

V

This basic recipe can be modified to your taste — note the variations below.

45 | **6 side-dish servings** (about ½ cup each)

	Per Serving:
3 cups water	Calories: 63
¾ cup yellow cornmeal	% of calories from fat: 4
Salt and pepper, to taste	Fat (gm): 0.3

Per Serving:
Calories: 63
% of calories from fat: 4
Fat (gm): 0.3
Saturated fat (gm): 0.0
Cholesterol (mg): 0.0
Sodium (mg): 0.5
Protein (gm): 1.5
Carbohydrate (gm): 13

1. Heat water to boiling; gradually stir in cornmeal. Cook over medium to medium-low heat, stirring constantly, until polenta thickens enough to hold its shape but is still soft, 5 to 8 minutes.

Exchanges:
Milk: 0.0;
Vegetable: 0.0
Fruit: 0.0
Bread: 1.0
Meat: 0.0
Fat: 0.0

Variations

Blue Cheese Polenta — Stir ½ cup (2 ounces) crumbled blue cheese, or other blue veined cheese, into the cooked polenta.

Goat Cheese Polenta — Stir ¼ to ½ cup (1 to 2 ounces) crumbled goat cheese into the cooked polenta.

Garlic Polenta — Sauté ¼ cup finely chopped onion and 4 to 6 cloves minced garlic in 1 tablespoon olive oil; add water, as above, and complete recipe.

SAUTÉED POLENTA WEDGES

V

45

❄

Gently seasoned with onions, garlic, and basil, the polenta can be served immediately after cooking, or cooled in a pan as the recipe directs.

4–6 side-dish servings (about ⅔ cup each)

2 green onions, sliced

1 clove garlic, minced

1 teaspoon dried basil leaves

2½ cups reduced-sodium vegetable broth

¾ cup yellow cornmeal

½ teaspoon salt

Per Serving:
Calories: 118
% of calories from fat: 6
Fat (gm): 0.8
Saturated fat (gm): 0.1
Cholesterol (mg): 0.0
Sodium (mg): 580.4
Protein (gm): 3.1
Carbohydrate (gm): 24.2

Exchanges:
Milk: 0.0;
Vegetable: 0.0
Fruit: 0.0
Bread: 1.5
Meat: 0.0
Fat: 0.0

1. Sauté onions, garlic, and basil in lightly greased large saucepan until tender, about 5 minutes. Add broth and heat to boiling; gradually stir in cornmeal and salt. Cook over low heat, stirring constantly, until thickened, about 10 minutes. Pour into lightly greased 8-inch cake pan; cool to room temperature. Refrigerate, covered, until firm, 3 to 4 hours.

2. Cut polenta into wedges; cook in lightly greased large skillet over medium heat until browned, 3 to 4 minutes on each side.

YELLOW GRITS

V

45

Versatile yellow grits can be served at any meal. Unlike polenta, the grits remain creamy, even when refrigerated.

6 side-dish servings (about ⅔ cup each)

4 cups water

¾ teaspoon salt

1 cup stone-ground yellow grits

Per Serving:
Calories: 97
% of calories from fat: 3
Fat (gm): 0.3
Saturated fat (gm): 0.0
Cholesterol (mg): 0.0
Sodium (mg): 294
Protein (gm): 2
Carbohydrate (gm): 21

Exchanges:
Milk: 0.0
Vegetable: 0.0
Fruit: 0.0
Bread: 1.5
Meat: 0.0
Fat: 0.0

1. Heat water and salt to boiling in large saucepan; gradually stir in grits. Reduce heat and simmer, stirring frequently until thickened to desired consistency, 20 to 25 minutes.

Variations

Cheddar-Garlic Grits — Make recipe as above, adding 1½ teaspoons minced garlic to the grits. Remove from heat; add 1 cup (4 ounces) shredded reduced-fat Cheddar cheese, stirring until melted.

Yellow Grits with Wild Mushroom Sauté — Make recipe as above. While grits are cooking, sauté 3 cups sliced wild mushrooms (shiitake, oyster, portobello, cremini) in 2 tablespoons margarine until tender, about 8 minutes; season to taste with salt and pepper. Spoon over cooked grits.

Tex-Mex Breakfast Grits — Make any of the grits recipes above. Top each serving with a fried egg; serve with Serrano Tomato Sauce (see p. 602) and vegetarian sausage links.

SPICY GRITS WITH BLACKEYE SALSA

L

45

Try these spicy grits with habanero or serrano chilies if you want to increase the heat!

4 main-dish servings

2 cups water
1–2 tablespoons chopped jalapeño chili
½ teaspoon each: ground cumin, salt
⅔ cup quick-cooking grits
1 cup (4 ounces) shredded reduced-fat Monterey Jack cheese
½ can (15-ounce size) black-eyed peas, rinsed, drained, coarsely chopped
Blackeye Salsa (recipe follows)

Per Serving:
Calories: 258
% of calories from fat: 22
Fat (gm): 5.6
Saturated fat (gm): 4.1
Cholesterol (mg): 20
Sodium (mg): 1007
Protein (gm): 14.8
Carbohydrate (gm): 36.8

Exchanges:
Milk: 0.0
Vegetable: 1.0
Fruit: 0.0
Bread: 2.0
Meat: 1.0
Fat: 1.0

1. Combine water, jalapeño chili, cumin, and salt in medium saucepan; heat to boiling. Gradually stir in grits; reduce heat and simmer, stirring occasionally until thickened, about 5 minutes. Add cheese and black-eyed peas, stirring until cheese is melted. Serve with Blackeye Salsa.

Blackeye Salsa

Makes about 1¾ cups

½ can (15-ounce size) black-eyed peas, rinsed, drained, coarsely chopped
1 cup chopped tomatoes
¼ cup chopped green onions
1–2 teaspoons minced jalapeño chili
1 tablespoon lime juice
½ teaspoon each: ground cumin, salt

1. Combine all ingredients.

45-MINUTE PREP TIP: Make Blackeye Salsa before preparing the rest of the recipe.

CORNMEAL AND MILLET MUSH

V

45

A breakfast favorite! Other grains, such as kasha, millet, or wheat berries, can be combined with the cornmeal too.

8 main-dish servings (about ¾ cup each)

4 cups water
1 cup yellow, or white, cornmeal
1 teaspoon salt
2 cups cooked millet
6 tablespoons brown sugar

1. Heat water to boiling in large saucepan; gradually stir in cornmeal and salt. Reduce heat to medium-low and cook 5 minutes, stirring constantly. Stir in millet and cook until mixture is thick, 3 to 5 minutes longer, stirring constantly. Sprinkle each bowl with brown sugar.

Per Serving:
Calories: 283
% of calories from fat: 8
Fat (gm): 2.7
Saturated fat (gm): 0.4
Cholesterol (mg): 0
Sodium (mg): 278
Protein (gm): 6.7
Carbohydrate (gm): 58.3

Exchanges:
Milk: 0.0
Vegetable: 0.0
Fruit: 0.0
Bread: 4.0
Meat: 0.0
Fat: 0.0

Variation

Fried Mush — Make cornmeal mixture as above, deleting brown sugar; pour into greased 8½ x 4½ inch loaf pan and cool. Refrigerate until firm, several hours or overnight. Loosen sides of cornmeal mixture with sharp knife; invert onto cutting board. Cut into slices and fry in lightly greased large skillet over medium heat until browned, 3 to 4 minutes on each side. Serve with warm maple syrup.

BEST BREAKFAST CEREAL

L

45

Delicious and nutritious! Although we all appreciate a breakfast that is fast to make, this cereal is even more delicious made with slow-cooking steel-cut oats. Treat yourself!

6 main-dish servings (about ⅔ cup each)

3 cups water

Pinch salt

1½ cups each: quick-cooking oats, cooked wheat berries

¼ cup chopped toasted pecans, or walnuts

½ cup dried fruit bits, or raisins

¼ cup packed dark brown sugar

1 cup fat-free milk

Per Serving:
Calories: 313
% of calories from fat: 13
Fat (gm): 4.9
Saturated fat (gm): 0.6
Cholesterol (mg): 0.7
Sodium (mg): 55
Protein (gm): 9.7
Carbohydrate (gm): 61.4

Exchanges:
Milk: 0.0
Vegetable: 0.0
Fruit: 0.5
Bread: 3.5
Meat: 0.0
Fat: 0.5

1. Heat water and salt to boiling in medium saucepan; stir in oats, wheat berries, pecans, and dried fruit bits. Reduce heat and simmer to desired consistency, about 5 minutes. Serve with brown sugar and milk.

TWELVE

Smart Carb Entrées

CREAM OF ARTICHOKE AND MUSHROOM SOUP WITH PARMESAN TOAST

L

45

Shiitake or cremini mushrooms can be substituted for the portobello mushrooms.

4 servings (about 1 cup each)

¾ cup chopped portobello mushrooms

2 tablespoons chopped onion

1 tablespoon all-purpose flour

3 cups reduced-fat milk

¼ cup nonfat dry milk

1 vegetable bouillon cube

1 package (9 ounces) frozen artichoke hearts, thawed, finely chopped

Salt and white pepper, to taste

Paprika, as garnish

4 slices Parmesan Toast (recipe follows)

Per Serving:
Net carbohydrate (gm): 29
Calories: 274
% of calories from fat: 30
Fat (gm): 9
Saturated fat (gm): 5
Cholesterol (mg): 28
Sodium (mg): 752
Protein (gm): 20
Carbohydrate (gm): 30

Exchanges:
Milk: 0.0
Vegetable: 0.0
Fruit: 0.0
Bread: 2.0
Meat: 1.0
Fat: 0.5

1. Sauté mushrooms and onion in lightly greased medium saucepan until tender, about 5 minutes. Stir in flour; cook 1 minute. Stir in milk, dry milk, and bouillon cube; heat to boiling, stirring. Add artichoke hearts; reduce heat and simmer, uncovered, 5 minutes. Season to taste with salt and white pepper. Sprinkle with paprika; serve with Parmesan Toast.

Parmesan Toast

Makes 4 servings

4 slices low-carb whole wheat bread, diagonally halved

½ cup (1 ounce) shredded Parmesan cheese

1. Sprinkle bread slices with cheese; broil 6 inches from heat source until browned, 2 to 3 minutes.

KIDNEY BEAN AND CABBAGE SOUP

0

45

The beans that are lowest in carbohydrates include kidney, black, and pinto — use any of these in this nutritious soup.

6 servings (about 1½ cups each)

3 cups thinly sliced cabbage

⅓ cup coarsely chopped onion

3 cloves garlic, minced

1 teaspoon crushed caraway seeds

1 tablespoon olive oil

1 quart vegetable broth

2 cups drained, rinsed, canned kidney beans

6 ounces uncooked low-carb whole wheat macaroni

Salt and pepper, to taste

Per Serving:
Net carbohydrate (gm): 22
Calories: 229
% of calories from fat: 14
Fat (gm): 4
Saturated fat (gm): 0.4
Cholesterol (mg): 0.0
Sodium (mg): 696
Protein (gm): 14
Carbohydrate (gm): 36

Exchanges:
Milk: 0.0
Vegetable: 0.0
Fruit: 0.0
Bread: 2.0
Meat: 1.5
Fat: 0.0

1. Sauté cabbage, onion, garlic, and caraway seeds in oil in large saucepan until cabbage begins to wilt, 8 to 10 minutes. Add broth and beans; heat to boiling. Stir in pasta; reduce heat and simmer, uncovered, until pasta is al dente, 10 to 15 minutes. Season to taste with salt and pepper.

TEMPEH PASTA SOUP

0

45

Tempeh contains about 2 times more protein than tofu, making it a nutritious choice for this soup.

4 servings (about 1¼ cups each)

2 cups sliced celery

1 cup each: sliced carrots, onion

3½ cups vegetable broth

1 package (8 ounces) tempeh, or firm tofu, coarsely chopped

1 teaspoon dried marjoram leaves

1 bay leaf

1 cup uncooked low-carb pasta shells

Salt and pepper, to taste

Per Serving:
Net carbohydrate (gm): 25
Calories: 275
% of calories from fat: 23
Fat (gm): 7
Saturated fat (gm): 1
Cholesterol (mg): 0.0
Sodium (mg): 568
Protein (gm): 21
Carbohydrate (gm): 34

Exchanges:
Milk: 0.0
Vegetable: 0.0
Fruit: 0.0
Bread: 2.0
Meat: 2.0
Fat: 0.5

1. Sauté celery, carrots, and onion in lightly greased large saucepan until crisp-tender, 5 to 8 minutes. Add broth, tempeh, and herbs; heat to boiling. Add pasta; reduce heat and simmer, covered, 5 minutes. Heat to boiling; add pasta, reduce heat and simmer, uncovered, until vegetables are tender and pasta is al dente, 7 to 10 minutes. Discard bay leaf. Season to taste with salt and pepper.

TWO-SEASON SQUASH AND BEAN SOUP WITH CHEESE MELTS

L *Winter and summer squash are combined with beans in this flavorful soup.*

45 **6 servings** (about 1¼ cups each)

1 cup chopped onion

2 cloves garlic, minced

3 cups vegetable broth

2 cups each: cubed, seeded butternut squash, sliced zucchini

1 can (28 ounces) reduced-sodium whole tomatoes, undrained, chopped

1 can (15 ounces) pinto, or black beans, rinsed, drained

1 teaspoon each: dried marjoram and rosemary leaves

1 bay leaf

Salt and pepper, to taste

6 slices low-carb whole wheat bread

1¼ cups (6 ounces) shredded reduced-fat Swiss cheese

Per Serving:
Net carbohydrate (gm): 28
Calories: 284
% of calories from fat: 23
Fat (gm): 8
Saturated fat (gm): 3
Cholesterol (mg): 14
Sodium (mg): 633
Protein (gm): 20
Carbohydrate (gm): 40

Exchanges:
Milk: 0.0
Vegetable: 0.0
Fruit: 0.0
Bread: 2.5
Meat: 2.0
Fat: 0.0

1. Sauté onion and garlic in lightly greased large saucepan until tender, about 5 minutes. Add remaining ingredients, except salt and pepper, bread, and cheese. Heat to boiling; reduce heat and simmer, covered, until squash is tender, about 10 minutes. Discard bay leaf; season to taste with salt and pepper.

2. Sprinkle bread slices with cheese; broil 6 inches from heat source until cheese is melted, 2 to 3 minutes. Serve with soup.

CHILI SIN CARNE

L

45

For a southwestern version of this chili, substitute black or pinto beans for the kidney beans and add 1 minced jalapeño chili. Garnish each serving with a sprinkling of finely chopped cilantro leaves.

6 servings (about 1⅓ cups each)

¾ cup each: chopped green bell pepper, sliced green onions

½ cup chopped onion

2 cloves garlic, minced

1 tablespoon olive oil

½ package (12-ounce size) vegetarian ground beef

2 cans (14½ ounces each) reduced-sodium diced tomatoes, undrained

1 can (15 ounces) red kidney beans, rinsed, drained

½ can (6 ounce-size) reduced-sodium tomato paste

¾ cup low-carb beer, or water

1–2 tablespoons chili powder

2 teaspoons ground cumin

1 teaspoon dried oregano leaves

Salt and pepper, to taste

½ cup each: reduced-fat sour cream, shredded reduced-fat Cheddar cheese (2 ounces)

Per Serving:
Net carbohydrate (gm): 22
Calories: 249
% of calories from fat: 24
Fat (gm): 7
Saturated fat (gm): 3
Cholesterol (mg): 12
Sodium (mg): 610
Protein (gm): 15
Carbohydrate (gm): 33

Exchanges:
Milk: 0.0
Vegetable: 0.0
Fruit: 0.0
Bread: 2.0
Meat: 2.0
Fat: 0.0

1. Sauté bell pepper, green onions, onion, and garlic in oil in large saucepan until vegetables are tender, 5 to 8 minutes. Add remaining ingredients, except salt, pepper, sour cream, and cheese; heat to boiling. Reduce heat and simmer, covered, 20 to 30 minutes. Season to taste with salt and pepper; top each bowl of chili with sour cream and cheese.

GARDEN MINESTRONE WITH PARMESAN CROUTONS

L

45

For a great nutrition boost, stir 1 cup kale or lightly packed baby spinach leaves into the soup during the last 2 to 3 minutes of cooking time.

6 servings (about 1⅔ cups each)

½ cup each: sliced carrot, green onions, celery, fennel bulb

2 cloves garlic, minced

1 tablespoon olive oil

5 cups vegetable broth

1 can (19 ounces) garbanzo beans, rinsed, drained

1 cup each: snap peas, sliced zucchini, broccoli florets

¾ teaspoon each: dried basil and oregano leaves

2 ounces uncooked low-carb whole wheat macaroni

1 cup halved cherry tomatoes

Salt and pepper, to taste

1½ cups Parmesan Croutons (½ recipe) (see pp. 560)

Per Serving:
Net carbohydrate (gm): 31
Calories: 257
% of calories from fat: 18
Fat (gm): 5
Saturated fat (gm): 0.7
Cholesterol (mg): 1.5
Sodium (mg): 805
Protein (gm): 13
Carbohydrate (gm): 42

Exchanges:
Milk: 0.0
Vegetable: 1.0
Fruit: 0.0
Bread: 2.0
Meat: 1.5;
Fat: 0.0

1. Sauté carrot, green onions, celery, fennel, and garlic in oil in large saucepan until vegetables are tender, 5 to 8 minutes. Add remaining ingredients, except salt, pepper, and Parmesan Croutons, and heat to boiling; reduce heat and simmer, covered, until vegetables are tender and pasta al dente, about 10 minutes. Season to taste with salt and pepper. Sprinkle each bowl of soup with Parmesan Croutons.

45-MINUTE PREP TIP: Make Parmesan Croutons before preparing the rest of the recipe.

VEGETARIAN MEATBALL SOUP

LO *The perfect soup when you expect a crowd! Purchased Vegetarian Meatballs can be substituted for the homemade.*

12 servings (about 2 cups each)

8 ounces hubbard, or butternut, squash, peeled, seeded, cubed (¾-inch)

½ cup chopped onion

2 cloves garlic, minced

1 tablespoon olive oil

5 cups reduced-sodium vegetable broth

1 can (15 ounces) garbanzo beans, rinsed, drained

1 can (16 ounces) reduced-sodium diced tomatoes, undrained

½ cup frozen peas

1 teaspoon dried Italian seasoning

Vegetarian Meatballs (recipe follows)

4 ounces uncooked low-carb whole wheat rotini

Salt and pepper, to taste

Per Serving:
Net carbohydrate (gm): 19
Calories: 207
% of calories from fat: 18
Fat (gm): 4
Saturated fat (gm): 0.8
Cholesterol (mg): 54
Sodium (mg): 650
Protein (gm): 16
Carbohydrate (gm): 27

Exchanges:
Milk: 0.0
Vegetable: 0.0
Fruit: 0.0
Bread: 1.5
Meat: 2.0
Fat: 0.0

1. Sauté squash, onion, and garlic in oil in large saucepan until onion is tender, about 5 minutes. Add broth, beans, tomatoes with liquid, peas, and Italian seasoning; heat to boiling. Reduce heat and simmer, covered, 10 minutes. Add Vegetarian Meatballs and pasta; simmer, uncovered, until pasta is al dente, 7 to 10 minutes. Season to taste with salt and pepper.

Vegetarian Meatballs

Makes 36

1 slice low-carb whole wheat bread

1 package (16 ounces) vegetarian ground beef

2 eggs, lightly beaten

3 cloves garlic, minced

4 tablespoons grated Parmesan cheese

1 teaspoon dried Italian seasoning

½ teaspoon fennel seeds, crushed

1. Process bread in food processor until finely ground; combine with remaining ingredients, mashing vegetarian ground beef lightly with fork. Shape into 36 balls.

HOT SOUR SOUP

The contrast in hot and sour flavors makes this Mandarin soup a unique offering. The hot chili sesame oil and Sour Sauce are intensely flavored, so use sparingly.

6 servings (about 1 cup each)

1 ounce dried Chinese black mushrooms (shiitake)

¾ cup boiling water

1 quart vegetable broth

2 cups (8 ounces) cubed tempeh or extra-firm tofu

½ cup bamboo shoots

¼ cup distilled white vinegar

2 tablespoons reduced-sodium tamari soy sauce

1 tablespoon each: finely chopped gingerroot,
   brown sugar, cornstarch

3 tablespoons water

Salt, cayenne, and black pepper, to taste

1 egg, lightly beaten

1 teaspoon Asian sesame oil

12–18 drops hot chili sesame oil, or Szechwan
   chili sauce

Sour Sauce (recipe follows)

Per Serving:
Net carbohydrate (gm): 14
Calories: 176
% of calories from fat: 28
Fat (gm): 6
Saturated fat (gm): 0.8
Cholesterol (mg): 35
Sodium (mg): 630
Protein (gm): 11
Carbohydrate (gm): 21

Exchanges:
Milk: 0.0
Vegetable: 0.0
Fruit: 0.0
Bread: 1.5
Meat: 1.5
Fat: 0.0

1. Combine mushrooms and boiling water in small bowl; let stand until mushrooms are softened, 15 to 20 minutes. Drain, reserving liquid. Slice mushrooms, discarding tough stems.

2. Heat broth, mushrooms and reserved liquid, tempeh, bamboo shoots, vinegar, soy sauce, gingerroot, and sugar to boiling in large saucepan. Reduce heat and simmer, uncovered, 10 minutes. Heat soup to boiling; stir in combined cornstarch and water; boil until thickened, stirring, about 1 minute. Season to taste with salt, cayenne, and black pepper. Stir egg slowly into soup; stir in sesame oil. Serve with hot chili oil and Sour Sauce.

Sour Sauce

Makes about ⅓ cup

3 tablespoons distilled white vinegar
1 tablespoon reduced-sodium tamari soy sauce
2 tablespoons packed light brown sugar

1. Mix all ingredients.

ASIAN MUSHROOM SOUP WITH NOODLES

V *Two kinds of mushrooms contribute rich flavor to this soup.*

6 servings (about 1½ cups each)

2 pounds cremini mushrooms, sliced, divided
½ cup minced onion
1 clove garlic, minced
½ teaspoon dried thyme leaves
2 tablespoons canola oil
1½ quarts vegetable broth
½ cup dry white wine, or vegetable broth
1 ounce dried shiitake mushrooms
4 ounces uncooked low-carb whole wheat linguini, or soba noodles
1 cup snow peas
⅓ cup thinly sliced radishes
1 tablespoon red wine vinegar
Salt and pepper, to taste

Per Serving:
Net carbohydrate (gm): 16
Calories: 215
% of calories from fat: 23
Fat (gm): 5
Saturated fat (gm): 0.3
Cholesterol (mg): 0.0
Sodium (mg): 431
Protein (gm): 14
Carbohydrate (gm): 25

Exchanges:
Milk: 0.0
Vegetable: 0.0
Fruit: 0.0
Bread: 1.5
Meat: 2.0
Fat: 0.0

1. Sauté half the cremini mushrooms, onion, garlic, and thyme in oil in large saucepan until soft, 5 to 8 minutes. Add broth, wine, and shiitake mushrooms; heat to boiling. Reduce heat and simmer, covered, 30 minutes. Strain soup, discarding mushrooms; return broth to saucepan. Add remaining ingredients, except salt and pepper; simmer, uncovered, until pasta is al dente, about 8 minutes. Season to taste with salt and pepper.

BEAN GAZPACHO

V

45

❄

Pureed beans contribute nutritional value, plus a velvety texture, to this delicious gazpacho.

6 servings (about 1½ cups each)

2 cans (15½ ounces each) pinto beans,
  rinsed, drained
1 quart reduced-sodium tomato juice
3–4 tablespoons lime juice
2 teaspoons chopped garlic
1 cup each: thick and chunky salsa, peeled, seeded,
  chopped cucumber, sliced celery
½ cup each: sliced green onions, chopped green
  bell pepper
½ small avocado, peeled, chopped
½ cup sour cream
¾ cup (¼ recipe) Herb Croutons (see p 561)

Per Serving:
Net carbohydrate (gm): 32
Calories: 266
% of calories from fat: 25
Fat (gm): 8
Saturated fat (gm): 3
Cholesterol (mg): 8
Sodium (mg): 833
Protein (gm): 11
Carbohydrate (gm): 42

Exchanges:
Milk: 0.0
Vegetable: 0.0
Fruit: 0.0
Bread: 2.5
Meat: 1.0
Fat: 1.0

1. Process beans, tomato juice, lime juice, Worcestershire sauce, and garlic in food processor or blender until smooth; pour into large bowl. Mix in remaining ingredients, except avocado, sour cream, and Herb Croutons. Refrigerate until chilled, 3 to 4 hours.

2. Mix avocado into soup; garnish each bowl of soup with a dollop of sour cream and sprinkle with croutons.

45-MINUTE PREP TIP: Make Herb Croutons before preparing the rest of the recipe.

PASILLA BLACK BEAN SOUP

L

45

For a hot and smoky flavor accent, add 1 to 2 teaspoons chopped canned chipotle peppers in adobo sauce to the soup.

4 servings (about 1½ cups each)

1 cup each: chopped onion, carrots
2 teaspoons each: minced jalapeño chili, garlic
¾ teaspoon each: dried oregano leaves, ground cumin

¼ teaspoon dried thyme leaves

1 tablespoon olive oil

1 quart vegetable broth

6 dried pasilla chilies, stems and seeds removed, torn into pieces

1 can (14½ ounces) diced tomatoes, undrained

1 can (15 ounces) black beans, rinsed, drained

Salt and pepper, to taste

1 cup (4 ounces) shredded reduced-fat Mexican cheese blend

Chopped cilantro, as garnish

Per Serving:
Net carbohydrate (gm): 26
Calories: 291
% of calories from fat: 23
Fat (gm): 7
Saturated fat (gm): 4
Cholesterol (mg): 15
Sodium (mg): 1234
Protein (gm): 16
Carbohydrate (gm): 40

Exchanges:
Milk: 0.0
Vegetable: 0.0
Fruit: 0.0
Bread: 2.5
Meat: 2.0
Fat: 0.0

1. Sauté onion, carrots, jalapeño chili, garlic, and herbs in oil in large saucepan until onion is tender, about 5 minutes. Add broth, pasilla chilies, tomatoes with liquid, and beans; heat to boiling. Reduce heat and simmer, covered, 10 minutes. Process soup in food processor or blender until smooth. Season to taste with salt and pepper. Sprinkle each bowl of soup with cheese and cilantro.

BLACK BEAN AND OKRA GUMBO

V

45

For easier preparation, substitute 2 cans (15 ounces each) rinsed and drained black beans for the dried.

8 servings (about 1 cup each)

2 cups small mushrooms

1 cup each: chopped onion, sliced carrots

¾ cup each: chopped red and green bell peppers

1 tablespoon olive oil

2 cups vegetable broth

1 can (16 ounces) tomatoes with chilies, undrained

3 cups cooked dried black beans

2 cups cut okra

1 package (10 ounces) vegetarian sausage, cut into ½-inch pieces

1 tablespoon chili powder

1 teaspoon gumbo file

Salt and pepper, to taste

Per Serving:
Net carbohydrate (gm): 17
Calories: 191
% of calories from fat: 24
Fat (gm): 5
Saturated fat (gm): 0.4
Cholesterol (mg): 0.0
Sodium (mg): 240
Protein (gm): 12
Carbohydrate (gm): 28

Exchanges:
Milk: 0.0
Vegetable: 0.0
Fruit: 0.0
Bread: 2.0
Meat: 1.0
Fat: 0.0

1. Sauté mushrooms, onion, carrots, and bell peppers in oil in large skillet until onions are tender, about 5 minutes. Add remaining ingredients, except salt and pepper; heat to boiling. Reduce heat and simmer, covered, until vegetables are tender, about 10 minutes. Simmer, uncovered, until thickened to desired consistency, 5 to 10 minutes. Season to taste with salt and pepper.

SOUTHERN STEWED BLACK EYES

V

45

You can find vegetarian sausage links in the refrigerated produce and frozen sections of the grocery store.

6 servings (about 1¼ cups each)

½ cup chopped onion

2 cloves garlic, minced

½ package (10-ounce size) vegetarian sausage links, quartered

1 tablespoon olive oil

2 cups halved small okra

1 can (16 ounces) reduced-sodium stewed tomatoes, undrained

2 cans (15 ounces each) black-eyed peas, rinsed, drained

½ package (10-ounce size) frozen spinach, partially thawed

1 teaspoon each: dried marjoram and thyme leaves

¼ teaspoon hot pepper sauce

Salt and pepper, to taste

Per Serving:
Net carbohydrate (gm): 20
Calories: 234
% of calories from fat: 22
Fat (gm): 6
Saturated fat (gm): 1
Cholesterol (mg): 0.0
Sodium (mg): 760
Protein (gm): 16
Carbohydrate (gm): 30

Exchanges:
Milk: 0.0
Vegetable: 0.0
Fruit: 0.0
Bread: 2.0
Meat: 2.0
Fat: 0.0

1. Sauté onion, garlic, and vegetarian sausage in oil in large saucepan until onion is tender, about 5 to 8 minutes. Stir in remaining ingredients, except salt and pepper; heat to boiling. Reduce heat and simmer, covered, until okra is tender, about 10 minutes. Season to taste with salt and pepper.

EASY CREOLE SKILLET STEW

V

Serve over rice or another favorite grain, if desired.

45 **4 servings**

1 package (10 ounces) vegetarian sausage links

¾ cup chopped onion

4 cloves garlic, minced

1 tablespoon olive oil

2 tablespoons flour

2 cups whole-kernel corn

1½ cups sliced zucchini

2 cans (14½ ounces each) reduced-sodium stewed tomatoes

½ teaspoon each: dried thyme and sage leaves

Salt and pepper, to taste

Per Serving:
Net carbohydrate (gm): 27
Calories: 285
% of calories from fat: 27
Fat (gm): 9
Saturated fat (gm): 1
Cholesterol (mg): 0.0
Sodium (mg): 562
Protein (gm): 20
Carbohydrate (gm): 34

Exchanges:
Milk: 0.0
Vegetable: 0.0
Fruit: 0.0
Bread: 2.0
Meat: 2.0
Fat: 0.5

1. Cook vegetarian sausage, onion and garlic in oil in large skillet over medium heat until onion is tender, about 5 minutes; stir in flour and cook 1 minute. Add corn, zucchini, tomatoes, and herbs; heat to boiling. Reduce heat and simmer, covered, 15 minutes. Season to taste with salt and pepper.

GREEK LENTIL STEW

L

Lentils and fresh vegetables partner in this easy stew.

45

6 servings (about 1¼ cups each)

1 cup each: chopped onion, green bell pepper

2 teaspoons minced garlic

1 tablespoon olive oil

1 cup peeled, diced potatoes

1 cup dried lentils

1 can (14½ ounces) reduced-sodium diced
tomatoes, undrained

3 cups reduced-sodium vegetable broth

1 teaspoon each: dried oregano and mint leaves

½ teaspoon each: ground turmeric, coriander

1 cup sliced zucchini

2 cups halved green beans

Salt and pepper, to taste

Feta Toast (recipe follows)

Per Serving:
Net carbohydrate (gm): 28
Calories: 298
% of calories from fat: 21
Fat (gm): 7
Saturated fat (gm): 2.5
Cholesterol (mg): 12.5
Sodium (mg): 526
Protein (gm): 17
Carbohydrate (gm): 45

Exchanges:
Milk: 0.0
Vegetable: 0.0
Fruit: 0.0
Bread: 3.0
Meat: 1.5
Fat: 0.0

1. Sauté onion, bell pepper, and garlic in oil in large saucepan until tender, about 5 minutes. Add potatoes, lentils, tomatoes and liquid, broth, and seasonings; heat to boiling. Reduce heat and simmer, covered, 15 minutes. Add zucchini and green beans; simmer, uncovered, until lentils are tender and stew is thickened, about 10 minutes. Season to taste with salt and pepper. Serve with Feta Toast.

Feta Toast

Makes 6 servings

6 slices low-carb or thick-sliced whole wheat bread

1 cup (4 ounces) crumbled feta cheese

1. Sprinkle bread with cheese; broil 4 inches from heat source until cheese is softened, 2 to 3 minutes. Cut bread slices diagonally into halves.

CABBAGE AND SAUERKRAUT CASSEROLE

LO *Cabbage leaves are stuffed, then layered and baked with sauerkraut and tomatoes.*

6 servings

1 small head cabbage (about 1¼ pounds), cored
⅔ package (12-ounce size) vegetarian ground beef
1 cup cooked brown rice
2 cloves garlic, minced
1½–2 teaspoons paprika
Salt and pepper, to taste
1–2 eggs
1 can (16 ounces) each: drained sauerkraut, undrained, coarsely chopped reduced-sodium whole tomatoes
1 cup thinly sliced onion
1½ teaspoons caraway seeds, crushed
¾ cup fat-free sour cream

Per Serving:
Net carbohydrate (gm): 20
Calories: 246
% of calories from fat: 28
Fat (gm): 8
Saturated fat (gm): 4
Cholesterol (mg): 81
Sodium (mg): 893
Protein (gm): 15
Carbohydrate (gm): 30

Exchanges:
Milk: 0.0
Vegetable: 0.0
Fruit: 0.0
Bread: 2.0
Meat: 2.0
Fat: 0.0

1. Remove 12 outside leaves from cabbage; thinly slice or shred remaining cabbage and reserve. Place cabbage leaves in large saucepan with water to cover; heat to boiling. Reduce heat and simmer, covered, until cabbage leaves are pliable but not too soft, 2 to 3 minutes. Drain.

2. Mix vegetarian ground beef, rice, garlic, and paprika; season to taste with salt and pepper. Mix in egg, using 2 if necessary for mixture to hold together. Place about ¼ cup mixture in center of each cabbage leaf; fold in sides and roll up.

3. Mix sauerkraut, tomatoes and liquid, reserved shredded cabbage, onion, and caraway seeds; spoon half the mixture into large Dutch oven. Place cabbage rolls on sauerkraut mixture; spoon remaining sauerkraut mixture on top. Heat to boiling; transfer to oven and bake, covered, until cabbage is tender, 1 to 1½ hours. Serve with sour cream.

SPINACH PASTA BAKE

LO

45

Jalapeño chili is an unexpected ingredient — add more if you enjoy really hot flavor.

6 servings (about 1⅓ cups each)

2 cups sliced mushrooms
1 medium onion, chopped
1 jalapeño chili, minced
1 cup reduced-fat ricotta cheese
½ cup (2 ounces) fat-free Parmesan cheese
¼–½ cup fat-free milk
2 packages (10 ounces each) frozen chopped
    spinach, thawed, well drained
¾ teaspoon ground nutmeg
Salt and pepper, to taste
1 egg
2 cups low-carb whole wheat elbow macaroni, cooked
½ cup (2 ounces) reduced-fat Monterey Jack cheese

Per Serving:
Net carbohydrate (gm): 19
Calories: 273
% of calories from fat: 20
Fat (gm): 6
Saturated fat (gm): 3
Cholesterol (mg): 56
Sodium (mg): 473
Protein (gm): 24
Carbohydrate (gm): 30

Exchanges:
Milk: 0.0
Vegetable: 0.0
Fruit: 0.0
Bread: 2.0
Meat: 2.0
Fat: 0.0

1. Sauté mushrooms, onion, and jalapeño chili in lightly greased large skillet until mushrooms are lightly browned, 3 to 5 minutes. Combine with ricotta and Parmesan cheese, milk, spinach, and nutmeg in bowl; season to taste with salt and pepper and stir in egg. Spoon half the macaroni into lightly greased 2-quart casserole; top with half the spinach mixture. Repeat layers; sprinkle with Monterey Jack cheese. Bake, uncovered, at 350 degrees until hot, 20 to 30 minutes.

45-MINUTE PREP TIP: Begin cooking macaroni before preparing the rest of the recipe.

CHEESY WILD RICE AND VEGETABLE CASSEROLE

Delicious, with a generous amount of melted cheese.

4 servings (about 1 cup each)

½ package (6¼ ounce-size) wild and white rice mix, cooked without spice packet

1½ cups each: cut asparagus spears, halved small Brussels sprouts, blanched

1 package (3 ounces) fat-free cream cheese, cubed

1 cup (4 ounces) shredded fat-free mozzarella cheese

Salt and pepper, to taste

Per Serving:
Net carbohydrate (gm): 20
Calories: 169
% of calories from fat: 4
Fat (gm): 0.7
Saturated fat (gm): 0.3
Cholesterol (mg): 7
Sodium (mg): 337
Protein (gm): 18
Carbohydrate (gm): 24

Exchanges:
Milk: 0.0
Vegetable: 1.0
Fruit: 0.0
Bread: 1.0
Meat: 2.0
Fat: 0.0

1. Mix rice, vegetables, and cheeses in greased 1½-quart casserole; season to taste with salt and pepper. Bake, covered, at 350 degrees until casserole is hot and cheese is melted, about 30 minutes.

EGGPLANT AND ZUCCHINI CASSEROLE

Herb-seasoned and baked with tomato, cheese, and bread crumb toppings, this casserole is both flavorful and healthful.

4 servings

1 eggplant (1¼ pounds), unpeeled, sliced (½-inch)

4 medium zucchini, halved lengthwise

1 medium red bell pepper, sliced

Vegetable cooking spray

½ teaspoon each: dried marjoram and oregano leaves, garlic powder

Pinch crushed red pepper

Salt and pepper, to taste

¼ cup sliced ripe olives

4 medium tomatoes, coarsely chopped

1 package (8 ounces) fat-free cream cheese, cubed

¼ cup fat-free milk

2 tablespoons reduced-sodium tomato paste

2 teaspoons sugar

½ cup (2 ounces) shredded reduced-fat mozzarella cheese

Per Serving:
Net carbohydrate (gm): 20
Calories: 210
% of calories from fat: 18
Fat (gm): 5
Saturated fat (gm): 2
Cholesterol (mg): 12
Sodium (mg): 509
Protein (gm): 17
Carbohydrate (gm): 30

Exchanges:
Milk: 0.0
Vegetable: 0.0
Fruit: 0.0
Bread: 2.0
Meat: 1.5
Fat: 0.0

1. Arrange eggplant, zucchini, and bell pepper in single layer in greased foil-lined jellyroll pan; spray with cooking spray and sprinkle with marjoram, oregano, garlic powder, and crushed red pepper. Roast at 475 degrees until beginning to brown, 15 to 20 minutes; sprinkle lightly with salt and pepper. Spoon into greased 11 x 7-inch baking dish; sprinkle with olives and tomatoes.

2. Heat cream cheese, milk, tomato paste, and sugar in small saucepan over low heat until cheese is melted, stirring; season to taste with salt and pepper. Pour over vegetables and sprinkle with mozzarella cheese. Bake, uncovered, at 350 degrees until casserole is hot and cheese melted, about 15 minutes.

EGGPLANT PROVENÇAL

This dish can be assembled several hours in advance; sprinkle with the bread crumb mixture just before baking.

4 servings (1½ cups each)

2 pounds eggplant, peeled, cubed (¾-inch)
2 medium green bell peppers, sliced
4 cups chopped tomatoes
1 cup chopped onion
1 clove garlic, minced
¼ cup sliced ripe, or pimiento-stuffed, olives
1 tablespoon drained capers
½–¾ teaspoon each: dried basil and oregano leaves
Salt and pepper, to taste
1½ cups (6 ounces) shredded fat-free
    mozzarella cheese

Per Serving:
Net carbohydrate (gm): 14
Calories: 176
% of calories from fat: 8
Fat (gm): 1.7
Saturated fat (gm): 0.3
Cholesterol (mg): 7.6
Sodium (mg): 466
Protein (gm): 18
Carbohydrate (gm): 26

Exchanges:
Milk: 0.0
Vegetable: 1.0;
Fruit: 0.0
Bread: 1.0
Meat: 2.0
Fat: 0.0

1. Sauté eggplant, bell peppers, tomatoes, onion, and garlic in lightly greased large skillet 3 to 4 minutes; cook, covered, over medium heat, until vegetables are tender, 8 to 10 minutes, stirring occasionally. Stir in olives, capers, and herbs; season to taste with salt and pepper. Spoon mixture into 11 x 7-inch baking dish; sprinkle with cheese. Bake, uncovered, at 350 degrees, until bubbly and browned, about 30 minutes.

CANNELLONI CASSEROLE

LO *Lasagne noodles are filled, rolled, sauced, and baked to perfection.*

8 servings

2 packages (10 ounces each) frozen, chopped
    spinach, thawed, well drained

2 cups fat-free small-curd cottage cheese

½ cup (2 ounces) grated fat-free Parmesan cheese

1½ teaspoons dried basil leaves

¼ teaspoon ground nutmeg

Salt and pepper, to taste

3 eggs

12 lasagne noodles, cooked, halved crosswise

1 cup fat-free milk, divided

2 tablespoons margarine, or butter

¼ cup all-purpose flour

⅓ cup coarsely crushed garlic croutons

Per Serving:
Net carbohydrate (gm): 24
Calories: 227
% of calories from fat: 23
Fat (gm): 6
Saturated fat (gm): 1
Cholesterol (mg): 84
Sodium (mg): 450
Protein (gm): 17
Carbohydrate (gm): 26

Exchanges:
Milk: 0.0
Vegetable: 2.0
Fruit: 0.0
Bread: 1.0
Meat: 2.0
Fat: 0.0

1. Mix spinach, cheeses, basil, and nutmeg in bowl; season to taste with salt and pepper. Stir in eggs. Spread each lasagne noodle with about 2 tablespoons cheese mixture; roll up. Place rolls, seams side down, in greased 11 x 7-inch baking pan.

2. Heat ½ cup milk and margarine to boiling in small saucepan. Whisk in combined flour and remaining ½ cup milk; boil, whisking, until thickened, about 1 minute. Season to taste with salt and pepper. Pour over pasta rolls; sprinkle with croutons. Bake, uncovered, at 350 degrees until hot, about 30 minutes.

PASTITSIO

LO

Sweet cinnamon and nutmeg season this Greek favorite.

45

6 servings

1 package (12 ounces) vegetarian ground beef

1 cup chopped onion

1 can (8 ounces) reduced-sodium tomato paste

⅓ cup water

Salt and pepper, to taste

2 cups macaroni, cooked

½ cup (2 ounces) grated fat-free Parmesan cheese

½ teaspoon ground cinnamon

¼ teaspoon ground nutmeg

2⅓ cups fat-free milk

2 tablespoons margarine, or butter

4 eggs, lightly beaten

Per Serving:
Net carbohydrate (gm): 29
Calories: 315
% of calories from fat: 23
Fat (gm): 8
Saturated fat (gm): 2
Cholesterol (mg): 144
Sodium (mg): 601
Protein (gm): 26
Carbohydrate (gm): 37

Exchanges:
Milk: 0.0
Vegetable: 0.0
Fruit: 0.0
Bread: 2.5
Meat: 2.5
Fat: 0.0

1. Sauté vegetarian ground beef and onion in lightly greased large skillet until onion is tender, 5 to 8 minutes. Stir in tomato paste and water; season to taste with salt and pepper. Spoon over ½ the macaroni in 13 x 9-inch baking pan; sprinkle with combined cheese and spices. Top with remaining macaroni.

2. Heat milk and margarine in medium saucepan, stirring until margarine is melted. Whisk mixture into eggs; pour over macaroni. Bake, uncovered, until casserole is bubbly, 50 to 60 minutes.

45-MINUTE PREP TIP: Begin cooking macaroni before preparing the rest of the recipe.

SERBIAN LEEK CAKES

LO *Flavorful leek pancakes are layered and baked with creamy vegetables.*

6 servings

1½ cups chopped leeks (white parts only)

1½ cups reduced-sodium vegetable broth

1 cup all-purpose flour

1 egg, beaten

¼–½ teaspoon salt

1 package (12 ounces) vegetarian sausage links, or patties, crumbled

½ cup each: chopped onion, green bell pepper

2 cloves garlic, minced

⅛ teaspoon crushed red pepper

Salt, to taste

½ cup fat-free sour cream

½ cup (2 ounces) shredded reduced-fat Swiss cheese

Per Serving:
Net carbohydrate (gm): 24
Calories: 219
% of calories from fat: 25
Fat (gm): 6
Saturated fat (gm): 0.6
Cholesterol (mg): 42
Sodium (mg): 390
Protein (gm): 15
Carbohydrate (gm): 28

Exchanges:
Milk: 0.0
Vegetable: 0.0
Fruit: 0.0
Bread: 2.0
Meat: 1.5
Fat: 0.0

1. Heat leeks and broth to boiling in medium saucepan; reduce heat and simmer, uncovered, 5 minutes. Strain, reserving 1 cup liquid. Mix leeks, flour, reserved broth, egg, and salt. Pour ⅓ of the batter into lightly greased medium skillet, spreading into 8-inch circle. Cook over medium heat until brown on the bottom, 3 to 5 minutes. Turn and cook until brown on other side. Repeat, making 2 more pancakes.

2. Cook vegetarian sausage, onion, bell pepper, and garlic in lightly greased medium saucepan until onion is tender, about 5 minutes. Add crushed red pepper; season to taste with salt. Spread ⅓ of the mixture over a leek pancake in a greased 9-inch pie plate. Repeat layers 2 times. Spread sour cream over the top; sprinkle with cheese. Bake at 375 degrees, uncovered, until browned, about 20 minutes. Cut into wedges.

SPINACH CHEESE CREPES

LO *For variation, add ½ cup sautéed chopped portobello mushrooms to the cottage cheese mixture.*

4 servings (2 crepes each)

¼ cup chopped onion

1 package (10 ounces) frozen chopped spinach, thawed, well drained

1 cup fat-free cottage cheese

½ teaspoon dried thyme leaves

2–3 pinches ground nutmeg

Salt and pepper, to taste

8 slices (½ ounce each) fat-free mozzarella, or Swiss, cheese

8 Crepes (see p. 575), warm

1½ cups (½ recipe), Fresh Tomato and Herb Sauce (see p. 584)

Per Serving:
Net carbohydrate (gm): 20
Calories: 342
% of calories from fat: 28
Fat (gm): 11
Saturated fat (gm): 2.6
Cholesterol (mg): 123
Sodium (mg): 905
Protein (gm): 36
Carbohydrate (gm): 27

Exchanges:
Milk: 0.0
Vegetable: 0.0
Fruit: 0.0;
Bread: 1.5
Meat: 4.0
Fat: 0.0

1. Sauté onion in lightly greased medium skillet until tender, 3 to 4 minutes. Add spinach and cook until very dry, about 5 minutes. Mix with cottage cheese, thyme, and nutmeg; season to taste with salt and pepper.

2. Place cheese slices on crepes; top with spinach-cheese mixture. Roll up crepes and place, seam sides down, in greased baking dish. Bake, loosely covered, at 325 degrees until hot, about 10 minutes. Serve with Fresh Tomato and Herb Sauce.

VEGETABLES AND TEMPEH MARENGO

V *Flavors of the Mediterranean accent this colorful dish.*

6 servings (about 1 cup each)

1½ packages (8-ouce size) tempeh or firm tofu, cubed (¾-inch)

2 cups cubed zucchini

1 cup each: onion wedges, halved small mushrooms

2 cloves minced garlic

1 tablespoon flour

1 can (16 ounces) reduced-sodium diced
   tomatoes, undrained

¾ cup vegetable broth

1 strip orange zest (3 x 1-inch)

½ teaspoon each: dried thyme and oregano leaves

1 bay leaf

Salt and pepper, to taste

2 cups cooked brown rice, warm

Per Serving:
Net carbohydrate (gm): 27
Calories: 228
% of calories from fat: 26
Fat (gm): 7
Saturated fat (gm): 1.4
Cholesterol (mg): 0.0
Sodium (mg): 101
Protein (gm): 14
Carbohydrate (gm): 31

Exchanges:
Milk: 0.0
Vegetable: 0.0
Fruit: 0.0
Bread: 2.0
Meat: 1.0
Fat: 0.5

1. Sauté tempeh, vegetables, and garlic in lightly greased large skillet until tempeh is beginning to brown, 5 to 8 minutes; stir in flour and cook 1 minute longer. Add remaining ingredients, except salt, pepper, and rice; heat to boiling; reduce heat and simmer, covered, until vegetables are tender, about 5 minutes. Discard bay leaf; season to taste with salt and pepper. Serve over rice.

GARDEN VEGETABLES AND TEMPEH SAUTÉ

V

Excellent served over rice, fresh Chinese-style noodles, or pasta!

45

❄

4 servings (about 1¼ cups each)

Tamari Marinade (see p. 613)

2 tablespoons red wine vinegar

1 teaspoon dried Italian seasoning

1 package (8 ounces) tempeh

½ cup each: sliced onion, red bell pepper

1 teaspoon minced garlic

1 cup reduced-sodium tomato juice, sliced zucchini

2 cups sliced mushrooms, tomato wedges

1 teaspoon each: dried basil and oregano leaves

¼ teaspoon cayenne pepper

Salt and pepper, to taste

Per Serving:
Net carbohydrate (gm): 16
Calories: 180
% of calories from fat: 30
Fat (gm): 6.8
Saturated fat (gm): 1.4
Cholesterol (mg): 0.0
Sodium (mg): 323
Protein (gm): 15
Carbohydrate (gm): 20

Exchanges:
Milk: 0.0
Vegetable: 1.0
Fruit: 0.0
Bread: 1.0
Meat: 1.5
Fat: 0.0

1. Make marinade, substituting red wine vinegar for the cider vinegar and Italian seasoning for the chili powder. Pour over tempeh in shallow glass bowl. Refrigerate, covered, 4 hours or overnight. Drain; reserve marinade. Cut tempeh into ½-inch cubes.

2. Sauté tempeh, onion, bell pepper, and garlic in lightly greased large skillet until vegetables are crisp-tender, about 5 minutes. Stir in reserved marinade and remaining ingredients, except salt and pepper; heat to boiling. Reduce heat and simmer, covered, until vegetables are tender, 5 to 8 minutes; season to taste with salt and pepper.

GRILLED TEMPEH WITH POBLANO SOUR CREAM SAUCE

L *Tempeh is marinated in Fajita Marinade for a flavor of the Southwest.*

4 entree servings

1 package (12 ounces) tempeh, halved crosswise
Fajita Marinade (see p. 182)
Vegetable cooking spray
Poblano Sour Cream Sauce (see p. 603)

1. Pour Fajita Marinade over tempeh in glass baking dish; refrigerate 1 to 2 hours, turning occasionally; drain. Spray tempeh on both sides with cooking spray; grill over medium-hot coals until browned, 4 to 6 minutes on each side. Serve with Poblano Sour Cream Sauce.

Per Serving:
Net carbohydrate (gm): 28
Calories: 272
% of calories from fat: 30
Fat (gm): 10
Saturated fat (gm): 2
Cholesterol (mg): 11
Sodium (mg): 68
Protein (gm): 22
Carbohydrate (gm): 29

Exchanges:
Milk: 0.0
Vegetable: 0.0
Fruit: 0.0
Bread: 2.0
Meat: 3.0
Fat: 0.0

ITALIAN-STYLE VEGETARIAN MEATBALLS WITH PEPERONATA

LO *Flavorful Vegetarian Meatballs are teamed with classic Italian peperonata.*

6 servings

2 cups each: sliced onions, green and red bell peppers

6 cloves garlic, minced

1 tablespoon olive oil

¼ cup water

Salt and pepper, to taste

Vegetarian Meatballs (see p. 437)

Per Serving:
Net carbohydrate (gm): 13
Calories: 225
% of calories from fat: 26
Fat (gm): 7
Saturated fat (gm): 2
Cholesterol (mg): 108
Sodium (mg): 606
Protein (gm): 22
Carbohydrate (gm): 21

Exchanges:
Milk: 0.0
Vegetable: 1.0
Fruit: 0.0
Bread: 1.0
Meat: 2.5
Fat: 0.0

1. Sauté onions, bell peppers, and garlic in oil in large skillet 5 minutes. Add water to skillet, cook, covered, over medium to medium-low heat until vegetables are very tender, 20 to 25 minutes, stirring occasionally. Season to taste with salt and pepper. Serve with Vegetarian Meatballs.

ROASTED EGGPLANT WITH PASTA

L
45

Cook the eggplant on a charcoal grill for a wonderful smoky flavor. The eggplant can be roasted or grilled up to 2 days in advance.

6 servings

1 pound eggplant

1 cup coarsely chopped tomato

3 green onions, sliced

7 ounces low-carb whole wheat spaghetti, cooked, room temperature

½ cup (2 ounces) shredded Parmesan cheese

2 tablespoons balsamic, or red wine vinegar

1 tablespoon olive oil

1–2 teaspoons lemon juice

Salt and pepper, to taste

Per Serving:
Net carbohydrate (gm): 21
Calories: 221
% of calories from fat: 15
Fat (gm): 4
Saturated fat (gm): 0.7
Cholesterol (mg): 2
Sodium (mg): 242
Protein (gm): 16
Carbohydrate (gm): 32

Exchanges:
Milk: 0.0
Vegetable: 0.0
Fruit: 0.0
Bread: 2.0
Meat: 1.5
Fat: 0.0

1. Pierce eggplant 6 to 8 times with fork; place in baking pan. Bake at 425 degrees until tender, about 30 minutes; cool. Cut eggplant in half; scoop out pulp and cut into ¾-inch pieces. Toss eggplant, tomato, onions, pasta, cheese, and combined vinegar, oil, and lemon juice; season to taste with salt and pepper.

ROASTED SUMMER VEGETABLES WITH PASTA

V

45

For attractive serving, the pasta can be shaped into small nests to contain the medley of roasted vegetables.

8 servings

3 tablespoons olive oil

2 tablespoons balsamic, or red wine vinegar

1 teaspoon lemon juice

3 cloves garlic, minced

2 teaspoons crushed caraway seeds

¼ teaspoon each: salt, pepper

1 medium eggplant (12 ounces), peeled, cut into 1-inch pieces

1 cup each: sliced zucchini, red, or green bell pepper, red onion wedges

16 ounces low-carb whole wheat linguine, cooked, warm

Per Serving:
Net carbohydrate (gm): 24
Calories: 275
% of calories from fat: 21
Fat (gm): 6
Saturated fat (gm): 0.7
Cholesterol (mg): 0.0
Sodium (mg): 258
Protein (gm): 17
Carbohydrate (gm): 38

Exchanges:
Milk: 0.0
Vegetable: 1.0
Fruit: 0.0
Bread: 2.0
Meat: 2.0
Fat: 0.0

1. Mix oil, vinegar, lemon juice, garlic, caraway seeds, salt, and pepper; pour over combined vegetables in shallow glass baking dish. Arrange vegetables in single layer on greased foil-lined jelly roll pan. Bake at 425 degrees until vegetables are browned and tender, 30 to 40 minutes. Toss with pasta.

LINGUINE WITH FENNEL AND SUN-DRIED TOMATO PESTO

L

Fennel, sometimes called anise, lends a fragrant flavor to this light entrée. Fennel tops can be used as an attractive garnish.

6 servings

1 cup each: thinly sliced onion, fennel bulb

¼ cup dry white wine, or water

12 ounces low-carb whole wheat linguine, cooked, warm

Sun-Dried Tomato Pesto (recipe p. 606)

Salt and pepper, to taste

Per Serving:
Net carbohydrate (gm): 26
Calories: 312
% of calories from fat: 24
Fat (gm): 24
Saturated fat (gm): 1
Cholesterol (mg): 0.3
Sodium (mg): 318
Protein (gm): 18
Carbohydrate (gm): 41

Exchanges:
Milk: 0.0
Vegetable: 2.0
Fruit: 0.0
Bread: 2.0
Meat: 2.0
Fat: 0.0

1. Sauté onion and fennel in lightly greased large skillet 2 to 3 minutes. Cook, covered, over medium-low heat until onion is very soft, 10 to 15 minutes. Stir in wine and simmer, covered, 15 to 20 minutes or until wine is almost gone. Toss with pasta and Sun-Dried Tomato Pesto; season to taste with salt and pepper.

PASTA SKILLET CAKES

O

A great recipe for using leftover pasta!

4 servings

1 cup cooked low-carb whole wheat linguine, or spaghetti, cut into ½-inch pieces

5 eggs

½ cup plain dry bread crumbs

½ cup each: shredded sweet potato, zucchini, chopped red bell pepper

¼ cup finely chopped onion

¾ teaspoon dried tarragon leaves

1 small jalapeño chili, finely chopped

¼ teaspoon each: salt, pepper

⅛ teaspoon cayenne pepper

Lemon Herb Mayonnaise (see p. 611)

Per Serving:
Net carbohydrate (gm): 29
Calories: 258
% of calories from fat: 15
Fat (gm): 4
Saturated fat (gm): 1
Cholesterol (mg): 110
Sodium (mg): 549
Protein (gm): 17
Carbohydrate (gm): 37

Exchanges:
Milk: 0.0
Vegetable: 1.0
Fruit: 0.0
Bread: 2.0
Meat: 1.0
Fat: 0.5

1. Mix all ingredients, except Lemon Herb Mayonnaise, in bowl. Spoon half the mixture into greased 7- or 8-inch skillet, pressing into an even layer with a pancake turner. Cook over medium heat until browned on the bottom, 3 to 4 minutes. Invert cake onto plate; slide cake back into skillet and cook until browned on the bottom, 3 to 4 minutes. Repeat with remaining mixture. Cut cakes into halves; serve with Lemon Herb Mayonnaise.

BRUSSELS SPROUTS AND PASTA SHELL SALAD

L *Make this colorful salad to celebrate the first summer harvest of Brussels sprouts.*

4 servings (about 1½ cups each)

6 ounces low-carb whole wheat pasta shells, cooked
2 cups halved small Brussels sprouts, cooked
1 cup each: chopped tomato, sliced green bell pepper
¼ cup thinly sliced red onion
Sun-Dried Tomato-Goat Cheese Dressing
   (recipe follows)
Salt and pepper, to taste
¼ cup (1 ounce) shredded Romano cheese

Per Serving:
Net carbohydrate (gm): 22
Calories: 268
% of calories from fat: 22
Fat (gm): 6.8
Saturated fat (gm): 2
Cholesterol (mg): 8
Sodium (mg): 424
Protein (gm): 18
Carbohydrate (gm): 35

Exchanges:
Milk: 0.0
Vegetable: 0.0
Fruit: 0.0
Bread: 2.5
Meat: 1.0
Fat: 0.5

1. Toss pasta, vegetables, and Sun-Dried Tomato-Goat Cheese Dressing in salad bowl; season to taste with salt and pepper. Sprinkle with cheese.

Sun-Dried Tomato and Goat Cheese Dressing

Makes about ½ cup

3 sun-dried tomato halves (not in oil), softened, finely chopped
1 tablespoon olive oil
2 tablespoons each: white wine vinegar, lemon juice
2–3 tablespoons goat cheese
2 cloves garlic, minced
½ teaspoon dried marjoram leaves

1. Mix all ingredients.

SUMMER FRUIT SALAD WITH LIME CILANTRO DRESSING

L

Take advantage of the season's ripest fruit for this salad.

45 **4 servings**

1 cup each: sliced strawberries, blueberries,
   cantaloupe balls, peeled kiwi
Lime Cilantro Dressing (recipe follows), divided
3 cups cottage cheese
4 large bibb lettuce leaves
2 tablespoons grated orange zest

1. Toss fruit and ¼ cup Lime Cilantro Dressing. Spoon fruit and cottage cheese onto lettuce-lined plates; drizzle with remaining ¼ cup dressing and sprinkle with grated orange zest.

Per Serving:
Net carbohydrate (gm): 28
Calories: 284
% of calories from fat: 22
Fat (gm): 7
Saturated fat (gm): 2
Cholesterol (mg): 14
Sodium (mg): 698
Protein (gm): 25
Carbohydrate (gm): 32

Exchanges:
Milk: 0.0
Vegetable: 0.0
Fruit: 2.0
Bread: 0.0
Meat: 3.0
Fat: 0.0

Lime Cilantro Dressing

Makes about ½ cup

¼ cup lime juice
2 tablespoons orange juice
2–3 tablespoons canola oil
¼ cup chopped cilantro
1 tablespoon honey

1. Mix all ingredients.

LENTIL SALAD WITH FETA CHEESE

L *There are lots of flavor, texture, and color contrasts in this salad.*

6 servings (about 1⅓ cups each)

1¼ cups dried brown lentils
2½ cups reduced-sodium vegetable broth
1½ cups each: coarsely chopped iceberg
    lettuce, tomatoes
½ cup each: thinly sliced celery, yellow bell pepper,
    onion, chopped cucumber
¾ cup (2–3 ounces) crumbled fat-free feta cheese
Balsamic Dressing (recipe follows)
Salt and pepper, to taste

Per Serving:
Net carbohydrate (gm): 19
Calories: 253
% of calories from fat: 28
Fat (gm): 8
Saturated fat (gm): 2
Cholesterol (mg): 8
Sodium (mg): 367
Protein (gm): 15
Carbohydrate (gm): 33

Exchanges:
Milk: 0.0
Vegetable: 0.0
Fruit: 0.0
Bread: 2.0
Meat: 1.0
Fat: 1.0

1. Heat lentils and broth to boiling in large saucepan; reduce heat and simmer, covered, until lentils are just tender, about 25 minutes. Drain; cool. Combine lentils, vegetables, and cheese; drizzle Balsamic Dressing over and toss. Season to taste with salt and pepper.

Balsamic Dressing

Makes about ⅓ cup

3 tablespoons balsamic, or red wine, vinegar
2 tablespoons each: olive oil, lemon juice
2 cloves garlic, minced
½ teaspoon dried thyme leaves

1. Mix all ingredients.

BLACK BEAN AND SMOKED TOFU SALAD

V *The smoky flavor of the tofu is a pleasant contrast to the picante chili, fresh cilantro, and Mustard-Honey Dressing. Purchased smoked tofu can be used.*

4 servings (about 1¼ cups each)

2 cans (15 ounces each) black beans, rinsed, drained
Mesquite-Smoked Tofu (see p. 191), cubed
1 cup each: chopped tomato, red bell pepper
½ cup sliced red onion
¼ cup each: finely chopped cilantro, parsley
2 teaspoons each: finely chopped jalapeno chili,
    roasted garlic
Mustard-Honey Dressing (recipe follows)

Per Serving:
Net carbohydrate (gm): 30
Calories: 309
% of calories from fat: 30
Fat (gm): 12
Saturated fat (gm): 2
Cholesterol (mg): 0.0
Sodium (mg): 1024
Protein (gm): 19
Carbohydrate (gm): 42

Exchanges:
Milk: 0.0
Vegetable: 0.0
Fruit: 0.0
Bread: 2.5
Meat: 2.5
Fat: 0.0

1. Combine all ingredients in salad bowl and toss.

Mustard-Honey Dressing

Makes about ½ cup

3–4 tablespoons each: olive oil, cider vinegar
1 tablespoon Dijon mustard
1–2 tablespoons honey
½ teaspoon dried oregano leaves
1–2 dashes red pepper sauce

1. Mix all ingredients.

TACOS PICADILLO

V *This Mexican favorite is seasoned with raisins, almonds, sweet spices, and jalapeno chili.*

6 servings (1 taco each)

¼ cup chopped onion

2 cloves garlic, minced

½ small jalapeno chili, minced

1 teaspoon canola oil

¾ package (12-ounce size) vegetarian ground beef

½ cup chopped tomato

¼ cup each: dark raisins, toasted slivered almonds

1–2 teaspoons cider vinegar

1 teaspoon ground cinnamon

¼ teaspoon each: dried oregano leaves, ground cloves and allspice

Salt and pepper, to taste

6 low-carb whole wheat tortillas, warm

Tomato Poblano Salsa (recipe follows)

Per Serving:
Net carbohydrate (gm): 14
Calories: 188
% of calories from fat: 24
Fat (gm): 6
Saturated fat (gm): 0.3
Cholesterol (mg): 0.0
Sodium (mg): 469
Protein (gm): 16
Carbohydrate (gm): 27

Exchanges:
Milk: 0.0
Vegetable: 0.0
Fruit: 0.0
Bread: 1.5
Meat: 2.0
Fat: 0.0

1. Sauté onion, garlic, and jalapeno chili in oil in medium skillet until tender, about 5 minutes. Add remaining ingredients, except salt, pepper, tortillas, and Tomato Poblano Salsa. Cook over medium heat until mixture is hot, about 5 minutes; season to taste with salt and pepper. Spoon about ⅓ cup mixture on each tortilla and roll up. Serve with Tomato Poblano Salsa.

Tomato Poblano Salsa

Makes about 1 cup

¾ cup chopped tomato

¼ cup each: chopped poblano chili, cilantro

2 tablespoons finely chopped onion

1 teaspoon finely chopped jalapeno chili

1 clove garlic, minced

Salt, to taste

1. Mix all ingredients, except salt; season to taste with salt.

GRINDERS

LO *Serve these fun sandwiches with New England Baked Beans and Roasted Potato Salad (see pp. 368, 210).*

6 servings

3 cups sliced green bell peppers

3 cloves garlic, minced

1–2 tablespoons olive oil

Salt and pepper, to taste

Vegetarian Meatballs (see p. 437)

3 cups reduced-sodium spaghetti sauce, warm

6 Italian, or Hoagie, rolls, toasted

4 tablespoons grated fat-free Parmesan cheese

Per Serving:
Net carbohydrate (gm): 24
Calories: 371
% of calories from fat: 28
Fat (gm): 13
Saturated fat (gm): 3
Cholesterol (mg): 112
Sodium (mg): 1103
Protein (gm): 23
Carbohydrate (gm): 40

Exchanges:
Milk: 0.0
Vegetable: 0.0
Fruit: 0.0
Bread: 2.5
Meat: 3.5
Fat: 0.0

1. Sauté bell peppers and garlic in oil 5 minutes; reduce heat to medium-low and cook, uncovered, until peppers are very soft, 15 to 20 minutes. Season to taste with salt and pepper. Heat Vegetarian Meatballs and spaghetti sauce in large saucepan until hot, 5 to 8 minutes. Spoon meatball and bell pepper mixture into rolls; sprinkle with cheese.

SUN-DRIED TOMATO PESTO AND CHEESE GRILL

L

45

Purchased sun-dried tomato or basil pesto can also be used. Thin onion slices can be added to the sandwich or substituted for the tomato slices.

4 servings

Sun-Dried Tomato Pesto (see p. 606)
8 slices sourdough bread
8 slices (6 ounces) fat-free mozzarella cheese
8 thin slices ripe tomato
Vegetable cooking spray

Per Serving:
Net carbohydrate (gm): 5
Calories: 281
% of calories from fat: 31
Fat (gm): 10
Saturated fat (gm): 1
Cholesterol (mg): 8
Sodium (mg): 749
Protein (gm): 24
Carbohydrate (gm): 27

Exchanges:
Milk: 0.0
Vegetable: 0.0
Fruit: 0.0
Bread: 2.0
Meat: 2.0
Fat: 0.5

1. Make Sun-Dried Tomato Pesto, using only 2 tablespoons olive oil; spread on bread slices. Top 4 slices bread with a cheese slice and 2 tomato slices; top with remaining cheese and bread. Spray both sides of sandwiches with cooking spray. Cook in large skillet over medium to medium-low heat until browned, about 5 minutes on each side.

CRANBERRY CHEESE MELT

L

Lots of melted cheese, with cranberry and walnut accents.

45 **4 servings**

¼ package (8-ounce size) fat-free cream
    cheese, room temperature
¼ cup (1 ounce) shredded reduced-fat Swiss cheese
¼ cup chopped walnuts
8 slices low-carb whole wheat bread
½ medium onion, thinly sliced
¼ cup whole-berry cranberry sauce
½ cup (2 ounces) shredded fat-free Cheddar cheese
Vegetable cooking spray

Per Serving:
Net carbohydrate (gm): 23
Calories: 246
% of calories from fat: 28
Fat (gm): 8
Saturated fat (gm): 0.6
Cholesterol (mg): 1
Sodium (mg): 654
Protein (gm): 16
Carbohydrate (gm): 30

Exchanges:
Milk: 0.0
Vegetable: 0.0
Fruit: 0.0
Bread: 2.0
Meat: 1.5
Fat: 0.5

1. Mix cheeses and walnuts; spread on 4 slices bread. Top with onion slices, cranberry sauce,

Cheddar cheese, and remaining bread. Spray both sides of sandwiches lightly with cooking spray; cook sandwiches in large skillet over medium heat until browned, 3 to 5 minutes on each side.

SCRAMBLED EGG PIZZA

LO

For those who love pizza for breakfast! Hearty enough for any time of the day.

45 **6 servings**

Whole Wheat Pizza Dough (see p. 299)

1 cup pizza sauce

4 ounces vegetarian sausage, crumbled

½ cup sliced green bell pepper

¼ cup thinly sliced onion

1½ cups (6 ounces) mozzarella cheese

2–3 eggs

Per Serving:
Net carbohydrate (gm): 20
Calories: 229
% of calories from fat: 29
Fat (gm): 8
Saturated fat (gm): 1
Cholesterol (mg): 76
Sodium (mg): 837
Protein (gm): 17
Carbohydrate (gm): 24

Exchanges:
Milk: 0.0
Vegetable: 0.0
Fruit: 0.0
Bread: 1.5
Meat: 2.0
Fat: 0.0

1. Spread Whole Wheat Pizza Dough on lightly greased 12-inch pizza pan, making rim around edge; spread evenly with pizza sauce. Sprinkle pizza with vegetarian sausage, green pepper, onion, and cheese. Bake at 425 degrees until pizza is lightly browned, 15 to 20 minutes.

2. Remove pizza from oven. Break eggs into center of pizza; stir with a fork and quickly spread over pizza; return to oven and bake until eggs are cooked, 3 to 4 minutes, stirring with a fork occasionally.

WILD MUSHROOM PIZZA

L

45

Regular mushrooms can be used for this pizza, but wild mushrooms are more flavorful.

6 slices

5 cups sliced wild mushrooms (cremini, portobello, shiitake)

¼ cup finely chopped shallots, or onions

1 teaspoon minced garlic

½ teaspoon dried thyme leaves

2 tablespoons water

Salt and pepper, to taste

Low-Carb Pizza Dough (see p. 467)

⅓ cup basil pesto

1½ cups (6 ounces) shredded fat-free mozzarella cheese, divided

Per Serving:
Net carbohydrate (gm): 19
Calories: 206
% of calories from fat: 27
Fat (gm): 6
Saturated fat (gm): 1
Cholesterol (mg): 10
Sodium (mg): 436
Protein (gm): 16
Carbohydrate (gm): 23

Exchanges:
Milk: 0.0
Vegetable: 0.0
Fruit: 0.0
Bread: 1.5
Meat: 2.0
Fat: 0.0

1. Cook mushrooms, shallots, garlic, thyme, and water in lightly greased large skillet, covered, over medium heat until mushrooms are wilted, about 5 minutes. Cook, uncovered, until mushrooms are tender and liquid is gone, 10 to 12 minutes; season to taste with salt and pepper.

2. Spread dough on greased 12-inch pizza pan, making rim around edge. Spread pesto on dough and sprinkle with ½ cup cheese. Top with mushroom mixture; sprinkle with remaining ½ cup cheese. Bake at 350 degrees until crust is browned, about 30 minutes.

45-MINUTE PREP TIP: Make pizza dough and begin the rest of the recipe while the dough is rising.

PIZZA, SOUTHWEST-STYLE

L *Vegetarian Chorizo (see pg. 287) would be an excellent addition to this pizza.*

6 slices

1 medium poblano chili, sliced
¾ cup each: sliced red bell pepper, onion
1 small jalapeño chili, finely chopped
2 cloves garlic, minced
⅔ cup whole kernel corn
1 teaspoon dried marjoram leaves
Salt and pepper, to taste
Low-Carb Pizza Dough (recipe follows)
Pizza Sauce (see p. 582)
½ teaspoon ground cumin
1½ cups (6 ounces) shredded fat-free
  mozzarella cheese

Per Serving:
Net carbohydrate (gm): 27
Calories: 183
% of calories from fat: 4
Fat (gm): 0.8
Saturated fat (gm): 0.1
Cholesterol (mg): 5
Sodium (mg): 323
Protein (gm): 14
Carbohydrate (gm): 32

Exchanges:
Milk: 0.0
Vegetable: 1.0
Fruit: 0.0
Bread: 1.0
Meat: 1.0
Fat: 0.0

1. Sauté poblano chili, bell pepper, onion, jalapeño chili, and garlic in lightly greased large skillet until tender, about 8 minutes. Stir in corn and marjoram; season to taste with salt and pepper.

2. Spread dough on greased 12-inch pizza pan, making rim around edge. Mix Pizza Sauce and cumin; spread on dough. Top with vegetable mixture and sprinkle with cheese. Bake at 425 degrees until crust is browned, 15 to 20 minutes.

Low-Carb Pizza Dough

Makes one 12-inch crust

1 cup whole wheat pastry flour, divided
1 package fast-rising yeast
¼ teaspoons salt
½ cup very hot water (120 degrees)
2 teaspoons honey

1. Combine ¾ cup flour, yeast, and salt in bowl; add hot water and honey, stirring until smooth. Mix in enough remaining flour to make soft dough. Knead dough on floured surface until smooth and elastic, about 5 minutes. Cover and let stand 15 minutes.

THIRTEEN

Vegetable
Side Dishes

BRAISED WHOLE ARTICHOKES

V

*The artichokes are cooked slowly until the bottoms are browned and crusty
—the resulting flavor is marvelous!*

4 servings

4 medium artichokes, stems removed

Salt

2–4 teaspoons extra-virgin olive oil

Per Serving:
Calories: 80
% of calories from fat: 24
Fat (gm): 2.4
Saturated fat (gm): 0.3
Cholesterol (mg): 0
Sodium (mg): 114
Protein (gm): 4.2
Carbohydrate (gm): 13.4

Exchanges:
Milk: 0.0
Vegetable: 2.0
Fruit: 0.0
Bread: 0.0
Meat: 0.0
Fat: 0.5

1. Cut 1 inch from tops of artichokes and discard.
Place artichokes in medium saucepan and sprinkle
lightly with salt; add 1 inch water to pan. Heat to
boiling; reduce heat and simmer, covered, until
artichokes are tender, about 30 minutes (bottom
leaves will pull out easily). Drain. Holding artichokes with a towel, brush bottoms with olive
oil; return to saucepan. Cook, uncovered, over
medium to medium-low heat until bottoms of
artichokes are deeply browned, 10 to 15 minutes.

ARTICHOKES WITH HOLLANDAISE SAUCE

L

45

*The Mock Hollandaise Sauce is excellent served over steamed asparagus
spears, broccoli, or cauliflower. Also see the recipe for delicious Eggs
Benedict (p. 338).*

4–6 servings

4–6 whole artichokes, stems removed

Mock Hollandaise Sauce (see p. 595)

Per Serving:
Calories: 114
% of calories from fat: 2
Fat (gm): 0.3
Saturated fat (gm): 0.1
Cholesterol (mg): 0.2
Sodium (mg): 396
Protein (gm): 11.9
Carbohydrate (gm): 17.5

Exchanges:
Milk: 0.5
Vegetable: 2.0
Fruit: 0.0
Bread: 0.0
Meat: 0.5
Fat: 0.0

1. Cut 1 inch from tops of artichokes and discard. Place artichokes in medium saucepan and
sprinkle lightly with salt; add 1 inch water to
pan. Heat to boiling; reduce heat and simmer,
covered, until artichokes are tender, about 30
minutes (bottom leaves will pull out easily).
Serve with Mock Hollandaise Sauce.

45-MINUTE PREP TIP: Make Mock Hollandaise Sauce before
preparing the rest of the recipe.

ASPARAGUS WITH LEMON-WINE SAUCE

L

45

This rich sauce is also delicious served with crisp-tender broccoli, cauliflower, green beans, or Brussels sprouts.

4 servings

2 tablespoons minced shallots, or green onions

¼ cup dry white wine, or water

¾ cup fat-free half-and-half, or fat-free milk

2 tablespoons flour

½ teaspoon each: dried thyme and marjoram leaves

1 tablespoon lemon juice

Salt and white pepper, to taste

1 pound asparagus spears, cooked crisp-tender, warm

Per Serving:
Calories: 85
% of calories from fat: 4
Fat (gm): 0.4
Saturated fat (gm): 0.1
Cholesterol (mg): 0
Sodium (mg): 59
Protein (gm): 4.8
Carbohydrate (gm): 13.4

Exchanges:
Milk: 0.0
Vegetable: 2.0
Fruit: 0.0
Bread: 0.5
Meat: 0.0
Fat: 0.0

1. Sauté shallots in lightly greased small saucepan until tender, 2 to 3 minutes. Add wine and heat to boiling; reduce heat and simmer, uncovered, until wine is evaporated, 3 to 4 minutes. Stir in combined half-and-half, flour, and herbs; heat to boiling. Boil, stirring, until thickened, about 1 minute. Stir in lemon juice; season to taste with salt and pepper. Serve with asparagus.

ASPARAGUS WITH PEANUT SAUCE

V

45

Asian flavors are the perfect complement to spring's freshest asparagus. The asparagus can be served warm or chilled.

6 servings

2 tablespoons reduced-fat peanut butter

¼ cup sugar

2–3 tablespoons reduced-sodium tamari soy sauce

3–4 teaspoons rice wine (sake), dry sherry, or water

1 teaspoon grated gingerroot

1½ pounds asparagus spears, cooked crisp-tender

Per Serving:
Calories: 95
% of calories from fat: 21
Fat (gm): 2.3
Saturated fat (gm): 0.5
Cholesterol (mg): 0
Sodium (mg): 246
Protein (gm): 4.8
Carbohydrate (gm): 15

Exchanges:
Milk: 0.0
Vegetable: 3.0
Fruit: 0.0
Bread: 0.0
Meat: 0.0
Fat: 0.5

1. Mix peanut butter, sugar, soy sauce, rice wine, and gingerroot until smooth. Serve with asparagus.

GREEK-STYLE GREEN BEANS

V

Fresh green beans are long simmered with tomatoes, herbs, and garlic in traditional Greek style.

4–6 servings

½ cup chopped onion

4 cloves garlic, minced

¾ teaspoon each: dried oregano and basil leaves

1 tablespoon olive oil

1 can (28 ounces) reduced-sodium tomatoes, undrained, coarsely chopped

1 pound green beans

Salt and pepper, to taste

Per Serving:
Calories: 123
% of calories from fat: 28
Fat (gm): 4.3
Saturated fat (gm): 0.6
Cholesterol (mg): 0
Sodium (mg): 30
Protein (gm): 4.5
Carbohydrate (gm): 20.5

Exchanges:
Milk: 0.0
Vegetable: 4.0
Fruit: 0.0
Bread: 0.0
Meat: 0.0
Fat: 0.5

1. Sauté onion, garlic, and herbs in oil in large skillet until onion is until tender, 3 to 4 minutes. Add tomatoes with liquid and green beans and heat to boiling; reduce heat and simmer, covered, until beans are very tender, 30 to 40 minutes. Season to taste with salt and pepper.

ORIENTAL GREEN BEANS

V

45

Serve these beans as an accompaniment to grilled tofu or portobello mushrooms.

4 servings

¼ cup each: chopped onion, red bell pepper
2 teaspoons each: finely chopped gingerroot, garlic
2 cups halved green beans
½ cup sliced water chestnuts
1 cup cooked dried, or drained, rinsed, canned, adzuki, or black, beans
1 tablespoon rice wine vinegar
1–2 teaspoons reduced-sodium tamari soy sauce
Salt and pepper, to taste

Per Serving:
Calories: 109
% of calories from fat: 2
Fat (gm): 0.2
Saturated fat (gm): 0
Cholesterol (mg): 0
Sodium (mg): 64
Protein (gm): 5.8
Carbohydrate (gm): 22.5

Exchanges:
Milk: 0.0
Vegetable: 1.5
Fruit: 0.0
Bread: 1.0
Meat: 0.0
Fat: 0.0

1. Stir-fry onion, bell pepper, gingerroot, and garlic in lightly greased large wok or saucepan until tender, 3 to 4 minutes. Add green beans and water chestnuts; stir-fry until beans are crisp-tender, 5 to 8 minutes. Add adzuki beans, vinegar, and soy sauce; stir-fry 1 to 2 minutes longer. Season to taste with salt and pepper.

GREEN BEAN CASSEROLE

L

45

◊

Reduced-fat cream of mushroom soup and fat-free sour cream make this old favorite possible in a healthier, low-fat form. We've used fresh green beans, but canned or frozen may be used.

6 servings

1 can (10¾ ounces) reduced-fat cream of mushroom soup
½ cup fat-free sour cream
¼ cup fat-free milk
1¼ pounds green beans, cut into 1½-inch pieces, cooked crisp-tender
½ cup canned French-fried onions

Per Serving:
Calories: 81
% of calories from fat: 31
Fat (gm): 2.9
Saturated fat (gm): 0.8
Cholesterol (mg): 1.3
Sodium (mg): 172
Protein (gm): 3
Carbohydrate (gm): 11.6

Exchanges:
Milk: 0.0
Vegetable: 2.0
Fruit: 0.0
Bread: 0.0
Meat: 0.0
Fat: 0.5

1. Mix soup, sour cream, and milk in 2-quart casserole; stir in beans. Bake, uncovered, at 350 degrees until mixture is bubbly, about 45 minutes; sprinkle with onions during last 5 minutes of baking time.

EL PASO SUCCOTASH

L

Delicious served over rice or with warm corn bread.

45   **4 servings**

½ cup each: chopped onion, poblano chili, or green bell pepper

1 teaspoon each: minced jalapeño chili, garlic

2 teaspoons chili powder

1 teaspoon ground cumin

1 tablespoon each: margarine, or butter, flour

1 cup fat-free milk

1 can (15 ounces) each: lima beans, black-eyed peas, rinsed, drained

1 cup whole-kernel corn

Salt and pepper, to taste

1 medium tomato, chopped

2 tablespoons chopped cilantro

2–3 teaspoons lime juice

Per Serving:
Calories: 280
% of calories from fat: 12
Fat (gm): 3.9
Saturated fat (gm): 0.8
Cholesterol (mg): 1.2
Sodium (mg): 484
Protein (gm): 15.2
Carbohydrate (gm): 48.8

Exchanges:
Milk: 0.0
Vegetable: 0.0
Fruit: 0.0
Bread: 3.0
Meat: 1.0
Fat: 0.0

1. Sauté onion, chilies, garlic, chili powder, and cumin in margarine in large saucepan until tender, about 5 minutes. Stir in flour and cook 1 minute. Stir in milk; heat to boiling, stirring until thickened, about 1 minute. Stir in beans, black-eyed peas, and corn; cook over medium heat 2 to 3 minutes. Season to taste with salt and pepper. Stir in remaining ingredients.

BEETS DIJON

L *The easiest way to peel beets is to cook them with the skins on; after cooking, the skins slip off easily!*

4 servings

¹⁄₃ cup finely chopped onion
2 cloves garlic, minced
¹⁄₃ cup fat-free sour cream
2 tablespoons Dijon mustard
2–3 teaspoons lemon juice
Salt and white pepper, to taste
1¹⁄₂ pounds beets, cooked, cubed, or sliced, warm

Per Serving:
Calories: 71
% of calories from fat: 7
Fat (gm): 0.6
Saturated fat (gm): 0.1
Cholesterol (mg): 0
Sodium (mg): 185
Protein (gm): 3.5
Carbohydrate (gm): 13.8

Exchanges:
Milk: 0.0
Vegetable: 3.0
Fruit: 0.0
Bread: 0.0
Meat: 0.0
Fat: 0.0

1. Sauté onion and garlic in lightly greased small saucepan until tender, 3 to 4 minutes. Stir in sour cream, mustard, and lemon juice; heat over low heat until hot, 2 to 3 minutes. Season to taste with salt and pepper. Spoon sauce over beets.

HARVARD BEETS

V *Sweet yet tart, the sauce can also be served over cooked carrots or pearl onions. Vary the amount of vinegar for the right amount of tartness.*

4 servings

3 tablespoons sugar
1¹⁄₂ tablespoons cornstarch
³⁄₄ cup water
3–4 tablespoons cider vinegar
2 teaspoons margarine
Salt and white pepper, to taste
1 pound beets, cooked, sliced, warm

Per Serving:
Calories: 94
% of calories from fat: 18
Fat (gm): 1.9
Saturated fat (gm): 0.4
Cholesterol (mg): 0
Sodium (mg): 70
Protein (gm): 1.1
Carbohydrate (gm): 19.3

Exchanges:
Milk: 0.0
Vegetable: 2.0
Fruit: 0.0
Bread: 0.5
Meat: 0.0
Fat: 0.0

1. Mix sugar and cornstarch in small saucepan; whisk in water and vinegar. Heat to boiling; boil, whisking, until thickened, about 1 minute. Add margarine, whisking until melted; season to taste with salt and pepper. Pour sauce over beets and toss.

HONEY-ROASTED BEETS

V

The beets are cooked briefly before roasting so they are easier to peel and cut.

45

6 servings

1½ pounds medium beets
2 medium red onions, cut into wedges
Vegetable cooking spray
¼ cup currants, or raisins
3–4 tablespoons toasted walnuts
4 tablespoons honey
2–3 tablespoons red wine vinegar
1 tablespoon canola oil
4 cloves garlic, minced
Salt and pepper, to taste

Per Serving:
Calories: 94
% of calories from fat: 18
Fat (gm): 1.9
Saturated fat (gm): 0.4
Cholesterol (mg): 0
Sodium (mg): 70
Protein (gm): 1.1
Carbohydrate (gm): 19.3

Exchanges:
Milk: 0.0
Vegetable: 2.0
Fruit: 0.0
Bread: 0.5
Meat: 0.0
Fat: 0.0

1. Arrange beets and onions on greased foil-lined jelly roll pan; spray with cooking spray. Roast at 425 degrees until beets are tender, about 40 minutes. Peel beets and cut into 1-inch pieces. Combine beets, onions, currants, and walnuts; pour combined remaining ingredients, except salt and pepper, over and toss. Season to taste with salt and pepper.

HERB-CRUMBED BROCCOLI

V

Herb-seasoned bread crumbs and pecans offer new flavor and texture contrasts in this favorite broccoli dish.

45

6 servings

2–4 tablespoons chopped pecans
¼ cup dry unseasoned bread crumbs
½ teaspoon dried marjoram leaves
¼ teaspoon dried chervil leaves
1½ pounds broccoli, cut into florets and stalks
  sliced, cooked
Salt and pepper, to taste

Per Serving:
Calories: 61
% of calories from fat: 28
Fat (gm): 2.1
Saturated fat (gm): 0.2
Cholesterol (mg): 0
Sodium (mg): 64
Protein (gm): 3.7
Carbohydrate (gm): 8.7

Exchanges:
Milk: 0.0
Vegetable: 1.5
Fruit: 0.0
Bread: 0.0
Meat: 0.0
Fat: 0.5

1. Sauté pecans in lightly greased small skillet over medium heat until toasted, 2 to 3 minutes, stirring frequently. Add bread crumbs, marjoram, and chervil; cook until crumbs are toasted, 3 to 4 minutes, stirring frequently. Season broccoli to taste with salt and pepper; spoon crumb mixture over.

BROCCOLI RABE SAUTÉED WITH GARLIC

V

45

A simple but flavorful vegetable recipe that can also be made with broccoli or asparagus.

4–6 servings

1 pound broccoli rabe, cooked crisp-tender
4 cloves garlic, minced
Salt and pepper, to taste

1. Sauté broccoli rabe and garlic in lightly greased large skillet until broccoli rabe is beginning to brown, 4 to 5 minutes. Season to taste with salt and pepper.

Per Serving:
Calories: 32
% of calories from fat: 8
Fat (gm): 0.4
Saturated fat (gm): 0.1
Cholesterol (mg): 0
Sodium (mg): 25
Protein (gm): 3.1
Carbohydrate (gm): 5.9

Exchanges:
Milk: 0.0
Vegetable: 1.0
Fruit: 0.0
Bread: 0.0
Meat: 0.0
Fat: 0.0

BROCCOLI TERRINE WITH LEMON HERB MAYONNAISE

LO

45

◊

❄

The terrine can also be served with Roasted Red Pepper Sauce or Fresh Tomato-Basil Sauce (see pp. 590, 584).

8 servings

1 pound broccoli, cut into 1-inch pieces, cooked
½ cup fat-free sour cream
¼ cup (1 ounce) grated fat-free Parmesan cheese
2–3 teaspoons lemon juice
½ teaspoon each: dried tarragon, thyme, and
   basil leaves
Salt and pepper, to taste
4 eggs
Lemon-Herb Mayonnaise (see p. 611)

Per Serving:
Calories: 103
% of calories from fat: 28
Fat (gm): 3
Saturated fat (gm): 1
Cholesterol (mg): 111
Sodium (mg): 227
Protein (gm): 7
Carbohydrate (gm): 11.5

Exchanges:
Milk: 0.0
Vegetable: 2.0
Fruit: 0.0
Bread: 0.0
Meat: 0.0
Fat: 1.0

1. Process broccoli in food processor until mixture is almost smooth; mix in sour cream, cheese, lemon juice, and herbs. Season to taste with salt and pepper. Mix in eggs.

2. Pour mixture into greased loaf pan, 7½ x 3½ inches. Place pan in large roasting pan on middle oven rack; add 2 inches hot water to roasting pan. Bake, covered with foil, at 350 degrees until set, about 1 hour. Remove loaf pan from roasting pan and uncover. Let stand 10 minutes. Loosen sides of loaf with sharp knife and invert onto serving plate, smoothing edges with knife, if necessary. Slice and serve warm or chilled with Lemon Herb Mayonnaise.

SUGAR-GLAZED BRUSSELS SPROUTS AND PEARL ONIONS

V

45

If Brussels sprouts are large, cut them into halves for easier eating. The pearl onions can be fresh, frozen, or canned.

4–6 servings

1 tablespoon margarine

¼ cup sugar

8 ounces each: small Brussels sprouts, pearl onions, cooked until crisp-tender, warm

Salt and white pepper, to taste

Per Serving:
Calories: 107
% of calories from fat: 25
Fat (gm): 3.2
Saturated fat (gm): 0.6
Cholesterol (mg): 0
Sodium (mg): 48
Protein (gm): 2.3
Carbohydrate (gm): 19.7

Exchanges:
Milk: 0.0
Vegetable: 2.0
Fruit: 0.0
Bread: 0.5
Meat: 0.0
Fat: 0.5

1. Heat margarine in medium skillet until melted; stir in sugar and cook over medium heat until mixture is bubbly. Add vegetables and toss to coat. Season to taste with salt and white pepper.

WINE-BRAISED CABBAGE

V

45

You'll enjoy the combination of aromatic anise and caraway seeds in this cabbage dish.

4–6 servings

¾ cup chopped onion

½ cup chopped green bell pepper

3 cloves garlic, minced

½ teaspoon each: crushed caraway and anise seeds

1 medium head cabbage, thinly sliced

½ cup each: canned reduced-sodium vegetable broth, dry white wine

2 tablespoons crumbled, cooked vegetarian bacon

Salt and pepper, to taste

Per Serving:
Calories: 118
% of calories from fat: 10
Fat (gm): 1.5
Saturated fat (gm): 0.1
Cholesterol (mg): 0
Sodium (mg): 148
Protein (gm): 6.4
Carbohydrate (gm): 19.3

Exchanges:
Milk: 0.0
Vegetable: 3.0
Fruit: 0.0
Bread: 0.5
Meat: 0.0
Fat: 0.0

1. Sauté onion, green pepper, garlic, caraway, and anise seeds in lightly greased large saucepan 3 to 4 minutes. Add cabbage, vegetable broth, and wine; heat to boiling. Reduce heat and simmer, covered, until cabbage is wilted, about 5 minutes. Simmer, uncovered, until cabbage is tender, 10 to 15 minutes. Stir in vegetarian bacon; season to taste with salt and pepper.

GINGERED CARROT PUREE

L

Cooked until thick, this intensely flavored puree owes its creamy texture to the additions of Idaho potato and fat-free half-and-half.

6 servings (about ½ cup each)

2 pounds carrots, sliced, cooked

2 cups cubed, peeled Idaho potato, cooked

1–2 tablespoons margarine, or butter

¼–½ cup fat-free half-and-half, or fat-free milk, warm

½ teaspoon ground ginger

Salt and white pepper, to taste

Ground nutmeg, as garnish

1 tablespoon chopped candied ginger

Per Serving:
Calories: 122
% of calories from fat: 16
Fat (gm): 2.2
Saturated fat (gm): 0.4
Cholesterol (mg): 0
Sodium (mg): 132
Protein (gm): 2.4
Carbohydrate (gm): 24.1

Exchanges:
Milk: 0.0
Vegetable: 2.5
Fruit: 0.0
Bread: 0.5
Meat: 0.0
Fat: 0.5

1. Process carrots and potato in food processor until smooth; transfer to large skillet and cook over medium to medium-low heat, stirring frequently, until mixture is the consistency of thick mashed potatoes (do not brown), about 15 minutes. Beat margarine and enough half-and-half into carrot mixture to make creamy consistency. Stir in ground ginger; season to taste with salt and white pepper. Sprinkle with nutmeg and candied ginger.

Variations

Cauliflower-Fennel Puree — Make recipe as above, substituting cauliflower for the carrots and deleting the ground nutmeg and candied ginger, and adding 1–1½ teaspoons crushed fennel or caraway seeds.

Celery Root Puree — Make recipe as above substituting celery root for the carrots and deleting the candied ginger.

Fennel Puree — Make recipe as above, substituting fennel bulbs for the carrots and deleting the ground nutmeg and candied ginger. Add ½ cup cooked onion to the fennel bulbs and potatoes when pureeing.

ORANGE-GLAZED BABY CARROTS

V

The sweet-spiced orange glaze is also delicious over sweet potatoes or beets.

45   **4 servings**

¾ cup orange juice

½ cup packed light brown sugar

2 tablespoons cornstarch

½ teaspoon ground cinnamon

¼ teaspoon each: ground allspice, mace

1 tablespoon margarine

Salt and white pepper, to taste

1 pound baby carrots, cooked crisp-tender, warm

Per Serving:
Calories: 191
% of calories from fat: 13
Fat (gm): 3
Saturated fat (gm): 0.6
Cholesterol (mg): 0
Sodium (mg): 145
Protein (gm): 1.8
Carbohydrate (gm): 42.4

Exchanges:
Milk: 0.0
Vegetable: 2.0
Fruit: 2.0
Bread: 0.0
Meat: 0.0
Fat: 0.5

1. Mix orange juice, brown sugar, cornstarch, and spices in small saucepan; heat to boiling. Boil, stirring, until thickened, about 1 minute. Stir in margarine until melted; season to taste with salt and pepper. Pour over carrots and toss.

45-MINUTE PREP TIP: Begin cooking carrots before preparing the rest of the recipe.

CARROT PUDDING

LO

45

This recipe is served as a dessert in Mexico — we think it makes an excellent side dish!

8 servings

2 pounds carrots, cooked, mashed

½ cup sugar

1½ tablespoons margarine, or butter, melted

½ cup all-purpose flour

1½ teaspoons baking powder

½ teaspoon each: ground cinnamon, salt

½ cup each: raisins, shredded fat-free
  Cheddar cheese

4 egg whites, beaten to stiff peaks

¼ cup sliced almonds (optional)

Per Serving:
Calories: 191
% of calories from fat: 11
Fat (gm): 2.5
Saturated fat (gm): 0.5
Cholesterol (mg): 1.3
Sodium (mg): 339
Protein (gm): 6.3
Carbohydrate (gm): 37.9

Exchanges:
Milk: 0.0
Vegetable: 1.5
Fruit: 0.5
Bread: 1.5
Meat: 0.0
Fat: 0.5

1. Mix carrots, sugar, and margarine in bowl; mix in combined flour, baking powder, cinnamon, and salt. Mix in raisins and cheese; fold in beaten egg whites. Spoon mixture into greased 8-inch-square baking pan; sprinkle with almonds (if using). Bake at 475 degrees 10 minutes; reduce temperature to 350 degrees and bake until browned and set, 50 to 60 minutes. Cut into squares; serve warm.

CAULIFLOWER WITH CREAMY CHEESE SAUCE

L

45

For flavor variations, make the cheese sauce with other reduced-fat cheeses, such as Havarti, Gruyère, American, or blue.

6 servings

1 large head cauliflower (2 pounds)
Creamy Cheese Sauce (recipe follows)
Paprika, as garnish

Per Serving:
Calories: 102
% of calories from fat: 31
Fat (gm): 3.6
Saturated fat (gm): 1.5
Cholesterol (mg): 5.7
Sodium (mg): 194
Protein (gm): 6.5
Carbohydrate (gm): 11.7

Exchanges:
Milk: 0.0
Vegetable: 2.0
Fruit: 0.0
Bread: 0.0
Meat: 0.5
Fat: 0.5

1. Simmer cauliflower in saucepan with 2 inches of water, covered, until tender, 20 to 25 minutes. Drain and place on serving plate; spoon Creamy Cheese Sauce over and sprinkle with paprika.

Creamy Cheese Sauce

Makes about 1¼ cups

2 tablespoons minced onion
1 tablespoon margarine, or butter
2 tablespoons flour
1 cup fat-free milk
½ cup (2 ounces) cubed reduced-fat pasteurized processed
   cheese
¼ teaspoon dry mustard
2–3 drops red pepper sauce
Salt and white pepper, to taste

1. Sauté onion in margarine in small saucepan 2 to 3 minutes. Stir in flour; cook, stirring, 1 minute. Whisk in milk and heat to boiling; boil, stirring, until thickened, about 1 minute. Reduce heat to low; add cheese, dry mustard, and pepper sauce, whisking until cheese is melted. Season to taste with salt and white pepper.

SUCCOTASH

L

45

Fat-free half-and-half contributes richness without adding fat calories in this old-fashioned favorite. Fresh crisp-tender cooked or frozen green beans can be substituted for the baby lima beans.

4 servings (about ¾ cup each)

1 small onion, chopped

1 tablespoon margarine, or butter

2 cups each: baby lima beans, whole kernel corn

½ cup each: canned reduced-sodium vegetable broth, fat-free half-and-half

Salt and pepper, to taste

Per Serving:
Calories: 146
% of calories from fat: 13
Fat (gm): 2.1
Saturated fat (gm): 0.4
Cholesterol (mg): 0
Sodium (mg): 69
Protein (gm): 6.6
Carbohydrate (gm): 26.7

Exchanges:
Milk: 0.0
Vegetable: 0.0
Fruit: 0.0
Bread: 1.5
Meat: 0.0
Fat: 0.5

1. Sauté onion in margarine in medium saucepan until tender, 5 to 8 minutes. Stir in lima beans, corn, broth, and half-and-half; heat to boiling. Reduce heat and simmer, covered, until vegetables are tender, about 5 minutes. Season to taste with salt and pepper.

FRIED CORN

V

Absolutely delicious! Use fresh corn, if you can.

4 servings (about ¾ cup each)

3 cups fresh, or frozen whole-kernel corn

¾ cup each: sliced green and red bell pepper

3 cloves garlic, minced

¼ cup water

Salt and pepper, to taste

Per Serving:
Calories: 127
% of calories from fat: 2
Fat (gm): 0.3
Saturated fat (gm): 0
Cholesterol (mg): 0
Sodium (mg): 7
Protein (gm): 4.9
Carbohydrate (gm): 31.6

Exchanges:
Milk: 0.0
Vegetable: 1.0
Fruit: 0.0
Bread: 1.5
Meat: 0.0
Fat: 0.0

1. Combine corn, bell peppers, and garlic in lightly greased large skillet; cook, covered, over medium-low heat until vegetables are very tender and browned, about 25 minutes, stirring occasionally. Add water and cook, covered, over low heat until water is absorbed, about 15 minutes. Season to taste with salt and pepper.

TEX-MEX SWEET CORN

V

Flavors of the Southwest make corn-on-the-cob better than ever!

45   6 servings

2–3 tablespoons margarine

½ teaspoon each: chili powder, ground cumin

¼ teaspoon each: dried oregano leaves, garlic powder

⅛ teaspoon cayenne pepper

6 ears fresh corn, cooked, warm

Salt, to taste

Chopped cilantro, as garnish

Per Serving:
Calories: 153
% of calories from fat: 25
Fat (gm): 4.8
Saturated fat (gm): 0.9
Cholesterol (mg): 0
Sodium (mg): 52
Protein (gm): 4.1
Carbohydrate (gm): 28.5

Exchanges:
Milk: 0.0
Vegetable: 0.0
Fruit: 0.0
Bread: 1.5
Meat: 0.0
Fat: 1.0

1. Melt margarine in small saucepan; stir in chili powder, cumin, oregano, garlic powder, and cayenne pepper. Brush on corn; sprinkle lightly with salt and cilantro.

FRESH CORN PUDDING

LO

Best made with fresh corn cut from the cob, but frozen corn will substitute nicely.

45

4–6 servings

2 tablespoons unseasoned dry bread crumbs

2 cups whole kernel corn

½ cup each: fat-free half-and-half, or fat-free milk, fat-free sour cream

1 tablespoon margarine, or butter, melted

2 eggs

½ teaspoon each: baking powder, dried savory and thyme leaves, salt

¼ teaspoon cayenne pepper

Per Serving:
Calories: 182
% of calories from fat: 25
Fat (gm): 5
Saturated fat (gm): 1
Cholesterol (mg): 59
Sodium (mg): 524
Protein (gm): 9
Carbohydrate (gm): 27

Exchanges:
Milk: 0.0
Vegetable: 0.0
Fruit: 0.0
Bread: 2.0
Meat: 0.0
Fat: 1.0

1. Coat greased 1-quart soufflé dish with bread crumbs; coat with bread crumbs. Process corn and remaining ingredients in blender or food processor until coarsely chopped. Pour into soufflé dish and bake at 350 degrees until puffed and set in the center, 45 to 50 minutes. Serve immediately.

SEASONED EGGPLANT SAUTÉ

V

Simply delicious and easy to make!

45

4 servings

1½ pounds eggplant, unpeeled, cubed (¾-inch)
1 cup chopped onions
½ cup chopped red bell pepper
6 cloves garlic, minced
¾ teaspoon each: dried oregano and thyme leaves
¼ teaspoon crushed red pepper
½ cup reduced-sodium vegetable broth
Salt and pepper, to taste

Per Serving:
Calories: 83
% of calories from fat: 6
Fat (gm): 0.6
Saturated fat (gm): 0.1
Cholesterol (mg): 0
Sodium (mg): 18
Protein (gm): 2.8
Carbohydrate (gm): 19.3

Exchanges:
Milk: 0.0
Vegetable: 3.0
Fruit: 0.0
Bread: 0.0
Meat: 0.0
Fat: 0.0

1. Sauté vegetables, herbs, and red pepper in lightly greased large skillet 5 minutes. Add broth and heat to boiling; reduce heat and simmer, covered, until vegetables are tender and broth absorbed, 15 to 20 minutes. Season to taste with salt and pepper.

EGGPLANT AND TOMATO CASSEROLE

LO

Assemble the casserole up to a day in advance, then bake before serving — perfect potluck fare!

45
◊

8 servings

1 large eggplant (2 pounds), peeled, cut into
    1-inch cubes
½ cup seasoned dry bread crumbs
⅓ cup chopped onion
3 cloves garlic, minced
2 teaspoons dried Italian seasoning
Salt and pepper, to taste
2 eggs
3 medium tomatoes, sliced
¼ cup grated fat-free Parmesan cheese

Per Serving:
Calories: 98
% of calories from fat: 16
Fat (gm): 1.9
Saturated fat (gm): 0.5
Cholesterol (mg): 53.3
Sodium (mg): 245
Protein (gm): 5.1
Carbohydrate (gm): 16.9

Exchanges:
Milk: 0.0
Vegetable: 2.0
Fruit: 0.0
Bread: 0.5
Meat: 0.0
Fat: 0.5

1. Cook eggplant in 2 inches simmering water in medium sauce-pan, covered, until tender, 5 to 8 minutes; drain. Mash eggplant with fork; mix in bread crumbs, onion, garlic, and Italian seasoning. Season to taste with salt and pepper; mix in eggs. Spoon into greased 11 x 7-inch baking dish; arrange tomatoes over top and sprinkle with cheese. Bake, uncovered, at 350 degrees until casse-role is hot and tomatoes tender, about 20 minutes.

LEMON-SPIKED GARLIC GREENS

Kale, collard, turnip, or beet greens make excellent choices for this quick and easy healthful dish.

4 servings

¼ cup each: finely chopped onion, red bell pepper

4 cloves garlic, minced

1½ pounds greens, coarsely chopped

⅓ cup water

1–2 tablespoons lemon juice

Salt and pepper, to taste

1 hard-cooked egg, chopped

Per Serving:
Calories: 58
% of calories from fat: 23
Fat (gm): 1.7
Saturated fat (gm): 0.4
Cholesterol (mg): 53.3
Sodium (mg): 43
Protein (gm): 5.9
Carbohydrate (gm): 7

Exchanges:
Milk: 0.0
Vegetable: 2.0
Fruit: 0.0
Bread: 0.0
Meat: 0.0
Fat: 0.0

1. Sauté onion, bell pepper, and garlic in lightly greased large saucepan until tender, 3 to 4 minutes. Add greens and water; heat to boiling. Reduce heat and simmer, covered, until greens are wilted and tender, about 5 minutes, adding more water if necessary. Season to taste with lemon juice, salt, and pepper. Spoon into bowl; sprinkle with egg.

BRAISED KALE

L

45

Packed with vitamins and minerals, kale and other dark leafy greens offer a nutritional bonus. Try other greens such as beet, turnip, or mustard with this recipe too.

4 servings

1 medium leek (white part only), or 6 green
   onions, sliced

2–3 teaspoons olive oil

1 pound kale, torn into pieces

½ cup water

½–1 teaspoon vegetable bouillon crystals

½ cup fat-free sour cream

1 teaspoon Dijon mustard

1–2 tablespoons crumbled cooked vegetarian bacon

Salt and pepper, to taste

Per Serving:
Calories: 109
% of calories from fat: 27
Fat (gm): 3.5
Saturated fat (gm): 0.5
Cholesterol (mg): 0
Sodium (mg): 232
Protein (gm): 5.7
Carbohydrate (gm): 15.8

Exchanges:
Milk: 0.0
Vegetable: 3.0
Fruit: 0.0
Bread: 0.0
Meat: 0.0
Fat: 0.5

1. Sauté leek in oil in large saucepan until tender, 3 to 4 minutes. Add kale, water, and bouillon crystals; heat to boiling. Reduce heat and simmer, covered, until kale is tender, about 5 minutes; cook uncovered until greens are almost dry. Stir in sour cream, mustard, and vegetarian bacon; cook over low heat 2 to 3 minutes. Season to taste with salt and pepper.

SMASHED POTATOES AND GREENS

L

45

The potatoes are not peeled, giving this dish a rustic character.

4 servings

¼ cup finely chopped onion

3 cloves garlic, minced

1½ cups thinly sliced greens (kale, mustard, or
   turnip greens)

¼ cup water

3 medium Idaho potatoes, cubed, cooked

¼ cup fat-free sour cream

2–4 tablespoons fat-free milk

1–2 tablespoons margarine, or butter

Salt and pepper, to taste

Per Serving:
Calories: 141
% of calories from fat: 19
Fat (gm): 3.1
Saturated fat (gm): 0.6
Cholesterol (mg): 0.1
Sodium (mg): 60
Protein (gm): 3.8
Carbohydrate (gm): 25.4

Exchanges:
Milk: 0.0
Vegetable: 2.0
Fruit: 0.0
Bread: 1.0
Meat: 0.0
Fat: 0.5

1. Sauté onion and garlic in lightly greased medium skillet until tender, 3 to 4 minutes. Add greens and water; heat to boiling. Cook, covered, until greens are tender about 5 minutes; cook, uncovered, until water has evaporated and greens are almost dry.

2. Mash potatoes with sour cream, milk, and margarine; stir into greens mixture and cook over low heat until hot, about 5 minutes. Season to taste with salt and pepper.

45-MINUTE PREP TIP: Begin cooking potatoes before preparing the rest of the recipe.

SAUTÉED LEEKS AND PEPPERS

V

A colorful side dish that will brighten any meal!

45   **6 servings**

3 medium leeks (white parts only), sliced (½-inch)
½ cup each: sliced yellow, red, and green
  bell pepper
½ teaspoon dried bouquet garni
Salt and pepper, to taste

1. Cook vegetables and bouquet garni in lightly greased large skillet, covered, over medium heat until wilted, 5 to 8 minutes. Cook, uncovered, until vegetables are tender and beginning to brown, about 5 minutes. Season to taste with salt and pepper.

Per Serving:
Calories: 63
% of calories from fat: 5
Fat (gm): 0.4
Saturated fat (gm): 0
Cholesterol (mg): 0
Sodium (mg): 13
Protein (gm): 2
Carbohydrate (gm): 14.6

Exchanges:
Milk: 0.0
Vegetable: 2.5
Fruit: 0.0
Bread: 0.0
Meat: 0.0
Fat: 0.0

MUSHROOMS WITH SOUR CREAM

L

Cooking the mushrooms very slowly until deeply browned intensifies their flavor. Especially delicious served with pierogi, ravioli, or grilled eggplant slices!

45

4 servings

12 ounces shiitake, or cremini, mushrooms, stems discarded, sliced
¼ cup finely chopped onion
1 teaspoon minced garlic

¼ cup dry white wine, or reduced-sodium
  vegetable broth
¼ teaspoon dried thyme leaves
½ cup fat-free sour cream
Salt and cayenne pepper, to taste

Per Serving:
Calories: 80
% of calories from fat: 2
Fat (gm): 0.2
Saturated fat (gm): 0.1
Cholesterol (mg): 0
Sodium (mg): 24
Protein (gm): 3.5
Carbohydrate (gm): 16.5

Exchanges:
Milk: 0.0
Vegetable: 2.0
Fruit: 0.0
Bread: 0.5
Meat: 0.0
Fat: 0.0

1. Sauté mushrooms, onion, and garlic in lightly greased large skillet 3 to 4 minutes. Add wine and thyme; heat to boiling. Reduce heat and simmer, covered, until mushrooms are very tender, 8 to 10 minutes. Cook, uncovered, on low heat until mushrooms are dry and well browned, 20 to 25 minutes. Stir in sour cream; season to taste with salt and pepper.

GULFPORT OKRA

V

Select small okra for best flavor and tenderness.

45 **6 servings**

1½ pounds fresh, or frozen, thawed, okra
Garlic powder, to taste
Salt and pepper, to taste

Per Serving:
Calories: 37
% of calories from fat: 4
Fat (gm): 0.2
Saturated fat (gm): 0.1
Cholesterol (mg): 0
Sodium (mg): 6
Protein (gm): 2.1
Carbohydrate (gm): 8.2

Exchanges:
Milk: 0.0
Vegetable: 1.5
Fruit: 0.0
Bread: 0.0
Meat: 0.0
Fat: 0.0

1. Cook okra in boiling water 1 to 2 minutes; drain. Cook okra in lightly greased large skillet over medium heat until well browned, almost black, about 10 minutes, stirring occasionally. Sprinkle generously with garlic powder; season to taste with salt and pepper.

QUARTET OF ONIONS

V

45

Cooked slowly until caramelized, the onion mixture is scented with a combination of mint and sage.

6 servings

2 pounds sweet onions, sliced

1 small leek (white part only), thinly sliced

½ cup each: chopped shallots, sliced green onions, reduced sodium vegetable broth

1–1½ teaspoons dried mint leaves

¼ teaspoon dried sage leaves

Salt and white pepper, to taste

Per Serving:
Calories: 90
% of calories from fat: 4
Fat (gm): 0.4
Saturated fat (gm): 0.1
Cholesterol (mg): 0
Sodium (mg): 16
Protein (gm): 2.7
Carbohydrate (gm): 20.1

Exchanges:
Milk: 0.0
Vegetable: 4.0
Fruit: 0.0
Bread: 0.0
Meat: 0.0
Fat: 0.0

1. Sauté onions, leek, shallots, and green onions in lightly greased large skillet 3 to 4 minutes, stirring frequently. Stir in broth and herbs and heat to boiling; reduce heat and simmer, covered, 5 minutes. Cook, uncovered, over medium-low heat until onion mixture is golden, about 15 minutes. Season to taste with salt and white pepper.

FRUIT-STUFFED VIDALIA ONIONS

V

45

◊

The onions can be poached and filled with fruit up to 1 day in advance; bake until hot through and tender, 30 to 35 minutes.

4 servings

2 large Vidalia onions, cut crosswise into halves

½ cup each: water, dry white wine

4 each: whole peppercorns, allspice

1 teaspoon mustard seeds

2 bay leaves

Salt, to taste

1 small apple, unpeeled, finely chopped

¼ cup each: chopped dried fruit, golden raisins

2–3 teaspoons sugar

Per Serving:
Calories: 142
% of calories from fat: 4
Fat (gm): 0.6
Saturated fat (gm): 0.1
Cholesterol (mg): 0
Sodium (mg): 7
Protein (gm): 1.9
Carbohydrate (gm): 30.5

Exchanges:
Milk: 0.0
Vegetable: 2.0
Fruit: 1.5
Bread: 0.0
Meat: 0.0
Fat: 0.0

1. Cut small slices off bottoms of onion halves so that onions can stand securely. Remove centers of onions, leaving scant ¾-inch shells; chop onion centers and reserve. Stand onions in medium skillet; add water, wine, and seasonings; heat to boiling. Reduce heat and simmer, covered, until crisp-tender, about 10 minutes. Remove onions with slotted spoon and transfer to baking pan; sprinkle lightly with salt. Reserve ¼ cup cooking liquid.

2. Sauté reserved onion centers and apple in lightly greased small skillet until tender, about 5 minutes. Stir in reserved ¼ cup cooking liquid, dried fruit, raisins, and sugar; cook over medium-low heat until liquid is absorbed. Spoon into onion halves. Bake, covered, at 375 degrees until onions are tender, 20 to 30 minutes.

BRAISED PARSNIPS AND WINTER VEGETABLES

V

45

Idaho or sweet potatoes, winter squash, or Brussels sprouts would be flavorful additions to this colorful vegetable dish.

6 servings

¼ cup minced onion

2 teaspoons minced garlic

1 cup each: cubed parsnips, sliced carrots, julienned celery root, or celery, and shredded red, or green, cabbage

½ cup dry red wine, or vegetable broth

2 tablespoons light brown sugar

1 teaspoon balsamic, or red wine, vinegar

¾ teaspoon each: dried sage and thyme leaves

Salt and pepper, to taste

Per Serving:
Calories: 92
% of calories from fat: 3
Fat (gm): 0.3
Saturated fat (gm): 0.1
Cholesterol (mg): 0
Sodium (mg): 47
Protein (gm): 1.5
Carbohydrate (gm): 19.3

Exchanges:
Milk: 0.0
Vegetable: 2.0
Fruit: 0.0
Bread: 0.5
Meat: 0.0
Fat: 0.0

1. Sauté onion and garlic in lightly greased large skillet 2 to 3 minutes; add remaining vegetables and sauté until beginning to brown, 4 to 5 minutes. Add remaining ingredients, except salt and pepper, and heat to boiling; reduce heat and simmer, covered, until vegetables are tender, 8 to 10 minutes. Season to taste with salt and pepper.

TINY PEAS AND ONIONS

V

45

The refreshing flavors of mint and dill are often used together in Mediterranean dishes.

6 servings

½ package (16-ounce size) frozen pearl onions
1 package (8 ounces) frozen tiny peas
¼ cup water
2–3 teaspoons margarine, or butter
½ teaspoon each: dried mint leaves, dill weed
Salt and pepper, to taste

1. Heat onions and water to boiling in medium saucepan; reduce heat and simmer until tender, 8 to 10 minutes, adding peas during the last 5 minutes. Drain. Add margarine and herbs, stirring until melted. Season to taste with salt and pepper.

Per Serving:
Calories: 63
% of calories from fat: 20
Fat (gm): 1.4
Saturated fat (gm): 0.3
Cholesterol (mg): 0
Sodium (mg): 57
Protein (gm): 2.5
Carbohydrate (gm): 10.4

Exchanges:
Milk: 0.0
Vegetable: 0.0
Fruit: 0.0
Bread: 1.0
Meat: 0.0
Fat: 0.0

PEPERONATA

V

45

Sweet bell peppers and onions are slowly cooked until tender and creamy in this Italian-inspired dish.

8 servings

2 cups sliced onions
1 cup each: sliced green and red bell pepper
6 cloves garlic, minced
¼ cup water
Salt and pepper, to taste

1. Cook onions, bell peppers, and garlic in lightly greased medium skillet over medium heat 5 minutes, stirring occasionally. Add water and cook, covered, over medium-low heat until vegetables are very tender and creamy, 20 to 25 minutes, stirring occasionally. Season to taste with salt and pepper.

Per Serving:
Calories: 29
% of calories from fat: 4
Fat (gm): 0.1
Saturated fat (gm): 0.0
Cholesterol (mg): 0.0
Sodium (mg): 2.5
Protein (gm): 1
Carbohydrate (gm): 7

Exchanges:
Milk: 0.0
Vegetable: 1.0
Fruit: 0.0
Bread: 0.0
Meat: 0.0
Fat: 0.0

REAL MASHED POTATOES

L

45

Just like grandma used to make! For a country-style variation, leave potatoes unpeeled.

6 servings (about ⅔ cup each)

2 pounds Idaho potatoes, peeled, quartered, cooked until tender

½ cup fat-free sour cream

¼ cup fat-free milk, hot

2 tablespoons margarine, or butter

Salt and pepper, to taste

Per Serving:
Calories: 112
% of calories from fat: 19
Fat (gm): 2
Saturated fat (gm): 0.5
Cholesterol (mg): 2.1
Sodium (mg): 44
Protein (gm): 3
Carbohydrate (gm): 20

Exchanges:
Milk: 0.0
Vegetable: 0.0
Fruit: 0.0
Bread: 1.5
Meat: 0.0
Fat: 0.5

1. Mash potatoes, or beat until smooth, in medium bowl, adding sour cream, milk, and margarine. Season to taste with salt and pepper.

Variations

Garlic Mashed Potatoes — Cook 10 peeled cloves of garlic with the potatoes. Follow recipe above, mashing garlic with potatoes.

Horseradish Mashed Potatoes — Make Real or Garlic Mashed Potatoes, beating in 2 teaspoons horseradish.

Potato Pancakes — Make any of the mashed potato recipes above; refrigerate until chilled. Mix in 1 egg, 4 chopped green onions, and ¼ cup grated fat-free Parmesan cheese. Form mixture into 8 patties, using about ½ cup mixture for each. Coat patties in flour, dip in beaten egg white, and coat with plain dry bread crumbs. Cook over medium heat in lightly greased large skillet until browned, 3 to 5 minutes on each side.

CREAMY POTATO AND BEAN MASHERS

L

Beans boost flavor and nutrition in this great dish!

45 **6 servings** (about ⅔ cup each)

1 pound Idaho potatoes, unpeeled, quartered, cooked

1 can (15½ ounces) Great Northern, or navy, beans, rinsed, drained

1–2 teaspoon minced roasted garlic

2 tablespoons margarine, or butter

¼–½ cup fat-free milk, hot

Salt and pepper, to taste

Per Serving:
Calories: 187
% of calories from fat: 20
Fat (gm): 4
Saturated fat (gm): 0.9
Cholesterol (mg): 0.2
Sodium (mg): 55
Protein (gm): 7
Carbohydrate (gm): 31

Exchanges:
Milk: 0.0
Vegetable: 0.0
Fruit: 0.0
Bread: 2.0
Meat: 0.0
Fat: 1.0

1. Mash potatoes, beans, garlic, and margarine in medium bowl, adding enough milk for desired consistency; season to taste with salt and pepper. Heat in saucepan over medium heat until hot, about 5 minutes.

Variations

Cheesy Bean and Onion Mashers — Sauté 1 cup chopped onion in 1 tablespoon margarine in small skillet until tender, about 5 minutes. Make recipe as above, adding onion and remaining 1 tablespoon margarine.

Lima Bean and Mushroom Mashers — Sauté 1 cup quartered cremini mushrooms in 2 tablespoons margarine in small skillet until tender, about 5 minutes. Make recipe as above, substituting lima beans for the Great Northern beans and deleting margarine; stir in mushrooms.

POTATOES GRATIN

These potatoes taste so rich and creamy you'll never imagine they were made without heavy cream!

8 servings (about ½ cup each)

2 tablespoons margarine, or butter

3 tablespoons flour

1¾ cups fat-free milk

2 ounces light pasteurized processed cheese, cubed

½ cup (2 ounces) shredded reduced-fat
  Cheddar cheese

Salt and pepper, to taste

2 pounds Idaho potatoes, peeled, sliced (¼-inch)

¼ cup thinly sliced onion

Ground nutmeg, to taste

Per Serving:
Calories: 202
% of calories from fat: 23
Fat (gm): 5.1
Saturated fat (gm): 1.7
Cholesterol (mg): 8.5
Sodium (mg): 259
Protein (gm): 7.6
Carbohydrate (gm): 31.7

Exchanges:
Milk: 0.0
Vegetable: 0.0
Fruit: 0.0
Bread: 2.0
Meat: 0.5
Fat: 0.5

1. Melt margarine in medium saucepan; stir in flour and cook over medium heat, stirring, 2 minutes. Whisk in milk and heat to boiling; boil, whisking, until thickened, about 1 minute. Remove from heat; add cheeses, stirring until melted. Season to taste with salt and pepper.

2. Layer ⅓ of the potatoes and onion in greased 2-quart casserole; sprinkle lightly with salt, pepper, and nutmeg. Spoon ⅔ cup sauce over. Repeat layers 2 times. Bake, covered, at 350 degrees for 45 minutes; uncover and bake until potatoes are fork-tender and browned, 20 to 30 minutes.

Variation

Scalloped Potatoes — Make sauce as above, increasing margarine to 3 tablespoons, flour to ¼ cup, and milk to 2¼ cups; delete cheeses. Assemble and bake as directed.

TWICE-BAKED POTATOES WITH CHEESE

L

45

These stuffed bakers are always a favorite! The potatoes can be prepared and refrigerated 24 hours in advance; increase baking time to 20 to 25 minutes.

4 servings

2 large Idaho potatoes (8 ounces each)

¼ cup each: fat-free sour cream, fat-free milk

¾ cup (3 ounces) shredded reduced-fat sharp, or mild Cheddar cheese, divided

Salt and pepper, to taste

Paprika, as garnish

Per Serving:
Calories: 177
% of calories from fat: 16
Fat (gm): 3.2
Saturated fat (gm): 1.6
Cholesterol (mg): 11.6
Sodium (mg): 314
Protein (gm): 8.4
Carbohydrate (gm): 29.2

Exchanges:
Milk: 0.0
Vegetable: 0.0
Fruit: 0.0
Bread: 2.0
Meat: 0.5
Fat: 0.0

1. Pierce potatoes with a fork; grease lightly and bake at 400 degrees until tender, about 1 hour. Cut lengthwise into halves; let stand until cool enough to handle. Scoop out potatoes, being careful to leave shells intact. Mash potatoes in medium bowl, adding sour cream, milk, and ½ cup cheese; season to taste with salt and pepper. Spoon into potato shells; sprinkle with remaining ¼ cup cheese and paprika. Bake, uncovered, at 400 degrees until hot, 15 to 20 minutes.

VEGGIE-STUFFED BAKERS

L

45

The potatoes are greased and baked for a crispy skin; for a softer skin, wrap in aluminum foil.

6 servings

2 large Idaho potatoes (8–10 ounces each)

⅓ cup fat-free sour cream, or plain yogurt

¾ cup (3 ounces) shredded fat-free Cheddar cheese, divided

1 cup each: chopped onion, green bell pepper

½ cup whole-kernel corn

4 cloves garlic, minced

Salt and pepper, to taste

1 cup broccoli florets, cooked crisp-tender

Per Serving:
Calories: 160
% of calories from fat: 2
Fat (gm): 0.3
Saturated fat (gm): 0
Cholesterol (mg): 0
Sodium (mg): 119
Protein (gm): 9
Carbohydrate (gm): 32.4

Exchanges:
Milk: 0.0
Vegetable: 1.0
Fruit: 0.0
Bread: 1.5
Meat: 0.5
Fat: 0.0

1. Pierce potatoes with a fork; grease lightly and bake at 400 degrees until tender, about 1 hour. Cut lengthwise into halves; let stand until cool enough to handle. Scoop out potatoes, being careful to leave shells intact. Mash potatoes in medium bowl, adding sour cream and half the Cheddar cheese.

2. Sauté onion, bell pepper, corn, and garlic in lightly greased medium skillet until tender, about 5 minutes. Mix into potatoes; season to taste with salt and pepper. Spoon into potato shells; arrange broccoli on top and sprinkle with remaining cheese. Bake, uncovered, at 350 degrees until hot, 20 to 30 minutes.

CRISPY FRENCH "FRIES"

V

45

Golden brown, delicious, and crisp, these potatoes look and taste like they've been deep-fried: the secret is salting the raw potatoes!

4–6 servings

1 pound Idaho potatoes, unpeeled
2 teaspoons salt
Vegetable cooking spray
Salt and pepper, to taste

Per Serving:
Calories: 166
% of calories from fat: 1
Fat (gm): 0.2
Saturated fat (gm): 0
Cholesterol (mg): 0
Sodium (mg): 12
Protein (gm): 3.5
Carbohydrate (gm): 38.6

Exchanges:
Milk: 0.0
Vegetable: 0.0
Fruit: 0.0
Bread: 2.5
Meat: 0.0
Fat: 0.0

1. Cut potatoes into sticks 3 to 4 inches long and a scant ½ inch wide. Sprinkle lightly with 2 teaspoons salt and let stand 10 minutes. Rinse in cold water and dry on paper toweling. Arrange potatoes in single layer on greased foil-lined jelly roll pan; spray with cooking spray, tossing to coat all sides. Sprinkle lightly with salt and pepper. Bake at 350 degrees until golden brown and crisp, 40 to 45 minutes, turning halfway through cooking time.

NOTE: Potatoes can be kept warm in a 200-degree oven for up to 1 hour.

Variations

Parmesan "Fries" — Follow recipe, sprinkling potatoes lightly with grated fat-free Parmesan cheese before baking.

Steak Fries — Cut potatoes into wedges 4 inches long and 1 inch wide. Follow recipe as above, baking until golden brown and crisp, 1 to 1¼ hours.

POTATOES WITH POBLANO CHILIES

V

Serve with a fried egg and salsa for brunch.

45

4 servings (about ⅔ cup each)

4 medium poblano chilies, halved

1 medium onion, sliced

1 pound Idaho potatoes, unpeeled, cooked,
    cubed (½-inch)

Salt and pepper, to taste

Per Serving:
Calories: 147
% of calories from fat: 2
Fat (gm): 0.3
Saturated fat (gm): 0.1
Cholesterol (mg): 0
Sodium (mg): 11
Protein (gm): 3.7
Carbohydrate (gm): 34

Exchanges:
Milk: 0.0
Vegetable: 1.0
Fruit: 0.0
Bread: 1,5
Meat: 0.0
Fat: 0.0

1. Place chilies, skin sides up, on broiler pan; broil 6 inches from heat source until skin is blackened and blistered. Place chilies in plastic bag or paper toweling 5 minutes; peel off skin and discard. Cut chilies into strips.

2. Sauté onion in lightly greased large skillet 2 to 3 minutes; add chilies and potatoes. Cook over medium heat until onion is tender and potatoes browned, 5 to 8 minutes. Season to taste with salt and pepper.

CANDIED YAMS

V

Whether they are called yams or sweet potatoes in your family, the sweet goodness of this dish is the same! If marshmallows are a must, add them 10 minutes before the end of baking time.

45

8–10 servings

⅓ cup packed light brown sugar

2 tablespoons light corn syrup

1 tablespoon each: flour, margarine

1 can (40 ounces) cut sweet potatoes in syrup, drained, sliced

1. Combine brown sugar, corn syrup, flour, and margarine in small saucepan; heat just to boiling, stirring. Layer sweet potatoes in 10 x 6-inch baking dish, spooning sugar mixture between each layer and over the top. Bake, uncovered, at 350 degrees until hot, 25 to 30 minutes.

NOTE: Two pounds fresh sweet potatoes can be substituted for the canned. Peel and slice potatoes. Cook, covered, in medium saucepan in 2 to 3 inches of simmering water until fork-tender, about 10 minutes. Drain well, cool slightly, and proceed with recipe.

Per Serving:
Calories: 176
% of calories from fat: 8
Fat (gm): 1.5
Saturated fat (gm): 0.3
Cholesterol (mg): 0
Sodium (mg): 63
Protein (gm): 1.5
Carbohydrate (gm): 39.5

Exchanges:
Milk: 0.0
Vegetable: 0.0
Fruit: 0.0
Bread: 2.5
Meat: 0.0
Fat: 0.0

HOLIDAY SWEET POTATO LOAF WITH APPLE-CRANBERRY RELISH

Perfect for the winter holidays — but this loaf is so delicious and easy to make, you'll want to serve it year-round.

12 servings

2½ cups coarsely grated, peeled sweet potatoes
1 each: finely chopped onion, tart cooking apple
½ cup raisins
1 teaspoon dried thyme leaves
½ teaspoon ground cinnamon
¼ teaspoon ground nutmeg
½ cup all-purpose flour
¼ cup orange juice
Salt and pepper, to taste
2 eggs
1 egg white
Apple-Cranberry Relish (see p. 609)

Per Serving:
Calories: 421
% of calories from fat: 12
Fat (gm): 5.6
Saturated fat (gm): 1
Cholesterol (mg): 71
Sodium (mg): 63.6
Protein (gm): 7.3
Carbohydrate (gm): 88.9

Exchanges:
Milk: 0.0
Vegetable: 0.0
Fruit: 3.0
Bread: 3.0
Meat: 0.0
Fat: 0.5

1. Mix sweet potatoes, onion, apple, raisins, seasonings, flour, and orange juice in bowl; season to taste with salt and pepper. Mix in eggs and egg white. Pack mixture in greased 7½ x 3¾-inch loaf pan. Bake, covered, at 350 degrees until loaf is set, about 1 hour.

Let stand 10 minutes before serving. Loosen sides of loaf with sharp knife; unmold onto serving plate. Slice loaf and serve with Apple-Cranberry Relish.

ORANGE-LIME SWEET POTATOES

V

45

Sweet potatoes are gently sauced with citrus juices; use freshly squeezed juices for best flavor.

4 servings (about ⅔ cup each)

1 cup chopped onion
1 teaspoon minced garlic
1 pound sweet potatoes, peeled, cubed (1-inch)
1 cup orange juice
¼ cup lime juice
Salt and pepper, to taste

1. Sauté onion and garlic in lightly greased medium skillet 3 to 4 minutes. Add sweet potatoes and juices; heat to boiling. Reduce heat and simmer, covered, until potatoes are tender, about 10 minutes. Cook, uncovered, until sauce is thickened, 8 to 10 minutes. Season to taste with salt and pepper.

Per Serving:
Calories: 143
% of calories from fat: 3
Fat (gm): 0.5
Saturated fat (gm): 0.1
Cholesterol (mg): 0
Sodium (mg): 14
Protein (gm): 2.6
Carbohydrate (gm): 33.5

Exchanges:
Milk: 0.0
Vegetable: 0.0
Fruit: 0.5
Bread: 1.5
Meat: 0.0
Fat: 0.0

SWEET POTATO PONE

LO *More of a country-style pudding than a soufflé, this comfort food will become a favorite. Drizzle with warm maple syrup, if you like.*

6 servings

1 small onion, finely chopped

1 tablespoon margarine, or butter

3 tablespoons flour

1 cup fat-free milk

2 eggs

2 cups cubed sweet potato, cooked, coarsely mashed

2 tablespoons packed light brown sugar

¼ teaspoon each: ground cinnamon, cloves, salt

2–3 dashes white pepper

4 egg whites, beaten to stiff peaks

Per Serving:
Calories: 208
% of calories from fat: 24
Fat (gm): 5.6
Saturated fat (gm): 1.5
Cholesterol (mg): 107
Sodium (mg): 330
Protein (gm): 11
Carbohydrate (gm): 29

Exchanges:
Milk: 0.0
Vegetable: 0.0
Fruit: 0.0
Bread: 2.0
Meat: 1.0
Fat: 0.0

1. Sauté onion in margarine in small saucepan until tender, 3 to 5 minutes. Stir in flour; cook 2 to 3 minutes. Stir in milk and heat to boiling; boil, stirring, until thickened, about 1 minute. Remove from heat.

2. Beat eggs in small bowl until thick and lemon colored, 3 to 4 minutes. Slowly whisk about half the milk mixture into egg; whisk egg mixture back into saucepan. Cook over low heat, whisking, 1 minute; transfer to large bowl. Mix in sweet potato, brown sugar, spices, salt, and pepper; fold in egg whites. Spoon into greased 1-quart soufflé dish or casserole. Bake at 375 degrees until puffed and golden and a sharp knife inserted halfway between center and edge comes out almost clean, 30 to 35 minutes.

CREAMED SPINACH

L

Try this recipe with other healthful greens, such as Swiss chard or kale.

45 **4 servings**

2 packages (10 ounces each) spinach, stems trimmed
¼ cup finely chopped onion
2 teaspoons margarine, or butter
2 tablespoons flour
1 cup fat-free milk, or fat-free half-and-half
¼ cup fat-free sour cream
Ground nutmeg, to taste
Salt and pepper, to taste

Per Serving:
Calories: 92
% of calories from fat: 20
Fat (gm): 2.2
Saturated fat (gm): 0.5
Cholesterol (mg): 1
Sodium (mg): 145
Protein (gm): 6.6
Carbohydrate (gm): 13.3

Exchanges:
Milk: 0.0
Vegetable: 2.5
Fruit: 0.0
Bread: 0.0
Meat: 0.0
Fat: 0.5

1. Rinse spinach and place in large saucepan; cook, covered, over medium-high heat until wilted, 3 to 4 minutes; drain.

2. Sauté onion in margarine in small saucepan until tender, 3 to 5 minutes. Stir in flour; cook 1 minute, stirring. Whisk in milk; heat to boiling. Boil, whisking, until thickened, about 1 minute. Remove from heat and stir in sour cream. Pour sauce over spinach and mix lightly; season to taste with nutmeg, salt, and pepper.

Variation

Spinach au Gratin — Prepare recipe as directed above, reserving ¼ cup sauce; mix spinach and remaining sauce and spoon into a small casserole. Spread reserved ¼ cup sauce over spinach; sprinkle with ¼ cup (1 ounce) grated fat-free Parmesan or Cheddar cheese. Bake, uncovered, at 375 degrees until cheese is melted, 5 to 8 minutes.

APPLE-PECAN ACORN SQUASH

V *Fruit and maple flavors complement sweet, baked winter squash.*

45

4 servings

1 large acorn squash, quartered, seeded
½ cup coarsely chopped mixed dried fruit
1 small sweet apple, cored, coarsely chopped
¼–½ cup coarsely chopped, toasted pecans
½ teaspoon ground cinnamon
⅛ teaspoon each: ground nutmeg, mace
¼–½ cup maple syrup

Per Serving:
Calories: 187
% of calories from fat: 1
Fat (gm): 0.3
Saturated fat (gm): 0.1
Cholesterol (mg): 0
Sodium (mg): 39
Protein (gm): 1.7
Carbohydrate (gm): 47

Exchanges:
Milk: 0.0
Vegetable: 0.0
Fruit: 2.0
Bread: 1.0
Meat: 0.0
Fat: 0.0

1. Place squash quarters, cut sides up, in baking pan; add ½ inch hot water. Bake, covered, at 400 degrees until squash is fork-tender, about 30 minutes. Spoon combined fruit, pecans, and spices into squash; drizzle with maple syrup. Bake, loosely covered, at 350 degrees until apples are tender, about 10 minutes.

ZUCCHINI FANS PROVENÇAL

V *Zucchini are thinly sliced, then spread out to form "fans."*

45

4 servings

2 medium sweet onions, thinly sliced
6 cloves garlic, minced
4 small zucchini, halved lengthwise
3 medium tomatoes, thinly sliced
½ cup dry white wine, or reduced-sodium
   vegetable broth, warm
Salt and pepper, to taste
1½ teaspoons dried Italian seasoning

Per Serving:
Calories: 89
% of calories from fat: 6
Fat (gm): 0.6
Saturated fat (gm): 0.1
Cholesterol (mg): 0
Sodium (mg): 16
Protein (gm): 3.4
Carbohydrate (gm): 15.3

Exchanges:
Milk: 0.0
Vegetable: 3.0
Fruit: 0.0
Bread: 0.0
Meat: 0.0
Fat: 0.0

1. Separate onions into rings; arrange half the onions and garlic in bottom of 11 x 7-inch baking pan. Cut zucchini halves lengthwise into scant ¼-inch slices, cutting to, but not through, small ends. Alternate zucchini and tomato slices in rows over onions, spreading zucchini slices into "fans." Arrange remaining onions and garlic on top; pour wine over. Sprinkle lightly with salt, pepper and Italian seasoning. Bake, covered, at 350 degrees until zucchini is tender, about 25 minutes.

ZUCCHINI FROM PUEBLO

L

45

If the Mexican white cheese "queso blanco" is not available, farmer's cheese can be easily substituted.

6 servings (about ½ cup each)

1 cup chopped onion

2 pounds zucchini, diagonally sliced (¼-inch)

4 roasted red bell peppers, sliced

½ cup reduced-sodium vegetable broth

½–1 teaspoon ground cumin

½ cup fat-free milk

Salt and pepper, to taste

2 tablespoons crumbled Mexican white cheese

Per Serving:
Calories: 62
% of calories from fat: 14
Fat (gm): 1
Saturated fat (gm): 0.1
Cholesterol (mg): 2.6
Sodium (mg): 32
Protein (gm): 2.9
Carbohydrate (gm): 11.8

Exchanges:
Milk: 0.0
Vegetable: 2.0
Fruit: 0.0
Bread: 0.0
Meat: 0.0
Fat: 0.0

1. Sauté onion in lightly greased large skillet until tender, 5 to 8 minutes. Add zucchini, roasted peppers, broth, and cumin. Heat to boiling. Reduce heat and simmer, covered, just until zucchini is crisp-tender, 5 to 8 minutes. Add milk; cook until hot, 1 to 2 minutes. Season to taste with salt and pepper; sprinkle with cheese.

SPAGHETTI SQUASH PARMESAN

L

45

The delicate flavor of the squash is complemented by the combination of Italian seasoning and Parmesan cheese.

4 servings

1 spaghetti squash (2½–3 pounds), cut lengthwise into halves, seeded

2 tablespoons sliced green onions

1 teaspoon minced garlic

1–2 tablespoons margarine, or butter

¼ cup reduced-sodium vegetable broth

1 teaspoon dried Italian seasoning

½ cup (2 ounces) fat-free Parmesan cheese

Salt and pepper, to taste

Per Serving:
Calories: 99
% of calories from fat: 29
Fat (gm): 3.6
Saturated fat (gm): 0.7
Cholesterol (mg): 0
Sodium (mg): 102
Protein (gm): 5.1
Carbohydrate (gm): 14.3

Exchanges:
Milk: 0.0
Vegetable: 2.0
Fruit: 0.0
Bread: 0.0
Meat: 0.5
Fat: 0.5

1. Place squash, cut sides down, in baking pan; add ½ inch hot water. Bake, covered, at 400 degrees until fork-tender, 30 to 40 minutes. Fluff strands of squash with tines of fork, leaving squash in shells.

2. Sauté green onions and garlic in margarine in small saucepan until tender, 3 to 4 minutes. Stir in broth and Italian seasoning; heat to boiling. Spoon half the mixture into each squash half and toss; sprinkle with Parmesan cheese and toss. Season to taste with salt and pepper.

CHAYOTE WITH PUMPKIN SEEDS

V

45

To toast the pumpkin seeds ("pepitas"), cook over medium heat in a lightly greased skillet. They will begin to pop and jump in the skillet, signaling that they are toasted!

4 servings

½ cup finely chopped onion

2 cloves garlic, minced

1 chayote squash, peeled, pitted, cubed (½-inch)

4 teaspoons pumpkin seeds, toasted

Salt and pepper, to taste

Per Serving:
Calories: 35
% of calories from fat: 16
Fat (gm): 0.7
Saturated fat (gm): 0.1
Cholesterol (mg): 0
Sodium (mg): 2
Protein (gm): 1.1
Carbohydrate (gm): 7

Exchanges:
Milk: 0.0
Vegetable: 1.5
Fruit: 0.0
Bread: 0.0
Meat: 0.0
Fat: 0.0

1. Sauté onion and garlic in lightly greased large skillet until tender, 3 to 5 minutes. Add squash and cook over medium heat until squash is crisp-tender, about 20 minutes, stirring occasionally. Stir in pumpkin seeds; season to taste with salt and pepper.

SAUTÉED SUMMER SQUASH WITH SNOW PEAS

V

45

The vegetables are best when crisp-tender, so don't overcook! Zucchini or chayote squash may also be used in the recipe.

4 servings

2 each: sliced green onions, minced garlic cloves

1½ cups yellow summer squash

2 ounces snow peas

1 tablespoon finely chopped fresh, or 1 teaspoon dried, tarragon, or basil leaves

Salt and white pepper, to taste

Per Serving:
Calories: 27
% of calories from fat: 10
Fat (gm): 0.3
Saturated fat (gm): 0.1
Cholesterol (mg): 0
Sodium (mg): 2
Protein (gm): 1.4
Carbohydrate (gm): 5.7

Exchanges:
Milk: 0.0
Vegetable: 1.0
Fruit: 0.0
Bread: 0.0
Meat: 0.0
Fat: 0.0

1. Sauté green onions and garlic in lightly greased large skillet 2 to 3 minutes. Add squash, snow peas, and tarragon to skillet and cook over medium heat until vegetables are crisp-tender, about 5 minutes. Season to taste with salt and pepper.

TOMATO PUDDING

V

45

Dry stuffing cubes can be substituted for the croutons. Two cups coarsely chopped fresh tomatoes can be substituted for the canned tomatoes; simmer until tomatoes wilt and release juices, 5 to 8 minutes.

4 servings

½ cup each: thinly sliced celery, chopped onion, green bell pepper

1 can (16 ounces) reduced-sodium whole tomatoes, undrained, coarsely chopped

½ teaspoon each: celery seeds, dried marjoram leaves

1 tablespoon light brown sugar

Salt and pepper, to taste

1½ cups (½ recipe) Sourdough Croutons (see p. 560)

Per Serving:
Calories: 85
% of calories from fat: 9
Fat (gm): 0.9
Saturated fat (gm): 0.1
Cholesterol (mg): 0
Sodium (mg): 88
Protein (gm): 2.6
Carbohydrate (gm): 17.9

Exchanges:
Milk: 0.0
Vegetable: 2.0
Fruit: 0.0
Bread: 0.5
Meat: 0.0
Fat: 0.0

1. Sauté celery, onion, and bell pepper in lightly greased medium skillet until tender, about 8 minutes. Add tomatoes, celery seeds, marjoram, and brown sugar; cook over medium heat until hot, about 5 minutes. Spoon into 1-quart soufflé dish or casserole; season to taste with salt and pepper. Stir in Sourdough Croutons, leaving some of the croutons on the top. Bake, uncovered, at 425 degrees until hot, about 20 minutes.

45-MINUTE PREP TIP: Make Sourdough Croutons before preparing the rest of the recipe.

HERBED TOMATO HALVES

L

45

Select ripe, yet firm, tomatoes, and vary the herbs to complement the main dish you're serving.

4 servings

4 medium tomatoes, halved

¼ cup (1 ounce) grated fat-free Parmesan cheese

1 tablespoon unseasoned dry bread crumbs

½ teaspoon each: dried basil, marjoram, and thyme leaves

⅛–¼ teaspoon garlic powder

2–3 pinches pepper

Per Serving:
Calories: 45
% of calories from fat: 9
Fat (gm): 0.5
Saturated fat (gm): 0.1
Cholesterol (mg): 0
Sodium (mg): 60
Protein (gm): 2.8
Carbohydrate (gm): 8.8

Exchanges:
Milk: 0.0
Vegetable: 2.0
Fruit: 0.0
Bread: 0.0
Meat: 0.0
Fat: 0.0

1. Place tomatoes, cut sides up, in baking pan; sprinkle with combined remaining ingredients. Bake at 375 degrees until tomatoes are hot and topping is browned, 15 to 20 minutes.

FRIED TOMATOES

V

Either green or red tomatoes can be used in this recipe — try both!

4 servings

4 medium green, or red, tomatoes, sliced (¼-inch)

¼ cup all-purpose flour

Salt and pepper, to taste

Per Serving:
Calories: 58
% of calories from fat: 5
Fat (gm): 0.3
Saturated fat (gm): 0
Cholesterol (mg): 0
Sodium (mg): 16
Protein (gm): 2.3
Carbohydrate (gm): 12.2

Exchanges:
Milk: 0.0
Vegetable: 1.0
Fruit: 0.0
Bread: 0.5
Meat: 0.0
Fat: 0.0

1. Coat tomato slices lightly with flour; cook over medium heat in lightly greased large skillet until browned, 2 to 3 minutes on each side. Sprinkle lightly with salt and pepper.

Variations

Sugar-Glazed Fried Tomatoes — Cook tomatoes as above, but do not coat with flour. After tomatoes are browned, sprinkle lightly with sugar and cook until caramelized, about 1 minute on each side. Do not season with salt and pepper.

Cornmeal-Fried Tomatoes — Cook tomatoes as above, substituting yellow cornmeal for the flour.

GREENS-STUFFED BAKED TOMATOES

We've used turnip greens, but any other flavorful greens, such as kale, mustard greens, or spinach, may be substituted.

6 servings

6 medium tomatoes

10 ounces fresh, or frozen, turnip greens, cooked, coarsely chopped

½ teaspoon each: dried chervil and marjoram leaves

Salt and pepper, to taste

1 tablespoon each: grated fat-free Parmesan cheese, unseasoned dry bread crumbs

1. Cut thin slice from tops of tomatoes; scoop pulp from tomatoes, discarding seeds. Chop pulp and mix with turnip greens and herbs; season to taste with salt and pepper. Spoon into tomatoes and sprinkle with combined cheese and bread crumbs. Place in baking pan and bake at 350 degrees until tender, about 20 minutes.

Per Serving:
Calories: 42
% of calories from fat: 11
Fat (gm): 0.6
Saturated fat (gm): 0.1
Cholesterol (mg): 0
Sodium (mg): 42
Protein (gm): 2.1
Carbohydrate (gm): 9

Exchanges:
Milk: 0.0
Vegetable: 2.0
Fruit: 0.0
Bread: 0.0
Meat: 0.0
Fat: 0.0

FOURTEEN

Salads and Dressings

SPINACH AND MELON SALAD

V *An unusual salad, with melon adding color and flavor contrasts.*

45 **6 side-dish servings** (about 1½ cups each)

8 cups torn spinach
1 cup each: watermelon, honeydew, and
  cantaloupe balls
⅓ cup each: thinly sliced cucumber, red onion
Honey Dressing (recipe follows)

1. Combine all ingredients and toss.

Honey Dressing

Makes ¼ cup

1–2 tablespoons honey
1 tablespoon each: red wine vinegar, olive oil
1–2 tablespoons each: orange and lime juice
½ teaspoon dried tarragon leaves
2–3 dashes each: salt, pepper

1. Mix all ingredients.

45-MINUTE PREP TIP: Make Honey Dressing before preparing the rest of the recipe.

Per Serving:
Calories: 67
% of calories from fat: 31
Fat (gm): 2.5
Saturated fat (gm): 0.3
Cholesterol (mg): 0.0
Sodium (mg): 61
Protein (gm): 2
Carbohydrate (gm): 11

Exchanges:
Milk: 0.0
Vegetable: 0.0
Fruit: 1.0
Bread: 0.0
Meat: 0.0
Fat: 0.0

WILTED SPINACH SALAD

O

45

A delicious favorite that includes crumbled vegetarian bacon for traditional flavor.

4 side-dish servings (about 1 cup each)

1 package (10 ounces) spinach
4 green onions, sliced
2 tablespoons crumbled, cooked vegetarian bacon
1 cup fat-free French dressing, or sweet-sour salad dressing
1 hard-cooked egg, chopped
Salt and pepper, to taste

Per Serving:
Calories: 142
% of calories from fat: 17
Fat (gm): 3
Saturated fat (gm): 0.6
Cholesterol (mg): 53
Sodium (mg): 647
Protein (gm): 5
Carbohydrate (gm): 25

Exchanges:
Milk: 0.0
Vegetable: 0.0
Fruit: 0.0
Bread: 1.5
Meat: 0.0
Fat: 0.5

1. Combine spinach, onions, and vegetarian bacon in salad bowl. Heat French dressing to boiling in small saucepan; immediately pour over salad and toss. Sprinkle egg over salad and toss; season to taste with salt and pepper.

CAESAR SALAD

LO

45

For food safety, use a pasteurized egg or ¼ cup real egg product in the salad.

4 side-dish servings (about 1½ cups each)

4 thick slices French, or Italian, bread
1 clove garlic, cut in half
6 cups torn romaine lettuce
2 tablespoons each: lemon juice, beaten egg
1 tablespoon olive oil
2 tablespoons grated fat-free Parmesan cheese
⅛ teaspoon dry mustard
Dash red pepper sauce
Salt and freshly ground pepper, to taste

Per Serving:
Calories: 127
% of calories from fat: 30
Fat (gm): 4.4
Saturated fat (gm): 0.6
Cholesterol (mg): 0
Sodium (mg): 200
Protein (gm): 5.3
Carbohydrate (gm): 17.1

Exchanges:
Milk: 0.0
Vegetable: 1.0
Fruit: 0.0
Bread: 1.0
Meat: 0.0
Fat: 0.5

1. Rub both sides of bread slices with cut sides of garlic; mince remaining garlic and reserve. Cut bread into ½ to ¾-inch cubes. Bake on jelly roll pan at 425 degrees until toasted, about 5 minutes.

2. Toss lettuce with combined lemon juice, egg, olive oil, reserved garlic, cheese, dry mustard, and red pepper sauce; season to taste with salt and pepper. Add croutons and toss.

GREAT GREEK SALAD

LO

45

Tofu adds a healthy twist to this classic salad. Fresh herbs lend a flavor accent.

4 main-dish servings (about 1½ cups each)

1 package (10 ounces) light extra-firm tofu, cut into ½-inch cubes

1 cup sliced, seeded cucumber

¼ cup each: thinly sliced red onion, sun-dried tomato (not in oil, softened)

½ cup fat-free Italian salad dressing

2–3 tablespoons chopped fresh, or 1 tablespoon dried, oregano, or basil leaves

¼ cup chopped parsley

4 cups sliced romaine lettuce

¼ cup crumbled fat-free feta cheese

8 pitted Kalamata olives, halved

1 hard-cooked egg, sliced

Per Serving:
Calories: 102
% of calories from fat: 23
Fat (gm): 2.7
Saturated fat (gm): 0.6
Cholesterol (mg): 53.1
Sodium (mg): 774
Protein (gm): 9.3
Carbohydrate (gm): 10.6

Exchanges:
Milk: 0.0
Vegetable: 2.0
Fruit: 0.0
Bread: 0.0
Meat: 1.0
Fat: 0.0

1. Combine tofu, cucumber, onion, sun-dried tomatoes, dressing, and herbs in large bowl; toss well. Add lettuce and toss. Spoon onto salad plates; top with remaining ingredients.

45-MINUTE PREP TIP: Begin cooking the hard-cooked eggs before preparing the rest of the recipe.

12-LAYER SALAD

LO

45

❄

A new look at an old favorite! Assemble, topped with dressing, up to a day in advance, and refrigerate.

6 main-dish servings (about 2 cups each)

2 cups sliced spinach leaves

2 medium carrots, sliced

1½ cups sliced celery

2 cups each: thinly sliced red cabbage, small broccoli florets, chopped iceberg lettuce

⅔ cup each: sliced yellow bell pepper, tomato

1½ cups cut green beans, cooked until crisp-tender

1 cup finely chopped parsley, divided

1 can (15 ounces) dark red kidney beans, rinsed, drained

1 medium red onion, thinly sliced

Garlic Dressing (recipe follows)

3 hard-cooked eggs, cut into wedges

Per Serving:
Calories: 214
% of calories from fat: 14
Fat (gm): 3.7
Saturated fat (gm): 0.9
Cholesterol (mg): 106.5
Sodium (mg): 637
Protein (gm): 14.8
Carbohydrate (gm): 37.8

Exchanges:
Milk: 0.0
Vegetable: 3.0
Fruit: 0.0
Bread: 1.0
Meat: 1.0
Fat: 0.0

1. Layer spinach, carrots, celery, cabbage, broccoli, lettuce, pepper, tomato, green beans, ½ cup parsley, kidney beans, and onion in 2½-quart glass salad bowl. Spread dressing over top and sprinkle with remaining ½ cup parsley. Before serving, toss salad and garnish with egg wedges.

Garlic Dressing

Makes about 1½ cups

¾ cup each: fat-free mayonnaise, fat-free sour cream

4 cloves garlic, minced

1 teaspoon each: dried basil and oregano leaves

¾ teaspoon dried tarragon

1. Mix all ingredients.

45-MINUTE PREP TIP: Begin cooking the hard-cooked eggs before preparing the rest of the recipe.

FREEZER COLESLAW

V *A colorful slaw that's easy to make and convenient to have on hand.*

8 side-dish servings (about ¾ cup each)

1½ pounds red cabbage, thinly sliced

½ cup each shredded carrots, chopped red
   bell pepper

¼ cup thinly sliced onion

Salt, to taste

1 cup water

¾ cup cider vinegar

1⅔ cups sugar

1 teaspoon caraway seeds

Per Serving:
Calories: 205
% of calories from fat: 1
Fat (gm): 0.4
Saturated fat (gm): 0
Cholesterol (mg): 0
Sodium (mg): 20
Protein (gm): 1.9
Carbohydrate (gm): 53.1

Exchanges:
Milk: 0.0
Vegetable: 2.0
Fruit: 0.0
Bread: 2.0
Meat: 0.0
Fat: 0.0

1. Layer cabbage, carrots, bell pepper, and onion in colander, sprinkling each layer lightly with salt; let stand 1 hour. Rinse and drain.

2. Heat remaining ingredients to boiling in small saucepan; reduce heat and simmer, uncovered, 5 minutes. Cool. Mix with cabbage and pack in freezer containers or bags and freeze. To serve, thaw in refrigerator or at room temperature.

PASTA COLESLAW

LO *The addition of pasta updates a traditional cabbage slaw.*

45 **4 side-dish servings** (about 1 cup each)

1½ cups (4 ounces) fusilli (spirals), or farfalle
   (bow ties), cooked

1 cup thinly sliced green cabbage

⅔ cup each: chopped tomato, green bell pepper

¼ cup sliced celery

Creamy Dressing (recipe follows)

Per Serving:
Calories: 139
% of calories from fat: 8
Fat (gm): 1.2
Saturated fat (gm): 0.3
Cholesterol (mg): 0.9
Sodium (mg): 156
Protein (gm): 5.4
Carbohydrate (gm): 27.3

Exchanges:
Milk: 0.0
Vegetable: 1.0
Fruit: 0.0
Bread: 1.5
Meat: 0.0
Fat: 0.0

1. Combine all ingredients and toss.

Creamy Dressing

Makes about ½ cup

¼ cup each: fat-free mayonnaise, low-fat plain yogurt
1 tablespoon lemon juice
2 cloves garlic, minced
½ teaspoon dried tarragon leaves
¼ teaspoon each: salt, pepper

1. Mix all ingredients.

45-MINUTE PREP TIP: Begin cooking the fusilli before preparing the rest of the recipe.

BROCCOLI SALAD

LO

45

Serve this nutrient-packed salad on a bed of salad greens, spinach, thinly sliced red cabbage, or in scooped-out tomato halves.

6 side-dish servings (about 1¼ cups each)

4½ cups sliced broccoli florets and stalks
1½ cups each: sliced zucchini, mushrooms, chopped green bell peppers
12 cherry tomatoes, halved
3 green onions, sliced
2 tablespoons dark raisins
Sour Cream-Mayonnaise Dressing (recipe follows)

1. Combine all ingredients and toss.

Per Serving:
Calories: 100
% of calories from fat: 13
Fat (gm): 1.7
Saturated fat (gm): 0.8
Cholesterol (mg): 2.7
Sodium (mg): 257
Protein (gm): 5.8
Carbohydrate (gm): 18.8

Exchanges:
Milk: 0.0
Vegetable: 4.0
Fruit: 0.0
Bread: 0.0
Meat: 0.0
Fat: 0.0

Sour Cream-Mayonnaise Dressing

Makes about 1¼ cups

⅓ cup each: fat-free sour cream, fat-free mayonnaise
3 cloves garlic, minced
3 tablespoons each: fat-free milk, crumbled blue cheese

1. Mix all ingredients.

CARROT-RAISIN SALAD

O

45

Comfort food at its best! A small can of drained pineapple tidbits can be added, if you like.

6 side-dish servings (about ⅓ cup each)

2½ cups shredded carrot
¾ cup chopped celery
⅓ cup each: raisins, coarsely chopped walnuts
¾ cup fat-free mayonnaise
½ teaspoon Dijon mustard
1–2 teaspoons sugar
⅛ teaspoon salt

Per Serving:
Calories: 115
% of calories from fat: 30
Fat (gm): 4.1
Saturated fat (gm): 0.3
Cholesterol (mg): 0
Sodium (mg): 460
Protein (gm): 2.6
Carbohydrate (gm): 19.2

Exchanges:
Milk: 0.0
Vegetable: 2.0
Fruit: 0.5
Bread: 0.0
Meat: 0.0
Fat: 1.0

1. Combine carrot, celery, raisins, and walnuts in medium bowl; mix in combined remaining ingredients.

GERMAN POTATO SALAD

V

45

Tart and tangy in flavor, this salad is best served warm from the skillet.

6 side-dish servings (about ⅔ cup each)

1 cup chopped onion
1 tablespoon flour
½ cup reduced-sodium canned vegetable broth
1¼ cups cider vinegar
1 tablespoon sugar
½ teaspoon celery seeds
1½ pounds peeled potatoes, cooked, sliced, warm
Salt and pepper, to taste
2 tablespoons each: crumbled cooked vegetarian
  bacon, chopped parsley

Per Serving:
Calories: 125
% of calories from fat: 5
Fat (gm): 0.7
Saturated fat (gm): 0.1
Cholesterol (mg): 0
Sodium (mg): 69.3
Protein (gm): 3
Carbohydrate (gm): 30.7

Exchanges:
Milk: 0.0
Vegetable: 0.0
Fruit: 0.0
Bread: 2.0
Meat: 0.0
Fat: 0.0

1. Sauté onion in lightly greased medium skillet until tender and browned, about 5 minutes. Stir in flour; cook 1 minute. Add broth, vinegar, sugar, and celery seeds and heat to boiling; boil, stirring, until thickened, 1 minute. Add potatoes and toss. Season to taste with salt and pepper; sprinkle with vegetarian bacon and parsley. Serve warm.

45-MINUTE PREP TIP: Begin cooking the potatoes before preparing the rest of the recipe.

CREAMY POTATO SALAD

LO

45

For the creamiest salad, toss the potatoes with the dressing while they're still slightly warm.

10 side-dish servings (about ⅔ cup each)

1½ pounds russet potatoes, peeled, cut into ¾-inch cubes, cooked, warm

1 cup sliced celery

½ cup each: sliced green onions, sweet pickle relish

¼ cup each: chopped green and red bell pepper

2 hard-cooked eggs, chopped

2–3 tablespoons crumbled, cooked vegetarian bacon

1 cup fat-free mayonnaise

½ cup fat-free sour cream

2 tablespoons cider vinegar

1 tablespoon yellow mustard

½ teaspoon celery seeds

Salt and pepper, to taste

Per Serving:
Calories: 119
% of calories from fat: 11
Fat (gm): 1.5
Saturated fat (gm): 0.4
Cholesterol (mg): 42.6
Sodium (mg): 464
Protein (gm): 3.9
Carbohydrate (gm): 23.4

Exchanges:
Milk: 0.0
Vegetable: 0.0
Fruit: 0.0
Bread: 1.5
Meat: 0.0
Fat: 0.0

1. Combine potatoes, celery, green onions, pickle relish, bell peppers, eggs, and vegetarian bacon in bowl. Add combined remaining ingredients, except salt and pepper and toss. Season to taste with salt and pepper.

CARIBBEAN POTATO SALAD

LO

45

Sweet and white potatoes combine with a creamy cumin and lime mayonnaise dressing; olives provide a pungent accent.

8 side-dish servings (about ¾ cup each)

¾ cup fat-free mayonnaise

½ cup fat-free milk

2 teaspoons lime juice

2 green onions, sliced

1 teaspoon ground cumin

⅛ teaspoon red cayenne pepper

1½ pounds each: sweet and russet, potatoes, peeled, cubed (1 inch), cooked

¼ cup small pimiento-stuffed olives

Salt, to taste

Per Serving:
Calories: 167
% of calories from fat: 5
Fat (gm): 1
Saturated fat (gm): 0.2
Cholesterol (mg): 0.3
Sodium (mg): 416
Protein (gm): 3.1
Carbohydrate (gm): 37.2

Exchanges:
Milk: 0.0
Vegetable: 0.0
Fruit: 0.0
Bread: 2.5
Meat: 0.0
Fat: 0.0

1. Mix mayonnaise, milk, lime juice, green onions, cumin, and cayenne pepper; mix gently into combined potatoes and olives in bowl. Season to taste with salt. Refrigerate 2 to 3 hours for flavors to blend.

FRUIT SALAD WITH RASPBERRY YOGURT DRESSING

L

45

Use sliced, unpeeled apples and ripe pears in fall and winter months when fresh berries are not available. Serve with Brown Sugar Banana Bread (see p. 563).

4 main-dish servings (about 1¼ cups each)

1½ cups halved strawberries

1 cup each: blueberries, raspberries

1 each: peeled, sliced medium papaya, or mango, kiwi

4 slices fresh pineapple, halved

1 orange, cut into segments

12 bibb lettuce leaves

Raspberry Yogurt Dressing (recipe follows)

Poppy seeds, as garnish

Per Serving:
Calories: 257
% of calories from fat: 4
Fat (gm): 1.2
Saturated fat (gm): 0.1
Cholesterol (mg): 0
Sodium (mg): 48
Protein (gm): 5.2
Carbohydrate (gm): 60.1

Exchanges:
Milk: 0.0
Vegetable: 0.0
Fruit: 4.0
Bread: 0.0
Meat: 0.0
Fat: 0.0

1. Arrange fruit on lettuce-lined plates. Serve Raspberry Yogurt Dressing on the side, or drizzle over the fruit; sprinkle with poppy seeds.

Raspberry Yogurt Dressing

Makes about 1 cup

1 cup fat-free raspberry yogurt
2 tablespoons honey
Lime juice, to taste

1. Mix yogurt and honey, adding lime juice to taste.

45-MINUTE PREP TIP: Make Raspberry Yogurt Dressing before preparing the rest of the recipe.

WALDORF SALAD

LO

45

Using both red and green apples adds color and flavor interest. Add miniature marshmallows, if you like!

4 side-dish servings (about ¾ cup each)

2 cups unpeeled, cubed red and green apples
1 cup sliced celery
¼ cup each: chopped, toasted walnuts,
    raisins, fat-free mayonnaise, sour cream
2–3 teaspoons lemon juice
1–2 tablespoons honey

1. Combine apples, celery, walnuts, and raisins in bowl. Mix in combined remaining ingredients.

Per Serving:
Calories: 149
% of calories from fat: 26
Fat (gm): 4.7
Saturated fat (gm): 0.3
Cholesterol (mg): 0
Sodium (mg): 227
Protein (gm): 3.5
Carbohydrate (gm): 26.5

Exchanges:
Milk: 0.0
Vegetable: 0.5
Fruit: 1.5
Bread: 0.0
Meat: 0.0
Fat: 1.0

SPROUTS AND VEGETABLE SALAD

L

Use any sprouted beans or grains you like in this salad; feel free to mix flavors and textures.

4 side-dish servings (about 1 cup each)

1 cup broccoli florets, chopped tomato
½ cup each: sprouted wheat berries, chick peas, and
   lentils (see next recipe for sprouting directions)
2 green onions, sliced
½ cup fat-free blue cheese, or other desired
   salad dressing
¼ cup (1 ounce) crumbled blue cheese

1. Combine all ingredients, except blue cheese, and toss; sprinkle with blue cheese.

Per Serving:
Calories: 129
% of calories from fat: 16
Fat (gm): 2.5
Saturated fat (gm): 1.4
Cholesterol (mg): 5.2
Sodium (mg): 452
Protein (gm): 5.7
Carbohydrate (gm): 23.5

Exchanges:
Milk: 0.0
Vegetable: 1.5
Fruit: 0.0
Bread: 1.0
Meat: 0.0
Fat: 0.5

SPROUTED LENTIL SALAD

V

All kinds of dried beans and grains can be sprouted. Sprouts are delicious for salads, as garnishes on main dishes and side dishes, or just to eat as snacks. Any favorite sprouted bean or grain can be used in this salad; any fat-free or reduced-fat salad dressing can be substituted for the Tofu Aioli.

4 side-dish servings (about 1 cup each)

Sprouted Lentils (recipe follows)
1 cup each: torn radicchio leaves, chopped tomato
½ cup each: chopped cucumber, yellow bell pepper
½ cup (⅔ recipe) Tofu Aioli (see p. 161)
Salt and pepper, to taste

1. Combine lentils, vegetables, and Tofu Aioli; toss. Season to taste with salt and pepper.

Per Serving:
Calories: 86
% of calories from fat: 18
Fat (gm): 1.9
Saturated fat (gm): 0.2
Cholesterol (mg): 0
Sodium (mg): 41
Protein (gm): 6.3
Carbohydrate (gm): 14.3

Exchanges:
Milk: 0.0
Vegetable: 3.0
Fruit: 0.0
Bread: 0.0
Meat: 0.0
Fat: 0.5

Sprouted Lentils

Makes about 2 cups

½ cup dried lentils
Water

1. Place lentils in quart jar; add water to cover lentils by 2 to 3 inches and soak overnight. Drain. Return drained lentils to jar and cover with cheesecloth. Let stand at room temperature until lentils have sprouted, about 2 days, rinsing lentils with cold water and draining 3 to 4 times a day.

2. Refrigerate sprouted lentils. Check sprouts daily; if they appear dry, rinse, drain, and return to refrigerator.

NOTES: All grains and beans can be sprouted according to the directions above, although they may require shorter or longer times to sprout. The various grains and beans will also yield different amounts.

Wheat berries: ½ cup dry wheat berries yield about 1½ cups sprouted wheat berries.

Chick peas: ½ cup dry chick peas yield about 1½ cups sprouted chick peas.

MANGO AND BLACK BEAN SALAD

V

45

Any tropical fruit, such as pineapple, kiwi, papaya, or star fruit, can be used in this refreshing salad.

4 main-dish servings (about 1 cup each)

4 large ripe mangoes, peeled, pitted, cubed
1 cup cubed pineapple
½ medium cucumber, seeded, sliced
¼ cup finely chopped red bell pepper
4 small green onions, thinly sliced
1 can (15 ounces) black beans, rinsed, drained
Honey-Lime Dressing (recipe follows)
Mint sprigs, as garnish

Per Serving:
Calories: 328
% of calories from fat: 20
Fat (gm): 8.6
Saturated fat (gm): 1.1
Cholesterol (mg): 0
Sodium (mg): 338
Protein (gm): 10.4
Carbohydrate (gm): 65.4

Exchanges:
Milk: 0.0
Vegetable: 0.0
Fruit: 2.0
Bread: 2.0
Meat: 0.0
Fat: 1.5

1. Combine all ingredients, except mint, and toss. Garnish with mint.

Honey-Lime Dressing

Makes about ⅓ cup

2 tablespoons each: olive oil, water
1 tablespoon each: honey, tarragon wine vinegar, grated lime zest
3–4 teaspoons lime juice
½ teaspoon dried mint leaves
Pinch salt

1. Mix all ingredients.

45-MINUTE PREP TIP: Make Honey-Lime Dressing before preparing the rest of the recipe.

SUMMER FRESH BEAN SALAD

A garden pick of vegetables and herbs team with beans in this perfect-for-potluck salad.

8 main-dish servings (about 1 cup each)

1 can (15 ounces) each: dark kidney, pinto, navy,
   and black beans, rinsed, drained
3 cups halved cherry tomatoes
½ cup each: chopped red onion, parsley, cilantro
¾ cup fat-free honey mustard vinaigrette
Salt and pepper, to taste

1. Combine all ingredients, except salt and pepper, and toss. Season to taste with salt and pepper.

Per Serving:
Calories: 211
% of calories from fat: 4
Fat (gm): 1.0
Saturated fat (gm): 0.2
Cholesterol (mg): 0
Sodium (mg): 992.1
Protein (gm): 12.2
Carbohydrate (gm): 41.6

Exchanges:
Milk: 0.0
Vegetable: 1.0
Fruit: 0.0
Bread: 2.0
Meat: 1.0
Fat: 0.0

CACTUS SALAD

V

45

The tender cactus paddles called "nopales" are readily available in large supermarkets today — be sure all the thorns have been removed! If not, they can be pulled out easily with tweezers.

6 side-dish servings (about ½ cup each)

2 quarts water

1½ pounds cactus paddles, cut into ½-inch pieces

1 tablespoon salt

¼ teaspoon baking soda

1½ cups cherry tomato halves

½ cup thinly sliced red onion

Lime Dressing (recipe follows)

Per Serving:
Calories: 78
% of calories from fat: 28
Fat (gm): 2.5
Saturated fat (gm): 0.3
Cholesterol (mg): 0
Sodium (mg): 131
Protein (gm): 2.4
Carbohydrate (gm): 12.5

Exchanges:
Milk: 0.0
Vegetable: 2.0
Fruit: 0.0
Bread: 0.0
Meat: 0.0
Fat: 0.5

1. Heat water to boiling in large saucepan; add cactus, salt, and baking soda. Reduce heat and simmer, uncovered, until cactus is crisp-tender, about 20 minutes. Rinse well in cold water; drain. Combine cactus and remaining ingredients and toss.

Lime Dressing

Makes about ¼ cup

2 tablespoons lime juice

1–2 tablespoons olive, or canola, oil

1 tablespoon water

1 teaspoon cider vinegar

2 teaspoons sugar

½ teaspoon dried oregano leaves

Combine all ingredients.

45-MINUTE PREP TIP: Make Lime Dressing before preparing the rest of the recipe.

JICAMA SALAD

V

45

Jicama adds a marvelous crispness to salads, complementing both fruits and vegetables.

6 side-dish servings (about ⅔ cup each)

12 ounces jicama, peeled, cut into 1½- x
   ½-inch pieces
½ cup sliced zucchini
1 small orange, cut into segments
2–3 thin slices red onion
Cilantro Lime Dressing (recipe follows)
Salt and pepper, to taste

1. Combine all ingredients, except salt and pepper, and toss. Season to taste with salt and pepper.

Per Serving:
Calories: 77
% of calories from fat: 27
Fat (gm): 2.4
Saturated fat (gm): 0.3
Cholesterol (mg): 0
Sodium (mg): 1
Protein (gm): 1.3
Carbohydrate (gm): 13.5

Exchanges:
Milk: 0.0
Vegetable: 1.0
Fruit: 0.5
Bread: 0.0
Meat: 0.0
Fat: 0.5

Cilantro Lime Dressing

Makes about ¼ cup

2 tablespoons lime juice, chopped cilantro
1 tablespoon orange juice
1–2 tablespoons olive, or canola, oil
2 teaspoons sugar

1. Combine all ingredients.

MACARONI SALAD

O

45

Fourth of July signals family picnics, which must include, of course, home-made macaroni salad! Add 1 cup halved cherry tomatoes for festive color.

6 side-dish servings (about ⅔ cup each)

2 cups cooked elbow macaroni
1 cup frozen baby peas, thawed
½ cup each: chopped onion, celery
⅓ cup shredded carrot
¼ cup each: chopped red bell pepper, sliced ripe, or pimiento-stuffed, olives
¾ cup fat-free mayonnaise
2 teaspoons yellow mustard
1 teaspoon sugar
Salt and pepper, to taste

Per Serving:
Calories: 129
% of calories from fat: 9
Fat (gm): 1.3
Saturated fat (gm): 0.2
Cholesterol (mg): 0
Sodium (mg): 583
Protein (gm): 4
Carbohydrate (gm): 25.6

Exchanges:
Milk: 0.0
Vegetable: 0.0
Fruit: 0.0
Bread: 1.5
Meat: 0.0
Fat: 0.0

1. Combine macaroni, peas, onion, celery, carrot, bell pepper, and olives in medium bowl. Mix in combined mayonnaise, mustard, and sugar. Season to taste with salt and pepper.

45-MINUTE PREP TIP: Begin cooking the macaroni before preparing the rest of the recipe.

MACARONI-BLUE CHEESE SALAD

LO

45

A not-so-traditional macaroni salad with blue cheese pizzazz!

8 side-dish servings (about ¾ cup each)

1 cup (4 ounces) elbow macaroni, cooked
⅔ cup each: chopped red bell pepper, cucumber, shredded carrots
¼ cup sliced green onions
Blue Cheese Dressing (recipe follows)

Per Serving:
Calories: 82
% of calories from fat: 9
Fat (gm): 0.9
Saturated fat (gm): 0.4
Cholesterol (mg): 1.3
Sodium (mg): 159
Protein (gm): 2.6
Carbohydrate (gm): 16.3

Exchanges:
Milk: 0.0
Vegetable: 2.0
Fruit: 0.0
Bread: 0.5
Meat: 0.0
Fat: 0.0

1. Combine macaroni, bell pepper, cucumber, carrots, and green onions in bowl; mix in Blue Cheese Dressing.

Blue Cheese Dressing

Makes about ½ cup

½ cup fat-free mayonnaise, or salad dressing
2 tablespoons crumbled blue cheese
1 tablespoon red wine vinegar
1 teaspoon celery seeds
½ teaspoon salt
⅛ teaspoon each: cayenne and black pepper

1. Mix all ingredients.

45-MINUTE PREP TIP: Begin cooking the macaroni before preparing the rest of the recipe.

ORZO WITH SUN-DRIED TOMATOES AND MUSHROOMS

V

45

A simple salad that is intensely flavored with sun-dried tomatoes, fresh rosemary, and sherry. If desired, the sherry can be omitted.

4 side-dish servings (about ¾ cup each)

2 sun-dried tomatoes, softened, sliced
1½ cups sliced mushrooms
¼ cup sliced green onions
2 cloves garlic, minced
½ cup canned vegetable broth
2 tablespoons dry sherry (optional)
½ cup (4 ounces) orzo, cooked
2 tablespoons each: finely chopped rosemary, parsley
¼ teaspoon each: salt, pepper

Per Serving:
Calories: 135
% of calories from fat: 6
Fat (gm): 0.8
Saturated fat (gm): 0.1
Cholesterol (mg): 0
Sodium (mg): 218
Protein (gm): 5.1
Carbohydrate (gm): 27.2

Exchanges:
Milk: 0.0
Vegetable: 0.0
Fruit: 0.0
Bread: 2.0
Meat: 0.0
Fat: 0.0

1. Sauté sun-dried tomatoes, mushrooms, green onions, and garlic in lightly greased large skillet until mushrooms are tender, 5 to 7 minutes. Add broth and sherry; heat to boiling. Reduce heat and simmer, uncovered, until liquid is reduced by half, about 5 minutes; cool. Toss with orzo, herbs, salt and pepper.

45-MINUTE PREP TIP: Begin cooking the orzo before preparing the rest of the recipe.

MIXED VEGETABLES AND ORZO VINAIGRETTE

V

45

The turmeric used in the salad dressing gives this salad its unusual yellow color. Curry powder can be used instead to impart the same color and add a delicate curry flavor.

8 side-dish servings (about 1 cup each)

2 cups cut asparagus (1½-inch pieces) cooked
   crisp-tender
1½ cups thinly sliced zucchini
1 cup frozen peas, thawed
½ cup sliced carrots, cooked crisp-tender
8 cherry tomatoes, halved
¾ cup (6 ounces) orzo, cooked
Mustard-Turmeric Vinaigrette (recipe follows)

Per Serving:
Calories: 142
% of calories from fat: 27
Fat (gm): 4.2
Saturated fat (gm): 0.6
Cholesterol (mg): 0
Sodium (mg): 112
Protein (gm): 5.5
Carbohydrate (gm): 20.9

Exchanges:
Milk: 0.0
Vegetable: 1.0
Fruit: 0.0
Bread: 1.0
Meat: 0.0
Fat: 1.0

1. Combine all ingredients and toss.

Mustard-Turmeric Vinaigrette

Makes about ½ cup

¼ cup red wine vinegar
¼ teaspoon ground turmeric
2–3 tablespoons lemon juice
2 tablespoons olive, or canola, oil
2 teaspoons Dijon mustard
2 cloves garlic, minced
¼ teaspoon each: salt, pepper

1. Heat vinegar and turmeric in small saucepan over medium heat until turmeric is dissolved, stirring, 2 to 3 minutes; cool. Combine with remaining ingredients.

45-MINUTE PREP TIP: Begin cooking the orzo and carrots before preparing the rest of the recipe.

CHILI-DRESSED SALAD WITH RADIATORE

V

45

A fun pasta, radiatore look like the tiny radiators for which they are named! Other shaped pastas can be used, if preferred.

4 main-dish servings (about 1½ cups each)

3 cups (8 ounces) radiatore, cooked
1½ cups broccoli florets
2 medium tomatoes, cut into wedges
½ cup cooked whole-kernel corn
½ medium avocado, cut into ¾-inch pieces
2 tablespoons finely chopped cilantro
Chili Dressing (recipe follows)

1. Combine all ingredients and toss.

Per Serving:
Calories: 361
% of calories from fat: 30
Fat (gm): 12.3
Saturated fat (gm): 1.1
Cholesterol (mg): 0
Sodium (mg): 25
Protein (gm): 10.6
Carbohydrate (gm): 54.6

Exchanges:
Milk: 0.0
Vegetable: 0.0
Fruit: 0.0
Bread: 4.0
Meat: 0.0
Fat: 2.0

Chili Dressing

Makes about ¼ cup

3 tablespoons lemon juice
2 tablespoons olive oil
½ teaspoon chili powder
¼ teaspoon salt
¼ teaspoon crushed red pepper

1. Mix all ingredients.

45-MINUTE PREP TIP: Begin cooking the radiatore and make the Chili Dressing before preparing the rest of the recipe.

FARFALLE SALAD WITH MINTED PESTO

L

The Minted Pesto provides a refreshing flavor counterpoint to the pasta and vegetables.

6 main-dish servings (about 1¼ cups each)

¼ cup finely chopped shallots, or onions

3 green onions, sliced

2 cloves garlic, minced

½ cup dry white wine, or vegetable broth

2 tablespoons lemon juice

Minted Pesto (see p. 608)

12 ounces farfalle, or rotini, cooked

⅔ cup each: sliced cucumber, yellow and red bell pepper, halved cherry tomatoes

Per Serving:
Calories: 316
% of calories from fat: 17
Fat (gm): 5.9
Saturated fat (gm): 0.7
Cholesterol (mg): 0
Sodium (mg): 24
Protein (gm): 9.9
Carbohydrate (gm): 53.4

Exchanges:
Milk: 0.0
Vegetable: 2.0
Fruit: 0.0
Bread: 3.0
Meat: 0.0
Fat: 0.6

1. Sauté shallots, green onions, and garlic in lightly greased medium skillet until tender, 3 to 5 minutes. Add wine and lemon juice; heat to boiling. Reduce heat and simmer, uncovered, until liquid has evaporated, 8 to 10 minutes. Spoon over pasta and remaining ingredients and toss. Refrigerate 1 to 2 hours for flavors to blend.

CURRIED PASTA SALAD

V

45

Especially delicious with flavored specialty pastas such as curry, lemon, sesame, or tomato.

4 main-dish servings (about 1¼ cups each)

⅓ cup chopped mango chutney

¼ cup chopped mixed dried fruit

2 tablespoons Dijon mustard

1 tablespoon each: olive oil, lime juice

8 ounces fettuccine, cooked

1 cup frozen stir-fry blend vegetables, cooked

Salt, cayenne, and black pepper, to taste

¼ cup sliced green onions

2–4 tablespoons chopped cashews

Per Serving:
Calories: 321
% of calories from fat: 22
Fat (gm): 8.1
Saturated fat (gm): 0.9
Cholesterol (mg): 0
Sodium (mg): 207
Protein (gm): 9.3
Carbohydrate (gm): 55.1

Exchanges:
Milk: 0.0
Vegetable: 0.0
Fruit: 1.5
Bread: 2.5
Meat: 0.0
Fat: 1.5

1. Combine chutney, dried fruit, mustard, oil, and lime juice; spoon over fettuccine and vegetables and toss. Season to taste with salt and pepper. Sprinkle with green onions and cashews.

45-MINUTE PREP TIP: Begin cooking the fettuccine and stir-fry vegetables before preparing the rest of the recipe.

ANGEL HAIR AND GOAT CHEESE SALAD

L

Goat cheese adds a creamy texture and piquant accent to this flavorful pasta dish.

45

6 main-dish servings (about 1½ cups each)

2 cups each: halved snow peas, sliced mushrooms

3 medium carrots, julienned

4 large plum tomatoes, sliced

2 teaspoons dried oregano leaves

1 teaspoon dried tarragon leaves

½ cup each: reduced-sodium vegetable broth, fat-free milk

2 teaspoons tomato paste

¼ teaspoon each: salt, pepper

12 ounces capellini (angel hair), or thin spaghetti, cooked, warm

3 ounces goat cheese, or reduced-fat cream cheese

Per Serving:
Calories: 328
% of calories from fat: 13
Fat (gm): 4.7
Saturated fat (gm): 2.3
Cholesterol (mg): 6.8
Sodium (mg): 197
Protein (gm): 13.9
Carbohydrate (gm): 58.5

Exchanges:
Milk: 0.0
Vegetable: 2.0
Fruit: 0.0
Bread: 3.0
Meat: 0.0
Fat: 1.0

1. Sauté vegetables and herbs in lightly greased large skillet until snow peas are crisp-tender, 6 to 8 minutes. Stir in broth, milk, and tomato paste; heat to boiling. Reduce heat and simmer, uncovered, until thickened to sauce consistency, about 10 minutes, stirring occasionally. Stir in salt and pepper. Toss with pasta and goat cheese.

45-MINUTE PREP TIP: Begin cooking the capellini before preparing the rest of the recipe.

GARDEN PASTA SALAD WITH CROSTINI

L

45

Serve this salad warm or chilled. Breadsticks can be substituted for the crostini.

6 main-dish servings (about 1 cup each)

3 cups broccoli florets

2 cups cut asparagus (1-inch)

1 medium yellow bell pepper, thickly sliced

¼ cup sliced green onions, red onion

½ cup whole-kernel corn

1 clove garlic, minced

1½ cups small pasta shells, cooked, warm

1 can (15 ounces) dark red kidney beans, rinsed, drained

1½ cups halved cherry tomatoes

3 tablespoons chopped fresh, or 1½ teaspoons dried, basil leaves

1½ tablespoons each: olive oil, red wine vinegar

2 tablespoons crumbled feta cheese

4 slices Italian bread

1 clove garlic, cut in half

Per Serving:
Calories: 319
% of calories from fat: 16
Fat (gm): 6.2
Saturated fat (gm): 1.1
Cholesterol (mg): 2.1
Sodium (mg): 297
Protein (gm): 15.5
Carbohydrate (gm): 57.4

Exchanges:
Milk: 0.0
Vegetable: 2.0
Fruit: 0.0
Bread: 3.0
Meat: 0.0
Fat: 1.0

1. Sauté broccoli, asparagus, bell pepper, green and red onions, corn, and garlic in lightly greased large skillet until crisp-tender, about 5 minutes. Toss with warm pasta, beans, tomatoes, and basil. Drizzle with oil and vinegar and toss. Sprinkle with cheese.

2. To make crostini, rub both sides of bread with cut clove of garlic; broil 4 inches from heat source until golden on both sides. Serve with the salad.

45-MINUTE PREP TIP: Begin cooking the pasta shells before preparing the rest of the recipe.

ORIENTAL NOODLE SALAD

V *Use Asian sesame oil for the fullest flavor.*

4 main-dish servings (about 2 cups each)

1 package (3 ounces) ramen noodles, cooked
   (discard spice packet)
1 cup each: halved snow peas, Brussels sprouts,
   cooked until crisp-tender
1 cup each: bean sprouts, sliced mushrooms
½ cup each: sliced red bell pepper, carrots,
   thawed frozen peas
1 can (11 ounces) mandarin orange segments, drained
¼ cup finely chopped cilantro
Orange-Sesame Salad Dressing (recipe follows)
2 teaspoons toasted sesame seeds

Per Serving:
Calories: 252
% of calories from fat: 25
Fat (gm): 7.5
Saturated fat (gm): 0.8
Cholesterol (mg): 13.3
Sodium (mg): 497
Protein (gm): 9.2
Carbohydrate (gm): 41.6

Exchanges:
Milk: 0.0
Vegetable: 3.5
Fruit: 0.5
Bread: 1.0
Meat: 0.0
Fat: 1.5

1. Combine all ingredients, except sesame seeds, and toss. Sprinkle with sesame seeds.

Orange-Sesame Salad Dressing

Makes about 1⅓ cups

⅓ cup orange juice
1 tablespoon Asian sesame oil
2 cloves garlic, minced
½ teaspoon five-spice powder
¼ teaspoon each: salt, white pepper

1. Mix all ingredients.

ASIAN NOODLE SALAD

LO

45

Enjoy the wonderful blend of flavors in this salad. Thin spaghetti or linguine can be substituted for the fresh Chinese egg noodles.

4 main-dish servings (about 1¼ cups each)

8 ounces fresh Chinese egg noodles, cooked
Yogurt Dressing (recipe follows)
1 cup each: shredded carrot, seeded, cubed cucumber
½ cup chopped red bell pepper
¼ cup each: sliced green onions, chopped cilantro

1. Combine all ingredients and toss.

Per Serving:
Calories: 388
% of calories from fat: 17
Fat (gm): 7.7
Saturated fat (gm): 1.5
Cholesterol (mg): 1
Sodium (mg): 242
Protein (gm): 14.3
Carbohydrate (gm): 67.3

Exchanges:
Milk: 0.0
Vegetable: 3.0
Fruit: 0.0
Bread: 3.5
Meat: 0.0
Fat: 1.5

Yogurt Dressing

Makes about 1½ cups

1 cup fat-free plain yogurt
¼ cup reduced-fat peanut butter
2 tablespoons rice wine vinegar
1 tablespoon each: reduced-sodium tamari soy sauce, sugar,
    minced gingerroot
1 teaspoon Asian sesame oil
½ teaspoon each: 5-spice powder, minced garlic, cayenne pepper

1. Mix all ingredients.

45-MINUTE PREP TIP: Begin cooking the noodles and making the Yogurt Dressing before preparing the rest of the recipe.

FIFTEEN

Breads

POTATO BREAD

L *Breads made with mashed potatoes are very moist and retain their freshness well. This dough can be made in advance and refrigerated up to 5 days.*

2 loaves (16 servings each)

1 package active dry yeast

1½ cups warm water (110–115 degrees)

2 tablespoons sugar

3 tablespoons margarine, or butter, room temperature

2 eggs

1 cup mashed potatoes, lukewarm

5½–6½ cups all-purpose flour, divided

1 cup whole wheat flour

1 teaspoon salt

Fat-free milk

Per Serving:
Calories: 121
% of calories from fat: 13
Fat (gm): 1.7
Saturated fat (gm): 0.4
Cholesterol (mg): 13.4
Sodium (mg): 103
Protein (gm): 3.6
Carbohydrate (gm): 22.7

Exchanges:
Milk: 0.0
Vegetable: 0.0
Fruit: 0.0
Bread: 1.5
Meat: 0.0
Fat: 0.5

1. Mix yeast and warm water in large bowl; let stand 5 minutes. Mix in sugar, margarine, eggs, and mashed potatoes until blended; mix in 5½ cups all-purpose flour, whole wheat flour, and salt. Mix in enough remaining 1 cup all-purpose flour to make smooth dough.

2. Knead dough on floured surface until smooth and elastic, about 5 minutes. Place in greased bowl; let rise, covered, in warm place until double in size, 1 to 1½ hours. Punch dough down.

3. Divide dough into halves; shape into loaves and place in greased 9 x 5-inch loaf pans. Let stand, loosely covered, until double in size, about 45 minutes. Brush tops of loaves with milk. Bake at 375 degrees until loaves are golden and sound hollow when tapped, about 45 minutes. Remove from pans; cool on wire racks.

PEASANT BREAD

V *Five grains and ground pecans combine in this hearty dense-textured country-style bread. Wonderful toasted, this bread is also delicious with honey.*

2 small loaves (8–10 servings each)

2 packages active dry yeast

½ cup warm water (110–115 degrees)

1¼ cups whole wheat flour

½ cup each: millet, cracked wheat, yellow cornmeal, bulgur wheat, quick cooking oats, ground pecans

1 teaspoon salt

1¼ cups lukewarm water

¼ cup honey

2 tablespoons canola oil

1–2 cups unbleached all-purpose flour

Per Serving:
Calories: 197
% of calories from fat: 22
Fat (gm): 5
Saturated fat (gm): 0.6
Cholesterol (mg): 0
Sodium (mg): 137
Protein (gm): 5.4
Carbohydrate (gm): 34.2

Exchanges:
Milk: 0.0
Vegetable: 0.0
Fruit: 0.0
Bread: 2.0
Meat: 0.0
Fat: 1.0

1. Mix yeast and ½ cup warm water in large bowl; let stand 5 minutes. Mix in remaining ingredients, except all-purpose flour; mix in enough all-purpose flour to make smooth dough.

2. Knead dough on floured surface until smooth and elastic, about 5 minutes (dough will be heavy and difficult to maneuver). Place in greased bowl; let rise, covered, in warm place until double in size, about 1½ hours. Punch dough down.

3. Divide dough into halves; shape into round loaves on greased baking sheet. Let stand, loosely covered, until double in size, about 1½ hours. Bake at 350 degrees until loaves are deep golden brown and sound hollow when tapped, about 40 minutes. Transfer to wire racks to cool.

HEARTY VEGETABLE-RYE BREAD

V | *Cauliflower adds moistness and subtle flavor to this aromatic rye loaf.*

1 loaf (10–12 servings)

1 package active dry yeast

⅓ cup warm water (110–115 degrees)

1 teaspoon sugar

1 cup pureed cooked cauliflower

1 tablespoon each: melted margarine, light molasses, spicy brown mustard

2–3 cups all-purpose flour, divided

1 cup rye flour

½ teaspoon salt

1½ teaspoons each: caraway and fennel seeds, crushed, divided

1 teaspoon dried dill weed

Melted margarine

Per Serving:
Calories: 177
% of calories from fat: 9
Fat (gm): 1.9
Saturated fat (gm): 0.3
Cholesterol (mg): 0
Sodium (mg): 149
Protein (gm): 5.3
Carbohydrate (gm): 34.8

Exchanges:
Milk: 0.0
Vegetable: 0.0
Fruit: 0.0
Bread: 2.0
Meat: 0.0
Fat: 0.5

1. Mix yeast, warm water, and sugar in large bowl; let stand 5 minutes. Mix in cauliflower, 1 tablespoon margarine, molasses, and mustard until blended. Mix in 2 cups all-purpose flour, rye flour, salt, 1 teaspoon each caraway and fennel seeds, and dill weed. Mix in enough remaining 1 cup all-purpose flour to make smooth dough.

2. Knead dough on floured surface until smooth and elastic, about 5 minutes. Place in greased bowl; let stand, covered, in warm place until double in size, about 1 hour. Punch dough down.

3. Shape dough into long or round loaf on greased cookie sheet. Let rise, loosely covered, until double in size, 45 to 60 minutes. Make 3 or 4 slits in top of loaf with sharp knife; brush with melted margarine and sprinkle with remaining ½ teaspoon each caraway and fennel seeds. Bake at 350 degrees until bread is golden and sounds hollow when tapped, 40 to 50 minutes. Transfer to wire rack to cool.

ROASTED RED PEPPER BREAD

LO *Bake this loaf in a freeform long or round shape, or in a pan. For convenience, use jarred roasted red pepper.*

1 loaf (16 servings)

2¼–2¾ cups all-purpose flour, divided

¾ cup whole wheat flour

¼ cup grated fat-free Parmesan cheese

1½ teaspoons dried Italian seasoning, divided

½ teaspoon salt

1 package fast-rising active dry yeast

1¼ cups very hot water (125–130 degrees)

1 tablespoon olive oil

4 ounces reduced-fat mozzarella cheese, cut into
   ½-inch cubes

½ cup coarsely chopped roasted red pepper

1 egg white, beaten

Per Serving:
Calories: 119
% of calories from fat: 16
Fat (gm): 2.2
Saturated fat (gm): 0.9
Cholesterol (mg): 3.8
Sodium (mg): 133
Protein (gm): 5.6
Carbohydrate (gm): 19

Exchanges:
Milk: 0.0
Vegetable: 0.0
Fruit: 0.0
Bread: 1.5
Meat: 0.0
Fat: 0.5

1. Combine 2¼ cups all-purpose flour, whole wheat flour, Parmesan cheese, 1 teaspoon Italian seasoning, salt, and yeast in large bowl; add hot water and oil, mixing until blended. Mix in mozzarella cheese, red pepper, and enough remaining ½ cup all-purpose flour to make smooth dough.

2. Knead dough on floured surface until smooth and elastic, about 5 minutes. Place in greased bowl; let rise, covered, in warm place until double in size, about 30 minutes. Punch dough down.

3. Shape dough into loaf and place in greased 9 x 5-inch loaf pan. Let stand, covered, until double in size, about 30 minutes. Make 3 or 4 slits in top of loaf with sharp knife. Brush egg white over dough and sprinkle with Italian seasoning. Bake at 375 degrees until loaf is golden and sounds hollow when tapped, 35 to 40 minutes. Remove from pan and cool on wire rack.

LIMA BEAN WHEAT BREAD

L *Actually, any kind of pureed bean can be used in this moist, dense bread.*

3 loaves (10–12 servings each)

2 packages active dry yeast

¼ cup warm water (110–115 degrees)

1 cup each: cooked dried lima beans, or rinsed, drained canned lima beans, cold water

2 cups fat-free milk

4–6 tablespoons melted margarine, or butter

⅓ cup sugar

4½–5½ cups all-purpose flour, divided

1½ cups whole wheat flour

1½ teaspoons salt

Fat-free milk, for glaze

Per Serving:
Calories: 125
% of calories from fat: 13
Fat (gm): 1.9
Saturated fat (gm): 0.4
Cholesterol (mg): 0.3
Sodium (mg): 133
Protein (gm): 4
Carbohydrate (gm): 23.2

Exchanges:
Milk: 0.0
Vegetable: 0.0
Fruit: 0.0
Bread: 1.5
Meat: 0.0
Fat: 0.5

1. Mix yeast and warm water in small bowl; let stand 5 minutes. Process beans and 1 cup cold water in food processor or blender until smooth. Mix bean puree, fat-free milk, margarine, and sugar in large bowl. Mix in yeast mixture, 4½ cups all-purpose flour, whole wheat flour, and salt. Mix in enough remaining 1 cup all-purpose flour to make soft dough.

2. Knead dough on floured surface until smooth and elastic, about 5 minutes. Place in greased bowl and let rise, covered, in warm place until double in size, about 1 hour. Punch dough down.

3. Divide dough into 3 equal pieces. Shape each into oval loaf on greased cookie sheet. Let rise, loosely covered, until double in size, about 45 minutes; brush with fat-free milk. Bake at 375 degrees until loaves are golden and sound hollow when tapped, about 1 hour. Transfer to wire racks and cool.

SWEET POTATO BRAIDS

LO *Canned pumpkin can be substituted for the sweet potatoes, if desired. For variation, add ½ cup raisins and/or ½ cup coarsely chopped walnuts or pecans to the bread dough.*

2 loaves (12 servings each)

2 packages active dry yeast

¼ cup warm fat-free milk (110–115 degrees)

1 cup mashed cooked sweet potatoes

1¾ cups fat-free milk

¼ cup canola oil

1 egg

3–4 cups all-purpose flour, divided

2 cups whole wheat flour

1 teaspoon salt

Per Serving:
Calories: 156
% of calories from fat: 17
Fat (gm): 2.9
Saturated fat (gm): 0.5
Cholesterol (mg): 9.2
Sodium (mg): 105
Protein (gm): 4.9
Carbohydrate (gm): 27.7

Exchanges:
Milk: 0.0
Vegetable: 0.0
Fruit: 0.0
Bread: 2.0
Meat: 0.0
Fat: 0.5

1. Mix yeast and warm milk in large bowl; let stand 5 minutes. Mix in sweet potatoes, 1¾ cups milk, oil, and egg until blended; mix in 3 cups all-purpose flour, whole wheat flour, and salt. Mix in enough remaining 1 cup all-purpose flour to make smooth dough.

2. Knead dough on floured surface until smooth and elastic, about 5 minutes. Place in greased bowl; let rise, covered, in warm place until double in size, about 1 hour. Punch dough down.

3. Divide dough into halves; divide each half into thirds. Roll pieces of dough into strips, 12 inches long. Braid 3 strips; fold ends under and place on greased cookie sheet. Repeat with remaining dough. Let rise, loosely covered, until double in size, 30 to 45 minutes. Bake at 375 degrees until breads are golden and sound hollow when tapped, 45 to 55 minutes. Transfer to wire racks and cool.

CRANBERRY-NUT WHEAT LOAF

Dried cranberries and walnuts make this bread a perfect fall and winter offering.

1 loaf (16 servings)

1 package active dry yeast

¾ cup warm water (110–115 degrees)

3 tablespoons honey

2–3 tablespoons margarine, or butter, room temperature

1 egg

1–2 cups all-purpose flour, divided

1 cup whole wheat flour

1 teaspoon salt

1 cup dried cranberries

⅔ cup coarsely chopped walnuts

Per Serving:
Calories: 153
% of calories from fat: 27
Fat (gm): 4.7
Saturated fat (gm): 0.6
Cholesterol (mg): 0
Sodium (mg): 141
Protein (gm): 4.1
Carbohydrate (gm): 24.6

Exchanges:
Milk: 0.0
Vegetable: 0.0
Fruit: 0.5
Bread: 1.0
Meat: 0.0
Fat: 1.0

1. Mix yeast, warm water, and honey in large bowl; let stand 5 minutes. Add margarine, egg, 1 cup all-purpose flour, whole wheat flour, and salt, mixing until blended. Mix in cranberries, walnuts, and enough remaining 1 cup all-purpose flour to make smooth dough.

2. Knead dough on floured surface until smooth and elastic, about 5 minutes. Place in greased bowl; let rise, covered, in warm place until double in size, 1 to 1½ hours. Punch dough down.

3. Shape into loaf and place in greased 9 x 5-inch loaf pan. Let stand, covered, until double in size, about 45 minutes. Brush top of loaf with fat-free milk. Bake at 375 degrees until loaf is golden and sounds hollow when tapped, 35 to 40 minutes. Remove from pan and cool on wire rack.

THREE KINGS' BREAD

LO *In Mexico, this rich fruit-studded bread is traditionally served to celebrate Twelfth Night on January 6. A tiny china doll is often baked into the dough; the person receiving the piece of bread with the doll must give a party on February 2 to celebrate the Feast of the Candles!*

1 loaf (12 servings)

1 package active dry yeast
⅓ cup warm fat-free milk (110–115 degrees)
2¼–2¾ cups all-purpose flour, divided
6 tablespoons margarine, or butter, room temperature
¼ cup plus 2 tablespoons sugar, divided
2 eggs
½ teaspoon salt
¼ cup dark raisins
½ cup candied fruit, divided
¼ cup chopped walnuts
1–2 tablespoons fat-free milk

Per Serving:
Calories: 205
% of calories from fat: 28
Fat (gm): 6.3
Saturated fat (gm): 1.3
Cholesterol (mg): 17.9
Sodium (mg): 174
Protein (gm): 4.2
Carbohydrate (gm): 33.1

Exchanges:
Milk: 0.0
Vegetable: 0.0
Fruit: 0.5
Bread: 1.5
Meat: 0.0
Fat: 1.5

1. Mix yeast, warm milk, and ½ cup flour in small bowl; beat well. Let stand, covered, in warm place for 30 minutes. Beat margarine and ¼ cup sugar in medium bowl until fluffy. Beat in eggs, salt, and yeast mixture, mixing well. Mix in raisins, ¼ cup candied fruit, walnuts, and 1¾ cups flour; mix in remaining ½ cup flour, if necessary, to make soft dough.

2. Knead on floured surface until smooth and elastic, about 5 minutes. Place in greased bowl; let stand, covered, in warm place until dough is double in size, about 1 hour. Punch dough down.

3. Form dough into a round on greased cookie sheet. Make a hole in center of dough, then stretch with fingers into a ring 8 inches in diameter. Let rise, covered, in warm place until double in size, about 30 minutes. Decorate with remaining ¼ cup candied fruit. Bake at 375 degrees until bread is golden, 25 to 30 minutes. Brush with 1 to 2 tablespoons of milk and sprinkle with remaining 2 tablespoons sugar. Bake until glazed, 3 to 5 minutes longer. Transfer to wire rack and cool.

ORANGE MARMALADE CRESCENTS

L *These fragrant coffeecakes for special occasions are drizzled with a warm honey and orange topping.*

2 loaves (12 servings each)

Potato Bread (see p. 538)

¼ cup sugar

2 tablespoons margarine, or butter, room temperature

¾ cup orange marmalade

½ cup raisins

¼–½ cup sliced almonds, divided

¼ cup each: light rum, or 1–2 teaspoons rum extract

¼ cup honey

2 tablespoons orange juice

Per Serving:
Calories: 229
% of calories from fat: 13
Fat (gm): 3.2
Saturated fat (gm): 0.7
Cholesterol (mg): 17.9
Sodium (mg): 151
Protein (gm): 4.9
Carbohydrate (gm): 44.7

Exchanges:
Milk: 0.0
Vegetable: 0.0
Fruit: 0.0
Bread: 3.0
Meat: 0.0
Fat: 0.5

1. Make recipe for Potato Bread through step 2, adding ¼ cup sugar. Divide dough into halves; roll each on floured surface into 15 x 6 inch rectangle. Spread each rectangle with 1 tablespoon margarine and place on greased cookie sheets.

2. Make 2-inch cuts at 1-inch intervals along the long sides of rectangles. Mix orange marmalade, raisins, half the almonds, and rum; spread half the mixture down center of each rectangle. Crisscross the cut strips over filling; pinch ends of coffeecakes to seal. Curve each coffeecake into a crescent shape. Let rise, covered, until impression of finger remains in dough, 1 to 1½ hours. Bake at 375 degrees until coffeecakes are golden, about 20 minutes. Transfer coffeecakes to wire racks and cool.

3. Heat honey and orange juice in small saucepan until hot; brush over warm coffeecakes and sprinkle with remaining almonds. Serve warm.

APPLE HONEY KUCHEN

LO *Use your favorite baking apple, tart or sweet, for this brunch bread.*

2 kuchens (8–10 servings each)

1 package active dry yeast

¾ cup warm fat-free milk (110–115 degrees)

6 tablespoons granulated sugar, divided

4 tablespoons margarine, or butter, divided

1 egg

2–3 cups all-purpose flour

¾ teaspoon salt

1 pound tart, or sweet, baking apples, peeled, sliced

½ cup raisins

¼ cup packed light brown sugar

2 tablespoons grated orange zest

¼ teaspoon ground cinnamon

⅛ teaspoon ground nutmeg

2–4 tablespoons honey

Fat-free milk

Per Serving:
Calories: 162
% of calories from fat: 19
Fat (gm): 3.4
Saturated fat (gm): 0.7
Cholesterol (mg): 13.5
Sodium (mg): 145
Protein (gm): 2.8
Carbohydrate (gm): 30.9

Exchanges:
Milk: 0.0
Vegetable: 0.0
Fruit: 0.0
Bread: 2.0
Meat: 0.0
Fat: 0.5

1. Mix yeast, milk, and 2 tablespoons granulated sugar in large bowl; let stand 5 minutes. Add 2 tablespoons margarine, egg, 2 cups flour, and salt, mixing until blended. Mix in enough remaining 1 cup flour to make smooth dough.

2. Knead dough on floured surface until smooth and elastic, about 5 minutes. Place in greased bowl; let rise, covered, in warm place until double in size, 1 to 1½ hours. Punch dough down.

3. Heat remaining 2 tablespoons margarine in large skillet until melted; add apples and raisins and cook over medium heat until apples are tender, 5 to 8 minutes. Remove from heat. Sprinkle combined brown sugar, orange zest, cinnamon, and nutmeg over apple mixture and toss.

4. Divide dough into halves. Roll each on floured surface into a 12-inch round. Arrange apple mixture on half of each round; drizzle each with 1 to 2 tablespoons honey. Brush edges of dough with milk; fold dough over filling and press edges with tines of fork to seal. Transfer to greased cookie sheets; sprinkle with remaining 4 tablespoons granulated sugar. Let rise, covered, until impression of finger remains in dough when touched, about 1 hour. Reseal edges, if necessary. Bake at 375 degrees until golden, about 20 minutes. Transfer to wire racks and cool; serve warm.

STICKY BUNS

LO *Impossible to resist, especially when the buns are fresh from the oven! Finger licking permitted!*

24 buns (1 each)

2–3½ cups all-purpose flour, divided

⅓ cup plus 2 tablespoons sugar, divided

1 package active dry yeast

1 tablespoon plus 1 teaspoon ground cinnamon, divided

1 teaspoon salt

1 cup warm fat-free milk (110–115 degrees)

¼ cup fat-free sour cream

1 egg, beaten

Grated zest from 1 orange

Sticky Bun Topping (recipe follows)

½ cup pecan pieces

Per Serving:
Calories: 199
% of calories from fat: 17.5
Fat (gm): 4.0
Saturated fat (gm): 0.6
Cholesterol (mg): 9.4
Sodium (mg): 138
Protein (gm): 3.1
Carbohydrate (gm): 38.8

Exchanges:
Milk: 0.0
Vegetable: 0.0
Fruit: 0.0
Bread: 2.5
Meat: 0.0
Fat: 0.5

1. Combine 2 cups flour, ⅓ cup sugar, yeast, 1 tablespoon cinnamon, and salt in large bowl. Stir in milk, sour cream, egg, and orange zest until blended. Stir in enough remaining 1½ cups flour to make soft dough.

2. Knead dough on floured surface until smooth and elastic, about 5 minutes. Place in greased bowl and let stand, covered, in warm place until double in size, 30 to 45 minutes. Punch dough down.

3. Spoon about ½ cup hot Sticky Bun Topping into 3 lightly greased 9-inch round cake pans; sprinkle with pecan pieces. Combine remaining 2 tablespoons sugar and 1 teaspoon cinnamon in small bowl. Divide dough into halves. Roll one half on floured surface into rectangle 12 x 7 inches; sprinkle with half the sugar mixture. Roll dough up, beginning with long side; cut into 12 equal slices.

4. Repeat with remaining dough and sugar mixture. Place 8 rolls, cut sides up, in each pan, over the topping. Let rise, covered, in warm place, until double in size, about 30 minutes. Bake at 375 degrees until rolls are golden, 15 to 20 minutes. Immediately invert rolls onto aluminum foil; serve warm.

Sticky Bun Topping

Makes about 1½ cups

4 tablespoons margarine, or butter
1½ cups packed light brown sugar
½ cup light corn syrup
¼ cup all-purpose flour

1. Melt margarine in small saucepan; stir in remaining ingredients and cook until bubbly.

Variation

Cinnamon Rolls — Delete Sticky Bun Topping. Make dough as above, mixing in ½ cup raisins. Let dough rise, then roll and shape as above, sprinkling with double the amount of sugar and cinnamon. Place rolls, cut sides up, in greased muffin cups. Bake as above, and invert rolls onto wire racks. Mix 2 cups powdered sugar with enough fat-free milk to make a thick glaze; drizzle over slightly warm rolls.

GRANOLA BREAD

L

A wonderful breakfast bread — serve with plenty of Spiced Rhubarb Jam (see p. 578). For convenience, this bread is made with an electric mixer and has only 1 rise.

2 loaves (16 servings each)

2 packages active dry yeast

¾ cup warm water (110–115 degrees)

2 tablespoons light brown sugar

1¼ cups buttermilk

3 cups all-purpose flour

¾–1½ cups whole wheat flour, d ivided

2 teaspoons baking powder

1 teaspoon salt

2–3 tablespoons margarine, or butter,
    room temperature

1½ cups low-fat granola

Buttermilk

Per Serving:
Calories: 200
% of calories from fat: 17
Fat (gm): 3.8
Saturated fat (gm): 0.6
Cholesterol (mg): 9
Sodium (mg): 131
Protein (gm): 3.1
Carbohydrate (gm): 38.9

Exchanges:
Milk: 0.0
Vegetable: 0.0
Fruit: 0.0
Bread: 2.5
Meat: 0.0
Fat: 0.5

1. Mix yeast, warm water, and brown sugar in large mixer bowl; let stand 5 minutes. Mix in buttermilk, all-purpose flour, ¾ cup whole wheat flour, baking powder, salt, and margarine on low speed until smooth. Mix in granola and enough remaining ¾ cup whole wheat flour to make a smooth dough (dough will be slightly sticky.) Knead dough on floured surface until smooth and elastic, about 5 minutes.

2. Divide dough into halves. Roll each into a rectangle 18 x 10 inches. Roll up, beginning at short ends; press ends to seal. Place loaves, seam sides down, in greased 9 x 5-inch loaf pans. Let rise, covered, in warm place until double in size, about 1 hour; brush with buttermilk. Bake at 375 degrees until loaves are golden and sound hollow when tapped, 40 to 45 minutes. Remove from pans and cool on wire racks.

ENGLISH MUFFIN BREAD

L *This quick and easy single-rise bread has a coarse texture similar to English muffins. Delicious warm from the oven, or toasted, with Gingered Honey (see p. 580).*

1 loaf (16 servings)

1½–2½ cups all-purpose flour, divided
½ cup quick-cooking oats
1 package active dry yeast
¼ teaspoon baking soda
1 teaspoon salt
1¼ cups warm fat-free milk (110–115 degrees)
1 tablespoon honey
Cornmeal

Per Serving:
Calories: 79
% of calories from fat: 4
Fat (gm): 0.4
Saturated fat (gm): 0.1
Cholesterol (mg): 0.3
Sodium (mg): 163
Protein (gm): 2.9
Carbohydrate (gm): 15.9

Exchanges:
Milk: 0.0
Vegetable: 0.0
Fruit: 0.0
Bread: 1.0
Meat: 0.0
Fat: 0.0

1. Combine 1½ cups flour, oats, yeast, baking soda, and salt in large bowl. Add milk and honey, mixing until smooth. Stir in enough of remaining 1 cup flour to make a thick batter. Pour into greased, cornmeal-coated 8 x 4-inch loaf pan. Let rise, covered, in warm place until double in size, 45 to 60 minutes. Bake at 400 degrees until bread is golden and sounds hollow when tapped, 25 to 30 minutes. Remove from pan and cool on wire rack.

Variation

Raisin Bread — Make recipe as above, adding 1 teaspoon ground cinnamon and ½ cup raisins to the batter; do not coat loaf pan with cornmeal.

BUBBLE LOAF

LO *Also called Bath Buns and Monkey Bread, this pull-apart loaf is easy to make, fun to eat, and perfect for potluck offerings and parties. The recipe can be halved and baked in a 6-cup fluted cake pan.*

1 loaf (16 servings)

2 packages active dry yeast
1 cup fat-free milk, warm (110–115 degrees)
6 tablespoons margarine, or butter,
    room temperature
¼ cup sugar
3 eggs
4 cups all-purpose flour
½ teaspoon salt

Per Serving:
Calories: 186
% of calories from fat: 27
Fat (gm): 5.5
Saturated fat (gm): 1.2
Cholesterol (mg): 40.2
Sodium (mg): 137
Protein (gm): 5.3
Carbohydrate (gm): 28.3

Exchanges:
Milk: 0.0
Vegetable: 0.0
Fruit: 0.0
Bread: 2.0
Meat: 0.0
Fat: 1.0

1. Stir yeast into milk in bowl; let stand 2 to 3 minutes. Beat margarine and sugar until fluffy in large bowl; beat in eggs, 1 at a time. Mix in combined flour and salt alternately with milk mixture, beginning and ending with dry ingredients and beating well after each addition. Let stand, covered, in warm place until dough is double in size, about 1 hour. Punch dough down.

2. Drop dough by large spoonfuls into greased 10-inch tube pan. Let rise, covered, until dough is double in size, about 30 minutes. Bake at 350 degrees until browned, 25 to 30 minutes. Cool in pan on wire rack 10 minutes; remove from pan. Serve warm.

MULTIGRAIN BATTER BREAD

L *Batter bread preparation is quick and easy, requiring no kneading and only one rise.*

2 loaves (16 servings each)

3¼ cups all-purpose flour
1 cup whole wheat flour
¼ cup soy flour, or quick-cooking oats
¾ cup quick-cooking oats
¼ cup sugar

½ teaspoon salt
2 packages fast-rising yeast
1 cup cooked brown rice
2¼ cups fat-free milk, hot (125–130 degrees)
2 tablespoons vegetable oil

Per Serving:
Calories: 97
% of calories from fat: 13
Fat (gm): 1.4
Saturated fat (gm): 0.2
Cholesterol (mg): 0.3
Sodium (mg): 43
Protein (gm): 3.5
Carbohydrate (gm): 17.9

Exchanges:
Milk: 0.0
Vegetable: 0.0
Fruit: 0.0
Bread: 1.0
Meat: 0.0
Fat: 0.5

1. Combine flours, oats, sugar, salt, and yeast in large bowl; add rice, milk, and oil, mixing until smooth. Spoon into 2 greased 8 x 4-inch bread pans; let stand, covered, until double in size, about 30 minutes. Bake at 375 degrees until loaves are browned and sound hollow when tapped, 35 to 40 minutes. Remove from pans and cool on wire racks.

SOFT PRETZELS

To achieve their typical dense, chewy texture, pretzels are cooked in boiling water before baking.

12 pretzels (1 each)

1 package active dry yeast
½ cup warm water (110–115 degrees)
1 tablespoon sugar
1 cup fat-free milk, heated to simmering, cooled
2–4 cups all-purpose flour, divided
1 teaspoon salt
2 quarts water
1 tablespoon baking soda
1 egg, beaten
1 tablespoon cold water
Toppings: poppy seeds, sesame seeds, coarse salt, herbs, dried onion flakes, etc. (optional)

Per Serving:
Calories: 152
% of calories from fat: 5
Fat (gm): 0.8
Saturated fat (gm): 0.2
Cholesterol (mg): 18.1
Sodium (mg): 509
Protein (gm): 5.2
Carbohydrate (gm): 30.2

Exchanges:
Milk: 0.0
Vegetable: 0.0
Fruit: 0.0
Bread: 2.0
Meat: 0.0
Fat: 0.0

1. Mix yeast, warm water, and sugar in large bowl; let stand 5 minutes. Add fat-free milk, 2 cups flour, and salt, beating until smooth. Mix in enough remaining 2 cups flour to make smooth dough. Knead dough on floured surface until smooth and elastic, about 5 minutes. Place in greased bowl; let rise, covered, in warm place until double in size, 45 to 60 minutes. Punch dough down.

2. Roll dough on floured surface to rectangle 16 x 12 inches. Cut dough lengthwise into 12 strips, 1 inch wide. Roll one strip dough with palms of hands until rounded and 18 to 20 inches long. Form loop, holding ends of strip and twisting strip 2 times. Bring ends of strip down and fasten at opposite sides of loop to form pretzel shape. Repeat with remaining dough, transferring pretzels to floured surface. Let pretzels stand, lightly covered, 30 minutes (they may not double in size).

3. Heat 2 quarts water to boiling in large saucepan; stir in baking soda. Transfer pretzels, a few at a time, into boiling water; boil until dough feels firm, about 1 minute. Remove pretzels from boiling water with slotted spoon, draining well. Place on generously greased foil-lined cookie sheets. Brush pretzels with combined egg and cold water; sprinkle with desired toppings. Bake at 400 degrees until golden, 18 to 20 minutes. Remove to wire racks and cool.

SQUASH DINNER ROLLS

L

Use pumpkin, Hubbard, or acorn squash for these rolls; mashed sweet potatoes can be used also. If a loaf is preferred, shape and bake the dough in a greased 8½ x 4½-inch loaf pan.

24 rolls (1 each)

1½–2½ cups all-purpose flour, divided

1 cup whole wheat flour

2 packages fast-rising yeast

1–2 teaspoons salt

½ cup fat-free milk

¼ cup honey

1–2 tablespoons margarine, or butter

¾ cup mashed cooked winter squash

1 egg

Per Serving:
Calories: 70
% of calories from fat: 11
Fat (gm): 0.9
Saturated fat (gm): 0.2
Cholesterol (mg): 9
Sodium (mg): 100
Protein (gm): 2.2
Carbohydrate (gm): 13.5

Exchanges:
Milk: 0.0
Vegetable: 0.0
Fruit: 0.0
Bread: 1.0
Meat: 0.0
Fat: 0.0

1. Combine 1½ cups all-purpose flour, whole wheat flour, yeast, and salt in large bowl. Heat milk, honey, and margarine in small saucepan to 125–130 degrees; add to flour mixture, mixing until smooth. Mix in squash, egg, and enough remaining 1 cup all-purpose flour to make smooth dough.

2. Knead dough on floured surface until smooth and elastic, about 5 minutes. Place in greased bowl; let stand, covered, in warm place until double in size, 30 to 45 minutes. Punch dough down.

3. Divide dough into 24 pieces; shape into round rolls and place in greased muffin tins. Bake at 375 degrees until browned, 20 to 25 minutes.

BOLILLOS

L

Bolillos are the crusty, "bobbin-shaped" yeast rolls popular throughout Mexico. The dough is similar to French bread dough.

12 rolls (1 each)

1 package active dry yeast
½ teaspoon sugar
1 cup hot water (110–115 degrees)
2 tablespoons vegetable shortening, room temperature
3½–4 cups all-purpose flour
½ teaspoon salt
2 tablespoons fat-free milk

Per Serving:
Calories: 155
% of calories from fat: 15
Fat (gm): 2.5
Saturated fat (gm): 0.6
Cholesterol (mg): 0
Sodium (mg): 91
Protein (gm): 4.1
Carbohydrate (gm): 28.4

Exchanges:
Milk: 0.0
Vegetable: 0.0
Fruit: 0.0
Bread: 2.0
Meat: 0.0
Fat: 0.5

1. Mix yeast, sugar, and hot water in medium bowl; add shortening, stirring until melted. Let stand 5 minutes. Mix in 3½ cups flour and salt; mix in enough remaining ½ cup flour to make soft dough.

2. Knead dough on floured surface until smooth and elastic, about 5 minutes. Place in greased bowl; let stand, covered, in warm place until dough is double in size, 1 to 1½ hours. Punch dough down.

3. Divide dough into 12 equal pieces. Roll or pat 1 piece into an oval shape, a scant ½ inch thick. Fold ⅓ of the dough along the long edge toward the center and flatten with palm of hand; fold dough in half in same direction and flatten with palm of hand. Roll dough lightly with hand to make a rounded oval shape. Place, seam side up, on lightly greased cookie sheet. Repeat with remaining dough. Let rolls stand, loosely covered, until double in size, about 1 hour; brush with milk. Bake at 375 degrees until lightly browned, about 25 minutes.

PITA BREADS

V *Also called Syrian bread or pocket breads, pitas can be eaten plain or split and filled. The breads freeze well, so make lots!*

12 pitas (1 each)

1 package active dry yeast
1⅓ cups warm water (110–115 degrees)
¼ teaspoon sugar
1½ tablespoons olive oil
3–4 cups all-purpose flour, divided
1 teaspoon salt

Per Serving:
Calories: 131
% of calories from fat: 14
Fat (gm): 2
Saturated fat (gm): 0.3
Cholesterol (mg): 0
Sodium (mg): 178
Protein (gm): 3.5
Carbohydrate (gm): 24.2

Exchanges:
Milk: 0.0
Vegetable: 0.0
Fruit: 0.0
Bread: 2.0
Meat: 0.0
Fat: 0.0

1. Combine yeast, warm water, and sugar in large bowl; let stand 5 minutes. Add oil, 3 cups flour, and salt, mixing until smooth. Mix in enough remaining 1 cup flour to make smooth dough.

2. Knead dough on floured surface until smooth and elastic, about 5 minutes. Place in greased bowl; let stand, covered, in warm place until double in size, about 1 hour. Punch dough down.

3. Shape dough into 12 balls; let stand, covered, 30 minutes (dough will not double in size). Roll balls of dough on floured surface into rounds 5 to 6 inches in diameter; place 2 to 3 inches apart on greased cookie sheets; let stand 30 minutes. Bake, 1 pan at a time, at 500 degrees until pitas are puffed and brown, 3 to 5 minutes. Remove to wire racks and cool.

WHOLE WHEAT LAVOSH

L *A flat cracker bread that is perfect to serve with dips and spreads, or as an accompaniment to soups and salads.*

8 lavosh (1 each)

½ cup fat-free milk, warm (110–115 degrees)
1 package active dry yeast
2⅓ cups whole wheat flour
½–1 cup all-purpose flour, divided

½ teaspoon salt

1 egg white

1 tablespoon water

Per Serving:
Calories: 186
% of calories from fat: 4
Fat (gm): 0.8
Saturated fat (gm): 0.2
Cholesterol (mg): 0.3
Sodium (mg): 150
Protein (gm): 7.7
Carbohydrate (gm): 38.5

Exchanges:
Milk: 0.0
Vegetable: 0.0
Fruit: 0.0
Bread: 2.5
Meat: 0.0
Fat: 0.0

1. Mix milk and yeast in large bowl; let stand 5 minutes. Mix in whole wheat flour, ½ cup all-purpose flour, and salt; mix in enough remaining ½ cup all-purpose flour to make a smooth dough. Let stand, covered, 15 to 20 minutes.

2. Divide dough into 8 equal pieces. Roll each on lightly floured surface into a 3-inch round; place on greased cookie sheet. Beat egg white and water; brush over top of dough. Bake at 425 degrees until crisp and browned, 5 to 8 minutes, turning over halfway through baking time. (Lavosh will become crisper upon cooling, so do not overbake.) Cool on wire rack.

FOCACCIA

L

This delicious Italian bread is very versatile — see Leek and Onion Focaccia and Fruit Focaccia (pp. 318, 318). Focaccia can be frozen, so bake extra to have on hand.

2 focaccia (10 servings each)

4–5½ cups bread or all-purpose flour, divided

1 package (¼ ounce) fast-rising yeast

1 teaspoon each: sugar, salt

1¾ cups very hot water (125–130 degrees)

Olive oil cooking spray

¼ cup (1 ounce) grated Parmesan cheese

Per Serving:
Calories: 139
% of calories from fat: 5
Fat (gm): 0.8
Saturated fat (gm): 0.2
Cholesterol (mg): 1
Sodium (mg): 131
Protein (gm): 5.2
Carbohydrate (gm): 28.2

Exchanges:
Milk: 0.0
Vegetable: 0.0
Fruit: 0.0
Bread: 2.0
Meat: 0.0
Fat: 0.0

1. Combine 4 cups flour, yeast, sugar, and salt in large mixing bowl. Add water, mixing until smooth. Mix in enough remaining 1½ cups flour to make soft dough.

2. Knead dough on floured surface until dough is smooth and elastic, about 5 minutes. Place in greased bowl; turn greased side up and let rise, covered, in warm place until double in size, about 1 hour. Punch dough down.

3. Divide dough into halves. Roll 1 piece dough on floured surface to fit jelly roll pan, 15 x 10 inches; ease dough into greased pan. Repeat with remaining dough. Let dough rise until double in size, 45 to 60 minutes. Make ¼-inch-deep indentations with fingers to "dimple" the dough; spray lightly with cooking spray and sprinkle with Parmesan cheese. Bake at 425 degrees until browned, about 30 minutes. Cool in pans on wire racks. Serve warm or at room temperature.

SPINACH-MUSHROOM FLATBREAD

L *This attractive bread is made in a freeform shape and topped with spinach and Parmesan cheese. The bread can be made in advance and reheated at 300 degrees, loosely wrapped in foil, for 15 to 20 minutes.*

1 loaf (12–16 servings)

2½–3½ cups all-purpose flour, divided

1½ cups whole wheat flour

2 tablespoons sugar

1½ teaspoons dried rosemary leaves, crushed

½ teaspoon each: dried thyme leaves, salt

1 package fast-rising yeast

2 cups very hot water (125–130 degrees)

¼ cup sliced onion

3 cloves garlic, minced

2 cups torn spinach leaves

1 cup sliced cremini, or white, mushrooms

¼ cup (2 ounces) shredded reduced-fat
mozzarella cheese

2–3 tablespoons grated fat-free Parmesan cheese

Per Serving:
Calories: 190
% of calories from fat: 5
Fat (gm): 1
Saturated fat (gm): 0.4
Cholesterol (mg): 1.3
Sodium (mg): 123
Protein (gm): 7
Carbohydrate (gm): 38.8

Exchanges:
Milk: 0.0
Vegetable: 0.0
Fruit: 0.0
Bread: 2.5
Meat: 0.0
Fat: 0.0

1. Combine 2½ cups all-purpose flour, whole wheat flour, sugar, herbs, salt, and yeast in large bowl; add water, mixing until smooth. Mix in enough remaining 1 cup all-purpose flour to make soft dough.

2. Knead dough on floured surface until smooth and elastic, about 5 minutes. Place in greased bowl; let rise, loosely covered, in warm place until double in size, 30 to 45 minutes. Punch dough down.

3. Pat dough into a round on floured surface. Pull the edges of the dough into a freeform shape, about 10 x 14 inches. Transfer dough to greased cookie sheet and let stand 20 minutes (dough will rise, but will not double in size). Bake at 350 degrees until golden, about 20 minutes.

4. While bread is baking, sauté onion and garlic in lightly greased skillet until tender, 3 to 4 minutes. Add spinach and mushrooms; cook, covered, over medium until spinach is wilted, about 5 minutes. Cook, uncovered, until mushrooms are tender, about 5 minutes. Remove from heat. Arrange spinach mixture over top of baked bread; sprinkle with cheeses. Return to oven until cheese is melted, 5 to 10 minutes. Transfer to wire rack and cool.

GARLIC BREAD

Select a good quality French or Italian loaf for this aromatic bread, or use sourdough bread for a flavorful variation.

4 servings

4 thick slices French, or Italian, bread
Olive oil cooking spray
2 cloves garlic, cut into halves

Per Serving:
Calories: 71
% of calories from fat: 10
Fat (gm): 0.8
Saturated fat (gm): 0.2
Cholesterol (mg): 0
Sodium (mg): 152
Protein (gm): 2.3
Carbohydrate (gm): 13.5

Exchanges:
Milk: 0.0
Vegetable: 0.0
Fruit: 0.0
Bread: 1.0
Meat: 0.0
Fat: 0.0

1. Spray both sides of bread generously with cooking spray. Broil on cookie sheet 4 inches from heat source until browned, about 1 minute on each side.

2. Rub both sides of hot toast with cut sides of garlic.

Variation

Parmesan Garlic Bread — Combine 2 tablespoons grated Parmesan cheese and 4 teaspoons minced garlic. Spray bread with cooking spray as above and spread top of each slice with cheese mixture. Broil as above, or wrap loosely in and bake at 350 degrees until warm, about 10 minutes.

CROUTONS

Croutons can brighten a soup, add crunch to a salad, and provide a flavor accent for many dishes.

12 servings (¼ cup each)

3 cups cubed firm, or day-old, French, or Italian, bread (½–¾ inch)
Vegetable cooking spray

1. Spray bread cubes with cooking spray; arrange in single layer on jelly roll pan. Bake at 375 degrees until browned, 8 to 10 minutes, stirring occasionally. Cool; store in airtight container up to 2 weeks.

Per Serving:
Calories: 20
% of calories from fat: 13
Fat (gm): 0.3
Saturated fat (gm): 0.1
Cholesterol (mg): 0
Sodium (mg): 39
Protein (gm): 0.6
Carbohydrate (gm): 3.7

Exchanges:
Milk: 0.0
Vegetable: 0.0
Fruit: 0.0
Bread: 0.0
Meat: 0.0
Fat: 0.0

Variations

Italian-Style Croutons — Spray bread cubes with vegetable cooking spray; sprinkle with combined 1 teaspoon garlic powder and 1 teaspoon Italian seasoning and toss. Bake as above.

Sourdough Croutons — Spray sourdough bread cubes with vegetable cooking spray; sprinkle with 2 teaspoons bouquet garni and toss. Bake as above.

Parmesan Croutons — Spray bread cubes with vegetable cooking spray; sprinkle with 1 to 2 tablespoons grated fat-free Parmesan cheese and toss. Bake as above.

Rye Caraway Croutons — Spray rye bread cubes with vegetable cooking spray; sprinkle with 2 teaspoons crushed caraway seeds and toss. Bake as above.

Sesame Croutons — Spray bread cubes with vegetable cooking spray; sprinkle with 2 to 3 teaspoons sesame seeds and toss. Bake as above.

Herb Croutons — Spray multigrain or whole wheat bread cubes with vegetable cooking spray; sprinkle with 2 teaspoons dried herbs or herb combinations, and toss. Bake as above.

GREEN CHILI CORN BREAD

Corn bread, Southwest-style! If using mild canned chilies, consider adding a teaspoon or so of minced jalapeño chili for a piquant accent.

9 servings

¼ cup chopped red bell pepper

2 cloves garlic, minced

½ teaspoon cumin seeds, crushed

1¼ cups yellow cornmeal

¾ cup all-purpose flour

2 teaspoons baking powder

1 teaspoon sugar

½ teaspoon each: baking soda, salt

1¼ cups buttermilk

½ cup canned cream-style corn

1 can (4 ounces) chopped hot, or mild, green chilies, well drained

2 eggs

3½ tablespoons margarine, or butter, melted

Per Serving:
Calories: 184
% of calories from fat: 29
Fat (gm): 6.1
Saturated fat (gm): 1.3
Cholesterol (mg): 24.9
Sodium (mg): 563
Protein (gm): 5.6
Carbohydrate (gm): 27.6

Exchanges:
Milk: 0.0
Vegetable: 0.0
Fruit: 0.0
Bread: 2.0
Meat: 0.0
Fat: 1.0

1. Sauté bell pepper, garlic, and cumin seeds in lightly greased small skillet until pepper is tender, 2 to 3 minutes.

2. Combine cornmeal, flour, baking powder, sugar, baking soda, and salt in large bowl. Mix in bell pepper mixture, buttermilk, and remaining ingredients; spread in greased 8-inch-square baking pan. Bake at 425 degrees until golden, about 30 minutes. Cool in pan on wire rack; serve warm.

THREE-GRAIN MOLASSES BREAD

V

Molasses and brown sugar give this hearty quick bread a special flavor.

45

◊

1 loaf (16 servings)

1 cup each: all-purpose flour, whole wheat flour,
   yellow cornmeal
1 teaspoon baking soda
½ teaspoon salt
1¼ cups water
½ cup each: light molasses, packed light brown sugar
3 tablespoons vegetable oil

1. Mix all ingredients in bowl; pour into greased
9 x 5-inch loaf pan. Bake at 350 degrees until
wooden pick comes out clean, about 1 hour.
Remove bread from pan and cool on wire rack.

Per Serving:
Calories: 155
% of calories from fat: 17
Fat (gm): 3
Saturated fat (gm): 0.4
Cholesterol (mg): 0
Sodium (mg): 153
Protein (gm): 2.5
Carbohydrate (gm): 30.5

Exchanges:
Milk: 0.0
Vegetable: 0.0
Fruit: 0.0
Bread: 2.0
Meat: 0.0
Fat: 0.5

FRUITED BRAN BREAD

L

*Use any combination of dried fruit you want in this quick, healthy, no-rise
batter bread.*

45

◊

1 loaf (16 servings)

1¼ cups all-purpose flour
½ cup whole wheat flour
2 teaspoons baking powder
½ teaspoon each: baking soda, salt
1½ cups whole bran cereal
1⅓ cups buttermilk
¾ cup packed light brown sugar
3 tablespoons margarine, or butter, melted
1 egg
1 cup coarsely chopped mixed dried fruit
¼–½ cup chopped walnuts

Per Serving:
Calories: 169
% of calories from fat: 20
Fat (gm): 4.2
Saturated fat (gm): 0.8
Cholesterol (mg): 14.1
Sodium (mg): 261
Protein (gm): 4.1
Carbohydrate (gm): 33.1

Exchanges:
Milk: 0.0
Vegetable: 0.0
Fruit: 0.0
Bread: 2.0
Meat: 0.0
Fat: 0.5

1. Combine flours, baking powder, baking soda, salt, and bran cereal
in medium bowl. Add buttermilk, brown sugar, margarine, and

egg, mixing just until dry ingredients are moistened. Gently fold in dried fruit and walnuts. Pour into greased and floured 9 x 5-inch loaf pan. Bake at 350 degrees until wooden pick inserted in center comes out clean, about 1 hour. Remove from pan; cool on wire rack before slicing.

BROWN SUGAR BANANA BREAD

Brown sugar gives this banana bread a caramel flavor; the applesauce adds moistness. It's the best!

1 loaf (16 servings)

4 tablespoons margarine, or butter, room temperature

¼ cup applesauce

2 eggs

2 tablespoons fat-free milk, or water

¾ cup packed light brown sugar

1 cup mashed banana (2–3 medium bananas)

1¾ cups all-purpose flour

2 teaspoons baking powder

½ teaspoon baking soda

¼ teaspoon salt

¼ cup coarsely chopped walnuts, or pecans

Per Serving:
Calories: 151
% of calories from fat: 28
Fat (gm): 4.8
Saturated fat (gm): 0.9
Cholesterol (mg): 26.7
Sodium (mg): 160
Protein (gm): 2.9
Carbohydrate (gm): 24.9

Exchanges:
Milk: 0.0
Vegetable: 0.0
Fruit: 0.5
Bread: 1.0
Meat: 0.0
Fat: 1.0

1. Beat margarine, applesauce, eggs, milk, and brown sugar in large mixer bowl until smooth. Add banana and mix at low speed; beat at high speed 1 to 2 minutes. Mix in combined flour, baking powder, baking soda, and salt; mix in walnuts. Pour into greased loaf pan, 8 x 4-inch. Bake at 350 degrees until bread is golden and toothpick inserted in center comes out clean, 55 to 60 minutes. Cool in pan 10 minutes; remove from pan and cool on wire rack.

MINT AND CITRUS TEA BREAD

LO

45

A delicious addition to any meal, this bread is fine textured and lightly scented with mint, orange, and lemon.

1 loaf (16 servings)

½ cup fat-free milk

2 tablespoons each: finely chopped fresh, or 2 teaspoons dried mint leaves, grated orange zest

1 tablespoon grated lemon zest

¼ cup orange juice

5 tablespoons margarine, or butter, room temperature

¾ cup sugar

2 eggs

1½ cups all-purpose flour

½ cup whole wheat flour

1½ teaspoons baking powder

½ teaspoon salt

½ cup powdered sugar

Fat-free milk

Ground nutmeg

Per Serving:
Calories: 153
% of calories from fat: 25
Fat (gm): 4.4
Saturated fat (gm): 0.9
Cholesterol (mg): 26.8
Sodium (mg): 151
Protein (gm): 2.9
Carbohydrate (gm): 26

Exchanges:
Milk: 0.0
Vegetable: 0.0
Fruit: 0.0
Bread: 1.5
Meat: 0.0
Fat: 1.0

1. Heat milk, mint, and citrus zest in small saucepan to simmering; strain, discarding mint and zest. Add orange juice; cool.

2. Beat margarine and sugar until smooth in medium bowl; beat in eggs. Mix in combined flours, baking powder, and salt alternately with milk mixture, beginning and ending with dry ingredients. Pour into greased 8 x 4-inch loaf pan. Bake at 325 degrees until bread is golden and toothpick inserted in center comes out clean, about 45 minutes. Remove from pan and cool on wire rack.

3. Mix powdered sugar with enough fat-free milk to make medium glaze consistency; drizzle over bread and sprinkle lightly with nutmeg.

SOUR CREAM COFFEECAKE WITH APPLE-DATE FILLING

LO *An irresistible offering, this moist cake is filled with apples, dates, sugar, and spices.*

1 coffeecake (24 servings)

½ cup margarine, or butter, room temperature

¼ cup unsweetened applesauce

1 cup granulated sugar

⅓ cup packed light brown sugar

3 eggs

1½ teaspoons vanilla

3 cups all-purpose flour

1½ teaspoons each: baking powder, baking soda

1 teaspoon ground cinnamon

½ teaspoon salt

1½ cups fat-free sour cream

Apple-Date Filling (recipe follows)

Cream Cheese Glaze (recipe follows)

Per Serving:
Calories: 198
% of calories from fat: 21
Fat (gm): 4.6
Saturated fat (gm): 1
Cholesterol (mg): 26.6
Sodium (mg): 235
Protein (gm): 3.8
Carbohydrate (gm): 36.1

Exchanges:
Milk: 0.0
Vegetable: 0.0
Fruit: 0.0
Bread: 2.0
Meat: 0.0
Fat: 1.0

1. Beat margarine, applesauce, and sugars in large bowl until smooth. Beat in eggs, 1 at a time; beat in vanilla. Mix in combined flour, baking powder, baking soda, cinnamon, and salt alternately with sour cream, beginning and ending with dry ingredients.

2. Spoon ⅓ of the batter into greased and floured 12-cup fluted cake pan; spoon ½ the Apple-Date Filling over batter. Repeat layers, ending with batter. Bake at 325 degrees until toothpick inserted in center of cake comes out clean, about 1 hour. Cool in pan on wire rack 10 minutes; remove from pan and cool until just warm. Spoon Cream Cheese Glaze over.

Apple-Date Filling

Makes about 1 cup

½ cup dried apples, coarsely chopped
¼ cup chopped dates
⅔ cup water
⅓ cup packed light brown sugar
1 tablespoon flour
¼ teaspoon ground nutmeg
⅛ teaspoon salt

1. Heat all ingredients to boiling in small saucepan; reduce heat and simmer, uncovered, until apples are tender and mixture is thick, 5 to 8 minutes. Cool.

Cream Cheese Glaze

Makes ½ cup

2 ounces fat-free cream cheese, room temperature
1 cup powdered sugar

1. Beat cream cheese and powdered sugar in bowl until smooth.

CRANBERRY COFFEECAKE

LO

45

Quick and easy to make, this sweet-tart coffeecake can be ready to bake in less than 10 minutes.

1 coffeecake (12 servings)

1½ cups fresh, or frozen, thawed, cranberries
1 cup sugar, divided
1 teaspoon grated orange zest
1½ cups all-purpose flour
2 teaspoons baking powder
½ teaspoon salt
1 egg
¼ cup each: orange juice, fat-free milk

3 tablespoons margarine, or butter,
room temperature

¼–½ cup chopped pecans

1. Arrange cranberries in greased 8-inch-square baking pan; sprinkle with ½ cup sugar and orange zest. Mix remaining ingredients until just moistened in medium bowl; drop by spoonfuls over cranberries, spreading batter evenly to sides of pan. Bake at 400 degrees until wooden pick inserted in center comes out clean, 25 to 30 minutes. Immediately invert onto serving plate; serve warm.

Per Serving:
Calories: 180
% of calories from fat: 25
Fat (gm): 5
Saturated fat (gm): 0.8
Cholesterol (mg): 17.8
Sodium (mg): 185
Protein (gm): 2.6
Carbohydrate (gm): 31.8

Exchanges:
Milk: 0.0
Vegetable: 0.0
Fruit: 0.0
Bread: 2.0
Meat: 0.0
Fat: 1.0

VINEGAR BISCUITS

L

45

Vegetable shortening contributes to the fine texture of these biscuits. Vegetable shortening with no trans fats is now available.

12 biscuits (1 each)

¾ cup fat-free milk

¼ cup cider vinegar

3 tablespoons vegetable shortening, melted

2 cups all-purpose flour

1½ teaspoons baking soda

1 teaspoon cream of tartar

½ teaspoon salt

1. Mix milk, vinegar, and shortening; mix into combined flour, baking soda, cream of tartar, and salt in medium bowl. Knead dough on generously floured surface 1 to 2 minutes. Pat dough into ½ inch thickness; cut into 12 biscuits with 3-inch-round cutter. Bake on greased cookie sheet at 425 degrees until golden, 10 to 12 minutes.

Per Serving:
Calories: 109
% of calories from fat: 27
Fat (gm): 3.2
Saturated fat (gm): 0.8
Cholesterol (mg): 0.3
Sodium (mg): 255
Protein (gm): 2.7
Carbohydrate (gm): 17.1

Exchanges:
Milk: 0.0
Vegetable: 0.0
Fruit: 0.0
Bread: 1.0
Meat: 0.0
Fat: 0.5

QUICK SELF-RISING BISCUITS

L

45

Two cups all-purpose flour combined with 1 tablespoon baking powder and ½ teaspoon salt can be substituted for the self-rising flour.

18 biscuits (1 each)

1 tablespoon vegetable shortening
2 2 cups self-rising flour
¾–1 cup fat-free milk
1 tablespoon margarine, or butter, melted

Per Serving:
Calories: 65
% of calories from fat: 21
Fat (gm): 1.4
Saturated fat (gm): 0.3
Cholesterol (mg): 0.2
Sodium (mg): 189
Protein (gm): 1.7
Carbohydrate (gm): 10.8

Exchanges:
Milk: 0.0
Vegetable: 0.0
Fruit: 0.0
Bread: 1.0
Meat: 0.0
Fat: 0.0

1. Cut shortening into flour in medium bowl until mixture resembles coarse crumbs. Stir in enough milk to make a soft dough. Roll dough on floured surface to ½ inch thickness; cut into 18 biscuits with 2-inch cutter. Place in greased 13 x 9-inch baking pan; brush with melted margarine. Bake at 425 degrees until golden, about 15 minutes.

Variations

Chive Biscuits — Make biscuits as above, mixing 3 tablespoons snipped fresh or dried chives into the dough.

Parmesan Biscuits — Make biscuits as above; sprinkle with 2 tablespoons grated fat-free Parmesan cheese before baking.

SWEET POTATO BISCUITS

L

45

Sweet potatoes offer moistness and a delicate sweetness to these biscuits. For a nonsweet biscuit, white potatoes can be substituted.

18 biscuits (1 each)

¾ cup mashed, cooked sweet potatoes
3–4 tablespoons margarine, or butter, melted
⅔ cup fat-free milk

2 cups all-purpose flour, divided

4 teaspoons baking powder

1 tablespoon brown sugar

½ teaspoon salt

Fat-free milk

Ground nutmeg

Per Serving:
Calories: 82
% of calories from fat: 23
Fat (gm): 2.1
Saturated fat (gm): 0.4
Cholesterol (mg): 0.1
Sodium (mg): 161
Protein (gm): 1.8
Carbohydrate (gm): 14

Exchanges:
Milk: 0.0
Vegetable: 0.0
Fruit: 0.0
Bread: 1.0
Meat: 0.0
Fat: 0.5

1. Mix sweet potatoes and margarine in medium bowl; stir in ⅔ cup milk. Mix in 1¾ cups flour, baking powder, brown sugar, and salt. Mix in remaining ¼ cup flour if dough is too sticky to handle easily.

2. Knead dough on floured surface 5 to 6 times. Roll on floured surface to ½ inch thickness; cut into 18 biscuits with 2-inch biscuit cutter and place close together on greased baking sheet. Brush biscuits lightly with milk and sprinkle with nutmeg. Bake at 425 degrees until golden, 12 to 15 minutes.

"LITTLE PANTS" BISCUITS

L

45

These Mexican-inspired sugar and cinnamon-topped breads are cross between a biscuit and a cookie. They are usually made into "pants" shapes but can be cut into rounds or squares if you prefer.

18 biscuits (1 each)

¼ cup vegetable shortening

½ cup sugar, divided

2 cups all-purpose flour

2 teaspoons baking powder

½ teaspoon salt

½ cup plus 2 tablespoons fat-free milk, divided

½ teaspoon ground cinnamon

Per Serving:
Calories: 101
% of calories from fat: 27
Fat (gm): 3
Saturated fat (gm): 0.8
Cholesterol (mg): 0.1
Sodium (mg): 100
Protein (gm): 1.7
Carbohydrate (gm): 16.7

Exchanges:
Milk: 0.0
Vegetable: 0.0
Fruit: 0.0
Bread: 1.0
Meat: 0.0
Fat: 0.5

1. Beat shortening and 6 tablespoons sugar in medium bowl until smooth. Beat in combined flour, baking powder, and salt alternately with ½ cup milk to form soft dough.

2. Roll dough on floured surface into a rectangle, a scant ½ inch thick. Cut dough into 18 trapezoid shapes, 2½ inches on the bottom, 1½ inches on the top, and 3 inches on the sides. Cut out a small wedge of dough from the bottom, center of each piece to form "pants legs."

3. Brush biscuits with remaining 2 tablespoons milk; sprinkle with combined remaining 2 tablespoons sugar and cinnamon. Bake at 350 degrees on greased cookie sheet until browned, 15 to 20 minutes.

WILD RICE MUFFINS

LO *Wild rice adds crunchy texture and a nutritional boost to these muffins.*

12 muffins (1 each)

1 cup fat-free milk

4 tablespoons margarine, or butter, melted

1 egg

½ cup wild rice, cooked, room temperature

1 cup all-purpose flour

½ cup whole wheat flour

3 tablespoons baking powder

1 tablespoon sugar

½ teaspoon salt

Per Serving:
Calories: 136
% of calories from fat: 30
Fat (gm): 4.5
Saturated fat (gm): 0.9
Cholesterol (mg): 18.1
Sodium (mg): 494
Protein (gm): 4.6
Carbohydrate (gm): 19.4

Exchanges:
Milk: 0.0
Vegetable: 0.0
Fruit: 0.0
Bread: 1.5
Meat: 0.0
Fat: 0.5

1. Mix milk, margarine, egg, and rice in large bowl. Add combined flours, baking powder, sugar, and ½ teaspoon salt, mixing just until dry ingredients are moistened.

2. Spoon batter into 12 greased muffin cups. Bake at 400 degrees until browned, 20 to 25 minutes. Remove from pans and cool on wire racks.

CARDAMOM-PEAR MUFFINS

LO

45

Any dried fruit can be substituted for the pears, and cinnamon can be substituted for the cardamom.

12 muffins (1 each)

1 cup fat-free milk

4 tablespoons margarine, or butter, melted

1 egg

2 cups all-purpose flour

⅓ cup plus 2 tablespoons sugar, divided

3 teaspoons baking powder

½ teaspoon salt

1 cup chopped dried pears

1 teaspoon grated orange, or lemon, zest

½ teaspoon ground cardamom

Per Serving:
Calories: 193
% of calories from fat: 21
Fat (gm): 4.5
Saturated fat (gm): 1
Cholesterol (mg): 18.1
Sodium (mg): 232
Protein (gm): 3.7
Carbohydrate (gm): 35.4

Exchanges:
Milk: 0.0
Vegetable: 0.0
Fruit: 0.0
Bread: 2.0
Meat: 0.0
Fat: 1.0

1. Mix milk, margarine, and egg in medium bowl. Add combined flour, ⅓ cup sugar, baking powder, and salt, mixing just until dry ingredients are moistened. Gently mix in pears and orange zest.

2. Spoon batter into 12 greased muffin cups; sprinkle with remaining 2 tablespoons sugar and cardamom. Bake at 400 degrees until muffins are browned and toothpick inserted in centers of muffins comes out clean, 20 to 25 minutes. Remove from pans and cool on wire racks.

HIGH-ENERGY MUFFINS

LO

45

These muffins have a nutritional bonus, thanks to the addition of pureed beans.

24 muffins (1 each)

3 cups cooked, dried red kidney beans, or 2 cans
   (15 ounces each) red kidney beans, rinsed, drained
⅓ cup fat-free milk
4 tablespoons margarine, or butter, room temperature
¾ cup packed light brown sugar
3 eggs
1 teaspoon vanilla
1 cup all-purpose flour
½ cup whole wheat flour
1 teaspoon each: baking soda, cinnamon
¼ teaspoon each: ground allspice, mace
½ teaspoon salt
¾ cup raisins
Cinnamon Streusel (recipe follows)
Vanilla Glaze (recipe follows)

Per Serving:
Calories: 174
% of calories from fat: 19
Fat (gm): 3.7
Saturated fat (gm): 0.8
Cholesterol (mg): 26.7
Sodium (mg): 146
Protein (gm): 4.1
Carbohydrate (gm): 31.9

Exchanges:
Milk: 0.0
Vegetable: 0.0
Fruit: 0.0
Bread: 2.0
Meat: 0.0
Fat: 0.5

1. Process beans and milk in food processor until smooth. Beat margarine, brown sugar, eggs, and vanilla until smooth in medium bowl; beat in bean mixture. Add combined flours, baking soda, spices, and salt, mixing just until blended. Mix in raisins.

2. Spoon batter into 24 greased muffin cups and sprinkle with Cinnamon Streusel. Bake at 375 degrees until toothpick inserted in centers of muffins comes out clean, 20 to 25 minutes. Cool muffins in pans 5 minutes; remove and cool on wire racks. Drizzle with Vanilla Glaze.

Cinnamon Streusel

Makes about ¾ cup

½ cup packed light brown sugar
2 tablespoons each: quick-cooking oats, flour
¼ teaspoon ground cinnamon
2 tablespoons cold margarine, or butter, cut into pieces

1. Combine brown sugar, oats, flour, and cinnamon in small bowl; cut in margarine until mixture resembles coarse crumbs.

Vanilla Glaze

Makes about ⅓ cup

1 cup powdered sugar
1 teaspoon vanilla
2–3 tablespoons fat-free milk

1. Mix powdered sugar, vanilla and enough milk to make medium glaze consistency.

BLUEBERRY PANCAKES WITH BLUEBERRY MAPLE SYRUP

LO

45

For special occasions or just for fun, drizzle pancake batter into heart or other shapes in the skillet!

4 servings

¾ cup fat-free milk

1 egg

1 tablespoon margarine, or butter, melted

¾ cup all-purpose flour

¼ cup whole wheat flour

1–2 tablespoons sugar

2 teaspoons baking powder

½ teaspoon salt

⅛ teaspoon ground nutmeg

¾ cup fresh, or frozen, thawed, blueberries

Blueberry Maple Syrup (recipe follows), or light
  pancake syrup, warm

Per Serving:
Calories: 308
% of calories from fat: 14
Fat (gm): 4.7
Saturated fat (gm): 1.1
Cholesterol (mg): 54
Sodium (mg): 511
Protein (gm): 6.9
Carbohydrate (gm): 60.9

Exchanges:
Milk: 0.0
Vegetable: 0.0
Fruit: 2.0
Bread: 2.0
Meat: 0.0
Fat: 1.0

1. Mix milk, egg, and margarine in medium bowl; add remaining ingredients, except blueberries and syrup, beating until almost smooth. Gently mix in blueberries.

2. Pour batter into lightly greased large skillet, using about ¼ cup batter for each pancake. Cook over medium heat until bubbles form in pancakes and they are browned on the bottoms, 3 to 5 minutes. Turn pancakes; cook until browned on other side, 3 to 5 minutes. Serve with Blueberry Maple Syrup.

Blueberry Maple Syrup

Makes about 1 cup

½–¾ cup maple syrup
½ cup fresh, or frozen, blueberries
1 teaspoon each: grated orange and lemon zest

1. Heat all ingredients in small saucepan over medium heat until hot, 3 to 5 minutes.

BUTTERMILK BUCKWHEAT PANCAKES

LO

Whole wheat flour can be substituted for the buckwheat flour.

45   **4 servings**

1 cup buttermilk
1 egg
1–2 tablespoons vegetable oil
½ cup each: all-purpose flour, buckwheat flour
1 tablespoon sugar
1 teaspoon each: baking powder, orange zest
½ teaspoon each: baking soda, salt
½–1 cup maple syrup, light pancake syrup, or
   Blueberry Maple Syrup (see recipe above), warm

Per Serving:
Calories: 291
% of calories from fat: 18
Fat (gm): 5.8
Saturated fat (gm): 1.3
Cholesterol (mg): 55.5
Sodium (mg): 593
Protein (gm): 7.1
Carbohydrate (gm): 54

Exchanges:
Milk: 0.0
Vegetable: 0.0
Fruit: 1.5
Bread: 2.0
Meat: 0.0
Fat: 1.0

1. Mix buttermilk, egg, and oil in medium bowl; add remaining ingredients, except syrup, beating until almost smooth.

2. Pour batter into lightly greased large skillet, using about ¼ cup batter for each pancake. Cook over medium heat until bubbles form in pancakes and they are browned on the bottoms, 3 to 5 minutes. Turn pancakes; cook until browned on other side, 3 to 5 minutes. Serve with warm syrup.

CREPES

LO

45

Cooked crepes can be kept warm in a 200-degree oven while cooking remaining crepes. Crepes can also be made in advance and frozen; layer crepes in plastic wrap and wrap in aluminum foil. To heat, place unwrapped crepes on cookie sheet; bake at 325 degrees until hot, 5 to 8 minutes.

4 servings (2 each)

½ cup each: all-purpose flour, fat-free milk

2 eggs

1 tablespoon margarine, melted, or canola oil

¼ teaspoon salt

Per Serving:
Calories: 120
% of calories from fat: 33
  (will decrease when filled)
Fat (gm): 4.3
Saturated fat (gm): 1
Cholesterol (mg): 53.8
Sodium (mg): 226
Protein (gm): 6
Carbohydrate (gm): 13.8

Exchanges:
Milk: 0.0
Vegetable: 0.0
Fruit: 0.0
Bread: 1.0
Meat: 0.0
Fat: 1.0

1. Beat all ingredients in small bowl until smooth (batter will be thin). Pour scant ¼ cup batter into lightly greased 8-inch crepe pan or small skillet, tilting pan to coat bottom evenly with batter. Cook over medium heat until browned on the bottom, 2 to 3 minutes. Turn crepe and cook until browned on other side, 2 to 3 minutes. Repeat with remaining batter.

Variation

Dessert Crepes — Make crepes as above, adding 1 to 2 tablespoons sugar to the batter.

MANDARIN PANCAKES

V

These delicious pancakes are worth the effort of making. Serve with Moo-Shu Tempeh (see pg. 176).

12 pancakes

⅓ cup boiling water

1 cup all-purpose flour

1. Stir water into flour in small bowl, mixing until crumbly; shape into a ball. Knead on lightly floured surface until smooth and satiny, about 10 minutes. Let stand, covered, 30 minutes.

2. Divide dough into 12 equal pieces; shape into balls. Roll 2 balls into 3-inch circles; spray 1 circle lightly with cooking spray and cover with second circle. Roll both circles together into a 6-inch pancake, being careful not to wrinkle dough when rolling. Cook pancake in lightly greased medium skillet over medium to medium-high heat until pancake blisters and is the color of parchment paper, turning frequently with chopsticks or tongs. Remove from skillet; carefully separate 2 pancakes with pointed knife.

3. Repeat rolling and cooking with remaining dough, making only 1 or 2 pancakes at a time. As pancakes are cooked and separated, keep warm, covered, in a 200-degree oven.

NOTE: Pancakes can be cooled, stacked with plastic wrap, and frozen in a freezer bag or aluminum foil for up to 2 months.

Per Serving:
Calories: 0
% of calories from fat: 0
Fat (gm): 0
Saturated fat (gm): 0
Cholesterol (mg): 0
Sodium (mg): 0
Protein (gm): 0
Carbohydrate (gm): 0

Exchanges:
Milk: 0.0
Vegetable: 0.0
Fruit: 0.0
Bread: 0.0
Meat: 0.0
Fat: 0.0

STUFFED FRENCH TOAST

LO

45

A rich breakfast entrée with a sweet surprise inside! Serve with warm maple syrup or a drizzle of honey.

4 servings

4 thick slices sourdough, or Italian, bread (1-inch)
4 tablespoons fat-free cream cheese
4 teaspoons strawberry, or other flavor, fruit preserves
2 eggs
¼ cup fat-free half-and-half, or fat-free milk
1 teaspoon ground cinnamon
¼ teaspoon ground nutmeg
1–2 tablespoons margarine, or butter
1 cup maple syrup, or light pancake syrup, warm

Per Serving:
Calories: 383
% of calories from fat: 16
Fat (gm): 7
Saturated fat (gm): 2
Cholesterol (mg): 108
Sodium (mg): 334
Protein (gm): 8
Carbohydrate (gm): 74

Exchanges:
Milk: 0.0
Vegetable: 0.0
Fruit: 0.0
Bread: 5.0
Meat: 0.0
Fat: 0.5

1. Cut a pocket in the side of each bread slice; fill with each with 1 tablespoon cream cheese and 1 teaspoon preserves. Lightly beat eggs, half-and-half, and spices in shallow bowl. Dip bread in egg mixture, turning to coat both sides.

2. Cook bread slices in margarine in large skillet on medium to medium-low heat until browned, about 5 minutes on each side. Serve with warm syrup.

SPICED PEAR BUTTER

V *Use ripe pears that are still firm for this gently spiced spread.*

Makes 1½ pints (1 tablespoon per serving)

2½ pounds firm, ripe pears, peeled, cored, chopped
½ cup water
1 tablespoon lemon juice
¾ teaspoon each: ground cinnamon, ginger
⅛ teaspoon ground nutmeg
2 cups sugar

Per Serving:
Calories: 47
% of calories from fat: 2
Fat (gm): 0.1
Saturated fat (gm): 0
Cholesterol (mg): 0
Sodium (mg): 0
Protein (gm): 0.1
Carbohydrate (gm): 12

Exchanges:
Milk: 0.0
Vegetable: 0.0
Fruit: 0.75
Bread: 0.0
Meat: 0.0
Fat: 0.0

1. Heat pears and water to boiling in large saucepan; reduce heat and simmer, covered, until pears are very tender, about 10 minutes. Process pears and liquid in food processor or blender until smooth. Return pear puree to saucepan; stir in remaining ingredients and heat to boiling. Reduce heat and simmer, uncovered, stirring frequently, until mixture thickens to desired consistency, 10 to 20 minutes. Pour pear butter into sterilized jars; cool and cover with lids. Refrigerate up to 2 weeks.

SPICED RHUBARB JAM

V *Cook this jam to desired consistency, as it is not made with pectin.*

Makes 2 pints (1 tablespoon per serving)

1½ pounds rhubarb, cut into 1 to 2-inch pieces

2 cups sugar

1 cup water

2 pieces gingerroot (each 1 inch), cut lengthwise
    into halves

1 cinnamon stick

¼ teaspoon ground cardamom

Per Serving:
Calories: 27
% of calories from fat: 1
Fat (gm): 0
Saturated fat (gm): 0
Cholesterol (mg): 0
Sodium (mg): 1
Protein (gm): 0.1
Carbohydrate (gm): 6.8

Exchanges:
Milk: 0.0
Vegetable: 0.0
Fruit: 0.5
Bread: 0.0
Meat: 0.0
Fat: 0.0

1. Heat rhubarb, sugar, and water to boiling in large saucepan;
reduce heat and simmer, covered, until rhubarb is tender, about
10 minutes. Strain rhubarb, returning juice to saucepan; reserve
rhubarb. Add spices to juice and heat to boiling. Reduce heat and
simmer rapidly, stirring occasionally, until very thick, 10 to 15
minutes. Discard cinnamon stick and gingerroot.

2. Stir rhubarb into juice mixture; simmer longer, if necessary to
achieve desired thickness, stirring to prevent sticking and burning.
Pour jam into sterilized jars; cool and cover with lids. Refrigerate
up to 2 weeks.

ORANGE-ROSEMARY JELLY

V *A subtle herb-flavored jelly that's especially wonderful with biscuits.*

45

Makes 2 pints (1 tablespoon per serving)

1 cup boiling water

2 tablespoons rosemary leaves, crushed

1 can (6 ounces) frozen orange juice concentrate

1 package (1¾ ounces) powdered fruit pectin

¼ cup lemon juice

1 tablespoon distilled white vinegar

Pinch salt

3⅓ cups sugar

1. Pour boiling water over rosemary in small bowl; let stand until cool. Strain; discard rosemary. Combine rosemary water and orange juice concentrate in 2-cup measure; add water to measure 2 cups.

2. Combine orange juice mixture and remaining ingredients, except sugar, in large saucepan; heat to boiling. Stir in sugar and return to boiling, stirring constantly. Boil hard 1 minute, stirring constantly. Pour jelly into sterilized jars; seal and cool. Store in refrigerator.

Per Serving:
Calories: 47
% of calories from fat: 0
Fat (gm): 0
Saturated fat (gm): 0
Cholesterol (mg): 0
Sodium (mg): 2
Protein (gm): 0.1
Carbohydrate (gm): 12.2

Exchanges:
Milk: 0.0
Vegetable: 0.0
Fruit: 0.75
Bread: 0.0
Meat: 0.0
Fat: 0.0

Variations

Rose Geranium Jelly — Make recipe as above, substituting ½ cup packed, torn rose geranium leaves for the rosemary and apple juice concentrate for the orange. Decrease lemon juice to 2–3 tablespoons.

Apple-Mint Jelly — Make recipe as above, substituting ½ cup loosely packed mint leaves, or 3 tablespoons dried mint leaves, for the rosemary and apple juice concentrate for the orange. Decrease lemon juice to 2–3 tablespoons.

TARRAGON WINE JELLY

V

A delicious jelly for biscuits or scones!

45

Makes 3 pints (1 tablespoon per serving)

4 cups dry white wine
2 tablespoons dried tarragon leaves
6 cups sugar
1 package (6 ounces) liquid pectin

1. Heat wine and tarragon to boiling in medium saucepan; reduce heat and simmer, covered, 10 minutes. Strain; discard tarragon. Return wine to saucepan; add sugar and heat to boiling,

Per Serving:
Calories: 58
% of calories from fat: 0
Fat (gm): 0
Saturated fat (gm): 0
Cholesterol (mg): 0
Sodium (mg): 10
Protein (gm): 0
Carbohydrate (gm): 14.1

Exchanges:
Milk: 0.0
Vegetable: 0.0
Fruit: 1.0
Bread: 0.0
Meat: 0.0
Fat: 0.0

stirring occasionally. Stir in pectin and heat to boiling; boil hard 1 minute, stirring constantly. Pour jelly into sterilized jars; seal and cool. Store in refrigerator.

EASY GINGER JELLY

V

45

❄

For best flavor, refrigerate 3 days before serving. Serve on crackers, home-made bread, or biscuits.

Makes 2 half-pints (1 tablespoon per serving)

2 jars (8 ounces each) apple jelly
4–6 quarter-size slices gingerroot (⅛ inch),
   finely chopped

1. Heat jelly and ginger to boiling over medium heat in small saucepan; cool. Pour jelly and ginger into sterilized jars; cool and cover with lids. Store in refrigerator.

Per Serving:
Calories: 39
% of calories from fat: 0
Fat (gm): 0
Saturated fat (gm): 0
Cholesterol (mg): 0
Sodium (mg): 2
Protein (gm): 0
Carbohydrate (gm): 10.1

Exchanges:
Milk: 0.0
Vegetable: 0.0
Fruit: 0.5
Bread: 0.0
Meat: 0.0
Fat: 0.0

GINGERED HONEY

V

45

❄

For best flavor, make this aromatic honey 2 weeks in advance of serving. Serve on toast, crackers, biscuits, or pancakes, or spoon over ice cream or fruit!

Makes 1 pint (1 tablespoon per serving)

4 ounces gingerroot, peeled, sliced paper-thin
1⅓ cups honey, clover or other flavor, warm

1. Loosely fill sterilized pint jar with gingerroot; fill to top with warm honey, covering ginger completely. Cool and cover with lid. Store in refrigerator.

Per Serving:
Calories: 46
% of calories from fat: 0
Fat (gm): 0
Saturated fat (gm): 0
Cholesterol (mg): 0
Sodium (mg): 1
Protein (gm): 0
Carbohydrate (gm): 11.9

Exchanges:
Milk: 0.0
Vegetable: 0.0
Fruit: 0.75
Bread: 0.0
Meat: 0.0
Fat: 0.0

SIXTEEN

Sauces
and
Condiments

PIZZA SAUCE

V *A simple sauce that can also be used on burgers, loaves, or other entrées.*

45   **4 servings** (¼ cup each)

¼ cup each: chopped onion, green bell pepper
2 cloves garlic, minced
1 can (8 ounces) reduced-sodium tomato sauce
½ teaspoon each: dried basil and oregano leaves
Salt and pepper, to taste

1. Sauté onion, bell pepper, and garlic in lightly greased medium saucepan until tender, about 5 minutes. Stir in tomato sauce and herbs; heat to boiling. Reduce heat and simmer, uncovered, until sauce thickens, about 5 minutes. Season to taste with salt and pepper.

Per Serving:
Calories: 37
% of calories from fat: 2
Fat (gm): 0.1
Saturated fat (gm): 0
Cholesterol (mg): 0
Sodium (mg): 18
Protein (gm): 1.5
Carbohydrate (gm): 7.8

Exchanges:
Milk: 0.0
Vegetable: 1.5
Fruit: 0.0
Bread: 0.0
Meat: 0.0
Fat: 0.0

MARINARA SAUCE

V *A classic Italian tomato sauce, seasoned very simply.*

45   **8 servings** (about ½ cup each)

2 medium onions, chopped
6–8 cloves garlic, minced
1–2 tablespoons olive oil
2 cans (16 ounces each) plum tomatoes,
    drained, chopped
½ cup dry white wine, or tomato juice
¼ cup tomato paste
2–3 tablespoons lemon juice
½ teaspoon salt
¼ teaspoon pepper

Per Serving:
Calories: 62
% of calories from fat: 28
Fat (gm): 2.1
Saturated fat (gm): 0.3
Cholesterol (mg): 0
Sodium (mg): 384
Protein (gm): 1.9
Carbohydrate (gm): 10.1

Exchanges:
Milk: 0.0
Vegetable: 2.0
Fruit: 0.0
Bread: 0.0
Meat: 0.0
Fat: 0.5

1. Sauté onions and garlic in oil in large saucepan until tender, about 5 minutes. Stir in tomatoes, wine, and tomato paste; heat to boiling. Reduce heat and simmer, uncovered, until mixture is medium sauce consistency, about 20 minutes. Stir in lemon juice, salt, and pepper.

TOMATO AND VEGETARIAN MEAT SAUCE

V *A perfect sauce for pasta, lasagne, and tomato sauce-based casseroles.*

45 **8 servings** (about ½ cup each)

1 medium onion, chopped

3 cloves garlic, minced

2 cans (14½ ounces each) reduced-sodium
diced tomatoes

½ package (12-ounce size) vegetarian ground beef

⅓ cup finely chopped parsley

¼ cup water

1 teaspoon dried Italian seasoning

⅛ teaspoon ground nutmeg

Salt and pepper, to taste

Per Serving:
Calories: 61
% of calories from fat: 5
Fat (gm): 0.3
Saturated fat (gm): 0.1
Cholesterol (mg): 0
Sodium (mg): 110
Protein (gm): 6.2
Carbohydrate (gm): 9.2

Exchanges:
Milk: 0.0
Vegetable: 2.0
Fruit: 0.0
Bread: 0.0
Meat: 0.5
Fat: 0.0

1. Sauté onion and garlic in lightly greased large saucepan until tender, 3 to 5 minutes. Add remaining ingredients, except salt and pepper; heat to boiling. Reduce heat and simmer, uncovered, until thickened, about 20 minutes, stirring occasionally. Season to taste with salt and pepper.

FRESH TOMATO-BASIL SAUCE

V

This fresh tomato sauce has an intense basil flavor. For interesting variations, other fresh herbs such as rosemary, tarragon, or sage can be substituted for the basil.

8 servings (about ½ cup each)

5 cups chopped tomatoes

1 small onion, chopped

5 cloves garlic, minced

½ cup dry red wine, or tomato juice

2 tablespoons tomato paste

1 tablespoon sugar

2 tablespoons chopped fresh, or 1½ teaspoons dried, thyme leaves

2 bay leaves

¼ cup chopped fresh, or 1 tablespoon dried, basil leaves

½ teaspoon salt

⅛ teaspoon crushed red pepper

¼ teaspoon ground black pepper

Per Serving:
Calories: 58
% of calories from fat: 8
Fat (gm): 0.6
Saturated fat (gm): 0.1
Cholesterol (mg): 0
Sodium (mg): 122
Protein (gm): 1.7
Carbohydrate (gm): 10.9

Exchanges:
Milk: 0.0
Vegetable: 2.0
Fruit: 0.0
Bread: 0.0
Meat: 0.0
Fat: 0.0

1. Combine all ingredients, except basil, salt, and peppers, in medium saucepan; heat to boiling. Reduce heat and simmer, covered, 5 minutes. Simmer, uncovered, until sauce is reduced to medium consistency, about 20 minutes. Stir in basil, salt, and peppers; simmer 5 to 10 minutes longer. Discard bay leaves.

FRESH TOMATO AND HERB SAUCE

V

45

Prepare and enjoy this sauce when garden-ripe tomatoes are at peak flavor. Use fresh herbs if possible.

6 servings (about ½ cup each)

¼ cup finely chopped onion

3 cloves garlic, minced

1 tablespoon olive oil

5 cups peeled, seeded, chopped tomatoes

2 tablespoons chopped fresh, or 2 teaspoons dried basil leaves

1 tablespoon each: chopped fresh, or ½ teaspoon
   dried oregano and thyme leaves

2 bay leaves

½ teaspoon each: salt, pepper

Per Serving:
Calories: 66
% of calories from fat: 36
   (10% with 2 oz. pasta)
Fat (gm): 2.9
Saturated fat (gm): 0.4
Cholesterol (mg): 0
Sodium (mg): 106
Protein (gm): 1.8
Carbohydrate (gm): 10.1

Exchanges:
Milk: 0.0
Vegetable: 2.0
Fruit: 0.0
Bread: 0.0
Meat: 0.0
Fat: 0.5

1. Sauté onion and garlic in oil in large saucepan
until tender, about 5 minutes. Add tomatoes and
herbs; cook, covered, over medium-high heat
until tomatoes release liquid, about 5 minutes.
Reduce heat and simmer, uncovered, until
mixture is very thick, about 20 minutes.
Discard bay leaves; stir in salt and pepper.

NOTE: If a smooth sauce is desired, process in
food processor or blender until smooth.

TOMATO SAUCE WITH MUSHROOMS AND SHERRY

V

45

*Flavors of mushrooms, sherry, rosemary, and oregano meld in a delicious
tomato sauce.*

4 servings (about ½ cup each)

1 small onion, finely chopped

2 cloves garlic, minced

1 tablespoon olive oil

4 cups sliced mushrooms

3 tablespoons dry sherry, or water

1 can (28 ounces) crushed tomatoes, undrained

½ teaspoon each: dried rosemary and oregano leaves

1 teaspoon sugar

¼ teaspoon each: salt, pepper

Per Serving:
Calories: 118
% of calories from fat: 29
Fat (gm): 4.2
Saturated fat (gm): 0.6
Cholesterol (mg): 0
Sodium (mg): 462
Protein (gm): 3.8
Carbohydrate (gm): 16.3

Exchanges:
Milk: 0.0
Vegetable: 3.0
Fruit: 0.0
Bread: 0.0
Meat: 0.0
Fat: 1.0

1. Sauté onions and garlic in oil in medium saucepan 2 to 3 minutes.
Add mushrooms and sherry; cook, covered, over medium-high heat
until mushrooms are wilted and release liquid. Reduce heat and
cook, uncovered, stirring occasionally, until mushrooms are soft
and have darkened. Stir in tomatoes, herbs, and sugar; heat to
boiling. Reduce heat and simmer, covered, 10 to 15 minutes. Stir
in salt and pepper.

BOLOGNESE-STYLE TOMATO SAUCE

V

45

Vegetarian ground beef or sausage are great substitutes for the meats traditionally used in a Bolognese sauce.

4 servings (about ½ cup each)

1 small onion, finely chopped

¼ cup each: chopped carrot, celery

3 cloves garlic, minced

½ teaspoon each: dried oregano, tarragon, and thyme leaves

⅛ teaspoon ground nutmeg

1 can (8 ounces) each: reduced-sodium tomato sauce, reduced-sodium whole tomatoes, drained, chopped

¼ cup dry white wine, or tomato juice

⅔ package (12-ounce size) vegetarian ground beef, or sausage

Salt and pepper, to taste

Per Serving:
Calories: 145
% of calories from fat: 2
Fat (gm): 0.3
Saturated fat (gm): 0.1
Cholesterol (mg): 0
Sodium (mg): 286
Protein (gm): 15.2
Carbohydrate (gm): 18.3

Exchanges:
Milk: 0.0
Vegetable: 2.0
Fruit: 0.0
Bread: 0.0
Meat: 2.0
Fat: 0.0

1. Sauté onion, carrot, celery, and garlic in lightly greased medium saucepan until crisp-tender, about 5 minutes; stir in herbs and cook 1 minute longer. Add tomato sauce, tomatoes, wine, and vegetarian ground beef; heat to boiling. Reduce heat and simmer, uncovered, until a thick sauce consistency, about 15 minutes. Season to taste with salt and pepper.

TOMATO AND VEGETARIAN MEATBALL SAUCE

V

45

You'll savor the full-bodied herb flavors in this streamlined version of a traditional pasta sauce. Serve with spaghetti, a shaped pasta, or gnocchi.

6 servings (about 1⅓ cups each)

1 cup chopped onion

3 cloves garlic, minced

1 tablespoon olive oil

1 can each: (16 ounces) reduced-sodium whole tomatoes, drained, chopped, (8 ounces) reduced-sodium tomato sauce

1 tablespoon tomato paste

2 teaspoons dried basil leaves

1 teaspoon each: dried tarragon and oregano leaves

⅛ teaspoon crushed red pepper

½ teaspoon salt

¼ teaspoon black pepper

1 package (12 ounces) vegetarian
  meatballs

Per Serving:
Calories: 169
% of calories from fat: 30
Fat (gm): 6
Saturated fat (gm): 1
Cholesterol (mg): 0.0
Sodium (mg): 556
Protein (gm): 13
Carbohydrate (gm): 17

Exchanges:
Milk: 0.0
Vegetable: 0.0
Fruit: 0.0
Bread: 1.0
Meat: 1.5
Fat: 0.5

1. Sauté onion and garlic in oil in large saucepan 2 to 3 minutes. Stir in tomatoes, tomato sauce, tomato paste, herbs, and red pepper; heat to boiling. Reduce heat and simmer, uncovered, 10 minutes; stir in salt and pepper. Add meatballs and simmer, uncovered, until medium sauce consistency, 10 to 15 minutes.

PEASANT BEAN SAUCE WITH TOMATOES AND SAGE

V *Hearty and chunky, with 2 types of beans, this sauce is so easy to make!*

45 **8 servings** (about ½ cup each)

1 can (15 ounces) each: red kidney beans,
  cannellini, or Great Northern beans, rinsed,
  drained

½ cup each: chopped onion, celery

2 cloves garlic, minced

1 can (16 ounces) plum tomatoes, drained, chopped

2 cups reduced-sodium vegetable broth

1 teaspoon dried sage leaves

¼ teaspoon salt

⅛ teaspoon pepper

Per Serving:
Calories: 121
% of calories from fat: 4
Fat (gm): 1.2
Saturated fat (gm): 0.5
Cholesterol (mg): 0
Sodium (mg): 300
Protein (gm): 9.2
Carbohydrate (gm): 25.1

Exchanges:
Milk: 0.0
Vegetable: 1.0
Fruit: 0.0
Bread: 1.0
Meat: 0.5
Fat: 0.0

1. Heat all ingredients to boiling in large saucepan. Reduce heat and simmer, covered, 5 minutes; simmer, uncovered, until mixture is desired sauce consistency, about 20 minutes.

CREOLE SAUCE

V

45

Creole flavors accent this substantial sauce. If you enjoy okra, it would be an excellent addition.

8 servings (about ½ cup each)

1½ cups sliced green bell peppers

⅔ cup each: sliced carrots, onion, celery

3 cloves garlic, minced

2 tablespoons olive oil

1 medium tomato, chopped

1 teaspoon each: dried basil and oregano leaves, paprika

½ teaspoon each: dried thyme leaves, gumbo file powder, salt

1 bay leaf

¼ teaspoon cayenne pepper

1 can each: (14½ ounces) reduced-sodium vegetable broth, (8 ounces) reduced-sodium tomato sauce

Per Serving:
Calories: 77
% of calories from fat: 40
  (14% with 2 oz. pasta)
Fat (gm): 3.6
Saturated fat (gm): 0.5
Cholesterol (mg): 0
Sodium (mg): 173
Protein (gm): 1.7
Carbohydrate (gm): 10.6

Exchanges:
Milk: 0.0
Vegetable: 2.0
Fruit: 0.0
Bread: 0.0
Meat: 0.0
Fat: 0.5

1. Sauté bell peppers, carrots, onion, celery, and garlic in oil until peppers are tender, 8 to 10 minutes. Stir in remaining ingredients, except broth and tomato sauce; cook over medium heat 2 to 3 minutes, stirring frequently. Add broth and tomato sauce; heat to boiling. Reduce heat and simmer, uncovered, until vegetables are tender and sauce is thickened to desired consistency, about 20 minutes. Discard bay leaf.

PEPERONATA-TOMATO SAUCE

V

Italian peperonata, a slow-cooked mixture of bell peppers and onions, is combined with tomato sauce — perfect for a pasta topping or vegetarian meatball sauce.

4 servings (about ½ cup each)

1 each: sliced red, green, and yellow bell pepper, onion

3 cloves garlic, minced

2 tablespoons each: olive oil, water

2 cans (8 ounces each) reduced-sodium tomato sauce

½ teaspoon salt

¼ teaspoon pepper

1. Sauté bell peppers, onion, and garlic in oil in medium saucepan 2 to 3 minutes. Add water; cook, covered, over medium to medium-high heat until peppers are wilted. Cook, uncovered, over medium-low heat until peppers and onions are very soft and browned, about 20 minutes. Stir in tomato sauce, salt and pepper; heat to boiling. Reduce heat and simmer, uncovered, until mixture is thick sauce consistency, 10 to 15 minutes.

Per Serving:
Calories: 135
% of calories from fat: 45
(18% with 2 oz. pasta)
Fat (gm): 6.9
Saturated fat (gm): 0.9
Cholesterol (mg): 0
Sodium (mg): 302
Protein (gm): 3
Carbohydrate (gm): 16

Exchanges:
Milk: 0.0
Vegetable: 3.0
Fruit: 0.0
Bread: 0.0
Meat: 0.0
Fat: 1.5

EGGPLANT SAUCE

V *This sauce, with flavors of the Mediterranean is perfect to serve over pasta or use as a sauce in lasagne.*

12 servings (about ½ cup each)

1 pound eggplant, unpeeled, cut into 1½-inch pieces

1 cup chopped onion

½ cup chopped green bell pepper

6 cloves garlic, minced

2 tablespoons olive oil

3 cups chopped tomatoes

1 can (28 ounces) crushed tomatoes, undrained

½ cup dry red wine, or water

2 tablespoons drained capers

1 teaspoon each: dried tarragon and thyme leaves

2 teaspoons sugar

½ teaspoon salt

¼ teaspoon pepper

Per Serving:
Calories: 83
% of calories from fat: 26
Fat (gm): 2.6
Saturated fat (gm): 0.4
Cholesterol (mg): 0
Sodium (mg): 317
Protein (gm): 2.2
Carbohydrate (gm): 12.5

Exchanges:
Milk: 0.0
Vegetable: 2.5
Fruit: 0.0
Bread: 0.0
Meat: 0.0
Fat: 0.5

1. Sauté eggplant, onion, bell pepper, and garlic in oil in large saucepan until onion is tender, about 5 minutes. Add remaining ingredients and heat to boiling. Reduce heat and simmer, covered, until eggplant is tender, about 20 minutes. Simmer, uncovered, until desired sauce consistency, about 10 minutes more.

MEDITERRANEAN TOMATO-CAPER SAUCE

V

45
❄

This fragrant sauce is not cooked; make it in advance for flavors to meld. The sauce can also be served hot.

4 servings (about ½ cup each)

2 cans (8 ounces each) reduced-sodium tomato sauce
2 teaspoons minced garlic
1 teaspoon each: dried oregano leaves, ground cumin and coriander, paprika
Pinch each: ground cardamom, cinnamon, cloves
2 teaspoons lime juice
¼ cup raisins
2–3 teaspoons drained capers
Salt and pepper, to taste

Per Serving:
Calories: 83
% of calories from fat: 3
Fat (gm): 0.3
Saturated fat (gm): 0
Cholesterol (mg): 0
Sodium (mg): 88
Protein (gm): 2.7
Carbohydrate (gm): 18.3

Exchanges:
Milk: 0.0
Vegetable: 2.0
Fruit: 0.5
Bread: 0.0
Meat: 0.0
Fat: 0.0

1. Combine all ingredients; refrigerate at least 2 hours for flavors to blend.

ROASTED RED PEPPER SAUCE

V

45

Fast and easy to make, this is a sauce you'll want to prepare often. No time to roast the peppers? 1 jar (12 ounces) roasted red peppers can be used.

8 servings (3 tablespoons each)

4 large red bell peppers, cut into halves
1 teaspoon sugar

Per Serving:
Calories: 41
% of calories from fat: 7
Fat (gm): 0.4
Saturated fat (gm): 0
Cholesterol (mg): 0
Sodium (mg): 0
Protein (gm): 1.6
Carbohydrate (gm): 9.4

Exchanges:
Milk: 0.0
Vegetable: 1.5
Fruit: 0.0
Bread: 0.0
Meat: 0.0
Fat: 0.0

1. Place peppers, skin sides up, on broiler pan. Broil 4 to 6 inches from heat source until skins are blistered and blackened. Place peppers in plastic bag for 5 minutes; peel off skins and discard. Process peppers and sugar in food processor or blender until smooth. Refrigerate until ready to use.

MANY-CLOVES GARLIC SAUCE

V

Cooked slowly until caramelized, the garlic becomes very sweet in flavor.

45 | **4 servings** (about ½ cup each)

25 cloves garlic, peeled
2 teaspoons olive oil
1¾ cups reduced-sodium vegetable broth, divided
¼ cup dry white wine, or vegetable broth
2 tablespoons each: flour, finely chopped parsley
⅛ teaspoon salt
2 dashes white pepper

Per Serving:
Calories: 78
% of calories from fat: 29
Fat (gm): 2.6
Saturated fat (gm): 0.4
Cholesterol (mg): 0
Sodium (mg): 76
Protein (gm): 0.5
Carbohydrate (gm): 2.5

Exchanges:
Milk: 0.0
Vegetable: 2.0
Fruit: 0.0
Bread: 0.0
Meat: 0.0
Fat: 1.0

1. Cook garlic in oil in medium skillet, covered, over medium to medium-low heat until tender, about 10 minutes. Cook, uncovered, over medium-low to low heat until garlic cloves are golden brown, about 10 minutes. Mash cloves slightly with a fork. Add broth and heat to boiling. Stir in combined wine and flour; boil, stirring, until thickened, about 1 minute. Stir in parsley, salt, and pepper.

ALFREDO SAUCE

L

Serve this favorite Parmesan-flavored sauce over traditional fettuccine noodles.

45 | **4 servings** (about ½ cup each)

3 tablespoons margarine, or butter
¼ cup all-purpose flour
2½ cups fat-free milk
¼ cup (1 ounce) grated Parmesan cheese
⅛ teaspoon ground nutmeg
½ teaspoon salt
¼ teaspoon pepper

Per Serving:
Calories: 187
% of calories from fat: 52
  (24% with 2 oz. pasta)
Fat (gm): 10.7
Saturated fat (gm): 3.1
Cholesterol (mg): 7.4
Sodium (mg): 561
Protein (gm): 8.7
Carbohydrate (gm): 13.9

Exchanges:
Milk: 0.5
Vegetable: 0.0
Fruit: 0.0
Bread: 0.5
Meat: 0.5
Fat: 2.0

1. Melt margarine in medium saucepan; add flour and cook, stirring 1 minute. Whisk in milk; heat to boiling. Boil, whisking, until thickened, about 1 minute. Reduce heat to low and whisk in remaining ingredients; cook 1 to 2 minutes longer.

GORGONZOLA SAUCE

L

45

Although higher in fat content than some of the other blue cheeses, Gorgonzola lends richness of flavor to this creamy sauce.

6 servings (about ⅓ cup each)

3 tablespoons margarine, or butter
¼ cup all-purpose flour
2 cups fat-free milk
¼ cup dry white wine, or fat-free milk
3 ounces Gorgonzola cheese, crumbled
¼ teaspoon pepper

1. Melt margarine in medium saucepan; add flour and cook, stirring, over medium heat 1 minute. Whisk in milk and wine; heat to boiling. Boil, whisking, until thickened, about 1 minute. Stir in cheese and pepper; cook over low heat until melted, 1 to 2 minutes.

Per Serving:
Calories: 138
% of calories from fat: 55
  (24% with 2 oz. of pasta)
Fat (gm): 9
Saturated fat (gm): 3
Cholesterol (mg): 10
Sodium (mg): 230
Protein (gm): 5
Carbohydrate (gm): 8

Exchanges:
Milk: 0.0
Vegetable: 0.0
Fruit: 0.0
Bread: 0.5
Meat: 0.5
Fat: 1.5

THREE-ONION SAUCE

V

This onion mixture is cooked very slowly, until the onions are caramelized.

4 servings (about ½ cup each)

1½ cups each: sliced leeks (white part only),
  chopped red onions
6 shallots, sliced
3 tablespoons olive oil
¼ cup all-purpose flour
1 can (14½ ounces) reduced-sodium vegetable broth
½ teaspoon dried thyme leaves
½ teaspoon salt
¼ teaspoon pepper

Per Serving:
Calories: 196
% of calories from fat: 47
  (25% with 2 oz. pasta)
Fat (gm): 10.5
Saturated fat (gm): 1.4
Cholesterol (mg): 0
Sodium (mg): 317
Protein (gm): 3
Carbohydrate (gm): 23.9

Exchanges:
Milk: 0.0
Vegetable: 1.0
Fruit: 0.0
Bread: 1.0
Meat: 0.0
Fat: 2.0

1. Sauté leeks, onions, and shallots in oil in medium saucepan 2 to 3 minutes. Reduce heat to medium-low and cook slowly until onions are golden brown, 20 to 25 minutes. Stir in flour; cook over medium heat 1 minute longer. Stir in broth, thyme, salt, and pepper; heat to boiling. Boil, stirring, until thickened, about 1 minute.

CREAMED SPINACH SAUCE

L

45

This sauce clings nicely, so serve over a substantial pasta such as farfalle (bow ties), radiatore, or tortellini.

6 servings (about ½ cup each)

2 cloves garlic, minced

2 tablespoons margarine, or butter

¼ cup all-purpose flour

3 cups 2% reduced-fat milk

1½ pounds spinach, cleaned, chopped

2 teaspoons dried basil leaves

⅛–¼ teaspoon ground nutmeg

4–6 dashes red pepper sauce

¼–½ teaspoon salt

Per Serving:
Calories: 141
% of calories from fat: 40
  (17% with 2 oz. pasta)
Fat (gm): 6.6
Saturated fat (gm): 2.8
Cholesterol (mg): 9
Sodium (mg): 284
Protein (gm): 8
Carbohydrate (gm): 14.4

Exchanges:
Milk: 0.5
Vegetable: 2.0
Fruit: 0.0
Bread: 0.0
Meat: 0.0
Fat: 1.0

1. Sauté garlic in margarine in large saucepan 1 to 2 minutes. Stir in flour and cook over medium heat 1 to 2 minutes. Whisk in milk; heat to boiling. Boil, whisking until thickened, about 1 minute. Stir in remaining ingredients. Cook, uncovered, over medium heat until spinach is cooked, 2 to 3 minutes.

ARTICHOKE SAUCE

L

45

Minced jalapeño chilies add a hint of piquancy to this sauce — add more if you want!

4 servings (about ½ cup each)

1 cup sliced onion

2 cloves garlic, minced

¼ teaspoon minced jalapeño chili

1 tablespoon olive oil

2 tablespoons flour

1 cup reduced-sodium
  vegetable broth

1 can (14 ounces) artichoke hearts, drained, sliced

¼ cup (1 ounce) grated Parmesan cheese

2 tablespoons chopped parsley

¼ teaspoon each: salt, pepper

Per Serving:
Calories: 149
% of calories from fat: 32
  (16% with 2 oz. pasta)
Fat (gm): 5.7
Saturated fat (gm): 1.7
Cholesterol (mg): 4.9
Sodium (mg): 372
Protein (gm): 7.3
Carbohydrate (gm): 20.4

Exchanges:
Milk: 0.0
Vegetable: 4.0
Fruit: 0.0
Bread: 0.0
Meat: 0.0
Fat: 1.0

1. Sauté onion, garlic, and jalapeno chili in oil in medium saucepan until tender, about 5 minutes. Stir in flour; cook 1 minute longer. Whisk in broth and heat to boiling. Boil, whisking, until thickened, about 1 minute. Stir in remaining ingredients; cook until hot, 3 to 4 minutes.

PRIMAVERA SAUCE

L *Select vegetables from the season's bounty for this rich, flavorful sauce.*

6 servings (about 1 cup each)

3 tablespoons margarine, or butter

¼ cup all-purpose flour

2 cups 2% milk

¼ cup dry white wine, or canned reduced-sodium vegetable broth

2 cups each: broccoli and cauliflower florets, cooked crisp-tender

1 cup diagonally sliced carrots, cooked crisp-tender

1 medium red bell pepper, sliced

¼ cup (1 ounce) grated Parmesan cheese

¼ teaspoon each: ground nutmeg, salt, and pepper

Per Serving:
Calories: 174
% of calories from fat: 44
   (26% with 2 oz. pasta)
Fat (gm): 8.9
Saturated fat (gm): 2.9
Cholesterol (mg): 9.3
Sodium (mg): 298
Protein (gm): 7.4
Carbohydrate (gm): 16.4

Exchanges:
Milk: 0.5
Vegetable: 2.0
Fruit: 0.0
Bread: 0.0
Meat: 0.0
Fat: 2.0

1. Melt margarine in medium saucepan; stir in flour and cook 1 to 2 minutes longer. Whisk in milk and wine; heat to boiling. Boil, whisking, until thickened, 1 to 2 minutes. Stir in vegetables; cook over medium heat until hot, 2 to 3 minutes. Reduce heat to low and stir in cheese, nutmeg, salt, and pepper; cook 1 to 2 minutes longer.

CURRY SAUCE

V *Delicious tossed with pasta, or served over cooked cauliflower or broccoli.*

45   **4 servings** (about ½ cup each)

¼ cup finely chopped onion

4 cloves garlic, minced

2 tablespoons flour

2 teaspoons curry powder

¼ teaspoon cayenne pepper

2 cups reduced-sodium vegetable broth

1 tablespoon cornstarch

¼ cup dry white wine, or water

Salt and pepper, to taste

Per Serving:
Calories: 50
% of calories from fat: 8
Fat (gm): 0.4
Saturated fat (gm): 0
Cholesterol (mg): 0
Sodium (mg): 8
Protein (gm): 1.1
Carbohydrate (gm): 8.3

1. Sauté onion and garlic in lightly greased medium saucepan 2 to 3 minutes; stir in flour, curry powder, and cayenne pepper. Cook 1 minute, stirring. Add broth and heat to boiling. Stir in combined cornstarch and wine; boil, stirring, until thickened, about 1 minute. Season to taste with salt and pepper.

Exchanges:
Milk: 0.0
Vegetable: 0.5
Fruit: 0.0
Bread: 0.5
Meat: 0.0
Fat: 0.0

MOCK HOLLANDAISE SAUCE

L

45

This creamy-textured Hollandaise Sauce is almost too good to be true. Enjoy it with Eggs Benedict and Artichokes with Hollandaise Sauce (see pp. 338, 470).

6 servings (about ¼ cup each)

2 packages (3 ounces each) fat-free cream cheese

⅓ cup fat-free sour cream

3–4 tablespoons fat-free milk

1–2 teaspoons lemon juice

½–1 teaspoon Dijon mustard

⅛ teaspoon ground turmeric

Per Serving:
Calories: 36
% of calories from fat: 1
Fat (gm): 0
Saturated fat (gm): 0
Cholesterol (mg): 0.1
Sodium (mg): 188
Protein (gm): 5.1
Carbohydrate (gm): 2.8

Exchanges:
Milk: 0.0
Vegetable: 0.0
Fruit: 0.0
Bread: 0.0
Meat: 0.5
Fat: 0.0

1. Heat all ingredients in small saucepan over medium-low to low heat until melted and smooth, stirring constantly. Serve immediately.

MUSHROOM GRAVY

V

45

Serve over vegetarian burgers, potato pancakes, eggplant slices, or bowls of warm polenta.

6 servings (about ¼ cup each)

1 cup sliced cremini, or white mushrooms

⅓ cup finely chopped onion

1 clove garlic, minced

1 cup reduced-fat vegetable broth

2 tablespoons flour

Salt and pepper, to taste

Per Serving:
Calories: 27
% of calories from fat: 7
Fat (gm): 0.2
Saturated fat (gm): 0
Cholesterol (mg): 0
Sodium (mg): 10
Protein (gm): 0.8
Carbohydrate (gm): 4.6

Exchanges:
Milk: 0.0
Vegetable: 1.0
Fruit: 0.0
Bread: 0.0
Meat: 0.0

1. Sauté mushrooms, onion, and garlic in lightly greased medium saucepan until tender, about 5 minutes. Sir in combined broth and flour; heat to boiling. Boil, stirring, until thickened, about 1 minute. Season to taste with salt and pepper.

WILD MUSHROOM SAUCE

V

45

Rich in flavor, this versatile sauce will complement many dishes. Serve over grilled tempeh, eggplant, or vegetarian burgers.

8 servings (about ⅓ cup each)

¼ cup finely chopped shallots

2 cloves garlic, minced

2 cups chopped or sliced wild mushrooms
   (portobello, shiitake, cremini, etc.)

⅓ cup dry sherry, or water

2–3 tablespoons lemon juice

½ teaspoon dried thyme leaves

2 cups reduced-sodium vegetable broth

2 tablespoons cornstarch

Salt and pepper, to taste

Per Serving:
Calories: 34
% of calories from fat: 5
Fat (gm): 0.2
Saturated fat (gm): 0
Cholesterol (mg): 0
Sodium (mg): 5
Protein (gm): 0.7
Carbohydrate (gm): 5.3

Exchanges:
Milk: 0.0
Vegetable: 1.0
Fruit: 0.0
Bread: 0.0
Meat: 0.0
Fat: 0.0

1. Sauté shallots, garlic, and mushrooms in lightly greased medium saucepan until tender, 5 to 8 minutes. Stir in sherry, lemon juice, and thyme; heat to boiling. Reduce heat and simmer, uncovered, until mushrooms are tender and excess liquid is gone, about 5 minutes. Stir in combined broth and cornstarch; heat to boiling. Boil, stirring, until thickened, about 1 minute. Season to taste with salt and pepper.

PAPRIKASH SAUCE

Use hot or sweet paprika in this recipe. Reduced-fat sour cream adds creamy texture and richness to the sauce. Serve over any kind of pasta.

6 servings (about ½ cup each)

1 cup each: sliced red and green bell pepper, onion

1 tablespoon margarine

2 tablespoons flour

1 tablespoon sweet Hungarian paprika

½ teaspoon salt

¼ teaspoon pepper

1 can (8 ounces) reduced-sodium tomato sauce

½ cup each: reduced-sodium vegetable broth, dry white wine, reduced-fat sour cream

Per Serving:
Calories: 97
% of calories from fat: 17
Fat (gm): 1.9
Saturated fat (gm): 0.1
Cholesterol (mg): 7.6
Sodium (mg): 230
Protein (gm): 2.9
Carbohydrate (gm): 14.2

Exchanges:
Milk: 0.0
Vegetable: 0.0
Fruit: 0.0
Bread: 1.0
Meat: 0.0
Fat: 0.5

1. Sauté bell peppers and onion in margarine in large skillet over medium heat until peppers are very soft, 10 to 15 minutes. Stir in flour, paprika, salt, and pepper; cook 1 to 2 minutes longer. Stir in tomato sauce, broth, and wine; heat to boiling. Boil, stirring, until thickened, about 1 minute. Reduce heat to low; stir in sour cream and cook 2 to 3 minutes.

CINCINNATI CHILI SAUCE

V

5-Way Cincinnati Chili gained fame in the chili parlors of Cincinnati. The vegetarian meat sauce is seasoned with sweet spices and has a hint of dark chocolate. The chili sauce is served 1 way, alone; 2 ways, over spaghetti; 3 ways, with added beans; 4 ways, with chopped onions; 5 ways, with shredded cheese!

8 servings (about ½ cup each)

½ cup chopped onion

4 cloves garlic, minced

1 can (28 ounces) reduced-sodium crushed tomatoes, undrained

1 can (8 ounces) reduced-sodium tomato sauce

½ cup water

½ package (12-ounce size) vegetarian ground beef

2–3 tablespoons chili powder

1 tablespoon cocoa

2 teaspoons dried oregano leaves

1 teaspoon each: ground cinnamon, allspice

½ teaspoon each: paprika, salt, pepper

Per Serving:
Calories: 79
% of calories from fat: 8
Fat (gm): 0.7
Saturated fat (gm): 0.1
Cholesterol (mg): 0
Sodium (mg): 269
Protein (gm): 7
Carbohydrate (gm): 12.9

Exchanges:
Milk: 0.0
Vegetable: 1.0
Fruit: 0.0
Bread: 0.0
Meat: 1.0
Fat: 0.0

1. Sauté onion and garlic in lightly greased medium saucepan until tender, about 5 minutes. Stir in remaining ingredients and heat to boiling. Reduce heat and simmer, covered, 15 minutes; simmer, uncovered, until sauce is thickened, about 15 minutes.

CHILI TOMATO SAUCE

V

45

A very simple but versatile sauce that can be used with tacos, enchiladas, and other favorite Mexican dishes.

8 servings (about ¼ cup each)

1 can (16 ounces) reduced-sodium tomato sauce
¼ cup water
2–2½ tablespoons chili powder
2 cloves garlic, minced
Salt and pepper, to taste

Per Serving:
Calories: 30
% of calories from fat: 10
Fat (gm): 0.3
Saturated fat (gm): 0
Cholesterol (mg): 0
Sodium (mg): 36
Protein (gm): 1.3
Carbohydrate (gm): 5.9

Exchanges:
Milk: 0.0
Vegetable: 0.8
Fruit: 0.0
Bread: 0.0
Meat: 0.0
Fat: 0.0

1. Heat all ingredients, except salt and pepper, to boiling in small saucepan. Reduce heat and simmer, uncovered, 2 to 3 minutes. Season to taste with salt and pepper.

ENCHILADA SAUCE

V

45

Many Mexican sauces are a simple combination of pureed ingredients that are then cooked or "fried" until thickened to desired consistency.

8 servings (about ¼ cup each)

1 ancho chili, seeds and veins discarded
2 medium tomatoes, chopped
⅓ cup each: chopped red bell pepper, onion
2 cloves garlic, minced
½ teaspoon dried marjoram leaves
⅛ teaspoon ground allspice
1 bay leaf
Salt, to taste

Per Serving:
Calories: 15
% of calories from fat: 8
Fat (gm): 0.2
Saturated fat (gm): 0
Cholesterol (mg): 0
Sodium (mg): 3.6
Protein (gm): 0.6
Carbohydrate (gm): 3.4

Exchanges:
Milk: 0.0
Vegetable: 0.0
Fruit: 0.0
Bread: 0.0
Meat: 0.0
Fat: 0.0

1. Cover ancho chili with boiling water in small bowl; let stand until softened, 10 to 15 minutes. Drain. Process chili, and remaining ingredients, except bay leaf and salt, in food processor or blender until almost smooth. Cook sauce and bay leaf in lightly greased small skillet over medium heat until thickened to a medium consistency; about 5 minutes. Discard bay leaf; season to taste with salt.

MOLE SAUCE

V *Mole is the most popular and traditional of all the Mexican sauces (see Enchiladas Mole, p. 179). Piquant with chilies and fragrant with sweet spices, the sauce is also flavored with unsweetened chocolate. Even this simplified version of the delicious mole is somewhat time-consuming to make, so double the recipe and freeze half!*

8 servings (about ⅓ cup each)

3 mulato chilies

4 each: ancho and pasilla chilies

1 tablespoon sesame seeds

4 whole peppercorns

2 whole cloves

⅛ teaspoon coriander seeds

Cinnamon stick (½-inch piece)

2 tablespoons each: raisins, pumpkin seeds,

whole, or slivered, almonds, and ¼ cup chopped onion

2 cloves garlic, finely chopped

1 small corn tortilla

1 medium tomato, chopped

1–2 tablespoons unsweetened cocoa

1–1½ cups canned reduced-sodium vegetable broth

Salt, to taste

Per Serving:
Calories: 68
% of calories from fat: 25
Fat (gm): 1.9
Saturated fat (gm): 0.2
Cholesterol (mg): 0
Sodium (mg): 101
Protein (gm): 1.5
Carbohydrate (gm): 11.2

Exchanges:
Milk: 0.0
Vegetable: 2.0
Fruit: 0.0
Bread: 0.0
Meat: 0.0
Fat: 0.5

1. Cook all chilies in ungreased large skillet over medium heat until softened, 2 to 3 minutes; remove and discard stems, seeds, and veins (if chilies are already soft, the cooking step can be omitted). Pour boiling water over chilies to cover in bowl; let stand 10 to 15 minutes. Drain, reserving ¾ cup liquid.

2. Cook sesame seeds and spices in ungreased small skillet over medium heat until toasted, 1 to 2 minutes, stirring; remove from skillet. Add raisins, pumpkin seeds, and almonds to skillet and cook until toasted, 1 to 2 minutes, stirring; remove from skillet. Add onion and garlic to skillet; cook until tender, 2 to 3 minutes; remove from skillet. Cook tortilla in lightly greased skillet until browned, about 1 minute on each side; cool and cut into 1-inch pieces.

3. Process chilies, reserved liquid, tomato, and cocoa in blender until smooth. Add 1 cup broth and remaining ingredients, except salt, and process, adding enough remaining vegetable broth to make smooth, thick mixture. Transfer to lightly greased large skillet and heat to boiling; reduce heat and simmer, uncovered, 5 minutes, stirring frequently. Season to taste with salt.

POBLANO CHILI SAUCE

Fast and easy to make, this sauce will vary in hotness depending upon the individual poblano chili and the amount of chili powder used.

8 servings (about ¼ cup each)

2 medium tomatoes, chopped
½ medium poblano chili, seeds and veins
   discarded, chopped
1 small onion, chopped
2 cloves garlic, minced
1–2 tablespoons chili powder
Salt and pepper, to taste

1. Cook all ingredients, except salt and pepper, in lightly greased large skillet until poblano chili and onion are very tender, 8 to 10 minutes. Process in food processor or blender until smooth; season to taste with salt and pepper.

Per Serving:
Calories: 18
% of calories from fat: 12
Fat (gm): 0.3
Saturated fat (gm): 0.1
Cholesterol (mg): 0.0
Sodium (mg): 12
Protein (gm): 0.7
Carbohydrate (gm): 4

Exchanges:
Milk: 0.0
Vegetable: 0.0
Fruit: 0.0
Bread: 0.0
Meat: 0.0
Fat: 0.0

SERRANO TOMATO SAUCE

V

Use garden ripe tomatoes for best flavor; any hot chili can be substituted for the serrano chili.

6 servings (about ⅓ cup each)

1 each: finely chopped small onion, clove garlic, serrano chili
2 large tomatoes, cut into wedges, pureed
Salt, to taste

1. Sauté onion, garlic, and serrano chili in lightly greased medium skillet until tender, 3 to 4 minutes. Add tomatoes and heat to boiling; cook over medium to medium-high heat until mixture thickens to a medium sauce consistency, 5 to 8 minutes. Season to taste with salt.

Per Serving:
Calories: 18
% of calories from fat: 8
Fat (gm): 0.2
Saturated fat (gm): 0
Cholesterol (mg): 0
Sodium (mg): 4
Protein (gm): 0.6
Carbohydrate (gm): 4

Exchanges:
Milk: 0.0
Vegetable: 1.0
Fruit: 0.0
Bread: 0.0
Meat: 0.0
Fat: 0.0

TOMATILLO SAUCE

V

45

Made with Mexican green tomatoes (tomatillos), this sauce is very fast and easy to make. It can be served over flautas, enchiladas, and tacos.

8 servings (about ¼ cup each)

1½ pounds tomatillos, husks removed
½ medium onion, chopped
1 clove garlic, minced
½ small serrano chili, minced
3 tablespoons chopped cilantro
2–3 teaspoons sugar
Salt and white pepper, to taste

1. Simmer tomatillos, covered, in 1 inch water in large saucepan until tender, 5 to 8 minutes. Cool; drain. Process with onion, garlic, serrano chili, and cilantro in food processor or blender until almost smooth. Cook sauce in lightly greased large skillet over medium heat until slightly thickened, about 5 minutes. Season to taste with sugar, salt, and pepper.

Per Serving:
Calories: 35
% of calories from fat: 20
Fat (gm): 1
Saturated fat (gm): 0.1
Cholesterol (mg): 0.0
Sodium (mg): 1
Protein (gm): 1
Carbohydrate (gm): 7

Exchanges:
Milk: 0.0
Vegetable: 1.0
Fruit: 0.0;
Bread: 0.0
Meat: 0.0
Fat: 0.0

POBLANO SOUR CREAM SAUCE

L

45

This versatile sauce is excellent served with vegetable fajitas or enchiladas or over Vegetable Crepes (see p. 159).

4 servings (about ⅓ cup each)

1 each: thinly sliced large poblano chili, chopped
   small onion
2 cloves garlic, minced
1 cup fat-free sour cream
¼–½ teaspoon ground cumin
Salt and pepper, to taste

1. Sauté poblano chili, onion, and garlic in lightly greased small saucepan until very tender, about 10 minutes. Stir in sour cream and cumin; cook over low heat until hot, 2 to 3 minutes. Season to taste with salt and pepper.

Per Serving:
Calories: 85
% of calories from fat: 2
Fat (gm): 0.2
Saturated fat (gm): 0.0
Cholesterol (mg): 10
Sodium (mg): 53
Protein (gm): 5
Carbohydrate (gm): 16

Exchanges:
Milk: 0.0
Vegetable: 0.0
Fruit: 0.0;
Bread: 1.0
Meat: 0.0
Fat: 0.0

JALAPEÑO CON QUESO SAUCE

L

45

A versatile sauce to enhance enchiladas and other tortilla dishes. This is especially delicious with Potatoes with Poblano Chilies (see p. 498).

8 servings (about ¼ cup each)

1 teaspoon each: finely chopped jalapeño chili,
   ground cumin
½ teaspoon dried oregano leaves
8 ounces reduced-fat pasteurized processed
   cheese, cubed
1¼ cups (5 ounces) shredded fat-free Cheddar cheese
⅓–½ cup fat-free milk

1. Sauté jalapeño chili in lightly greased medium saucepan until tender, about 2 minutes; stir in cumin and oregano. Add processed cheese and cook over low heat, stirring frequently, until melted. Stir in Cheddar cheese and enough milk to make desired consistency; cook until hot, 1 to 2 minutes.

Per Serving:
Calories: 92
% of calories from fat: 30
Fat (gm): 3.2
Saturated fat (gm): 2
Cholesterol (mg): 13.4
Sodium (mg): 562
Protein (gm): 12.2
Carbohydrate (gm): 4.4

Exchanges:
Milk: 0.0
Vegetable: 0.0
Fruit: 0.0
Bread: 0.0
Meat: 2.0
Fat: 0.0

GARBANZO SALSA

V

45

A colorful salsa with fresh flavors that will complement vegetarian burgers, loaves, and many other entrées.

8 servings (about ⅓ cup each)

1 can (15½ ounces) garbanzo beans, rinsed, drained
¾ cup each: chopped, seeded cucumber, quartered cherry tomatoes
3 green onions and tops, thinly sliced
¼ cup chopped yellow bell pepper
2 tablespoons each: finely chopped mint, cilantro
2–3 cloves minced garlic
2–3 teaspoons olive oil
Lemon juice, to taste

Per Serving:
Calories: 76
% of calories from fat: 29
Fat (gm): 2.5
Saturated fat (gm): 0.3
Cholesterol (mg): 0
Sodium (mg): 221
Protein (gm): 2.9
Carbohydrate (gm): 11

Exchanges:
Milk: 0.0
Vegetable: 1.0
Fruit: 0.0
Bread: 0.5
Meat: 0.0
Fat: 0.5

1. Combine all ingredients, except lemon juice, in bowl and toss; season to taste with lemon juice.

TROPICAL SALSA

V

45

A fruit and vegetable salsa with a cool refreshing flavor!

6 servings (about ¼ cup each)

½ cup each: cubed pineapple, tomato, papaya, or mango
¼ cup each: rinsed, drained canned black beans, chopped, seeded cucumber
½ teaspoon minced jalapeño chili
2 tablespoons finely chopped cilantro
¼ cup orange juice
1 tablespoon lime juice
2–3 teaspoons sugar

Per Serving:
Calories: 32
% of calories from fat: 6
Fat (gm): 0.2
Saturated fat (gm): 0
Cholesterol (mg): 0
Sodium (mg): 30.4
Protein (gm): 1
Carbohydrate (gm): 7.6

Exchanges:
Milk: 0.0
Vegetable: 0.0
Fruit: 0.5
Bread: 0.0
Meat: 0.0
Fat: 0.0

1. Combine all ingredients in bowl and toss.

MIXED HERB PESTO

V

45

If using packaged fresh herbs, each ½-ounce package yields about ¼ cup of packed herb leaves. Serve pesto sauces at room temperature, mixing with hot pasta.

4 servings (about 2 tablespoons each)

½ cup each: packed basil and parsley leaves
¼ cup packed oregano leaves
3 cloves garlic
2 tablespoons grated Parmesan cheese
¼ cup walnuts
2 tablespoons olive oil
2 teaspoons lemon juice
½ teaspoon salt
¼ teaspoon pepper

Per Serving:
Calories: 134
% of calories from fat: 77
 (31% with 2 oz. pasta)
Fat (gm): 12
Saturated fat (gm): 1.9
Cholesterol (mg): 2.4
Sodium (mg): 330
Protein (gm): 4
Carbohydrate (gm): 4.9

Exchanges:
Milk: 0.0
Vegetable: 1.0
Fruit: 0.0
Bread: 0.0
Meat: 0.0
Fat: 2.5

1. Process all ingredients in food processor or blender until very finely chopped. Serve at room temperature.

SPINACH PESTO

V

45

Serve with any favorite pasta, or as a topping for sliced tomato or vegetable salads.

4 servings (about 2 tablespoons each)

1 cup loosely packed spinach
¼ cup loosely packed basil leaves
1–2 cloves garlic
1 tablespoon grated fat-free Parmesan cheese
2 tablespoons olive oil
1–2 teaspoons lemon juice
Salt and pepper, to taste

Per Serving:
Calories: 68
% of calories from fat: 86
(16% with 2 oz. pasta)
Fat (gm): 6.8
Saturated fat (gm): 0.9
Cholesterol (mg): 0
Sodium (mg): 22
Protein (gm): 1
Carbohydrate (gm): 1.4

Exchanges:
Milk: 0.0
Vegetable: 0.0
Fruit: 0.0
Bread: 0.0
Meat: 0.0
Fat: 1.5

1. Process all ingredients, except lemon juice, salt, and pepper, in food processor or blender until almost smooth. Season to taste with lemon juice, salt, and pepper. Serve at room temperature.

SUN-DRIED TOMATO PESTO

L

Use yellow or red sun-dried tomatoes in this flavorful pesto.

45   **4 servings** (2 tablespoons each)

½ cup each: packed basil leaves, sun-dried tomatoes (not in oil), boiling water

2 cloves garlic

3 tablespoons olive oil

2 tablespoons grated fat-free Parmesan cheese

Salt and pepper, to taste

Per Serving:
Calories: 90
% of calories from fat: 68
  (26% with 2 oz. of pasta)
Fat (gm): 7
Saturated fat (gm): 1
Cholesterol (mg): 0.5
Sodium (mg): 171
Protein (gm): 2
Carbohydrate (gm): 6

Exchanges:
Milk: 0.0
Vegetable: 1.0
Fruit: 0.0
Bread: 0.0
Meat: 0.0
Fat: 1.5

1. Soak tomatoes in boiling water in bowl until softened, about 10 minutes. Drain, reserving liquid.

2. Process tomatoes, basil, garlic, oil, and cheese in food processor or blender, adding enough reserved liquid to make a smooth, spoonable mixture. Season to taste with salt and pepper. Serve at room temperature.

FENNEL PESTO

L

Perfect with pasta, or sliced tomatoes. Or stir into fat-free sour cream for a marvelous veggie dip.

45

6 servings (scant ¼ cup each)

1 tablespoon fennel seeds

1 cup chopped fennel bulb, or celery

½ cup loosely packed parsley

2 cloves garlic

3 tablespoons water

1 tablespoon olive oil

¼ cup (1 ounce) grated fat-free Parmesan cheese, walnuts

Salt and pepper, to taste

Per Serving:
Calories: 71
% of calories from fat: 61
  (17% with 2 oz. pasta)
Fat (gm): 5
Saturated fat (gm): 0.6
Cholesterol (mg): 0
Sodium (mg): 42
Protein (gm): 2.6
Carbohydrate (gm): 4.6

Exchanges:
Milk: 0.0
Vegetable: 1.0
Fruit: 0.0
Bread: 0.0
Meat: 0.0
Fat: 1.0

1. Soak fennel seeds in hot water in small bowl; let stand 10 minutes; drain. Process fennel seeds and remaining ingredients, except salt and pepper, in food processor or blender until almost smooth. Season to taste with salt and pepper. Serve at room temperature.

RED PEPPER PESTO

L

45

Make this pesto with jarred roasted peppers, or roast your own, following step 1 in the recipe for Roasted Red Pepper Sauce (see p. 590).

4 servings (about 2 tablespoons each)

1 cup each: roasted red peppers, packed basil leaves
2 cloves garlic
¼ cup grated fat-free Parmesan cheese
1 teaspoon each: sugar, balsamic vinegar
3 tablespoons olive oil
Salt and pepper, to taste

1. Process all ingredients, except salt and pepper, in food processor or blender until smooth. Season to taste with salt and pepper. Serve at room temperature.

Per Serving:
Calories: 124
% of calories from fat: 71
  (30% with 2 oz. pasta)
Fat (gm): 10.3
Saturated fat (gm): 1.4
Cholesterol (mg): 0
Sodium (mg): 46
Protein (gm): 2.7
Carbohydrate (gm): 6.8

Exchanges:
Milk: 0.0
Vegetable: 1.0
Fruit: 0.0
Bread: 0.0
Meat: 0.0
Fat: 2.0

CILANTRO PESTO

L

45

Delightful on pasta, or with tomato and cucumber salad!

6 servings (about 2 tablespoons each)

1½ cups packed cilantro leaves
½ cup packed parsley
1 clove garlic
¼ cup (1 ounce) grated Parmesan cheese
3 tablespoons pine nuts, or walnuts
1 tablespoon each: olive oil, lemon juice
Salt and pepper, to taste

1. Process all ingredients, except salt and pepper, in food processor or blender until almost smooth. Season to taste with salt and pepper. Serve at room temperature.

Per Serving:
Calories: 70
% of calories from fat: 73
  (20% with 2 oz. pasta)
Fat (gm): 6.1
Saturated fat (gm): 1.1
Cholesterol (mg): 3.3
Sodium (mg): 173
Protein (gm): 3.5
Carbohydrate (gm): 1.7

Exchanges:
Milk: 0.0
Vegetable: 0.5
Fruit: 0.0
Bread: 0.0
Meat: 0.0
Fat: 1.5

SPINACH-CILANTRO PESTO

L

Any favorite herb can be substituted for the cilantro.

45

4 servings (about 2 tablespoons each)

1 cup loosely packed spinach
¼ cup packed cilantro leaves
3 cloves garlic
¼ teaspoon ground cumin
1 tablespoon grated fat-free Parmesan cheese
1–2 teaspoons each: olive oil, lime juice
1–2 tablespoons water
Salt and pepper, to taste

Per Serving:
Calories: 22
% of calories from fat: 47
  (9% with 2 oz. pasta)
Fat (gm): 1.2
Saturated fat (gm): 0.2
Cholesterol (mg): 0
Sodium (mg): 24
Protein (gm): 1.2
Carbohydrate (gm): 1.9

Exchanges:
Milk: 0.0
Vegetable: 0.0
Fruit: 0.0
Bread: 0.0
Meat: 0.0
Fat: 0.5

1. Process all ingredients, except water, salt, and pepper, in food processor or blender until almost smooth; add water if necessary for consistency. Season to taste with salt and pepper. Serve at room temperature.

MINTED PESTO

L

Try this pesto using different mints, such as peppermint, spearmint, lemon mint, and so on. The refreshing flavor is a complement to vegetables and salads, as well as pasta dishes.

45

8 servings (about 2 tablespoons each)

1 cup packed mint leaves
½ cup packed parsley
2 cloves garlic, minced
2 tablespoons each: grated fat-free Parmesan
  cheese, walnut pieces
2–3 tablespoons each: olive oil, water
Salt and pepper, to taste

Per Serving:
Calories: 51
% of calories from fat: 78
  (19% with 2 oz. pasta)
Fat (gm): 4.6
Saturated fat (gm): 0.5
Cholesterol (mg): 0
Sodium (mg): 15
Protein (gm): 1.2
Carbohydrate (gm): 1.7

Exchanges:
Milk: 0.0
Vegetable: 0.0
Fruit: 0.0
Bread: 0.0
Meat: 0.0
Fat: 1.0

1. Process all ingredients, except salt and pepper, in food processor or blender until almost smooth. Season to taste with salt and pepper. Serve at room temperature.

GREMOLATA

V

45

Gremolata is a pungent seasoning mixture that can be added to soups, pasta, or rice as a flavor accent.

4 servings (about 2 tablespoons each)

1 cup packed parsley
1–2 teaspoons grated lemon zest
4 large cloves garlic
Salt, to taste

1. Process all ingredients, except salt, in food processor until minced; season to taste with salt. Stir into sauces and soups as desired.

Per Serving:
Calories: 10
% of calories from fat: 10
Fat (gm): 0.1
Saturated fat (gm): 0
Cholesterol (mg): 0
Sodium (mg): 9
Protein (gm): 0.6
Carbohydrate (gm): 2

Exchanges:
Milk: 0.0
Vegetable: 0.0
Fruit: 0.0
Bread: 0.0
Meat: 0.0
Fat: 0.0

APPLE CRANBERRY RELISH

V

45

A delicious relish for the winter holidays!

6 servings (about ¼ cup each)

1 cup whole berry cranberry sauce
½ cup each: coarsely chopped tart apple, segmented orange
¼ cup each: chopped pecans, or walnuts, sugar
1 tablespoon grated lemon zest

1. Heat all ingredients in small saucepan over medium heat until sugar is dissolved and apple is tender, 3 to 5 minutes. Cool.

Per Serving:
Calories: 148
% of calories from fat: 20
Fat (gm): 3
Saturated fat (gm): 0.3
Cholesterol (mg): 0.0
Sodium (mg): 7
Protein (gm): 0.6
Carbohydrate (gm): 30

Exchanges:
Milk: 0.0
Vegetable: 0.0
Fruit: 2.0
Bread: 0.0
Meat: 0.0
Fat: 0.5

GINGERED TOMATO RELISH

V

Served warm, this relish is a delicious accompaniment to any veggie entree.

45 **12 servings** (about 2 tablespoons each)

1½ cups chopped tomatoes
½ cup finely chopped zucchini
¼ cup each: finely chopped carrot, onion
1 tablespoon grated gingerroot
Salt and pepper, to taste

1. Combine all ingredients, except salt and pepper, in lightly greased medium skillet; cook over medium heat until tomatoes are soft and mixture is bubbly. Simmer, uncovered, until excess liquid is gone, about 10 minutes. Season to taste with salt and pepper. Serve warm.

Per Serving:
Calories: 15
% of calories from fat: 7
Fat (gm): 0.1
Saturated fat (gm): 0.1
Cholesterol (mg): 0.0
Sodium (mg): 7
Protein (gm): 0.6
Carbohydrate (gm): 3.4

Exchanges:
Milk: 0.0
Vegetable: 0.0
Fruit: 0.0
Bread: 0.0
Meat: 0.0
Fat: 0.0

CRANBERRY COULIS

V

This mildly tart sauce is used as a flavor accent in White Bean and Sweet Potato Soup with Cranberry Coulis (see p. 64). It is also excellent served over fruit, cake, or ice cream.

45

6 servings (about 3 tablespoons each)

1½ cups fresh, or frozen, cranberries
1 cup orange juice
2–3 tablespoons sugar
1–2 tablespoons honey

1. Heat cranberries and orange juice to boiling in small saucepan; reduce heat and simmer, covered, until cranberries are tender, 5 to 8 minutes. Process with sugar and honey in food processor or blender until almost smooth. Serve warm or room temperature.

Per Serving:
Calories: 57
% of calories from fat: 2
Fat (gm): 0.1
Saturated fat (gm): 0.0
Cholesterol (mg): 0.0
Sodium (mg): 1
Protein (gm): 0.4
Carbohydrate (gm): 15

Exchanges:
Milk: 0.0
Vegetable: 0.0
Fruit: 1.0;
Bread: 0.0
Meat: 0.0
Fat: 0.0

LEMON-HERB MAYONNAISE

LO

45

Delicious served with Pasta Skillet Cakes (p. 457), with vegetable salads, or as a dip with vegetable relishes.

6 servings (about 2 tablespoons each)

½ cup fat-free mayonnaise
¼ cup fat-free sour cream
1–2 teaspoons lemon juice
1 teaspoon grated lemon zest
½ teaspoon dried tarragon leaves
¼ teaspoon dried thyme leaves

1. Mix all ingredients.

Per Serving:
Calories: 29
% of calories from fat: 18
Fat (gm): 0.6
Saturated fat (gm): 0.1
Cholesterol (mg): 3.6
Sodium (mg): 176
Protein (gm): 0.7
Carbohydrate (gm): 5

Exchanges:
Milk: 0.0;
Vegetable: 0.0
Fruit: 0.0
Bread: 0.0
Meat: 0.0;
Fat: 0.0

YOGURT-CUCUMBER SAUCE

L

45

Serve with tortellini or ravioli for a pasta salad, with sliced summer vegetables, or spoon into pita sandwiches.

6 servings (¼ cup each)

1 cup fat-free yogurt
¼ cup fat-free sour cream
⅓ cup finely chopped, seeded, peeled cucumber
2 cloves garlic, minced
2–3 teaspoons dried dill weed
Salt and white pepper, to taste

1. Combine all ingredients, except salt and pepper; season to taste with salt and pepper.

Per Serving:
Calories: 30 %
% of calories from fat: 3
Fat (gm): 0.1
Saturated fat (gm): 0
Cholesterol (mg): 0.7
Sodium (mg): 36
Protein (gm): 3
Carbohydrate (gm): 4.5

Exchanges:
Milk: 0.0
Vegetable: 1.0
Fruit: 0.0
Bread: 0.0
Meat: 0.0
Fat: 0.0

MUSTARD SAUCE

L

45

Serve this spicy sauce with Baked Spinach Balls or Mixed Vegetable Egg Rolls (see pp. 37, 40).

8 servings (about 2 tablespoons each)

¾ cup fat-free sour cream

3–4 teaspoons Dijon mustard

1½–2 tablespoons honey

1 tablespoon chopped chives

1. Mix all ingredients.

Per Serving:
Calories: 27
% of calories from fat: 4
Fat (gm): 0.1
Saturated fat (gm): 0
Cholesterol (mg): 0
Sodium (mg): 39
Protein (gm): 1.5
Carbohydrate (gm): 5.4

Exchanges:
Milk: 0.0
Vegetable: 1.0
Fruit: 0.0
Bread: 0.0
Meat: 0.0
Fat: 0.0

PLUM SAUCE

V

45

A fragrant and flavorful sauce to serve with oriental appetizers, or with baked or broiled tofu kabobs.

8 servings (about 2 tablespoons each)

¾ cup Asian plum sauce

2–3 tablespoons tamari, or reduced-sodium, soy sauce

2 tablespoons rice wine vinegar, or cider vinegar

1 tablespoon grated gingerroot

1–2 teaspoons brown sugar

1 green onion, thinly sliced

2 cloves garlic, minced

1. Mix all ingredients.

Per Serving:
Calories: 37
% of calories from fat: 1
Fat (gm): 0
Saturated fat (gm): 0
Cholesterol (mg): 0
Sodium (mg): 258
Protein (gm): 0.6
Carbohydrate (gm): 9

Exchanges:
Milk: 0.0
Vegetable: 0.0
Fruit: 0.0
Bread: 0.5
Meat: 0.0
Fat: 0.0

TAMARI DIPPING SAUCE

V *An excellent sauce for egg rolls, wontons, and potstickers!*

45 **12 servings** (1 tablespoon each)

½ cup reduced-sodium tamari, or soy, sauce
2 tablespoons rice wine vinegar
4 teaspoons lemon juice
2 teaspoons honey

1. Mix all ingredients.

Per Serving:
Calories: 15
% of calories from fat: 0
Fat (gm): 0
Saturated fat (gm): 0
Cholesterol (mg): 0
Sodium (mg): 405
Protein (gm): 1.2
Carbohydrate (gm): 2.1

Exchanges:
Milk: 0.0
Vegetable: 0.0
Fruit: 0.0
Bread: 0.0
Meat: 0.0
Fat: 0.0

TAMARI MARINADE

V *A simple but flavorful marinade that is especially nice for tofu or tempeh. Use as a dipping sauce, too.*

45

4 servings (1 tablespoon each)

2 tablespoons each: reduced-sodium tamari soy
  sauce, cider vinegar
1½ teaspoons minced garlic
½–1 teaspoon chili powder

1. Mix all ingredients.

Per Serving:
Calories: 11
% of calories from fat: 5
Fat (gm): 0.1
Saturated fat (gm): 0
Cholesterol (mg): 0
Sodium (mg): 307
Protein (gm): 1
Carbohydrate (gm): 1.7

Exchanges:
Milk: 0.0
Vegetable: 0.0
Fruit: 0.0
Bread: 0.0
Meat: 0.0
Fat: 0.0

FRAGRANT BASTING SAUCE

V

Delicious with broiled or grilled tofu, tempeh, and vegetable kabobs.

45

6 servings (about 2 tablespoons each)

2 tablespoons reduced-sodium soy sauce

¼ cup each: packed light brown sugar, rice wine, or dry sherry

1 tablespoon finely chopped green onion

1 teaspoon grated lemon zest, black bean sauce

2 teaspoons sesame oil

1–2 dashes hot chili sesame oil

1. Combine all ingredients.

Per Serving:
Calories: 55
% of calories from fat: 24
Fat (gm): 1.5
Saturated fat (gm): 0.2
Cholesterol (mg): 0
Sodium (mg): 197
Protein (gm): 0.6
Carbohydrate (gm): 10.3

Exchanges:
Milk: 0.0
Vegetable: 0.0
Fruit: 0.0
Bread: 0.5
Meat: 0.0
Fat: 0.5

SEVENTEEN

Desserts

RHUBARB STREUSEL CAKE

LO

45

A rich and crispy streusel and a light orange glaze top this wonderfully moist cake.

12 servings

½ cup margarine, or butter, room temperature

1⅓ cups sugar

1 egg, beaten

1 teaspoon vanilla

2 cups all-purpose flour

1 teaspoon each: baking soda, ground cinnamon

½ teaspoon each: ground nutmeg, salt

1 cup buttermilk

2 cups sliced fresh, or frozen, thawed, rhubarb (1-inch)

⅓ cup raisins

2 teaspoons grated orange zest

Crisp Streusel (recipe follows)

Orange Glaze (recipe follow)

Per Serving:
Calories: 342
% of calories from fat: 27
Fat (gm): 10.4
Saturated fat (gm): 2.2
Cholesterol (mg): 18.5
Sodium (mg): 336
Protein (gm): 4.1
Carbohydrate (gm): 59.3

Exchanges:
Milk: 0.0
Vegetable: 0.0
Fruit: 1.0
Bread: 3.0
Meat: 0.0
Fat: 1.5

1. Beat margarine and sugar until smooth in large bowl; beat in egg and vanilla. Mix in combined flour, baking soda, cinnamon, nutmeg, and salt alternately with buttermilk, beginning and ending with dry ingredients. Mix in rhubarb, raisins, and orange zest. Pour into greased and floured 13 x 9-inch baking pan; sprinkle with Crisp Streusel.

2. Bake at 350 degrees until toothpick inserted in center comes out clean, 35 to 40 minutes. Cool in pan on wire rack 15 minutes; drizzle with Orange Glaze.

Crisp Streusel

½ cup packed light brown sugar

2 tablespoons each: quick-cooking oats, flour, cold margarine, or butter, cut into pieces

1. Combine brown sugar, oats, and flour in small bowl; cut in margarine to form crumbly mixture.

Orange Glaze

½ cup powdered sugar
1 teaspoon grated orange zest
2–4 teaspoons orange juice

1. Mix powdered sugar and orange zest with enough orange juice to make glaze consistency.

45-MINUTE PREP TIP: Make Crisp Streusel before preparing the rest of the recipe.

GLAZED ORANGE CHIFFON CAKE

Sometimes called Sunshine Cake, this cake has a perfect, tender texture and delicate orange flavor.

12 servings

2¼ cups cake flour
1⅔ cups granulated sugar
1 tablespoon baking powder
¼ teaspoon salt
¾ cup orange juice, or water
⅓ cup canola oil
5 egg yolks
1 teaspoon vanilla
2 teaspoons grated orange zest
7 egg whites
½ teaspoon cream of tartar
2 cups powdered sugar
2–3 tablespoons orange juice
Ground nutmeg

Per Serving:
Calories: 358
% of calories from fat: 21
Fat (gm): 8.4
Saturated fat (gm): 1.5
Cholesterol (mg): 88.8
Sodium (mg): 163
Protein (gm): 5
Carbohydrate (gm): 66.3

Exchanges:
Milk: 0.0
Vegetable: 0.0
Fruit: 0.0
Bread: 4.0
Meat: 0.0
Fat: 1.5

1. Combine flour, granulated sugar, baking powder, and salt in large mixing bowl. Add combined orange juice, oil, egg yolks, vanilla, and orange zest, beating at medium speed until smooth.

2. Beat egg whites until foamy in large bowl; add cream of tartar and beat to stiff, but not dry, peaks. Stir about ¼ of egg whites into cake batter; fold batter back into remaining egg whites. Pour into ungreased 10-inch tube pan.

3. Bake at 325 degrees until cake is golden and springs back when touched (cracks in top of cake will appear dry), 55 to 60 minutes. Invert cake pan on a funnel or bottle until cake is completely cool. Loosen side of cake and invert onto serving plate. Mix powdered sugar with enough orange juice to make glaze consistency, spoon glaze over cake and sprinkle with nutmeg.

CHOCOLATE BUTTERMILK CAKE WITH MOCHA FROSTING

LO

45

A chocolate dream come true, this cake is 3 layers high and generously covered with creamy mocha frosting!

16 servings

6 tablespoons vegetable shortening

1 cup granulated sugar

½ cup packed light brown sugar

3 eggs

1 teaspoon vanilla

2 cups cake flour

½ cup unsweetened cocoa

2 teaspoons baking powder

½ teaspoon each: baking soda, salt

1 cup buttermilk

Mocha Frosting (recipe follow)

Per Serving:
Calories: 287
% of calories from fat: 17
Fat (gm): 6
Saturated fat (gm): 1
Cholesterol (mg): 32
Sodium (mg): 172
Protein (gm): 3
Carbohydrate (gm): 57

Exchanges:
Milk: 0.0
Vegetable: 0.0
Fruit: 0.0
Bread: 4.0
Meat: 0.0
Fat: 0.5

1. Beat shortening, sugars, eggs, and vanilla in large bowl until smooth. Mix in combined flour, cocoa, baking powder, baking soda, and salt alternately with buttermilk, beginning and ending with dry ingredients. Pour into 3 greased and floured 8-inch round cake pans.

2. Bake at 350 degrees until toothpicks inserted in centers of cakes come out clean, 25 to 30 minutes. Cool in pans on wire racks 10 minutes; invert onto wire racks and cool. Place 1 cake layer on serving plate; frost with about ½ cup frosting. Repeat with second cake layer; top with third layer, frosting top and side.

Mocha Frosting

Makes about 2½ cups

5 cups powdered sugar
½ cup unsweetened cocoa
2–3 teaspoons instant coffee crystals
1 tablespoons margarine, or butter, room temperature
1 teaspoon vanilla
4–5 tablespoons fat-free milk

1. Combine powdered sugar, cocoa, coffee crystals, and margarine in large bowl; beat in vanilla and enough milk to make the consistency spreadable .

FLOURLESS CHOCOLATE CAKE

LO

It's hard to believe a cake so sinfully rich and wonderful can actually be low-fat! Although regular cocoa can be used, the Dutch process cocoa lends a special flavor.

8 servings

½ cup Dutch process cocoa
¾ cup packed light brown sugar
3 tablespoons flour
2 teaspoons instant coffee crystals
⅛ teaspoon salt
Pinch pepper
¾ cup fat-free milk
1 teaspoon vanilla
2 ounces each: chopped unsweetened and semisweet chocolate
1 egg, lightly beaten
3 egg whites
⅛ teaspoon cream of tartar
⅓ cup granulated sugar
Rich Chocolate Frosting (recipe follows)

Per Serving:
Calories: 335
% of calories from fat: 22
Fat (gm): 8.9
Saturated fat (gm): 3.6
Cholesterol (mg): 27.1
Sodium (mg): 107
Protein (gm): 6.3
Carbohydrate (gm): 66.1

Exchanges:
Milk: 0.0
Vegetable: 0.0
Fruit: 0.0
Bread: 4.0
Meat: 0.0
Fat: 1.0

1. Combine cocoa, brown sugar, flour, coffee crystals, salt, and pepper in medium saucepan; add milk and vanilla, stirring until smooth. Heat over medium heat, stirring frequently, until mixture is hot and sugar dissolved (do not boil). Remove from heat; add chocolate, stirring until melted. Whisk about ½ cup chocolate mixture into egg; whisk mixture back into saucepan. Cool.

2. Beat egg whites to soft peaks in medium bowl; add cream of tartar and beat, adding sugar gradually, until stiff, but not dry, peaks form. Stir about ¼ of the egg whites into chocolate mixture; fold chocolate mixture back into egg whites. Pour into greased and floured parchment-lined 9-inch round cake pan.

3. Place cake pan in large roasting pan on center oven rack; add 1 inch hot water to pan. Bake cake at 350 degrees until just firm when touched, 25 to 30 minutes (do not test with toothpick as cake will still be soft in the center). Cool in pan on wire rack; refrigerate, covered, 8 hours or overnight.

4. Loosen side of cake from pan with sharp knife. Remove from pan and place on serving plate. Frost with Rich Chocolate Frosting.

Rich Chocolate Frosting

Makes about ¾ cup

1–2 tablespoons margarine, or butter, room temperature
1½ cups powdered sugar
¼ cup Dutch process cocoa
½ teaspoon vanilla
3–4 tablespoons fat-free milk

1. Mix all ingredients, adding enough milk to make the consistency spreadable.

COFFEE-FROSTED COCOA CAKE

LO

A perfect cake for shared dinners and picnics.

45

16 servings

1½ cups sugar

½ cup margarine, or butter, room temperature

2 eggs

1 teaspoon vanilla

2 cups all-purpose flour

¾ cup unsweetened cocoa

2 teaspoons baking soda

1 teaspoon salt

1 cup fat-free milk

Coffee Frosting (recipe follows)

Per Serving:
Calories: 240
% of calories from fat: 27
Fat (gm): 7.6
Saturated fat (gm): 1.6
Cholesterol (mg): 26.9
Sodium (mg): 385
Protein (gm): 3.9
Carbohydrate (gm): 41.6

Exchanges:
Milk: 0.0
Vegetable: 0.0
Fruit: 0.0
Bread: 2.5
Meat: 0.0
Fat: 1.5

1. Beat sugar and margarine in large bowl until fluffy. Add eggs one at a time, beating well after each addition; mix in vanilla. Mix in combined flour, cocoa, baking soda, and salt alternately with milk, beginning and ending with dry ingredients. Spread batter in greased and floured 13 x 9-inch cake pan.

2. Bake cake at 350 degrees 25 to 35 minutes or until toothpick inserted in center comes out clean and sides begin to pull away from pan. Cool in pan on wire rack. Frost with Coffee Frosting.

Coffee Frosting

Makes about ½ cup

1 tablespoon each: instant coffee granules, hot water, margarine, or butter, room temperature

1 cup powdered sugar

2–3 tablespoons fat-free milk

1. Dissolve coffee in hot water in medium bowl. Beat in margarine, powdered sugar, and enough milk to make the consistency spreadable.

CHOCOLATE-CHERRY PUDDING CAKE

L

Served warm, this fudgy favorite will bring smiles to kids of all ages.

45

14 servings

1¾ cups all-purpose flour

1¼ cups granulated sugar

⅓ cup plus ¼ cup unsweetened cocoa, divided

3 tablespoons baking powder

¾ cup fat-free milk

½ cup unsweetened applesauce

1 cup fresh, or frozen, thawed, sweet cherries, pitted

¼ cup chopped pecans

1¼ cups packed dark brown sugar

3 cups hot water

Per Serving:
Calories: 242
% of calories from fat: 7
Fat (gm): 1.9
Saturated fat (gm): 0.2
Cholesterol (mg): 0
Sodium (mg): 264
Protein (gm): 3
Carbohydrate (gm): 55.1

Exchanges:
Milk: 0.0
Vegetable: 0.0
Fruit: 1.5
Bread: 2.0
Meat: 0.0
Fat: 0.0

1. Combine flour, granulated sugar, ⅓ cup cocoa, and baking powder in large bowl; stir in milk and applesauce just until dry ingredients are moistened. Fold in cherries and pecans. Spoon into greased and floured 13 x 9-inch baking pan. Mix brown sugar, hot water, and ¼ cup cocoa in medium bowl, until smooth; pour over batter.

2. Bake at 350 degrees 35 to 40 minutes or until set (cake will have a pudding-like texture). Serve warm or at room temperature.

CARROT CAKE WITH CREAM CHEESE FROSTING

LO

Moist and sweetly spiced, this cake is one you'll want to make over and over again.

45

16 servings

3 cups shredded carrots

½ cup raisins

1 cup packed light brown sugar

⅓ cup vegetable oil

3 eggs

2 cups all-purpose flour

1 teaspoon each: baking powder, baking soda, ground cinnamon

Per Serving:
Calories: 346
% of calories from fat: 24
Fat (gm): 9.7
Saturated fat (gm): 2.7
Cholesterol (mg): 44.9
Sodium (mg): 255
Protein (gm): 4.7
Carbohydrate (gm): 62.2

Exchanges:
Milk: 0.0
Vegetable: 1.0
Fruit: 0.0
Bread: 5.0
Meat: 0.0
Fat: 2.0

¼ teaspoon each: ground allspice, nutmeg, salt
Cream Cheese Frosting (recipe follows)

1. Mix carrots, raisins, brown sugar, oil, and eggs in large bowl. Mix in combined remaining ingredients, except Cream Cheese Frosting. Pour into 2 greased and floured 8-inch-round cake pans.

2. Bake at 350 degrees until toothpicks inserted in cakes come out clean, 25 to 30 minutes. Cool in pans on wire rack 10 minutes; remove from pans and cool. Place 1 cake layer on serving plate and frost. Top with second cake layer, frosting top and side of cake.

Cream Cheese Frosting

Makes about 3 cups

1 package (8 ounces) reduced-fat cream cheese, room temperature
2 tablespoons margarine, or butter, room temperature
1 teaspoon vanilla
4–5 cups powdered sugar

1. Beat cream cheese, margarine, and vanilla in medium bowl until smooth; beat in enough powdered sugar to make the consistency spreadable.

SPICE CAKE WITH PENUCHE FROSTING

LO

45

The flavor combination of sweet spices and creamy caramel fudge (penuche) frosting is too good to be true!

10 servings

4 tablespoons margarine, or butter, room temperature

¾ cup sugar

1 egg

½ teaspoon vanilla

1⅓ cups all-purpose flour

2 teaspoons baking powder

¾ teaspoon ground cinnamon

¼ teaspoon each: ground nutmeg, ginger, salt

⅔ cup fat-free milk

Penuche Frosting (recipe follows)

Per Serving:
Calories: 342
% of calories from fat: 23
Fat (gm): 8.7
Saturated fat (gm): 1.8
Cholesterol (mg): 21.6
Sodium (mg): 233
Protein (gm): 3.1
Carbohydrate (gm): 63.6

Exchanges:
Milk: 0.0
Vegetable: 0.0
Fruit: 0.0
Bread: 4.0
Meat: 0.0
Fat: 1.5

1. Beat margarine, sugar, egg, and vanilla in large bowl until smooth. Mix in combined flour, baking powder, spices, and salt alternately with milk, beginning and ending with dry ingredients. Pour into greased and floured 8- or 9-inch-round cake pan.

2. Bake at 350 degrees until cake springs back when touched, about 40 minutes. Cool in pan on wire rack 10 minutes; remove from pan and cool. Place cake on serving plate; spread top and side with Penuche Frosting.

Penuche Frosting

Makes about 2½ cups

3 tablespoons margarine, or butter

½ cup packed light brown sugar

2–2½ cups powdered sugar

½ teaspoon vanilla

2–4 tablespoons fat-free milk

1. Melt margarine in medium saucepan; stir in brown sugar and cook over medium heat until bubbly. Stir in powdered sugar, vanilla, and enough milk to make spreadable consistency.

NOTE: Use the frosting immediately as it tends to thicken quickly. If frosting becomes too thick, thin with a few drops of hot water.

PINEAPPLE UPSIDE-DOWN CAKE

L

45

Invert the cake immediately after baking so all the warm caramel topping releases from the pan.

8–10 servings

3 tablespoons light corn syrup

5 tablespoons margarine, or butter, room temperature, divided

⅔ cup packed light brown sugar

2–3 tablespoons chopped pecans

1 can (8 ounces) sliced pineapple in juice, drained, slices halved

4 maraschino cherries, halved

⅔ cup granulated sugar

1 egg

½ teaspoon pineapple, or vanilla extract

1⅓ cups all-purpose flour

2 teaspoons baking powder

¼ teaspoon salt

⅔ cup fat-free milk

Light whipped topping, as garnish

Per Serving:
Calories: 347
% of calories from fat: 23
Fat (gm): 9.1
Saturated fat (gm): 1.7
Cholesterol (mg): 27
Sodium (mg): 264
Protein (gm): 4
Carbohydrate (gm): 63.8

Exchanges:
Milk: 0.0
Vegetable: 0.0
Fruit: 0.5
Bread: 3.5
Meat: 0.0
Fat: 1.5

1. Heat corn syrup and 1 tablespoon margarine until melted in small skillet. Stir in brown sugar and pecans and cook over medium heat until bubbly, 2 to 3 minutes; pour into ungreased 9-inch-round cake pan; arrange pineapple slices and cherries on top.

2. Beat remaining 4 tablespoons margarine, granulated sugar, egg, and pineapple extract in medium bowl until smooth. Mix in combined flour, baking powder, and salt alternately with milk, beginning and ending with dry ingredients. Pour over topping in pan.

3. Bake at 350 degrees until cake springs back when touched, about 40 minutes. Loosen side of cake with sharp knife and invert onto serving plate. Serve warm with whipped topping.

BOSTON CREAM CAKE

LO *A comfort food, with chocolatey glaze and a luxurious cream filling. Although sometimes called a "pie," it is, indeed, a cake.*

12 servings

8 tablespoons margarine, or butter,
   room temperature
1¼ cups sugar
2 eggs
1 teaspoon vanilla
2⅔ cups all-purpose flour
3 teaspoons baking powder
½ teaspoon salt
1⅔ cups fat-free milk
Vanilla Cream Filling (recipe follows)
Chocolate Glaze (recipe follows)

Per Serving:
Calories: 353
% of calories from fat: 23
Fat (gm): 9.3
Saturated fat (gm): 2
Cholesterol (mg): 54.2
Sodium (mg): 305
Protein (gm): 6.6
Carbohydrate (gm): 61.3

Exchanges:
Milk: 0.0
Vegetable: 0.0
Fruit: 0.0
Bread: 4.0
Meat: 0.0
Fat: 1.5

1. Beat margarine, sugar, eggs, and vanilla until smooth in medium bowl. Mix in combined flour, baking powder, and salt alternately with milk, beginning and ending with dry ingredients. Pour into 2 greased and floured 8- or 9-inch-round cake pans.

2. Bake at 350 degrees until cakes spring back when touched, about 40 minutes. Cool in pans on wire rack 10 minutes; remove from pans and cool.

3. Place 1 cake layer on serving plate; spread with Vanilla Cream Filling. Top with second cake layer and spoon Chocolate Glaze over.

Vanilla Cream Filling

Makes about ¼ cup

¼ cup sugar
2 tablespoons cornstarch
1 cup fat-free milk
1 egg, beaten
½ teaspoon vanilla

1. Mix sugar and cornstarch in small saucepan; whisk in milk and heat to boiling. Boil, whisking, until thickened, about 1 minute.

Whisk about ½ the milk mixture into beaten egg in small bowl; whisk back into saucepan. Whisk over low heat 30 to 60 seconds. Stir in vanilla and cool.

Chocolate Glaze

1 cup powdered sugar

2 tablespoons unsweetened cocoa

½ teaspoon vanilla

1–2 tablespoons fat-free milk

1. Mix all ingredients, using enough milk to make glaze consistency.

PUMPKIN-GINGER CAKE WITH WARM RUM SAUCE

LO

45

Moist with pumpkin and savory with spices, this cake is a perfect choice for fall and winter holidays.

8 servings

½ cup each: canned pumpkin, packed light brown sugar

¼ cup each: margarine, or butter, room temperature, light molasses

1 egg

1½ cups all-purpose flour

½ teaspoon each: baking powder, baking soda, ground allspice, cloves, ginger

Warm Rum Sauce (recipe follows)

Per Serving:
Calories: 245
% of calories from fat: 28
Fat (gm): 8
Saturated fat (gm): 2
Cholesterol (mg): 22
Sodium (mg): 196
Protein (gm): 4
Carbohydrate (gm): 39

Exchanges:
Milk: 0.0
Vegetable: 0.0
Fruit: 0.0
Bread: 2.5
Meat: 0.0;
Fat: 1.5

1. Combine pumpkin, brown sugar, margarine, molasses, and egg in large bowl; beat at medium speed until fluffy. Mix in combined flour, baking powder, baking soda, allspice, cloves, and ginger until moistened. Pour into greased and floured 8-inch-square baking pan.

2. Bake 350 degrees until toothpick inserted in center of cake comes out clean, 30 to 40 minutes. Cool in pan on wire rack 10 minutes; remove from pan and cool. Serve with Warm Rum Sauce.

Warm Rum Sauce

Makes 1½ cups

¼ cup sugar
1 tablespoon cornstarch
1¼ cups fat-free milk
2 tablespoons each: rum, or ½ teaspoon rum extract, margarine, or butter
½ teaspoon vanilla
⅛ teaspoon ground nutmeg

1. Mix sugar and cornstarch in small saucepan; whisk in milk and rum. Heat to boiling, whisking until thickened, about 1 minute. Remove from heat; stir in margarine, vanilla, and nutmeg. Serve warm.

BANANA-CINNAMON CAKE

LO *Bananas add flavor and moistness to this picnic-perfect cake.*

45 **10 servings**

1 package (6 ounces) reduced-fat custard-style
  banana yogurt
1 cup mashed ripe banana
2 tablespoons margarine, or butter,
  room temperature
1 egg
1 teaspoon vanilla
1½ cups all-purpose flour
½ cup packed light brown sugar
2 teaspoons baking powder
1 teaspoon each: baking soda, ground cinnamon
¼ teaspoon salt
Powdered Sugar Frosting (recipe follows)

Per Serving:
Calories: 235
% of calories from fat: 19
Fat (gm): 5
Saturated fat (gm): 0.9
Cholesterol (mg): 0.1
Sodium (mg): 326
Protein (gm): 3.7
Carbohydrate (gm): 44.4

Exchanges:
Milk: 0.0
Vegetable: 0.0
Fruit: 0.5
Bread: 2.5
Meat: 0.0
Fat: 0.5

1. Mix yogurt, banana, margarine, egg, and vanilla in large bowl until smooth; mix in combined remaining ingredients, except Powdered Sugar Frosting. Pour into greased and floured 9-inch baking pan.

2. Bake at 375 degrees 25 to 30 minutes or until cake springs back when touched in center. Cool in pan on wire rack 10 minutes; invert onto wire rack and cool. Spread with Powdered Sugar Frosting.

Powdered Sugar Frosting

Makes about ½ cup

1 cup powdered sugar
2 tablespoons margarine, or butter, melted
2–3 tablespoons fat-free milk

1. Mix all ingredients, adding enough milk to make spreadable consistency.

LEMON POUND CAKE

LO

45

◊

Savor the rich flavor of this cake. It may also be served with Tart Lemon Sauce (p. 675), if desired.

12 servings

¾ cup sugar
⅓ cup margarine, or butter, room temperature
1 cup reduced-fat sour cream
3 egg whites
2 teaspoons lemon juice
1 tablespoon grated lemon zest
2½ cups cake flour
1 teaspoon baking soda
¼ teaspoon salt
Lemon Syrup (recipe follows)
Powdered sugar, as garnish

Per Serving:
Calories: 230
% of calories from fat: 26
Fat (gm): 6.5
Saturated fat (gm): 1
Cholesterol (mg): 6.3
Sodium (mg): 235
Protein (gm): 3.5
Carbohydrate (gm): 38.8

Exchanges:
Milk: 0.0
Vegetable: 0.0
Fruit: 0.0
Bread: 2.5
Meat: 0.0
Fat: 1.0

1. Beat sugar and margarine in large bowl until fluffy. Beat in sour cream, egg whites, lemon juice and zest until smooth. Mix in combined flour, baking soda, and salt, beating until smooth, about 1 minute. Spoon into greased and floured 6-cup fluted cake pan.

2. Bake 40 to 50 minutes or until toothpick inserted in center of cake comes out clean. Cool in pan on wire rack 20 minutes; pierce cake at 1-inch intervals with skewer or tines of a fork. Spoon warm Lemon Syrup over and let stand 30 minutes. Invert onto serving plate; sprinkle generously with powdered sugar.

Lemon Syrup

Makes about ⅔ cup

⅔ cup powdered sugar
¼ cup lemon juice
3 tablespoons water

1. Heat all ingredients to boiling in small saucepan, stirring until sugar is dissolved. Cool slightly.

ORANGE POPPY SEED CAKE

LO

This citrus-fresh cake is a perfect addition to any brunch menu.

45

12 servings

½ cup sugar
6 tablespoons margarine, or butter, room temperature
2 eggs
¾ cup fat-free sour cream
2 tablespoons frozen orange juice concentrate, thawed
2 cups cake flour
2 tablespoons poppy seeds
1 teaspoon baking powder
½ teaspoon baking soda
¼ teaspoon salt
Citrus Glaze (recipe follows)

Per Serving:
Calories: 278
% of calories from fat: 33
Fat (gm): 10
Saturated fat (gm): 3
Cholesterol (mg): 48
Sodium (mg): 277
Protein (gm): 5
Carbohydrate (gm): 42

Exchanges:
Milk: 0.0
Vegetable: 0.0
Fruit: 0.0
Bread: 2.5
Meat: 0.0
Fat: 2.0

1. Beat sugar and margarine in large bowl until fluffy. Beat in eggs, sour cream, and orange juice; add combined flour, poppy seeds, baking powder, baking soda, and salt, beating on medium-high speed until smooth, 1 to 2 minutes. Pour into greased and floured 6-cup fluted cake pan.

2. Bake at 350 degrees 40 to 55 minutes, or until toothpick inserted in center of cake comes out clean. Cool in pan on wire rack 25 to 30 minutes; invert onto wire rack and cool. Spoon Citrus Glaze over cake.

Citrus Glaze

1 cup powdered sugar
3–4 tablespoons orange juice

1. Combine sugar and enough orange juice to make glaze consistency.

RASPBERRY-ORANGE SWIRL CAKE

LO

A swirl of raspberry puree enhances the flavor and appearance of this delectable cake.

45

14 servings

2 cups fresh, or frozen, thawed, raspberries
1 package (18½ ounces) yellow cake mix
1 cup water
2 tablespoons frozen orange juice
   concentrate, thawed
3 egg whites
1 teaspoon orange extract, divided
2 teaspoons grated orange zest
2 cups powdered sugar
½ teaspoon orange extract
3–4 tablespoons fat-free milk

Per Serving:
Calories: 173
% of calories from fat: 16
Fat (gm): 3
Saturated fat (gm): 0.5
Cholesterol (mg): 0.6
Sodium (mg): 182
Protein (gm): 2
Carbohydrate (gm): 35

Exchanges:
Milk: 0.0
Vegetable: 0.0
Fruit: 0.0
Bread: 2.0
Meat: 0.0
Fat: 0.5

1. Process raspberries in food processor or blender until smooth; strain and discard seeds.

2. Combine cake mix, water, orange juice, egg whites, ½ teaspoon orange extract, and zest in large bowl; beat on medium-high speed until smooth, about 2 minutes. Pour half the batter into greased and floured 12-cup fluted cake pan; spoon raspberry puree over and top with remaining batter. Cut through batter a few times with a knife to marbleize.

3. Bake at 350 degrees 40 to 45 minutes or until toothpick inserted in center of cake comes out clean. Cool in pan on wire rack 20 minutes; remove from pan and cool. Mix powdered sugar, remaining ½ teaspoon orange extract, and enough milk to make glaze consistency; spoon over cake.

PINEAPPLE-LEMON TRIFLE

LO *Select your prettiest glass bowl for this attractive dessert. A fruit puree replaces the more traditional preserves, enhancing the use of fresh fruits in this recipe.*

12 servings

1 package (18¼ ounces) white cake mix
1½ cups water
3 egg whites
1½ cups pineapple chunks in juice, drained
Lemon Custard (recipe follows)
1 pint strawberries, sliced
2 medium bananas, sliced
¾ cup light whipped topping

Per Serving:
Calories: 289
% of calories from fat: 19
Fat (gm): 6
Saturated fat (gm): 2
Cholesterol (mg): 36
Sodium (mg): 321
Protein (gm): 5
Carbohydrate (gm): 54

Exchanges:
Milk: 0.0
Vegetable: 0.0
Fruit: 0.0
Bread: 3.5
Meat: 0.0
Fat: 1.0

1. Prepare cake mix according to package directions, using 1½ cups water and 3 egg whites. Pour into lightly greased and floured 13 x 9-inch baking pan.

2. Bake at 350 degrees 28 to 30 minutes, or until cake springs back when touched. Cool on wire rack. Cut half the cake into 1-inch cubes. (Reserve or freeze remaining cake for another use.)

3. Process pineapple chunks in blender or food processor until smooth. Layer ⅓ of cake cubes in bottom of 2-quart glass serving bowl. Spoon ⅓ of the Lemon Custard and pineapple puree over cake cubes; top with ⅓ of the strawberries and bananas. Repeat layers twice. Refrigerate until chilled, about 1 hour. Garnish with whipped topping.

Lemon Custard

Makes about 2 cups

¼ cup sugar

2 tablespoons each: cornstarch, flour

1 cup fat-free milk

½ cup lemon juice

2 eggs, lightly beaten

¼ teaspoon ground nutmeg

1. Mix sugar, cornstarch, and flour in medium saucepan; stir in milk and lemon juice. Cook over medium heat, stirring, until mixture boils and thickens, about 1 minute. Stir about ½ cup milk mixture into eggs; stir egg mixture back into saucepan. Cook over low heat, stirring, 1 minute. Remove from heat and cool; stir in nutmeg. Refrigerate until chilled, 1 to 2 hours.

CASSATA SICILIANA

L

45

Filled with ricotta cheese, candied fruit, and chocolate chips, cassata is an Italian dessert traditionally served during the Christmas holidays.

10 servings

1 package (6.95 ounces) angel food loaf cake mix

½ cup water

1 cup low-fat ricotta cheese

¼ cup sugar

2 tablespoons finely chopped mixed candied fruit

1 ounce semisweet chocolate, finely chopped

1 teaspoon grated lemon zest

¼ cup dark rum, or water and ½ teaspoon
  rum extract

Chocolate Sauce (recipe follows)

Per Serving:
Calories: 183
% of calories from fat: 12
Fat (gm): 2.5
Saturated fat (gm): 0.2
Cholesterol (mg): 0.5
Sodium (mg): 270
Protein (gm): 4.4
Carbohydrate (gm): 34.2

Exchanges:
Milk: 0.0
Vegetable: 0.0
Fruit: 0.0
Bread: 2.5
Meat: 0.0
Fat: 0.0

1. Mix cake mix according to package instructions, using ½ cup water. Pour into ungreased 9 x 5-inch loaf pan.

2. Bake at 375 degrees 25 to 30 minutes, or until cracks on top of cake appear dry. Cool completely in pan tipped on side on wire rack.

Remove cake from pan. Slice cake horizontally into three equal layers with serrated knife

3. Combine remaining ingredients, except rum and Chocolate Sauce in small bowl. Place 1 cake layer, crust side down, in a 9 x 5-inch loaf pan lined with plastic wrap. Brush cake with 1 tablespoon rum; spread with half of the ricotta mixture. Top with second cake layer, brush with 1 tablespoon rum, and spread with remaining ricotta mixture. Top with remaining cake layer, and brush with remaining rum. Cover with plastic wrap, pressing firmly to compact layers. Refrigerate overnight, weighted with two 16-ounce cans. Remove cake and slice; drizzle with Chocolate Sauce.

Chocolate Sauce

Makes about 1 cup

¼ cup unsweetened cocoa
2 tablespoons sugar
1 tablespoon cornstarch
⅓ cup dark corn syrup
¼ cup 2% reduced-fat milk
1 teaspoon margarine, or butter
2 teaspoons vanilla

1. Combine cocoa, sugar, and cornstarch in small saucepan. Whisk in corn syrup and milk until smooth. Heat over medium heat, whisking, until mixture boils and thickens, about 1 minute. Stir in margarine and vanilla. Cool.

BASIC PIE PASTRY

L

45

This pastry contains a minimum of margarine yet is not difficult to handle or roll. Use cold margarine and ice water, as the recipe directs.

8 servings (one 8- or 9-inch pie crust)

1¼ cups all-purpose flour

2 tablespoons sugar

¼ teaspoon salt

3 tablespoons cold margarine, or butter

4–5 tablespoons ice water

Per Serving:
Calories: 121
% of calories from fat: 33
(will decrease in pie
servings)
Fat (gm): 4.4
Saturated fat (gm): 0.9
Cholesterol (mg): 0
Sodium (mg): 117
Protein (gm): 2.1
Carbohydrate (gm): 18.1

Exchanges:
Milk: 0.0
Vegetable: 0.0
Fruit: 0.0
Bread: 1.0
Meat: 0.0
Fat: 1.0

1. Combine flour, sugar, and salt in medium bowl. Cut in margarine with pastry blender or 2 knives until mixture resembles coarse crumbs. Sprinkle with water, 1 tablespoon at a time, mixing lightly with a fork after each addition until pastry just holds together. Flatten into a round, wrap in plastic wrap and refrigerate 30 minutes.

2. Roll dough on lightly floured surface into circle 2 inches larger than inverted pie pan. Wrap pastry around rolling pin and unroll into 8- or 9-inch pie or tart pan, easing it onto bottom and side of pan. Trim edge, fold under, and flute. Bake as recipe directs.

Variation

Double Crust Pie Pastry — Make recipe as above, using 2 cups flour, 3 tablespoons sugar, ½ teaspoon salt, 5 tablespoons margarine and 6–7 tablespoons ice water.

NOTE: When a pie crust is baked before filling, the recipe will indicate baking with weights so the bottom of the crust remains flat. Line bottom of pastry with foil and fill with a single layer of pie weights or dried beans. Remove weights and foil 5 minutes before end of baking time. If not using weights or dried beans, piercing the bottom of the pastry with the tines of a fork will help crust remain flat.

MERINGUE PIE CRUST

O

45

Light, airy, delicious, and versatile. Fill this crust with scoops of frozen low-fat yogurt or ice cream, and top with a light drizzle of Warm Rum Sauce or Bittersweet Chocolate Sauce (see pp.628, 661).

8 servings (one 8- or 9-inch pie crust)

4 egg whites
½ teaspoon cream of tartar
1 cup sugar

1. Beat egg whites and cream of tartar in medium bowl to soft peaks. Gradually beat in sugar, beating to stiff peaks. Spoon mixture into ungreased 8- or 9-inch glass pie pan, spreading on bottom and sides to form a large bowl shape. Bake at 350 degrees 40 minutes or until crust is firm to touch and very lightly browned. Cool on wire rack.

Per Serving:
Calories: 98
% of calories from fat: 0
Fat (gm): 0
Saturated fat (gm): 0
Cholesterol (mg): 0
Sodium (mg): 28
Protein (gm): 1.8
Carbohydrate (gm): 24.2

Exchanges:
Milk: 0.0
Vegetable: 0.0
Fruit: 1.0
Bread: 0.0
Meat: 0.5
Fat: 0.0

GRAHAM CRACKER CRUMB CRUST

L

45

Mix this crust right in the pie pan — quick and easy!

8 servings (one 8- or 9-inch pie crust)

1¼ cups graham cracker crumbs
2 tablespoons sugar
3 tablespoons margarine, or butter, melted

1. Combine graham crumbs, sugar, and margarine in 8- or 9-inch pie pan; pat mixture evenly on bottom and side of pan. Bake at 350 degrees 8 to 10 minutes or until edge of crust is lightly browned. Cool on wire rack.

Per Serving:
Calories: 131
% of calories from fat: 44
   (will decrease in pie
   servings)
Fat (gm): 6.4
Saturated fat (gm): 0.8
Cholesterol (mg): 0
Sodium (mg): 148
Protein (gm): 1.3
Carbohydrate (gm): 17.2

Exchanges:
Milk: 0.0
Vegetable: 0.0
Fruit: 0.0
Bread: 1.0
Meat: 0.0
Fat: 1.0

VANILLA CRUMB CRUST

L

A perfect recipe when a delicately flavored crust is desired.

45

8 servings (from 8- or 9-inch pie crust)

1 cup vanilla wafer cookie crumbs
2 tablespoons margarine, or butter, melted

1. Combine vanilla crumbs and margarine in 8- or 9-inch pie pan; pat mixture evenly on bottom and side of pan. Bake 8 to 10 minutes or until edge of crust is lightly browned. Cool on wire rack.

Per Serving:
Calories: 83
% of calories from fat: 51
  (will decrease in pie
  servings)
Fat (gm): 4.7
Saturated fat (gm): 0.9
Cholesterol (mg): 7.8
Sodium (mg): 64
Protein (gm): 0.6
Carbohydrate (gm): 9.4

Exchanges:
Milk: 0.0
Vegetable: 0.0
Fruit: 0.0
Bread: 0.5
Meat: 0.0
Fat: 1.0

GINGERSNAP CRUMB CRUST

L

Gingersnaps provide a zesty flavor accent in this crust.

45

8 servings (from 8- or 9-inch pie crust)

½ cup each: graham cracker crumbs, gingersnap
  cookie crumbs
2 tablespoons margarine, or butter

1. Combine graham and gingersnap crumbs and margarine in 8- or 9-inch pie pan; pat mixture evenly on bottom and sides of pan. Bake at 350 degrees 8 to 10 minutes or until edge of crust is lightly browned. Cool on wire rack.

Per Serving:
Calories: 84
% of calories from fat: 46
  (will decrease in pie
  servings)
Fat (gm): 4.3
Saturated fat (gm): 0.7
Cholesterol (mg): 0
Sodium (mg): 113
Protein (gm): 0.9
Carbohydrate (gm): 10.5

Exchanges:
Milk: 0.0
Vegetable: 0.0
Fruit: 0.0
Bread: 0.5
Meat: 0.0
Fat: 1.0

GRANDMA'S LEMON MERINGUE PIE

LO

45

◊

A perfect flavor combination of sweet and tart, topped with a mile-high meringue! Be sure to spread the meringue while filling is hot, sealing to the edge of the crust to prevent weeping.

10 servings

2 cups sugar, divided

½ cup cornstarch

1½ cups water

½ cup lemon juice

1 egg, lightly beaten

2 tablespoons margarine, or butter

Basic Pie Pastry (see p. 635), baked in 9-inch pie pan

4 egg whites

¼ teaspoon cream of tartar

Per Serving:
Calories: 318
% of calories from fat: 21
Fat (gm): 7
Saturated fat (gm): 2
Cholesterol (mg): 21
Sodium (mg): 168
Protein (gm): 4
Carbohydrate (gm): 60

Exchanges:
Milk: 0.0
Vegetable: 0.0
Fruit: 0.0
Bread: 4.0
Meat: 0.0
Fat: 1.0

1. Combine 1½ cups sugar and cornstarch in medium saucepan; whisk in water and lemon juice. Heat to boiling; boil, whisking, until thickened, about 1 minute. Whisk about 1 cup lemon mixture into egg; whisk mixture back into saucepan. Cook over very low heat, whisking, 30 to 60 seconds. Remove from heat; add margarine, stirring until melted. Pour into baked pastry.

2. Beat egg whites to soft peaks; add cream of tartar and beat to stiff peaks, adding remaining ½ cup sugar gradually. Spread meringue over hot filling, sealing well to edge of pie crust.

3. Bake at 400 degrees until meringue is browned, about 5 minutes. Cool completely on wire rack before cutting. Refrigerate leftover pie.

45-MINUTE PREP TIP: Make pie pastry before preparing the rest of the recipe.

DOUBLE-CRUST APPLE PIE

L

Nothing is more American than real homemade apple pie. Enjoy it warm with a generous scoop of fat-free frozen yogurt or a slice of reduced-fat Cheddar cheese.

10 servings

Double Crust Pie Pastry (see p. 635)
8 cups peeled, cored, sliced tart baking apples
1 cup sugar
4–5 tablespoons all-purpose flour
¾ teaspoon ground cinnamon
¼ teaspoon ground nutmeg
⅛ teaspoon each: ground cloves, salt
2 tablespoons margarine, or butter, cut into
    pieces (optional)

Per Serving:
Calories: 297
% of calories from fat: 19
Fat (gm): 6.3
Saturated fat (gm): 1.2
Cholesterol (mg): 0
Sodium (mg): 200
Protein (gm): 3.1
Carbohydrate (gm): 58.9

Exchanges:
Milk: 0.0
Vegetable: 0.0
Fruit: 1.0
Bread: 3.5
Meat: 0.0
Fat: 1.5

1. Roll ⅔ of the pastry on floured surface into circle 2 inches larger than inverted 9-inch pie pan; ease pastry into pan.

2. Toss apples with combined sugar, flour, spices, and salt in bowl; arrange in pastry and dot with margarine, if using. Roll remaining pastry to fit top of pie and place over apples. Trim edges of pastry to within ½ inch of pan; fold top pastry over bottom pastry and flute. Cut vents in top crust.

3. Bake at 425 degrees until apples are tender and pastry browned, 40 to 50 minutes. Cover pastry with foil if becoming too brown. Cool 10 to 15 minutes before cutting.

TARTE TATIN

L *Caramelized sugar contributes special flavor to this French-style upside-down apple tart.*

8 servings

Basic Pie Pastry (see p. 635)

5 cups sliced, peeled Granny Smith apples (½-inch)

¾ cup sugar, divided

¼ teaspoon ground nutmeg

1 tablespoon lemon juice

2 tablespoons margarine, or butter

Per Serving:
Calories: 279
% of calories from fat: 24
Fat (gm): 7.6
Saturated fat (gm): 1.5
Cholesterol (mg): 0
Sodium (mg): 83.1
Protein (gm): 1.4
Carbohydrate (gm): 53.8

Exchanges:
Milk: 0.0
Vegetable: 0.0
Fruit: 1.5
Bread: 2.0
Meat: 0.0
Fat: 1.0

1. Roll chilled pastry into 11-inch circle; cover loosely with plastic wrap and reserve.

2. Toss apples with combined ½ cup sugar and nutmeg in bowl; sprinkle with lemon juice. Heat remaining ¼ cup sugar in 10-inch oven-proof skillet over medium heat until melted and golden brown, about 5 minutes, stirring occasionally (watch carefully as the sugar can burn easily). Add apple mixture and margarine; cook until apples are just tender, about 5 minutes, stirring occasionally. Arrange apples in skillet so they are slightly mounded in the center. Place reserved pastry on top, tucking edges around apples. Cut slits in pastry.

3. Bake at 425 degrees 20 to 25 minutes or until pastry is lightly browned. Invert onto serving plate. Serve warm or at room temperature.

OLD-FASHIONED BUTTERMILK PIE

LO *Carry on Grandma's best tradition with this pie!*

45 **8 servings**

Gingersnap Crumb Crust (see p. 637)

¾ cup sugar

1 tablespoon margarine, or butter, room temperature

2 eggs

3 tablespoons flour

¼ teaspoon salt

1 cup buttermilk

Ground nutmeg, as garnish

Per Serving:
Calories: 202
% of calories from fat: 31
Fat (gm): 7
Saturated fat (gm): 2
Cholesterol (mg): 54
Sodium (mg): 263
Protein (gm): 4
Carbohydrate (gm): 31

Exchanges:
Milk: 0.0
Vegetable: 0.0
Fruit: 0.0
Bread: 2.0
Meat: 0.0
Fat: 1.5

1. Make Gingersnap Crumb Crust, using 8-inch pie pan; do not bake. Mix sugar and margarine in medium bowl until blended; beat in eggs. Mix in flour, salt, and buttermilk; pour into crust.

2. Bake at 350 degrees 40 minutes or until sharp knife inserted near center of pie comes out clean. Sprinkle with nutmeg; serve warm or chilled.

SPICED SWEET POTATO PIE

LO

45

A change from traditional pumpkin, this pie will brighten any winter holiday table.

10 servings

1½ cups mashed, cooked, peeled sweet potatoes

¾ cup packed light brown sugar

2 eggs

1½ cup fat-free milk

1 teaspoon each: ground cinnamon, ginger

½ teaspoon ground mace

¼ teaspoon salt

Basic Pie Pastry (see p. 635), baked in 8-inch pie pan

Light whipped topping (optional)

Per Serving:
Calories: 215
% of calories from fat: 24
Fat (gm): 6
Saturated fat (gm): 1
Cholesterol (mg): 43
Sodium (mg): 217
Protein (gm): 5
Carbohydrate (gm): 37

Exchanges:
Milk: 0.0
Vegetable: 0.0
Fruit: 0.0
Bread: 2.5
Meat: 0.0
Fat: 1.0

1. Beat sweet potatoes and remaining ingredients, except pastry and whipped topping, in bowl; pour into baked pastry.

2. Bake at 350 degrees until sharp knife inserted near center of pie comes out clean, about 45 minutes. Serve warm or room temperature with whipped topping.

45-MINUTE PREP TIP: Make pie pastry before preparing the rest of the recipe.

BANANA-STRAWBERRY CREAM PIE

LO

Strawberries add a new twist to this old favorite.

45

8 servings

Graham Cracker Crumb Crust (see p. 636)

¼ cup graham cracker crumbs

1 tablespoon margarine, or butter

⅓ cup sugar

¼ cup cornstarch

2 tablespoons flour

¼ teaspoon salt

2½ cups fat-free milk

3 egg yolks

1 teaspoon vanilla

¼ teaspoon each: ground cinnamon, nutmeg

1 cup sliced strawberries

2 medium bananas

Per Serving:
Calories: 250
% of calories from fat: 30
Fat (gm): 8.5
Saturated fat (gm): 1.7
Cholesterol (mg): 81.1
Sodium (mg): 226
Protein (gm): 5.4
Carbohydrate (gm): 38.9

Exchanges:
Milk: 0.0
Vegetable: 0.0
Fruit: 0.5
Bread: 2.0
Meat: 0.0
Fat: 1.5

1. Make pie crust, adding ¼ cup graham crumbs and 1 tablespoon margarine to recipe and using 9-inch pie pan.

2. Mix sugar, cornstarch, flour, and salt in medium saucepan; whisk in milk and heat to boiling over medium-high heat. Boil, whisking, until thickened, about 1 minute. Whisk about ½ cup mixture into egg yolks; whisk egg mixture back into saucepan. Cook over low heat, whisking, 30 to 60 seconds. Stir in vanilla, cinnamon, and nutmeg; cool, stirring frequently. Refrigerate until chilled, 1 to 2 hours.

3. Reserve 8 strawberry slices. Slice 1½ bananas and arrange in crust with remaining strawberries. Spoon custard over fruit; refrigerate until set, 4 to 6 hours. Slice remaining banana and garnish top of pie with banana and strawberry slices.

TOASTED COCONUT CREAM TART

LO

45

❄

Tucked in a tart pan for a new look, you'll enjoy this updated version of an old favorite.

8 servings

⅓ cup sugar

2 tablespoons cornstarch

1½ cups 2% milk

1 egg, slightly beaten

¼ cup flaked, toasted, unsweetened coconut

Basic Pie Pastry (see p. 635), baked in a 9-inch
  tart pan

Per Serving:
Calories: 170
% of calories from fat: 26
Fat (gm): 4.9
Saturated fat (gm): 1.1
Cholesterol (mg): 30
Sodium (mg): 85
Protein (gm): 3.8
Carbohydrate (gm): 28

Exchanges:
Milk: 0.0
Vegetable: 0.0
Fruit: 0.0
Bread: 2.0
Meat: 0.0
Fat: 1.0

1. Mix sugar and cornstarch in small saucepan; whisk in milk and heat to boiling over medium-high heat. Boil, whisking, until thickened, about 1 minute. Whisk about ½ cup mixture into egg; whisk egg mixture back into saucepan. Whisk over low heat 30 to 60 seconds. Stir in 3 tablespoons coconut; pour into baked pastry, spreading evenly. Sprinkle with remaining 1 tablespoon coconut; cool. Refrigerate until set, 2 to 4 hours.

45-MINUTE PREP TIP: Make pie pastry before preparing the rest of the recipe.

KIWI TART

LO

45

❄

Add other sliced spring or summer fruit to this tart if you wish.

8 servings

¼ cup sugar

2 tablespoons cornstarch

1¼ cups 2 % milk

1 tablespoon lemon juice

1 egg, slightly beaten

Basic Pie Pastry (see p. 635), baked in 9-inch tart pan

5 medium kiwi, peeled, sliced

1. Mix sugar and cornstarch in small saucepan; whisk in milk and lemon juice and heat to boiling over medium-high heat. Boil, whisking, until thickened, about 1 minute. Whisk about ½ cup milk mixture into egg; whisk egg mixture back into saucepan. Whisk over low heat 30 to 60 seconds. Pour into baked pastry, spreading evenly; cool to room temperature. Lightly cover custard with plastic wrap; refrigerate 2 to 4 hours, or until set. Arrange kiwi slices in overlapping circles on custard.

45-MINUTE PREP TIP: Make pie pastry before preparing the rest of the recipe.

Per Serving:
Calories: 168
% of calories from fat: 20
Fat (gm): 3.8
Saturated fat (gm): 1
Cholesterol (mg): 29
Sodium (mg): 78
Protein (gm): 3.7
Carbohydrate (gm): 30.4

Exchanges:
Milk: 0.0
Vegetable: 0.0
Fruit: 1.0
Bread: 1.0
Meat: 0.0
Fat: 1.0

LEMON CLOUD PIE

LO

45

Other flavors of this wonderful dessert are easy — just substitute another low-fat fruit yogurt, such as strawberry, raspberry, or cherry.

8 servings

1½ cups each: light whipped topping, low-fat custard-style lemon yogurt
2 tablespoons grated lemon zest
Meringue Pie Crust (see p. 636), baked in 9-inch pie plate
Lemon slices, as garnish

Per Serving:
Calories: 170
% of calories from fat: 17
Fat (gm): 3.5
Saturated fat (gm): 0.3
Cholesterol (mg): 2
Sodium (mg): 62
Protein (gm): 3.6
Carbohydrate (gm): 35.5

Exchanges:
Milk: 0.5
Vegetable: 0.0
Fruit: 2.0
Bread: 0.0
Meat: 0.0
Fat: 0.5

1. Combine whipped topping, yogurt, and lemon zest in small bowl; spoon into center of Meringue Pie Crust. Garnish with lemon slices. Serve immediately or refrigerate until ready to serve.

45-MINUTE PREP TIP: Make pie pastry before preparing the rest of the recipe.

RASPBERRY-GLAZED BLUEBERRY TART

L

Top slices with a small scoop of frozen low-fat vanilla or lemon yogurt.

45

❄

8 servings

3 cups fresh blueberries

Basic Pie Pastry (see p. 635), baked in a 9-inch
  tart pan

¾ cup raspberry spreadable fruit

1 tablespoon raspberry-flavor liqueur (optional)

2 teaspoons cornstarch

¼ teaspoon each: ground cinnamon, nutmeg

Per Serving:
Calories: 169
% of calories from fat: 13
Fat (gm): 2.6
Saturated fat (gm): 0.4
Cholesterol (mg): 0
Sodium (mg): 70
Protein (gm): 2
Carbohydrate (gm): 13

Exchanges:
Milk: 0.0
Vegetable: 0.0
Fruit: 1.0
Bread: 1.0
Meat: 0.0
Fat: 0.5

1. Arrange blueberries in baked pastry. Heat
combined remaining ingredients to boiling in
small saucepan, stirring; spoon over blueberries.
Refrigerate until glaze is slightly firm, about
30 minutes.

45-MINUTE PREP TIP: Make pie pastry before
preparing the rest of the recipe.

PEAR TART WITH CRÈME ANGLAISE

LO

Select pears that are just ripe, but not soft, for this elegant and delicate tart.

8 servings

2 pounds (4 large) pears, peeled, cored, and sliced
  ¼ inch thick

¼ cup all-purpose flour

3 tablespoons sugar

½ teaspoon ground cinnamon

¼ teaspoon ground nutmeg

Basic Pie Pastry (see p. 635), baked in a 9-inch
  tart pan

Crème Anglaise (recipe follows)

Per Serving:
Calories: 210
% of calories from fat: 14
Fat (gm): 3.5
Saturated fat (gm): 0.6
Cholesterol (mg): 25
Sodium (mg): 66
Protein (gm): 3.6
Carbohydrate (gm): 42

Exchanges:
Milk: 0.0
Vegetable: 0.0
Fruit: 1.0
Bread: 2.0
Meat: 0.0
Fat: 0.5

1. Toss pears with combined flour, sugar, cinnamon, and nutmeg; arrange in overlapping circles

in baked pastry. Bake at 375 degrees until pears are tender, 20 to 25 minutes. Serve warm with Crème Anglaise.

Crème Anglaise

Makes about 1 cup

1 tablespoon cornstarch
2 teaspoons sugar
1 cup fat-free milk
1 egg yolk
⅛–¼ teaspoon ground nutmeg

1. Mix cornstarch and sugar in small saucepan; whisk in milk and heat to boiling over medium-high heat. Boil, whisking, until thickened, about 1 minute. Whisk about ½ cup milk mixture into egg yolk; whisk egg yolk mixture back into saucepan. Whisk over low heat 30 to 60 seconds (mixture will coat back of spoon). Remove from heat; stir in nutmeg. Serve warm or chilled.

45-MINUTE PREP TIP: Make pie pastry before preparing the rest of the recipe.

RUSTIC COUNTRY FRUIT TART

L

45

Perfect for a lazy-day summer picnic, this tumble of garden fruits is lightly glazed and encased in a free-form pastry.

8 servings

Basic Pie Pastry (see p. 635)
¼ cup all-purpose flour, divided
2 tablespoons cold margarine, or butter
2 cups each: raspberries, sliced strawberries
1 cup seedless grapes
4 each: halved peeled medium apricots, peaches
⅓ cup sugar
½ teaspoon ground cinnamon
¼ cup apricot spreadable fruit
2 tablespoons water

Per Serving:
Calories: 295
% of calories from fat: 23
Fat (gm): 7.8
Saturated fat (gm): 1.5
Cholesterol (mg): 0
Sodium (mg): 152
Protein (gm): 4
Carbohydrate (gm): 54.4

Exchanges:
Milk: 0.0
Vegetable: 0.0
Fruit: 1.0
Bread: 2.5
Meat: 0.0
Fat: 1.0

1. Make Basic Pie Pastry, adding ¼ cup flour and 2 tablespoons margarine to recipe. Roll pastry on lightly floured surface into a 12-inch circle (edges do not need to be even). Transfer pastry to a 12-inch pizza pan.

2. Toss fruits with combined remaining ¼ cup flour, sugar, and cinnamon. Arrange fruits in center of pastry, leaving a 2- to 3-inch border around outer edge. Gently gather and fold outer edge of pastry over fruits (fruits will not be completely enclosed).

3. Bake at 425 degrees 20 to 25 minutes, or until crust is lightly browned and fruit is tender. Heat spreadable fruit and water in small saucepan until warm; brush over fruit.

SPRING BERRY CHEESECAKE

LO

You won't believe how delicious this cheesecake is!

45

16 servings

Vanilla Crumb Crust (see p. 637)

1 cup low-fat cottage cheese

1 package (8 ounces) fat-free cream cheese, room temperature

1 cup fat-free sour cream

⅓ cup plus ¼ cup sugar, divided

3 eggs

½ cup fat-free milk

2 tablespoons lemon juice

3 tablespoons each: finely grated lemon zest, all-purpose flour

1 teaspoon vanilla

⅛ teaspoon salt

1 quart strawberries, or blueberries, sliced

Per Serving:
Calories: 122
% of calories from fat: 23
Fat (gm): 3.1
Saturated fat (gm): 0.8
Cholesterol (mg): 42.6
Sodium (mg): 209
Protein (gm): 6.7
Carbohydrate (gm): 16.6

Exchanges:
Milk: 0.0
Vegetable: 0.0
Fruit: 0.5
Bread: 0.5
Meat: 0.5
Fat: 0.5

1. Make Vanilla Crumb Crust and press in bottom of 9-inch spring-form pan.

2. Process cottage cheese in food processor or blender until smooth. Transfer to large bowl and beat in cream cheese, sour cream, and ⅓ cup sugar until fluffy. Add eggs one at a time, beating well after each addition. Mix in milk, lemon juice and zest, flour, vanilla, and salt. Pour over crust.

3. Bake at 325 degrees until the cheesecake is set, but still slightly soft in the center, about 50 minutes. Cool on wire rack; carefully loosen side of pan. Refrigerate, covered, 8 hours or overnight. Combine berries and remaining ¼ cup sugar; serve over cheese-cake slices.

NEW YORK-STYLE CHEESECAKE

LO

There's only one word for this cheesecake — spectacular!

45

12 servings

Graham Cracker Crumb Crust (see p. 636)

3 packages (8 ounces each) fat-free cream cheese, room temperature

¾ cup sugar

2 eggs

2 tablespoons cornstarch

1 teaspoon vanilla

1 cup reduced-fat sour cream

Per Serving:
Calories: 209
% of calories from fat: 28
Fat (gm): 6.2
Saturated fat (gm): 3.2
Cholesterol (mg): 45
Sodium (mg): 452
Protein (gm): 10.4
Carbohydrate (gm): 258

Exchanges:
Milk: 0.0
Vegetable: 0.0
Fruit: 0.0
Bread: 1.5
Meat: 1.0
Fat: 1.0

1. Make Graham Cracker Crumb Crust, patting mixture on bottom and ½ inch up sides of 9-inch springform pan.

2. Beat cream cheese and sugar in large bowl until fluffy; beat in remaining ingredients; pour into crust.

3. Bake at 325 degrees until cheesecake is set but still slightly soft in the center, 45 to 50 minutes. Turn oven off; let cheesecake cool in oven with door ajar for 2 hours. Carefully loosen side of pan; refrigerate, covered, 8 hours or overnight.

LEMON MERINGUE CHEESECAKE

LO

45

Never has a cheesecake filling been quite as velvety smooth as this. The filling is slightly soft, so chill very well before cutting.

12 servings

3 packages (8 ounces each) fat-free cream cheese, room temperature

4 egg yolks

⅔ cup lemon juice

2 tablespoons flour

1 cup sugar

⅓ cup cornstarch

⅔ cup water

2 teaspoons grated lemon zest

Basic Pie Pastry (see p. 635), baked in 9-inch pie pan

4 egg whites

¼ teaspoon cream of tartar

⅓ cup powdered sugar

Per Serving:
Calories: 224
% of calories from fat: 13
Fat (gm): 3.3
Saturated fat (gm): 0.8
Cholesterol (mg): 81
Sodium (mg): 441
Protein (gm): 11.6
Carbohydrate (gm): 35.4

Exchanges:
Milk: 0.0
Vegetable: 0.0
Fruit: 0.0
Bread: 2.5
Meat: 1.0
Fat: 0.0

1. Beat cream cheese and egg yolks in medium bowl until smooth; beat in lemon juice and flour.

2. Mix sugar and cornstarch in medium saucepan; whisk in water and lemon zest. Heat over medium-high heat to boiling; boil, whisking, until mixture thickens, about 1 minute. Remove from heat. Whisk in cheese mixture, blending well. Pour into baked crust.

3. Beat egg whites and cream of tartar in large bowl to soft peaks; gradually add powdered sugar, beating to stiff, but not dry, peaks. Spread meringue over top of pie, sealing to edge of crust. Bake at 425 degrees until meringue is golden, about 10 minutes. Cool on wire rack; refrigerate at least 4 hours.

45-MINUTE PREP TIP: Make pie pastry before preparing the rest of the recipe.

CHOCOLATE FILLO CHEESECAKE

LO

Crisp, golden layers of fillo make a delicate crust for this cheesecake.

45

12 servings

2 tablespoons unseasoned dry bread crumbs
6 sheets frozen fillo pastry, thawed
Vegetable cooking spray
3 packages (8 ounces each) fat-free cream cheese, room temperature
1 cup reduced-fat sour cream
⅔ cup sugar
⅓ cup Dutch process cocoa
2 eggs
3 tablespoons flour
½ teaspoon ground cinnamon

Per Serving:
Calories: 159
% of calories from fat: 8
Fat (gm): 1.4
Saturated fat (gm): 0.3
Cholesterol (mg): 45
Sodium (mg): 358
Protein (gm): 12.3
Carbohydrate (gm): 22.4

Exchanges:
Milk: 0.0
Vegetable: 0.0
Fruit: 0.0
Bread: 1.0
Meat: 1.5
Fat: 0.0

1. Coat 9-inch greased springform pan with bread crumbs. Spray each fillo sheet lightly with cooking spray. Layer fillo in bottom of pan, turning each sheet slightly so that corners are staggered. Bake at 375 degrees until lightly browned, 6 to 8 minutes. Cool on wire rack.

2. Reduce oven temperature to 350 degrees. Beat cream cheese until fluffy in large bowl; mix in sour cream, sugar, and cocoa. Beat in eggs; mix in flour and cinnamon. Pour into fillo crust; gently fold sides of fillo inward so they do not extend outside edge of pan.

3. Bake until cheesecake is set, but still slightly soft in the center, about 50 minutes. Cover edges of fillo crust with foil during last 15 or 20 minutes of baking time if beginning to get too brown. Cool on wire rack 10 minutes. Carefully loosen side of pan; cool to room temperature. Cover loosely and refrigerate 8 hours or overnight.

CHOCOLATE CHIP COOKIES

LO *America's favorite cookie!*

45 **5 dozen cookies** (1 per serving)

8 tablespoons margarine, or butter, room temperature

1 cup packed light brown sugar

½ cup granulated sugar

1 egg

1 teaspoon vanilla

2½ cups all-purpose flour

½ teaspoon each: baking soda, salt

⅓ cup fat-free milk

½ package (12-ounce size) reduced-fat semisweet chocolate morsels

Per Serving:
Calories: 66
% of calories from fat: 27
Fat (gm): 2
Saturated fat (gm): 0.7
Cholesterol (mg): 3.6
Sodium (mg): 70
Protein (gm): 0.8
Carbohydrate (gm): 11.2

Exchanges:
Milk: 0.0
Vegetable: 0.0
Fruit: 0.0
Bread: 0.5
Meat: 0.0
Fat: 0.5

1. Beat margarine and sugars in medium bowl until fluffy; beat in egg and vanilla. Mix in combined flour, baking soda, and salt alternately with milk, beginning and ending with dry ingredients. Mix in chocolate morsels. Drop cookies by tablespoonfuls onto greased cookie sheets. Bake at 375 degrees until browned, about 10 minutes. Cool on wire racks.

RAISIN OATMEAL COOKIES

LO *Moist and chewy, just the way they should be!*

45 **2½ dozen cookies** (1 per serving)

6 tablespoons margarine, or butter, room temperature

¼ cup fat-free sour cream

1 egg

1 teaspoon vanilla

1 cup packed light brown sugar

1½ cups quick-cooking oats

1 cup all-purpose flour

½ teaspoon baking soda

¼ teaspoon baking powder

1 teaspoon ground cinnamon

½ cup raisins

Per Serving:
Calories: 90
% of calories from fat: 27
Fat (gm): 2.7
Saturated fat (gm): 0.5
Cholesterol (mg): 7.1
Sodium (mg): 57
Protein (gm): 1.5
Carbohydrate (gm): 15.3

Exchanges:
Milk: 0.0
Vegetable: 0.0
Fruit: 0.0
Bread: 1.0
Meat: 0.0
Fat: 0.5

1. Mix margarine, sour cream, egg, and vanilla in large bowl; beat in brown sugar. Mix in combined oats, flour, baking soda, baking powder, and cinnamon. Mix in raisins. Drop dough onto greased cookie sheets, using 2 tablespoons for each cookie. Bake at 350 degrees until browned, 12 to 15 minutes. Cool on wire racks.

FROSTED SUGAR COOKIES

Rich, crisp, and generously frosted, these cookies will flatter any holiday or special occasion.

LO

45

6 dozen cookies (1 per serving)

10 tablespoons margarine, or butter, room temperature

2 tablespoons fat-free sour cream

1 egg

1 teaspoon lemon extract

1 cup powdered sugar

2 cups all-purpose flour

1 teaspoon baking powder

¼ teaspoon salt

Sugar Frosting (recipe follows)

Ground cinnamon or nutmeg

Per Serving:
Calories: 48
% of calories from fat: 31
Fat (gm): 1.7
Saturated fat (gm): 0.3
Cholesterol (mg): 3
Sodium (mg): 45
Protein (gm): 0.5
Carbohydrate (gm): 7.7

Exchanges:
Milk: 0.0
Vegetable: 0.0
Fruit: 0.0
Bread: 0.5
Meat: 0.0
Fat: 0.5

1. Beat margarine, sour cream, egg, and lemon extract in medium bowl until smooth; mix in powdered sugar. Mix in combined flour, baking powder, and salt. Refrigerate 4 to 6 hours.

2. Roll dough on floured surface to ¼ inch thickness. Cut out shapes with 2-inch cookie cutters. Bake at 375 degrees on greased cookie sheets until lightly browned, 8 to 10 minutes. Cool on wire racks. Frost with Sugar Frosting; sprinkle lightly with cinnamon.

Sugar Frosting

Makes about ¾ cup

2 cups powdered sugar

½ teaspoon lemon extract, or vanilla

2–3 tablespoons fat-free milk

1. Mix powdered sugar, lemon extract, and enough milk to make the consistency spreadable.

GLAZED CHOCOLATE SHORTBREAD SQUARES

LO

Rich, chocolatey, and crisp!

45

5 dozen squares (1 per serving)

1½ cups all-purpose flour

¼ cup unsweetened cocoa

¾ cup sugar

¼ teaspoon salt

8 tablespoons margarine, or butter, room temperature

1 egg

2 teaspoons vanilla

Sugar Glaze (recipe follows)

Per Serving:
Calories: 44
% of calories from fat: 31
Fat (gm): 1.6
Saturated fat (gm): 0.3
Cholesterol (mg): 0
Sodium (mg): 29
Protein (gm): 0.5
Carbohydrate (gm): 7.2

Exchanges:
Milk: 0.0
Vegetable: 0.0
Fruit: 0.0
Bread: 0.5
Meat: 0.0
Fat: 0.5

1. Combine flour, cocoa, sugar, and salt in medium-size bowl; cut in margarine with pastry blender or 2 knives until mixture resembles coarse crumbs. Mix in egg and vanilla, stirring just enough to form a soft dough. Pat and spread dough in greased 15 x 10-inch jelly roll pan, using fingers and small spatula, until bottom of pan is evenly covered. Pierce dough with tines of fork.

2. Bake at 350 degrees until firm to touch, 20 to 25 minutes. Cool slightly on wire rack. Spoon glaze over and cut into squares while warm.

Sugar Glaze

Makes about 1 cup

1 cup powdered sugar
tablespoons fat-free milk

1. Mix powdered sugar with enough milk to make glaze consistency.

Variations

Cocoa-Glazed Cookie Crisps — Make recipe as above, using 1¾ cups flour, deleting the cocoa, and substituting packed light brown sugar for the granulated sugar. Brush dough with 1 beaten egg white before baking. Add 2 tablespoons unsweetened cocoa to the glaze.

Spiced Cookie Crisps — Make recipe as above, using 1¾ cups flour, deleting the cocoa, and adding 1½ teaspoons ground cinnamon or cardamom. Brush dough with 1 beaten egg white before baking. Add 1 teaspoon vanilla to the Sugar Glaze.

FROSTED COCOA BROWNIES

LO

45

You'll never guess these very chocolatey and slightly chewy brownies are low in fat.

25 brownies (1 per serving)

1 cup each: all-purpose flour, sugar

¼ cup unsweetened cocoa

5 tablespoons margarine, or butter, melted

¼ cup fat-free milk

2 eggs

¼ cup honey

1 teaspoon vanilla

Cocoa Frosting (recipe follows)

Per Serving:
Calories: 111
% of calories from fat: 24
Fat (gm): 3.1
Saturated fat (gm): 0.6
Cholesterol (mg): 8.6
Sodium (mg): 42
Protein (gm): 1.5
Carbohydrate (gm): 20.4

Exchanges:
Milk: 0.0
Vegetable: 0.0
Fruit: 1.5
Bread: 0.0
Meat: 0.0
Fat: 0.5

1. Combine flour, sugar, and cocoa in medium bowl; mix in margarine, milk, eggs, honey, and vanilla, blending well. Pour into greased and floured 8-inch-square baking pan. Bake at 350 degrees until brownies spring back when touched, about 30 minutes. Cool in pan on wire rack; spread with Cocoa Frosting.

Cocoa Frosting

Makes about ½ cup

1 cup powdered sugar
2–3 tablespoons unsweetened cocoa
1 tablespoon margarine, or butter, room temperature
2–3 tablespoons fat-free milk

1. Mix all ingredients, adding enough milk to make the consistency spreadable.

SUGARED LEMON SQUARES

LO *Just like the favorites you remember, but with a low-fat bonus!*

45

25 squares (1 per serving)

¾ cup all-purpose flour
4 tablespoons margarine, or butter, room temperature
2 tablespoons each: reduced-fat sour cream,
  granulated sugar
1 cup granulated sugar
2 eggs
1 tablespoon grated lemon zest
tablespoons lemon juice
½ teaspoon baking powder
¼ teaspoon salt
Powdered sugar

Per Serving:
Calories: 71
% of calories from fat: 27
Fat (gm): 2.1
Saturated fat (gm): 0.4
Cholesterol (mg): 8.9
Sodium (mg): 57
Protein (gm): 1
Carbohydrate (gm): 12.2

Exchanges:
Milk: 0.0
Vegetable: 0.0
Fruit: 0.0
Bread: 1.0
Meat: 0.0
Fat: 0.5

1. Mix flour, margarine, sour cream, and 2 tablespoons granulated sugar in bowl to form soft dough; pat into bottom and ¼ inch up sides of an 8 x 8-inch baking pan. Bake at 350 degrees until lightly browned, about 20 minutes. Cool on wire rack.

2. Mix 1 cup granulated sugar and remaining ingredients, except powdered sugar, in small bowl; pour over baked pastry. Bake at 350 degrees until no indentation remains when touched in the center, 20 to 25 minutes. Cool on wire rack; cut into squares. Sprinkle lightly with powdered sugar.

CHOCOLATE FUDGE MERINGUES

o

Better bake several batches, as these won't last long!

45

24 cookies (1 per serving)

3 egg whites
½ teaspoon cream of tartar
¼ teaspoon salt
2 cups powdered sugar
½ cup unsweetened cocoa
1 ounce semisweet chocolate, finely chopped

Per Serving:
Calories: 43
% of calories from fat: 11
Fat (gm): 0.5
Saturated fat (gm): 0
Cholesterol (mg): 0
Sodium (mg): 29
Protein (gm): 0.8
Carbohydrate (gm): 9.1

Exchanges:
Milk: 0.0
Vegetable: 0.0
Fruit: 0.0
Bread: 0.5
Meat: 0.0
Fat: 0.0

1. Beat egg whites to soft peaks in large bowl; add cream of tartar and salt and beat, adding sugar gradually, until stiff, but not dry, peaks form. Fold in cocoa and chocolate. Drop by tablespoons onto parchment or foil-lined cookie sheets. Bake at 300 degrees until cookies feel crisp when touched, 20 to 25 minutes. Cool on pans on wire racks.

Variation

Orange-Almond Meringues — Make recipe as above, substituting ¾ cup granulated sugar for the powdered sugar, and adding ½ teaspoon orange extract. Delete cocoa and semisweet chocolate. Fold ½ cup chopped almonds into beaten egg white mixture.

Peppermint Clouds — Make Orange-Almond Meringue, deleting orange extract and substituting crushed peppermint candies for the almonds.

HAZELNUT MACAROONS

o

Use any favorite nuts in these moist and crunchy macaroons.

45

30 cookies (1 per serving)

4 egg whites
⅛ teaspoon cream of tartar
¼ teaspoon salt

1 cup each: sugar, sweetened flaked coconut

¼ cup finely chopped hazelnuts, or pecans

1. Beat egg whites to soft peaks in large bowl; add cream of tartar and salt and beat to stiff, but not dry, peaks, adding sugar gradually. Fold in coconut and hazelnuts. Drop mixture by table-spoons onto parchment or foil-lined cookie sheets. Bake at 300 degrees until cookies begin to brown and feel crisp when touched, 20 to 25 minutes. Cool in pans on wire racks.

Per Serving:
Calories: 44
% of calories from fat: 28
Fat (gm): 1.4
Saturated fat (gm): 0.8
Cholesterol (mg): 0
Sodium (mg): 25.6
Protein (gm): 0.7
Carbohydrate (gm): 7.6

Exchanges:
Milk: 0.0
Vegetable: 0.0
Fruit: 0.0
Bread: 0.5
Meat: 0.0
Fat: 0.5

ANISE-ALMOND BISCOTTI

Crisp because they're baked twice, biscotti are perfect for dunking into coffee, tea, or Vin Santo, the Italian way!

60 bars (1 per serving)

4 tablespoons margarine, or butter, room temperature

¾ cup sugar

3 eggs

2½ cups all-purpose flour

2 teaspoons crushed anise seeds

1½ teaspoons baking powder

½ teaspoon baking soda

¼ teaspoon salt

⅓ cup (1 ounce) whole blanched almonds

Per Serving:
Calories: 41
% of calories from fat: 26
Fat (gm): 1.2
Saturated fat (gm): 0.2
Cholesterol (mg): 7.1
Sodium (mg): 40
Protein (gm): 1
Carbohydrate (gm): 6.7

Exchanges:
Milk: 0.0
Vegetable: 0.0
Fruit: 0.0
Bread: 0.5
Meat: 0.0
Fat: 0.0

1. Beat margarine, sugar, and eggs until smooth. Mix in combined flour, anise seeds, baking powder, baking soda, and salt. Mix in almonds. Shape dough on greased cookie sheets into 4 slightly flattened rolls, 1½ inches in diameter.

2. Bake at 350 degrees until lightly browned, about 20 minutes. Let stand on wire rack until cool enough to handle, then cut into ½-inch slices. Arrange slices, cut sides down, on ungreased cookie sheets. Bake at 350 degrees until toasted and almost dry, 7 to 10 minutes on each side. Cool on wire racks.

APRICOT-SESAME BISCOTTI

O

Biscotti become crisper as they cool, so bake only until almost dry.

45

60 bars (1 per serving)

2½ cups all-purpose flour

1 teaspoon baking powder

½ teaspoon baking soda

¾ cup packed light brown sugar

2 tablespoons each: grated orange zest, toasted
 sesame seeds

3 eggs

½ cup finely chopped dried apricots

Per Serving:
Calories: 37
% of calories from fat: 9
Fat (gm): 0.4
Saturated fat (gm): 0.1
Cholesterol (mg): 7.1
Sodium (mg): 21
Protein (gm): 1
Carbohydrate (gm): 7.4

Exchanges:
Milk: 0.0
Vegetable: 0.0
Fruit: 0.0
Bread: 0.5
Meat: 0.0
Fat: 0.0

1. Combine all ingredients, except eggs and dried apricots, in large
bowl; mix in eggs and dried apricots. Shape dough on greased
cookie sheets into 4 slightly flattened rolls, 1½ inches in diameter.

2. Bake at 350 degrees until lightly browned, about 20 minutes. Let
stand on wire rack until cool enough to handle, then cut into ½-
inch slices. Arrange slices, cut sides down, on ungreased cookie
sheets. Bake at 350 degrees until toasted and almost dry, 7 to 10
minutes on each side. Cool on wire racks.

SPICED ORANGE COMPOTE

V

*A perfect dessert for winter, when other fresh fruits are not available. Serve
with cookies. such as Spiced Cookie Crisps (see p. 654).*

45

❄

8 servings

5 oranges, peeled, sliced

⅓ cup orange juice

3 tablespoons packed light brown sugar

2–3 tablespoons orange-flavored liqueur (optional)

4 whole allspice

1 cinnamon stick

Mint sprigs, as garnish

Per Serving:
Calories: 72
% of calories from fat: 1
Fat (gm): 0.1
Saturated fat (gm): 0
Cholesterol (mg): 0
Sodium (mg): 2
Protein (gm): 0.8
Carbohydrate (gm): 16.8

Exchanges:
Milk: 0.0
Vegetable: 0.0
Fruit: 1.0
Bread: 0.0
Meat: 0.0
Fat: 0.0

1. Place oranges in shallow glass bowl. Heat remaining ingredients, except mint, to boiling in small saucepan; pour over orange slices. Refrigerate, covered, 8 hours or overnight for flavors to blend. Garnish with mint.

HONEY-LIME MELON WEDGES

A recipe that is so simple, but so very good.

45

4 servings

1 small cantaloupe, or other melon, cut into wedges
3–4 tablespoons honey
4 lime wedges
Ground nutmeg

1. Drizzle melon with honey and squeeze lime juice over; sprinkle with nutmeg.

Per Serving:
Calories: 112
% of calories from fat: 3
Fat (gm): 0.5
Saturated fat (gm): 0
Cholesterol (mg): 0
Sodium (mg): 15
Protein (gm): 1.5
Carbohydrate (gm): 28.1

Exchanges:
Milk: 0.0
Vegetable: 0.0
Fruit: 2.0
Bread: 0.0
Meat: 0.0
Fat: 0.0

HONEY-BROILED PINEAPPLE SLICES

This dessert beckons a selection of cookie accompaniments. Choose among Frosted Cocoa Brownies, Frosted Sugar Cookies, or Hazelnut Macaroons (see pp. 654, 652, 656).

45

4 servings (2 pineapple slices each)

1 medium pineapple (1½ pounds), peeled, cored, and cut into eight ½-inch slices
3 tablespoons honey
2 tablespoons each: thawed frozen orange juice concentrate, minced fresh cilantro, or mint

1. Arrange pineapple rings on broiler pan; brush with combined honey and orange concentrate. Broil 6 inches from heat source 3 minutes on each side, basting with honey mixture. Sprinkle with cilantro.

Per Serving:
Calories: 143
% of calories from fat: 4
Fat (gm): 0.7
Saturated fat (gm): 0
Cholesterol (mg): 0
Sodium (mg): 3
Protein (gm): 0.8
Carbohydrate (gm): 36.5

Exchanges:
Milk: 0.0
Vegetable: 0.0
Fruit: 2.5
Bread: 0.0
Meat: 0.0
Fat: 0.0

FRESH BERRY RHUBARB

V

Frozen fruit can also be used, so this light dessert can be enjoyed all year.

45 **6 servings** (½ cup each)

3 cups sliced rhubarb (about 1 pound)
½ cup each: water, sugar
¼ teaspoon ground cinnamon
1 cup each: sliced strawberries, blueberries

1. Heat rhubarb, water, and sugar to boiling in medium saucepan; reduce heat and simmer until rhubarb is tender, about 10 minutes. Stir in cinnamon and cool. Stir in berries.

Per Serving:
Calories: 103
% of calories from fat: 3
Fat (gm): 0.3
Saturated fat (gm): 0.1
Cholesterol (mg): 0
Sodium (mg): 5.3
Protein (gm): 1
Carbohydrate (gm): 25.6

Exchanges:
Milk: 0.0
Vegetable: 0.0
Fruit: 1.5
Bread: 0.0
Meat: 0.0
Fat: 0.0

CARAMEL APPLE SLICES

V

Serve these fragrant apple slices over frozen low-fat vanilla yogurt for a sumptuous sundae, or serve over pancakes, waffles, or crepes.

45

4 servings

2 large sweet or tart apples, peeled, cored, sliced (¼-inch)
½ cup apple cider
¼ cup packed light brown sugar
Ground cinnamon and nutmeg

1. Heat apples, cider, and brown sugar to boiling in medium saucepan; reduce heat and simmer, uncovered, until apples are crisp-tender, 3 to 4 minutes. Remove apples to serving dish with slotted spoon. Heat cider mixture to boiling; boil until mixture is reduced to a syrup consistency. Pour over apples, and sprinkle lightly with cinnamon and nutmeg.

Per Serving:
Calories: 104
% of calories from fat: 2
Fat (gm): 0.3
Saturated fat (gm): 0
Cholesterol (mg): 0
Sodium (mg): 5
Protein (gm): 0.1
Carbohydrate (gm): 24.1

Exchanges:
Milk: 0.0
Vegetable: 0.0
Fruit: 1.5
Bread: 0.0
Meat: 0.0
Fat: 0.0

PEARS BELLE HÉLÈNE

Cocoa-Glazed Cookie Crisps (see p. 654) would compliment this elegant offering.

4 servings

4 cups water
¼ cup sugar
4 small pears, peeled, with stems intact
1 cup frozen low-fat vanilla yogurt
Bittersweet Chocolate Sauce (recipe follows)

Per Serving:
Calories: 183
% of calories from fat: 5
Fat (gm): 1.1
Saturated fat (gm): 0
Cholesterol (mg): 0
Sodium (mg): 0
Protein (gm): 2.3
Carbohydrate (gm): 43.9

Exchanges:
Milk: 0.0
Vegetable: 0.0
Fruit: 2.0
Bread: 1.0
Meat: 0.0
Fat: 0.0

1. Heat water and sugar to boiling in small saucepan; add pears, reduce heat, and simmer, covered, until pears are tender, 10 to 15 minutes. Cool pears in syrup; refrigerate until chilled, 1 to 2 hours. Drain.

2. Flatten scoops of frozen yogurt in 4 shallow dishes; place pears on top and drizzle with Bittersweet Chocolate Sauce.

Bittersweet Chocolate Sauce

Makes about 1½ cups

¾ cup unsweetened cocoa
½ cup sugar
¾ cup fat-free milk
2 tablespoons margarine, or butter
1 teaspoon vanilla
¼–½ teaspoon ground cinnamon

1. Mix cocoa and sugar in small saucepan; stir in milk and margarine. Heat to boiling, stirring; reduce heat and simmer until sauce is smooth and slightly thickened, 3 to 4 minutes. Stir in vanilla and cinnamon. Serve warm or at room temperature.

Variation

Pears with Raspberry Sauce — Make recipe as above, deleting Bittersweet Chocolate Sauce. Process 1 pint fresh, or frozen, thawed, raspberries and ⅓ cup sugar in blender or food processor until smooth. Strain, discarding seeds. Makes about 1 cup Raspberry Sauce.

STRAWBERRY-KIWI SHORTCAKE

LO

45

This moist, nutritious whole wheat shortcake is made to order for a duo of fresh fruit.

8 servings

1 cup each: all-purpose flour, whole wheat flour

⅓ cup sugar

1½ teaspoons baking powder

½ teaspoon baking soda

¼ teaspoon salt

⅔ cup buttermilk

4 tablespoons margarine, or butter, melted

2 eggs, lightly beaten

1½ teaspoons vanilla

3 cups sliced strawberries

1 cup peeled, sliced kiwi

Per Serving:
Calories: 227
% of calories from fat: 29
Fat (gm): 7.3
Saturated fat (gm): 1.5
Cholesterol (mg): 27.4
Sodium (mg): 319
Protein (gm): 6.5
Carbohydrate (gm): 39.1

Exchanges:
Milk: 0.0
Vegetable: 0.0
Fruit: 1.0
Bread: 2.0
Meat: 0.0
Fat: 1.0

1. Combine flours, sugar, baking powder, baking soda, and salt in medium bowl. Add combined buttermilk, margarine, eggs, and vanilla, mixing only until dry ingredients are moistened. With floured hands, lightly pat dough into greased 8-inch round or square baking pan.

2. Bake at 400 degrees 12 to 15 minutes, or until toothpick inserted near center of cake comes out clean. Cool in pan on wire rack 10 minutes. Slice cake into wedges or squares and top with fruit.

DUTCH PANCAKE WITH SPICED FRUIT MÉLANGE

LO *A spectacular dessert or brunch entree that will win raves!*

45 **8 servings**

Dutch Pancake (recipe follows)
3 medium cooking apples, peeled, cored, sliced
1¼ cups mixed dried fruit
¼ cup each: dried cranberries, or cherries, sugar
½ cup orange juice
1 teaspoon ground cinnamon
Maple syrup, warm

Per Serving:
Calories: 225
% of calories from fat: 22
Fat (gm): 6
Saturated fat (gm): 1
Cholesterol (mg): 106
Sodium (mg): 154
Protein (gm): 6
Carbohydrate (gm): 40

Exchanges:
Milk: 0.0
Vegetable: 0.0;
Fruit: 0.5
Bread: 2.0
Meat: 0.0
Fat: 1.0

1. Make Dutch Pancake. While Dutch Pancake is baking, sauté apples in lightly greased large skillet 2 to 3 minutes. Add remaining ingredients, except maple syrup, and cook, covered, over medium heat until apples are crisp-tender, about 5 minutes. Heat to boiling and cook, uncovered, until liquid is syrupy, 2 to 3 minutes. Spoon into warm Dutch Pancake; cut into wedges and serve with maple syrup.

Dutch Pancake

4 eggs
¾ cup each: fat-free milk, all-purpose flour
1 tablespoon sugar
¼ teaspoon salt
2 tablespoons margarine, or butter

1. Whisk all ingredients, except margarine, in large bowl until almost smooth (batter will be slightly lumpy). Heat margarine in 12-inch ovenproof skillet until melted and bubbly; pour in batter. Bake, uncovered, at 425 degrees until pancake is puffed and browned, 20 to 25 minutes (do not open door during first 15 minutes).

FRAN'S RHUBARB CRUNCH

L

45

◊

Recipes from neighbors are the best. With a crunchy sweet crust on top and bottom, you'll lick your bowl clean and ask for more! The recipe can be halved and baked in a 9-inch-square baking pan.

16 servings

1 cup each: all-purpose flour, whole wheat flour

1½ cups packed light brown sugar

1 cup quick-cooking oats

½ cup bran, or quick-cooking oats

2 teaspoons ground cinnamon

10 tablespoons margarine, or butter, melted

2 pounds fresh, or frozen, thawed, rhubarb, cut into 1-inch pieces

2 cups granulated sugar

¼ cup cornstarch

2 cups water

2 teaspoons vanilla

Per Serving:
Calories: 341
% of calories from fat: 10
Fat (gm): 7.9
Saturated fat (gm): 1.5
Cholesterol (mg): 0
Sodium (mg): 94
Protein (gm): 3.8
Carbohydrate (gm): 66.9

Exchanges:
Milk: 0.0
Vegetable: 0.0
Fruit: 1.0
Bread: 3.0
Meat: 0.0
Fat: 1.5

1. Combine flours, brown sugar, oats, bran, and cinnamon in large bowl; stir in margarine to make a crumbly mixture. Press half the mixture evenly on bottom of 13 x 9-inch baking pan. Arrange rhubarb evenly over crust.

2. Combine granulated sugar and cornstarch in medium saucepan; stir in water and heat to boiling. Boil, stirring, until thickened, about 1 minute. Stir in vanilla; pour over rhubarb. Sprinkle remaining crumb mixture over rhubarb. Bake at 350 degrees, uncovered, until bubbly around the edges, 55 to 60 minutes.

APPLE-CRANBERRY CRISP

V

45

◊

Apples and cranberries are happy companions in this streusel-topped fruit crisp.

6 servings

2½ pounds cooking apples, peeled, cored, sliced

1 cup fresh, or frozen, thawed cranberries

½ cup packed light brown sugar

2 tablespoons flour

1 teaspoon finely chopped crystallized ginger

Streusel Topping (recipe follows)

1. Combine all ingredients, except Streusel Topping, in a 1-quart glass casserole; sprinkle with Streusel Topping. Bake, uncovered, at 350 degrees until apples are tender, 30 to 40 minutes. Serve warm.

Per Serving:
Calories: 283
% of calories from fat: 12
Fat (gm): 3.9
Saturated fat (gm): 0.7
Cholesterol (mg): 0
Sodium (mg): 43
Protein (gm): 1.9
Carbohydrate (gm): 64

Exchanges:
Milk: 0.0
Vegetable: 0.0
Fruit: 2.0
Bread: 2.0
Meat: 0.0
Fat: 0.5

Streusel Topping

⅓ cup quick-cooking oats

3 tablespoons each: flour, packed light brown sugar

1½ tablespoons cold margarine, or butter

1. Combine oats, flour, and brown sugar in small bowl; cut in margarine until mixture resembles coarse crumbs.

45-MINUTE PREP TIP: Make Streusel Toping before preparing the rest of the recipe.

BANANAS FOSTER

L *A real taste of New Orleans!*

45 **4 servings**

¼ cup packed light brown sugar

1½ teaspoons cornstarch

½ cup water

1 tablespoon rum, or ½ teaspoon rum extract

1 teaspoon vanilla

2 medium bananas, sliced

¼ cup toasted pecan halves

1⅓ cups frozen low-fat vanilla yogurt

Per Serving:
Calories: 236
% of calories from fat: 20
Fat (gm): 5.5
Saturated fat (gm): 0.5
Cholesterol (mg): 0
Sodium (mg): 5
Protein (gm): 3.4
Carbohydrate (gm): 43

Exchanges:
Milk: 0.0
Vegetable: 0.0
Fruit: 2.0
Bread: 1.0
Meat: 0.0
Fat: 1.0

1. Mix brown sugar and cornstarch in small saucepan; stir in water and heat to boiling. Boil, stirring, until thickened, about 1 minute. Stir in rum and vanilla; add bananas and simmer until warm, 1 to 2 minutes. Stir in pecans; serve warm over frozen yogurt.

PRALINE SUNDAES

L

45

Fresh peach slices would make a delicious addition to the sundaes, or serve with one of the cookies from this chapter.

4 servings

¼ cup packed light brown sugar

1½ teaspoons cornstarch

½ cup water

1 tablespoon bourbon, or ½ teaspoon brandy extract

1 teaspoon margarine, or butter

½ teaspoon vanilla

2 tablespoons chopped pecans

1 pint frozen low-fat vanilla yogurt

Per Serving:
Calories: 256
% of calories from fat: 20
Fat (gm): 5.7
Saturated fat (gm): 1.9
Cholesterol (mg): 45
Sodium (mg): 72
Protein (gm): 8.3
Carbohydrate (gm): 41.1

Exchanges:
Milk: 0.0
Vegetable: 0.0
Fruit: 0.0
Bread: 3.0
Meat: 0.0
Fat: 1.0

1. Mix sugar and cornstarch in small saucepan; stir in water. Heat to boiling over medium heat; boil, stirring, until thickened, about 1 minute. Add bourbon, margarine, vanilla and pecans, stirring until margarine is melted. Serve warm over frozen yogurt.

ORANGE-PINEAPPLE SHERBET

L

45

❄

Use an ice cream maker to produce the smoothest texture in sherbets and ices. Add orange segments just before freezing is completed to keep them whole.

8 servings

½ cup sugar

⅓ cup water

1 can (15¼ ounces) unsweetened crushed
   pineapple, undrained

1¼ cups buttermilk

¼ cup orange juice

1 can (11 ounces) mandarin orange
   segments, drained

Per Serving:
Calories: 67
% of calories from fat: 5
Fat (gm): 0.4
Saturated fat (gm): 0.2
Cholesterol (mg): 1
Sodium (mg): 42
Protein (gm): 1.6
Carbohydrate (gm): 15.4

Exchanges:
Milk: 0.0
Vegetable: 0.0
Fruit: 1.0
Bread: 0.0
Meat: 0.0
Fat: 0.0

1. Heat sugar and water to boiling in medium saucepan, stirring until sugar is dissolved; cool. Process sugar syrup, pineapple, buttermilk, and orange juice in food processor or blender until smooth.

2. Freeze mixture in ice cream maker according to manufacturer's directions, adding oranges just before sherbet is frozen. Or pour into 8-inch-square baking pan and freeze until slushy, about 2 hours; spoon into bowl and beat until fluffy, then stir in oranges, return to pan, and freeze until firm, 6 hours or overnight.

GINGER-CITRUS SORBET

V

Slightly tart, slightly zesty, very refreshing!

45

6 servings

3½ cups water

1½ cups sugar

¼ cup peeled, minced gingerroot

2 teaspoons finely grated orange zest

⅓ cup orange juice

2 tablespoons lemon juice

Per Serving:
Calories: 190
% of calories from fat: 0
Fat (gm): 0.1
Saturated fat (gm): 0
Cholesterol (mg): 0
Sodium (mg): 1
Protein (gm): 0.2
Carbohydrate (gm): 50.6

Exchanges:
Milk: 0.0
Vegetable: 0.0
Fruit: 3.0
Bread: 0.0
Meat: 0.0
Fat: 0.0

1. Heat water, sugar, gingerroot, and orange zest to boiling in medium saucepan, stirring until sugar is dissolved. Reduce heat and simmer 7 to 10 minutes; cool. Stir in orange and lemon juices.

2. Freeze mixture in ice cream maker according to manufacturer's directions. Or pour into 8-inch-square baking pan and freeze until slushy, 2 to 4 hours; spoon into bowl and beat until fluffy, then return to pan and freeze until firm, 6 hours.

LEMON ICE

V

Serve this sweet-and-tart ice as a dessert or as a refreshing palate cleanser between dinner courses.

45
❄

8 servings

2 cups water
1 cup each: sugar, lemon juice
½ cup grated lemon zest

Per Serving:
Calories: 101
% of calories from fat: 0
Fat (gm): 0
Saturated fat (gm): 0
Cholesterol (mg): 0
Sodium (mg): 1.3
Protein (gm): 0.2
Carbohydrate (gm): 27.6

Exchanges:
Milk: 0.0
Vegetable: 0.0
Fruit: 0.0
Bread: 1.5
Meat: 0.0
Fat: 0.0

1. Heat water, sugar, lemon juice, and zest to boiling in medium saucepan, stirring until sugar is dissolved. Reduce heat and simmer, uncovered, 5 minutes; cool.

2. Freeze mixture in ice cream maker according to manufacturer's directions. Or pour into 8-inch-square baking pan and freeze until slushy, about 2 hours; spoon into bowl and beat until fluffy, then return to pan and freeze until firm, 6 hours or overnight.

PINEAPPLE-CHAMPAGNE ICE

V

Champagne-inspired for a touch of elegance.

45
❄

8 servings

2½ cups unsweetened pineapple juice
½ cup dry champagne, or sparkling wine
⅓ teaspoon ground nutmeg
8 slices fresh pineapple (½-inch)
Mint sprigs, as garnish

Per Serving:
Calories: 99
% of calories from fat: 4
Fat (gm): 0.5
Saturated fat (gm): 0.1
Cholesterol (mg): 0
Sodium (mg): 2
Protein (gm): 0.6
Carbohydrate (gm): 22.4

Exchanges:
Milk: 0.0
Vegetable: 0.0
Fruit: 1.5
Bread: 0.0
Meat: 0.0
Fat: 0.0

1. Mix pineapple juice, champagne, and nutmeg; freeze in ice cream maker according to manufacturer's directions. Or pour mixture into 9-inch-square baking pan and freeze until slushy, about 2 hours; spoon into bowl and beat until fluffy, then return to pan and freeze until firm, 6 hours or overnight. Top pineapple slices with scoops of Pineapple-Champagne Ice; garnish with mint.

MIXED FRUIT TORTONI

L

45

❄

Traditionally made with heavy cream and candied fruits, our version of this Italian favorite uses fresh seasonal fruits and low-fat topping.

12 servings

1½ cups fresh, or frozen, thawed, raspberries

½ cup pitted, halved sweet cherries, divided

⅓ cup each: cubed peeled apricots, pineapple

¼ cup sugar

3 envelopes (1.3 ounces each) low-fat whipped topping mix

1½ cups 2% milk

¼ cup chopped pistachio nuts, or slivered almonds, divided

Per Serving:
Calories: 126
% of calories from fat: 28
Fat (gm): 3.5
Saturated fat (gm): 0.7
Cholesterol (mg): 2
Sodium (mg): 32
Protein (gm): 2.1
Carbohydrate (gm): 18.2

Exchanges:
Milk: 0.0
Vegetable: 0.0
Fruit: 1.5
Bread: 0.0
Meat: 0.0
Fat: 0.5

1. Process raspberries in food processor or blender until smooth; strain and discard seeds.

2. Reserve 12 cherry halves. Combine remaining cherries, apricots, pineapple and sugar in small bowl.

3. Beat whipped topping and milk in large bowl at high speed until topping forms soft peaks, about 4 minutes; fold in raspberry puree, sugared fruits, and 2 tablespoons nuts. Spoon into 12 paper-lined muffin cups; garnish tops of each with reserved cherry halves and remaining nuts. Freeze until firm, 6 hours or overnight.

NOTE: If desired, 1 tablespoon sherry or ½ teaspoon sherry extract can be folded into the whipped topping mixture.

ORANGE BAKED ALASKA PIE

LO

45

Orange Baked Alaska Pie can be frozen overnight — or, freeze with unbaked meringue and bake just before serving.

8 servings

Gingersnap Crumb Crust (see p. 637)

½ cup graham cracker crumbs

1 tablespoon margarine, or butter

1 quart frozen low-fat vanilla yogurt, slightly softened

2 tablespoons orange-flavored liqueur, or orange juice concentrate

½ teaspoon ground nutmeg

3 egg whites

⅛ teaspoon cream of tartar

¼ cup sugar

Per Serving:
Calories: 332
% of calories from fat: 25
Fat (gm): 9.2
Saturated fat (gm): 2.5
Cholesterol (mg): 45
Sodium (mg): 245
Protein (gm): 10.7
Carbohydrate (gm): 50

Exchanges:
Milk: 0.0
Vegetable: 0.0
Fruit: 0.0
Bread: 3.5
Meat: 0.0
Fat: 2.0

1. Make crumb crust, adding ½ cup graham cracker crumbs and 1 tablespoon margarine, and using 8-inch pie pan. Spoon combined frozen yogurt, liqueur, and nutmeg into cooled crust. Cover with plastic wrap and freeze until firm, 8 hours or overnight.

2. Beat egg whites and cream of tartar to soft peaks in large bowl; beat to stiff but not dry peaks, adding sugar gradually. Spread meringue over frozen pie, carefully sealing to edge of crust. Bake at 500 degrees 3 to 5 minutes or until meringue is golden. Serve immediately.

Variation

Chocolate Baked Alaska — Make recipe above, using Vanilla Crumb Crust (see p. 637), and adding ½ cup vanilla wafer crumbs and 1 tablespoon margarine. Substitue low-fat frozen chocolate yogurt for the vanilla, and delete orange liqueur and nutmeg.

FROZEN PEPPERMINT CAKE ROLLS

LO

45

This beautiful dessert is deceptively easy to prepare using cake mix. The cake rolls can be frozen, wrapped in foil, for up to 1 month.

20 servings

4 eggs

1 package (18¾ ounces) yellow cake mix

½ cup water

Powdered sugar

¾ cup crushed peppermint candies

1½ quarts frozen low-fat vanilla yogurt, slightly softened

Bittersweet Chocolate Sauce (see p. 661)

Per Serving:
Calories: 249
% of calories from fat: 16
Fat (gm): 4.4
Saturated fat (gm): 1
Cholesterol (mg): 42.4
Sodium (mg): 212
Protein (gm): 5.1
Carbohydrate (gm): 47

Exchanges:
Milk: 0.0
Vegetable: 0.0
Fruit: 0.0
Bread: 3.0
Meat: 0.0
Fat: 1.0

1. Lightly grease two 15 x 10-inch jelly roll pans. Line bottom of pan with parchment or waxed paper; grease and flour paper.

2. Beat eggs in medium bowl at high speed until thick and lemon-colored, about 5 minutes. Mix in cake mix and water; pour into prepared pans. Bake at 375 degrees until cakes spring back when touched, about 15 minutes. Immediately invert cakes onto clean kitchen towels sprinkled generously with powdered sugar. Peel off parchment; roll cakes up in towels, starting at short ends. Cool on wire racks just until cool, about 30 minutes.

3. Mix peppermint candies into frozen yogurt. Unroll cakes; spread with frozen yogurt mixture. Reroll cakes and wrap in plastic wrap; freeze until firm, 8 hours or overnight. Trim ends from cake and place on serving plate. Sprinkle generously with powdered sugar; drizzle slices with Bittersweet Chocolate Sauce.

ICE CREAM JELLY ROLL CAKE

LO

45

A versatile cake that can be filled with your flavor choice of fat-free ice cream, frozen yogurt, or light whipped topping and sliced fruit.

8 servings

3 egg yolks

½ teaspoon vanilla

¾ cup sugar, divided

3 egg whites

¾ cup cake flour

1 teaspoon baking powder

¼ teaspoon salt

1–1½ quarts strawberry, or other flavor, fat-free
  ice cream, slightly softened

Powdered sugar, as garnish

Whole strawberries, as garnish

Per Serving:
Calories: 229
% of calories from fat: 8
Fat (gm): 2
Saturated fat (gm): 0.6
Cholesterol (mg): 79.9
Sodium (mg): 197
Protein (gm): 7.2
Carbohydrate (gm): 47.2

Exchanges:
Milk: 0.0
Vegetable: 0.0
Fruit: 0.0
Bread: 2.5
Meat: 0.0
Fat: 0.0

1. Grease 15 x 10-inch jelly roll pan. Line bottom of pan with parchment or waxed paper; grease and flour paper.

2. Beat egg yolks and vanilla in medium bowl until thick and lemon colored, 3 to 5 minutes. Gradually beat in ¼ cup sugar. Using clean beaters and large bowl, beat egg whites to soft peaks; gradually beat in remaining ½ cup granulated sugar, beating to stiff but not dry peaks. Fold egg whites into yolks; fold in combined flour, baking powder, and salt. Spread evenly in prepared pan.

3. Bake at 375 degrees until cake is golden and springs back when touched, 10 to 12 minutes. Immediately invert cake onto large kitchen towel sprinkled generously with powdered sugar; peel off parchment; roll cake up in towel, starting at short end. Cool on wire rack just until cool, about 30 minutes.

4. Unroll cake; spread with ice cream. Reroll cake, wrap in plastic wrap, and freeze until firm, 8 hours or overnight. Trim ends from cake and place on serving plate. Sprinkle generously with powdered sugar and garnish with strawberries.

Variation

Chocolate Ice Cream Jelly Roll Cake — Make cake as above, adding ¼ cup unsweetened cocoa to the flour mixture. Fill cake with chocolate chip or chocolate fudge fat-free ice cream.

RICH CHOCOLATE PUDDING

This cake is unbelievably rich in flavor and smooth in texture. Use Dutch or European process cocoa for fullest flavor. Serve with Hazelnut Macaroons (see p. 656).

4 servings

½ cup sugar
⅓ cup unsweetened cocoa
3 tablespoons cornstarch
⅛ teaspoon salt
2 cups 2% reduced-fat milk
1 egg yolk, slightly beaten
2 teaspoons vanilla

Per Serving:
Calories: 216
% of calories from fat: 17
Fat (gm): 4.3
Saturated fat (gm): 2
Cholesterol (mg): 62.3
Sodium (mg): 135
Protein (gm): 6.2
Carbohydrate (gm): 41.2

Exchanges:
Milk: 0.5
Vegetable: 0.0
Fruit: 0.0
Bread: 2.0
Meat: 0.0
Fat: 0.5

1. Mix sugar, cocoa, cornstarch, and salt in medium saucepan; whisk in milk and heat to boiling. Boil, whisking, until thickened, about 1 minute. Whisk about ½ cup milk mixture into egg yolk; whisk egg yolk mixture back into saucepan. Whisk over low heat 30 to 60 seconds. Stir in vanilla; cool. Spoon into dessert bowls. Refrigerate, covered with plastic wrap, 1 to 2 hours.

BAKED CEREAL PUDDING

LO

45

Eat warm from the oven, or refrigerate for a chilled dessert. Either way, this comfort food is delicious.

6 servings (½ cup each)

3 eggs

¼ cup each: sugar, packed brown sugar

¾ cup natural wheat and barley cereal (Grape-Nuts)

2 cups fat-free milk

2 tablespoons margarine, or butter, melted

1 teaspoon vanilla

⅛ teaspoon salt

Per Serving:
Calories: 214
% of calories from fat: 24
Fat (gm): 5.8
Saturated fat (gm): 1.4
Cholesterol (mg): 72.3
Sodium (mg): 262
Protein (gm): 7.9
Carbohydrate (gm): 33.2

Exchanges:
Milk: 0.0
Vegetable: 0.0
Fruit: 0.0
Bread: 2.0
Meat: 0.5
Fat: 1.0

1. Beat eggs and sugars in medium bowl until blended; mix in remaining ingredients. Pour into greased 1-quart soufflé dish or casserole. Place dish in roasting pan on oven rack; pour 2 inches hot water into pan. Bake, uncovered, at 375 degrees until pudding is set, about 50 minutes, stirring well halfway through baking time. Cool on wire rack; serve warm or chilled.

OLD-FASHIONED BAKED RICE PUDDING

L

45

Serve warm with Tart Lemon Sauce or Raspberry Sauce (see pp. 675, 662).

6 servings

½ cup uncooked rice

3 cups fat-free milk

⅓ cup sugar

¼ cup golden raisins

½ teaspoon ground cinnamon

2 dashes ground nutmeg

Per Serving:
Calories: 158
% of calories from fat: 2
Fat (gm): 0.3
Saturated fat (gm): 0.2
Cholesterol (mg): 2
Sodium (mg): 65
Protein (gm): 5.4
Carbohydrate (gm): 34

Exchanges:
Milk: 0.5
Vegetable: 0.0
Fruit: 0.5
Bread: 1.0
Meat: 0.0
Fat: 0.0

1. Combine all ingredients in 2-quart casserole. Bake, uncovered, at 350 degrees until rice is tender and milk is absorbed, about 2½ hours, stirring occasionally. Serve warm or chilled.

BLUEBERRY BREAD PUDDING WITH TART LEMON SAUCE

LO

45

Serve this pudding with Raspberry Sauce (p. 662) for a double-berry treat!

8 servings

3 tablespoons margarine, or butter, room temperature

6 slices whole wheat bread

1 cup fresh, or frozen, blueberries

2 cups fat-free milk

2 eggs, lightly beaten

½ cup sugar

¼ teaspoon salt

1 teaspoon vanilla

Tart Lemon Sauce (recipe follows)

Per Serving:
Calories: 302
% of calories from fat: 29
Fat (gm): 10
Saturated fat (gm): 2.2
Cholesterol (mg): 80.9
Sodium (mg): 332
Protein (gm): 7.7
Carbohydrate (gm): 47.7

Exchanges:
Milk: 0.0
Vegetable: 0.0
Fruit: 0.0
Bread: 3.0
Meat: 0.0
Fat: 2.0

1. Spread margarine on one side of each bread slice; cut into 2-inch squares and place in greased 9-inch baking dish or 1-quart casserole. Add blueberries and toss. Heat milk in small saucepan until just boiling; whisk in combined eggs, sugar, salt, milk, and vanilla; pour over bread cubes.

2. Place baking dish in a 15 x 10-inch roasting pan; pour 1 inch hot water into pan. Bake, uncovered, at 350 degrees 35 to 40 minutes or until knife inserted near center comes out clean. Serve warm with Tart Lemon Sauce.

Tart Lemon Sauce

Makes 1½ cups

2 tablespoons margarine, or butter

⅔–1 cup sugar

1 cup lemon juice

2 eggs, slightly beaten

1. Melt margarine over low heat in small saucepan; stir in sugar and lemon juice. Cook over medium heat until sugar is dissolved. Whisk about ½ cup the hot lemon mixture into eggs. Whisk egg mixture back into saucepan; cook over low heat, whisking until thickened, 2 to 3 minutes. Serve warm or room temperature.

Variation

Raisin-Pecan Bread Pudding — Make recipe above, substituting ⅓ cup each raisins and toasted pecan halves for the blueberries.

WARM INDIAN PUDDING

L

Molasses and sweet spices signal the welcome flavors of fall.

45

6 servings

3 cups milk, divided

¼ cup yellow cornmeal

¾ cup light molasses

⅓ cup packed light brown sugar

¼ teaspoon salt

3 tablespoons margarine, or butter

¼ cup dark raisins

½ teaspoon ground cinnamon

¼ teaspoon ground nutmeg

⅛ teaspoon each: ground cloves, ginger

Per Serving:
Calories: 277
% of calories from fat: 19
Fat (gm): 6.1
Saturated fat (gm): 1.3
Cholesterol (mg): 2
Sodium (mg): 143
Protein (gm): 5.3
Carbohydrate (gm): 35

Exchanges:
Milk: 0.5
Vegetable: 0.0
Fruit: 0.5
Bread: 2.5
Meat: 0.0
Fat: 0.5

1. Heat 2¾ cups milk just to boiling in medium saucepan; reduce heat and gradually stir in cornmeal. Simmer until thickened, about 15 minutes, stirring occasionally. Stir in remaining ingredients, except remaining ¼ cup milk. Pour into greased 1½-quart casserole; pour remaining ¼ cup milk over top. Bake, uncovered, until knife inserted near center comes out clean, about 1¼ hours. Serve warm.

BROWN SUGAR APPLE PUDDING

LO *Topped and baked with a batter and brown sugar syrup, this is the best apple pudding you will ever eat!*

10 servings

6 cups sliced, cored peeled apples (¼- inch)

½ cup packed light brown sugar

¼ cup margarine, or butter, room temperature

1 egg

½ teaspoon vanilla

1½ teaspoons ground cinnamon

¾ cup all-purpose flour

teaspoons baking powder

¼ teaspoon salt

½ cup fat-free milk

Brown Sugar Syrup (recipe follows)

Per Serving:
Calories: 220
% of calories from fat: 23
Fat (gm): 5.8
Saturated fat (gm): 1.2
Cholesterol (mg): 21.5
Sodium (mg): 198
Protein (gm): 2.4
Carbohydrate (gm): 41.1

Exchanges:
Milk: 0.0
Vegetable: 0.0
Fruit: 0.5
Bread: 2.0
Meat: 0.0
Fat: 1.0

1. Arrange apple slices in lightly greased 1½-quart casserole. Mix brown sugar, margarine, egg, vanilla, and cinnamon in medium bowl until blended; mix in combined flour, baking powder, and salt alternately with milk, stirring only until blended. Spread over apple slices; pour Brown Sugar Syrup over. Bake, uncovered, at 375 degrees until apples are tender, 50 to 55 minutes. Serve warm.

Brown Sugar Syrup

½ cup packed light brown sugar

2 tablespoons flour

1 teaspoon margarine, or butter

1 cup water

½ teaspoon vanilla

1. Combine brown sugar, flour, and margarine in small saucepan. Stir in water and heat to boiling. Boil 2 to 3 minutes, stirring constantly; stir in vanilla.

LEMON VELVET PUDDING

LO

45

❄

Top this velvet-textured custard with fresh fruit; serve with a plate of Apricot-Sesame Biscotti (see p. 658).

4 servings

½ cup sugar

3 tablespoons cornstarch

⅛ teaspoon salt

2 cups 2% milk

1 egg yolk, slightly beaten

2 tablespoons lemon juice

1 teaspoon lemon extract

Per Serving:
Calories: 200
% of calories from fat: 16
Fat (gm): 3.6
Saturated fat (gm): 1.9
Cholesterol (mg): 62.3
Sodium (mg): 130
Protein (gm): 4.8
Carbohydrate (gm): 37.4

Exchanges:
Milk: 0.5
Vegetable: 0.0
Fruit: 0.0
Bread: 2.0
Meat: 0.0
Fat: 0.5

1. Mix sugar, cornstarch, and salt in medium saucepan; whisk in milk. Heat to boiling over medium-high heat; boil, stirring, until thickened, about 1 minute. Whisk about ½ cup milk mixture into egg yolk; whisk mixture back into saucepan. Add lemon juice and extract; whisk over low heat 30 to 60 seconds. Cool. Spoon into dessert dishes; refrigerate, covered, until chilled, 1 to 2 hours.

FRESH APRICOT CUSTARD

LO

45

❄

A delicate custard with fresh apricots gently folded in. Serve with cookies — Spiced Cookie Crisps (see p. 654) would be nice.

6 servings

½ cup sugar

3 tablespoons cornstarch

2 cups fat-free milk

½ cup apricot nectar

2 egg yolks, slightly beaten

2 tablespoons margarine, or butter

1½ cups peeled, coarsely chopped fresh apricots

Per Serving:
Calories: 193
% of calories from fat: 26
Fat (gm): 5.8
Saturated fat (gm): 1.4
Cholesterol (mg): 72.3
Sodium (mg): 90
Protein (gm): 4.4
Carbohydrate (gm): 32

Exchanges:
Milk: 0.0
Vegetable: 0.0
Fruit: 0.5
Bread: 1.5
Meat: 0.0
Fat: 1.0

1. Mix sugar and cornstarch in medium saucepan; whisk in milk and apricot nectar. Heat to boiling over medium-high heat; boil, whisking, until thickened, about 1 minute. Whisk about ½ cup milk mixture into egg yolks; whisk mixture back into saucepan. Whisk over low heat, 30 to 60 seconds. Stir in margarine; cool. Refrigerate, covered with plastic wrap, until chilled, 1 to 2 hours.

2. Stir custard until fluffy; stir in apricots. Spoon into dessert dishes.

CARAMEL FLAN

Unbelievably delicate and fine in texture, this flan is one you'll serve over and over again.

8 servings

½ cup sugar, divided
4 cups fat-free milk
5 eggs, lightly beaten
2 teaspoons vanilla

Per Serving:
Calories: 140
% of calories from fat: 14
Fat (gm): 2.1
Saturated fat (gm): 0.7
Cholesterol (mg): 81.9
Sodium (mg): 114
Protein (gm): 8.3
Carbohydrate (gm): 21.3

Exchanges:
Milk: 0.5
Vegetable: 0.0
Fruit: 0.0
Bread: 1.0
Meat: 0.0
Fat: 0.5

1. Heat ¼ cup sugar in small skillet over medium-high heat until sugar melts and turns golden, stirring occasionally (watch carefully as the sugar can burn easily!). Quickly pour caramel into bottom of 2-quart soufflé dish, tilting to spread caramel over bottom. Cool.

2. Mix milk and remaining ¼ cup sugar in medium saucepan; heat until beginning to bubble at the edges. Whisk milk mixture gradually into eggs in bowl; stir in vanilla. Pour mixture through strainer into soufflé dish.

3. Place soufflé dish in roasting pan on middle oven rack. Cover dish with lid or foil. Pour 2 inches hot water into roasting pan. Bake at 350 degrees until sharp knife inserted halfway between center and edge of custard comes out clean, about 1 hour. Cool soufflé dish on wire rack. Refrigerate 8 hours or overnight. To unmold, loosen edge of custard with sharp knife. Place rimmed serving dish over soufflé dish and invert.

Variation

Orange Flan — Make recipe above, substituting ¼ cup orange juice concentrate for ¼ cup of the milk, and adding 1 egg and 1 teaspoon orange extract.

HERBED CUSTARD BRULÉE

LO

45

Scented with herbs, the delicate custard is topped with a sprinkling of caramelized sugar.

6 servings

3 cups fat-free milk

2 tablespoons each: chopped fresh, or ½ teaspoon dried, basil, cilantro, and tarragon leaves

5 eggs

½ cup granulated sugar

3 tablespoons packed light brown sugar

Per Serving:
Calories: 191
% of calories from fat: 20
Fat (gm): 4
Saturated fat (gm): 1
Cholesterol (mg): 179
Sodium (mg): 113
Protein (gm): 9
Carbohydrate (gm): 29

Exchanges:
Milk: 0.5
Vegetable: 0.0
Fruit: 0.0
Bread: 1.0
Meat: 1.0
Fat: 0.5

1. Heat milk and herbs in medium saucepan to boiling; remove from heat, cover, and let stand 10 minutes. Strain; discard herbs.

2. Beat eggs and granulated sugar in medium bowl until thick and pale yellow, about 5 minutes. Gradually whisk milk mixture into eggs; strain and pour into 8 custard cups.

3. Place cups in 15 x 10-inch roasting pan on center oven rack; pour 2 inches hot water into pan. Bake, uncovered, at 350 degrees until knife inserted halfway between center and edge of custard cups comes out clean, about 20 minutes. Cool custard cups on wire rack. Refrigerate until chilled, 2 to 4 hours.

4. Sprinkle brown sugar evenly in small baking dish and bake at 200 degrees until moisture is evaporated, about 10 minutes (do not melt sugar). Sprinkle brown sugar evenly over custards in baking pan; broil, 4 inches from heat source, until sugar is melted and caramelized, 2 to 3 minutes. Serve immediately.

PEACH-ALLSPICE SOUFFLÉS

O

Fresh or frozen drained peaches can be used for this recipe.

45

6 servings

◊

1½ cups chopped fresh, or canned, drained peaches

2 teaspoons lemon juice

1 teaspoon vanilla

¼ cup plus 1 teaspoon sugar, divided

⅛ teaspoon ground allspice

2 egg yolks

4 egg whites

⅛ teaspoon cream of tartar

Powdered sugar, as garnish

Per Serving:
Calories: 85
% of calories from fat: 18
Fat (gm): 1.7
Saturated fat (gm): 0.5
Cholesterol (mg): 71
Sodium (mg): 39
Protein (gm): 3.6
Carbohydrate (gm): 14.1

Exchanges:
Milk: 0.0
Vegetable: 0.0
Fruit: 1.0
Bread: 0.0
Meat: 0.5
Fat: 0.0

1. Process peaches, lemon juice, vanilla, 1 teaspoon sugar, and allspice in food processor or blender until smooth. Add egg yolks, one at a time, processing until smooth.

2. Beat egg whites and cream of tartar to soft peaks in large bowl; gradually beat in ¼ cup sugar, beating to stiff but not dry peaks. Fold in peach mixture. Spoon into 6 greased 1-cup soufflé dishes; arrange in baking pan.

3. Bake, uncovered, at 450 degrees 7 minutes; reduce heat to 425 degrees and bake until soufflés are lightly browned and a sharp knife inserted halfway between center and edge of dishes comes out clean, about 7 minutes. Sprinkle with powdered sugar; serve immediately.

NOTE: Soufflé can be baked in a 1-quart soufflé dish. Bake at 450 degrees for 10 minutes; reduce heat to 425 degrees and bake until sharp knife inserted halfway between center and edge of dish comes out clean about 10 minutes.

INDEX

A

Adzuki Bean Pastitsio, 366
Adzuki Bean Stir-Fry, 381
Alfredo Sauce, 591
All-Season Risotto, 409
Alsatian Peasant Soup, 100
Angel Hair and Goat Cheese Salad, 532
Anise-Almond Biscotti, 657
Appetizers and Snacks
  Bread, Artichoke-Stuffed, 33
  Bruschetta, 46
  Bruschetta, Mushroom, 35
  Calzones, 44
  Cheese and Spinach Squares, 36
  Croustades, 47
  Croustades, Curried Onion, 32
  Curried Pinwheels, 34
  Dips and Spreads
    Artichoke, Baked, 6
    Artichoke Pâté, 18
    Bean
      Herb Cannellini, 14
      Mexican, 8
      Pinto and Avocado, 9
      Roasted Garlic and Cannellini, 14
    Cheese Spread, Chutney, 21
    Chili Con Queso, 10
    Cream Cheese
      Cranberry-Pistachio, 23
      Pepper-Onion Relish, 23
      Raisin Marmalade, 24
    Curry Dip, 6
    Eggplant Caviar, 17
    Eggplant Marmalade, 20
    Faux "Liver," Chopped, 20
    Guacamole, 12
    Hummus
      Black Bean, 16
      Spicy Orange, 16
      Sun-Dried Tomato, 15
    Mushroom Spread, Garden, 19
    Onion Dip, Toasted, 5
    Parthenon Platter, 15
    Pâté, Pine Nut Spinach, 12
    Pâté, Wild Mushroom, 13
    Queso Fundido, 10
    Roasted Garlic and Three-Cheese, 22
    Salsa
      Med-Mex Fusion, 8
      Red Tomato, 8
      Tomatillo, 7
    Sombrero Dip, 11
    Soybean and Vegetable Spread, 13
    Zucchini and Garlic, Roasted, 18
  Edamame Snackers, 4
  Egg Rolls, Mixed Vegetable, 40
  Empanadas, Fruit, 30
  Foccaccia, Onion and Blue Cheese, 44
  Fruit Nuggets, 4
  Gorp, By Golly!, 2
  Hot Stuff!, 2
  Jicama with Lime and Cilantro, 29
  Lavosh, Easy Herb, 45
  Mushrooms, Cheese and Spinach
    Stuffed, 32
  Mushrooms, Orzo Stuffed, 32
  Nachos, 28
  Pita Chips, 46
  Pita Chips, Seasoned, 46
  Plantains, Fried Ripe, 29
  Plantains, Sweetened, 29
  Potstickers, Five-Spice, 38
  Quesadillas
    Black Bean, 26
    Goat Cheese with Tropical Fruit Salsa, 25
    Poblano, 26
  Quiches, Mini-, Spinach and Cheese, 36
  Shells, Ricotta-Stuffed, with Spinach
    Pesto, 31
  Soy Noshers, 3
  Spinach Balls, Baked, 37
  Strudel, Apple-Cabbage, 43
  Tofu Satay, Indonesian-Style, 41
  Tortellini Kabobs with Many-Cloves
    Garlic Sauce, 42
  Tortilla Wedges, 27
  Wasabi Potato Slices, 38
  Wonton, Cranberry-Cheese, 39
  Wonton, Sesame Cups, 25
Apple
  -Cabbage Strudels, 43
  -Cranberry Crisp, 664
  Cranberry Relish, 500, 609
  -Date Filling, 566
  -Mint Jelly, 579
  -Pecan Acorn Squash, 503
  Pie, Double-Crust, 639
  -Cranberry Relish, 609
  Honey Kuchen, 547
  Pudding, Brown Sugar, 677
  Salad Pizza, 317
Apricot-Sesame Biscotti, 658
Apricot Custard, Fresh, 678
Artichoke(s)
  -Stuffed Appetizer Bread, 33
  and Roasted Pepper Pizza, 306
  Baked, Dip, 6
  Braised, Whole, 470

Hearts and Vegetables, Millet with, 398
Hearts, Mushrooms, and Peppers, "Little
    Ears" with, 248
Lasagne, 268
Pâté, 18
Pie, 328
Roasted Tomato-Herb Sauce and,
    Spaghetti Squash with, 202
Sauce, 593
Soup, Cream of, and Mushroom with
    Parmesan Toast, 432
Tortellini Bake, 259
with Hollandaise Sauce, 470
Asian
-Style Pizza, 304
Fried Rice, 404
Mushroom Soup with Noodles, 439
Noodle Salad, 535
Asparagus
and Plum Tomatoes, Penne with, 235
and White Beans, Italian-Style, 382
Pilaf, Mushroom and, 404
Sesame Stir-Fry, 152
Wine-Glazed Ravioli and, 262
with Lemon-Wine Sauce, 471
with Peanut Sauce, 472
Autumn Vegetable Pie, 325
Avocado Dip, Pinto Bean and, 9
Avocado Sour Cream, 95

B
Baked
Artichoke Dip, 6
Cereal Pudding, 674
Spinach Balls, 37
Tart Crust, 330
Tortilla Strips, 103
Bakers, Veggie-Stuffed, 496
Balsamic Dressing, 460
Banana(s)
-Cinnamon Cake, 628
-Strawberry Cream Pie, 642
Brown Sugar Bread, 563
Foster, 665
Barley
-Vegetable Chowder, 392
Bowl, Wheat and, 394
Moussaka, Vegetable-, 146
with Peppers and Potatoes, 394
Soup, Savory Mushroom and, 77
and Vegetable Mélange, 395
Basic
Pie Pastry, 635
Pizza Dough, 298
Vegetable Stock, 52
Basil
Dressing, 237
Pizza, Tomato and, 305
Sauce, Tomato-, 584
Vinaigrette, 223
Bean(s) and Legume(s) (see also Salads,
Sandwiches and Patties, Soups, and Stews)
-Thickened Soup, 64
-Thickened Vegetable Stew, 116
Adzuki, Pastitsio, 366

Adzuki, Stir-Fry, 381
Bake, Tuscan, 371
Baked
Ginger-, 368
New England, 368
Santa Fe, 370
Black
Brazilian Bake, 372
Cheesecake with Salsa, 352
Eggs Rancheros with, and 2 Salsas, 348
Hummus, 16
and Jalapeno Pizza, 310
Meatballs, Vegetarian, 383
and Okra Gumbo, 441
Quesadillas, 26
and Rice, 374
and Rice Salad, 389
Salad, Mango and, 523
Seasoned Mashed, 373
and Smoked Tofu Salad, 461
Soup
    with Sun-Dried Tomatoes and
        Cilantro Cream, 66
    Classic, 67
    Pasilla, 440
Tostados, Picante, 288
Blackeye Salsa, 428
Black-Eyed Peas and Greens with Millet,
    396
Butter and Sprouts Stir-Fry, 380
Cannellini
Dip, Herb, 14
Patties with Fresh Tomato Relish, 285
Roasted Garlic and, Dip, 14
Casserole of Roasted Vegetables and, 199
and Cheese, Chilies Rellenos, 351
Cheesy, and Onion Mashers, 494
Chili, Yellow and White, 362
Creamy Potato and, Mashers, 494
Curried
Soup, 361
Soybeans and Potatoes, 382
Tortellini with, and Squash, 260
Dip, Mexican, 8
Edamame Snackers, 4
Eggplant and, Curry Stew, 367
Fava Bean
Bruschetta, 358
Salad Platter, 390
Spread, 358
Four-, and Vegetable Soup, 62
Garbanzo
Burgers with Fennel Goat Cheese
    Relish, Greek-Style, 284
Mafalde with, Tomatoes and Croutons,
    249
Salsa, 604
Soup, 68
Gazpacho, 440
Green Bean(s)
Casserole, 473
Greek-Style, 472
Oriental, 473
Herbed, and Sweet Potato Hash, 339
Hot 'N Spicy, and Vegetable Stew, 122

Hummus
  Black, 16
  Spicy Orange, 16
  Sun-Dried Tomato, 15
Italian-Style, and Vegetables, 378
Jerk Tempeh with Black, and Rice, 191
Just Peachy, Pot, 369
Kidney, and Cabbage Soup, 433
Lentil
  Fried, 372
  Ravioli with Gingered Tomato Relish,
    167
  Salad with Feta Cheese, 460
Lima, and Mushroom Mashers, 494
Lima, Wheat Bread, 542
Mexi-Beans, Greens, and Rice, 375
Mexican, Dip, 8
and Onion Mashers, Cheesy, 494
Orange-Marinated, Salad, 388
Pasta
  with Greens and, 232
  Mean, 384
  Salad with White, Dressing, 385
  Salad, White, and Red Cabbage, 386
Pastitsio, 450
Pinto, and Avocado Dip, 9
Pot, Just Peachy, 369
Red, and Rice, Bourbon Street, 376
Refried, 374
Roasted Vegetables with, and Fruit, 198
Rotini and, Niçoise, 252
Salad
  Sprouted Lentil, 522
  Sprouts and Vegetable, 522
  Summer, 524
  Vegetable with 2, 388
Sauce with Tomatoes and Sage, Peasant,
  587
Soup
  Black-Eyed Pea and Lentil, Easiest, 360
  with Cheese Melts, Two-Season Squash
    and, 434
  Lima, Garlicky, 359
  Lentil, Country, 113
  Lentil, Indian, 114
  Navy, 63
  Tuscan, 65
  Two-, and Pasta, 107
  Veggie, and Burger, 100
Soy Noshers, 3
Soybean and Vegetable Spread, 13
Soybean-Veggie Burgers, 286
Sprouted Lentils, 522
Stew
  and Squash, 120
  with Fusilli, Spiced, 131
  Ginger, and Blackeye, 128
  Greek Lentil, 444
  with Polenta, Three-, 130
  Vegetable, Hot 'N Spicy, 122
  and Vegetable, Very Quick, 364
  Vegetable, Winter, 365
  Wheat Berry and Lentil, with
    Dumplings, 392
Stir-Fried, and Greens, 379

and Sweet Potato Hash, Herbed, 339
Tomato, and Bread Salad, 387
Tortellini and 2-, Vegetable Soup, 260
Veggie Tamales with, 184
White Bean
  and Sweet Potato Soup with Cranberry
    Coulis, 64
  Dressing, 385
  Mashers with Sautéed Vegetables, 152
  and Vegetable Stew, Winter, 365
Beet(s)
Borscht, 59
  Dijon, 475
  Grilled Puree, 208
  Harvard, 475
  Honey-Roasted, 476
  Soup, Dilled, 58
Best Breakfast Cereal, 429
Beverages
  Blueberry Breeze, 49
  Cantaloupe Cooler, 49
  Pomegranate Passion, 49
  Tofruity, 48
  Very Berry Smoothie, 48
Bittersweet Chocolate Sauce, 661
Black Mushroom Soup, 77
Blackeye Salsa, 428
Black-Eyed Peas and Greens with Millet, 396
Blue Cheese
  and Pear Melt, 293
  Dressing, 528
  Focaccia, Onion and , 44
  Macaroni- Salad, 527
  Polenta, 425
Blueberry
  Bread Pudding with Tart Lemon Sauce,
    675
  Breeze, 49
  Maple Syrup, 574
  Pancakes with Blueberry Maple Syrup,
    573
  Tart, Raspberry-Glazed, 645
Blues Veggie Burgers, 276
Bolillos, 555
Bolognese-Style Tomato Sauce, 586
Boston Cream Cake, 626
Bourbon Street Red Beans and Rice, 376
Braised, 587
  Kale, 487
  Parsnips and Winter Vegetables, 491
  Whole Artichokes, 470
Brazilian Black Bean Bake, 372
Bread(s)
  Artichoke-Stuffed Appetizer, 33
  Banana, Brown Sugar, 563
  Biscuits,
    Chive, 568
    "Little Pants", 569
    Parmesan, 568
    Quick Self-Rising, 568
    Sweet Potato, 568
    Vinegar, 567
  Bolillos, 555
  Buns, Sticky, 548
  Coffeecake, Cranberry, 566

Coffeecake, Sour Cream with Apple-Date
  Filling, 565
Corn, Green Chili, 561
Corn, Roasted Chili, 216
Crepes, 575
Crepes, Dessert, 575
Crescents, Orange Marmalade, 546
Croutons, 560
  Herb, 561
  Italian-Style, 560
  Parmesan, 560
  Rye Caraway, 560
  Sesame, 560
  Sourdough, 560
English Muffin, 551
Flatbread, Spinach-Mushroom, 558
Focaccia, 557
French Toast, Stuffed, 576
Fruited Bran, 562
Garlic, 559
Granola, 550
Kuchen, Apple Honey, 547
Lavosh, Whole Wheat, 556
Lima Bean Wheat, 542
Loaf, Bubble, 552
Mint And Citrus Tea, 564
Muffins
  Cardamom-Pear, 571
  High-Energy , 572
  Wild Rice, 570
Multigrain Batter, 552
Pancakes
  Blueberry with Blueberry Maple Syrup,
    573
  Buttermilk Buckwheat, 574
  Dutch, with Spiced Fruit Mélange, 663
  Mandarin, 575
Parmesan Garlic, 559
Pastry, Empanada, 30
Pastry Dough, Galette, 335
Peasant, 539
Pita, 556
Pizza Dough
  Basic, 298
  Cheese, 299
  Cornmeal, 298
  Rye, 299
  Whole Wheat, 299
Potato, 538
Pretzels, Soft, 553
Raisin, 551
Roasted Red Pepper, 541
Rolls, Cinnamon, 549
Rolls, Squash Dinner, 554
-Rye, Hearty Vegetable, 540
Sweet Potato Braids, 543
Tamale Dough, 183
Three Kings', 545
Three-Grain Molasses, 562
Wheat Loaf, Cranberry-Nut, 544
Breakfast Burritos, 348
Breakfast Pizza, 302
Broccoli
  and Cheese Rotolo with Many-Cloves
    Garlic Sauce, 143

and Mushroom Pizza, 312
Herb-Crumbed, 476
Manicotti, Mushroom-, 258
Rabe Sauteed with Garlic, 477
Risotto, 411
Salad, 517
Soup
  Cream of, 60
  Dilled, 60
  Dilled Zucchini and, 89
  Herbed and Pasta, 61
  -Kale, 60
Terrine with Lemon Herb Mayonnaise,
  477
Brown Sugar Apple Pudding, 677
Brown Sugar Syrup, 677
Bruschetta, 46
  Fava Bean, 358
  Mushroom, 35
Brussels Sprouts
  and Gnocchi Salad, 225
  and Pasta Shell Salad, 458
  and Pearl Onions, Sugar-Glazed, 478
  Bucatini with, and Walnuts, 238
  Fettuccine with Fresh Fennel and, 229
Burgers, Vegetarian (see Sandwiches)
Burritos with Poblano Chili Sauce, 178
Burritos, Breakfast, 348
Butter Bean and Sprouts Stir-Fry, 380
Buttermilk Pie, Old-Fashioned, 640

C

Cabbage
  and Potato Hash, 155
  and Potatoes, Pasta with, 251
  and Sauerkraut Casserole, 445
  Ragout With Real Mashed Potatoes, 119
  Salad, Pasta, White Bean, and Red, 386
  Soup, Kidney Bean and, 433
  Soup, Russian, 68
  Strudel, -Fennel, 153
  Strudels, Apple-, 43
  Stuffed with Chili Tomato Sauce, 154
  Sweet-Spiced with Quinoa, 150
  Wine-Braised, 479
Cactus Salad, 525
Caesar Salad, 513
Cajun Eggplant, 208
Cajun Seasoning, 209
Cake(s)
  Banana-Cinnamon, 628
  Boston Cream, 626
  Carrot with Cream Cheese Frosting, 622
  Cassata Siciliana, 633
  Cheesecake
    Chocolate Fillo, 650
    Lemon Meringue, 649
    New York-Style, 648
    Spring Berry, 647
  Chiffon, Glazed Orange, 617
  Chocolate
    Buttermilk with Mocha Frosting, 618
    Ice Cream Jelly Roll, 673
    -Cherry Pudding, 622
  Coffee-Frosted Cocoa, 621

Flourless Chocolate, 619
Frozen Peppermint Rolls, 671
Jelly Roll
    Chocolate Ice Cream, 673
    Ice Cream, 672
    Peppermint, 671
Orange Poppy Seed, 630
Pineapple Upside-Down, 625
Pound, Lemon, 629
Pumpkin-Ginger with Warm Rum Sauce, 627
Raspberry-Orange Swirl, 631
Rhubarb Streusel, 616
Shortcake, Strawberry-Kiwi, 662
Spice with Penuche Frosting, 624
Calzones, 44
    Cheese and Mushroom, 320
    Sweet Fennel, 321
    Vegetarian Sausage, 319
Candied Yams, 498
Canned Vegetable Stock, 56
Cannellini
    Bean Patties with Fresh Tomato Relish, 285
    Dip, Herb, 14
    Dip, Roasted Garlic and, 14
Cannelloni Casserole, 449
Cantaloupe Cooler, 49
Capellini, Molded Carbonara, 255
Caramel Apple Slices, 660
Caramel Flan, 679
Caraway Dressing, 386
Cardamom-Pear Muffins, 571
Caribbean Potato Salad, 520
Caribbean Sweet-and-Sour Stew, 127
Carrot(s)
    and Ginger Cream, Star Pasta with, 240
    Cake with Cream Cheese Frosting, 622
    Orange-Glazed, Baby, 480
    Pudding, 481
    Puree, Gingered, 479
    Salad, -Raisin, 518
    Soup, Dilled, 69
    Soup, Ginger Spiced-Orange, 70
Cassata Siciliana, 633
Casseroles
    Artichoke Tortellini Bake, 259
    Baked Beans (see Beans)
    Cabbage and Sauerkraut, 445
    Cabbage, Sweet-Spiced with Quinoa, 150
    Cannelloni, 449
    Eggplant
        Lasagne, 142
        Parmesan Torte, Spaghetti and, 145
        Souffle, 149
        and Tomato, 485
        and Tomato Sauce Parmesan, 146
        and Zucchini, 447
    Green Bean, 473
    Lasagne
        Artichoke, 268
        Eggplant, 142
        Mexican-Style, 139
        Roasted Red Pepper and Spinach, 267
        Squash and Mushroom, 266

Vegetarian Sausage, 141
Veggie with Eggplant Sauce, 140
Macaroni and Cheese, 136
Macaroni and Cheese Primarvera, 136
Manicotti, Mushroom-Broccoli, 258
Meatballs, Vegetarian, in Tomato Chili Sauce, 124
Meatballs, Vegetarian, Italian-Style with Peperonata, 455
Noodles Florentine, 346
Pastitsio, 450
Pastitsio, Adzuki Bean, 366
Potatoes Gratin, 495
Potatoes, Scalloped, 495
Pudding
    Carrot, 481
    Fresh Corn, 484
    Tomato, 507
Ratatouille, 148
of Roasted Vegetables and Beans, 199
Rotolo, Broccoli and Cheese with Many-Cloves Garlic Sauce, 143
Rotolo, Spinach-Mushroom with Marinara Sauce, 144
Spinach au Gratin, 502
Spinach Pasta Bake, 446
Sweet Potato Pone, 501
Tajine, Oven-Baked Vegetable, 135
Tetrazzini, Vegetarian, 138
Torta Rustica, 322
Vegetable(s)
    and Mixed Rice, 138
    Cheesy Wild Rice and, 447
    Mexican-Style Grain and, 397
    Moussaka, -Barley, 146
    Puff, 344
    Roasted and Beans, 198
Veggie Kugel, 346
Veggie, Mixed Grain and, 137
Wild Rice, Cheesy and Vegetable, 447
Zucchini Fans Provençal, 50
Zucchini from Pueblo, 50
Cauliflower
    Puree, -Fennel, 480
    Soup with Cheese, Cream of, 70
    with Creamy Cheese Sauce, 482
Celery Root Puree, 480
Cereal, Best Breakfast, 429
Chayote Squash Soup with Cilantro Sour Cream, 87
Chayote with Pumpkin Seeds, 506
Cheese
    and Mushroom Calzones, 320
    and Spinach Squares, 36
    and Spinach Stuffed Mushrooms, 32
    and Vegetable Rarebit, 355
    Rotolo with Many-Cloves Garlic Sauce, Broccoli and, 143
    Burgers, Gourmet Veggie, 275
    Cake, Black Bean with Salsa, 352
    Cheddar-Garlic Grits, 427
    Cheesy Bean and Onion Mashers, 494
    Cheesy Wild Rice and Vegetable Casserole, 447
    Chiles Rellenos, Beans and, 351

Chili con Queso, 10
Cream Cheese
   Cranberry-Pistachio, 23
   Frosting, 623
   Glaze, 566
   Pepper-Onion Relish and, 23
   Raisin-Marmalade, 24
Crepes, Spinach, 452
Dressing
   Blue, 528
   Sun-Dried Tomato-Goat, 458
   Sun-Dried Tomato and Goat, 226
Dumplings, Chili-, 364
Focaccia, Onion and Blue, 44
Fondue, 354
Grill, Sun-Dried Tomato Pesto and, 464
Lasagne
   Artichoke, 268
   Eggplant, 142
   Mexican-Style, 139
   Roasted Red Pepper and Spinach, 267
   Sausage, Vegetarian, 141
   Squash and Mushroom, 266
   Veggie with Eggplant Sauce, 140
Macaroni and, 527
Macaroni and Primarvera, 527
and Mushroom Calzones, 320
Pasta with Goat, and Onion Confit, 231
Pizza Dough, 299
Pizza, 4-, Spinach and, 300
Pizza, Roasted Red Pepper and, 306
Polenta, Blue, 425
Polenta, Goat, 425
Potatoes, Twice-Baked with, 496
Quesadillas, Black Bean, 26
Quesadillas, Goat with Tropical Fruit
   Salsa, 25
Queso Fundido, 10
Quiche(s)
   Lorraine, 356
   Mini-, Spinach and, 36
   Spinach, 356
Ravioli, Feta, and Sun-Dried Tomato, 265
Ravioli, Herbed with Wild Mushroom
   Sauce, 263
Relish, Fennel Goat, 284
Risotto, Two-, 413
Salad
   Angel Hair and Goat, 532
   Lentil with Feta, 460
   Macaroni-Blue, 527
Sauces
   Alfredo, 591
   Creamy, 482
   Gorgonzola, 592
   Jalapeno con Queso, 603
   Welsh Rarebit, 355
Soufflé, Cheddar, 353
and Spinach Squares, 36
and Spinach Stuffed Mushrooms, 32
Spread, Chutney, 21
Spread, Roasted Garlic and Three-, 22
-Stuffed Pasta Shells with Simple Tomato
   Sauce, 168
-Stuffed Shells with Spinach Pesto, 31

Welsh Rarebit, 355
Wontons, Cranberry-, 39
Cheesecakes (see under Cakes)
Cherry, Pudding Cake, Chocolate-, 622
Cherry, Soup Sweet, 57
Chick Pea and Pasta Soup, 106
Chick Peas, Sprouted, 523
Chili
   -Cheese Dumplings, 363
   Chipotle, Sweet Potato, 80
   Con Queso, 10
   Corn Bread, Green, 561
   Corn Bread, Roasted, 216
   -Dressed Salad with Radiatore, 530
   Dressing, 530
   Poblano, Potatoes with, 498
   Poblano, Stuffed, 274
   Sauce
      Cincinnati, 598
      Poblano, 601
      Tomato, 599
   Sin Carne, 435
   Soup, Poblano, 102
   Stew, 121
   Stew, Mexican, Ancho, 123
   Tamales, Three- , 183
   Yellow and White Bean, 362
Chilled Pea Soup, 82
Chinese Noodles with Sweet Potatoes and
   Snow Peas, 246
Chive Biscuits, 568
Chocolate (see under Cakes, Cookies,
   Frostings, Pies, Puddings, Sauces)
Chop Suey, 174
Chutney Cheese Spread, 21
Cilantro
   Cream, 67,
   Cream, Sour, 88
   Dressing, Lime, 526
   Dressing, Lime, Summer Fruit with, 459
   Jicama with Lime and, 29
   Pesto, 607
   Pesto, Spinach-, 608
   Rice, Orange, 420
   Tomatillo Soup with, 103
Cincinnati Chili Sauce, 598
Cinnamon
   Cake, Banana-, 628
   Rolls, 549
   Soup, -Spiced Pumpkin, 90
   Streusel, 572
   Vinaigrette, Lemon- Citrus Glaze, 417
Citrus Vinaigrette, 227
Citrus Vinaigrette, 388
Classic Black Bean Soup, 67
Cocoa Frosting, 655
Cocoa-Glazed Cookie Crisps, 654
Coffee Frosting, 621
Coffee-Frosted Cocoa Cake, 621
Condiments
   Butter, Spiced Pear, 577
   Compote, Spiced Orange, 658
   Coulis, Cranberry, 610
   Jelly
      Apple-Mint, 579

Ginger, Easy, 580
Orange-Rosemary, 578
Rose Geranium, 579
Spiced Rhubarb Jam, 578
Tarragon Wine, 579
Relish
Apple-Cranberry, 609
Fennel Goat Cheese, 284
Fresh Tomato, 285
Gingered Tomato, 610
Grilled Pepper, 200
Onion-Chutney, 400
Pepper-Onion and Cream Cheese, 23
Salsa (see under Appetizers and Sauces)
Cookies
Biscotti, Anise-Almond, 657
Biscotti, Apricot-Sesame, 658
Chocolate Chip, 651
Crisps, Cocoa-Glazed, 654
Crisps, Spiced, 654
Lemon Squares, Sugared, 655
Macaroons, Hazelnut, 656
Meringues
Chocolate Fudge, 656
Orange-Almond, 656
Peppermint Clouds, 656
Raisin Oatmeal, 651
Shortbread Squares, Glazed Chocolate, 653
Sugar, Frosted, 652
Corn
Chowder, Hearty and Potato Chowder, 86
Chowder, Roasted and Potato Chowder, 186
Fried, 483
Fusilli with Tomatoes and, 237
Pudding, Fresh, 484
Soup with Epazote, 74
Soup, Creamed, 73
Tex-Mex Sweet, 484
Corn Bread, Green Chili, 561
Corn Bread, Roasted Chili, 216
Cornmeal
and Millet Mush, 428
-Fried Tomatoes, 509
Pizza Dough, 298
Country Lentil Soup, 113
Couscous
Curried, 399
Curried Sweet Potato, 400
Fruited with Smoked Tofu, 401
Garden Stew with, 133
Cranberry
Apple Relish, 500, 609
Cheese Melt, 464
-Cheese Wontons, 39
Coffeecake, 566
Coulis, 610
Crisp, Apple-Cranberry, 664
-Nut Wheat Loaf, 544
-Pistachio Cream Cheese, 23
Cream
of Artichoke and Mushroom Soup with Parmesan Toast, 432
of Broccoli Soup, 60
of Cauliflower Soup with Cheese, 70

Cilantro, 67
Filling, Vanilla, 626
Ginger, Star Pasta with Carrots and, 240
of Mushroom Soup, 76
Pie, Banana-Strawberry, 642
Sage, Potato Gnocchi with, 253
Tart, Toasted Coconut, 643
of Tomato Soup, 92
Crème Anglaise, 646
Creamed
Corn Soup, 73
Spinach Sauce, Vegetable Manicotti with, 257
Vegetable Soup, Lightly, 97
Creamy
Cheese Sauce, 482
Dressing, 517
Fettuccine Primavera, 227
Peanut Butter Soup, 111
Potato and Bean Mashers, 494
Potato Salad, 519
Creole Sauce, 588
Creole Skillet Stew, Easy, 443
Crepes, 575
Dessert, 575
Spinach Cheese, 452
Vegetable, 159
Crisp Streusel, 616
Crispy French "Fries", 497
Croustades, 47
Croustades, Curried Onion, 32
Croutons, 560
Herb, 561
Italian-Style, 560
Parmesan, 560
Rye Caraway, 560
Sesame, 560
Sourdough, 560
Cucumber
Cheese Melt, 293
Dressing, -Sour Cream, 417
Sauce, Yogurt, 28, 61
Soup, Herbed, 71
Soup, and Sorrel, 72
Yogurt, 400
Curried
Bean Soup, 361
Butternut Squash Soup, 90
Couscous, 399
Couscous, Sweet Potato, 400
Onion Baklava, 333
Onion Croustades, 32
Pasta and Vegetables, 232
Pasta Salad, 531
Pinwheels, 34
Soybeans and Potatoes, 382
Stew, Mediterranean, 134
Tofu and Vegetables, 166
Tortellini with Beans and Squash, 260
Vietnamese Coconut Soup, 112
Curry
Dip, 6
Sauce, 594
Stew, Eggplant and Bean, 367
Vegetable, 165

Custard
Apricot, Fresh, 678
Brulée, Herbed, 680
Lemon, 633
Topping, 147

D
Deep-Pan Spinach Pizza, 301
Desserts (see also Cakes, Cookies, Fillings
and Toppings, Frostings and Glazes, Pies,
Puddings and Custards, Sauces)
Apple Slices, Caramel, 660
Apple-Cranberry Crisp, 664
Bananas Foster, 665
Frozen
Ice, Lemon, 668
Ice, Pineapple-Champagne, 668
Sherbet, Orange-Pineapple, 666
Sorbet, Ginger-Citrus, 667
Sundaes, Praline, 666
Tortoni, Mixed Fruit, 669
Honey-Lime Melon Wedges, 659
Orange Compote, Spiced, 658
Peach-Allspice Soufflés, 681
Pears Belle Hélène, 661
Pears with Raspberry Sauce, 662
Pineapple Slices, Honey-Broiled, 659
Pineapple-Lemon Trifle, 632
Rhubarb Crunch, Fran's, 664
Rhubarb, Fresh Berry, 660
Dilled
Beet Soup, 58
Broccoli Soup, 60
Carrot Soup, 69
Mayonnaise Dressing, 210
Zucchini and Broccoli Soup, 89
Dips and Spreads (see under Appetizers)
Dressings (see Salad Dressings)
Dumplings, Chili-Cheese, 364
Dumplings, Herb, 118

E
Easiest Black-Eyed Pea and Lentil Soup, 360
Easy
Creole Skillet Stew, 443
Ginger Jelly, 580
Herb Lavosh, 45
Edamame Snackers, 4
Egg(s)
Bean and Cheese Chiles Rellenos, 351
Bean, Black Cheesecake with Salsa, 352
Benedict, 338
Burritos, Breakfast, 348
Cheesecake with Salsa, Black Bean, 352
Chilies Rellenos, Bean and Cheese, 351
Frittata, Pasta, 342
Frittata, Vegetable with Parmesan
Toast, 343
Hash, 339
Sweet Potato, with Poached, 340
Sweet Potato, Herbed Bean and, 339
Huevos Rancheros, 347
and Mushrooms À La King, 340
Noodles Florentine, 346

Omelet Puff with Vegetable Mélange, 345
Piperade, 338
Quiche(s)
Lorraine, 356
Mini-, Spinach and Cheese, 36
Spinach, 356
Rancheros with Black Beans and 2 Salsas,
348
Salad, Pasta, 341
Scrambled
with Cactus, 350
with Crisp Tortilla Strips, 350
with Vegetarian Chorizo, 349
Soufflé(s)
Cheddar Cheese, 353
Eggplant Casserole, 149
Peach-Allspice, 681
Wild Rice, 424
Vegetable Puff, 344
Veggie Kugel, 346
Eggplant
and Bean Curry Stew, 367
Cajun, 208
Casserole Soufflé, 149
Caviar, 17
Filling, 264
Greek with Feta,
Lasagne, 142
Loaf with Simple Tomato Sauce, 265
Marmalade, 20
Mediterranean Roasted and Tomatoes, 204
Parmesan Sandwiches, 286
Parmesan Torte, Spaghetti and, 145
Persillade, Fettuccine with, 230
Polenta Stack, 156
Provençal, 448
Ravioli, 264
Roasted
and Squash, Farfalle with, 238
and Squash, Quinoa with, 402
with Pasta, 455
Sauce, 589
Saute, Seasoned, 485
Soup with Roasted Red Pepper Sauce, 74
and Tomato Casserole, 485
and Tomato Sauce Parmesan, 146
and Vegetable Sauté, 156
and Zucchini Casserole, 447
El Paso Succotash, 474
Empanada Pastry, 30
Empanadas, Fruit, 30
Enchilada Sauce, 599
Enchiladas Mole, 179
English Muffin Bread, 551
Entrees (see also Casseroles, Cheese, Eggs,
Beans and Legumes, Grains, Grilled and
Roasted Dishes, Loaves, Pasta, Salads,
Sandwiches and Patties, Soups, and Stews)
Burritos with Poblano Chili Sauce, 178
Cabbage and Potato Hash, 155
Cabbage, Stuffed, with Chili Tomato
Sauce, 154
Chop Suey, 174
Crepes, Spinach Cheese, 452
Crepes, Vegetable, 159

Eggplant and Vegetable Sauté, 156
Eggplant Polenta Stack, 156
Enchiladas Mole, 179
Enchiladas, Vegetable, 180
Flautas with Tomatillo Sauce, 181
Grapevine Leaves, Stuffed, 164
Loaf, Teem Seem, 175
Mushrooms, Portobello, Stuffed, 157
Niçoise Platter, 160
Polenta, Italian Vegetarian Meatballs
    with, 169
Ravioli, Lentil with Gingered Tomato
    Relish, 167
Shells, Cheese-Stuffed Pasta with Simple
    Tomato Sauce, 168
Spaghetti and Spaghetti!, 166
Spaghetti Squash with Vegetable Sauté,
    158
Stir-Fry(ied)
    Five-Spice, 172
    Sesame Asparagus, 152
    Spring Vegetable, 170
    Thai, 171
    with Tofu, Green on Green, 170
    Vegetable, Szechuan, 173
Strudel
    Cabbage-Fennel, 153
    Leek and Mushroom, 162
    Vegetable with Wild Mushroom Sauce,
        161
Sweet Potato Cakes, 158
Tamales, Three-Chili, 183
Tamales, Veggie, with Beans, 184
Tempeh
    Fajitas, 182
    Moo-Shu, 176
    Steak with Red and Green Stir-Fry, 177
Tofu and Vegetables, Curried, 166
Vegetable(s)
    Curry, 165
    Paprikash, 163
    Sautéed, White Bean Mashers with, 152

F
45-Minute Preparation Tips, vi
Fajita(s)
    Grilled Vegetable, 214
    Marinade, 182
    Tempeh, 182
Falafel Burgers, Vegetarian, 280
Falafel Pitas with Tahini Dressing, 281
Farfalle Salad with Minted Pesto, 531
Farfalle with Roasted Eggplant and Squash,
    238
Faux Chopped "Liver", 20
Fava
    Bean Bruschetta, 358
    Bean Salad Platter, 390
    Bean Spread, 358
Fennel
    Calzones, Sweet, 321
    Fettuccine with Fresh, and Brussels
        Sprouts, 229
    Goat Cheese Relish, 284
    Pesto, 606

Puree, 480
Puree, Cauliflower-, 480
Strudel, Cabbage-, 153
Feta Cheese and Sun-Dried Tomato Ravioli,
    265
Feta Toast, 444
Fettuccine
    Primavera, Creamy, 227
    with Eggplant Persillade, 230
    with Fresh Fennel and Brussels Sprouts,
        229
    with Greens and Caramelized Onions, 228
    with Roasted Garlic, Onions, and
        Peppers, 228
    with Roasted Vegetable Sauce, 194
Five-Spice Potstickers, 38
Five-Spice Stir-Fry, 172
Flautas with Tomatillo Sauce, 181
Flourless Chocolate Cake, 619
Focaccia, 557
    Fruit, 318
    Leek and Onion, 318
    Onion and Blue Cheese, 44
Four-Bean and Vegetable Soup, 62
Fragrant Basting Sauce, 614
Fran's Rhubarb Crunch, 664
Freezer Coleslaw, 516
French
    "Fries," Crispy, 497
    Onion Soup, 78
    -Style Onion Pizza, 304
    Toast, Stuffed, 576
Fried
    Corn, 483
    Lentils, 372
    Mush, 429
    Ripe Plantains, 29
    Tomatoes, 508
Frosted Cocoa Brownies, 654
Frosted Sugar Cookies, 652
Frostings and Glazes
    Chocolate, 627
    Chocolate, Rich, 620
    Citrus, 631
    Cocoa, 655
    Coffee, 621
    Cream Cheese, 566, 623
    Mocha, 619
    Orange, 617
    Penuche, 624
    Powdered Sugar, 629
    Sugar, 652, 653
    Vanilla, 573
Frozen Peppermint Cake Rolls, 671
Fruit
    Empanadas, 30
    Focaccia, 318
    Mélange, Spiced, Dutch Pancake with, 663
    Nuggets, 4
    Orchard Pizza, 316
    Pilaf, 405
    Salad with Raspberry Yogurt Dressing, 520
    Salad, Summer, with Lime Cilantro
        Dressing, 459
    Salsa, Tropical, 25

-Stuffed Vidalia Onions, 490
Tart, Rustic Country, 646
Tofruity, 48
Tortoni, Mixed Fruit, 669
Fruited Bran Bread, 401
Fruited Couscous with Smoked Tofu, 490
Fusilli, Spiced Bean Stew with, 131
Fusilli with Tomatoes and Corn, 237

G

Galette Pastry Dough, 335
Garbanzo
Bean Soup, 68
Burgers, Greek-Style, with Fennel Goat
Cheese Relish, 284
Salsa, 604
Tomatoes, and Croutons, Mafalde with,
249
Garden
Harvest Soup, 99
Minestrone with Parmesan Croutons, 436
Mushroom Spread, 19
Pasta Salad with Crostini, 533
Patch Pizza, 314
Quinoa, 403
Stew with Couscous, 133
Vegetable and Pasta Salad, 222
Vegetables and Tempeh Saute, 453
Garlic
Bread, 559
Bread, Parmesan, 559
Burgers, Smothered Onion-, Veggie, 275
Dressing, 515
Grits, Cheddar-, 427
Mashed Potatoes, 493
Pasta, Great, 234
Polenta, 425
Roasted
and Cannellini Dip, 14
and Three-Cheese Spread, 22
Onions, and Peppers, Fettuccine with,
228
Sauce, Many-Cloves, 591
Soup with Toast, 75
Soup, Garlicky Lima Bean, 359
Spread, Roasted Zucchini and, 18
Vinaigrette, 222
Vinaigrette, Roasted, 419
Guacamole, 12
Gazpacho, 94
Bean, 440
Pizza, 316
German Potato Salad, 518
Ginger(ed)
-Baked Beans, 368
Bean and Blackeye Stew, 128
Cake, Pumpkin-, with Warm Rum Sauce,
627
Carrot Puree, 479
Cream, Star Pasta with Carrots and, 240
Honey, 580
Jelly, Easy, 580
Sorbet, -Citrus, 667
Spiced-Orange Carrot Soup, 70

Squash Stew, Orange and, 126
Tomato Relish, 610
Gingersnap Crumb Crust, 637
Glaze(s) (See under Frostings and Glazes)
Glazed Chocolate Shortbread Squares, 653
Glazed Orange Chiffon Cake, 617
Goat Cheese
Dressing, Sun-Dried Tomato and, 226, 458
Hoagies, 291
and Onion Confit, Pasta with, 231
Polenta, 425
Relish, Fennel, 284
Quesadillas with Tropical Fruit Salsa, 25
Salad, Angel Hair and, 532
Gorgonzola Sauce, 592
Gorp, By Golly!, 2
Gourmet Cheese Veggie Burgers, 275
Graham Cracker Crumb Crust, 636
Grains
Barley
and Vegetable Mélange, 395
Bowl, Wheat and, 394
Chowder, -Vegetable, 392
Soup, Savory Mushroom and, 77
Vegetable-, Moussaka, 146
with Peppers and Potatoes, 394
Casserole, Mexican-Style, and
Vegetable, 397
Casserole, Mixed, and Veggie, 137
Cereal, Best Breakfast, 429
Couscous
Curried, 399
Curried Sweet Potato, 400
Fruited, with Smoked Tofu, 401
Garden Stew with, 133
Kasha
Burgers, -Veggie, 283
Loaf Baked In Squash Halves, 273
with Green Veggies, 396
Millet
Black-Eyed Peas and Greens with, 396
Mush, Cornmeal and, 428
Vegetable Salad with, 417
with Artichoke Hearts and Vegetables,
398
Mush, Fried, 429
Pilaf
Fruit, 405
Garden, 403
Oriental, 407
Mushroom and Asparagus, 404
Quinoa and Wheat Berry, 402
Sweet Bulgur, 406
Polenta
Blue Cheese, 425
Eggplant Stack, 156
Garlic, 25
Goat Cheese, 425
Grill-Roasted Vegetables with, 197
Italian-Style Veggie Meatballs with, 169
Portobello Mushrooms with Grilled
Pepper Relish and, 169
Stack, Eggplant, 156
Three-Bean Stew with, 130
Wedges, Sauteed, 426

Pudding, Baked Cereal, 674
Quinoa
    and Wheat Berry Pilaf, 402
    Garden, 403
    Sweet-Spiced Cabbage with, 150
    with Roasted Eggplant and Squash, 402
Rice
    Black Beans and, 374
    Bourbon Street Red Beans and, 376
    Casserole, Vegetable and Mixed, 138
    Casserole, Cheesy Wild, and
        Vegetable, 447
    Fried, Asian, 404
    Fried, Thai, 423
    Loaf, Mesquite-Smoked Tofu and
        Brown, 272
    Mexi-Beans, Greens, and, 375
    Mexican Red, 421
    Muffins, Wild, 570
    Noodles, with Vegetables, 245
    Orange Cilantro, 420
    Pudding, Old-Fashioned Baked, 674
    Salad
        Black Bean and, 389
        Noodle, 226
        Vegetable and Wild, 211
    Soufflé, Wild, 424
    Soup, Greek Lemon-, 110
    Spicy, 422
    Tempeh with Black Beans and, Jerk, 191
    Turmeric, 423
    Yellow Salsa, 42
Risotto
    All-Season, 409
    Broccoli, 411
    Porcini, 410
    Risi Bisi, 413
    Summer Squash, 412
    Two-Cheese, 413
    -Vegetable Cakes, 414
    Winter Vegetable, 408
    with Roasted Tomatoes, 195
Tabbouleh, 415
Tabbouleh and Vegetable Salad Medley, 416
Tempeh, Tandoori, with Orange
    Cilantro, 192
Wheat and Barley Bowl, 394
Wheat Berry(-ies)
    and Garden Tomato Salad, 419
    and Lentil Stew with Dumplings, 392
    Pilaf, Quinoa and, 402
    Sprouted, 523
    Waldorf, 418
Grandma's Lemon Meringue Pie, 638
Granola Bread, 550
Great Garlic Pasta, 234
Great Greek Salad, 514
Greek
    Eggplant with Feta, 204
    Isle Veggie Burgers, 276
    Lemon-Rice Soup, 110
    Lentil Stew, 444
    -Style Garbanzo Burgers with Fennel
        Goat Cheese Relish, 284
    -Style Green Beans, 472

Green
    Bean Casserole, 473
    Chili Corn Bread, 561
    on Green Stir-Fry with Tofu, 170
Greens
    and Beans, Pasta with, 232
    and Caramelized Onions, Fettuccine
        with, 228
    Lemon-Spiked Garlic, 486
    Mexi-Beans, and Rice, 375
    with Millet, Black-eyed Peas and, 396
    Raisins, and Pine Nuts, Pasta with, 247
    Smashed Potatoes and, 487
    Stir-Fried Beans and, 379
    -Stuffed Baked Tomatoes, 509
Gremolata, 609
Grilled Foods (see Roasted and Grilled)
Grinders, 463
Guacamole, 12
Gulfport Okra, 489

H
Harvard Beets, 475
Hash
    and Eggs, 339
    Cabbage and Potato, 155
    Sweet Potato, Herbed Bean and, 339
    Sweet Potato, with Poached Eggs, 340
Hasty Stew, 116
Hazelnut Macaroons, 656
Hearty Corn and Potato Chowder, 86
Hearty Vegetable-Rye Bread, 540
Herb(ed)
    Bean and Sweet Potato Hash, 339
    Broccoli and Pasta Soup, 61
    Cannellini Dip, 14
    Cheese Ravioli with Wild Mushroom
        Sauce, 263
    Croutons, 561
    -Crumbed Broccoli, 476
    Cucumber Soup, 71
    Custard Brulée, 680
    Dip, Cannellini, 14
    Dumplings, 118, 393
    Lavosh, Easy, 45
    Mayonnaise, Lemon-, 611
    Pesto, Mixed, 605
    Potage, Fresh, Potato and, 84
    Sauce, Fresh Tomato and, 584
    Sauce, Roasted Tomato-, 202
    Soup, Savory Squash, 91
    Tomato Halves, 508
    Veggie Burgers, 282
    Vinaigrette, Mixed, 224
High-Energy Muffins, 572
Holiday Sweet Potato Loaf with Apple-
    Cranberry Relish, 499
Homemade Pasta, 220
Honey
    -Broiled Pineapple Slices, 659
    Dressing, 512
    Dressing, -Lime, 524
    Dressing, Mustard-, 461
    Gingered, 580
    Kuchen, Apple, 547

-Lime Melon Wedges, 659
-Roasted Beets, 476
Hopping John, 377
Horseradish Mashed Potatoes, 493
Hot 'N Spicy Bean and Vegetable Stew, 122
Hot Pepper Vichyssoise, 187
Hot Sour Soup, 438
Hot Stuff!, 2
Huevos Rancheros, 347
Huevos Rancheros Pizza, 311

I

Ices (see Desserts, Frozen)
Ice Cream (see Desserts, Frozen)
Indian Lentil Soup, 114
Indonesian-Style Tofu Satay, 41
Ingredient Information, ix
Italian,
  Meatballs, Vegetarian with Polenta, 169
  -Style
    Beans and Vegetables, 378
    Croutons, 560
    Vegetarian Meatballs with Peperonata, 455
  Vegetarian Meatball Stew, 132
  -Style Veggie Burger Pie, 323

J

Jalapeño Con Queso Sauce, 603
Jelly (see under Condiments)
Jerk Seasoning, 192
Jerk Tempeh with Black Beans and Rice, 191
Jicama Salad, 526
Jicama with Lime and Cilantro, 29
Just Peachy Bean Pot, 369

K

Kasha
  Loaf Baked In Squash Halves, 273
  -Veggie Burgers, 283
  with Green Veggies, 396
Kidney Bean and Cabbage Soup, 433
Kiwi Tart, 643
Kiwi, Shortcake, Strawberry-, 662

L

Lasagne (see under Pasta)
Lavosh, Easy Herb, 45
Lavosh, Whole Wheat, 556
Leek
  and Feta Pizza with Pesto, 309
  and Mushroom Strudel, 162
  and Onion Focaccia, 318
  Cake, Serbian, 451
  Pie, 331
  Sauteed, and Peppers, 488
  Soup, Onion and, with Pasta, 80
  Soup, Ripe Tomato and, 94
Lemon
  -Cinnamon Vinaigrette, 417
  Cloud Pie, 644
  Custard, 633
  -Herb Mayonnaise, 611

Ice, 668
Meringue Cheesecake, 649
Meringue Pie, Grandma's, 638
Pound Cake, 629
Sauce, Tart, 675
Sauce, Wine-, Asparagus with, 471
Soup, Greek -Rice, 110
-Spiked Garlic Greens, 486
Squares, Sugared, 655
Syrup, 630
Trifle, Pineapple-, 632
Velvet Pudding, 678
Lentil
  Country Soup, 113
  Fried, 372
  Indian Soup, 114
  Ravioli with Gingered Tomato Relish, 167
  Salad, Sprouted, 522
  Salad with Feta Cheese, 460
  Soup
    Country, 113
    Easiest Black-Eyed Pea and, 360
    Indian, 114
  Sprouted, 522
  Stew, Greek, 444
  Stew, Wheat Berry and, with Dumplings, 392
Lima Bean and Mushroom Mashers, 494
Lima Bean Wheat Bread, 542
Lime
  and Cilantro, Jicama with, 29
  Cilantro Dressing, 459
  Dressing, 525
  Honey-, Dressing, 524
  Honey-, Melon Wedges, 659
  -Scented Vegetable Soup, 98
  Sweet Potatoes, Orange-, 500
Linguine
  Soup, Sun-Dried Tomato and, 105
  with Fennel and Sun-Dried Tomato Pesto, 457
  with Julienne Vegetables and Red Pepper Pesto, 230
"Little Ears" with Artichoke Hearts, Mushrooms, and Peppers, 232
"Little Ears" with Smoked Tempeh and Vegetables, 236
"Little Pants" Biscuits, 569
Lo Mein, Vegetable, 244
Loaf(-ves)
  Bubble, 552
  Eggplant, with Simple Tomato Sauce, 265
  Kasha, Baked in Squash Halves, 273
  Oriental, 272
  Sweet Potato, with Apple-Cranberry Relish, Holiday, 499
  Teem Seem, 175
  Tofu and Brown Rice, Mesquite-Smoked, 272
  Wheat, Cranberry-Nut, 544
Low-Carb Pizza Dough, 467

M

Macaroni
  and Cheese, 136

and Cheese Primarvera, 136
Salad, 527
Salad, -Blue Cheese, 527
Macaroons, Hazelnut, 656
Mafalde with Garbanzo Beans, Tomatoes,
and Croutons, 249
Mafalde with Sweet Potatoes and Kale, 249
Mandarin Pancakes, 575
Mango and Black Bean Salad, 523
Many-Cloves Garlic Sauce, 591
Marinade (see under Sauces)
Marinara Sauce, 582
Mayonnaise
Dressing, 341
Dilled, 210
Lemon-Herb, 611
Sour Cream, 517
Mean Bean Pasta, 384
Meatballs
Black Bean, 383
Italian-Style Veggie, with Polenta, 169
Vegetarian, 437
Vegetarian, in Tomato Chili Sauce, 124
Meatless Sloppy Joes, 289
Med-Mex Fusion Salsa, 8
Mediterranean
Curried Stew, 134
Roasted Eggplant and Tomatoes, 204
Stock, 54
-Style Vegetable Soup, 101
Tomato-Caper Sauce, 590
Veggie Burgers, 276
Melon Salad, Spinach and, 512
Melon Wedges, Honey-Lime, 659
Meringue(s) (see under Cookies and Pies)
Mesquite-Smoked Tofu, 191
Mesquite-Smoked Tofu and Brown Rice
Loaf, 272
Mexi-Beans, Greens, and Rice, 375
Mexi-Veggie Burgers, 276
Mexicali Pie, 328
Mexican
Ancho Chili Stew, 123
Bean Dip, 8
Red Rice, 421
-Style
Grain and Vegetable Casserole, 397
Lasagne, 139
Vegetable Stew, 125
Millet
Mush, Cornmeal and, 428
Vegetable Salad and, 417
with Artichoke Hearts and Vegetables, 398
Minestrone
with Parmesan Croutons, Garden, 436
Roasted Vegetable, 189
Summer, 96
Mint and Citrus Tea Bread, 564
Mint Jelly, Apple-, 579
Minted Pesto, 608
Minted Sour Cream, 149
Mocha Frosting, 619
Mock Chicken Salad Sandwiches, 291
Mock Hollandaise Sauce, 595
Molded Capellini Carbonara, 255

Mole Sauce, 600
Mole, Enchiladas, 179
Moo-Shu Tempeh, 176
Moo-Shu Style, Roasted Vegetables, 201
Moroccan Style, Roasted Squash, 196
Moussaka, Vegetable-Barley, 146
Muffins (see under Bread)
Mush, Cornmeal and Millet, 428
Mush, Fried, 429
Mushroom(s)
and Asparagus Pilaf, 404
-Broccoli Manicotti, 258
Bruschetta, 35
Calzones, Cheese and, 320
Flatbread, Spinach-, 558
Galette, Squash and, 334
Gravy, 596
Lasagne, Squash and, 266
Pilaf, and Asparagus, 404
Pinwheels, Sliced, 295
Pizza, Broccoli and, 312
Pizza with Fillo Crust, Zucchini and, 31
Rotolo with Marinara Sauce, Spinach-, 144
Salad, Roasted, 212
Sandwiches, Grilled Portobello, 215
Sauce, Wild, 596
Soup
Asian, with Noodles, 439
Black, 77
Cream of, 76
Cream of Asparagus and, with
Parmesan Toast, 432
Savory, and Barley, 77
Tortellini and, 109
with Sour Cream, 488
Spread, Garden, 19
Stock, Rich, 54
Strudel, Leek and, 162
Tart, 330
Tortellini, Roasted Vegetables with, 193
Wild
Pâté, 13
Pizza, 466
Sauce, 596
Veggie Burgers, 275
Mustard
-Honey Dressing, 461
Sauce, 612
Seed Vinaigrette, 236
-Turmeric Vinaigrette, 529

N

Nachos, 28
Navy Bean Soup, 63
New England Baked Beans, 368
New York-Style Cheesecake, 648
Niçoise Platter, 160
Noodle(s)
Chinese, with Sweet Potatoes and Snow
Peas, 246
Florentine, 346
Salad
Asian, 439
Oriental, 534
Rice, 226

Sesame, Soup with Vegetables, 242
Stir-Fried Rice, with Vegetables, 245
Nutritional Data, vi-viii

O

Okra, Gulfport, 489
Old-Fashioned Baked Rice Pudding, 674
Old-Fashioned Buttermilk Pie, 640
Omelet Puff with Vegetable Mélange, 345
Onion(s)
Baklava, Curried, 333
Burgers, Smothered –Garlic Veggie, 275
Croustades, Curried, 32
Focaccia, and Blue Cheese, 44
Focaccia, Leek and, 318
Fruit-Stuffed Vidalia, 490
Peas and, Tiny, 492
Pizza, French-Style, 304
Quartet of, 490
Relish, -Chutney, 400
Relish, Pepper- and Cream Cheese, 23
Salad, Sweet, 212
Sauce, Three-, 592
Soup
and Leek, with Pasta, 80
French, 78
Three-, with Mushrooms, 79
Vidalia, 81
Tarte Tatin, Sweet, 332
Toasted Dip, 5
Orange
-Almond Meringue, 656
Cake
Chiffon, Glazed, 617
Poppy Seed, 630
Raspberry- Swirl, 631
Compote, Spiced, 658
Dressing, 389
Dressing, -Sesame Salad, 534
Flan, 680
Glaze, 617
-Glazed Baby Carrots, 480
Hummus, Spicy, 16
-Lime Sweet Potatoes, 500
-Marinated Bean Salad, 388
Marmalade Crescents, 546
Pie, Baked Alaska, 670
-Pineapple Sherbet, 666
Rice, Cilantro, 420
-Rosemary Jelly, 578
Salad, -Marinated Bean, 388
Soup, Ginger Spiced- Carrot, 70
Soup, -Scented Squash, 91
Stew, and Ginger Squash, 126
Sweet Potatoes, -Lime, 500
Oregano Vinaigrette, 418
Oriental
Green Beans, 473
Loaf, 272
Noodle Salad, 534
Pilaf, 407
Soup with Noodles, 243
Stock, 55
Vegetable Satay, 206

Vinaigrette, 214
Watercress Soup, 110
Orzo Stuffed Mushrooms, 32
Orzo with Sun-Dried Tomatoes and
Mushrooms, 528
Oven-Baked Vegetable Tajine, 135

P

Pancakes (see under Breads)
Pancakes, Mandarin, 575
Pancakes, Potato, 493
Paprikash Sauce, 597
Paprikash, Vegetables, 452
Parmesan
"Fries", 497
Biscuits, 568
Croutons, 560
Garlic Bread, 559
Toast, 432
Vinaigrette, 387
Parthenon Platter, 15
Pasilla Black Bean Soup, 440
Pasta (see also Casseroles, Salads)
Bucatini with Brussels Sprouts and
Walnuts, 238
with Cabbage and Potatoes, 251
Capellini Carbonara, Molded, 255
with Carrots and Ginger Cream, Star, 240
Chinese Noodles with Sweet Potatoes and
Snow Peas, 246
with Cilantro Pesto, Southwest, 240
Curried, and Vegetables, 232
Eggplant Loaf with Simple Tomato Sauce,
265
Farfalle with Roasted Eggplant and
Squash, 238
Fettuccine
Primavera, Creamy, 227
with Eggplant Persillade, 230
with Fresh Fennel and Brussels
Sprouts, 229
with Greens and Caramelized Onions,
228
with Roasted Garlic, Onions, and
Peppers, 228
from Pescia, 250
Fusilli with Tomatoes and Corn, 237
Garlic, Great, 234
Gnocchi
Potato with Sage Cream, 253
Salad, Brussels Sprouts and, 225
Spinach, with Gorgonzola Sauce, 254
with Goat Cheese and Onion Confit, 231
with Greens and Beans, 232
with Greens, Raisins, and Pine Nuts, 247
Homemade, 220
Lasagne
Artichoke, 268
Eggplant, 142
Mexican-Style, 139
Roasted Red Pepper and Spinach, 267
Sausage, Vegetarian, 141
Squash and Mushroom, 266
Veggie with Eggplant Sauce, 140

Linguine with Julienne Vegetables and
Red Pepper Pesto, 230
"Little Ears" with Artichoke Hearts,
Mushrooms, and Peppers, 248
"Little Ears" with Smoked Tempeh and
Vegetables, 236
Lo Mein, Vegetable, 244
Mafalde with Garbanzo Beans, Tomatoes,
and Croutons, 249
Mafalde with Sweet Potatoes and Kale, 249
Manicotti, Mushroom-Broccoli, 258
Manicotti with Creamed Spinach Sauce,
Vegetable, 257
Penne with Asparagus and Plum
Tomatoes, 235
Peperonata, 492
from Pescia, 250
Ravioli
20-Minute, 261
Eggplant, 264
Feta Cheese and Sun-Dried Tomato, 265
Herbed Cheese, with Wild Mushroom
Sauce, 263
Sweet Potato with Curry Sauce, 262
Wine-Glazed and Asparagus, 262
Rigatoni with Vegetarian Sausage and
Fennel Pesto, 252
Rotini and Beans Niçoise, 252
Santa Fe, 241
Shells Stuffed with Spinach and Tofu, 256
Soup,Oriental with, 243
Soup, Sesame Noodle with Vegetables, 242
Stir-Fried Rice with Vegetables, 245
Tortellini
Artichoke Bake, 259
Curried with Beans and Squash, 260
and 2-Bean Vegetable Soup, 260
Very Simple Primavera, 233
Ziti with Gremolata, 23
Pastitsio, 450
Pastitsio, Adzuki Bean, 366
Pâté
Artichoke, 18
Pine Nut Spinach, 12
Wild Mushroom, 13
Patties (see Sandwiches)
Pea(s)
and Onions, Tiny, 492
Soup
Chilled, 82
Snow, 82
Split, 83
Peach-Allspice Soufflés, 681
Peachy Bean Pot, Just, 369
Peanut Sauce, 206
Peanut Sauce, Thai, 423
Peanut Butter Soup, Creamy, 111
Peanutty and Jelly Sandwiches, 294
Pear(s)
Belle Hélène, 661
Butter, Spiced, 577
Melt, Blue Cheese and, 293
Muffins, Cardamom-, 571
Pizza, Dessert, 317

Tart with Crème Anglaise, 645
with Raspberry Sauce, 662
Peasant Bean Sauce with Tomatoes and
Sage, 587
Peasant Bread, 539
Penne with Asparagus and Plum Tomatoes,
235
Penuche Frosting, 624
Peperonata, 492
Pasta, 246
Roasted, 209
Roasted, Galette, 335
-Tomato Sauce, 588
Peppermint Clouds, 656
Peppermint Cake Rolls, Frozen, 671
Pepper-Onion Relish and Cream Cheese, 23
Pesto (see under Sauces)
Picante Black Bean Tostadas, 288
Pies (see also Pie Crusts)
Dessert
Apple, Double-Crust, 639
Buttermilk, Old-Fashioned, 640
Cream, Banana-Strawberry, 642
Lemon Cloud, 644
Meringue, Lemon, Grandma's, 638
Orange Baked Alaska, 670
Sweet Potato, Spiced, 641
Savory
Artichoke, 328
Baklava, Curried Onion, 333
Calzones, 44
Cheese and Mushroom, 320
Sausage, Vegetarian, 319
Sweet Fennel, 321
Galette, Roasted Peperonata, 335
Galette, Squash and Mushroom, 334
Italian-Style Veggie Burger, 323
Leek, 331
Mexicali, 328
Tart, Mushroom, 330
Tart, Rich Tomato, 329
Tarte Tatin, Sweet Onion, 332
Use-It-Up, 327
Vegetable, Autumn, 325
Veggie Pot, 324
Veggie Pot, Shepherd's, 326
Tart
Blueberry, Raspberry-Glazed, 645
Coconut Cream, Toasted, 643
Kiwi, 643
Pear, with Crème Anglaise, 645
Rustic Country Fruit, 646
Tarte Tatin, 640
Pie Crusts
Basic, 635
Crumb
Gingersnap, 637
Graham Cracker, 636
Vanilla, 637
Galette Dough, 335
Meringue, 636
Pastry
Double Crust, 635
Empanada, 30
Pot Pie, 325

Tart, Baked, 330
Pilaf (see under Grains)
Pine Nut Spinach Pâté, 12
Pineapple
    -Champagne Ice, 668
    -Lemon Trifle, 632
    Slices, Honey-Broiled, 659
    Upside-Down Cake, 625
Pinto Bean and Avocado Dip, 9
Piperade, 338
Pita Breads, 556
Pita Chips, 46
Pita Chips, Seasoned, 46
Pizza
    Apple Salad, 317
    Artichoke and Roasted Pepper, 306
    Asian-Style, 304
    Black Bean and Jalapeño, 310
    Breakfast, 302
    Broccoli and Mushroom, 312
    Egg, Scrambled, 465
    Fruit Orchard, 316
    Garden Patch, 314
    Gazpacho, 316
    Huevos Rancheros, 311
    Leek and Feta with Pesto, 309
    Mushroom, Wild, 466
    on Pasta, 308
    Onion, French-Style, 304
    Pear Dessert, 317
    Potato, Tuscan, 307
    Ranch-Style, 302
    Reuben, 303
    Roasted Red Pepper and Cheese, 306
    Sauce, 582
    Southwest-Style, 467
    Spinach
        and 4-Cheese, 300
        Deep-Pan, 301
        Salad, 315
    Taco, 309
    Tomato and Basil, Fresh, 305
    Tomato Fillo, 314
    with Yellow and Green Squash, 312
    Zucchini and Mushroom with Fillo Crust,
        31
Pizza Crusts and Dough
    Basic, 298
    Cheese, 299
    Cornmeal, 298
    Low Carb, 467
    Rye, 299
    Whole Wheat, 299
Plantains, Fried Ripe, 29
Plantains, Sweet, 29
Plum Sauce, 612
Poblano
    Chili Sauce, 601
    Chili Soup, 102
    Quesadillas, 26
    Sour Cream Sauce, 603
Polenta (see under Grains)
Pomegranate Passion, 49
Porcini Risotto, 410

Portobello Mushroom(s)
    with Grilled Pepper Relish and Polenta,
        200
    Grilled Sandwiches, 215
    Monte Cristo Grill, 292
    Pasta and, Vinaigrette, 223
    Roasted Stuffed with Spinach-Cilantro
        Pesto, 203
    Sandwiches, Grilled, 215
    Stuffed, 157
    Vinaigrette, Pasta and, 223
Pot Pie
    Pastry, 325
    Shepherd's Veggie, 326
    Veggie, 324
Potato(es)
    and Fresh Herb Potage, 84
    Bread, 538
    Chowder, 86
        Hearty Corn and, 86
        Roasted Corn and, 186
    Curried Soybeans and, 382
    Gnocchi with Sage Cream, 253
    Gratin, 495
    Hash, Cabbage and, 155
    Mashed,
        Garlic, 493
        Horseradish, 493
        Real, 493
        Real, Cabbage Ragout with, 119
        Root Veggies and, 205
    Mashers, Creamy, and Bean, 494
    Pancakes, 493
    Pasta with Cabbage and, 251
    Pizza, Tuscan, 307
    with Poblano Chilies, 498
    Salad
        Caribbean, 520
        Creamy, 519
        German, 518
        Roasted, 210
    Scalloped, 495
    Smashed, and Greens, 487
    Stew, Sweet-Sour Squash and, 128
    Twice-Baked, with Cheese, 496
    Wasabi, Slices, 38
Potstickers, Five-Spice, 38
Pound Cake, Lemon, 629
Powdered Sugar Frosting, 629
Pozole, 104
Praline Sundaes, 666
Primavera
    Creamy Fettuccine, 227
    Sauce, 594
    Very Simple, 233
Pumpkin
    Cake with Warm Rum Sauce, Ginger, 627
    Seeds, Chayote with, 506
    Soup, Cinnamon-Spiced, 90
Puddings and Custards
    Apple, Brown Sugar, 677
    Apricot, Fresh, 678
    Bread, Blueberry with Tart Lemon Sauce,
        675
    Bread, Raisin-Pecan, 676

Brulee, Herbed, 680
Cake, Chocolate-Cherry, 622
Carrot, 481
Cereal, Baked, 674
Chocolate, Rich, 673
Corn, 484
Cream Filling, Vanilla, 626
Crème Anglaise, 646
Flan, Caramel, 679
Flan, Orange, 680
Lemon, 633
Lemon Velvet, 678
Rice, Old-Fashioned Baked, 674
Tomato, 507
Topping, 147
Warm Indian, 676
Puree(d)
Cauliflower-Fennel, 480
Celery Root, 480
Fennel, 480
Gingered Carrot, 479
Grilled Beet, 208
Roasted Vegetable Soup, 188

Q

Quartet of Onions, 490
Quesadillas (see under Appetizers)
Queso Fundido, 10
Quiche (see under Eggs)
Quick Self-Rising Biscuits, 568
Quinoa
and Wheat Berry Pilaf, 402
Garden, 403
Sweet-Spiced Cabbage with, 150
with Roasted Eggplant and Squash, 402

R

Ragout, Cabbage, with Real Mashed
  Potatoes, 119
Raisin
Bread, 551
-Marmalade Cream Cheese, 24
Oatmeal Cookies, 651
-Pecan Bread Pudding, 676
Ranch-Style Pizza, 302
Raspberry
-Glazed Blueberry Tart, 645
-Orange Swirl Cake, 631
Sauce, Pears with, 662
Yogurt Dressing, 521
Ravioli (see under Pasta)
Red Beans and Rice, Bourbon Street, 376
Red Pepper
Bread, Roasted, 541
Lasagne, and Spinach, 267
Pesto, 607
Pizza, and Cheese, 306
Sauce, Roasted, 590
Soup, Sweet, 84
Red Tomato Salsa, 8
Refried Beans, 374
Relishes (see under Condiments)
Rellenos, Bean and Cheese Chiles, 351
Reuben Pizza, 303

Rhubarb
Cake, Streusel, 616
Crunch, Fran's, 664
Fresh Berry, 660
Jam, Spiced, 578
Rice (see under Grains)
Rice Noodle (see under Pasta)
Rich
Chocolate Frosting, 620
Chocolate Pudding, 673
Mushroom Stock, 54
Tomato Tart, 329
Ricotta-Stuffed Shells with Spinach Pesto, 31
Rigatoni with Vegetarian Sausage and
  Fennel Pesto, 252
Ripe Tomato and Leek Soup, 94
Risi Bisi, 413
Risotto (see under Grains)
Roasted and Grilled
Beet Puree, 208
Cajun Eggplant, 208
Casserole of Roasted Vegetables and
  Beans, 199
Chili Corn Bread, 216
Corn and Potato Chowder, 186
Eggplant,
  Greek with Feta, 204
  Mediterranean and Tomatoes, 204
  with Pasta, 455
Fettuccine with, Vegetable Sauce, 194
Garlic
  and Cannellini Dip, 14
  and Three-Cheese Spread, 22
  Vinaigrette, 419
Hot Pepper Vichyssoise, 187
Jerk Tempeh with Black Beans and Rice,
  191
Mushroom Salad, 212
Onion, Sweet, Salad, 212
Oriental
  Salad, 213
  Vegetable Satay, 206
  Vinaigrette, 214
Peperonata, 209
Peperonata Galette, 335
Pepper Relish, 200
Portobello Mushrooms with, Pepper
  Relish and Polenta, 200
Portobello Mushroom Sandwiches, 215
Portobello Mushrooms, Stuffed with
  Spinach-Cilantro Pesto, 203
Potato Salad, 210
Red Pepper,
  Bread, 541
  and Cheese Pizza, 306
  and Spinach Lasagne, 267
  Sauce, 590
Spaghetti Squash with, Tomato-Herb
  Sauce and Artichokes, 202
Squash, Moroccan Style, 196
Tandoori Tempeh with Orange Cilantro
  Rice, 192
Tofu, Mesquite-Smoked, 191
Tomatoes Stuffed with Pepper-Roasted
  Wild Mushrooms, 207

Tomatoes, Risotto with, 195
Tomato-Herb Sauce, 202
Vegetable(s)
  with Beans and Fruit, 198
  with Polenta, 197
  and Wild Rice Salad, 211
  with Mushroom Tortellini, 193
  Fajitas, 214
  Minestrone, 189
  Moo-Shu Style, 201
  Pureed Soup, 188
  Stock, 53
  Summer with Pasta, 456
Veggie(s)
  Many- Stew, 190
  Pocket Sandwiches, 216
  Root and Mashed Potatoes, 205
  Zucchini and Garlic Spread, 18
Rolls (see under Breads)
Rose Geranium Jelly, 579
Rotini and Beans Niçoise, 252
Rotolo (see under Pasta)
Rum Sauce, Warm, 628
Russian Cabbage Soup, 68
Rustic Country Fruit Tart, 646
Rye Caraway Croutons, 560
Rye Pizza Dough, 299

S

Salad(s) (see also Beans and Legumes)
  12-Layer, 515
  Bean, Black, Mango and, 523
  Bean, Black, and Smoked Tofu, 461
  Bean, Summer, 524
  Broccoli, 517
  Cactus, 525
  Caesar, 513
  Carrot-Raisin, 518
  Chili-Dressed with Radiatore, 530
  Coleslaw, Freezer, 516
  Coleslaw, Pasta, 516
  Fruit with Raspberry Yogurt Dressing, 520
  Fruit, Summer, with Lime Cilantro
    Dressing, 459
  Great Greek, 514
  Jicama, 526
  Lentil, with Feta Cheese, 460
  Lentil, Sprouted, 522
  Mushroom, 212
  Onion, Sweet, 212
  Oriental, Roasted, 213
  Pasta
    Angel Hair and Goat Cheese, 532
    Asian Noodle, 535
    Curried, 531
    Egg, 341
    Farfalle with Minted Pesto, 531
    Garden, with Crostini, 533
    Garden Vegetable and, 222
    Gnocchi, Brussels Sprouts and, 225
    Light Summer, 222
    Macaroni, 527
    Macaroni-Blue Cheese, 527
    Oriental Noodle, 534

    Orzo with Sun-Dried Tomatoes and
      Mushrooms, 528
    Rice Noodle, 226
    Sesame, with Summer Vegetables, 224
    Shell, Brussels Sprouts and, 468
  Potato
    Caribbean, 520
    Creamy, 519
    German, 518
    Roasted, 210
  Spinach and Melon, 512
  Spinach, Wilted, 513
  Sprouts and Vegetable, 522
  Vegetable and Wild Rice, 211
  Vegetables and Orzo Vinaigrette, Mixed,
    529
  Waldorf , 521
  Waldorf, Wheat Berry, 418
  Wheat Berry and Garden Tomato, 419
Salad Dressing
  Balsamic, 460
  Basil, Fresh, 237
  Blue Cheese, 528
  Caraway, 386
  Chili, 530
  Cilantro Lime, 526
  Creamy, 517
  Cucumber-Sour Cream, 417
  Garlic, 515
  Honey, 512
  Honey-Lime, 524
  Lime, 525
  Lime Cilantro, 459
  Mustard-Honey, 461
  Orange, 389
  Orange-Sesame Salad, 534
  Raspberry Yogurt, 521
  Sour Cream-Mayonnaise, 517
  Sun-Dried Tomato and Goat Cheese, 226,
    458
  Tahini, 281
  Vinaigrette
    Basil, 223
    Citrus, 227, 388
    Garlic, 222
    Lemon-Cinnamon, 417
    Mixed Herb, 224
    Mixed Vegetables and Orzo, 529
    Mustard Seed, 236
    Mustard-Turmeric, 529
    Oregano, 418
    Oriental, 214
    Parmesan, 387
    Pasta and Portobello Mushrooms, 223
    Roasted Garlic, 419
  White Bean, 385
  Yogurt, 53
Salsa (see under Appetizers and Sauces)
Sandwiches, Patties, and Loaves
  Burgers,
    Bonanza, Vegetarian 275
    Cannellini Bean with Fresh Tomato
      Relish, 285
    Falafel, Vegetarian, 280
    Falafel Pitas with Tahini Dressing, 281

Garbanzo, with Fennel Goat Cheese
   Relish, Greek-Style, 284
Squash and Tempeh, 279
Tofu, Smoked, 278
Veggie
   Blues, 276
   Cheese, Gourmet, 275
   Greek Isles, 276
   Herbed, 282
   Kasha-, 283
   Mediterranean, 276
   Mexi-, 276
   Mushroom, Wild, 275
   Onion-Garlic, Smothered, 275
   Soybean-, 286
   Swiss Kraut, 276
   -Tofu, 277
Chicken Salad, Mock, 291
Chilies, Stuffed Poblano, 274
Eggplant Parmesan, 286
Hoagies, Goat Cheese, 291
Loaf(ves)
   Brown Rice, Mesquite-Smoked Tofu
      and, 272
   Chilies, Stuffed Poblano, 274
   Kasha Baked In Squash Halves, 273
   Oriental, 272
Melts
   Blue Cheese and Pear, 293
   Cheese, Two-Season Squash and Bean
      Soup with, 434
   Cranberry Cheese, 464
   Cucumber Cheese, 293
   Monte Cristo Grill, Portobello, 292
   Peanutty and Jelly, 294
   Pinwheels, Swiss Cheese and Spinach, 294
   Pinwheels, Sliced Mushroom, 295
   Sloppy Joes, Meatless, 289
   Tostadas, Picante Black Bean, 288
   Vegetarian Chorizo, 287
   Veggie Joes, 290
Satay, Indonesian-Style Tofu, 41
Satay, Oriental Vegetable, 206
Sauces (see also Condiments and Jelly)
   Alfredo, 591
   Artichoke, 593
   Bean, Peasant with Tomatoes and Sage,
      587
   Chili Tomato, 599
   Chili, Cincinnati, 598
   Chili, Poblano, 601
   Creole, 588
   Curry, 594
   Dessert
      Chocolate, 634
      Chocolate, Bittersweet, 661
      Coulis, Cranberry, 610
      Lemon, Tart, 675
      Raspberry, 662
      Rum, Warm, 628
   Eggplant, 589
   Enchilada, 599
   Fragrant Basting, 614
   Garlic, Many-Cloves, 591
   Gorgonzola, 592

Gravy, Mushroom, 596
Gremolata, 609
Jalapeño Con Queso, 603
Marinades
   Fajita, 182
   Tandoori, 193
   Tamari, 613
Marinara, 582
Mayonnaise, Lemon-Herb, 611
Mock Hollandaise, 595
Mole, 600
Mushroom, Wild, 59
Mustard, 612
Onion, Three-, 592
Paprikash, 597
Peperonata-Tomato, 588
Pesto
   Cilantro, 607
   Fennel, 606
   Minted, 608
   Mixed Herb, 605
   Red Pepper, 607
   Spinach, 605
   Spinach-Cilantro, 608
   Sun-Dried Tomato, 606
Pizza, 582
Plum, 612
Poblano Sour Cream, 603
Primavera, 594
Raspberry, 662
Roasted Red Pepper, 590
Salsa
   Blackeye, 428
   Garbanzo, 604
   Med-Mex Fusion, 8
   Red Tomato, 8
   Tomatillo, 7
   Tomato Poblano, 462
   Tropical, 604
Sour, 439
Spinach, Creamed, 593
Tamari Dipping, 613
Tamari Marinade, 613
Tomatillo, 602
Tomato
   Bolognese-Style, 286
   -Caper, Mediterranean, 590
   and Vegetarian Meat, 583
   and Vegetarian Meatball, 586
   with Mushrooms and Sherry, 585
   Fresh and Herb, 584
   Fresh -Basil, 584
   Serrano, 602
   Yogurt-Cucumber, 61, 280
Sausage, Vegetarian
   Calzones, 319
   Lasagne, 141
   Rigatoni with, and Fennel Pesto, 252
Serbian Leek Cake, 451
Serrano Tomato Sauce, 602
Sesame
   Asparagus Stir-Fry, 152
   Croutons, 560
   Dressing, 225
   Noodle Soup with Vegetables, 242

Pasta Salad with Summer Vegetables, 224
Wonton Cups, 25
Shells Stuffed with Spinach and Tofu, 256
Shepherd's Veggie Pot Pie, 326
Sherbet, Orange-Pineapple, 666
Side Dishes
  Artichokes with Mock Hollandaise Sauce,
    470
  Artichokes, Braised Whole, 470
  Asparagus with Lemon-Wine Sauce, 471
  Asparagus with Peanut Sauce, 472
  Beets
    Dijon, 475
    Harvard, 475
    Honey-Roasted, 476
  Green Bean(s)
    Casserole, 473
    Greek-Style, 472
    Oriental, 473
  Broccoli
    Herb-Crumbed, 473
    Rabe Sauteed with Garlic, 477
    Terrine with Lemon Herb Mayonnaise,
      477
  Brussels Sprouts, Sugar-Glazed and Pearl
    Onions, 478
  Cabbage, Wine-Braised, 479
  Carrot(s)
    Gingered Puree, 479
    Orange-Glazed Baby, 480
    Pudding, 481
  Cauliflower with Creamy Cheese Sauce,
    482
  Cauliflower-Fennel Puree, 480
  Celery Root Puree, 480
  Corn
    Fried, 483
    Pudding, Fresh, 484
    Sweet, Tex-Mex, 484
  Eggplant, Seasoned Saute, 485
  Eggplant and Tomato Casserole, 485
  Fennel Puree, 480
  Greens, Lemon-Spiked Garlic, 486
  Kale, Braised, 487
  Greens, Smashed Potatoes and, 487
  Leeks and Peppers, Sauteed, 488
  Mushrooms with Sour Cream, 488
  Okra, Gulfport, 489
  Onions, Quartet of, 490
  Onions, Fruit-Stuffed Vidalia, 490
  Parsnips and Winter Vegetables, Braised,
    491
  Peas, Tiny and Onions, 492
  Peperonata, 492
  Potato(es)
    Cheesy Bean and Onion Mashers, 494
    Creamy, and Bean Mashers, 494
    "Fries", Crispy French, 497
    "Fries", Parmesan, 497
    "Fries", Steak, 498
    Garlic Mashed, 493
    Gratin, 495
    Horseradish Mashed, 493
    Lima Bean and Mushroom Mashers,
      494

  Pancakes, 493
    with Poblano Chilies, 498
    Real Mashed, 493
    Scalloped, 495
    Sweet Loaf, Holiday, with Apple-
      Cranberry Relish, 499
    Sweet, Orange-Lime, 500
    Sweet Pone, 501
    Twice-Baked with Cheese, 496
    Veggie-Stuffed Bakers, 496
    Yams, Candied, 498
  Spaghetti Squash Parmesan, 505
  Spinach, Creamed, 502
  Spinach Au Gratin, 502
  Squash, Acorn, Apple-Pecan, 503
  Squash, Chayote with Pumpkin Seeds, 506
  Squash, Summer, Sauteed, with Snow
    Peas, 506
  Succotash, 483
  Succotash, El Paso, 474
  Tomato(es)
    Baked, Greens-Stuffed, 509
    Cornmeal-Fried, 509
    Fried, 508
    Fried, Sugar-Glazed, 508
    Herbed Halves, 508
    Pudding, 507
  Zucchini Fans Provençal, 503
  Zucchini From Pueblo, 504
Sherbet (see under Desserts)
Sloppy Joes, Meatless, 289
Snow Pea Soup, 82
Soft Pretzels, 553
Sombrero Dip, 11
Sorbet (see Desserts)
Soufflés
  Cheddar Cheese, 353
  Eggplant Casserole, 149
  Peach-Allspice, 681
  Wild Rice, 424
Sour Cream
  Avocado, 95
  Cilantro, 88
  Coffeecake with Apple-Date Filling, 565
  Dressing, Cucumber-, 417
  Dressing, Mayonnaise, 517
  Minted, 149
  Mushrooms with, 488
  Sauce, Poblano, 603
  Sauce, Poblano, Grilled Tempeh with, 454
Soups
  Alsatian Peasant, 100
  Bean
    Black Classic, 67
    Black with Sun-Dried Tomatoes and
      Cilantro Cream, 66
    Four- and Vegetable, 62
    Garbanzo, 68
    Navy, 63
    -Thickened, 64
    Tuscan, 65
    Two- and Pasta, 107
    White and Sweet Potato with
      Cranberry Coulis, 64
  Beet Borscht, 59

Beet, Dilled, 58
Berry, Very, 57
Broccoli
  Cream of, 60
  Dilled, 60
  Herbed and Pasta, 61
  -Kale, 60
Cabbage, Russian, 68
Carrot, Dilled, 69
Carrot, Ginger Spiced-Orange, 70
Cauliflower, Cream of with Cheese, 70
Cherry, Sweet, 57
Chick Pea and Pasta, 106
Corn
  Creamed, 73
  with Epazote, 74
  Hearty and Potato Chowder, 86
Creamy Peanut Butter, 111
Cucumber and Sorrel, 72
Cucumber, Herbed, 71
Eggplant with Roasted Red Pepper Sauce,
  74
Garden Harvest, 99
Garlic with Toast, 75
Gazpacho, 94
Greek Lemon-Rice, 110
Lentil, Country, 113
Lentil, Indian, 114
Minestrone, Summer, 96
Mushroom
  Black, 77
  Cream of, 76
  Savory and Barley, 77
Onion
  French, 78
  and Leek with Pasta, 80
  Three-, with Mushrooms, 79
  Vidalia, 81
Oriental Watercress, 110
Pea, Chilled, 82
Pea, Split, 83
Poblano Chili, 102
Potato and Fresh Herb Potage, 84
Potato Chowder, 86
Pozole, 104
Pumpkin, Cinnamon-Spiced, 90
Red Pepper, Sweet, 84
Snow Pea, 82
Spinach and Tortellini, 108
Squash
  Chayote, with Cilantro Sour Cream, 87
  Curried Butternut, 90
  Orange-Scented, 91
  Savory Herbed, 91
  Summer, 88
  Winter, 92
Stock
  Mediterranean, 54
  Mushroom, Rich, 54
  Oriental, 55
  Vegetable, Basic, 52
  Vegetable, Canned,
  Vegetable, Roasted, 53
Sweet Potato Chipotle Chili, 80
Tomatillo with Cilantro, 103

Tomato
  Cream of, 92
  and Leek, Ripe, 94
  Sun-Dried, and Linguine, 105
  Two-, 93
Tortellini and Mushroom, 109
Tortellini with Kale, 108
Tortilla, 104
Vegetable
  Lightly Creamed, 97
  Lime-Scented, 98
  Mediterranean-Style, 101
  with Orzo, 96
  Veggie, Bean, and Burger, 100
  Vichyssoise, 85
  Vietnamese Curried Coconut, 112
  Zucchini and Broccoli, Dilled, 89
Sour Cream
  Avocado, 95
  Cilantro, 88
  Coffeecake with Apple-Date Filling, 565
  Cucumber Dressing, 417
  -Mayonnaise Dressing, 517
  Minted, 149
  Poblano, Sauce, 603
Sour Sauce, 439
Sourdough Croutons, 560
Southern Stewed Black Eyes, 442
Southwest Pasta with Cilantro Pesto, 240
Soy Noshers, 3
Soybean and Vegetable Spread, 13
Soybean-Veggie Burgers, 286
Spaghetti and Eggplant Parmesan Torte, 145
Spaghetti and Spaghetti!, 166
Spaghetti Squash
  Parmesan, 505
  with Roasted Tomato-Herb Sauce and
    Artichokes, 202
  with Vegetable Sauté, 158
Spicy Rice, 422
Spinach
  Balls, Baked, 37
  and 4-Cheese Pizza, 300
  and Cheese Mini-Quiches, 36
  and Melon Salad, 512
  and Tortellini Soup, 108
  Au Gratin, 502
  Cheese Crepes, 452
  Creamed, 502
  Gnocchi with Gorgonzola Sauce, 254
  Lasagne, Roasted Red Pepper and, 267
  -Mushroom Flatbread, 558
  -Mushroom Rotolo with Marinara Sauce,
    144
  Pasta Bake, 446
  Pesto, 605
  Pesto, -Cilantro, 608
  Pizza, Deep-Pan, 301
  Quiche, 356
  Salad Pizza, 315
  Salad, Wilted, 513
  Sauce, Creamed, 593
  Soup, and Tortellini, 108
  Squares, Cheese and, 36
Split Pea Soup, 83

Spring Berry Cheesecake, 647
Spring Vegetable Stir-Fry, 170
Sprouts and Vegetable Salad, 522
Squash
    Acorn, Apple-Pecan, 503
    Butternut, Curried, Soup, 90
    Chayote Soup with Cilantro Sour
      Cream, 87
    Dinner Rolls, 554
    Halves, Kasha Loaf Baked in, 273
    and Mushroom Galette, 334
    and Mushroom Lasagne, 266
    Pizza, with Yellow and Green, 312
    Risotto, Summer, 412
    Roasted, Moroccan-Style, 196
    Soup
      Savory Herbed, 91
      Orange-Scented, 91
      Summer, 88
    Stew, Bean and, 120
    Stew, Orange and Ginger, 126
    Summer Soup, 88
    Summer, Sauteed with Snow Peas, 506
    Sweet-Sour and Potato Stew, 128
    and Tempeh Patties, 279
    Two-Season and Bean Soup with Cheese
      Melts, 434
    Winter Soup, 92
Star Pasta with Carrots and Ginger Cream,
    240
Steak Fries, 498
Stews (see also Beans and Legumes)
    Bean
      and Squash, 120
      and Vegetable, Hot N' Spicy, 122
      -Thickened Vegetable, 116
    Cabbage Ragout with Real Mashed
      Potatoes, 119
    Caribbean Sweet-and-Sour, 127
    Chili, 121
    Chili, Mexican Ancho, 123
    Garden, with Couscous, 133
    Ginger Bean and Blackeye, 128
    Hasty, 116
    Italian Vegetarian Meatball, 132
    Mediterranean Curried, 134
    Orange and Ginger Squash, 126
    Roasted Many-Veggie, 190
    Spiced Bean, with Fusilli, 131
    Sweet-Sour Squash and Potato, 128
    Tofu and Vegetable, 129
    Three-Bean, with Polenta, 130
    Vegetable
      Bean-Thickened, 116
      Mexican-Style, 125
      Tex-Mex, 122
    Veggie, with Dumplings, 117
    Veggie Mélange with Bulgur, 118
Sticky Bun Topping, 549
Sticky Buns, 548
Stir-Fry(ied)
    Adzuki Bean, 381
    Beans and Greens, 379
    Butter Beans and Sprouts, 380
    Five-Spice, 172

Green on Green, with Tofu, 170
Red and Green, Tempeh Steak with, 177
Rice Noodles with Vegetables, 245
Sesame Asparagus, 152
Thai, 171
Vegetable, Spring, 170
Vegetable, Szechuan, 173
Stocks (see Soups)
Strawberry-Kiwi Shortcake, 662
Streusel
    Cake, 616
    Crisp, 616
    Rhubarb, 616
    Topping, 665
Succotash, 483
Succotash, El Paso, 474
Sugar Cookies, Frosted, 652
Summer Squash Risotto, 412
Summer Squash Soup, 88
Sun-Dried Tomato
    and Goat Cheese Dressing, 226, 458
    Hummus, 15
    and Linguine Soup, 105
    Pesto, 606
    Pesto and Cheese Grill, 464
Sweet Bulgur Pilaf, 406
Sweet Cherry Soup, 57
Sweet Fennel Calzones, 321
Sweet Onion Salad, 212
Sweet Onion Tarte Tatin, 332
Sweet Plantains, 29
Sweet Potato
    Biscuits, 568
    Braids, 543
    Cakes, 157
    Chipotle Chili, 80
    Hash with Poached Eggs, 340
    Pone, 501
    Ravioli with Curry Sauce, 262
Sweet Red Pepper Soup, 84
Sweet-Sour Squash and Potato Stew, 128
Sweet-Spiced Cabbage with Quinoa, 150
Swiss Cheese and Spinach Pinwheels, 294
Swiss-Kraut Veggie Burgers, 276
Szechuan Vegetable Stir-Fry, 173

T

12-Layer Salad, 515
20-Minute Ravioli, 261
Tabbouleh, 415
Tabbouleh and Vegetable Salad Medley, 416
Taco Pizza, 309
Tacos Picadillo, 462
Tahini Dressing, 281
Tamale(s)
    Dough, 183
    Three-Chili, 183
    Veggie, with Beans, 184
Tamari Dipping Sauce, 613
Tamari Marinade, 613
Tandoori Marinade, 193
Tandoori Tempeh with Orange Cilantro
    Rice, 192
Tarragon Wine Jelly, 579
Tart Crust, Baked, 330

Tarte Tatin, 640
Teem Seem Loaf, 175
Tempeh
  Fajitas, 182
  Grilled, with Poblano Sour Cream Sauce, 454
  Jerk, with Black Beans and Rice, 191
  Moo-Shu, 176
  Pasta Soup, 433
  Patties, Squash and, 279
  Saute, Garden Vegetables and, 453
  Steak with Red and Green Stir-Fry, 177
  Tandoori, with Orange Cilantro Rice, 192
  Smoked and Vegetables, "Little Ears" with, 236
  Vegetables and, Marengo, 452
Tetrazzini, Vegetarian, 138
Texas Stew with Chili-Cheese Dumplings, 363
Tex-Mex
  Breakfast Grits, 427
  Sweet Corn, 484
  Vegetable Stew, 122
Thai
  Fried Rice, 423
  Peanut Sauce, 423
  Stir-Fry, 171
Three Kings' Bread, 545
Tofruity 48
Tofu
  Aioli, 161
  Burgers, Smoked, 278
  Burgers, Veggie-, 277
  Curried, and Vegetables, 166
  Green on Green Stir-Fry with, 170
  Indonesian-Style, Satay, 41
  Loaf, Mesquite-Smoked, and Brown Rice, 272
  Mesquite-Smoked, 191
  Mesquite-Smoked and Brown Rice Loaf, 272
  Salad, Black Bean and Smoked, 461
  Shells Stuffed with Spinach and, 256
  Smoked, Fruited Couscous with, 401
  and Vegetable Stew, 129
Tomatillo
  Salsa, 7
  Sauce, 602
  Soup with Cilantro, 103
Tomato(es)
  Cornmeal-Fried, 509
  Eggplant and, Mediterranean Roasted, 204
  Eggplant and, Casserole, 485
  Fillo Pizza, 314
  Fried, 508
  Fried, Sugar-Glazed, 508
  Fusilli with, and Corn, 237
  Greens Stuffed Baked, 509
  Halves, Herbed, 508
  Penne with Asparagus and Plum, 235
  with Pepper-Roasted Wild Mushrooms, Stuffed, 207
  Pizza, Fillo, 314
  Pizza, Fresh, and Basil, 305
  Plum, Penne with Asparagus and, 235

Pudding, 507
Relish, Fresh, 285
Relish, Gingered, 610
Risotto with Roasted, 195
Salad, Bean, and Bread, 387
Salad, Garden, Wheat Berry and, 419
Sauce (see under Sauces)
Soup (see under Soups)
Tart, Rich, 329
Torta Rustica, 322
Tortellini
  and 2-Bean Vegetable Soup, 260
  and Mushroom Soup, 109
  Artichoke Bake, 259
  Curried, with Beans and Squash, 260
  Kabobs with Many-Cloves Garlic Sauce, 42
  Mushroom, Roasted Vegetables with, 193
  Soup with Kale, 108
  Soup, Spinach and, 108
Tortilla
  Baked Strips, 103
  Soup, 104
  Strips, Eggs Scrambled with Crisp, 350
  Wedges, 27
Tortoni, Mixed Fruit, 669
Tostadas, Picante Black Bean, 288
Trifle, Pineapple-Lemon, 632
Tropical Salsa, 604
Turmeric Rice, 423
Tuscan
  Bean Bake, 371
  Bean Soup, 65
  Potato Pizza, 307
Two-Bean and Pasta Soup, 107
Two-Cheese Risotto, 413
Two-Season Squash and Bean Soup with Cheese Melts, 434
Two-Tomato Soup, 93

U
Use-It-Up Pie, 327

V
Vanilla
  Cream Filling, 626
  Crumb Crust, 637
  Glaze, 573
Vegetable(s)
  -Barley Moussaka, 146
  Crepes, 159
  Curry, 165
  Enchiladas, 180
  Frittata with Parmesan Toast, 343
  Lo Mein, 244
  Manicotti with Creamed Spinach Sauce, 257
  Mélange, 345
  and Mixed Rice Casserole, 138
  Paprikash, 163
  Puff, 344
  Salad with 2 Beans, 388
  Salad with Millet, 417
  Soup with Orzo, 96
  Strudel with Wild Mushroom Sauce, 161

and Tempeh Marengo, 452
and Wild Rice Salad, 211
Vegetarian
  Chorizo, 287
  Falafel Burgers, 280
  Meatball Soup, 437
  Meatballs, 437
  Meatballs in Tomato Chili Sauce, 124
  Sausage Calzones, 319
  Sausange Lasagne, 141
  Tetrazzini, 138
Vegetarian Types/Symbols, viii
Veggie
  Bean, and Burger Soup, 100
  Joes, 290
  Kugel, 346
  Lasagne with Eggplant Sauce, 140
  Mélange with Bulgur, 118
  Pocket Sandwiches, 216
  Pot Pie, 324
  Stew with Dumplings, 117
  -Stuffed Bakers, 496
  Tamales with Beans, 184
  -Tofu Burgers, 277
Very Berry Smoothie, 48
Very Berry Soup, 57
Very Quick Bean and Vegetable Stew, 364
Very Simple Primavera, 233
Vichyssoise, 85
Vietnamese Curried Coconut Soup, 112
Vinegar Biscuits, 567

W

Waldorf Salad, 521
Warm Indian Pudding, 676
Warm Rum Sauce, 628
Wasabi Potato Slices, 38
Welsh Rarebit, 355
Wheat and Barley Bowl, 394
Wheat Berry
  and Garden Tomato Salad, 419

and Lentil Stew with Dumplings, 392
Waldorf, 418
White Bean
  Dressing, 385
  Mashers with Sautéed Vegetables, 152
  and Sweet Potato Soup with Cranberry
    Coulis, 64
Whole Wheat Lavosh, 556
Whole Wheat Pizza Dough, 299
Wild Rice Muffins, 570
Wild Rice Soufflé, 424
Wilted Spinach Salad, 513
Wine-Braised Cabbage, 479
Wine-Glazed Ravioli and Asparagus, 26
Winter
  Bean and Vegetable Stew, 36
  Squash Soup, 9
  Vegetable Risotto, 40
Wonton Cups, Sesame, 25
Wontons, Cranberry-Cheese, 39

Y

Yellow
  Grits, 42
  Grits with Wild Mushroom Saute, 42
  and White Bean Chili, 36
Yellow Salsa Rice, 42
Yogurt-Cucumber Sauce, 28
Yogurt Dressing, 53

Z

Ziti with Gremolata, 23
Zucchini
  and Broccoli Soup, Dilled, 89
  Casserole, Eggplant and, 447
  Fans Provençal, 50
  from Pueblo, 50
  and Mushroom Pizza with Fillo Crust, 31
  Roasted, and Garlic Spread, 18